Daily Prayer

Daily Prayer

NICK FAWCETT

Daily Prayer

**kevin
mayhew**

This edition first published in 2003 by

KEVIN MAYHEW LTD
Buxhall, Stowmarket, Suffolk, IP14 3BW
Email: info@kevinmayhewltd.com

KINGSGATE PUBLISHING INC
1000 Pannell Street, Suite G, Columbia, MO 65201
E-mail: sales@kingsgatepublishing.com

All scripture quotations are translated or paraphrased by
Nick Fawcett unless otherwise indicated. For permission
to quote marked passages we are grateful to:

The New Revised Standard Version of the Bible, copyright
© 1989, and the Revised Standard Version of the Bible,
copyright © 1946, 1952 and 1971 by the Division of
Christian Education of the National Council of Churches
of Christ in the USA.

The New English Bible, copyright © 1961 and 1970,
Oxford University and Cambridge University Presses.

The Authorised Version of the Bible, copyright © Oxford
University Press.

9 8 7 6 5 4 3 2 1 0

ISBN 1 84417 094 2
Catalogue No 1500601

Hardback edition:
ISBN 1 84003 771 7
Catalogue No 1500443

Cover design by Jonathan Stroulger
Edited by Katherine Laidler
Typesetting by Richard Weaver

Printed and bound in China

Contents

To Tom Elliott, Terry Brown, Alan Johnson and Sue Pells,
and all those with whom I was privileged
to work during my time with Toc H

Introduction

'When you pray, go into your room, shut the door, and pray privately to your Father who is hidden, and your Father who sees what is hidden will reward you' (Matthew 6:6). An unmistakable call from Jesus himself to private prayer – making time and space in the busyness of our lives to speak with God, listen for his answer and reflect on what he might be saying. So far, so good, only sometimes that discipline doesn't come easily. What should we say? How should we say it? What form should our reflection take? How do we begin? Above all, how do we prevent such times becoming a matter of routine, offered out of habit and repeated almost parrot fashion?

There are no easy answers to such questions, but there are tools that might be of help. Some time ago a friend bought me such a tool: a book of devotions that I used for several years. The format was very simple – a Bible verse, a comment and a prayer – but I found it enormously helpful. It offered me something to ponder each day, and often served to stimulate further prayer and reflection. That is the aim of this book of devotions. It cannot solve all the problems relating to prayer, still less serve as the sum total of anyone's prayer life, but it is offered as an aid to reflection, a springboard into what I hope will be a personal encounter with God.

I am conscious of many weaknesses in this material. Chief among them is that space has not permitted the inclusion of intercessions. I would urge you to build some time into your devotions to remember others, recognising that faith is not simply a private matter but concerned with all. Similarly, this book necessarily comprises words, but prayer is also about silence, listening to what God is saying to us. Again, then, do not rush through the material, but build in times for quiet reflection. Finally, I have tried as best I can to cover the many and varied aspects of life and Christian discipleship, but inevitably my choice of material and emphases will reflect my own moods, needs and understanding of faith. You may feel that some themes are unduly emphasised at the expense of others.

I have purposely followed the same format throughout the book. Each day begins with a passage of scripture, followed by a brief comment upon this. Take time to read and reread the Bible verses carefully, asking what God is saying to you through them. There follows a question or questions designed to stimulate further thought, and after this a prayer, drawing together the various issues raised. Finally, a second passage of scripture sums up the theme, after which I offer a brief prayer in conclusion. Because certain seasons of the Christian year, such as Holy Week and Easter, fall on variable dates, I have included supplementary material at the back of the book that you can turn to as appropriate. However, to keep this to a minimum, I have focused on Advent and Lent themes within the main body of the book at the appropriate times.

I would stress once again that this book is not a teach-yourself manual on prayer, still less a substitute for bringing your own thoughts and needs directly to God. Ultimately, our prayer life depends on a personal relationship with him, which alone makes it meaningful, but if this material can help strengthen that relationship, then it will more than have served its purpose.

I am indebted in the writing of this book to my family for the patience and support they have shown in what has turned out to be a mammoth project. Special thanks also to Katherine Laidler for the many hours she has put in editing the manuscript, and to Peter Dainty for his invariably helpful comments and criticisms. My thanks also go, once again, to Kevin Mayhew Publishers for the opportunity to put this and other material into print.

Nick Fawcett

JANUARY

Time's paces

Read

Lord, you have been our home across the centuries. Before the mountains were formed and before you fashioned this world we live in, from eternity to eternity you are God. You return us to dust, saying, 'Back to what you once were, you mortals!' A thousand years are like a passing day in your sight, as short-lived as the night-watch. Our fleeting span is seventy years, perhaps eighty if we are strong; throughout they are filled with struggle and sorrow, here today and gone tomorrow. Teach us to make the most of our days and so to discover the secret of inner wisdom.

Psalm 90:1-4, 10, 12

Ponder

There comes a time in our lives when it dawns on us that we are not as young as we used to be. Whereas the future once seemed to stretch out indefinitely, suddenly it appears all too short, the time left to fulfil our dreams far less than we thought. Time and tide, as they say, waits for no one.

It would be easy to move from here to a maudlin self-pity, but instead the psalmist turns to focus on God whose eternal nature stands in such contrast to our own transience. In the context of faith, the passage of time should not be seen as the years running out so much as life moving on, one more step along an unfolding journey in which there is always more to be discovered and new joys to be experienced. Of course, we will sometimes remember the past with a tinge of regret, and look to the future with a degree of anxiety, but we should also recognise each day as God's gift, and live each one of them in the assurance that nothing will ever separate us from his love made known in Christ.

Ask yourself

Are you brooding over the past or trusting in God's future? Do you begin this new year weighed down by a sense of hopelessness and futility, or uplifted by the certain realisation of God's promises?

Pray

Living God, I spend so much of my life in ceaseless striving, pursuing first this, then that. I labour, I fret, I fight, I struggle, all my thoughts so often focused on present gain and immediate satisfaction. Yet all the goals which consume me bring but a moment's pleasure, each destined to fade away.

Teach me to set my heart first on you, and to discover the fulfilment you long to give me in both this life and the next. Help me to live not just in the context of this brief span you have given here on earth, but in the light of your eternal purpose in which, by your grace, you invite us all to share. Amen.

Remember

All people are like grass, as short-lived as the flowers of the field. The grass shrivels, the flower goes over . . . but the word of our God continues for ever.   *Isaiah 40:6b, 8*

Close

Everlasting God, send me out into the coming year, confident that whatever it may bring you will be with me in it, and that your loving purpose will not fail. Through Jesus Christ my Lord. Amen.

A new creation

Read

Anyone united with Christ is a new creation; the old self has passed away in its entirety; everything is made new.

2 Corinthians 5:17

Ponder

Do you still make New Year resolutions? If you're anything like me, you used to once but you've long since come to realise that the chances of living up to them are remote if not non-existent. Is this a healthy realism or the counsel of despair, practical common sense or weary resignation? The answer is a bit of both. By ourselves, we *can* change to a point, but to change our spots completely is beyond us.

In Christ, however, it is a different story; the gospel, at its heart, is about new beginnings, a fresh start not of our own making but made possible by the grace of God. However frustrated you may be at your inability to live the life you want to, never lose sight of that fact: the life-changing power of God in Christ that is always striving to bring its new creation to perfection.

Ask yourself

Do you still greet each day as a new beginning, a fresh start? Do you still believe God is able to change your life?

Pray

Lord Jesus Christ, I am not good at letting go of the past, at recognising there are times when I need to move on in life and take a step forward in faith if I am ever truly to grow. I prefer the security of the familiar, the comfort of that which does not stretch or challenge me too far, and I am wary of the prospect of change, afraid that it might ask more of me than I am willing to give. I am not good at letting go of the old and putting on the new, at turning away from my former way of life and taking instead the way of the cross. I am reluctant to abandon old habits, fearful of being thought different, unwilling to deny myself the pleasures of this world for the promise of the world to come. So I try to keep a foot in both camps, to combine the old self with the new. I think I can balance the two, but, of course, I can't, the end result being to compromise both and embrace neither.

Help me to understand that, while the old has its place, there are some areas in life where a complete break is needed, a turning away from what *has been*, before I am ready to receive what *shall be*. Lord Jesus Christ, you want to work within me to finish the new creation you have begun. Give me courage to trust you completely, so that you may refashion my life to your glory. I ask it in your name. Amen.

Remember

No one patches an old cloak with an unshrunk cloth; otherwise, the new piece will pull away from the old and a worse tear will be made. Similarly, no one stores new wine in old wineskins, for the skins will burst and the wine will be lost along with the skins; but instead one puts new wine into fresh wineskins.

Mark 2:21-22

Close

Lord Jesus Christ, move within me and draw me closer to you, so that the newness of this year may be echoed in newness of life springing fresh within me every day, now and always. Amen.

Keeping faith

Read

There was a man called Simeon in Jerusalem who was upright and devout, eagerly awaiting the consolation of Israel, and the Holy Spirit was with him. The Spirit had disclosed to him that he would not taste death before he had seen the Lord's Messiah. Led by the Spirit, Simeon entered the temple; and when Jesus' parents brought in their child to honour the customs of the Law, Simeon cradled him in his arms and praised God, saying, 'Master, now let your servant go in peace, according to your promise. With my own eyes I have seen the salvation you have prepared before all the world – a light that will reveal you to the Gentiles and bring glory to your people Israel.' The child's parents were stunned at these words concerning him. Then Simeon blessed them and said to his mother Mary, 'This child is ordained to be a sign that many will reject; one through whom the inner thoughts of many will be revealed and even your own soul will be pierced. Many in Israel will stand or fall because of him.'   *Luke 2:25-35*

Ponder

It is not just our faith in ourselves that can take a knock as the years go by; it is our faith in God as well. As another natural catastrophe strikes, another country is plunged into violent conflict, another friend dies of cancer, or another person is raped, mugged or murdered, it is hard to reconcile the harsh realities of life with the picture of a loving and merciful Father. The fact that society as a whole generally dismisses any talk of God makes it all the harder to keep on believing, harder to withstand the drip-drip effect of scorn and scepticism or sheer disinterest.

Yet the example of Simeon, and of the prophetess Anna whose story follows his, urges us to keep trusting, confident that God is at work and that, in the fullness of time, his will shall be done. Both Simeon and Anna had the courage to stay true to their faith despite outward appearances. Have we?

Ask yourself

Does your faith in God's purpose burn as brightly as it once did? Have you lost sight of his ability to change the world?

Pray

Loving God, it is hard sometimes to continue believing when so much denies my convictions. It is harder still when those around me ridicule my faith and deride me for following you, and it is hardest of all when hopes are dashed and you seem far from me, my prayers for help seemingly unanswered.

Give me strength, despite adversity or disappointment, to stay true to you, trusting in your purpose, in the assurance that your way will finally prevail. Amen.

Remember

We rejoice in our present sufferings, because we know that suffering creates endurance, and endurance creates fortitude, and fortitude creates hope, and hope does not let us down, because God's love is poured into our innermost being through the Holy Spirit he has put within us.

Romans 5:3-5

Close

Sovereign God, renew my faith, revive my hope, restore my trust, rekindle my vision, and so may I serve you in quiet confidence, this day and always. Through Jesus Christ my Lord. Amen.

A time for everything

Read

There is a season for everything, and a time for every activity under heaven: a time to be born, and a time to die; a time to plant, and a time to uproot; a time to kill, and a time to heal; a time to pull down and a time to build up; a time to cry and a time to laugh; a time to grieve and a time to dance; a time to scatter stones and a time to gather them; a time to embrace and a time not to embrace; a time to seek and a time to lose; a time to keep and a time to throw away; a time to tear and a time to mend; a time for silence and a time for speech; a time to love and a time to hate; a time for war and a time for peace. *Ecclesiastes 3:1-8*

Ponder

Time's a funny thing, isn't it? One moment we can feel down in the dumps and the next on top of the world; today life can seem full of trouble but tomorrow it may appear full of promise. Our experience is always changing and life is constantly moving on. In some ways that is a sobering prospect, reminding us all too starkly of our mortality, yet where would we be without the variety that the passing of time brings: the passing of the seasons, the birth and growth of a child, the anticipation of a special event and, of course, our hope in Christ.

The secret, with time, is knowing how to respond to it; understanding what mood or action is appropriate for a particular occasion. Should we put the past behind us or hold on to it? Should we grasp the nettle or admit defeat? Should we stand up for our principles or be ready to bend? We face a host of questions like these every day, and no answer is uniformly correct. We need to seek God's guidance and help, for he is the one who holds all time in his hands; the one who in all the changes and chances of this life will not change.

Ask yourself

Are you always chasing after time? Are you burdened by a fear of the future or a weight from the past? Is it time you let go and trusted in God's timing?

Pray

Loving God, thank you for this day and all the opportunities it brings – moments to work and rest, give and receive, wonder and worship. Thank you for having been with me throughout my life – always there to guide my footsteps and lead me forward. Thank you for the assurance of your continuing guidance – the knowledge that whatever the future may bring, whatever challenges I may face or trials I may endure, you will be there to see me through, giving me the strength and resources I need, and a joy that cannot be shaken.

God of past, present and future; the same yesterday, today and tomorrow; I praise you for each and every moment, and consecrate them all to your service. In the name of Christ. Amen.

Remember

I trust in you, O Lord; I say, 'You are my God.' My times are in your hand.   *Psalm 31:14-15a*

Close

Eternal God, teach me to use each moment wisely, open to your guidance and so understanding what is right for each occasion. Teach me to see time not as a threat but as your gift, and so may I live life to the full, as you desire. Through Jesus Christ my Lord. Amen.

Behind the labels

Read

Now tax-collectors and sinners were all drawing near to him. And the scribes and Pharisees were scandalised, muttering among themselves, 'This man welcomes sinners and eats with them.'

Luke 15:1-2

Ponder

It was a conundrum: a tin without a label found in the murky depths of the kitchen cupboard. What was inside, I wondered? Beans? Peaches? Fish? Meat? There was only one way to find out and that, of course, was to open it and look inside. It brought home to me how important labels can be, for without them we may not know what's hidden underneath. On the other hand, labels can be misleading. Just because there's a brand name on the tin doesn't necessarily mean it contains a superior product; the supermarket cheap-label alternative may be just as good if not better.

When it comes to people, using labels is a dangerous thing for none of us fit easily into neat categories, each a complex mixture of good and bad, strong and weak, wise and foolish. Yet, as Jesus found throughout his ministry, it is human nature to pigeonhole people, despite the misery and division this causes. Can anything good come out of Nazareth? Has a tax-collector the right to see Jesus? Should a prostitute be forgiven? Is it possible to love a Samaritan? Could a home-grown boy possibly turn out to be the Messiah? Today it is no different; such prejudice all too easily finds a place in our own hearts. The barriers that keep us apart are as real as they have ever been. We need to look, as Jesus did, behind the label to the person beneath. Only then will we discover each individual's true worth and, as well as theirs, discover our own.

Ask yourself

In what ways are you guilty of labelling people? Are there prejudices and preconceptions that you still need to overcome?

Pray

Gracious God, I know that you value each one of us, not for what we might become but for what we are. Forgive me that, all too often, I forget that truth, full of my own importance, preoccupied with self, harbouring vain illusions about who I am and what I can achieve. I have not valued others as they deserve, allowing prejudices and preconceptions to colour my judgement and poison my attitudes. I have looked down on those around me, failing to see the good in them, closed to the contribution they can make to my life. For all those times when I have valued myself too much and others too little, Lord, forgive me. In the name of Christ. Amen.

Remember

You are all children of God through faith in Jesus Christ, for all who have been baptised in Christ have been clothed with him. There can neither be Jew or Greek, slave or free, male or female, for you are all one in Christ Jesus.

Galatians 3:26-28

Close

Gracious God, give me a proper sense of my own worth, a true appreciation of the worth of others, and, above all, an understanding of your greatness, beside which we are as nothing, yet through which you count us as your children. Amen.

Wise men still seek him

Read

Following the birth of Jesus in Bethlehem of Judea during the reign of King Herod, magi arrived in Jerusalem from the east, saying, 'Where is the one born king of the Jews, for we saw his star rising in the east and have come to pay our respects. As they entered the house they saw the child with his mother Mary, and, falling down in worship, they offered him their treasures: gifts of gold, frankincense and myrrh.   *Matthew 2:1-2, 11*

Ponder

There's a pithy little saying often still displayed around Christmas time on a church notice board, car windscreen or suchlike. The words? 'Wise men still seek him.' And, of course, that's perfectly true, for there are many today, just as there have always been, who still search in vain to find faith. It's not that they don't want to believe – quite the opposite – but there is so much in the world they cannot make sense of, so much that seems to contradict the God of love preached in the Christian faith. It would have been easy for the wise men to give up on their search, not least when they arrived in Bethlehem to find that no one had any idea who or what they were talking about. Could there have been some mistake? Had their journey been a waste of time? Yet they kept on searching and trusting until, finally, they came to the place where the child lay.

We, too, will reach our destination if we have the courage to keep on seeking. If we persevere on the journey, we will find our questions answered and the confusion resolved as we glimpse for ourselves the wonder of God revealed in Christ.

Ask yourself

Have you allowed obstacles of doubt and disappointment to impede your journey of faith? Is it time to commit yourself afresh to the path of Christian discipleship?

Pray

Lord Jesus Christ, you have told us to seek and we shall find. Yet that search is not always easy. As I look for meaning in my life, there is so much that puzzles and perplexes. The more I discover, the more I realise how little I have understood. Give me the determination of the wise men to keep on looking, despite all that obscures you, until at last I find my perseverance rewarded and I glimpse your glory and kneel before you in joyful worship. Amen.

Remember

For the moment we see but a riddle in a mirror, then we shall see face to face; now I see only in part, but then I will fully know just as I am fully known.   *1 Corinthians 13:12*

Close

Gracious God, may your light guide my footsteps along the pathway of life. May your hand be upon me and your love always enfold me, and so lead me safely onwards to know and love you better, to the glory of your name. Amen.

The God who seeks us out

Read

He told them this parable: 'If a man had a hundred sheep and lost one of them, wouldn't he leave the ninety-nine in the desert and go in search of the one that is lost until he finds it? And, when it is found, he places it over his shoulders rejoicing. And then, coming home, he calls together his friends and neighbours, saying, "Rejoice with me, for I have found my sheep that was lost." In exactly the same way, I assure you that there will be more joy in heaven over one sinner coming to repentance than over ninety-nine righteous people who have no need to repent.'

Luke 15:3-7

Ponder

Why is it that when you drop something it always falls into the most awkward and inaccessible of places? Instead of falling into the middle of the room, somehow it invariably ends up in some obscure nook or cranny, never to be found again. How long we are willing to keep on looking for it depends on the item in question. If it's a penny piece, we'll soon shrug and forget all about it; a gold ring, on the other hand, and we'll keep on looking for many weeks, probably always hoping that it will finally turn up. Few if any of us, however, will keep on looking for ever.

Yet that is the wonderful picture that Jesus paints of God in the three parables of Luke 15: the Lost Sheep, the Lost Coin and the Lost Son. God, we are told, is like the shepherd who goes on looking for his lost sheep 'until he has found it'! What a wonderful picture that is – a truly astonishing testimony to God's amazing grace! Here is the 'love that will not let me go' of which the hymn-writer George Matheson speaks; a love that goes on looking for us whenever we go astray; never resting and never giving up until we have been restored to the Father's side. It is a love unlike anything else we can ever know.

Ask yourself

Do you worry about what the future may hold, or have you learned to rest secure in the knowledge that, whatever may happen, God will be with you in it, nothing finally able to separate you from his love?

Pray

Lord Jesus Christ, thank you for the way you watch over me throughout my life, the way you are continually there to guard and guide me, whatever I may face. When I wander far from your side, you do not abandon me to my fate but instead come looking for me, your love refusing to let me go. Though I may forsake you, you never forsake me. Though I am faithless, you remain faithful. I praise you for that great truth, and ask forgiveness for the areas in my life in which I continue to go astray. Help me to follow you more closely in the days ahead, to the glory of your name. Amen.

Remember

This is what the Sovereign Lord says: 'I will personally search for my sheep and take care of them. Just as a shepherd searches for his sheep should his flock be scattered, so I will go in search of my sheep and rescue them, no matter where they have been scattered in dark and dismal days. I will search for the lost and bring back those who have strayed.'   *Ezekiel 34:11-12, 16a*

Close

Gracious God, I praise you for the assurance that though I may sometimes lose sight of you, you will never lose sight of me. Watch over me, and lead me safely through my journey of life. Through Jesus Christ my Lord. Amen.

Reflecting Christ

Read

Because the veil has been taken from our faces, we all reflect the Lord's glory like a mirror, and we are being transfigured to be ever more like him, from glory to glory, through the Lord who is Spirit.   *2 Corinthians 3:18*

Ponder

What do you get when you look in the mirror each morning? More likely than not, an unwelcome shock! Yet, where would we be without mirrors? Try shaving, combing your hair or cleaning your teeth without one and you'll soon realise how important they are to us. It's not, however, only glass that can reflect things; there's water, metal and plastic – and people too. We talk about actions reflecting well or badly on somebody, and we also recognise that the things we say and do may be taken as a reflection on others, whether parents, family, friends or associates.

It was very much this latter idea that Paul had in mind in his second letter to the Corinthians in what were, at once, both simple yet truly astounding words. We, he said, reflect Christ's glory! Is that true of us? Do people glimpse anything of Christ in our lives, let alone see his glory reflected in us? The trouble is, of course, that mirrors don't always do their job. They mist over, crack, even distort an image, so that what we see in them is a travesty of our true reflection. Too easily, the same is true in our lives – the picture of Jesus we present to the world unrecognisable from the Lord we are meant to be serving. So, next time you look in the mirror, as well as considering your own reflection, think also about how far your life is reflecting something of Jesus to those around you.

Ask yourself

Is the picture you give to the world the one you think you are giving? Are you conscious that the way you live is a daily reflection on Christ?

Pray

Almighty God, through Christ you have demonstrated the wonder of your goodness, the awesome extent of your love. You call me to follow in his footsteps – to reflect through my life and witness more of that same gracious love. Forgive me for failing to do that – for failing to show in my life the faith I profess with my lips. Forgive me that all too often the picture I give is a feeble caricature, a pathetic parody of the Lord I so hunger to serve.

Take, then, what I am and, by your grace, make me what I long to be, so that I may truly bring glory to you. Through Jesus Christ my Lord. Amen.

Remember

Let the light within you shine before others so that they may see the good deeds you do and give glory to your heavenly Father.   *Matthew 5:16*

Close

Lord Jesus Christ, may your grace redeem me, your power renew me, your example inspire me, and your love shine from me. Send me out, renewed in faith, to walk in your way and make you known, to the glory of your name. Amen.

Taken on trust

Read

Gideon said to God, 'To test whether you will indeed deliver Israel by my hand, as you have promised, I am going to put a fleece of wool down on the threshing-floor. If there is dew only on the fleece and the ground is entirely dry, then I shall know that you will deliver Israel through me, just as you have said.' Sure enough, that is what happened. When Gideon rose at dawn the next day and squeezed the fleece, he wrung enough dew from it to fill a bowl with water. Then Gideon said to God, 'Please don't lose your temper with me; permit me to speak again. Allow me to make one more trial with the fleece. This time may the fleece alone be dry and the ground be covered all over with dew.' And that night God did exactly what he asked. Only the fleece was dry; the ground everywhere was wet with dew.   *Judges 6:36-40*

Ponder

Few things are more difficult than living by faith. The idea sounds wonderful, but when it comes to the moment of decision most of us prefer certainties to promise. If that's true in our human relationships, it's equally so in our dealings with God. Which of us at some time or other hasn't asked for a sign: some clear, unmistakable indication that we have understood his will correctly and taken the right path? Such an attitude is perfectly natural – but it is not faith. It betrays, ultimately, a lack of assurance in God's sovereign purpose – a purpose that, for our own well-being, we must learn to take on trust.

Ask yourself

How often have you attempted to bargain with God? How ready are you to let God have his way in your life?

Pray

Gracious God, like your servant Gideon, I often feel uncertain about the way ahead. I see problems rather than opportunities. I remember failure instead of success. I am filled with doubt rather than faith. Like Gideon, once again, I crave a sign, some assurance that you will see me safely through. Forgive me for finding it so hard to trust you, for so easily forgetting all you have done for me. I do not deserve any proof, yet so often in your mercy you provide the sign I am looking for. Teach me at such times to follow without reserve, and grant that I may draw closer to you until I need no further confirmation of your purpose than the daily, living reality of your presence. Amen.

Remember

Now faith is the guarantee of things hoped for, the proof of things not seen. *Hebrews 11:1*

Close

Sovereign God, teach me to trust in you even when I cannot see the way ahead. Help me to walk in faith, even when faith seems foolish. Grant me grace to entrust myself into your everlasting arms in the assurance that you will be sufficient for all my needs. Through Jesus Christ my Lord. Amen.

The extra mile

Read

If anyone decides to sue you and take your coat, let them
have your cloak as well, and whoever forces you to go one
mile, go with them a second also. Give to whoever begs, and
do not turn away anyone wishing to borrow from you.

Matthew 5:40-41

Ponder

The sign was quite specific: Taunton 84 miles. Still a long
way to go, then, but having driven over one hundred miles
already, at least we were over half-way home. I set the mileo-
meter to nought so that I could keep track of our progress
and ploughed onwards, hoping that the children would stay
asleep in the back. Thirty miles further on (I'd counted every
one!) and another sign: Taunton 59 miles. To our dismay,
another five miles had crept in somewhere and, to cap it
all, Kate had woken up and started screaming in protest!

To go further than one expects is never easy, even if it's
only a car journey, but when Jesus spoke to the crowd in
the Sermon on the Mount he had in mind something far
more demanding than that. A Roman soldier had the right,
in law, to compel any subject to carry his armour and
accessories for one mile – no more, no less. It was a heavy
physical load to bear, but in Jewish eyes what was worse
was the way it brought home their status as an occupied
nation, an enslaved people. Yet here was Jesus telling them
not just to do what was required but to go far beyond it, to
fall over themselves to help. That advice applied not just
then but is equally valid now. Don't just do what you *have*
to do, Jesus tells us; look whenever you can to do more; to
do that little bit extra; to put yourself out for the sake of
others. It's not easy advice, is it? Most of us prefer to serve
ourselves before thinking of anyone else. But the way of

Christ is the way of sacrifice, of giving without counting the cost, of always being ready to go the extra mile.

Ask yourself
How ready are you to put yourself out for someone else? How far is your faith just talk and how far are you ready to put it into practice?

Pray
Living God, you challenge me through Jesus to go the extra mile, to do more than is asked or expected of me. Forgive me that I find that so hard: that more often than not I do as little as possible rather than as much; that I give my help, time, service and money grudgingly rather than cheerfully. I praise you for the readiness of Christ to go not just the extra mile but to give his all, identifying himself with my humanity, willingly experiencing suffering and death so that I might discover life in its fullness.

Thank you for all those I have known who have been prepared to go the extra mile – among family and friends, within the fellowship of the Church, or in the wider world – all those who go beyond the call of duty in the service of others. Touch my heart through their example and inspire me through the love of Christ, so that I may be more ready to live as one of his people. Teach me in turn to do that little bit extra, to go beyond people's expectations, to give as you have given to me in Christ. In his name I ask it. Amen.

Remember
The truth is this: whoever sows sparingly will also reap sparingly, while the one who sows liberally will also reap liberally.   *2 Corinthians 9:6*

Close
Lord Jesus Christ, you didn't just go the extra mile – you gave everything, enduring death on a cross so that I might live. Work within me and help me to be willing to give something of myself in the service of others. As I have received from you, so now teach me to give. For your name's sake. Amen.

First things first

Read

Consider how you have fared. You have sown much, but have harvested little. You eat, but never have as much as you would like. You drink, but never have your fill. You clothe yourselves, but are never warm. You earn wages, but it is as though you put them into a bag full of holes. You look for much, but it comes to little; and what you bring home, I blow away. Why? says the Lord of hosts. Because my house lies derelict while each of you rush off to your own houses.

Haggai 1:6, 9

Ponder

We live today, so we are told, in an age of rampant materialism, an era in which everyone is always grasping after the newest gadget, the latest fashion, the most up-to-date model.

It is difficult to argue with such an assessment of modern society, but is the phenomenon as new as we sometimes tend to make out? The book of Haggai suggests not. As we read through its pages, we could well be reading a socioeconomic analysis of Britain today, such are the similarities in tone. The technology and resources at our disposal may be far greater than those in Haggai's time, but the underlying cravings are no different. Greed, materialism – call it what you will – is an age-old, and probably universal, characteristic, yet the irony is that it rarely seems to bring happiness, all too often indeed the reverse. Creature comforts have their place, as Haggai would I'm sure have been the first to accept, but if we put these before our spiritual needs the result is a never-ending striving for an inner fulfilment which will forever remain tantalisingly out of reach.

Ask yourself

What comes first in your life? Where does God rank in your list of priorities? Does the way you live lend support to your answer?

Pray

Loving God, in all the stress and rush of life it is so easy to forget you and to lose my way. In the press of each day I allow you to be crowded out, preoccupied instead with my own problems and concerns, my own plans and needs. Only, suddenly I stop and find that I am alone, burdened and troubled, weighed down by guilt and uncertainty, unable to cope with the demands put upon me. My thoughts are turned in on myself rather than up towards you and out to the world. Teach me to untangle myself from the snare of self-interest and to put you at the centre of my life. Teach me to put first things first. Amen.

Remember

Do not be anxious, saying, 'What will we eat?' or 'What will we drink?' or 'What will we wear?' But seek first the kingdom and righteousness of God, and you shall be given all of these in addition.   *Matthew 6:31a, 33*

Close

Lord Jesus Christ, go with me now and help me to walk the way of discipleship. Equip me with the faith to offer my life to you, focusing on the things that really matter, and so may I discover life in all its fullness. In your name I pray. Amen.

Anger

Read

Give vent to anger, yet do not sin; never let the sun set on your anger, thus making room for the devil.

Ephesians 4:26-27

Ponder

There can be few of us who, at some time, do not lose our temper. For those cursed with a short fuse it can be a common occurrence, whilst for those of a more phlegmatic disposition it may be something of a rarity, but all of us have our threshold where something snaps inside and we fly into a rage.

There is, of course, a place for anger, as Jesus showed on more than one occasion during his ministry. Confronted with evil and injustice, actions or attitudes that prevent people from living life to the full, it is not only natural but necessary. Yet more often than not anger is sparked by very different motives – wounded pride, frustration, intolerance, an unwillingness to face the truth, or simply misunderstanding. It doesn't take much to send the blood rushing to our heads, but it can take a great deal to put right the consequences of one moment's madness.

Ask yourself

Do you tend to get angry about things which don't really matter? Do you ever get angry about the things that really do?

Pray

Lord, we are not good at showing anger; at least, not as it is meant to be shown. We are ready enough to show our temper, easily riled by the most innocuous of things, and capable, at our worst, of destructive fits of rage, but such anger is rarely justified, almost always serving merely to give vent to our own feelings at the cost of someone else's.

Your anger is so very different, being not about yourself but us. You see injustice and exploitation, and your blood boils for the oppressed. You see the peddling of drugs and pornography, and your heart burns within you at the innocent led astray. You see hatred, violence, cruelty, and your spirit seethes for those caught up in its wake. Whatever destroys hope, denies love or despoils life arouses wrath within you. Teach me to share that anger and to channel it in your service, committing myself to do all in my power to fight against evil, and striving for your kingdom. Through Jesus Christ my Lord. Amen.

Remember

Whoever controls their anger shows great understanding; a hot temper is the height of folly! Those who are short-tempered stir up discord, but those who are patient calm division. A foolish person gives their anger full rein, but the wise person gives it time to cool down.

Proverbs 14:29; 15:18; 29:11

Close

Living God, teach me when it is right to be angry: to rage against the things in life that demean and destroy; that feed injustice and further exploitation; that cheat, corrupt, wound and hurt; that lead the innocent astray and divide people from one another and from you. Yet, teach me also when anger is foolish and petty, more about my hurt pride than right and wrong, about myself than the cause I attribute anger to. Save me, then, from the errors it might lead me into – thoughtless words, careless deeds, and destructive attitudes – and help me to control such anger before it controls me. Through Jesus Christ my Lord. Amen.

An unexpected encounter

Read

Jacob left Beersheba and set off towards Haran. He reached a certain spot and stopped off there for the night, because the sun had gone down. Taking a stone he found there, he tucked it under his head and lay down in that place. And in his dreams he saw a ladder rising up from the ground, its top reaching into heaven, the angels of God climbing up and down it. And the Lord appeared, standing beside him, and said, 'I am the Lord, the God of your father Abraham and the God of Isaac . . .' Jacob woke and said, 'Surely the Lord is in this place, and I didn't know it!' And he was afraid, and said, 'How awe-inspiring is this place!' It is nothing less than the house of God, the very gate of heaven.'

Genesis 28:10-13a, 16-17

Ponder

Of all the great figures of the Old Testament, few showed less initial promise than Jacob. He comes across as an opportunist and a cheat, callously tricking his brother Esau out of his birthright, and then compounding this with the shameful deception of his father. As he made his way towards Haran, it was, no doubt, with a smug sense of self-satisfaction at having secured the prospect of a highly prosperous future. The last thing on his mind would have been God.

God, though, had other ideas, confronting him during the night in a vivid and unforgettable dream. It was the beginning of a gradual change in Jacob's life. No, he didn't change overnight – far from it. He continued in many ways to be the wily schemer of old. Yet the seeds had been sown; God had met with him and opened up a new perspective on life and the beginning of a new relationship. It was one, ultimately, that would see Jacob revered as one of the founding fathers of the Jewish faith and a celebrated 'man of God'.

Ask yourself
Are there times when you have been suddenly aware of God's presence? Is he trying to break into your life?

Pray
Living God, I thank you that before ever I thought of seeking you, you sought me. I praise you that you had time for me even when I lived only for myself. Teach me that you are always at work in my life, ready to confront me with your searching presence when I least expect it, and challenging me to consider who you are and what you mean in my life.

Grant me, then, eyes to see you and a heart to respond. Through Jesus Christ my Lord. Amen.

Remember
The Lord searches the mind, and understands every plan and thought.   *1 Chronicles 28:9b*

Close
Gracious God, though I forget you, do not forget me. Meet with me and help me to glimpse again your glory. Through Jesus Christ my Lord. Amen.

God is able

Read

Then in a blinding rage, Nebuchadnezzar ordered Shadrach, Meshach and Abednego to be brought in; so they were brought before the king. Nebuchadnezzar said to them, 'Is it true, Shadrach, Meshach and Abednego, that you do not serve my gods or worship the golden statue I have had erected?' Shadrach, Meshach and Abednego answered the king, 'O Nebuchadnezzar, we have no need to answer to you concerning this matter. If any god is able to deliver us from the fiery furnace, then it is our God, and he will deliver us from your hand, O king. But if not, let us tell you this, O king, we will not serve your gods and will not worship the golden image that you have set up.'   *Daniel 3:13-14, 16-18*

Ponder

The story of Shadrach, Meshach and Abednego is one of the great biblical classics, an unforgettable tale of courage and the triumph of good over evil that has captured the hearts of countless generations. Yet, as with all classics, there is a danger that familiarity may inure us to the full impact of the underlying message. We read the story, knowing the outcome of events – for Shadrach, Meshach and Abednego there was no such luxury. They staked all in the faith that God would deliver them, risking death itself rather than compromising their convictions.

Have we that same conviction of God's purpose? Do we have even a fraction of their astonishing trust? They knew that whatever trials they might face and whatever conspired against God's purpose, nothing finally could thwart his purpose. Remember that next time you feel up against it, the demands of life too great and your resources to meet them too small. Remember that we too can say with confidence, 'If any god is able to deliver us then it is our God.'

Ask yourself

Are you willing to put your trust in God, even though it may mean putting yourself at risk? Do you still have a sense of God's power at work, both in your life and the life of the world?

Pray

Sovereign God, I thank you that whatever I may face, whatever dangers may threaten me, you are able to deliver me from evil. In life and in death you are by my side, nothing able to separate me from the wonder of your love. Help me, then, to trust you always, to love you unswervingly and to honour you each day with faithful and committed service, to the glory of your name. Amen.

Remember

Now to the one who, through his sovereign power, is able to do incalculably more than we can begin to ask or even think of, to him be glory in the Church and in Christ Jesus in this and every generation. Amen.   *Ephesians 3:20*

Close

God of past, present and future, help me to remember all you have done, to rejoice in all you are doing, and to trust in all you shall yet do. Teach me to put my hand in yours and to walk with you wherever you may lead, knowing that you will walk by my side, this day and always. Amen.

A God of surprises

Read

You will have heard of my former conduct within Judaism
– how I vigorously persecuted and laid waste the church of
God and how I progressed in Judaism beyond most of my
contemporaries, defending the tradition of my fathers with
a fanatical zeal. But when the one who had set me apart in
my mother's womb graciously chose to reveal his Son
through me, calling me to proclaim him among all nations,
I did not consult with flesh and blood. I went into the
regions of Syria and Cilicia, though I was unknown by sight
to those in Christ in the churches of Judea. All they had
heard was this: 'The one who was previously persecuting us
is now preaching the very faith he aimed to destroy!' And
they glorified God concerning me.

Galatians 1:13-16, 21-24

Ponder

Imagine what it must have been like to be a Christian at the
time Saul was sweeping through Judea, intent on destroying
the Church. Assuming you had clung on to your faith despite
the knowledge that it might cost you your life, what would
your prayer have been? Would it have been for grace to bear
martyrdom with courage, or perhaps for Jesus to return
and establish his kingdom, or maybe for Saul to be struck
down? It might have been for all or any of those, but what
you probably wouldn't have prayed for is what actually
happened – that Saul, the arch-persecutor of the Church
would become, arguably, the greatest ambassador it has
ever had. Such a thing, you would have thought, was surely
too much to ask for.

Throughout the scriptures, God has a habit of springing
surprises, working in ways that defy human expectation or
understanding, and so it continues today. A situation may

seem beyond hope, a person beyond redemption, a problem beyond solution, but in each case that is to reckon without God. Never, ever underestimate his capacity to catch us unawares; what may seem impossible to us is always possible to him!

Ask yourself

Are you open to God overturning your expectations? Have you mistakenly set limits to the way you think God is able to work?

Pray

Loving God, I did not choose you – you chose me. You are the one who opens the way for me to know you, who breaks down the barriers that keep us apart, who holds the future in your hands. Help me to remember that and to be open to all the possibilities it presents. Save me from presumptuously limiting you to my own narrow expectations, or from thinking that I can map out my destiny. Teach me that you are a God of the unexpected, a God always waiting with new surprises to enrich my life. Amen.

Remember

O the depths of the riches and wisdom and knowledge of God; how unfathomable are his judgements and mysterious his ways. For who has known the Lord's mind, or who has been his counsellor, or who has given to him that they should be repaid? From him and to him and through him belong all things; to him be glory for all time. Amen.

Romans 11:33-36

Close

Sovereign God, go with me and continue to surprise me each day by the extent of your love, the awesomeness of your power, the generosity of your mercy and the graciousness of your purpose. Through Jesus Christ my Lord. Amen.

Living in peace

Read

How good and pleasant it is when kindred live together in unity! It is as fragrant as oil poured over the head and running down upon the beard, running down the beard of Aaron and over the collar of his robes. It is like the dew of Hermon falling on the mountains of Zion. There the Lord grants his blessing, life for all eternity.

Psalm 133

Ponder

There are few things more sad, yet more common, than a family divided amongst itself. Yet it's something we see over and over again: husbands who no longer speak to wives; children who have fallen out with their parents; brothers, sisters, cousins, nephews, aunts and uncles, each disowning the other and refusing to have any further dealings with them. As if that isn't sad enough, invariably the cause of such bad feeling is something trivial, blown up out of all proportion over the years because of an unwillingness to meet and resolve the issue. Unchecked, the poison festers, feeding on itself and destroying the lives of all concerned.

Whether it was a dispute such as this that inspired Psalm 133, or whether it was something more complex, I do not know. The reminder this simple psalm gives of the importance of living together in harmony is, however, one we would all do well to consider, whether at the level of our immediate family or the family of the Church. The relationships we are intended to enjoy in both are special; we simply cannot afford to waste them.

Ask yourself

Are you estranged from someone as the result of a dispute or disagreement? What's stopping you from mending the quarrel? Isn't it time you made your peace?

Pray

Lord, it's easy to start a quarrel, so much harder to end it. It's easy to see faults in others, far more difficult to see them in myself. It's easy to destroy relationships, almost impossible to build them again once they have been broken.

Forgive me the weaknesses that so often create divisions, that separate me not simply from my fellow human beings but sometimes even from my own family and friends. Help me, so far as it lies with me, to live in harmony with all, and when that harmony is broken teach me to act as peace-maker, healing hurts, restoring trust and breaking down barriers. In the name of Christ, who shall come to reconcile all things to himself. Amen.

Remember

If possible, and so far as it's down to you, live peaceably with everyone.   *Romans 12:18*

Close

Lord of all, forgive me everything that separates me from those around me – my pride, fear, envy and suspicion; my unwillingness to accept new ideas and refusal ever to countenance I could be wrong. Forgive me my share in the brokenness of this world, my contribution to its wounds, scars and continuing pain. Open my heart to others through being open to you, and so may I pursue all that makes for peace until that day when you come in Christ to establish your kingdom and make all things new. In his name I pray. Amen.

Getting the message

Read

The Lord called Samuel, and he answered, 'Here I am', and ran to Eli, saying, 'You called me. I'm here.' But Eli said, 'I didn't call; lie down again.' So he went and lay down. The Lord called Samuel again, and he got up and went to Eli once more, saying, 'Here I am, for you called me.' But he said, 'No, I didn't call, my son; lie down again.' At this time, Samuel had not yet come to know the Lord, and the word of the Lord had not been made known to him. The Lord called Samuel a third time, and once more he got up and went to Eli, and said, 'Here I am. You did call me.' Then Eli realised that the Lord was calling the boy, so he told Samuel, 'Go and lie down; and if he should call again, say, "Speak, Lord, for your servant is listening."' So Samuel went and lay down in his place.   *1 Samuel 3:4-9*

Ponder

What would have happened to Samuel, I wonder, had it not been for Eli? Would he finally have realised that the voice he heard was God calling him, or would he have gone on for ever imagining it was someone else speaking to him? It's an interesting thought, and one that highlights the on-going problem of recognising God's voice. Many people believe themselves called to something when it is patently clear to others that they are mistaken. Equally, there are some who appear manifestly called by God yet who, for reasons best known to themselves, cannot or will not believe it. Samuel's story reminds us that even the greatest spiritual leaders are by no means always certain when God is speaking to them. Equally important, they remind us that it can take a third party to help us recognise God's call. Sometimes others can see what he is saying to us more clearly than we can see it ourselves.

Ask yourself

Are you open to the guidance of others in relation to what God might be asking of you? Is he perhaps calling you to some area of service at present?

Pray

Living God, time and again I ask you to speak to me, to reveal your will and give me your guidance, but all too often when your call comes I fail to recognise it. Though I talk of prayer being a two-way encounter, the reality is usually different; I seldom seriously expect to hear your voice. Give me a readiness to be guided by the wisdom of others so that I may both recognise your voice and understand what you are saying. In the name of Christ. Amen.

Remember

If you hear my voice and open the door, I will come in and eat with you, and you with me.   *Revelation 3:20*

Close

Gracious God, speak to me now and help me to listen. Open my ears to all the ways your voice may come, and then, like Samuel, teach me to respond in faith. For Jesus' sake. Amen.

A small price to pay

Read

A certain ruler questioned him, 'Good Teacher, what do I need to do to inherit eternal life?' Jesus said to him, 'Why do you call me good? Only God is good, no one else. You know the commandments: "Do not commit adultery; do not murder; do not steal; do not bear false witness; honour your father and mother."' The man replied, 'I have kept all these since I was a boy.' Hearing this, Jesus said to him, 'There is one thing still missing. Sell everything you own and share the money among the poor, and you will have treasure in heaven; then come, follow me.' But, hearing this, the man became sad, for he was exceedingly wealthy. Jesus looked at him and said, 'How hard it is for the well-to-do to enter the kingdom of God! Truly, it is easier for a camel to pass through the eye of a needle than for a rich person to enter the kingdom of God.'   *Luke 18:18-25*

Ponder

Does the story of the rich ruler make you uneasy? It does me. Despite the fact that many rationalise its message, essentially suggesting that it should be understood today as a hypothetical challenge rather than a generally applicable principle, it is impossible to escape the feeling that these words of Jesus represent a forcible challenge to our comfortable twenty-first-century lifestyles. Of course money isn't everything, we tell ourselves. Of course we'd happily give it up if asked. But would we? I doubt it very much.

Thankfully, Jesus probably doesn't want us to give up all our possessions; the economic and social consequences, if we did, would be alarming. Yet, it is equally probable that he wants us to give up a lot more than we are usually prepared to sacrifice. In a world of massive poverty and suffering, in which the divide between rich and poor grows wider every day, can any of us really say we are doing enough? When we think of what Jesus gave for us, how does our giving to others compare? The price asked of the rich ruler may seem large but it is small contrasted to that. No wonder the story makes us uncomfortable.

Ask yourself

Have you ever given sacrificially? Would you be willing to go hungry so that another might be fed; to go without a little so that others may have much?

Pray

Gracious God, no one can ever give us more than you have given, for you have blessed us with life itself – life over-flowing with good things, life eternal – and to make that gift possible you gave of yourself, not just a little but all. You bore the limitations of human flesh; you endured rejection, humiliation and finally death on a cross; and, most awesome of all, through Christ you took on yourself the dreadful burden of this world's sinfulness, experiencing the despair and isolation that brings.

Forgive me that, despite all this, I give so grudgingly in return. Forgive me that though my words say one thing my life says another. Forgive me that so often my thoughts are little for you and still less for others. Help me to catch again a glimpse of the love that you have so freely given and so may I spontaneously give of myself in joyful and heartfelt thanksgiving. Through Jesus Christ my Lord. Amen.

Remember

The one who exploits the needy offends his Maker, but happy is the one who is kind to the poor.   *Proverbs 14:21*

Close

God of justice, quicken my conscience and stir my heart so that I may show my faith not simply in easy words but in costly actions. Teach me what it means to deny myself and, in doing so, may I bring joy, help and hope to others. Through Jesus Christ my Lord. Amen.

The Lord of life

Read

Jesus said, 'Remove the stone', but Mary, the sister of the deceased, exclaimed, 'Lord, there is already a stench because he has been dead for four days.' Jesus said to her, 'Didn't I tell you that you will see the glory of God if you believe?' So they took away the stone. He cried with a loud voice, 'Lazarus, come out!' The dead man came out, his hands and his feet bound with strips of cloth, and his face wrapped in a cloth. Jesus said to them, 'Release the bindings, and let him go.'

John 11:39-41a, 43-44

Ponder

What wouldn't I give to believe! When it comes to resurrection and eternal life, I've heard words like those countless times. Even the most avowed atheist or agnostic would like to believe there is something after this life; that death is not the end. Yet most, if they do not laugh derisively at such an idea, shake their heads wistfully at any suggestion it might be true.

So it was quite understandably for the family of Lazarus. They had watched him die and seen him sealed in his tomb; and with that, all hope had gone. Yet, suddenly, here was Jesus, ordering that the stone be rolled away, and, all at once, there was Lazarus before them, alive and well. It was a sign of things to come, a pointer to the empty tomb and the ultimate triumph over death in the resurrection of Christ – not just revival this time but resurrection, life for all eternity; and with it the promise of new life for all who follow him. We do not understand how it can be or what form that life will take, but, thankfully, it does not depend on our faith, but rests solely with Christ – the one who alone can say, 'I am the resurrection and the life.'

Ask yourself

Is your faith based on surmise and supposition or on the testimony of scripture and personal experience?

Pray

Lord Jesus Christ, you promise new life to those who follow you – not just a different quality of life here and now, though that is a part of it, but life beyond the grave, life eternal. Thank you for the way you foreshadowed that promise during your earthly ministry, demonstrating your sovereign, life-giving power. You raised Lazarus, you raised the daughter of Jairus, you raised the son of a widow, and finally after three days in the tomb, you rose yourself! Through word and deed, you have given us the assurance that nothing in life or in death can ever separate us from your love.

Lord Jesus Christ, the resurrection and the life, I praise you. Amen.

Remember

Jesus said, 'I am the resurrection and the life; anyone who believes in me, even though they should die, will live; and whoever lives and believes in me will never die.

John 11:25-26

Close

Lord Jesus Christ, may new life be born within me today and every day, and may your life-giving hope sustain me through the joys and sorrows of this world until that time I pass through the shadow of death into the light of your eternal kingdom. Amen.

Light in our darkness

Read

Job resumed his discourse, saying, 'If only I could go back to the way things were, to those days when God watched over me; when his lamp shone over my head and I walked by its light through the darkness. If it could be like when I was in my prime, when God encircled my tent; when the Almighty was still beside me and my children surrounded me; when my footsteps were awash with milk, and the rock gushed out streams of oil for me! Now my soul is empty within me; despair holds me each day in its grip. My bones are racked night after night by a remorseless pain. God himself has cast me into the mire, discarded like dust and ashes.'   *Job 29:1-6; 30:16, 19*

Ponder

The book of Job is one of the more unusual books of the Bible. It does not offer memorable promises or assurances of blessing. It does not deal with mighty deeds or glorious conquests. Instead, it wrestles with the age-old problem of suffering, and it does so in what is, at times, a brutally stark manner. Whatever else, the book does not pull its punches, Job speaking his mind with a frankness that can shock the unsuspecting reader. It is, though, perhaps for this reason that many have found the underlying message of Job so helpful, for it tackles a universal conundrum with a refreshing honesty. There are no pat answers, no simplistic attempts to explain the inexplicable. Instead, there is a blunt admission that some things in life are beyond our comprehension. We cannot and do not always understand the way God works.

Yet we are not left entirely high and dry. Despite the traumas he endured, Job ultimately found his faith deepened and his awareness of God enriched. The journey was undeniably painful, but he emerged stronger and wiser for it.

The mystery is not fully resolved, yet some sense is made of it: out of darkness God brings light; out of evil, something good; out of despair, hope. If that was true for the writer of Job, how much more so is it true for us today in the light of the suffering and death of Christ.

Ask yourself
Is yours a fair-weather faith, or one that will be able to stand in the storms of life? Are you able to see life at its darkest and still believe that somehow God is there?

Pray
Gracious God, you came to our world through Jesus Christ, and despite everything that conspires against you, your love continues to shine through him. You conquered the forces of evil, you overcame the sting of death, and you brought joy out of sorrow, hope out of despair.

Teach me, whatever I may face, to hold on to that truth, confident that you will always lead me out of darkness into your marvellous light. Hold on to me when life is hard, and assure me that you are present even in the bleakest moments, able to use every moment of each day in ways beyond my imagining. Amen.

Remember
In this rejoice, even if temporarily you have to endure a multitude of trials, so that the substance of your faith – more priceless than gold, which, even though it is perishable, is refined by fire – may be found to bring praise, glory and honour to God when Jesus Christ is revealed. *1 Peter 1:6-7*

Close
Sovereign God, hold on to me in all the changes and chances of life. Help me to put my hand in yours, knowing that you are there, sharing my experience and able to see me finally through. Through Jesus Christ my Lord. Amen.

The divine seal

Read

When you heard the word of truth, the good news of salvation, and believed in him, you likewise were marked with the seal of the Holy Spirit – the guarantee of our inheritance when God redeems his people, to the praise of his glory. *Ephesians 1:13-14*

Ponder

A while back I received a letter in the morning post, the seal of which had somehow come unstuck in transit. Whether it had gone to a wrong address and been opened by mistake or whether it had not been properly stuck in the first place wasn't clear, but what interested me was a sticker over the envelope bearing an apology from the Post Office. Clearly the fact that the seal had been broken was considered a serious thing, serious enough to merit some kind of formal acknowledgement. As it turned out, the contents of the letter were unimportant, just another of those innumerable circulars that turn up with such monotonous regularity, but the incident shed new light for me on the words of Paul to the Ephesians. If a seal is important today, it was ten times more so in his time, the personal seal of an important dignitary or official often bearing the impression of the sender and investing a document with that sender's authority. It guaranteed safe passage and the authenticity of what lay within.

So it is with the gift God has sent in Christ. The promise of mercy, renewal and new life in him is given by God's authority and with his guarantee. He has accomplished all that needs to be done, overcoming everything that comes between us. The promise is sure, the inheritance certain – signed and sealed.

Ask yourself
Do you lose sight sometimes of the assurance God has given to every Christian believer? Do you fail to show the trust in him that you should?

Pray
Gracious God, I praise you that in the shifting sands of time your purpose remains sure; that though all else may change, your love will never alter. For the assurance you give me of your love in Christ, and for making that new each day through the living presence of your Holy Spirit, receive my thanks. Teach me to live every moment in the light of your goodness, and so to be at one with you and myself, through Jesus Christ my Lord. Amen.

Remember
God's foundation stands sure, bearing this seal: The Lord knows those who are his.   *2 Timothy 2:19*

Close
Loving God, may the inner presence of your Holy Spirit convince me ever more each day of the certainty of your promises, and so may my faith be deepened, my knowledge of Christ be enriched, my soul rejoice and my heart be at peace. For his name's sake. Amen.

God's part

Read

He said, 'The kingdom of God is like this: as if someone scattered seed on the earth, and should then sleep and rise night and day; the seed sprouts and grows though that person has no idea how. The earth bears fruit without any further assistance; first a blade of grass, then an ear and then a full head of corn within the ear.'

Mark 4:26-28

Ponder

I will never forget the first time I tried my hand at horticulture. I had recently started at college, and my mother had given me some tradescantia cuttings from home. It seemed impossible that those spindly stems with just a couple of leaves attached could ever grow into new plants but, obediently, I planted them and placed them on a windowsill, more in hope than expectation. To my surprise, a couple of weeks later they had developed roots and, before I knew it, they had formed thriving bushy plants that went on to grace my mantelpiece for the remaining four years of my college course.

In that, alone, is a demonstration of God's creative power, but we can apply the principle far more widely. So often, he works behind the scenes in ways far beyond our imagining. Though we cannot see it, let alone understand how it happens, he takes the most unpromising of materials or situations and creates out of them something unrecognisable from that with which he started. If life were determined solely by human hands, and our own destiny shaped entirely by our own efforts, what a sorry state of affairs it would be. If we had to tackle the problems we face without any assistance, or respond to God's call in our own strength, how bleak the prospect would seem. Thank God, in his sovereign power he is able to work without any other assistance to fulfil his will and accomplish his purpose!

Ask yourself

Is life getting on top of you – the problems mounting up so that you feel unable to cope? Are you expecting too much of yourself? Are there things you need to leave in the hands of God?

Pray

Lord Jesus Christ, it is hard sometimes not to feel overwhelmed by the scale of the challenges I face and the obstacles that block my path. I am part of a world where faith is ridiculed and where your name is casually dismissed, a world in which people live for today with no thought of tomorrow and in which good seems overpowered by evil. Instead of truth, there is falsehood; instead of love, hatred; instead of peace, division; instead of joy, sorrow; the dawn of your kingdom apparently further away than ever rather than drawing near.

Teach me, despite everything, not to lose heart. Help me to understand that I have a part in your purpose but that the final victory is down to you. Give me strength to do what you ask of me as best I can and to leave the rest in your hands, confident that, though I may not see it, the seed you have sown is growing, and that the day will come when you will rule with the Father in your eternal kingdom – one God, world without end. Amen.

Remember

The Lord of Hosts has vowed: As I have planned, so shall it be; as I have designed, so shall it happen . . . the Lord of Hosts has devised his plan: who will frustrate it? His hand is extended, and who will turn it back?   *Isaiah 14:24, 27*

Close

The seed is sown, the kingdom is growing, the harvest will come. Loving God, I praise you for that knowledge, and in quiet trust I offer you my worship. Amen.

Our part

Read

Once sufficient time has been allowed for the fruit to develop, the farmer immediately sets to with the sickle, because the time for harvest has come. *Mark 4:29*

Ponder

It would be good if every horticultural endeavour were as successful as the one considered yesterday but, sadly, it is not always the case. A failure to qualify that first scenario would leave a dangerously unbalanced picture. There have been times when I have planted cuttings and they have failed to grow, when I have sown seeds and they have refused to germinate, when I have planted seedlings and they have curled up and died. Why? Because I have forgotten to water them or watered them too much; planted them in the wrong place or at the wrong time; overfed them or underfed them; and so I could go on. Although it is God, ultimately, who gives growth, there are times when he both needs and expects a helping hand. He could go it alone if he wanted to, but he invites us to share in his creative purpose, to be a part of his ongoing activity in human history. On the one hand, this is an awesome privilege; on the other, a daunting responsibility.

Before deciding that everything can be safely left in God's hand, consider an alternative possibility; maybe he's already done his bit and is depending on you to do yours!

Ask yourself

Do you see faith as being about what God can do for you rather than what you can do for him? Is it time you thought again about what Christian commitment entails?

Pray

Living God, I thank you that you are always at work in my life and in the world, constantly looking to fulfil your sovereign purpose. Forgive me that all too often I leave it at that, expecting you to do everything and forgetting the part I have to play if your will is to be done. Show me where you would have me serve, and help me to work with you for the growth of your kingdom and the sharing of your love. Through Jesus Christ my Lord. Amen.

Remember

You must become doers of the word rather than hearers only, thus misleading yourselves.   *James 1:22*

Close

Sovereign God, teach me not only how to pray but how to help make my prayers come true. Teach me to be your hands and feet, the agent of your purpose, and so work through me to the glory of your name. Through Jesus Christ my Lord. Amen.

OHMS

Read

Whatever you do, do it with all your being for the Lord rather than any person, since you know that you will receive an inheritance from the Lord as your reward. You serve the Lord Christ.   *Colossians 3:23-24*

Ponder

What does it mean to call Jesus 'Lord'? On the one hand, it means to honour him, to give him our praise and adoration, as summed up by the popular chorus 'Jesus, we enthrone you'. But it means more than that. It has something of the idea encapsulated in those four letters above: letters that stand, of course, for 'On her majesty's service'. Admittedly, when they are stamped on formal correspondence those initials are largely figurative: the Queen has no direct interest either way in our tax affairs, electoral intentions or other such matters. Yet, the efficient administration of such things is essential to the smooth running of any kingdom. No doubt the Queen would be highly gratified by the unbridled devotion of all her subjects, especially in an era when the monarchy is coming under ever-closer scrutiny, but I have no doubt also that what matters most to her is not adulation but service in its broadest sense.

I suspect the same may be true with Jesus. Of course, worship is vitally important, but if we leave it there, as we can so easily do, then it doesn't mean all that much. To call Jesus *Lord*, to honour him as king, ultimately means one thing: reaching out to the world 'on his majesty's service'!

Ask yourself

Can worship become an easy way out of offering service? Does the worship you offer show itself in the way you live?

Pray

Lord Jesus Christ, teach me what it means to acknowledge you as Lord. Help me to offer you the worship you deserve: to bring you my praise and homage, and to acknowledge you as King of kings and Lord of lords.

But help me also to offer you the service you deserve: to respond to everything you have done for me through working wholeheartedly for your kingdom, committing myself body, mind and soul to the fulfilment of your purpose and the making known of your love. Take me, and use me as you will, for your glory. Amen.

Remember

Not everyone saying to me, 'Lord, Lord' will enter the kingdom of heaven, but rather the one who does the will of my heavenly Father.   *Matthew 7:21*

Close

Lord Jesus Christ, help me to worship you not just for these few moments or in one small part of my life, but in all my words and deeds – through the person I am and the life I lead, the praise I bring you and the service I offer each day. In your name I ask it. Amen.

The unwelcome call

Read

The word of the Lord came to me, saying, 'Before I formed you in the womb I knew you, and before you were born I consecrated you; I appointed you to be a prophet to the nations.' Then I answered, 'Ah, Lord God! I don't know how to speak. I'm only a boy.' But the Lord responded, 'Do not say you're only a boy; for you will go to those I send you to, and you will speak to them the words I give you. Do not be afraid of them, for I will watch over you and protect you; you have my word.'   *Jeremiah 1:4-8*

Ponder

What would we give to have the faith of Moses or Samuel, Elijah or Isaiah? How much easier it would be to serve God then. How much clearer our path would be. Have you ever felt like that? If so, think again, for when you read the biblical accounts of God calling people to service, almost always the initial response is the same: not delight but dismay, not pleasure but panic, not thanksgiving but fear. Look closer, and it's hardly surprising, for, as we shall see later, the things God called people to do were onerous to say the least, nine times out of ten guaranteeing a less than enthusiastic reception. Few if any of those called considered themselves suited for the job, and most would have ducked it given the chance. Yet God was to equip each one to meet the task set before them.

We too may find ourselves facing challenges we believe beyond us, God's call a disturbing experience rather than the joyride we might have hoped for. But, if we are ready to respond, then we, like those before us, will discover that when God asks us to do something, he gives us the resources we need to finish the job.

Ask yourself
Is God calling you to something you feel is beyond your capacity to meet? Are we looking at the situation through your eyes or God's?

Pray
Gracious God, I thank you that you have spoken throughout history, calling people to your service. Thank you for those who have had the courage to respond, even when that call has involved unpopularity, ridicule and persecution. Thank you that they were ordinary everyday people, just like me, hesitant, fearful, uncertain of their ability to do what you asked of them, yet receiving the strength they needed when they needed it.

Still today you call your people to challenging areas of service – to jobs they would rather not do, issues they would rather not face and messages they would rather not deliver. Yet, once again, you promise that you will give each one of your people the resources they need to meet the task. Give me, then, courage to hear your voice and respond to your call. Through Jesus Christ my Lord. Amen.

Remember
Do not worry about what you should say: the words will be given to you when you need them – not your own words but those of the Spirit of your Father speaking through you.   *Matthew 10:19-20*

Close
Gracious God, give me strength to answer your call. May I be ready, like so many before me, to respond in faith and follow where you might lead, to the glory of your name. Amen.

Bearing fruit

Read

He told this parable: 'A man, having planted a fig tree in his vineyard, came looking for fruit on it but found none. So he said to the vinedresser, "Look here! I've been coming here looking for fruit on this fig tree for the last three years, but I've found nothing. Chop it down! Why carry on letting it be a waste of space?" He replied, "Sir, leave it for this year, until I've had the chance to dig in some manure around it, and then let's see if it bears fruit next season. If not, you can chop it down."'

Luke 13:6-9

Ponder

What sort of comments did you get on your school reports? For me there was one remark that seemed to reappear with depressing regularity: 'Shows promise, but could do better'. Does that ring a bell? I thought it might! But, more important, was it true? How many of us, I wonder, wish we had worked just that little bit harder while we had the chance? How much more could we have achieved? How different might life have been? If only, if only, if only!

Sadly, we don't often get the chance to make up for past mistakes, not in terms of academic qualifications anyway, but when it comes to what matters most of all, thankfully it's another story. In the parable above, the vinedresser asks for one year's reprieve, in which the fig tree might bear fruit. Jesus goes further still, asking the Father to give us not just *one* more chance but as many as it takes for us finally to fulfil our potential in his service. Though we repeatedly grieve him through our failure to grow and bear fruit, he never gives up believing that the harvest may yet come.

Ask yourself

Have you fulfilled your potential in the service of Christ? Are the fruits of the Spirit evident in your life?

Pray

Lord Jesus Christ, I know the fruits you want to see in my life: love, joy, peace, patience, kindness, generosity, faithfulness, gentleness and self-control. I know I ought to show these, but I know also how rarely I do, how all too often the fruits are anything but. Instead of living by the Spirit I live by the flesh, and the results are plain for all to see.

Forgive me, and by your grace grant me another chance to start again. Put your Spirit within me and nurture my faith so that the time will come when my life will bear a rich harvest to the glory of your name. Amen.

Remember

A solitary branch cannot bear fruit but only if it remains part of the vine; so it is with you unless you remain part of me. I am the vine, you are the branches – whoever remains in me and I in them will bear much fruit.   *John 15:4-5*

Close

Gracious God, nurture the seed of faith within me. Help me to grow closer to you and to Christ, and so cultivate within me the fruits you hunger to see, through the grace of Jesus Christ my Lord. Amen.

Salt of the earth

Read

You are the salt of the earth; but if salt is adulterated, how can its saltiness be restored? It no longer has any use, fit only to be thrown out and trampled underfoot.

Matthew 5:13

Ponder

The salt of the earth – how often have you heard that expression used of someone? What a wonderful compliment it is! To be somebody who adds that little bit extra to life, who brings help and happiness to others, who is trustworthy and dependable – what higher praise can there be? So would people describe us in those terms? They should do, according to Jesus. We should be those who exhibit precisely such qualities; those with a quality of life that makes people sit up and take notice.

Of course we can't please everyone all the time, and there will always be those hostile to the Christian faith who therefore have little time for us. Yet the principle holds nonetheless. Faith is not simply about ourselves: our own welfare, security and happiness. It's about making a difference to the world we live in, helping to change lives, showing compassion and offering love. If we're not doing that, then it's time to ask ourselves some serious questions.

Ask yourself

Has your faith become too much about you and too little about others? In what ways are you being 'salt of the earth'?

Pray

Lord Jesus Christ, I thank you for the difference you have made both to my own life and to the experience of so many people like me. Thank you for the difference you have made to the world, working through countless individuals and transforming innumerable situations across the centuries. You call us all, in turn, to make a difference – to bring joy, hope, help and healing to those who are hurting, to all who have lost their sense of purpose or faith in the future.

Forgive me for failing so often to honour that calling, my discipleship making such a feeble impact on those around me. Teach me to reach out in your name and to share in your renewing work. Teach me to be salt of the earth, fit for use in your service, to the glory of your name. Amen.

Remember

Do everything without arguing or complaint, so that you may be irreproachable beyond causing offence, above criticism in a decadent and corrupt generation, shining like stars in the world and thus holding up the word of life to all.

Philippians 2:14-16a

Close

Living God, send me out with love in my heart, light in my eyes and life in my soul, to proclaim what you have done for me and to share what you have given. For Christ's sake. Amen.

Bouncing back

Read

The Lord said to Moses, 'Pharaoh will not listen to you, so I will have to perform even more wonders in the land of Egypt.' Despite all the wonders Moses and Aaron showed to Pharaoh, the Lord hardened Pharaoh's heart, and he refused to let the people of Israel leave his land.

Exodus 11:9-10

Ponder

I read recently about a celebrated author whose first novel was rejected 97 times before finally being accepted for publication! That takes some doing, doesn't it? – to keep on bouncing back from disappointment after disappointment. How many of us, I wonder, would have shown anything like that same determination? It's a rare gift!

Yet that is precisely what we see in the story of Moses. Called to seek an audience with Pharaoh and demand the release of his fellow Israelites from slavery, he was to suffer repeated frustrations as his requests were either turned down flat or granted for a moment only to be denied later. It would have been hard enough for Moses to continue undeterred had he naturally warmed to the task in hand, but when we remember that every moment was an ordeal for him, so much so that his brother Aaron was needed for support, we realise the full extent of his dedication. No one could have blamed him had he washed his hands of the whole venture after the first few attempts; I suspect I would have done so in his place! Yet, with incredible resilience, he battled on until at last he achieved success. His story gives us a memorable glimpse not just of human perseverance, but also of the God who reaches out with equal devotion to his people in every place and time, determined to set them free from all that holds them captive.

Ask yourself

Are you feeling frustrated, disappointed or disillusioned about something? Is God calling you to try again?

Pray

Lord, it's hard to keep striving sometimes when all my efforts meet with failure; hard to keep praying when all my prayers seem to be unanswered; hard to keep believing when so much in life seems to undermine my faith. Yet it is at such times as those that I need to hold firmly to you, discovering the strength that you alone can give and trusting in your sovereign purpose.

Teach me to persevere even when the odds seem hopelessly stacked against me, confident that your will shall finally prevail despite everything that conspires against me. Help me to know that though I may be tempted to give up on you, you will never give up on me! Amen.

Remember

We are afflicted in every way, yet we are not pushed over the edge. We face continual difficulties, yet do not despair. We are persecuted, yet not abandoned. We are cast down, yet not destroyed, for we constantly carry the death of Jesus within us in order that the life of Jesus may be made visible within us as well.   *2 Corinthians 4:8-10*

Close

Sovereign God, equip me with faith, hope, courage, resilience, enthusiasm and dedication, and so may I walk the path of discipleship faithfully, through good or ill, to the glory of your name. Amen.

Why did I do it?

Read

I do not understand why I act as I do. For I end up doing the things I hate rather than the things I want to do. I do evil instead of the good I wish to do. Now if I do what I don't really want to do, it can no longer be I that do it, but must be the sin that dwells within me. I find it to be a law that whenever I intend to do good, evil is there as well, for, while I delight deep within in the law of God, I see a different law in my body that battles with the law of my mind, holding me captive to the law of sin that dwells in my members. What a wretched man I am! Who will deliver me from this body of death? Thanks be to God through Jesus Christ our Lord! *Romans 7:15, 19-25*

Ponder

Why did I do it? How often have you asked yourself that question? Time and again, just like the Apostle Paul, we find ourselves doing exactly the opposite of what we intended. The reasons, of course, are many and varied: greed, envy, lust and pride, to name but a few. Yet why is it that we struggle sometimes to control these, no matter how much we long to? That is a much deeper question, which people will answer in different ways according to their perspective on life. For Paul it pointed to the essentially fallen nature of humanity: what some might term original sin; what others would simply call human weakness. We could debate the issues involved for the rest of our days and still not exhaust them. We could struggle to overcome our faults with every fibre of our body, yet be no nearer success at the end than at the beginning.

Thankfully, as Paul reminds us, we can also spend the rest of our days, and those beyond, at peace with God and ourselves, for what we cannot deal with has been decisively dealt with by him through his living, dying and rising among us in Christ. No wonder Paul ended his outburst of frustration in an outpouring of praise: 'Thanks be to God through Jesus Christ our Lord!'

Ask yourself

Are you weighed down by a sense of guilt over past mistakes? Isn't it time you let go and trusted in God's forgiveness?

Pray

Merciful God, unlike me you don't dwell on past failures. Instead, you invite me to acknowledge them openly before you, to receive your pardon and then to move on.

Teach me to do just that – to accept your offer for what it is and, rather than wallow in my guilt, to rejoice in your mercy. Help me not simply to talk about new life but to live it joyfully, receiving each moment as your gracious gift. Through Jesus Christ my Lord. Amen.

Remember

If we confess our sins, he is just, and we can rely on him to forgive our sins and cleanse us from all evil.   *1 John 1:9*

Close

Merciful Lord, with my heart at peace I return to the journey of life, the past put behind me, the future full of promise. Receive my praise, in the name of Christ. Amen.

Studying the word

Read

On the first day of the first month Ezra fixed the day for the departure from Babylon, and on the first day of the fifth month he reached Jerusalem, for the gracious hand of his God was upon him. For Ezra had committed himself to study the law of the Lord, and to put it into practice, and to teach its statutes and ordinances in Israel.   *Ezra 7:9-10*

Ponder

Few people if asked to list their top ten characters of the Old Testament would include Ezra in their choice. Despite having a book named after him, he fails to capture the imagination quite as characters like Moses, Samson, David or Isaiah do. Some have called him dull; others have gone even further and accused him of being largely responsible for the narrow legalism which came to typify Judaism at the time of Jesus.

Yet this is to overlook the very real contribution Ezra made to his nation at a formative time in its history, and to undervalue the motivation that lay behind it. As a scribe and priest, his overriding concern was to nurture the faith of his people, and he did this in the way he knew best: by reading, learning and acting upon God's words. He knew that if past mistakes were not to be made again, the people's relationship with God needed to be deepened, and one of the best ways of ensuring that was through reflecting on scripture. There is much we can learn today from his example of single-minded devotion to the study of God's word if we too would grow in faith.

Ask yourself

How often do you make time to study the Word? How well do you know the Bible and what impact does it make on your life?

Pray

Living God, you have given your word in the scriptures but, all too often, I fail to read them. I dip in casually as the mood takes me, selecting those passages that suit me best and ignoring any that might prove difficult or demanding. Even the little I read is rarely applied to my life in a way that really touches me. Despite the claims I make for it, the reality is that much of the Bible is a closed book to me.

Forgive me, and help me make time and space to study your word, to hear you speaking, and to respond in faith. Amen.

Remember

Let the word of God dwell richly within you.

Colossians 3:16

Close

Sovereign God, guide me in the reading and understanding of your word, until it becomes so much a part of me that your voice is heard through all I am and do, to the glory of your name. Amen.

Unanswered prayer

Read

I call to you, O Lord my rock: do not refuse to listen, for if you keep silent I shall be like those who go down into the depths. Hear my entreaty as I beg you for help, and as I lift up my hands towards your dwelling place.   *Psalm 28:1-2*

Ponder

It was a frustrating business. We'd been connected and were enjoying a good chat when suddenly a fault developed on the line and although I could still hear my friend, he could no longer hear me. It felt suddenly as if I was talking to myself. On other occasions like this, the roles may be reversed, so that we are suddenly unable to hear the person we are speaking to even though they continue to hear us. Both scenarios can find an echo in prayer: one day we are blissfully aware of God's presence and the next it's as though we've been cut off; either our words unheard, unregistered, or the reply being blocked somewhere.

So it was, on more than one occasion, for David. In Psalm 28, he cries out to God, begging him to listen, patently aware that an answer does not always appear forthcoming. In Psalm 22, his prayer is even more poignant: 'O my God, I cry to you by day, yet you do not answer; and by night, yet find no relief' (verse 2). Those who have never had such an experience in prayer are fortunate indeed. Yet, for David this was not the end of the story. In both cases, he ends his psalm with an outpouring of praise, an expression of trust and thanksgiving, for it becomes clear that God has not only heard him but also responded. Remember that if ever you feel that the 'line has gone dead' and your prayers are unheard. The testimony of scripture is that ours is a God who always hears and who will always finally answer.

Ask yourself

Have you stopped believing God will answer your prayers? Have you given up praying as you once did? Are you still open to what God might have to say?

Pray

Living God, I bring to you those times when I call to you for help and you seem to be silent; those days when I do not hear your voice no matter how I listen for it. Help me to understand that even when I feel alone, you are listening, and even when you seem far away, you are always near.

Give me faith to hold on, courage to trust in your promises, and humility to recognise that your answer will come in your own time and your own way. May that knowledge sustain and inspire me, whatever I may face. Through Jesus Christ my Lord. Amen.

Remember

Blessed be the Lord, for he has heard my plea. The Lord is my strength and my shield; in him I trust with all my heart. So I am sustained; my heart dances for joy and my whole body gives praise to him!   *Psalm 28:6-7*

Close

Gracious God, draw close to me and help me to draw nearer to you. Speak to me and help me to hear. Challenge me and help me to respond. Enthuse me with the wonder of your love, and so may joy and peace fill my heart, now and for evermore. Amen.

FEBRUARY

A moment's madness

Read

As the afternoon was drawing on, David got up from his couch and, taking a stroll on the palace roof, he happened to spot from there a woman taking a bath; a woman who was very beautiful. David sent someone to find out who the woman was. The report came back: 'She is Bathsheba, daughter of Eliam, the wife of Uriah the Hittite.' So David sent messengers to summon her, and she came to him, and they made love.   *2 Samuel 11:2-4a*

Ponder

'On guard!' According to Hollywood at least, those are the words that used to precede a sword fight in years gone by. It would have been considered unchivalrous not to give one's prospective opponent due warning and time to prepare for battle. Unfortunately, when it comes to temptation the attack is often very different. It comes without warning, unsought, unexpected; nine times out of ten taking us by surprise.

So it was for David. One moment he was reclining on his rooftop enjoying the afternoon sun, and the next he was planning illicit sex. A great and devout king he may have been; it counted for nothing – like a moth drawn towards a candle he was unable to resist the pull of temptation. In one moment of madness he made a mistake that was to haunt him for the rest of his life. We cannot excuse David's actions, but we can learn from them. Like those swash-buckling 'heroes' of old, real or imagined, we too must be 'on guard'.

Ask yourself

Are you aware of your weaknesses? Is there anything you can do to guard against them?

Pray

Lord Jesus Christ, you were tempted just as I am and yet you did not sin. Forgive me that I find it so much harder to resist temptation, my spirit willing but the flesh weak. Forgive me that all my resolve can be undermined in just a few seconds as, time and again, temptation catches me unawares. Renew and refashion me in your image, so that when I am tempted to go astray – to indulge my desires, ignore your will and excuse what I know to be inexcusable – I will have the inner strength to say no. Touch my heart and put a right spirit within me, so that in the time of trial I too may stay true to your way, by your grace. Amen.

Remember

Be clear-headed, be vigilant, for your adversary the devil prowls about like a roaring lion, looking for someone to devour. *1 Peter 5:8*

Close

Almighty God, pardon me my past mistakes, deliver me from present folly, and lead me forward in the way of life eternal. Through Jesus Christ my Lord. Amen.

A new beginning

Read

When eight days had passed, the time came to circumcise the child; and they called him Jesus, the name the angel had given even before conception. When the time came for him to be purified according to the law of Moses, they brought him to Jerusalem to present him to the Lord (as it is written in the law of the Lord, 'Every firstborn male shall be designated as holy to the Lord'). They offered a sacrifice as prescribed in the law of the Lord, 'a pair of turtledoves or two young pigeons'. When they had done everything the law of the Lord required, they returned to their hometown of Nazareth in Galilee. The child grew in strength and wisdom; and God's favour rested on him.   *Luke 2:21-24, 39-40*

Ponder

'And it's from the old I travel to the new' – so runs the popular hymn and those words perfectly capture a truth at the heart of the gospel: that in Christ we see a new beginning. Yet, read the account of Jesus' presentation at the temple and you could be excused for thinking that nothing was going to change after all. Jesus was brought *according to the law of Moses*; presented at the temple *as it is written in the law of the Lord*, and a sacrifice offered *as prescribed in the law of the Lord*. It was only when *they had done everything the law of the Lord required* that Mary and Joseph felt able to return home.

Do not be fooled, however, for once Jesus began his ministry it became clear that he brought a decisive break with the old. 'You have heard it said', he told the crowd, concerning various points of the law, and then continued, 'but I say to you', after which he set out a new and revolutionary interpretation of established wisdom. This was a break with the past, a parting of the ways between old and new, but it was not a complete parting, for he was also able to say, 'Do not think I have come to abolish the law or the prophets; I have come not to abolish but to fulfil.' From the old had come something new. Turn from the birth to the death of Jesus, for thirty-three years later he was presented to God in Jerusalem once again, only this time there were to be no sacrifices offered on his behalf – *he* was the sacrifice! Here, supremely, is the Christ who brings new life out of old, transforming what *has been* into what *shall be*. He continues to do the same in our lives today, taking what we are and reshaping our lives day by day into a new creation.

Ask yourself
How far have you let go of the old self and put on the new? How open are you to Jesus refashioning your life?

Pray
Lord Jesus Christ, just as you brought new out of old through your fulfilment of the law and the prophets, so also continue to make me new, taking my old self and refashioning it by your grace into a new creation. Help me to let go of everything in my past that denies and destroys, separating me from your love.

Take what I am and re-create me by your power, so that I may be the person you would have me be, for I ask it in your name. Amen.

Remember
He said to them, 'A teacher of the law who is ready to learn of the kingdom of heaven is like the master of a household who can produce from his stores both new and old.'

Matthew 13:52

Close
Living God, from the unpromising material of my life, fashion your new creation, through Jesus Christ my Lord. Amen.

Good intentions

Read

'What do you make of this? A man had two children. Approaching the first, he said, "My child, go and work in the vineyard today." He answered, "I'll go", but he didn't. The father went to the second and asked the same thing; and he answered, "Sir, I won't go", but he had second thoughts and went. Which of the two did the father's will?' They said, 'The latter.'   *Matthew 21:28-31*

Ponder

How many times have you intended to do something and failed to do it? I expect it's been more often than you care to remember. It's easy to make a promise, much harder to honour it. The reasons, of course, are many. Sometimes we just forget or are too busy. At other times, we find we've taken on more than we bargained for, swept along on a tide of enthusiasm only to find, in the cold light of day, that the task we've committed ourselves to appears less attractive than we thought. On other occasions still, we can be guilty of sheer old-fashioned laziness.

With luck, our failure to honour our intentions may not matter all that much. On the other hand, it may matter a good deal, having consequences far greater than we might envisage possible. It may even be that the opportunity we have missed may never come our way again, so if God is calling you to do something and if the job needs doing, don't put it off. Act now before it's too late!

Ask yourself

Is your faith more talk than substance? How often do you fail to translate good intentions into action?

Pray

Gracious God, forgive me for those things I should have done but have left undone: the acts of kindness I never found time for, the thoughtful word never spoken, the message of encouragement or concern never sent, the helpful deed never attempted. Forgive me for all the opportunities I have missed: the plans I never made, the dreams I never brought to reality, the possibilities I never even imagined, the gifts I never used. Forgive me for my failure to serve you as I promised: the prayers I never offered, the sacrifices I never made, the faith I never had, the commitment I never gave. Forgive me for so often having time only for self: for being self-centred, self-important, self-righteous, self-interested, self-indulgent, self-opinionated. Forgive me for forgetting my friends, my neighbour, and, above all, you.

Gracious God, save me from being a person of unfulfilled intentions. Help me to translate my thoughts into actions, to put my preaching into practice and to turn my good intentions into good deeds, to the glory of your name. Amen.

Remember

What good is it, my brothers and sisters, if you claim to have faith but fail to show it in works? Can faith save you? If a brother or sister is naked and lacks sufficient food, and one of you says to them, 'Go in peace, keep warm and eat plenty', but fails to give them what they really need, what value is there in that? Mark my words, faith alone, without works, is dead.   *James 2:14-17*

Close

Lord Jesus Christ, save me from simply talking about faith, from meaning to do good. Help me to turn concern into compassion, sympathy into service, aim into action, resolve into reality, and so may I be the person you want me to be, to your glory. Amen.

The God beyond us

Read

My thoughts are not your thoughts, neither are your ways my ways, says the Lord. For as the heavens are higher than the earth, so are my ways higher than your ways and my thoughts higher than your thoughts.   *Isaiah 55:8-9*

Ponder

When did you last feel a sense of awe in the presence of God? How long is it since you caught your breath in wonder as you offered him your worship? It may be that such moments are still frequent but, if my experience is anything to go by, you may find that they have grown fewer and farther between. Partly that happens because we simply don't find time to worship as often as we should; partly it's because over-familiarity dulls our senses. See anything breathtakingly beautiful once and we gaze in amazement. See it several times and the chances are we'll pass it by without a second look.

Whether we're talking of a beautiful view or a sense of God's majesty, it can take a fresh pair of eyes to stir our imaginations once more and help us recapture that first-time sense of wonderment. For me, that fresh pair of eyes is given in those wonderful words of the prophet Isaiah. They are a constant reminder of the sheer 'otherness' of God whose greatness is beyond words, whose awesomeness defies expression; who is more powerful, more caring, more gracious, more good than the human mind can ever comprehend. Glimpse that, and once more we find ourselves catching our breath in sheer amazement and kneeling in joyful worship.

Ask yourself

Is your picture of God too small? Have you limited God to your own horizons, rather than allowed yours to be shaped by his greatness?

Pray

Sovereign God, all too often I lose sight of your greatness, settling instead for a picture of you I feel comfortable with. I have frustrated your will through the smallness of my vision. I have missed opportunities to serve you through the narrowness of my horizons. I have denied myself your mercy through the confines I place upon your grace. Repeatedly I have presumed that your ways are *my* ways and your thoughts *my* thoughts, forgetting that you are beyond words or human understanding. Forgive me, and teach me never to underestimate the awesomeness of your being or the extent of your love. Amen.

Remember

O Lord, you have searched me and known me. You know when I sit down and when I rise up; you discern my thoughts from far away. Such knowledge is too wonderful for me; it is so high that I cannot attain it.

Psalm 139:1-2, 6

Close

Almighty God, open my eyes afresh to your greatness, your power, your sovereignty over all. Give me again a glimpse of your glory, not just here but everywhere, not just today but every day, so that my heart may be overwhelmed by your splendour and my soul may soar in exultation, in joyful and reverent praise. Amen.

Going astray

Read

We have all gone astray like sheep; each going our own
way, but the Lord has laid on him the offences of us all.

Isaiah 53:6

Ponder

One of the television programmes I used to enjoy watching
was the BBC series *One man and his dog*. The skill of the
handlers and the devoted obedience of the sheepdogs never
ceased to amaze me. Equally fascinating were the actions
of the sheep: at times seeming plain stupid, at other times
wilfully stubborn.

It is little wonder that biblical writers so often drew an
analogy between sheep and people, because we too have a
penchant for displaying precisely those characteristics. We
blindly follow those around us instead of thinking for ourselves. We stumble from one mistake to another. We act on
impulse rather than from reason and can even on occasions
resist those who try to help us. Yet, however far we go astray,
ours is a God who comes looking for us; a God who has
given his all to restore us to his side. Give thanks for the
wonder of that love.

Ask yourself

In what ways do you tend to follow the crowd? Is there an
area in your life where you have gone astray at present?

Pray

Lord Jesus Christ, I thank you for the way you watch over
me throughout my life, the way you are continually there
to guard and guide me, whatever I may face. When I wander
far from your side you do not abandon me to my fate, but
instead come looking for me, your love refusing to let

me go. Though I may forsake you, you never forsake me. Though I may be faithless, you remain faithful.

I praise you for that great truth, I ask forgiveness for the areas in my life in which I continue to go astray, and I pray for help to follow you more closely in the days ahead, to the glory of your name. Amen.

Remember

You were like sheep that had lost their way, but now you have been brought back to follow the Shepherd and keeper of your souls.   *1 Peter 2:25*

Close

Gracious God, go with me now, protect me from evil, deliver me from temptation, and help me to walk in the way of Christ, this and every day, for his name's sake. Amen.

A place for all

Read

Are not five sparrows sold for a couple of pence? Yet God does not overlook a single one of them. Believe me, the very hairs of your head are numbered. Never fear, then, for you mean even more to him than many sparrows.

Luke 12:6-7

Ponder

We live today, as never before, in an impersonal society – a world in which increasingly we are treated as numbers rather than individuals. Instead of being people, we are a reference number on a tax form, a policy number with an insurance company, a national health service number on a waiting list, a telephone number to a double-glazing firm. Answerphones, automated messages, e-mails, the Internet – these have become the order of the day, personal contact reduced to the barest minimum. Disturbingly, many young people relate more easily to a computer screen than to real-life flesh and blood.

In such a world it is reassuring to know that, in God's eyes at least, we are still real people, each one of us unique and precious to him. He values us for what we are, inviting us to share in a meaningful personal relationship with him. More than that, he calls us to recognise the value of others and, in so doing, to resist the depersonalising forces that threaten to undermine society today. Whatever you do, never forget that each person you have dealings with is not a number or an object, but precisely that – a person!

Ask yourself

Do you realise how much you matter to God? Do others realise how much they matter to you? Do you make time to show how much you value them?

Pray

Father God, reach out to all who are lonely, deprived of human companionship through age or infirmity, or separated from others – even when they are with them – through fear, shyness, mistrust or prejudice. Reach out into our fragmented society in which so much of the feeling of community has been lost, where ties that once bound families together have been broken, where so many live only for themselves.

Father, give to me and to all a sense of worth and an understanding of the humanity that binds us all together, through Jesus Christ my Lord. Amen.

Remember

What are people, that you bother with them; mortals, that they matter to you? Yet you have made them scarcely less than divine, and crowned them with glory and honour.

Psalm 8:5

Close

Loving God, send me out rejoicing in the knowledge that you value me, and so help me to show how much I value others, expressing my concern and appreciation through word and deed, to the glory of your name. Amen.

Excuses, excuses

Read

The Lord God called to the man, and said to him, 'Where are you?' He answered, 'I heard your footfall in the garden, and I was ashamed because I was naked, so I hid myself.' He said, 'Who told you that you were naked? Have you eaten from the tree I told you not to eat from?' The man said, 'The woman you gave me as a companion, she gave me fruit from the tree, so I ate it.' Then the Lord God said to the woman, 'What have you done?' The woman said, 'The serpent misled me, and I ate.'   *Genesis 3:9-13*

Ponder

Are you good at admitting your mistakes? I wish I were. To hold up one's hand and candidly admit one has done wrong is a rare gift, taking courage that few of us possess. Our natural reaction is more like that of Adam and Eve, frantically trying to justify our actions. 'It wasn't my fault,' we claim. 'I was forced into it. My hands were tied.' Deep down, though, we know that the responsibility to choose is ours, no one else's. We are all answerable for our own actions. It isn't easy to admit our mistakes, but until we learn to do that, they will hang heavy upon us, impinging on our relationships with those we have wronged. Acknowledge our errors, and we pave the way to forgiveness and a new beginning.

Ask yourself

Have you sufficient courage and honesty to admit your mistakes? Is it time you stopped hiding behind excuses?

Pray

Lord, I don't like being wrong. It hurts my pride and goes against the grain to admit I've made a mistake. I prefer to blame somebody else, to look for an excuse that justifies my actions, but though I may fool myself, I can never fool you.

Forgive me, Lord, for those times I have shifted the blame on to others. Forgive me for hiding behind false-hoods and half-truths, letting excuses become so much part of me that I no longer realise I am making them. Teach me to act wisely and with integrity; and when I go wrong, give me courage to admit it and humility to accept my dependence on your unfailing grace. Amen.

Remember

Let no one, experiencing temptation, suggest that the temptation comes from God, for God has no interest in evil and would never tempt anyone. Each person is lured by their own desires, enticed and ensnared until desire spawns sin, which in turn leads on to death. My dear friends, do not be taken in.   *James 1:13-16*

Close

Loving God, grant me grace to be honest with you, with others and with myself. Through Jesus Christ my Lord. Amen.

A time to decide

Read

No one can serve two masters, for they will either hate the one and love the other, or cling to the one and spurn the other. You cannot simultaneously serve God and this world.

Matthew 6:24

Ponder

One of the things I have never succeeded in doing is learning to swim. I've tried many times, having had lessons in school and later in life as an adult but, though I've come close, I've never quite mastered it. The reason is simple enough – I try to keep a foot in both camps. Whereas I should trust myself completely to the water, I insist on keeping one foot firmly on the floor and the result is that I neither sink nor swim. I know I should leap out in faith but somehow I just can't bring myself to make that decisive step. The same, of course, can be true of life. To change the metaphor, there are times when sitting on the fence or hedging our bets means that we end up achieving nothing.

It is even truer when it comes to faith, as Jesus made plain in those often-quoted words from the Sermon on the Mount. We may like to think we can play it both ways, but there comes a point when we can't. This doesn't mean that we should live as reclusive eccentrics, still less that we should dismiss the very real joys this world has to offer. What it does mean is that when life throws up difficult choices, as it assuredly will, we have to be clear about our priorities; about who or what we are serving. Compromise then, in an attempt to secure the best of both worlds, and we may end up securing neither.

Ask yourself

How often do you stop to consider where your loyalties lie? Do your decisions reflect the way of the world or the way of Christ?

Pray

Lord Jesus Christ, I want to commit myself to your service and I do my best to follow you, but I am led astray so easily, my faith so weak and temptation so strong. I think I have turned my back on my old ways, only to find them resurfacing in another guise. I try to let go of self, only to discover it still holds me firmly in its grip. For all my good intentions, I find myself caught between two worlds, unable to embrace the one and unwilling to embrace the other.

Forgive me the many times I fail you, and give me strength, when my allegiance is tested, to put you first. Help me not simply to call you Lord, but to make you the Lord of my life, to the glory of your name. Amen.

Remember

A way can sometimes appear to be right, yet it is ultimately the path to death. *Proverbs 16:25*

Close

Gracious God, show me where I have lost my way and help me to learn from past mistakes. Show me where my loyalties are still divided and, by your grace, help me to change. Show me the path to life, and help me to walk it more faithfully. I commit myself again to your service, in the name of Christ. Amen.

Making a difference

Read

On some have compassion, making a difference.

Jude v. 22

Ponder

It was only the smallest of mistakes, a single letter inadvertently inserted in place of another, but it made all the difference. Instead of reading 'The bishop much enjoyed the singing' it read – you've guessed it – 'The bishop much enjoyed the sinning'! A potentially embarrassing mistake but a simple reminder that it doesn't take much to give a different result than expected. Indeed, the verse above is a case in point. The *New Revised Standard Version* translates it 'have mercy on some who are wavering', while the *New English Bible* goes for 'there are some doubting souls who need your pity'. My own rendering leans heavily on the King James translation of the Bible and is probably the least accurate of any, yet the message could hardly be more important, for if there is one thing that should characterise our lives as Christians it should surely be making a difference. It doesn't take much: a word here, a deed there, and the effects can be remarkable. Few of us will make an indelible impact through our discipleship, let alone change the world, but all of us, if our faith is what it ought to be, should make a difference somewhere. If it doesn't, something is badly wrong.

Ask yourself

In what ways does your faith affect the way you live? In what ways does it influence your dealings with those around you?

Pray

Living God, too easily I turn faith into a matter of personal devotion and fulfilment, forgetting that it must show itself in the way I live. I make time for prayer and worship, I read and study your word, but then I fail to go out into the world and make real there the truth of what I believe.

Forgive me, and help me to minister in your name, bringing peace, hope, help and healing, sharing your love and working to bring your kingdom closer here on earth. In the name of Christ I ask it. Amen.

Remember

Little children, do not let love be simply all talk, but show its authenticity in action. *1 John 3:18*

Close

Loving God, make a difference to me, so that I may make a difference to others. Amen.

Here, there and everywhere

Read

Where can I evade your spirit? Where can I flee from your presence? If I soar up to heaven, you are there; if I make my bed in Sheol, you are there. If I sail on the wings of the morning and settle at the uttermost limits of the sea, even there your hand will lead me, your right hand holding me firm. If I say, 'Surely darkness will steal over me, night will envelop me', darkness is not dark to you; the night is as bright as day; for you both dark and light are the same.

Psalm 139:7-10

Ponder

We seek him here, we seek him there, those Frenchies seek him everywhere. Is he in heaven? – Is he in hell? That demmed elusive Pimpernel?

So run the famous lines of Baroness Orczy concerning the renowned character of her novels: the so-called Scarlet Pimpernel. Come what may, the dashing hero invariably turns up at the right time and the right place; no one and nowhere, it seems, beyond his reach. Such, of course, is the prerogative of fictional heroes.

With God, though, it is no fiction. He is the one before and beyond all, yet the one who is with us, here and now; the ruler over space and time, yet the one constantly by our side. No one is outside his love, nowhere beyond his grace, no situation outside his concern – not even death itself can separate us from his sovereign purpose in Christ. Whether you see him or whether you don't, whether you sense he is close or feel he is far away, remember this: he is here, there and everywhere.

Ask yourself

Do you feel a sense of God's constant presence in every area of your life? Do you live in a way that reflects that awareness?

Pray

Sovereign God, higher than my highest thoughts, yet always close by my side; greater than I can ever imagine, yet made known to me in Christ; more powerful than words can express yet having a special concern for every one of us – I worship you. I praise you that, though I wander far from you, always you seek me out; though you sometimes seem distant, always you are near; though life seems to make no sense, still you are present, your purpose unchanging, your hand reaching out to bless. Sovereign God, I give you thanks for the assurance that brings, the hope for this life and the life to come. Hear my prayer, in the name of Christ. Amen.

Remember

The eyes of the Lord are everywhere, monitoring good and evil alike.   *Proverbs 15:3*

Close

Living God, I thank you that you are not just with me here in prayer but with me always in the daily round of life; as much there as anywhere, waiting to meet me, lead me and bless me. Help me to glimpse your presence, and to live each moment conscious that you are by my side, to your praise and glory. Amen.

The slippery slope

Read

Demas, in love with this present world, has deserted me
and gone to Thessalonica.   *2 Timothy 4:9*

Ponder

How often have you started something full of enthusiasm,
only to wonder a little later just what it is you have taken
on? It may have been a job round the house, an interest, a
hobby, a responsibility – the list is almost limitless – but,
whatever it was, we believed at the time that we'd see it
through with undiminished energy. Nine times out of ten,
the bubble soon bursts. Another job, another interest,
another hobby, another responsibility, and suddenly the
old is discarded in favour of the new.

The same, sadly, can all too easily happen with faith. How
many have started the course only to turn back, professed
faith in Christ only to lose interest in anything to do with
him? The commitment is real enough at the outset but, for
a variety of reasons, it is undermined. Make no mistake:
none of us is immune from the same befalling us. We all
have our weak spots; we can all grow cold. That which began
as a joyful privilege can end up as an empty duty, before
finally petering out into nothingness. Don't let what happened to Demas happen to you.

Ask yourself

Is your faith as real as it once was, or is it slowly slipping
away?

Pray

Living God, I pray for those who find faith hard, those who
want to believe but cannot get past their doubts. I pray for
those whose faith is wavering, undermined by the pressures
and temptations of life. I pray for those who have lost their

faith, the fire that once burned within them extinguished. I pray for myself, conscious that for me too faith can sometimes lose its spark. For all those facing the dark night of faith I pray: 'Lord, we do believe, help overcome our unbelief.' Amen.

Remember

Let us unswervingly hold fast to the hope we profess, for he who has promised is faithful.   *Hebrews 10:23*

Close

Gracious God, when the spark of faith starts to flicker and the fire of commitment grows cold, rekindle in me the joy with which I first started out, so that I may awake each day with hope in my heart and live each moment rejoicing in your love, to the glory of your name. Amen.

An outer veneer

Read

You who yearn for the day of the Lord are fools, for what will that day actually mean to you? It will be darkness, not light; as though you have fled from a lion only to be met by a bear; or taken refuge in a house only to be bitten by a snake as you rest a hand against the wall. That is what the day of the Lord will be like: unrelieved darkness, night with no prospect of dawn. I loathe and reject your festivals, and take no pleasure in your sacred rituals. Bring me your animal sacrifices and cereal offerings if you must – I will not accept them; I want nothing to do with the atoning sacrifices of your fatted animals. Take away from me the clamour of your songs; I will not listen to the tune of your harps. Instead, let justice cascade down like a mighty river, and righteousness like an inexhaustible stream.

Amos 5:18-24

Ponder

It looked a nice piece of furniture, nice enough, in fact, to take me in completely. I imagined it was solid wood, built to last, but time was to prove otherwise. Before long, the thin layer of veneer began to peel away, exposing the cheap chipboard beneath and, eventually, the whole surface cracked beyond repair.

It's not only furniture that superficially can look the part; it's people too. As Amos so powerfully observed, outwardly our practice of religion may be exemplary, yet this may mask a profound failure to serve God. He wasn't just talking about those who hide dark secrets behind a respectable public face; his words warn us all of the danger of fine-sounding words that are belied by our actions, of ostentatious show concealing a hollow interior.

Ask yourself

How far is your faith a matter of show? How far is it reflected in the way you live?

Pray

Lord, it's easy to go to church, hard to reach out to the world. It's easy to say my prayers, hard to act upon them. It's easy to offer my money, hard to give you my life. It's easy to sing your praises, hard to live to your glory. Forgive me for so often taking the easy way, the way of outward show rather than inner faith. Move within me, so that the words of my lips may show themselves in the thoughts of my heart, and the claims of my faith may be proven through the sincerity of my service. Amen.

Remember

A silky tongue masking an evil heart is like the glaze that covers an earthenware pot.   *Proverbs 25:23*

Close

Gracious God, you send me out to turn words into deeds, worship into service and vision into reality. I have heard your call; give me grace to act upon it. In the name of Christ. Amen.

Daring to trust

Read

There was a certain disciple in Damascus by the name of Ananias, and the Lord spoke to him in a vision, saying, 'Ananias.' He answered, 'I'm here, Lord.' The Lord said to him, 'Get up and go to the street known as The Straight, and there look in the house of Judas for a man called Saul of Tarsus. He is praying at this very moment, and in a vision he has seen a man called Ananias enter and lay hands on him so that he might recover his sight. But Ananias protested, 'Lord, I have heard from many people about this man, about all his cruelty to your saints in Jerusalem, and how he has come here now with authority from the chief priests to arrest all those who confess your name.'

Acts 9:10-14

Ponder

What would you do if you sensed danger looming? The answer is obvious: you'd do everything possible to avoid it. Should you be the adventurous type, it's possible that you might flirt with it for a moment but, if you felt your life was on the line, you'd ultimately want to ensure your own safety. That, no doubt, was paramount in the mind of Ananias, having heard that Saul, persecutor of the Church, was in town. Quite simply, he was keeping his head down until the danger had passed, hoping against hope that he would not hear the fateful knock on the door summoning him to imprisonment and almost certain death. Imagine his surprise, then, when another summons came, calling him to seek out this man who struck fear into the heart of every Christian, and to knock on his door! It was asking a lot, to say the least!

Would you have obeyed that call, or would you have made excuses to evade it, dismissed it as ridiculous, looked the other way? Had Ananias done any of those, who can say how different the history of the Christian Church might have been? It took his faith and courage to finish the transformation of Saul, enemy of the faith, into Paul, its greatest ambassador. When God asks you to step out in faith, will you have the courage, like Ananias, to say yes?

Ask yourself

Are you willing to trust God, even when he asks of you more than you feel able to do? Have you sufficient courage to take, if necessary, a step of faith?

Pray

Loving God, there are times when you call me to tasks that seem beyond me; responsibilities I would rather avoid. I hear your voice but I do not feel up to the challenge, my natural inclination to run away. Yet, if you ask anyone to do something you always give the strength to do it.

Give me courage, then, to respond when you call, knowing that however things may seem, you are always able to transform them in ways far beyond my expectations. Amen.

Remember

He himself has categorically said, I will never abandon or forsake you, so take heart and say, 'I will not be afraid – the Lord is my helper, so what can anyone do to me?'

Hebrews 13:5b-6

Close

Living Lord, when you ask me to go out in your name – to listen to your voice, to venture into the unknown, to let go of self and to reach out in love – teach me to be strong, courageous, obedient and faithful; teach me to say yes. Amen.

An affair of the heart

Read

During his time at Bethany, while he was dining at the house of Simon the leper, a woman came in carrying an alabaster jar of expensive ointment of nard, and, breaking open the jar, she poured the ointment on his head. Some there muttered angrily to each other, 'Why has she wasted the ointment like that? Such ointment could have been sold for over three hundred denarii, and the proceeds given to the poor.' And they reprimanded her. But Jesus said, 'Leave her be; why are you criticising her? She has done a wonderful thing for me.'

Mark 14:3-6

Ponder

How far should we allow our hearts to rule our heads? Not at all, you might well say, and, generally, you'd be right. Yet are there not occasions when we need to act on impulse? While it pays to look before we leap, it would be a sad business indeed if we felt it necessary to analyse the pros and cons of every action before ever doing anything. The impulsive gesture can be our undoing, but equally it can be the road to happiness, bringing joy to others and fulfilment to ourselves.

When it comes to relationships, this is all the more so. When we love someone, we want to show it. So it was for the woman who anointed Jesus' feet. She loved Jesus, not in the sense of being physically attracted to him but because of who he was and what he meant. She recognised he was someone special, offering a new dimension to life, and instinctively she responded. Do we still have that urge within us to show how much Jesus means to us? Do we find ourselves spontaneously offering our love, our lives, our money, our service? Is your faith still an affair of the heart?

Ask yourself

When did you last offer something to Jesus as a token of your love for him? Does your faith involve joyful response as well as intellectual assent?

Pray

Lord Jesus Christ, I can never repay all I owe you, nor even a fraction of what I have received from your loving hand. There are no words or deeds great enough to thank you for all your goodness, but I yearn to make some kind of response; to express my gratitude for all you have done for me. You have poured out your blessings upon me, day after day, filling my life with good things. You have met my needs and more than my needs.

Receive my worship, receive my faith, receive my love, for I bring them to you as a small but simple way of saying thank you. Amen.

Remember

I will give thanks to the Lord with all my heart.   *Psalm 9:1*

Close

Lord Jesus Christ, I offer you my life, not to settle a debt or buy your favour but as an expression of my love, a token of my gratitude, an outpouring of my worship and a symbol of my commitment. Accept me, and use me in your service, for your name's sake. Amen.

Judge not

Read

Why do you judge your brother or sister? How is it you presume to look down on them? We will all stand before the judgement seat of God. For it is written, 'As I live, says the Lord, every knee shall bend to me, and every tongue shall confess God's name.' Each of us, therefore, will have to account for our actions before God. So then, let us no longer pass judgement on one another, but let us instead make up our minds never to put an obstacle or impediment in anyone's way.   *Romans 14:10-13*

Ponder

How well do you know those you mix with – your family or friends, your colleagues at work or fellow church members? You may think you know them, but do you? There have been many times when, talking to a friend of long standing, I have unexpectedly learned something about them which gives a whole new insight into their character and history. Actions which before made no sense suddenly fit into place; words which left me puzzled find a simple explanation. The experience can be profoundly humbling, bringing home all too sharply how easily and often we make judgements about people based on the flimsiest of facts.

Perhaps more disturbing still is the realisation that others form conclusions about us in much the same way. No wonder, then, that the scriptures repeatedly warn us against judging others.

Ask yourself

Are you open to your own faults, rather than the faults of others? Have you been guilty of passing judgement on someone? Is it time you offered an apology?

Pray

Almighty God, I have set myself up in your place so often, presuming I have a right to judge others. I know it is wrong, and I try to stop myself, yet I fall into the same trap time and again, pointing the accusing finger in condemnation. I jump to conclusions that say more about myself than anyone; I see faults in others yet I am blind to my own innumerable failings.

Forgive me, and help me to change. Teach me to see the best rather than the worst, to look for good rather than evil, to build up rather than destroy. Teach me to forgive as you have forgiven me, and to leave final judgement where it belongs – with you. Amen.

Remember

Brothers and sisters, do not malign each other. There is one lawgiver and one judge who is able to save and to destroy, so who do you think you are to pass judgement on your neighbour?   *James 4:11a, 12*

Close

Gracious God, help me to see with your eyes, to reach out with your touch, to love with your heart, and to respond always with your gentleness. Through Jesus Christ my Lord. Amen.

A constant source of strength

Read

I labour and I struggle, exploiting the mighty strength of
Christ at work within me.   *Colossians 1:29*

Ponder

One of the television programmes that fascinates my
young son is the series *World's strongest man*. His interest is
understandable. Whereas I struggle nowadays even to carry
him, these heavyweights pick up a massive block of solid
concrete as though it's a mere pebble, and tow a mighty
juggernaut as though it's a child's toy. Impressive stuff, which
few of us could ever hope to match.

There's one source of strength, however, that we all have
access to, and that is the power of God, or, as Paul
describes it, the mighty strength of Christ. We may not be
able to hoist a car with our bare hands but, through faith,
we can move mountains! We can take on impossible odds,
we can persevere in adversity, we help to shape lives and
even transform the world, not in our own strength but
with God's help. It is, of course, a very different sort of
power than that which can be cultivated through exercise
and body-building routines, yet it is ultimately a greater
power than any, for it comes from the one who brought
the very universe into being.

Never underestimate what God can do, and never forget
what he can do through you.

Ask yourself

Are you guilty of underestimating the power of God? Are
there areas of life in which you are trusting solely in your
own strength?

Pray

Sovereign God, creator and ruler of all, forgive me that I lose sight sometimes of your greatness, forgetting the incredible resources you put at my disposal. I look at the difficulties I face and I feel overwhelmed, questioning my ability to get through. I look at the needs of the world, and I feel there is nothing I can do, no way I can make a difference. I look at your call to discipleship, your summons to make disciples of all nations, and I feel it is utterly beyond me, such a mission beyond all credibility. I measure the challenge against *my* ability to respond to it rather than *yours*. I think only in terms of my feebleness instead of your awesome strength.

Come to me afresh through your Holy Spirit, and fill me with your power – the power of faith, love, courage and mercy – and so use me to fulfil your will and bring nearer your kingdom. Through Jesus Christ my Lord. Amen.

Remember

Now to him who by his power at work within us is able to achieve inestimably more than anything we can ask or even dream of, to him be glory in the Church and in Christ Jesus in this and every generation, now and always. Amen.

Ephesians 3:20-21

Close

Lord Jesus Christ, I go in your strength, knowing that whatever I may face you will be sufficient for all my needs. In you I put my trust, now and always. Amen.

The gift of laughter

Read

A merry heart makes for a cheerful countenance, but a morose disposition crushes the spirit. Every day in life is wretched for the downtrodden, yet those with a cheerful heart feast continually. *Proverbs 15:13, 15*

Ponder

Towards the end of my ministry in Cheltenham I organised a special if rather unusual service – a celebration of laughter. We had held music services and songs of praise services, so why not a laughter service? The idea caught on and, through a series of such services, we thanked God for the ability to laugh. Not everybody, however, thought it was a good idea. Shortly after advertising the first service, I spotted a letter in the local paper roundly condemning my heretical idea and suggesting it would undermine the solemnity and reverence of worship. Others were intrigued, so much so that the service earned a mention in a national newspaper and led to a live telephone interview on Radio Newcastle.

Is the idea of God enjoying a good joke so shocking? I hope not, for heaven will be a dull place if it is! To my mind, laughter is one of God's most precious gifts: one that can be abused, it's true, but one that can also bring happiness and enrichment beyond measure.

Ask yourself

What place do you think laughter has in faith? Must faith be humourless?

Pray

Loving God, I thank you for the things in life that make me laugh, the things that bring a smile to my face. I thank you for a sense of humour helping me to see the funny side of life, enabling me to share a joke even when it is on me. I thank you for those with the special gift of bringing laughter to others, bringing a little light relief into the seriousness of our world.

I know that there is a time to weep and a time to laugh, a place for solemnity and a place for humour – help me to get the balance right in my life. Teach me to appreciate your gift of laughter, and to share it with those around me. In the name of Christ. Amen.

Remember

A sunny disposition is an excellent medicine, but a dejected spirit shrivels the bones. *Proverbs 17:22*

Close

Lord, send me out with laughter in my eyes, a smile on my lips, a song in my heart and merriment in my soul, and so may I share the joy that you have given me, to the glory of your name. Amen.

Reclaimed, renamed, retrained

Read

You are a chosen race, a royal priesthood, a holy nation, a people who God has set apart so that you may declare the goodness of him who called you out of darkness into his wonderful light. Once, you were not a people – now you are the people of God; once you had not obtained forgiveness – now you have received mercy.   *1 Peter 2:9-10*

Ponder

When I was a boy I often used to walk around the mudflats of Essex, spotting birds or simply enjoying the peace of the countryside. Although I prefer rugged cliffs and sandy bays, there is nonetheless something haunting about those desolate places, a peace and tranquillity to be had there rarely found elsewhere. Close to nature it all may seem, yet much of the land thereabouts would not be accessible but for human intervention, the bulk of it having been reclaimed earlier last century with the help of Dutch engineers skilled at land reclamation. For example, what we today call Canvey Island was, not so long ago, simply an area of mud exposed at low tide, and, but for the sea wall that surrounds it, would swiftly revert to that.

There is a parallel to this in the Christian life, made clear in those words from the first epistle of Peter. By his grace, God has reclaimed us from the stranglehold of our old nature, he has renamed his people, and he is constantly at work within us, helping to reshape and redirect our lives. Once again, it is a continuing process, the way of self constantly threatening to engulf us. Yet, thanks be to God, though we must play our part, the final victory is not down to us but to him.

Ask yourself

In what ways might God still be looking to shape your life?
Are there areas where your old nature is holding back his
purpose?

Pray

Loving God, I praise you for the way you have worked in
my life: the way you have offered me a new beginning, a
new identity and a new sense of purpose, constantly working
within me to refashion and redeem me. I thank you that,
despite my weakness, you are able to take and use me far
beyond my expectations. Forgive me everything within me
that frustrates your will and, by your grace, continue to
draw me to yourself, remaking me as a living testimony to
your sovereign saving love. Through Jesus Christ my Lord.
Amen.

Remember

Praise be to the God and Father of our Lord Jesus Christ, by
whose inestimable mercy we have been born again to a living
hope through the resurrection of Jesus Christ from the
dead, to an inheritance that is incorruptible, unspoiled and
unfading.   *1 Peter 1:3-4*

Close

To God who is always forgiving, always loving, always
offering a new beginning, be honour and glory, praise and
thanksgiving, this day and for ever. Amen.

The wilderness of despair

Read

Calling two of his disciples, John sent them to the Lord to ask, 'Are you the one we've been anticipating or should we await someone else?' Now Jesus had just healed many of diseases, afflictions and evil spirits, and given sight to many who were blind. He replied, 'Go and report to John the things you have seen and heard: how the blind see again, the lame walk, lepers become whole, the deaf hear, the dead are raised, the poor hear good news. Blessed is everyone who has no problem understanding this.' *Luke 7:19, 21-23*

Ponder

There are days when life seems utterly bleak. We listen to the news and it is another catalogue of disaster, tragedy, hatred and violence. We look around us, and we see greed, division and selfishness. We look within, and where once there was faith now there is doubt.

It felt like that for John the Baptist in the days following his arrest. Having spent his ministry as a voice in the desert, he found himself in a different sort of wilderness: the wilderness of despair. Had all his efforts been for nothing? Was Jesus an impostor, not the Messiah after all? Had he been taken in, naively putting his faith in a sovereign purpose that simply didn't exist? No wonder he sent messengers to Jesus seeking reassurance, asking what exactly was going on. Only then the message came back: news of a different sort, good things happening, signs of hope, new beginnings, new life. What that news meant to John back in the darkness of his cell we are not told, but I imagine it was all he needed to hear, giving him strength to face his imminent death with a quiet and calm assurance, the knowledge that God's will would triumph. His story is a reminder to all who find themselves in the wilderness of despair: stop and look again, for there, in the apparent barrenness all around you, you will see the seeds of God's kingdom, the proof of his love, bursting into new and irrepressible life.

Ask yourself

Have you found yourself drawn into the wilderness of despair? Are there signs of hope around you that you have lost sight of?

Pray

Sovereign God, despite all that conspires against your purpose, you are at work in our world and at work in my life. You came in Christ, making yourself known, demonstrating your faithfulness, revealing the awesome nature of your love, and, through his ministry, you sowed the seeds of your kingdom. You have worked since through countless generations of believers and you are working still, stirring hearts, quickening consciences, transforming lives, your light reaching out where there is darkness, your love offering new beginnings where the future had seemed hopeless.

Help me to glimpse your kingdom, to work for its fulfilment and to look forward in faith to that day when Christ shall come in glory to take up his throne and rule over all, to the glory of your name. Amen.

Remember

Now may the God of hope fill you with all joy and peace in believing, so that hope may blossom within you, through the power of the Holy Spirit. *Romans 15:13*

Close

Lord of all, when life seems dark, help me to put my trust in you. Inspire me with the knowledge that in the wilderness experiences of people's lives you have often been supremely at work – challenging, deepening and strengthening their faith, equipping them for new avenues of service and opening the way to a richer experience of your love. In that assurance, lead me forward, through Jesus Christ my Lord. Amen.

Recognising our limitations

Read

Elisha sent out a messenger to Naaman, saying, 'If you wash yourself in the Jordan seven times, your skin will be made whole and you will be clean.' But Naaman was incensed and stormed away, saying, 'At the very least I expected him to come out to me, stand and call on the name of the Lord his God, and then brandish his hand over the spot, and so cure me of my leprosy! Surely the rivers of Damascus, Abana and Pharpar are infinitely superior to all the waters of Israel? Why can't I wash in them, and be clean?' He stomped off in a rage, but his servants approached him and said to him, 'My Lord, if the prophet had told you to do something complicated, would you not have done it? How much more then, when all he asks you to do is "Wash, and be clean"?'

2 Kings 5:10-13

Ponder

The higher we rise, the harder we fall – so conventional wisdom tells us. But there is another side to that observation, for we could equally say we must be brought low before we can rise high. In the story of Naaman both of these truths are well demonstrated. Asked to bathe in the muddy waters of the Jordan, Naaman storms off in a fit of pique; the idea of so demeaning himself was complete anathema. It takes the gentle coaxing of his entourage to make him see reason. What does a dent to his pride matter if it leads finally to personal wholeness? To his credit, Naaman succeeds in swallowing his pride and taking their advice.

We can hardly miss the absurdity of Naaman's initial reaction, yet do we recognise with equal clarity the same foolishness in ourselves? How often do we allow a misplaced sense of our own importance to blind us to the right way forward? How many times have we rejected sorely required help rather than admit our need of others? It is a natural human tendency to believe we can go it alone – the story of Naaman reminds us that we can't.

Ask yourself

In what ways does pride have a foothold in your life? Are you ready to admit that you may be wrong and others right?

Pray

Sovereign God, I have been guilty of the sin of pride, thinking of myself more highly than I should, boasting of my own achievements and looking down on those around me. I have not listened to your voice or the voice of others, believing instead that I know best, and I have been guilty of pride in more subtle ways, hiding my frailties behind a mask of self-sufficiency, denying my weaknesses and refusing support when it has been offered.

Forgive me, and grant me true humility: a willingness to listen to your voice, to recognise my weaknesses and to acknowledge my need of others. Through Jesus Christ my Lord. Amen.

Remember

Fools imagine they are always right; wise is the one who heeds advice. *Proverbs 12:15*

Close

Sovereign God, give me a deeper awareness of your greatness and a fuller appreciation of the worth of those around me, and so help me to have a proper sense of my own importance, neither valuing myself too little nor too highly. In the name of Christ I ask it. Amen.

Set free from fear

Read

Though an army encamp against me, my heart shall not fear; though war rise up against me, yet will I be confident. Do not be afraid of sudden panic, or of the storm that strikes the wicked; for the Lord will be your confidence and will keep your foot from being caught. Even though I walk through the darkest of valleys, I fear no evil; for you are by my side; your staff and your crook continually there to reassure me. *Psalm 27:3; Proverbs 3:25-26; Psalm 23:4*

Ponder

Of all the destructive forces at work within us, few, I believe, are more powerful than fear. I don't mean the fear we all feel sometimes when confronted by danger, but rather that dull nagging anxiety which can creep into our lives almost unnoticed and then slowly take over. Such fear saps us of energy, drains us of self-confidence, and robs us of enthusiasm. At its most extreme it can result in inexplicable feelings of panic, even complete breakdown.

It is hardly surprising, then, that our natural instinct is to run away from our fears, and to stifle as best we can any such feeling within us. This, though, is a recipe for disaster. The only way to conquer fear is to confront it, in the knowledge that with God on our side nothing can finally harm us. We have his assurance that, whatever we may face, he will be there to see us through and set us free.

Ask yourself

Are you running away from your fears? Are you ready instead to face them, in God's strength?

Pray

Loving God, I thank you that in the turmoil of life you are always with me – your love reaching out, your hand supporting me and your grace giving me strength. Help me truly to believe that, not just in my mind but also in my heart; to put my trust wholly in you, confident that you will never fail me. Help me to let go of the fears and anxieties that weigh me down, that destroy my confidence and undermine my happiness, that alienate me from others and prevent me living life to the full. Help me to receive the freedom you offer, which comes from knowing you hold all things in your hands and that nothing can finally separate me from your love. In the name of Christ I ask it. Amen.

Remember
I sought the Lord, and he answered me, and set me free from all my fears.   *Psalm 34:4*

Close
Lord Jesus Christ, teach me that whatever today may hold and whatever tomorrow might bring, the future is secure, for you are with me, the same yesterday, today and for ever. Help me, then, to live each moment with you, in quiet confidence and joyful celebration, knowing that I am yours and you are mine, for all eternity. Amen.

Learning to say sorry

Read

If you are bringing a gift to the altar and, when you get there, you remember that someone has something against you, leave your gift there before the altar and, before anything else, make your peace with that person; then come and offer your gift.   *Matthew 5:23-24*

Ponder

There is one word that, could we learn to say it more often, has the power to change the world, but it is probably one of the hardest words to say. I refer, of course, to that little word 'sorry' – a word that should be so simple, yet which sticks in the throat as few others do. We can mean to say it and even look for the opportunity but, when the moment comes, so often we are unable to spit it out. The reason I suppose is our reluctance to lose face, our unwillingness to admit publicly our fallibility. Yet, although some might see saying sorry as a sign of weakness, it actually requires great humility and immense strength of character. If only more of us had the courage to give it a go.

Ask yourself

Have you wronged somebody recently? Have you the courage to admit your mistake to them and ask for forgiveness?

Pray

Loving God, I usually know when I have done wrong but I very rarely admit it. I am reluctant to lose face, so I go on pretending, adding one falsehood to another. Yet there can be no peace that way, no prospect of inner contentment. Give me the wisdom and the humility I need to recognise my mistakes, to acknowledge them openly, to seek forgiveness, and where possible to make amends. Through Jesus Christ my Lord. Amen.

Remember

Confess your sins to one another. *James 5:16*

Close

Gracious God, help me to acknowledge my sins not only to you but to those I sin against, and help me to say sorry not only through my words but through my actions. So may I pursue the way of peace, in the name of Christ. Amen.

An enduring kingdom

Read

I know that whatever God does endures for ever; nothing can be added to or taken away from it. God has done this, so that all must stand in wonder before him.

Ecclesiastes 3:14

Ponder

Last week I had the pleasure of copy-editing a book on archaeology. It was a fascinating read, documenting civilisations that existed centuries before Christ, some so technologically advanced that it has taken nearly seven millennia to rediscover the skills they took for granted. At the time they must have filled surrounding nations with awe, and the prospect of such mighty empires ever declining must have been quite unthinkable. Yet decline they did, to the point that, barely fifty years ago, we knew next to nothing about them.

There is one kingdom, and one kingdom only, which is different and that, of course, is the kingdom of God. When everything else has passed away, when the brief existence of this planet we call Earth is long since over, his kingdom will endure – unending, unchanging, unshakeable. All this is not to disparage the wonder of this world or the joys of this life. Rather it reminds us of the need to place our ultimate trust in what is of ultimate significance – in a hope that will never let us down.

Ask yourself

How far is your happiness dependent on things that will change?

Pray

Eternal God, in a world of constant flux I thank you that you remain the same – solid, unchanging, dependable – a

God in whom I can put my trust. Though all else fails, you will not. Though empires come and go, your kingdom will endure for ever. Teach me to base my life on that fact, celebrating the many blessings you give me now but recognising also where my eternal fulfilment lies. So may I rejoice in the light of your love, today, tomorrow and always. Amen.

Remember

Heaven and earth will pass away, but my words will never pass away. *Matthew 24:35*

Close

Sovereign God, before all, above all, within all, beyond all, go with me now and remain with me always, through Jesus Christ my Lord. Amen.

The key to it all

Read

Remember, then, what you have received and heard; observe it and repent. If you fail to keep watch, I will come upon you like a thief at an hour which you will have no way of knowing. Those who triumph will be clothed in white robes, and I guarantee that their name will not be erased from the book of life; I will acknowledge them before my Father and his angels. All who have ears to hear what the Spirit is saying to the churches, let them listen. And to the messenger of the church in Philadelphia, write this: These are the words of the holy and true one, the one having the key of David, who opens so that no one can shut and shuts so that no one can open.   *Revelation 3:3, 5-7*

Ponder

Have you ever lost or forgotten your house key? It's infuriating, isn't it? You can look through the letterbox, peer through the window, but you just can't get inside. If you're lucky, a neighbour or friend has a key; if not, you have to force the lock or smash a window to get in. For many, much of the Bible and the Christian faith feels rather similar – it gives a tantalising glimpse of a world they want to be part of, but which they cannot seem to get into. How can we believe in a loving Creator, they ask? What is meant by eternal life? Where and what is God? There are a multitude of questions that even the most committed of us struggle to answer. It has rightly been observed that no one has ever been argued into the kingdom of heaven. Even those of us who are Christians struggle to make sense of much in the scriptures, not least in the pages of the Old Testament. If we agonise over the problems and questions, valid though they may be, we will never reach a point of commitment and forever find ourselves on the outside looking in, and there is no way this time of forcing the lock to gain entry.

We need someone with the key, and that person is Jesus, the one who makes God real, the Word made flesh. It is only when we look at him that we are able to see what God is like, and it is through accepting his love and following his way that we find the door opened into the wonder of his kingdom.

Ask yourself
Do you lose yourself sometimes in trying to make sense of the mystery of God? Have you made faith too complicated?

Pray
Lord Jesus Christ, I thank you that you are the one who makes sense of it all – the one who enables me to grasp something of the mystery of God and to reconcile this with the riddle of life and the complexities of the world. I thank you that you are the key that unlocks the door, opening up for me the way to understanding and to life in all its fullness.

Save me from getting lost in all that I cannot understand, from barring the door once again by restricting faith to my own limited understanding. Help me always to look to you and, through receiving your grace, may I follow your way until that day when I pass through the gates of your kingdom into the glory of God – Father, Son and Holy Spirit. Amen.

Remember
No one has ever seen God; but he who is close to his heart, his one and only Son, has made him known.   *John 1:18*

Close
Sovereign God, for opening through Christ the way to know and love you, receive my praise. Amen.

121

Faith in action

Read

Some may argue, 'You have faith and I have works.' Show me your faith without works, and I will show you my faith by my works. You have sufficient faith to believe there is one God. Well done! Even demons believe that and tremble at the thought. Can't you get it into your head, you nitpicker, that faith divorced from works yields nothing?

James 2:18-20

Ponder

'Do as I say, not as I do.' It's easy to empathise with the sentiment behind those words, for probably most of us are all too aware of the gulf between the principles we claim to follow and those we actually live by. 'Don't be put off,' we want to tell people; 'look at the theory rather than the practice.' Only, of course, they don't – actions invariably speak louder than words. We can talk about faith all we like. We can speak of God's love and his care for all until we are blue in the face. It will count for nothing if the way we live puts across a different message.

Our faith needs to show itself in the things we do and the people we are; only then will people stop and take notice. To use another old saying: 'Precepts may lead, but examples draw.'

Ask yourself

What does your life say to others? Is it an expression or denial of your faith?

Pray

Lord Jesus Christ, I like to think that faith is enough to save me, for I know my deeds are poor and my witness is weak, incapable of earning salvation. I thank you that you see beyond my failures to the intentions beneath them, and that, when I acknowledge my faults, you are always willing to have mercy. Yet save me from using that as an excuse to abdicate my responsibilities, from imagining that the way I live and the service I offer are unimportant.

Help me to understand that, though faith does not depend on works, it must show itself through them; that the ultimate test of whether my life is rooted in you is whether it bears fruit in your service. Teach me, then, through the care I offer, the love I share and the service I give to express my commitment to you, faith showing itself in action, to the glory of your name. Amen.

To remember

Little children, let us love, not in word or empty promise, but in deed and reality.   *1 John 3:18*

Close

Living God, teach me to hear your cry in the groans of the hungry, the suffering of the sick, the plight of the homeless and the sorrow of the bereaved; to hear your call in the misery of the lonely, the despair of the oppressed, the plea of the weak and the helplessness of the poor. Teach me to listen and to respond, in the name of Christ. Amen.

Return to sender?

Read

As the rain and snow come down from heaven and do not return until they have watered the earth – making it blossom and sprout, and giving seed to be sown and bread for food – so it is with the word of my mouth; it will not return fruitless, but will accomplish my purpose, and achieve that for which I sent it.   *Isaiah 55:10-11*

Ponder

I'd posted my letter and was waiting eagerly for a reply, each day growing increasingly impatient at the delay. 'What could be keeping them?' I wondered. How much longer would it be? Three weeks later the letter arrived – not the letter I was anticipating but the one I had sent with a curt message scribbled across the front: 'Return to sender. Address not known.' Life can be like that sometimes, can't it? We think we've done something, only to find it's gone wrong. We believe we've completed a job only to discover it needs doing all over again.

With God, it's different. What he says he will do, he does. What he accomplishes is accomplished once and for all. We may frustrate him, impede him, even oppose him but, ultimately, his will shall be done. Hold on to his promises, trust in his word, for neither will return to him empty.

Ask yourself

Have you lost sight of God's assurance that his will shall triumph? Is it time you reminded yourself of his promises in the light of his faithfulness across the years?

Pray

Living God, I praise you for the assurance that your will shall be done and your purpose shall finally triumph. I thank you that in all the changing circumstances of life you are constantly active, day by day working to fulfil your sovereign purpose.

Teach me, then, to live each moment with total confidence, knowing that, though all else may fail, you will not. Teach me to leave all things in your hands, secure in your love, convinced of your faithfulness, and certain that what you have promised, you will deliver. Through Jesus Christ my Lord. Amen.

Remember

The Lord of hosts has affirmed, 'As I have designed, so it will be; as I have planned, so it will happen.'   *Isaiah 14:24*

Close

Eternal God, I put myself in your hands, knowing that your kingdom shall come and your will be done, through Jesus Christ my Lord. Amen.

A fitting response

Read

He rescued me from the slippery pit, out of the mud and the mire; he set my feet on a rock and gave me a sure footing. He has put a new song on my lips, a song of praise to our God.

Psalm 40:2-3

Ponder

Imagine going to a concert or a play in which the most superlative performance was given but after which the audience got up and left in stony silence. Or imagine going to a football match or some other sporting event in which the crowd sat motionless, with no sign of emotion or involvement whatsoever. It's unimaginable, isn't it? Each of these excites passion and appreciation, not only inviting but expecting some kind of response. To applaud, chant, cheer, leap out of one's seat – each denotes how much the event means to those experiencing it.

So it is with God. After everything he has done for us can we remain silent? In the light of his inexpressible love, his innumerable gifts and his inexhaustible grace, can we do anything less than respond? Of course not! Here is the essence of worship – a spontaneous outpouring of praise, thanksgiving, love and wonder; a way of telling God how much it all means to us. Is that what worship means to you? Is that your motivation behind these few moments you have set aside for prayer and reflection? It should be, and if it's not then maybe it's time you reminded yourself once again of who God is, what he has given, and what he continues to give.

Ask yourself

Is your response to God in worship what it used to be? Have you lost sight of all God has given and all you owe to him?

Pray

Great and wonderful God, you have blessed me in so much, showering me with your love and blessings. Your goodness is greater than I can ever hope to measure, your love beyond anything I can even begin to fathom, your gifts more than I can ever start to number, and yet I know you as a living reality in my heart, as the one who gives shape and purpose to all of life.

So I come to you with a grateful heart in joyful homage, seeking, as best I can, to make my response. I consecrate this time to pray, to read, to think and to learn. I acknowledge you as my creator, my Lord, my Father and my friend, and I thank you for your incredible and unfailing love. Accept now my worship, poor though it is and inadequate though my words may be, for I bring it to you as an expression of my gratitude and a sign of my commitment, through Jesus Christ my Lord. Amen.

To remember

I will sing unceasingly of your unfailing love, O Lord; I will declare your faithfulness to all generations. Your constant love is unchanged from the beginning of time, and your faithfulness is as permanent as the heavens. *Psalm 89:1-2a*

Close

Gracious God, you bless me beyond my imagining, love me beyond my dreaming, forgive me beyond my deserving and use me beyond my hoping. To you be praise and thanks-giving, honour and adoration, now and always. Amen.

A pause for thought

Read

Martha was preoccupied with her many tasks; so she came to him and asked, 'Lord, doesn't it matter to you that my sister has left me to do all the work by myself? Tell her to lend a hand.' But the Lord answered her, 'Martha, Martha, you are fretting and distracted by many things; only one thing is really important. Mary has chosen that more important thing, and it will not be taken away from her.'

Luke 10:40-42

Ponder

We live today at breakneck speed, rushing here, there and everywhere, yet forever chasing our tails. Despite having labour-saving gadgets such as our grandparents could only have dreamed of, we are part of a society ravaged by exhaustion and burn-out as we attempt to cram yet more activity into our already overcrowded lives. The material rewards are many, yet spiritually most of us are hopelessly impoverished.

We need sometimes to pause and ask ourselves where we are going and why. We need to consider the deeper things of life and to reflect on what actually matters most. Unless we pause to think now, we may reach the end of our days only to discover that we have frittered our lives away on much that is ultimately empty and meaningless trivia.

Ask yourself

Do you succeed in making time for quiet reflection, or are such moments crowded out by the demands and concerns of daily life?

Pray

Loving God, we live at such a hectic pace, our lives so busy and pressurised, with never a moment to spare. Yet so often we forget the one thing we really need: time to pause and ponder, to take stock of our lives and reflect on your good-ness so that we might understand what it is that you would say to us.

Draw near to me now in these few moments of quietness. Teach me to be still and to know your presence, through Jesus Christ my Lord. Amen.

Remember

Thus said the Lord God, the Holy One of Israel: Come back, be at peace, and you will be safe; your strength lies in quietness and being still.   *Isaiah 30:15*

Close

Lord of all, I have made time and space for quietness to hear your voice. Go with me now into the turmoil of life, with all its noise and confusion, all its demands and responsibilities, and may your peace rest with me there, this day and for evermore. Through Jesus Christ my Lord. Amen.

See page 804 for 29 February

MARCH

The beauty of creation

Read

The heavens extol the glory of God; the firmament testifies to his handiwork. Each day witnesses eloquently and each night communicates knowledge, without need of speech, language or any other voice. Their music pervades all the earth; the words of their mouth reach out to the furthest parts of the world.

Psalm 19:1-4

Ponder

Across the years, few things have spoken more powerfully of God's presence than the wonder of nature. Take the words of the poet William Wordsworth:

> The sun, above the mountain's head,
> a freshening lustre mellow
> through all the long green fields has spread,
> his first sweet evening yellow.
>
> Books! 'tis a dull and endless strife:
> come, hear the woodland linnet,
> how sweet his music! on my life,
> there's more of wisdom in it.
>
> And hark! how blithe the throstle sings!
> he, too, is no mean preacher:
> come forth into the light of things,
> let Nature be your teacher.
>
> One impulse from a vernal wood
> may teach you more of man,
> of moral evil and of good,
> than all the sages can.
>
> *From 'The Tables Turned'*

All this is not to idealise nature, for there is much within it that is harsh and even ugly. Yet this can never detract from the loveliness of so much around us: the awesomeness of the stars at night, the simple yet exquisite beauty of a bird singing or bud bursting into bloom, the evocative smell of the sea or scent of a wild flower. These speak not just of the wonder of this world but also of the splendour of God. We need to thank him for such treasures, but, more than that, we need to recognise our duty to safeguard these for future generations. Ecological responsibility in an age of global warming and unprecedented environmental exploitation is not just an optional extra – for the Christian it is central to faithful discipleship.

Ask yourself
What aspects of creation speak most powerfully to you of God? In what ways are you helping to preserve the environment and in what ways are you guilty of exploiting it?

Pray
Loving God, I thank you for the wonder of the universe and the infinite beauty of this world. I praise you for the loveliness that surrounds me, the inexhaustible splendour of creation. Forgive me for becoming overfamiliar with it all, exploiting and squandering your many gifts. Help me to rejoice in all you have given and to act as a faithful steward of creation, to the glory of your name. Amen.

Remember
Sing gratefully to the Lord; make a joyful melody on the harp in his honour. He shrouds the sky in cloud and prepares rain for the earth; he bedecks the hills with grass and foliage. He causes the snow to fall, white as wool, and sprinkles frost thick as ashes; he scatters hail like crumbs of bread; he sends cold, and pools of water freeze over; he speaks his word, and the ice melts; he makes the wind blow and the waters flow again.   *Psalm 147:7-8, 15-18*

Close
Gracious God, open my eyes to the loveliness of this world and in honouring your creation may I honour you. Amen.

The gift of hope

Read

My soul waits quietly for God; my confidence comes from him. He, and he alone, is my rock, my deliverance and my stronghold; nothing will shake me.   *Psalm 62:5-6*

Ponder

Of the three great Christian gifts spoken of by the Apostle Paul, the most neglected is surely 'hope'. We hear much in the Church of faith and love, but hope seems to be the poor relation, seldom getting much of a mention. Yet what would life be without it? I don't mean hope in the sense of wishful thinking – that is simply an illusion – nor in the sense of hoping against hope – that would be plain foolishness. No, the hope God gives us is a confidence in the future based upon the present experience of his love. We do not know the precise details of what that future holds, nor do we need to know. We have the assurance that God is at work in our lives, and that one day his purpose will be fulfilled. What more could we want?

Ask yourself

Does the thought of the future fill you with confidence or dread? Do you feel able to leave your ultimate destiny in the hands of God, confident that, whatever you may face, he will finally make all things work together for good?

Pray

Lord, it is hard sometimes not to lose faith in your purpose. When hopes are dashed, when dreams are shattered, when one disappointment piles up on another, it's difficult not to lose heart completely, not to retreat into a shell of despair. I want to believe I can change, but there seems little evidence to support it. I want to believe the world can be different, but experience appears to prove otherwise. My heart tells me one thing, my head says another, and it is the latter that finally wins the day.

Yet you have promised that nothing in heaven or on earth will finally overcome your purpose, and throughout history you have shown that to be true, constantly over-turning human expectations, hope returning like a phoenix from the ashes. Speak to me now through the faith and vision of those who have gone before, so that, however dark the world may seem, I too may dare to hope in turn, through Jesus Christ my Lord. Amen.

Remember

Why is my soul disheartened and my spirit troubled within me? I put my hope in you, O God, for I will again praise you, my help and my God.   *Psalm 42:5-6a*

Close

Loving God, send me back into the world renewed in hope and restored in faith, to live and work for you. Amen.

Celebrating the new morning

Read

Satisfy us each morning with your unswerving love, so that we may rejoice and celebrate all our days.   *Psalm 90:14*

Ponder

Mornings are not my favourite time, and I suspect many would say the same. We may occasionally greet the new day with a song in our hearts, but probably more often it is with a groan of dismay, the pressures and responsibilities of daily life weighing so heavily upon us that we wake with a sense of foreboding rather than anticipation. Yet every morning is God's gift, full of immeasurable potential and untold possibilities, if only we have eyes to see and ears to hear. Make time, when you wake, to acknowledge God's goodness and to commit the day ahead to him.

Ask yourself

Do you still welcome each day as a gift? Do you need to re-examine your sense of perspective?

Pray

Loving God, I thank you for the gift of this and every day. I praise you for all the possibilities each brings, the innumerable opportunities for love, joy, fascination and fulfilment that every one opens up. Teach me to count my blessings and to welcome this day as your gift, consecrating it to your service in grateful praise, through Jesus Christ my Lord. Amen.

Remember

The enduring love of the Lord never fades, his mercies can never be exhausted; each morning they are made new, such is his great faithfulness. 'The Lord is all I need,' declares my soul, 'and so I will trust in him.'   *Lamentations 3:22-24*

Close

God of life, may the promise of the sunrise be echoed in my mind, the warmth of the midday sun flow into my heart and the peace of the sunset touch my soul, and when life seems dark teach me to remember that still you are with me and that I will again see your light. In the name of Christ. Amen.

Cut it out!

Read

If your right eye is your weak spot, pluck it out and throw it
away; it is preferable for you to lose one part of your body
than for the whole of it to be thrown into hell. And if your
right hand is your weak spot, cut it off and throw it away; it
is preferable for you to lose one part of your body than for
the whole of it to go to hell.   *Matthew 5:29-30*

Ponder

We'd done a good job – or so I thought. We'd scrubbed the
walls until every last trace of mildew was gone and then
applied two layers of mould repellent before decorating once
again; surely this time our problems were at an end. Yet,
three months later, we were back to square one, the walls
black with mould, the room dank and stale. Where had we
gone wrong? The answer, of course, is that we hadn't tackled
the root problem: the lack of a damp course and adequate
ventilation. Without that, we could redecorate as often as
we wanted to and it would make no difference.

That experience helped me understand what Jesus was
talking about in those somewhat puzzling words of the
Sermon on the Mount. Would any of us really mutilate ourselves in the way he suggests? I hope not, for what Jesus
was doing here was using the typical rabbinic device of
hyperbole to get across the importance of his point. If you
want to conquer your weaknesses, he is saying, it's no good
simply papering over the cracks. You have to tackle the root
cause of the problem; otherwise the same old problem will
surface again and again. It's not finally a part of the body we
need to cut out but those things in our lives that expose our
weaknesses. Ignore those and, for all our good intentions,
we're asking for trouble.

Ask yourself

What are the areas of weakness in your life? Have you done anything to avoid them or do you actively put yourself in situations where you are tempted?

Pray

Living God, help me to be honest with myself: to see myself as I really am, with all my weaknesses, ugliness and sinfulness. Teach me to face all those things I usually push aside – the unpleasant truths I sweep under the carpet, pretending they are not there. Then, having done that, help me to be firm with myself, avoiding that which I know will lead me astray. Teach me that though I ultimately depend on you to change me from within, I also have a part to play within that, a responsibility that I must accept. So, as well as praying, 'Lead me not into temptation', may I do all in my power to keep temptation at bay. Through Jesus Christ my Lord. Amen.

Remember

Watch and pray, so that temptation does not find a hold: for though the spirit is willing, the flesh is weak.

Matthew 26:41

Close

Lord Jesus Christ, help me to turn from everything that leads me astray, and to focus on you and your will, for your name's sake. Amen.

A love that will not let us go

Read

When Israel was a child, I loved him, calling my son out of Egypt. I was the one who taught my people Ephraim to walk, who cradled them in my arms; but they did not know it was me who nurtured them. I restrained them with love and led them with cords of kindness. I was like a parent lifting an infant to their cheek, kneeling down to feed them. How can I let you go, Ephraim, and Israel, how can I relinquish you? How can I make you like Admah or treat you like Zeboiim? My heart flinches within me; my devotion burns tenderly within me. I will not give vent to my fury; I will not again destroy Ephraim; for I am God, not human, the Holy One among you, and I will not come in anger.

Hosea 11:1, 3-4, 8-9

Ponder

We talk a lot about the love of God but I wonder how many of us have even begun to grasp it. I suspect we think of God in terms of judgement as much as grace; as a somewhat stern and forbidding Father ready to reach out and punish the moment we step out of line.

Certainly there are times when discipline is necessary but, as the wonderful words of Hosea make clear, this is never something he delights in doing. Taking his own broken marriage as a model, the prophet paints a graphic and moving picture of the anguish God feels at the repeated rejection and betrayal of his people. Here is an unforgettable glimpse of a love that finally will not let us go, however much we may throw against it. There can be few passages that portray more beautifully the true nature of the God we serve.

Ask yourself

Do you think of God in the same way as Hosea or have you been guilty of underestimating his love?

Pray

Gracious God, I talk often about love, but I have little idea what it really is. The love I show to others is invariably flawed, corrupted by ulterior motives and self-interest. I can scarcely begin to fathom the immensity of the love you hold for me; a love that is inexhaustible, awesome in its intensity, devoted beyond measure.

Forgive me for losing sight of this one great reality at the heart of faith without which all else is as nothing. Forgive me for portraying you as a God of vengeance and justice when, above all, you are a God of love; a God who, despite my repeated disobedience, refuses to let me go. Teach me to open my heart to all you so freely give, and so may I love you and others with something of that same total commitment. In the name of Christ. Amen.

Remember

I have loved you with a never-ending love; therefore I have remained faithful to you always.   *Jeremiah 31:3*

Close

Merciful God, encircle me, nurture me, guide and protect me, for I am still a weak and foolish child. In your great love, stay close and watch over me always. Through Jesus Christ my Lord. Amen.

Recognising our faults

Read

He told a further parable to some who were so convinced of their own righteousness that they looked down dismissively on others. 'Two men went up to the temple to pray, the first a Pharisee and the second a tax-collector. The Pharisee, standing aloof, prayed like this, "God, I thank you that I am not like other people – corrupt, deceitful, adulterous – or even like this tax-collector. I fast twice weekly and tithe all my income." But the tax-collector, standing at a distance, could not even bring himself to lift his eyes to heaven, but rather beat his breast, saying, "God, be merciful to a miserable sinner like me!" Mark my words, it was this man rather than the other who went home at peace with God; for all who laud their own virtue will be humbled, but those who humble themselves will be exalted.'   *Luke 18:9-14*

Ponder

When I was a student I worked for a time in a factory. The work was dull but the camaraderie among the workers was fun and, although their language could be a little ripe at times, the majority were good-hearted people whose company I enjoyed. Then somebody asked me about my long-term plans and, when I told them of my intention to enter the ministry, her face fell. 'What do you want to do that for?' she said. 'It will ruin you!' For this lady, the church was synonymous with narrow-minded, holier-than-thou bigotry.

Was she right? Not entirely, no – generalisations only contain half a truth at best – but it's disturbing, isn't it, that someone can gain this impression of Christianity? There are many who, justified or otherwise, would echo her sentiments – a fact we would do well to reflect on. I'm sure we all like to think of ourselves as the humble sinner seeking repentance but we need to ask, honestly and prayerfully, are we guilty sometimes of being more like the smug, complacent Pharisee?

Ask yourself

Are there ways in which you come across as self-righteous? Is it possible that this impression might be justified?

Pray

Lord Jesus Christ, I do not mean to be self-righteous but I can be, more often than I realise. I claim to be accepting of others, but when they do not conform to my expectations I make little attempt to conceal my feelings. I claim to recognise my faults, but if anyone points them out to me I am quick to take offence. I see the speck in my neighbour's eye but repeatedly overlook the log in my own.

Forgive any tendency to assume that I am right and others are wrong. Help me, instead, to understand that I depend finally on your grace, and so, recognising the strengths and weaknesses of all, may I live in true humility, to the glory of your name. Amen.

Remember

Why is it you can see the speck in another's eye, yet cannot see the log in your own? How can you say to someone, 'Allow me to take that speck out of your eye', when there is still a log sticking out of your own? You hypocrite! Take the log out of your own eye first and then you will be in a position to take the speck out of someone else's.   *Matthew 7:3-5*

Close

Gracious God, for your gracious love that none deserves yet all can receive I give you my praise, and I ask for help to show that same accepting attitude in all my dealings. Through Jesus Christ my Lord. Amen.

The moment of truth

Read

The day dawned when the Lord planned to take Elijah up to heaven in a mighty wind. Elijah and Elisha were about to set off from Gilgal, and Elijah said to Elisha, 'Stay here; for the Lord has sent me to Bethel.' But Elisha said, 'By the Lord's life and yours, I will not leave you.' So they went down to Bethel together. A company of prophets there approached Elisha, saying, 'Are you not aware that the Lord is going to take your master from you today?' 'I'm aware of it,' he replied; 'say no more.' *2 Kings 2:1-3*

Ponder

To take responsibility for our lives and make our own decisions is a difficult and, at times, painful business, yet it is an essential part of reaching maturity. As children, we rely on parents for guidance, or, failing these, perhaps a close friend, another member of our family, or a teacher at school. Eventually, though, both they and we need to let go if we are to make our own way in the world.

In the case of Elisha, dependence was rooted in his friend and mentor Elijah, but suddenly his world fell apart as he found himself faced with the prospect of having to go it alone. No wonder he didn't want to talk about it. In his words and actions we see someone desperately trying to deny reality. Yet, when the moment of truth came, he found God had prepared him to meet the challenge.

An unhealthy sense of dependence can attach itself not only to people but also to God, such that we expect him to give us clear instructions in every situation. I've even heard of Christians earnestly praying as to what they should eat for breakfast: seriously wondering whether God prefers them to have cornflakes or shredded wheat! There is, of course, a place for seeking his will, but we can take it too far. He offers us the help and instruction we need but he has also given us common sense, which he fully expects us to use.

Ask yourself

Are you guilty sometimes of using God as a prop to avoid taking responsibility for your life?

Pray

Loving God, it is not easy to carry responsibilities. We prefer to share the burden with others, to have someone else we can lean on knowing that they will always be there to support us. But there are times when we have to stand on our own two feet and accept the challenges life brings.

Help me, when those moments come, to recognise that, however helpless I may feel, I am never alone, for you are always with me, giving me the help I need to meet those challenges head on. Teach me to trust in your strength, and, through the power of the Holy Spirit, faithfully to discharge the responsibilities you give me. Amen.

Remember

God has told you what is good; and what does he want of you but to act justly, to delight in showing kindness, and to walk in humility with your God.   *Micah 6:8*

Close

Living God, for the way you guide me and the way you give me freedom to make my own decisions, I praise you. Teach me when I need to listen and when I need to act in faith. Through Jesus Christ my Lord. Amen.

Your God needs you!

Read

How can they cry out to someone they have not believed in? How can they believe in someone they have never heard of? And how can they hear of him unless someone proclaims it to them? And how can anyone proclaim unless they are sent?   *Romans 10:14-15*

Ponder

If you had been out and about in the year 1914, you would have seen, wherever you went, a poster emblazoned with the words 'Your country needs you!' It was all part of the government's campaign to enlist new recruits to serve in the First World War and, incredible though it may seem to us today in the light of what we know about the horrors of that conflict, young men signed up in their thousands, eager to be part of this 'great adventure'. The reasons behind that are many: partly it reflected nationalistic fervour and partly dreams of glory and heroism, but perhaps the underlying reason – and one cleverly exploited by the poster – was the fact that all of us like to feel needed. This, more than anything, gives us a sense of worth and purpose in life.

So, when we read the words of Romans 10, we should catch our breath in praise and thanksgiving, for here we find God expressing his need of us! In Christ he has good news for all the world, a message he wants everyone to hear and rejoice in, but in order to spread the word and make real his love, he depends on our contribution. It may be a cliché, and one that sounds quite incredible, but it is nonetheless true that God requires us to be his hands and feet, his eyes and mouth, his agents here on earth. Quite simply, your God needs you!

Ask yourself

Have you taken seriously God's need of you? Are you guilty sometimes of wondering why he hasn't answered your prayers when the reality is that you have failed to help answer them yourself?

Pray

Lord, I need your love, your mercy, your guidance and your peace, for without you my soul is restless, my life impoverished and my destiny hopeless. But I thank you too that, incredibly, you are a God who has need of me, a God who has chosen to make yourself dependent on human co-operation. You need my faith and trust; my hands and feet; my willingness to speak in service and witness; my commitment to you in body, mind and soul.

Living God, I marvel that you need me as much as I need you, but I thank you for that great truth, that awesome privilege and that amazing responsibility. Help me to honour the trust you have placed in me, through Jesus Christ my Lord. Amen.

Remember

Go, then, and make disciples of all people, baptising them in the name of the Father, the Son and the Holy Spirit.

Matthew 28:19

Close

Lord Jesus Christ, you have touched my life, brought me joy and given me life in all its fullness. Equip me now, through your Spirit, to make you known and share with others the blessing I have found in you, for your name's sake. Amen.

Persevering in prayer

Read

He said to them, 'Imagine going to a friend at midnight and saying, "Friend, lend me three loaves of bread, for one of my friends has turned up and I haven't a scrap to feed him", only to receive the answer, "Stop bothering me; the door's fastened and we're all in bed; I'm not getting up to give you anything." I tell you, even though friendship may not be a sufficient spur to rouse your friend to help you, sheer persistence, if nothing else, will persuade him to get up and give you what it is you need.' *Luke 11:5-8*

Ponder

At first sight, the teaching of Jesus on prayer can seem confusing. On the one hand, he tells us not to go in for long-winded prayers as if God will hear us because of our many words; on the other, he urges us to persist in prayer until God hears and answers. There is, though, no contradiction here. The injunction to keep things simple still stands – after all, God knows our needs before we ask him, so we hardly need to labour the point. On occasions, however, God chooses for a variety of reasons not to answer our prayer immediately, or is unable to do so. It may be that we need to demonstrate our resolve, or that the time to grant our request is not yet right, or that we are asking for the wrong thing. Whatever the reason, this parable tells us not to lose heart; still less to worry that God might grow impatient with us. Unlike the friend at midnight, God is *always* anxious to meet our needs, at any and every moment. If the answer doesn't seem to come, then make no mistake, there is good reason.

Ask yourself

Do you hesitate sometimes to bother God again about a

recurring problem? Are you making the mistake of attributing your own lack of patience to him?

Pray

Lord Jesus Christ, I know that God hears my prayers, that he is ready to answer when I call to him, but I am still reluctant sometimes to ask for help, for I am conscious of having asked so many times before. I seek forgiveness for the same old mistakes. I ask for help with the same old problems. I look for guidance concerning the same old matters. I intercede for the same old people. Day after day, week after week, I bring the same list of requests, so familiar that even I have grown tired of them, let alone him. I am afraid of exhausting his patience, of becoming an irritation and a nuisance, and I wonder whether I am asking for the wrong things, or whether perhaps God has given his answer, only I have failed to hear.

Yet you tell me he is always ready to listen, always wanting to bless me, and that no matter how often I approach him he will make time to hear me and time to answer. Teach me, then, to approach with confidence and to bring all my needs in faith before him, assured that he longs to meet my need and that, in his own time and way, he *will* respond. In your name I ask it. Amen.

Remember

Do not brood over anything, but thankfully acquaint God with all your needs through your prayers and petitions.

Philippians 4:6

Close

Gracious God, I thank you for all the prayers you have answered over the years, and I bring you those that seem unanswered, knowing that you are always ready to hear me and that you always, finally, answer. Receive my praise, through Jesus Christ my Lord. Amen.

Consequences

Read

The stubborn get their just deserts; likewise the good get what they deserve. The simple believe anything but the wise think before they act. The wise are circumspect and avoid evil, but the fool acts without thought, discarding moderation. The hot-blooded act foolishly, and the conniver is despised. The simple are dressed up with folly, but the wise are crowned with understanding.   *Proverbs 14:14-18*

Ponder

In recent years, a fascinating school of thought has gained ground in scientific theory centred around so-called 'chaos theory'. The proposition behind this is that something as tiny as the fluttering of a butterfly's wings in Australia could have far-reaching consequences in Europe, or that a pebble falling in a Saharan oasis may ultimately affect conditions on the Antarctic ice-sheet.

How true the theory is remains to be demonstrated, but it is certainly indisputable that many actions have consequences far greater than we might expect. An angry word, an error of judgement or a split-second moment of carelessness can set in motion a catastrophic chain of cause and effect. Before we act, we need to think about where our action may lead. Above all, in our response to God – whether we obey his commandments and follow his guidance – we need to consider the consequences: for us, for others and for him.

Ask yourself

How often have you regretted a thoughtless action? Have you learned from your mistake?

Pray

Loving God, so often we act with little or no thought as to the potential repercussions, only to find later that the results of decisions taken, whether our own or those of others, are hard to bear. We act unkindly and cause untold hurt. We speak hastily, and sow a seed that grows beyond our control. We ignore your will and then find life has turned sour.

Help me to act wisely, carefully considering the future in all my decisions. Help me to put past mistakes right and to learn from them. Help me to think of the consequences before I do something, rather than afterwards when it is too late to change them. In the name of Christ. Amen.

Remember

Do not be taken in: God will not be made a fool of. Whatever someone sows, that person will also reap; the one who sows what the body wants will reap corruption but the one who sows what the Spirit desires will reap eternal life through that same Spirit. *Ephesians 6:7-8*

Close

Gracious God, take what is, reshape what has been and direct what shall be. Through Jesus Christ my Lord. Amen.

So much more to share

Read

On the first evening of the Sabbath, the disciples having assembled to break bread, Paul preached to them and, conscious that he was due to depart the next day, he talked on past midnight. Now there were a number of oil-lamps in the upstairs room where they had gathered and, as Paul continued still longer with his sermon, a young man called Eutychus, who was perched on a window sill, sank into a torpor and fell from the third storey, and was assumed to be dead. Paul rushed down and cradled him in his arms, saying, 'Don't be alarmed. He's still alive!' And he went back upstairs, broke bread, and, having eaten this, once more talked at length until dawn broke, after which he finally departed.

Acts 20:7-11

Ponder

When did you last hear a boring sermon? We've all sat through them, haven't we, and in my case I've probably preached a few as well! I doubt, though, that we've ever been involved in a situation quite like that recorded in Acts 20. Here we see none other than the Apostle Paul as the archetypal preacher who doesn't know when to stop, going on so long, in fact, that one of his unfortunate listeners dozes off and keels out of an upstairs window! Whether the sermon was dull we are not told – the mishap is charitably put down to the room being over-warm – but had I been sitting there for that length of time I think my eyes would have glazed over too. What is truly astonishing, however, is that when the young man turns out not to be seriously injured, or even dead as first feared, Paul gets back to his feet and carries on with his sermon! Is that thick-skinned, or what!

So what lay behind this mammoth homily? It wasn't that Paul liked the sound of his own voice; it was rather that the good news bubbled up within him so that he felt compelled to share it! His example isn't one I would recommend following too closely, but we all need something of that enthusiasm. If we had even a fraction of Paul's irrepressible desire to share his faith, what a difference we could make.

Ask yourself
When did you last communicate the joy you have found in Christ? In what ways, if any, do you share your faith?

Pray
Sovereign God, you have given me so much to share, more than I can ever begin to express. You have showered me with your blessings, touching my life in innumerable ways. You have given me joy that knows no bounds, mercy beyond all my deserving, hope that can never be exhausted, peace that passes understanding and love that exceeds anything I can ever ask or think of.

Teach me to share that with others, to tell joyfully and spontaneously of everything that you have done and all you mean to me, to the glory of your name. Amen.

Remember
We cannot help speaking of the things that we have seen and heard.   *Acts 4:20*

Close
Loving Lord, I have so much to share – save me from ever keeping it to myself. Amen.

Coming to faith

Read

He said to them, 'What about you – who do you say that I am?' Peter answered, 'You are the Christ.' Then he warned them to tell no one about him. And he began to teach them that it was necessary for the Son of man to suffer many things, to be rejected by the chief priests, the elders and the scribes, to be killed and on the third day to rise again. He made no secret of it. Then Peter, taking him aside, began to reproach him. But he spun round, and seeing the disciples there, he took Peter to task, saying, 'Get behind me, Satan: for you are preoccupied not with the things of God, but the things of man.'   *Mark 8:29-33*

Ponder

The moment when Peter confessed his faith in Christ tends to be portrayed as one of the most momentous events in the gospel narratives – a supreme moment of understanding and a corresponding expression of commitment. To me, though, it is also an enigmatic moment; as much a day Peter would have wanted to forget as remember. Certainly, he declared Jesus to be the Messiah, but was he alone in this perception or simply voicing the opinion held by his fellow Apostles. The idea that he understood who Jesus was more clearly than they did is given the lie in what follows, when far from being the rock of the Church, as he is described in other accounts of this incident, he is labelled 'Satan'. Strong stuff indeed!

Perhaps the greatest lesson we can draw from this story is that coming to faith is not the one-off event we sometimes imagine but an ongoing process that never ends. Peter thought he had understood the nature of Christ, and, to a point, he had. He was to imagine the same again when Jesus asked to wash his feet, only to deny his faith shortly afterwards. Later still, he was to recognise that his distinction between Jew and Gentile, clean and unclean, had no place in the Christian message. Faith was never a finished article but always on the production line, being shaped, added to, refined, polished. Beware the one who thinks they've arrived and who believes they have fathomed the depths of the gospel. Avoid such an error yourself. We may know the truth but, in this life at least, we will never know the whole truth.

Ask yourself
Have you lost sight of the need to grow in faith? Have you come to regard being a Christian as settling at a destination rather than progressing on a journey?

Pray
Loving God, I thank you for those moments in my life that have been milestones in my journey of faith – moments when I have been especially conscious of your presence, when faith has grown, when truth has dawned on me in an unmistakable way. I thank you for such times but I pray you will help me always to recognise that my journey is not ended but only just begun. Teach me that, however many answers I may have, there is always more to see, more to learn and more to understand. Amen.

Remember
Knowledge puffs up whereas love builds up. If someone imagines they have fully understood something, then they have not yet begun to understand it at all, but if anyone loves God then that person is fully known by him.

1 Corinthians 8:1-2

Close
Sovereign God, open my heart to all you have yet to say, yet to do and yet to teach. Help me to recognise that, far from being over, my journey has only just begun. Through Jesus Christ my Lord. Amen.

A glimpse of glory

Read

Six days after this, Jesus took Peter, James and John up on to a lofty mountain with him, where they were alone together, removed from all, and there Jesus was transfigured before them. His garments gleamed a dazzling white, such as no fuller on earth could ever whiten them; and alongside Jesus, in conversation with him, appeared Moses and Elijah.

Mark 9:2-4

Ponder

I've never found the story of the Transfiguration an easy one to understand. It calls to mind the words in *Alice in Wonderland*: 'curiouser and curiouser', and is even vaguely suggestive of the claims of certain soap powders to wash whiter than white. Yet the strangeness of the incident should not blind us to its underlying message. This was no sensational sideshow designed to dispel doubts among the inner circle of disciples. On the contrary, it was a glimpse of the extraordinary in what had seemed an ordinary moment, a blossoming of faith leading to a deeper vision. At least that's how I read it. The three disciples are walking with Jesus, listening to his words, reflecting on his ministry, and, suddenly, it's not just a mountain they ascend but a spiritual peak – a high spot in which the reality of who Jesus is dawns on them. They discern, albeit fleetingly, that he is the fulfilment of the law and the prophets, represented by Moses and Elijah. They realise he is sent from God, dazzling in his splendour. They catch a brief vision of Christ in all his glory. Life would never be quite the same for them again, for this is the moment in which faith came of age, their old picture of Jesus exposed as hopelessly inadequate.

We can imagine, in our turn, that, having committed ourselves to Christ, we are well advanced along the path of faith, but we should never underestimate the power of Jesus to surprise us. The message here is similar to that of Peter's confession of Christ – namely that our knowledge of Jesus and our understanding of his glory will never be complete until this life is over and we meet him face to face. Until then, let us make time to be alone in his presence – to listen, hear and reflect – so that perhaps we too may glimpse a little more of his awesome wonder.

Ask yourself
Do you ever imagine that you've grasped the full glory of Christ? Is there a danger of growing overfamiliar in your relationship with him, stressing the human side of his nature at the cost of the divine?

Pray
Omnipotent God, you are able to do more in my life than I can ever begin to imagine. Forgive me for losing sight of that fact – for being content to muddle along, frustrating your will and quenching your Spirit through the narrowness of my vision. Give me today a new sense of all you want to achieve and the many ways you are able to use me in achieving your purpose. Stir my imagination and send me out renewed in faith to live and work for your glory. Through Jesus Christ my Lord. Amen.

Remember
The word became flesh, residing among us, and we perceived his glory, the glory as the Father's only Son, full of grace and truth.
John 1:14

Close
Lord Jesus Christ, meet with me afresh each day, and open my eyes to see you, my ears to hear you, my mind to know you and my heart to love you. So may I glimpse a little more of your glory and my life sing your praises in joyful worship. Amen.

A tough decision

Read

Everything is allowable for me, but not everything is valuable. All things are permissible, but I will not allow anyone to dictate to me. Watch out, though, in case exercising your freedom should put a stumbling block in the way of the weak.

1 Corinthians 6:12; 8:9

Ponder

Was it a goal or wasn't it? The 'goal' scored by Geoff Hurst in England's victory against West Germany in the 1966 World Cup final must be one of the most frequently shown clips and widely debated incidents in the annals of sport. Even today, with the aid of slow-motion replays and computer simulation, nobody can be completely sure, so what hope did the unfortunate referee have on the day? Yet, of course, he had to come to a decision.

There are often moments like that in daily life; moments when we are faced by the need to decide even though the right choice is far from clear. So it was for the Corinthians in the days of the Apostle Paul, not least about whether it was permissible or otherwise for Christians to eat meat that had been dedicated to idols. Paul's answer, essentially, was that it depends on the circumstances – what's right in one situation may be wrong in another. There is a warning here we would do well to heed. Occasionally issues may be clear-cut, but there are times also when it is unwise to be dogmatic. We may prefer living with moral and ethical certainties, but that is not always the way of Christ.

Ask yourself

Are you sometimes more dogmatic than you should be? Does this reflect the strength of your faith or its underlying weakness?

Pray

Living God, day by day I have to choose, to make decisions about right and wrong, good and evil. Sometimes the choice is clear, sometimes confusing; sometimes easy, sometimes hard; sometimes mattering little, sometimes much, but, whatever the case, I need to seek your will and to make up my mind as to the best way forward.

Help me to decide wisely, for there is so much I do not understand, so many complicated and confusing areas of life. Grant me faith to wrestle with such matters, confident that you can use them to lead me to new insights and a deeper awareness of your sovereign purpose, to the glory of your name. Amen.

Remember

Jesus said to them, 'Give to Caesar the things that are Caesar's and to God the things that are God's.'　　　*Mark 12:17*

Close

Lord Jesus Christ, you tell me that the whole law is summed up in the command to love. Help me to understand what that means and so may that truth shape my decisions, my attitudes and my life, to your glory. Amen.

Seeing is believing

Read

Philip found Nathaniel and told him, 'We have found the one written about in the law of Moses and the prophets: Jesus of Nazareth, the son of Joseph.' Nathaniel responded, 'Can anything good come out of Nazareth?' Philip answered, 'Come and see.'

John 1:45-46

Ponder

If I were to tell you that I can tear a telephone directory in half with my bare hands, or that I can run a three-minute mile, or that I've just been voted the best-dressed man in Britain, would you believe me? Of course not! You'd either think I'm the most bigheaded or misguided person in the country, or the worst liar you've ever come across. If you could see me doing those things, on the other hand, it would be different: there would be no question then – after all, seeing is believing. Sadly I can lay no such claims to fame, but let me paint another scenario. If someone arrived claiming to be the Messiah, able to heal the sick, forgive sins and raise the dead, would you believe them? I doubt it. And neither did Nathaniel when his friend Philip told him that he had found the deliverer they had long waited for. After all those barren years of expectation, could it be true, and, if so, could he have come from Nazareth of all places?

Philip's reply was the best possible: 'Come and see.' His words remind us that the gospel is not about speculation or philosophy but is a testimony to the experience of innumerable people whose lives were directly touched by the ministry of Christ. It includes eyewitness accounts of concrete events and a flesh-and-blood person. Most important of all, it invites us to put our faith in Jesus, to respond to his promises, and so to see for ourselves the truth of who he is and all he means.

Ask yourself

Do you lose sight sometimes of the fact that the New Testament is based on the concrete experience of Christ's love? Have you shared that experience yourself?

Pray

Sovereign God, I thank you that you took on our humanity, walking our earth, experiencing our joy and sorrow, becoming part of our world of space and time. I thank you for the experience of those who met with you in Christ, and for their testimony to your life-changing power through him.

Above all, I thank you that I too can experience that same love and power within my life; that though I may not see Jesus in the flesh I can still know him as a living reality in my heart and so experience for myself the good news at the heart of the gospel. Receive my grateful praise, through Jesus Christ my Lord. Amen.

Remember

Concerning the Word of life – which was from the beginning, which we have heard and seen with our own eyes, and which we witnessed and touched with our own hands – this we now announce to you in order that you too may have fellowship with us.   *1 John 1:1, 3*

Close

Lord Jesus Christ, live in my heart, fill my soul, renew my mind, so that I may know and love you fully, just as you know and love me. Amen.

Confronting evil

Read

As we were on our way to a place of prayer, we were met by
a young girl possessed by some strange spirit, who brought
a wealthy living to her masters through her claims to foretell
the future. She followed us, crying out, 'These men are servants
of the most high God, and have come to announce to you
the way of salvation', and she did this for many days. Paul,
greatly troubled at what was going on, spun round and
said to the Spirit, 'I command you in the name of Jesus
Christ to come out of her'; and immediately it came out. Her
masters, seeing their comfortable livelihood disappearing,
seized Paul and Silas and dragged them to the marketplace
before the rulers and magistrates who, having heard the
charges, had them thrown into prison, their feet securely
fettered in the stocks.   *Acts 16:16-20a, 24*

Ponder

When a mass protest took place at the meeting of the
World Trade Organisation in Seattle in December 1999,
what was intended as a peaceful demonstration was taken
over by a small group of anarchists, and violence erupted
that was rightly condemned. The majority, however, had
come for one purpose – to voice their concern over what
they saw as the exploitation and oppression resulting from
unimpeded free trade. Whether they were right or wrong in
that assessment I am not sure, but I have to admire their
willingness to stand up for their convictions. It is all too
easy apathetically to turn a blind eye to injustice; to believe
something is wrong yet leave it to others to do something
about it.

The Apostle Paul could have done that with regard to
the young girl who was being unscrupulously exploited for
her supposed gifts of fortune-telling, but he recognised this

to be unequivocally evil and refused to walk by on the other side. Confronting evil may well prove costly, just as it did for Paul and his companions, but there are times when it is a necessary part of discipleship.

Ask yourself

Are there issues you feel strongly about yet which, through fear or complacency, you have done nothing about? Does ignoring evil make you an accessory to it?

Pray

Sovereign God, there is much in this world that is corrupt and so much in society that is unjust, but I am often afraid to speak out against it for fear of the consequences. Even when wrongdoing affects me personally I am reluctant to protest in case the result proves costly. I am cautious about throwing the first stone in case it turns out I have misunderstood the situation. I do not want to risk hostility or damage my credibility. I am afraid that once I nail my colours to the mast there may be no going back.

Sovereign God, you do not want me to judge, but you do want me to stand up for what is right and to oppose what is evil. Help me to recognise when those times are, and give me the courage then to be true to my convictions, and true to you. Amen.

Remember

Do not surrender to evil, but conquer evil with good.

Romans 12:21

Close

Lord Jesus Christ, you faced up to evil, even though it cost you your life. Give me wisdom to know when I must stand up for my principles, and then give me courage to stand firm, for your name's sake. Amen.

Against the grain

Read

Enter through the narrow gate. For wide is the gate and broad the way leading to destruction, and many are those who take that route, but the path leading to the gate of life is straight and narrow, and only a few find it.

Matthew 7:13-14

Ponder

Are you a DIY expert? I wish I was but, sadly, such skills have always eluded me. Take the time at school many years ago, when I was furiously planing a piece of wood that stubbornly insisted on splintering and snagging at every thrust of the blade. One look from my woodwork teacher told me I had gaffed again. 'Plane *with* the grain,' he told me, with a weary groan of despair, 'not *against* it!' There was a simple lesson in that, not just for woodwork but also for life. Attempt to go against the grain and you will have problems – guaranteed.

Yet, as the words of Jesus make clear, on occasions we must be willing to do just that; to go against the grain of self-interest and received wisdom, of force of habit and expected behaviour, of family loyalties and personal inclination. It is not that we rebel for the sake of it, but there will be times when faith brings us into conflict with accepted norms and when the call of Christ means renouncing the way of the world. Such a path is never easy and we will always face the temptation to take a less-demanding option, a course of less resistance, but though that way may seem attractive, its lure is ultimately deceptive, for in running from the challenge we run from life itself; the life God wants us to know in all its fullness.

Ask yourself

Are there areas in your life in conflict with the message of the gospel? Do you need to let go and surrender these to Christ?

Pray

Lord, there is so much in the gospel that goes against the grain: your call to deny ourselves and put others first; your command to love our enemies and turn the other cheek; your challenge to forgive and go on forgiving. All this, and so much else, runs contrary to my natural inclinations, contradicting the received wisdom of this world.

I do not find it easy and at times I resist, yet I know that in you and you alone is the path to life – the way to peace, joy and fulfilment. Take me, then, and fashion my life according to your pattern, until your will becomes my will and your way my way. In the name of Christ I ask it. Amen.

Remember

All your ways may seem pure in your own eyes, but the Lord weighs the spirit.   *Proverbs 16:2 (NRSV)*

Close

Loving God, when I pray, 'Your kingdom come, your will be done', teach me to mean it, however hard working towards that may be. Through Jesus Christ my Lord. Amen.

This is the day

Read

This is the day that the Lord has made; let us celebrate and
rejoice in it.

Psalm 118:24

Ponder

The other day I was looking back at a holiday scrapbook
compiled by my mother when I was nine years old. It had
been my first proper holiday and it was fascinating to recall
moments long since past. It's good sometimes to look back
just as it's good also to look forward, yet we must take care,
for both have their dangers. If we're not careful, we can end
up so preoccupied with the past or the future that we overlook the blessings of the present. We strive in the first half
of our lives to achieve first this, then that, only in later
years to look back to the good old days and wish we'd
made more of them while we had the chance.

What we need to learn is to enjoy each moment, recognising all it has to offer. Give thanks for the past, by all
means; anticipate the future, of course; but never forget that
this is the day the Lord has made – don't let it pass you by.

Ask yourself

How often do you stop and simply enjoy the present
moment? How often do you make a point of thanking
God for it?

Pray

Gracious God, this is the day that you have made and I
praise you for it.

Forgive me for so often failing to do that, frittering away
what I have now through my preoccupation with what
once was or what yet might be. Help me to recognise each
day as your gift, to be received with gratitude and lived to
the full. Teach me to welcome every moment as a new

beginning: the past put behind me, the future waiting to be grasped and the present mine to celebrate. Lord, this is the day that you have made; I will rejoice and be glad in it. Through Jesus Christ my Lord. Amen.

Remember

Do not fret about tomorrow, for tomorrow will take care of itself. Tackle your problems one day at a time.

Matthew 6:34

Close

Gracious God, teach me to take each moment as it comes and to live it to the full. Through Jesus Christ my Lord. Amen.

You shall!

Read

You shall know the truth, and the truth shall set you free. I have come so that you shall have life, and have it to the full. Ask and it shall be given to you; seek and you shall find; knock and the door shall be opened to you.

John 8:32; 10:10; Matthew 7:7

Ponder

'Don't do that!' 'Stop it!' 'Leave it alone!' There are times when being a parent feels like constantly nagging, forever saying no. The same, sadly, is the impression some people have of the Church; a view reinforced by those old Wayside Pulpit posters you still sometimes see, starkly proclaiming 'The wages of sin is death' or some other equally cheery message! Undeniably, there is a negative element in the Bible, epitomised by the majority of the Ten Commandments with their stern preface: 'Thou shalt not . . .'

This, however, is by no means the whole story, for in the teaching of Jesus the message is reversed. Instead of 'You shall not' it becomes 'You shall', all the negative commandments being summed up in one positive: 'A new commandment I give you: Love one another' (John 13:14). Repeatedly it is the same story: you *shall* have, you *shall* know, you *shall* find – the blind shall see, the lame walk, the imprisoned be set free, the pure in heart see God, the hungry and thirsty be satisfied, and so on and so on. Never think that being a Christian is about what you *can't* do, still less give that impression to others. Above all, it is about what you *can* do; about the possibilities the love of Christ opens up; about the sheer potential of life!

Ask yourself

Do we see Christianity as the imposition of boundaries or the offering of possibilities?

Pray

Sovereign God, I thank you that you came in Christ not to exact punishment but to show mercy; not to restrict but to liberate, not to deny but to affirm. Forgive me for sometimes turning joyful faith into sombre religion, the living gospel into lifeless dogma, a message of hope into a foretelling of doom. Teach me to receive the gifts you want me to enjoy and to turn life into a celebration of your goodness. So may the person I am, as well as the words I say, truly proclaim the good news of Jesus Christ. In his name I pray. Amen.

Remember

Anyone who follows me shall never walk in darkness but shall have the light of life.   *John 8:12*

Close

Lord Jesus Christ, as you have affirmed life for me, so may I affirm it for others, in word and deed, to the glory of your name. Amen.

Agreeing to disagree

Read

I beg Euodia and Syntyche to share a common mind in the Lord. And yes, I ask you, my trustworthy colleague, to help them both, for they struggled with me in the cause of the gospel, alongside Clement and my other fellow-workers, each of whose names is in the book of life.

Philippians 4:2-3

Ponder

When were you last involved in an argument? Probably more recently than you care to remember. Somehow, what begins as a healthy disagreement invariably seems to lead on to a full-blown quarrel. At times this may have good cause, but just as often it is about something futile, and the issues so hotly disputed are of little or no importance. What had come between Euodia and Syntyche we are not told, but it is clear that daggers were drawn and others were inexorably being drawn into the conflict. Sadly, once a quarrel starts, it develops a life of its own, the smallest of details magnified out of all proportion until the initial difference of opinion is lost behind a mountain of real or imagined slights. How many families have been divided, friendships broken and feuds started through the most trivial of disagreements? A quarrel is easy to start and hard to end – far better to avoid it in the first place.

Ask yourself

Is there a feud or argument you have become embroiled in? What is it really all about? Isn't it time you put the past behind you and made your peace?

Pray

Gracious God, forgive us the foolish divisions we allow to come between us, the petty disputes that grow out of all proportion until they destroy the fellowship we share. I know there will always be occasions when we disagree, for we are all different, each having our own way of looking at the world and our own unique experience of life, but in Christ we should be able to see such diversity as a blessing rather than a threat, a source of strength instead of a cause of weakness. Forgive me my own pride and insecurity that prevents that, leading me instead to nurse anger, bitterness and resentment in my heart.

Teach me to admit my mistakes whenever I am in the wrong, and when the fault lies with others, teach me to forgive freely as you have forgiven me. Grant me the mind of Christ so that I may live in harmony, for his name's sake. Amen.

Remember

Starting a quarrel is like springing a leak; stop, then, before a dispute turns nasty. Steer clear of stupid arguments, genealogies, disagreements, and debates concerning points of the law, for they are a waste of time and help no one.

Proverbs 17:14; Titus 3:9

Close

Lord Jesus Christ, give me grace to see the point of view of others, humility to accept when I am wrong and sensitivity in my attitude when I am right. Help me to pursue all that makes for peace, for your name's sake. Amen.

Do as you would be done by

Read

Laban had two daughters, the oldest called Leah, and the younger, Rachel. Leah had appealing eyes, but Rachel was both attractive and elegant. Jacob fell for Rachel, and so he said, 'I will give you seven years' service in return for your youngest daughter Rachel.' Laban answered, 'I'd rather give her to you than any other man. Stay and work for me, certainly.' So Jacob served his seven years for Rachel, and such was his love that they seemed just a few days. Then Jacob said to Laban, 'I've honoured my pledge. Give me my wife for I want to sleep with her.' So Laban invited everyone in the region and staged a banquet. That evening he took his daughter Leah and brought her to Jacob, and they slept together. When dawn came, he realised it was Leah!

Genesis 29:16-23

Ponder

Your sins, we are told, will find you out. Is that true? It was for Jacob. While it is hard not to feel sorry for him being duped so outrageously on his wedding day, there is a delicious irony in his being hoodwinked in much the same way as he had cynically deceived his father to filch the blessing intended for his brother Esau. Whether Laban had decided on a little restorative justice or whether we glimpse here God's sense of humour, I'm not sure. It would be wrong to draw simplistic conclusions from this, for much of the time cheats seem to prosper, corruption reaps handsome rewards and evil goes unpunished. Nonetheless, here is ample support for that old proverb, 'Do as you would be done by.' Jacob's experience offers a salutary reminder that there is accountability in this life as well as the next. If we spin a web of deceit, the chances are that we will end up getting caught in it ourselves.

Ask yourself

Do you deal with others in the way you would like them to deal with you? Are there areas in your life where your past actions are catching up with you? What can you learn from this?

Pray

Lord, there are times when life doesn't seem fair, when those who openly flout your will seem to prosper while those who follow you gain scant reward. I know this shouldn't matter – that my treasure should be in heaven rather than on earth, my heart set on things eternal rather than the riches of this world – yet it's hard sometimes not to feel frustrated, even resentful, at the apparent injustice of life.

Forgive me the times I have made that mistake, setting myself up as judge and jury. Forgive me the times I have doubted you in consequence, questioning your justice and resenting your grace. Teach me to understand that, whoever we are, our actions will finally catch up with us, and so help me to live faithfully as one of your people, rejoicing in the blessings you have given, and anticipating the joy yet to come. Amen.

Remember

A wicked person earns an illusory profit; the one who sows honestly reaps a certain reward.   *Proverbs 11:18*

Close

Loving God, teach me to see beneath the surface and to recognise that good and evil bring their own reward, and so may I live with integrity, intent on doing your will. Through Jesus Christ my Lord. Amen.

A mixed bag

Read

The names of the twelve Apostles were as follows: first, Simon, known as Peter, and his brother Andrew; then James son of Zebedee, and his brother John; Philip and Bartholomew; Thomas and Matthew, the tax-collector; James son of Alphaeus, and Thaddaeus; Simon the Cananaean, and Judas Iscariot, the one who was later to betray him.

Matthew 10:1-4

Ponder

I shall always be grateful for my time at college and university. I studied there with people of different characters, backgrounds and ideas, with contrasting ideas and attitudes, representing a variety of denominations and faiths or no faith at all. We were in many ways a mixed bag, yet we were united by a common cause, a shared goal. The same could be said of the Apostles, a motley crew if ever there was one. They included a tax-collector and a freedom-fighter; an impulsive firebrand who wore his heart on his sleeve and a man who was to sneak off into the darkness to betray Jesus; some who were models of faith yet one who is remembered as an example of doubt – hardly those you would expect to hit it off. Yet these were those Jesus called to share in his ministry and, with the exception of Judas, those who carried it on afterwards. They didn't always see eye to eye – in fact, at times they were clearly at loggerheads – yet God was able to use them.

There is a parallel in all this with the Church today. Despite the pious twaddle we sometimes come out with, myself included, we are not always a happy family, everything sweetness and light between us. We are a curious mixture of people with different temperaments and convictions, hopes and fears, joys and sorrows, likes and dislikes. Whether these prove a strength or a weakness depends on us and our shared commitment to serving Christ.

Ask yourself

Do you tend to gravitate towards those of a like mind and similar disposition? Could it be that God is looking to broaden your horizons through sharing with those you don't naturally get on with?

Pray

Lord Jesus Christ, there are some people I find it easy to relate to, others I find hard; some I am naturally drawn towards, others I shy away from; some I enjoy working with, others constantly rub me up the wrong way. Yet you have called me into a family in which all have their place, however different they may be. Teach me to see such differences as strengths, and help me to be ready to learn from others. Amen.

Remember

You are, therefore, no longer strangers and aliens, but fellow-citizens with the saints and members of God's family.

Ephesians 2:19

Close

Lord Jesus Christ, teach me that whatever might divide me from other Christians, far more unites me with them, and so may I be open to all, recognising the unity we share in you. Amen.

The call to conserve

Read

The earth is the Lord's and everything in it, the world and all those who live in it. In his hand are the innermost parts of the earth, and the mountain peaks belong to him. The sea is his, for he made it, and his hands shaped the dry land.

Psalm 24:1; 95:4

Ponder

I was reading an article in *The Ecologist* the other day that somehow gave me a new perspective on the story of Noah's flood. It was nothing revolutionary: simply the observation that God commanded Noah to take two of every living creature into the ark. What was the reason for that? The truth, surely, is that not only humankind but the whole of creation matters to God. It is not ours to exploit willy-nilly, as we sometimes seem to imagine; he has a place in his heart for everything he has made. Do we as Christians take that seriously? We may think we do, but how many of us show it in the way we live.

There seems little doubt that the world today is in the grip of a growing ecological crisis. Sadly, the response from the Church has typically been muted, one Christian even suggesting to me that such matters should not concern us since our future is in heaven rather than on earth. I, for one, cannot accept such a simplistic response. Indeed, I wonder sometimes if those who call us to wake up to our environmental responsibilities, whether they be Christian or otherwise, are the true prophets of our time. If the earth is the Lord's, as we claim, then do we not owe it to him to take care of it, if not for our sakes then for his?

Ask yourself

Have you adjusted your lifestyle to cut out unnecessary waste and pollution where possible? Should you be adding your voice to calls for international action on such issues as global warming and the overexploitation of global resources?

Pray

Lord of all, I praise you for the universe in all its wonder, for the world in all its beauty and for life itself in all its incredible variety. There is so much that gives me pleasure, that offers me fulfilment, that captures my imagination, that challenges and inspires, that gives me cause to look forward with anticipation, that speaks to me of your great love.

Forgive me for so often abusing all you have given – despoiling this world, failing to appreciate it as I should, treating it as mine by right rather than entrusted as your gift. Open my eyes to the countless blessings and inexhaustible riches you have so freely given, and help me to show my appreciation by being a faithful steward of your creation. In the name of Christ. Amen.

Remember

The earth dries up and withers; the world languishes and shrivels up and the heavens suffer with it. Its own inhabitants despoil the earth, for they have flouted the laws, violated the statutes and desecrated the eternal covenant.

Isaiah 24:3-4

Close

Sovereign God, teach me to see the world not as a trinket or a plaything but as a priceless treasure – an heirloom passed on to me and to be handed on intact to others. So teach me to live wisely and responsibly, in harmony with you and all you have made. Through Jesus Christ my Lord. Amen.

Shedding light

Read

You are the light of the world. Just as a city situated on a mountaintop cannot be hidden, so nobody lights a lamp and places it under a bushel basket, putting it instead on a lamp-stand in order that it might shed light throughout the house. Similarly, let your light shine before others, so that they may see the good deeds you do and give glory to your Father in heaven.

Matthew 5:14-16

Ponder

There is something reassuring about light, isn't there? I remember as a child how I always wanted a light left on and how scared I was of the dark; and my own children, in turn, like to have a nightlight left on throughout the hours of darkness. No wonder, then, that light is a symbol shared by almost every religion and by many movements and organisations that profess no faith at all. Within the Christian faith, there are few more enduring or better-loved images than that of Jesus coming as the Light of the World.

The picture Jesus paints here, however, is rather different, and one that comes as something of a shock, for it stands the image on its head. 'You are the light of the world', he tells us, and suddenly, as well as receiving light we are those called to illuminate the lives of others. It reminds us that faith involves give as well as take, responsibility as well as privilege, service as well as reward. It's not all down to us, of course – it is ultimately the light of Christ that must shine through us – but if we think we can have one without the other, then it's time to ask some searching questions of our faith, for we may just find that we've taken a step back into the darkness.

Ask yourself

In what ways do you bring light to others? In what way is the light of Christ seen in your life?

Pray

Lord Jesus Christ, the idea of hiding a lamp under a bushel basket does sound ridiculous, yet I do it all the time. Instead of sharing what you have done for me, I keep it to myself. Instead of looking to the interests of others, I focus on my own. Instead of reaching out to those in need, I shut my mind to their plight. Repeatedly, my words say one thing and my life another.

Forgive me my failure to honour your calling. Fill my heart once more with the joy of knowing you, and so may I shine like a star in the world, bringing glory to God the Father, for your name's sake. Amen.

Remember

You were formerly darkness, but now you are light in the Lord – walk then as children of the light.   *Ephesians 5:8b*

Close

Living God, as the dew falls in the morning, so may your grace descend upon me, and as the sun bathes all in its life-giving light, so may the radiance of Christ shine in my heart. Work in me, with me, and through me, to your glory. Amen.

'Who, me?!'

Read

Now in the sixth month the angel Gabriel was sent by God to a town in Galilee called Nazareth, to a virgin engaged to a man named Joseph, a member of the house of David. The virgin's name was Mary. Approaching her, he said, 'Greetings, you who have been highly favoured. The Lord is with you.' She was bewildered by his words, and contemplated what such a greeting might mean. The angel said to her, 'Don't be frightened, Mary, for you have found favour with God. You will conceive in your womb and bear a son, and you will give him the name "Jesus". He will be great, and will be called the Son of the Most High, and the Lord God will give him the throne of his ancestor David. He will reign over the house of Jacob for ever, and his kingdom will never end.' Mary said to the angel, 'How can this be, since I am a virgin?' The angel answered, 'The Holy Spirit will come upon you, and the power of the Most High will rest over you, so that the child you will bear will be called the Son of God, for with God nothing is impossible.' Mary responded, 'I am the Lord's servant. Let it be to me just as you say.'

Luke 1:26-35, 38

Ponder

Surely God can't use me? How often have we echoed that response of Mary when God has asked something of us? The response is all the more vociferous when what God is asking involves sacrifice on our part. Yet if Mary's initial response is perfectly understandable, how then do we account for her compliance with God's wishes just a few moments afterwards? The answer is simple – she measured what was being asked of her not against her own resources but against God's. So it was that she offered acceptance –

no doubt still confused, still wondering quite why she had been chosen, but ready to let God use her as he saw fit.

This story of Mary calls for a similar response from us today. We warm to accounts of the birth of Jesus, we celebrate his life and ministry, we give intellectual assent to the lordship of Christ, and we may be fascinated, even moved by it all, but God wants more. He wants us to be *changed*: our lives turned around, our very self re-created through his grace. He wants us to become part of his people and to use us in the work of his kingdom. 'Who, me?!' we may say – and that, of course, brings us back to where we started: to the quiet, trusting response of Mary to God's call. It is a response that resounds across the centuries, speaking loud and clear today: 'Yes, you!'

Ask yourself

Are there times when you have backed away from God's call? Do you judge from God's perspective or from your own?

Pray

Gracious God, you may not ask of us what you asked of Mary, but nonetheless your challenge comes to each one of us, calling us to avenues of service that we would never imagine possible. Whoever we are, we all have a part to play in your purposes.

Grant us the humility we need to hear your voice and the faith we need to respond. Like Mary, let us be ready to answer when you call: 'I am the Lord's servant. Let it be to me just as you say'. In Jesus' name I pray. Amen.

Remember

God did not give us a spirit of cowardice, but rather a spirit of power, love and self-control. *2 Timothy 1:7*

Close

Sovereign God, teach me to look not at my weakness but at your power, through Jesus Christ my Lord. Amen.

The courage of our convictions

Read

The administrators and satraps plotted together and then sought an audience with the king. They said to him, 'O King Darius, live forever! The administrators, prefects, satraps, counsellors and governors of the kingdom are all of the opinion that the king should pass and enforce a royal law decree that anyone caught praying, whether to God or man, over these next thirty days – unless, of course, it's to you, O king! – will be thrown into a den of lions. Now, O king, institute this law and sign a decree, so that it is irrevocably binding according to the law of the Medes and the Persians, which cannot be revoked.' So King Darius signed the decree. Daniel knew full well that the decree had been signed, but he followed his usual practice, going to his house, in which the upstairs windows faced towards Jerusalem, and there kneeling three times a day in prayer to offer praise to God, just as he had always done. The plotters came and found Daniel praying and asking God for help.   *Daniel 6:6-11*

Ponder

The story of Daniel in the lions' den must be one of the best known in the whole of the Old Testament; a tale that has been told and retold across the centuries, delighting countless generations. It is a classic example of good con-quering evil; a victory against all the odds. But, of course, it needed the faith and courage of Daniel for that triumph to happen, his willingness to make a stand for the things he believed in, never mind the consequences. Today, thank-fully, times are very different; there is little chance of us being fed to the lions, not literally anyway! Yet we need people of Daniel's stature as much as ever; people ready to risk all in the cause of truth, ready to hold firmly to their principles despite every attempt to sway them. Have we even a fraction of that courage and commitment?

Ask yourself

What pressures to compromise your beliefs do you face today? Have you given in to them?

Pray

Lord, I thank you for the privilege you have given me of being able to worship and witness to you freely. I thank you that I can read your word and declare your name without fear of recrimination. Save me, though, from ever imagining because of this that my faith is safe from challenge. I live in a world in which Christian values are constantly being undermined, where greed and selfishness are held up as virtues, where wealth and success have all too often replaced you as the real object of humankind's devotion. Every day the pressure is there to conform; to give a little ground – first here, then there, until little by little my convictions are diluted and the distinctiveness of my faith destroyed. Teach me to be awake to the dangers I face, and give me strength to resist them by holding fast to you. Amen.

Remember

Do not be conformed to the spirit of the age, but transformed by the renewing of your mind, so that your life might attest to the good, well-pleasing and perfect will of God.

Romans 12:2

Close

Sovereign God, when I am led astray, call me back and help me to walk your way more faithfully, to my journey's end. Amen.

The challenging word

Read

God's word is dynamic and alive, sharper than any two-edged sword, penetrating so deeply it divides soul from spirit, joints from marrow; able to discern the thoughts and objectives of the heart.

Hebrews 4:12

Ponder

Seeking God's will, if we take it seriously, involves risks – the risk, first, that we may be disappointed by God's answer or lack of it, and the risk, second, that it may lead to more than we had bargained for. Sometimes, for reasons we don't understand, no clear guidance seems forthcoming, while at other times the answer God gives is very different from the one we'd hoped for, bringing an awkward, disturbing challenge that we would rather not hear. The question then, of course, is: are we willing to listen, or do we close our ears?

Ask yourself

Are you open to what God might say to you, or do you expect him to fit in with your own expectations?

Pray

Loving God, I claim to be a seeker of truth, but the reality is that it sometimes scares me. It probes too deeply into areas I prefer kept hidden; it challenges me in ways I would rather not face; it exposes issues I find hard to deal with. Despite my fine-sounding words I am often less than honest with myself and with others.

Forgive me, and give me the courage and sensitivity I need both to face the truth and to speak it, in the name of Christ, the way, the truth, and the life. Amen.

Remember

It is a disturbing thing to fall into the hands of the living God. *Hebrews 10:31*

Close

Gracious God, go with me, and may your love continue to astonish me, your grace continue to captivate me, your strength continue to sustain me, and your call continue to surprise me. In Christ's name I ask it. Amen.

Will you be my friend?

Read

Only Luke is with me.

2 Timothy 4:11a

Ponder

What would you say is the greatest social problem of our time? Homelessness? Poverty? Unemployment? There can certainly be no denying the pain each of these causes, but let me suggest another problem, equally widespread and involving immeasurable pain. I speak of loneliness. We live in a world today where people are crying out for companionship, and I don't just mean the elderly or housebound, though for these the problem may be most acute. It is true of people from all walks of life and all ages, condemned to increasing isolation in an ever more fragmented society. For some this means the agony of scarcely meeting another human being from week to week; for others the equal, if not more intense, pain of feeling utterly alone, even when part of a crowd.

So how should we respond? If we are lonely, perhaps we need to reach out to another in friendship and break the ice – it may well be that he or she feels equally as lonely as us. If, on the other hand, we know someone else is lonely, perhaps we can do something to help. It needn't take much: a word of greeting, a solicitous phone call, even a cheery wave can mean far more than we might think.

Ask yourself

Is there someone you know who is feeling lonely? Is there something you can do about it?

Pray

Loving God, I pray for all who are lonely: those whose relationships have been broken or who have never enjoyed the relationships they might have had; those who feel rejected by society and unsure of their worth; those who spend day after day alone and those who feel hopelessly isolated even when they are in company. Give to each one the knowledge that you are with them always, and enrich their lives with companionship and friendship. In the name of Christ I ask it. Amen.

Remember

Even when we reached Macedonia, we knew no peace, for we were troubled in every way – outwardly by disputes and inwardly by fears. Yet God, the one who uplifts the down-hearted, encouraged us by the presence of Titus, not only by his arrival among us but also by the encouragement he had received in you – your yearning, remembrance and enthusiastic support for me, which he communicated until I rejoiced still more. *2 Corinthians 7:5-7*

Close

Lord Jesus Christ, friend of the friendless, reach out to me and help me to reach out in turn, through your grace. Amen.

The God of all comfort

Read

Comfort, comfort my people, says your God. He has sent me to comfort all who mourn, to decorate them with a garland of beauty instead of ashes, the oil of joy instead of sorrow, and a spirit clothed in praise instead of cloaked in despair. As a mother comforts her child, so will I comfort you.

Isaiah 40:1a; 61:1b, 2b-3; 66:13

Ponder

There are many joys in being a parent, and one is the privilege of being able to comfort a child in times of distress. It is astonishing how a sobbing, hysterical child can, in just a few moments, be laughing and smiling once more, simply through the reassuring warmth of a mother or father's embrace and words of reassurance. 'Let's kiss it better,' we say and, although it's nonsense, it works! The pain doesn't always go away, but the child knows that he or she is loved.

If we can do that for our children, how much more can God do it for us, and that is the picture we see time and again in the scriptures, not least in the words of the prophet Isaiah. Ours is a God who loves us more than the most devoted parent; who grieves when we grieve and suffers when we suffer. He doesn't lightly allow us to face such things but, like any good parent, he knows that it is the price of true freedom and the necessary corollary to experiencing joy and pleasure. Yet he always cares, always longs to encircle us in his arms, and, whatever we may face, he promises always to be there to bring us comfort. In the words of the Apostle Paul: 'Glory be to the God and Father of our Lord Jesus Christ: the God of all comfort, who comforts us in all our suffering so that we can comfort those experiencing any kind of suffering with the comfort God has given us' (2 Corinthians 1:3-4).

Ask yourself

Have you opened your heart to the comfort God longs to offer? Are you ready to let his love envelop you?

Pray

God of all comfort, I bring you this world of so much pain: my own and that of those around me. I bring you my own hurts and troubles, anxieties and fears, placing them into your hands, and I pray for those countless others facing sorrow or suffering: hopes dashed, dreams broken; let down by those they counted dear; betrayed; abused; wrestling with depression or illness; mourning loved ones.

Hold on to me and to all who walk through the valley of tears. Reach out and grant the knowledge that you are there, sharing our pain and moved by our sorrow. Minister the consolation that you alone can offer, and give the assurance that those who mourn shall be comforted and those who weep will laugh. Lord, in your mercy, hear my prayer, through Jesus Christ my Lord. Amen.

Remember

I will ask the Father, and he will give you another comforter to be with you for ever. I will not abandon you to your fate; I will come to you. *John 14:16, 18*

Close

Gracious God, when tears are my food day and night, and when my heart is breaking within me, assure me of your love, reach out with your comfort, and help me to know that joy will come again. Through Jesus Christ my Lord. Amen.

The God who takes hold of us

Read

I am the Lord your God, who takes hold of your right hand and says to you: Never fear: I will help you. I, the Lord, have called you in my goodness; I will take hold of your hand.

Isaiah 41:13; 42:6

Ponder

A while back I taught my son Samuel to ride a bicycle without stabilisers. It took him some time, but eventually, with much cajoling and encouragement, he cracked it. If it was hard for him, it was hard for me too, for the only way I could persuade him to have a go at first was to promise to be there alongside him, always there to support him should he lose his balance or start to wobble. I learned then that even a young child can go surprisingly fast, especially for one the wrong side of forty!

We all need a little support sometimes, don't we? Someone to hold on to us when the going gets tough, when we're unsure of our ground, when our confidence fails and we feel ourselves slipping. The message of scripture is that we have such a one in God. Across the ages he has reiterated his promise to support us along the journey of life; to stay close by our side so that, in times of crisis, we can rely upon him to keep us safe. There were moments when Samuel felt like giving up; there will be moments when we feel like that too. But just as my being there gave the reassurance needed for Samuel finally to succeed, so the knowledge of God's constant presence will give us the confidence we need, when we need it.

Ask yourself

Are you facing a challenge which you feel is beyond you? Do you find yourself in life questioning your ability to get through? Have you the faith to trust that God will be there to hold you?

Pray

Loving God, I thank you for your constant guidance throughout my life, for the assurance that you are always there to encourage, strengthen and support me. I praise you for the many ways I have found that to be true; the strength you have given in times of weakness, encouragement in times of fear, support in times of difficulty, faith in times of doubt.

Teach me through all I have experienced to trust you more completely in the future, confident that whatever may be asked of me, your hand will hold me firm and see me through. Amen.

Remember

When I thought, 'My foot is starting to slip', your love, O Lord, supported me. I am constantly with you; you hold my right hand. I will acclaim you, O Lord, for I was at rock bottom and you lifted me up. *Psalm 94:18; 73:23; 30:1*

Close

Loving God, when life is hard and days are dark, enfold me in your arms and surround me with your loving care, holding me close for all eternity. Amen.

Taking hold of Christ

Read

I want to know Christ, and the power of his resurrection, and the fellowship with him that comes through sharing his suffering, even identifying with his death. Not that I have yet received these or been made perfect, but I follow Christ so that I may take hold of them, even as Christ has taken hold of me.

Philippians 3:10, 12

Ponder

It may be a cliché but the old saying is true nonetheless: it takes two to tango. It's true in our human relationships and it's true in our relationship with God in Christ. He will not let go of us, but he needs us to take hold of him if we are to stand firm. We warm to that first truth, but find the second rather harder, don't we? We mean to stay close, but somehow we drift away, disentangling our hand from his to follow our own path and pursue our own interests. Christ is still there, reaching out, ready to respond the moment we ask him, but if we will not hold on then we limit what he can do. It goes further than that. The joy of faith, the peace of God, the hope of eternal life can all be lost so easily, not because they are taken away but because we lose our grip on them, intent on grasping other pleasures. Don't leave it all to him: each day take hold afresh of Christ and make him yours as you are his.

Ask yourself

Is your hold on Christ as sure as it once was, or have you let your hand slip from his grasp?

Pray

Lord Jesus Christ, forgive me for the way I have made my relationship with you one-sided, expecting you to be there for me but all too rarely there for you. Forgive me that I have let go of you so often, intent on going my own way, clinging to what ultimately can never satisfy. Forgive me for doubting you when times are hard, questioning your ability to lead me safely through; for reaching out only when I have need of you, asking you to lift me up from a mire of my own making and to set me on my feet again.

Help me to hold on to you more firmly, in simple trust, quiet confidence and eager expectation, knowing that whatever I face and wherever I may find myself, you will never let go of me. Amen.

Remember

Since we have a great high priest who has gone through the heavens, Jesus Christ the Son of God, let us hold firmly to the faith we profess. We are his house, if we hold on to our courage and the hope of which we boast. I am coming soon. Hold on to what you have, so that no one will take it from you. *Hebrews 4:14; 3:6; Revelation 3:3*

Close

Gracious God, day after day, year after year, you are there to hold on to me. Day after day, year after year, help me to hold on to you, by the grace of Christ. Amen.

APRIL

The God of mercy

Read

The scribes and Pharisees escorted a woman into the crowd who had been caught committing adultery and, setting her before Jesus, they said to him, 'Teacher, this woman was caught red-handed in the act of adultery. Now, in the law Moses commanded us to stone women like her, so what do you say we should do?' They said this to trap him, so that they might have some accusation to level against him. Jesus crouched down and wrote with his finger in the dust, but since they persisted in questioning him, he straightened up and said to them, 'If any of you are without sin, then you be the one to hurl the first stone at her.' He bent down once more and again wrote in the dust. Hearing his words, they melted away, one by one, starting with the oldest, until he was left alone with just the woman before him. Standing up again, he asked her, 'Woman, where are they? Has no one condemned you?' She said, 'No one, sir.' Then Jesus said, 'I do not condemn you, either. Off you go, and from now on do not sin again.'   *John 8:2-11*

Ponder

There's a wonderful old hymn, all too rarely sung nowadays, which begins 'There's a wideness in God's mercy', and which continues, in a later verse: 'But we make his love too narrow by false limits of our own; and we magnify his strictness with a zeal he will not own.'

How true those words are. We tend to assume that God will judge us in much the same way that we so readily judge others. Surely even *his* patience has its limits. Yet, that is the astonishing message at the heart of the gospel – that God is altogether different from us, his attitudes, goodness and forgiveness on a level we find hard to comprehend.

Never labour under a burden of guilt. Never imagine that you have committed some unforgivable sin. Whereas *we* are swift to point the accusing finger, even at ourselves, the nature of God is always to have mercy.

Ask yourself

Do you think of God primarily in terms of judgement or mercy? Have you begun to grasp the sheer magnitude of his grace?

Pray

Sovereign God, I thank you that you judge not by the outside but by the person underneath; not simply by my faithless actions but by my underlying desire to serve you. Where I am swift to condemn, you are looking to forgive. You are always ready to show mercy, to believe in my potential rather than dwell on my past record.

Save me from interpreting your judgement in terms of my own narrow horizons, from attributing to you a strictness that ultimately reflects my own intolerant attitudes and denies your grace. Teach me to receive your forgiveness and to rejoice in the newness of life you long to bring. Through Jesus Christ my Lord. Amen.

Remember

The Lord is merciful and gracious, abounding in steadfast love and not easily riled. He does not constantly accuse or forever nurse his anger, nor does he deal with us according to our sins or repay us for our mistakes. His unswerving love towards those that fear him is as great as the heavens are high above the earth; he banishes our faults from us as far as the east is from the west.   *Psalm 103:8-12*

Close

Gracious God, always watching, always loving, always caring, always ready to forgive and forget, I give you praise, in the name of Christ. Amen.

Working it out for ourselves

Read

You must work out your own salvation with fear and trembling, recognising that God is at work in you so that you will be able to understand and accomplish his good purpose.

Philippians 2:12

Ponder

Are you good at crossword puzzles? I used to have a whole book of them and, in my few spare moments, much enjoyed tackling them. But I discovered I have a fundamental weakness: I can't resist looking at the answers! The result was that I finished each crossword in good time but rather defeated the object of the exercise in the process! When it comes to learning something, there is a similar danger. A child can use a calculator to work out a complicated sum but this will do nothing to further his or her understanding of mathematics. A parent can help children with their homework, yet if they do the work for them, they are ultimately doing a disservice. To appreciate and understand something, we need to work it out for ourselves.

That surely is the point of Paul's words to the Philippians. He is not saying we can earn our salvation or find a way to achieve it through our own ingenuity. Rather he wants to stress the importance of working at our relationship with God, of growing each day in our faith, of striving to become more like Christ. We depend on grace but that does not excuse us our part. Learn about God parrot fashion, consider ourselves a Christian because we know about Jesus and have heard something of the gospel, and we will discover eventually that we have learned very little. Salvation involves commitment to an ongoing relationship and, in that sense, it is something no one else can do for us – we must work it out for ourselves.

Ask yourself

Have you grown casual in your discipleship? Has faith become a matter of theory rather than personal encounter?

Pray

Living God, all too often I leave it to you to make the running in our relationship. I am casual and complacent in discipleship, careless in making time to meet with you and forgetful of your love, yet I still expect you to be there when I need you, ready to answer my prayers and grant your blessing despite my slowness to serve you.

Forgive me for seeing faith as something given to me rather than as something I also need to work at. Forgive me for seeing it as a one-off moment of conversion rather than a continuing story of commitment. Teach me to make time to know you, to listen to your voice and to seek your will. Deepen my experience of you in Christ, and so may I come to know you as a living reality in my life and rejoice in all that you have done. In his name I pray. Amen.

Remember

I pray for this . . . that Christ may so dwell in your hearts through faith that you will be able to grasp with all the saints the breadth, length, height and depth of the love of Christ; and that you may know this all-surpassing love in such a way that you will be filled with the very fullness of God! *Ephesians 3:14a, 17–19*

Close

Sovereign God, by your grace help me to know you better, to love you more fully and to serve you more completely, day by day. Amen.

The God who has time for us

Read

As he walked by, Jesus spotted a man named Matthew sitting at the custom house, and he said to him, 'Follow me'. And, springing up, the man followed him.   *Matthew 9:9*

Ponder

There can be few events that have elicited such a massive display of grief as the death of Diana, Princess of Wales. Theories abound as to what it was about her that captured the public imagination, but the quality most often cited is the fact that she had time for people. Whether it was the victim of a landmine or an AIDS sufferer, she showed that she cared, and she did it in such a way that people believed they really mattered to her.

There was something very akin to that in the experience of Matthew. As a tax-collector, and thus a collaborator with the Romans, he was used to rejection and hatred, to people passing him by with a gesture of contempt or simply ignoring him altogether. Suddenly, though, here was Jesus, not just stopping to talk with him, not simply looking him in the eye, not even merely treating him as a person, but asking him to follow, to become his disciple. It must have been an astounding moment, and we can well imagine Matthew pinching himself to make sure he wasn't dreaming! Yet it was true, and not just for him but for us. God has time for every one of us. For all his splendour and sovereignty, he values us as individuals and wants us to be a part of his kingdom. That too is a mind-boggling fact, a truly astonishing invitation: have we begun to grasp it?

Ask yourself

Do you find it hard to believe anyone has time for you? Have you lost sight of the fact that you are important in God's eyes?

Pray

Almighty God, you are greater than my mind can imagine, sovereign over history, the creator of the ends of the earth, and yet you have time for each one of us. You are all good, all true, all holy, all righteous, and yet you accept me with my many imperfections. You are the source of love, the fount of knowledge, the giver of life, the one who gives meaning to the universe, and yet you delight in my companionship. Almighty God, such things are too wonderful for me, too awesome to take in, but I marvel at your grace, I rejoice in your goodness and I offer now my worship, through Jesus Christ my Lord. Amen.

Remember

Cast all your cares upon him, for he cares for you.

1 Peter 5:7

Close

Loving God, as you have time for me, help me to have time for others and for you. Amen.

Turning the other cheek

Read

You have heard that it was said, 'An eye for an eye and a tooth for a tooth.' Yet I say to you, do not resist an evildoer, but if someone strikes you on the right cheek, offer the other cheek too.

Matthew 5:38-39

Ponder

An eye for an eye and a tooth for a tooth – that is the rule we find in the Old Testament, and it is one some feel we should still live by today, not least the proponents of corporal and capital punishment. Most of us prefer a less extreme kind of justice, based, in theory at least, on reform and reintegration rather than retribution. Should we be the one wronged, however, the desire for revenge is not so far beneath the surface as we might like to think. What would we give to get our own back in such circumstances? If the chance were to present itself there is every possibility that we might just take it.

The law of Christ is different. It does not rule out some kind of retribution, for to do that would be to deny any kind of justice or morality in the universe, but it tells us to leave such matters in the hands of God. The best way to respond is with love, not hatred; to meet evil with good and inhumanity with compassion – a way exemplified by Gordon Wilson who, in November 1987, amazed the world by publicly forgiving the terrorists whose bomb at Enniskillen injured him and killed his daughter Marie. His humble Christian witness over the ensuing years, and that of others like him, has stirred hearts and quickened consciences, in no small part paving the way for new initiatives towards peace. I'm not sure that I could do what he did, for I know if someone harmed me or, worse still, my loved ones, the desire for vengeance would be overwhelming. Yet I know too that such a response leads only to an endless cycle of violence and hatred that ultimately destroys all. It is the Gordon Wilsons of this world who help us glimpse the logic of the way of Christ.

Ask yourself

Are you nursing a grudge against someone? Is it achieving anything? Who is it hurting most, them or you?

Pray

Gracious God, you tell me that as I forgive so I shall be forgiven, and the thought of that is frightening, for I find forgiving others so very difficult. When I am hurt, insulted, let down, my natural inclination is to want revenge, and I allow that thirst to fester within me until it grows out of all proportion to the wrong I have suffered.

Teach me to leave vengeance to you, knowing that in your own time justice will be done. Amen.

Remember

Never return evil for evil. Strive to show goodness to all. So far as it's down to you, seek to live in peace with everyone. Dear friends, do not try and avenge yourselves; leave that to divine retribution; for it is written 'Vengeance is mine, says the Lord, I will repay. But if your enemy is hungry, feed him and if thirsty, give him a drink; because through this you will heap live coals on his head.' Do not let evil overcome you, but use good to conquer evil.   *Romans 12:17-21*

Close

Gracious God, give me courage, faith and humility to let go of hatred and to follow the way of love, through Jesus Christ my Lord. Amen.

Don't forget it

Read

Hear, O Israel: The Lord is our God, the Lord alone. You shall love the Lord your God with all your heart, and with all your soul, and with all your might. Keep these words that I am commanding you today in your heart. Recite them to your children and talk about them when you are at home and when you are away, when you lie down and when you rise. Bind them as a sign on your hand, fix them as an emblem on your forehead, and write them on the doorposts of your house and on your gates.

Deuteronomy 6:4-9

Ponder

Are you the sort of person liable to forget your own head if it wasn't screwed on? I am! I've lost count of the various items I've mislaid on my travels. Last week it was a pair of trousers left in a hotel wardrobe; before that a pullover at a friend's house: and before that there was a succession of diaries, combs, wallets, utensils, books, umbrellas and countless other bits and pieces. You may not be quite so forgetful but we all have limits to what we can remember, whether trivial things or matters of greater importance.

That's why the writer of Deuteronomy laid such store on teaching God's commandments and recalling his marvellous deeds across the years. He knew that no matter what God does for us, we can all too easily forget it, singing his praises one moment and bitterly complaining the next. Don't fall into the trap. Don't lose sight of the many blessings you have received, the promises God has given, the help and strength he still longs to give, the future he has in store for you and all who love him.

Ask yourself

Have there been times when you have forgotten all you owe to God? What things can help you to remember better in future?

Pray

Almighty God, I remember again all you have done across the years: your creative acts, your mighty deeds throughout history, your gift of Jesus Christ. I remember all you have done for me: your sovereign love, your gracious mercy and your constant guidance every day of my life.

Forgive me that so often and so easily I forget those things, brooding instead over my troubles, coveting what I do not have, preoccupied with my own well-being rather than your kingdom. Help me each day to remind myself of your goodness, to recall the ways you have blessed me, and so to keep you at the forefront of my life, living and working for your glory. In Christ's name I ask it. Amen.

Remember

Take care and watch yourselves closely, so as neither to forget the things that your eyes have seen nor to let them slip from your mind all the days of your life; make them known to your children and your children's children.

Deuteronomy 4:9

Close

Gracious God, so dwell within me that I will rejoice each day at all your mercies and love you with heart and soul and mind. Through Jesus Christ my Lord. Amen.

The God who never forgets us

Read

Cry out for joy, O heavens; exult, O earth; burst into song, O mountains; for the Lord has comforted his people and shown compassion to them in their time of distress. Yet Zion claims, 'The Lord has abandoned me, God has forgotten me.' Is there any way a mother could forget the baby at her breast and fail to show compassion to the child she has borne? Even if she could possibly forget, I will not forget you! Look and see, I have engraved you on the palms of my hands.

Isaiah 49:13-16a

Ponder

Elephants, they say, never forget. Whether that's true or not, I've no idea, but one thing of which I'm fully convinced is that God never forgets us. It may seem otherwise sometimes; indeed, in several places in the Bible, and in the Psalms particularly, we often encounter the anguished cry of someone who feels utterly abandoned by God. The passage we shall look at tomorrow – part of the testimony of Job – is one such example. Yet, invariably, even the most heart-rending of these passages ends up with a realisation that God was present all along – a fact that leads to a spontaneous outburst of praise and thanksgiving.

At other times, we may feel God has justifiably forgotten us, not because he doesn't care but because we have forgotten him. A sense of guilt can lead us to dismiss any idea that he is still interested in us. When it comes to people, even those we may have counted valued friends, that may be true – it can often be a case of out of sight and out of mind – but with God never! No matter how often we fail, frustrate or deny him, how estranged we may feel or undeserving we may consider ourselves, we are always in his thoughts, his love reaching out to bless and his hand outstretched to lead. Even though *we* may forget him, *he* will not forget us.

Ask yourself

Have you ever felt abandoned by God? Are you even perhaps feeling it now? Have you forgotten God's promise and past faithfulness?

Pray

God of truth, justice and power, I praise you that you are also a God of love. Though I disobey your commandments and lose sight of your goodness, though I fail to love others and am forgetful of you, still you love me. Though I reject your guidance, betray my convictions and deny my calling, still you care. Always you are there, watching over me, calling me back, welcoming me home. Day after day I receive new blessings, mercy and strength from your loving hands.

Gracious God, I praise you for your awesome love and your great faithfulness, in the name of Christ. Amen.

Remember

The Lord your God is a merciful God; he will not abandon or destroy you or forget the covenant with your forefathers, which he confirmed to them by an oath. *Deuteronomy 4:31*

Close

Almighty God, through all things you remember me; help me to remember you, in Jesus' name. Amen.

Why?

Read

Why, O Lord, are you so distant? Why do you hide yourself from me in my hour of need? My God, my God, why have you abandoned me? Why are you so far from helping me, from heeding my groans? I cry to you by day, O God, but you do not answer; and by night, but gain no respite. Why did I not die at birth, expire when I was brought from my mother's womb? Why do those consumed by despair continue to see the light of day, and why is life given to the bitter in soul who long for death only for it not to come?

Psalm 10:1; 22:1-2; Job 3:11, 20-21a

Ponder

Of all the mysteries of life and faith, none is harder to reconcile than the problem of suffering. How is it, we ask, that a supposedly loving and caring God can allow so much pain and misery to rack our world? Across the centuries scholars have wrestled with that conundrum yet failed to come up with a satisfactory solution. It is all too easy to offer pat answers that serve only to add to the misery of those wrestling with inexplicable suffering.

The book of Job was written precisely to counter such simplistic responses, flatly contradicting the received wisdom of the time that suffering was God's punishment for sin and that a godly life goes hand in hand with health, happiness and prosperity. Yet, no alternative theory is offered in its place. That would have risked repeating the mistake. What Job offers instead is the ultimate conviction that even when we cannot begin to understand, and even when life flies in the face of all we believe, God is there.

Ask yourself

Are there times when you have felt overwhelmed by questions, unable to reconcile a God of love with sufferings you or your loved ones have faced? Does the story of Job, with its emphasis on the mystery of God, help you come to terms with such questions?

Pray

Living God, there is so much suffering in this world of ours, so much pain, so much sorrow, so much evil. It is hard sometimes to reconcile all this with it being your world too, created by you and precious in your sight. We search desperately for answers, clinging first to this and then to that, and underneath there are times when our faith begins to crumble.

Teach me, though I cannot always see it, that you are there, sharing in our anguish, carrying in yourself the agony of creation as it groans under the weight of imperfection. Teach me that you will not rest until that day when all suffering is ended, when evil is no more and your kingdom is established; and in that assurance give me strength to face each day, whatever it might bring. Amen.

Remember

Then the Lord answered Job out of the storm: 'Who is this that speaks in the dark and questions me out of ignorance? Listen now and I will ask the questions. Do you presume to put me in the wrong? Do you question my justice to justify yourself? Do you have an arm like God's arm, and can you thunder with a voice like his?' Then Job answered the Lord: 'I know that you can do anything, and that nothing is beyond you. I have spoken of mysteries I do not understand, things so wonderful they are beyond my comprehension.'

Job 38:1-2; 40:7-9; 42:1-3

Close

Sovereign God, in the puzzles and mysteries of life, and in all that seems to contradict my faith, help me to believe still that you are there and that your purpose will not be defeated. Amen.

Rock of ages!

Read

The Lord is my rock, my fortress and my deliverer. My God is my rock, in whom I take refuge, my shield and the horn of my salvation. He is my stronghold, my refuge and my saviour. He is a shield for all who take refuge in him. For who is the Rock except our God? The Lord lives! Praise be to my Rock! Exalted be God, the Rock, my Saviour!

2 Samuel 22:2-3, 31b-32, 47

Ponder

Some places live on in the memory long after you last visited them. For me such a place is Lindisfarne Castle up on the Northumberland Coast. No, it wasn't just the mead brewed locally by the monks, delicious though that was; it was the sight of that castle perched majestically on its rocky outcrop as the sea lapped across the causeway that separates its island location from the mainland at high tide. It is almost as though castle and rock are one, and it is easy to imagine the castle proudly standing there for centuries to come in defiance of the wind and the waves that batter against it.

The memory of the scene breathes life for me into the repeated references in scripture to God as our rock and our fortress, giving a vivid impression of the sort of qualities each writer was seeking to convey. Ours indeed is a rock who will endure not just for centuries but for all eternity; a stronghold that nothing shall ever overcome. Though all else may change, God remains the same. Though all else may fail, he will not!

Ask yourself

In what ways have you experienced God as a rock and a fortress? What image does this conjure up for you, and what does the picture mean?

Pray

Sovereign God, Lord of past, present and future, I thank you that in all the uncertainties of life I find in you one who is unchanging: a rock on which I can base my life, a fortress to protect me in times of danger and a shield to defend me in the journey of life. I praise you that nothing can ever overcome your purpose; that whatever may fight against you, your will shall finally triumph. In that assurance may I face each day, confident that you will deliver me from evil and lead me safely through into your eternal kingdom. Through Jesus Christ my Lord. Amen.

Remember

In times of trouble he will keep me safe beneath his roof; he will hide me in the shelter of his tent and set me high upon a rock. He and he alone is my rock, my mighty fortress: I cannot be shaken. Trust in him always, my people; pour out your hearts to him, for God is our refuge.

Psalm 27:5; 62:2, 8

Close

God of grace, forgive me; Lord of creation, remake me; ruler of history, direct my path. Be a rock to support me, a shield to protect me, and a fortress to surround me. Through Jesus Christ my Lord. Amen.

The cost of greed

Read

A voice called out of the crowd to him, 'Teacher, tell my brother to divide the family inheritance with me.' But he replied, 'Man, who appointed me to be a judge or arbiter over you?' And he warned them, 'Beware! Guard against all types of greed; for the value of a person's life cannot be measured in terms of the amount of their possessions.'

Luke 12:13-15

Ponder

I could hardly believe it, but there it was in black and white: 'Take as much as you can eat.' Well, I wasn't going to waste that chance, was I? So I set about piling up my plate, eyes wide with anticipation as I surveyed the bewildering range of delicacies before me. A bit of this, a bit of that, and a bit more just for luck. So it went on, until I was almost staggering under the mountain of food I had assembled. It seemed like a good idea at the time, but a short while later, with my belt tightening and every mouthful becoming more of an effort, I began to reconsider. For all my endeavours, the mountain had scarcely diminished and it was clear that there was no way I could eat it all. Yet I couldn't let everyone see that my eyes were bigger than my stomach – I had to do my best to clear my plate. The result was that what should have been a gourmet's delight turned out to be a gastronomic nightmare – one that I have never forgotten to this day.

I should, of course, have been content with enough but, sadly, I wasn't. We can all be guilty of that, wanting that little bit extra even though we probably already have too much. That extra possession we acquire, for example – does it really bring us happiness, or is it simply another insurance risk, another item to clutter up the home, another five-minute wonder soon to be discarded, another empty treasure that we will hoard away with scarcely a second glance? It is not only the stomach that pays the price of greed; body, mind and soul can pay also. Beware!

Ask yourself

Are there areas in your life where you are particularly vulnerable to greed? In what ways has greed proven destructive?

Pray

Gracious God, forgive me the greed within me that spoils and destroys, that always looks for more and is never content with what I have. Forgive me for being obsessed with instant satisfaction and material gain, for becoming sensitised to the spirit of this age and allowing my spirit to become dulled to the things in life that can really satisfy.

Teach me to hunger and thirst instead for the things of your kingdom. So shall I discover not just how much I have to be thankful for now but also the treasures in heaven that only you can give. In Christ's name I pray. Amen.

Remember

If you find honey, eat only what you need, or else, having too much, you will bring it all up.   *Proverbs 1:18-19*

Close

Living God, you have given me enough and more than enough. Receive my praise, in Christ's name. Amen.

Into the unknown

Read

The Lord said to Abram, 'Leave your country, your kinfolk and your father's house and head for a land that I will show you. I will make a great nation of you. I will bless you, and make your name celebrated, so that you will be a blessing. I will bless those who bless you, and curse whoever curses you; and through you all the families of the earth shall be blessed in turn.' So Abram set off, as the Lord had told him.

Genesis 12:1-5

Ponder

What are you most scared of? Spiders? Snakes? The dark? Possibly even all of these? According to those who claim to know, there is one thing probably all of us are scared of still more, and that, quite simply, is the unknown. Familiarity may breed contempt, but it also brings a sense of security, and the thought of venturing out into uncharted waters can be a daunting challenge which most of us prefer to avoid. It can be traumatic enough moving to a new house or starting a new job – any change more radical than that can be bewildering indeed.

This, though, was the challenge faced by Abram, later to be called Abraham. Comfortably settled in the town of Haran, he suddenly felt a call to move on. The destination was unclear, as were any details as to what he might find when he got there. This was to be a step into the unknown, a journey of faith. Few of us today will be asked to make a bold decision, yet there are times when we need to let go of the tried and trusted nonetheless. We may be called to a new venture, new responsibilities or a new lifestyle, not knowing where they might lead or what will be demanded of us. We may be asked to make new friends, embrace new ideas or explore new horizons that, once again, we have no way of quantifying. Will we be ready to respond if we believe God is speaking – not putting off a decision to weigh up all the implications or brushing aside what we would rather not hear, but following in faith? We may not know what the future holds, but we do know who holds it – let that be sufficient inspiration for us.

Ask yourself

Is God calling you to take a step into the unknown? Is it time to stop prevaricating and respond?

Pray

Lord, you do not call me to a destination but a journey – a journey of continual new discoveries and new experiences of your love. Save me from ever thinking I have arrived; from imagining I know all there is to know or that I have exhausted the riches of everything you would reveal to me.

Open my eyes to the great adventure of life and to the unfathomable mysteries of your purpose, and so help me to be a pilgrim, travelling in faith as Abraham travelled, until I reach at last the kingdom you hold in store for all your people. Amen.

Remember

By faith Abraham responded to the call to set off in search of a place God had promised to give him as an inheritance, even though he had no idea where he was going.

Hebrews 11:8

Close

Sovereign God, teach me to walk with you, confident that though I do not know the way, you will guide my footsteps to my journey's end. Through Jesus Christ my Lord. Amen.

The God who travels with us

Read

The Lord went ahead of them the whole time, a pillar of cloud to guide them by day and a pillar of fire to lighten their way by night, so that they could travel by day or night. Neither the pillar of cloud by day nor the pillar of fire by night moved from its place in front of the people.

Exodus 13:21-22

Ponder

The words of our reading today offer an important complement to the passage we explored yesterday. We left Abram then setting off into the unknown; now we find the Israelites engaged in another journey into uncharted waters, following Moses out of Egypt and into what was to become years of wandering in the wilderness. Yet, though the final destination was unclear, the route they had to take was not a matter of guesswork, for God was there to guide them. Just as he led Abraham, so now, through a pillar of cloud and fire, he directs their footsteps. They do not travel alone; God is travelling with them.

Few are privileged to receive such a clear sign of God's presence with them, but the principle is one that applies to each one of us. As we journey through life, God is always there to share our pilgrimage – leading, encouraging, equipping, providing. We have no more idea of where our path may take us than Abram or Moses had, but we have the assurance that wherever we are asked to travel, he will travel with us.

Ask yourself

Do you feel that you are travelling alone sometimes? Have you lost sight of the God who is travelling alongside you?

Pray

Living God, I do not find it easy to journey in faith. I want a clearer idea of what the future holds, a knowledge of where I am heading and how I am going to get there. Yet neither life nor faith is like that, few things as definite as I would like them to be. Inspire me, though, by the knowledge that you are journeying with me every step of the way. May that truth equip me with courage to step out into the unknown, with faith to follow wherever you lead, with trust to walk with humility and with commitment to travel on to my journey's end. Through Jesus Christ my Lord. Amen.

Remember

I guarantee that I will be with you every day, to the very end of time.   *Matthew 28:20*

Close

Loving God, go with me now, and through all the uncertainties of life may I glimpse your presence, a beacon of hope and a signpost along the way. Amen.

Honest prayer

Read

O God, smash the teeth in their mouths; rip out the fangs of the lions, O Lord! Let them disappear like water that trickles away; let them be trodden underfoot like grass and wither away. Let them be like a slug putrefying in their own slime, like a stillborn child that never sees the light of day. The faithful will rejoice when they see vengeance done; they will wash their feet in the blood of the wicked. Then people will say, 'Surely virtue is rewarded; there is indeed a God who judges the earth.'

Psalm 58:6-8, 10-11

Ponder

When did you last hear a sermon on a text like that! Frankly, I'll be astonished if you ever have. We rightly find such sentiments offensive, and the very idea that we might call these words prayer is utterly repugnant. Yet not so fast, for passages like this still have something to teach us. I don't claim that they're a paradigm of prayer – far from it – but what they do show is a remarkable candour before God. David, the writer of this Psalm, was clearly angry and frustrated; annoyed at the fact that evil seems to prosper, annoyed at the way he'd suffered because of it, and most of all annoyed that God appeared to be doing nothing about it. That's how he felt, so that's what he said.

Was that right or wrong? – you tell me. If we're thoroughly fed up with life, what point is served by dutifully offering our thanksgiving? If we're consumed by doubt, how genuine is it to praise God for his purpose? There's a danger of simply going through the motions in prayer, telling God what we think he wants to hear rather than expressing our true feelings. More damaging still, we can assume that prayer requires a special sort of language, almost a technical expertise, if God is to hear us, and that some matters cannot be aired. Personally, I believe God prefers an honest prayer, no matter how shocking, to one that is divorced from the heart. I'm not saying he will applaud our feelings, still less that he will answer as we would like, but he will respond nonetheless, and, if we listen, then we will learn and be equipped to grow, both as people and in faith.

Ask yourself

How often have you dared tell God how you really feel? Can prayer really be effective if it is not honest?

Pray

Gracious God, I thank you that I can open my heart to you, that I can pour out my innermost soul and share my deepest thoughts in the knowledge that you are there, always ready to listen and understand. So once more I lay my life before you, open to your gaze: the bad as well as the good, the doubt as well as the faith, the sorrow as well as the joy, the despair as well as the hope.

I bring my feelings of anger as well as peace, of hatred as well as love, of confusion as well as certainty, of fear as well as trust. I bring them honestly to you, so that I may discover the renewing love that only you can offer – a love that frees me to live as you would have me live, and that allows me to be the person you would have me be! Hear now my prayer, in the name of Christ. Amen.

Remember

I cry out to the Lord; I lift up my voice begging him for mercy. I pour out my grievance before him; I tell him openly of my trouble. *Psalm 142:1-2*

Close

Lord, I bring myself, not as I would like to be, nor as I know I should be, but as I am. Hear me as I pour out my soul to you, and answer me through your grace. Amen.

Keep it simple

Read

We proclaim Christ crucified, an offence to the Jews and plain folly to others, but to those who have been called, whether Jews or Greeks, it is the message of Christ, the power and wisdom of God.   *1 Corinthians 1:23-24*

Ponder

Read the small print. I expect we've lost count of the times we've been told that, but I wonder how many of us actually do. When we receive a policy document through the post, or when a licensing agreement for our latest computer program pops up on the screen, how many of us sit down and read it through word for word? The fact is that not only is this usually interminably dull but more often than not it is also incomprehensible. Little wonder that efforts have been made in recent years to cut down on official gobbledegook, even if it doesn't as yet show!

It's not just officialdom, though, that can be guilty of verbosity; we can all fall into that trap. In fact, according to my editor, I do it all the time! As Christians, we're particularly prone, repeatedly slipping into language that may mean much to us but says nothing to those outside the Church. Worse still, we complicate the gospel with all kinds of dogmas, doctrines and creeds, insisting that this is sound and that unsound, one point a central tenet of faith while another borders on heresy. I don't doubt that there is sometimes a need for theological niceties or a place for religious jargon, but I suspect we would all do well occasionally to get back to basics.

That's what we see in the words of Paul to the Corinthians. Derided as a public speaker in comparison to the great orators of his day, and condemned as a Jew for having supposedly blasphemed against his God, he didn't care. He summarised his message in one sentence; a sentence that says it all: 'Christ crucified . . . the power and wisdom of God.' Yes, of course that needs fleshing out, and of course what one person means by it may be different from the next, but it's there nonetheless, the heart of the matter in a nutshell. The success of Paul as a preacher speaks for itself, and it's a lesson we need to learn from. We often extol the virtue of a simple faith; sadly, we don't often practise it.

Ask yourself
In what ways do you feel the message of the gospel has been overcomplicated?

Pray
Gracious God, I thank you for the simplicity of the gospel: the message of your living, dying and rising among us in Christ. I thank you that it is not about clever words or subtle concepts, but speaks rather about a concrete expression of your love. Forgive us for complicating that message: for cluttering it up with our ideas and prejudices, our attempts to define and delimit, our interpretations and terminology.

Open my eyes again to the heart of what it all means and, through letting go of so much that is ultimately trivial, help me to communicate what really matters: the good news of forgiveness and new life in Jesus. I ask it for his sake. Amen.

Remember
Christ did not send me to baptise but to declare the gospel; not using clever words and concepts in case those should empty the cross of Christ of its power.   *1 Corinthians 1:17*

Close
Living God, such is your love that you lived and died among us, and rose again so that we might live. For that simple yet wonderful message, I thank you, in the name of Christ. Amen.

Strength in weakness

Read

He has said to me, 'My grace is enough for you, for my power is made perfect in weakness.' Therefore, I will gladly boast of my weaknesses that allow the power of Christ to work within me. I am more than happy to endure weakness, abuse, privation, persecution, and misfortune for the sake of Christ; for the weaker I am, the stronger I become.

2 Corinthians 12:9–10

Ponder

What does it mean to talk about strength in weakness? The idea sounds nonsensical, a contradiction in terms, and, wrongly understood, it is precisely that. If we imagine that every frailty is in fact a source of power, every Achilles' heel the secret of some Herculean endowment, then we are in for a rude surprise. No weakness in itself is something to be proud of. It is how we deal with it that matters: whether we persist nonetheless in attempting to prove ourselves, or whether we recognise our ultimate dependence on divine grace. God, and God alone, is able to turn weakness into strength. The more we understand that, the more he is able to work within us.

Ask yourself

In what areas of life do you feel at your weakest? Is there a way in which God might be able to turn this weakness into strength? Does he show his strength through it?

Pray

Sovereign God, you came to our world in Christ and you lowered yourself, taking the form of a servant, enduring suffering and humiliation, even finally death on a cross. Yet through that sacrifice you won the greatest of all victories, triumphing over evil, scattering darkness, defeating death itself. What appeared to be weakness was shown as strength. What seemed like disaster was revealed as triumph. What the world deemed failure proved to be glorious success.

Teach me to recognise that now, as then, you turn lives upside down, working in the most unexpected of ways through the most unexpected of people. Teach me that you can work in *my* life too, taking my frail faith and feeble commitment, and using my weakness to demonstrate your glory. Take me and use me for your kingdom. Through Jesus Christ, the Lord yet servant of all. Amen.

Remember

The foolishness of God is wiser than human wisdom and the weakness of God stronger than human strength.

1 Corinthians 1:25

Close

Jesus Christ, crucified Lord and servant King, take my weakness and my frailty and, by your grace, use me still to achieve great things for your kingdom. Amen.

The cost of discipleship

Read

He said to all, 'If any want to come after me, let them deny themselves and take up their cross daily, and then follow me. For those wishing to save their life will lose it, but those who lose their life for my sake will save it.

Luke 9:23-24

Ponder

'I'm delighted to tell you that you've won a free holiday in our prize draw competition.' Have you had a phone call like that recently? It's sales talk, of course; just one of the many marketing ploys used to convince us that we're getting something for nothing, whereas, in fact, the opposite is more likely true. Another tack is the one sometimes employed by book and music clubs: 'Buy any four for 99 pence each', only we then have to buy another four at full price during the next year. It's easy to be swept along by wonderful-sounding promises, without stopping to consider the commitment entailed.

In terms of the Christian faith, though, there should be no such danger, for Jesus never attempted to conceal the real cost of discipleship. If you want the reward, he tells us, there's a price to pay. To get something out of faith we must also put something in. There is no sales hype, no dressing things up with fantastic offers, yet the irony is that in this case the price is more than worth paying!

Ask yourself

Have you taken seriously the cost of discipleship? Does your faith involve give as well as take?

Pray

Lord Jesus Christ, it is easy to talk of taking up my cross and following you, but the reality is different. I find it hard to deny myself even a little, let alone to give my all. There is so much I want to enjoy, so much I want to achieve, and the thought of sacrificing any of that is one I would rather push aside. Yet, you have taught that it is in losing our lives we truly find them, and that we shall find lasting treasures not on earth but in heaven. Help me, then, instead of clinging slavishly to self-interest, to give of myself freely, just as you gave yourself for me. Amen.

Remember

Which of you, if you wanted to build a tower, would not first sit down and work out the cost, to make sure you were able to complete the job once you started it?   *Luke 14:28*

Close

Lord Jesus Christ, you gave your all so that I might have life; you counted yourself as nothing so that I might rejoice in the wonder of your love; you endured agony of body, mind and spirit, so that I might receive mercy and know the peace that only you can give. Help me today to recognise more clearly everything you did for me, and so inspire me to give a little of myself in return. Teach me to walk the way of the cross and to bear the cost gladly for the joy set before me, for your name's sake. Amen.

Songs of praise

Read

I will sing of your devoted love for ever, O Lord; my mouth
will declare your faithfulness to the end of time. Come, let
us lift up our joyful songs to the Lord; let us make a glad
sound to the rock of our salvation! Let us come gratefully
before him and make a joyful sound to him with songs of
praise! Come, let us bow down and worship, let us kneel
before the Lord our creator, for he is our God and we are
his people.   *Psalm 89:1; 95:1-2, 6-7a*

Ponder

There are few areas within the life of the Church more divisive
than music. Whereas in the past Christians were divided
over issues of doctrine, today it is often music that keeps us
apart. For some, traditional hymnody is like a distant
planet, unexplored and assumed to be barren. For others,
modern choruses are anathema, representing froth rather
than substance, superficial emotion rather than faith
rooted in history. The polarisation that can develop around
this never ceases to amaze me. Of course we each have our
preferences, just as we all have our own tastes in music, but
is one inherently better than another? One song may be
linguistically more polished than another or one tune
more catchy, but so far as God is concerned that counts for
nothing. What matters is the sincerity with which we sing,
and whether our lives measure up to our words. As David
reminds us, our songs are sung not for our own benefit but
as an offering of worship to God. Whether it is a chorus or
a hymn, a chant or an anthem, what matters is that we sing
to the Lord. Without that, our songs are meaningless and
our time is wasted.

Ask yourself

Do you get steamed up about music in church? Have you lost sight of what it is all about? Do you focus sometimes more upon the song than God?

Pray

Lord, I thank you for the gift of song; for its ability to move, challenge and inspire me, its power to express feelings of joy and sorrow, hope and despair; its capacity to sum up my feelings in grateful hymns of praise.

Teach me when I worship to use this gift thoughtfully, singing to you from the heart, and offering not just the song but myself with it. Teach me to reflect on the words I use so that they may speak *to* me of all that you have done and speak *for* me of all *I* would do for *you*. O Lord, open my lips, and my mouth shall declare your praise. Amen.

Remember

Sing psalms, hymns and spiritual songs among yourselves, singing and making music in your hearts to the Lord, giving thanks always to God the Father for everything, in the name of our Lord Jesus Christ. *Ephesians 5:19-20*

Close

Loving God, send me out not just with a song on my lips but with a song in my heart, to the glory of your name. Amen.

It's a promise!

Read

Was I vacillating when I wanted to do this? Do I make my plans according to ordinary human standards, ready to say 'Yes, yes' and 'No, no' at the same time? As surely as God is faithful, our word to you has not been 'Yes and No'; but in him it is always 'Yes'. For in him every one of God's promises is a 'Yes'. For this reason it is through him that we say the 'Amen', to the glory of God.   *2 Corinthians 1:17-20*

Ponder

How many of us can put our hand on our heart and say we have never broken a promise? I doubt anyone could make such a claim. It's not that we intend to go back on our word – not usually anyway; more that circumstances alter, unforeseen eventualities arise, or we are simply unable to deliver on our pledge. The Apostle Paul knew that as well as any, his second letter to the Corinthians revealing that they had taken him to task for failing to honour his promise to visit them. Yet, there is one, he says, whose promises are never broken, whose word is utterly reliable, and it is to him that Paul suddenly turns, almost in mid-sentence, bursting into a joyful celebration of God's faithfulness. What God has said he will do, shall be done – we have his word.

Ask yourself

Do you expect God to honour his promises, or has your faith succumbed to disillusionment in life?

Pray

Loving God, I thank you that you are a God I can depend on, a God in whom I can put my trust. What you promise is done; what you purpose is fulfilled. I remember your promise to Abraham that, through his offspring, all the world would be blessed; to Moses, that you would lead the Israelites out of Egypt; to Isaiah, that you would deliver your people from exile; to your prophets, that the Messiah would come; to the Apostles, that he would rise again on the third day.

I thank you that you fulfilled those promises, just as you said you would – your Son born from the line of Abraham; your chosen nation set free from slavery; your people returning joyfully to Jerusalem, your promised deliverer born in Bethlehem; your power seen in the resurrection of Christ. I thank you for what that means for me today – that I can live each moment with confidence, whatever my circumstances may be, whatever times of testing may befall me, knowing that, though all else may fail, you will not; though heaven and earth may pass away, your words will endure for ever.

So I look forward to that day when your purpose is fulfilled and you are all in all, and, until then, I will trust in you, secure in your love, confident in your eternal purpose, assured that your will shall be done. Receive my thanks, in the name of Christ. Amen.

Remember

His divine power has given us everything needed for life and godliness, through the knowledge of him who called us by his own glory and goodness. Thus he has given us, through these things, his precious and very great promises.

1 Peter 1:3-4

Close

Sovereign God, faithful and true, in you I put my trust, confident that what you have promised shall come to fruition. To you be praise and glory, now and always, through Jesus Christ my Lord. Amen.

Made for sharing

Read

Some give unreservedly, yet grow richer for it; others keep back what is due, yet end up suffering want. A generous person will find enrichment and the one who brings refreshment to others will be refreshed in turn.

Proverbs 11:24-25

Ponder

Do you remember the old advertising slogan, 'Quality Street, made for sharing'? It had a point, didn't it, for, like most pleasures, a box of chocolates is indeed all the better for being shared. To enjoy something on one's own simply doesn't bring the same satisfaction; it somehow feels more like indulgence, selfishness or greed. In much the same way as a problem shared is a problem halved, so a pleasure shared brings double the happiness. It's not just true of chocolates but of most things; in fact of people in general – we are all made for sharing. Receiving may bring happiness but giving brings a far greater joy; a jealously guarded possession loses its lustre yet one that is open to others to enjoy finds its sparkle polished anew every day. Generosity of spirit is a rare quality that doesn't come naturally to many of us, yet it is one of the most precious gifts we can ever have. Learn to let go of what you have, to share from your little or your plenty, and you will discover what enrichment really means.

Ask yourself

What things hold you back from sharing with others? Are you as generous as you know you ought to be?

Pray

Gracious God, forgive me my mean and selfish spirit – my desire so often to safeguard pleasures for myself, to provide for my own well-being and ignore the needs of others. Teach me that it is in giving I receive, in denying myself that I discover true riches. Help me not just to assent to that truth intellectually, but to believe it in my heart and show it in my life. Give me a heart overflowing with generosity, eager to share with others the good things you have given me, and so may I add to their joy and my own. Through Jesus Christ my Lord. Amen.

Remember

He himself said, 'It is more blessed to give than to receive.'

Acts 20:35

Close

Lord Jesus Christ, you know what it is to give, for you gave your all. Teach me that whatever *I* give, I shall receive far more, and so use me to show your love and bring your blessing, to the glory of your name. Amen.

A disfigured masterpiece

Read

So God created humankind in his likeness – he made both male and female in his own image. God looked at all he had made, and was satisfied that it was good. The Lord God commanded the man, 'You can eat freely of any tree in the garden except the tree of good and evil; the day you eat of that you shall die.' When the woman realised that the tree not only offered attractive and appetising food but was also able to make one wise, she took one of its fruits and ate; and she gave some of it to her husband, who was with her, and he ate too. Then their eyes were opened, and they understood that they were naked; and they sewed fig leaves together to make loincloths for themselves.

Genesis 1:26-27; 2:16-17; 3:6-7

Ponder

It was an act that shocked the nation: an internationally renowned painting wantonly vandalised by a knife-wielding madman in a frenzied and motiveless attack. What once had been a priceless masterpiece was suddenly a shredded piece of canvas hanging forlornly from its frame; a pathetic reminder of what should have been.

A similar act of desecration lies behind the creation stories in Genesis, only on a much broader scale, for we are talking here not about a human creation but God's, not about an abstract masterpiece but human lives. God made us in his likeness, each one of us designed as a unique and precious masterpiece, but such is our nature that we disfigure that creation, our faults and failings rendering the initial design almost unrecognisable. Think about that next time temptation comes: remember that each time we succumb we are not just betraying ourselves – we are destroying the work of God's hands, the people he intended us to be.

Ask yourself

What things within you prevent you being the person God wants you to be?

Pray

Loving God, I know what I should be and I know what I am; the gulf between the two so wide. So I come now in shame and sorrow before you, seeking your mercy. Forgive me everything that disfigures my life: the pride, greed, selfishness and envy that alienate me not only from myself and others but, above all, from you. Forgive me my unkind words, foolish deeds and unworthy thoughts, my weakness of will and carelessness in discipleship. Work within me and, by your grace, make me whole. Through Jesus Christ my Lord. Amen.

Remember

Live by the Spirit, I tell you, and do not indulge the desires of the flesh. For the desire of the flesh is opposed to the Spirit, and the desire of the Spirit is opposed to the flesh; for these are incompatible, to prevent you doing what you want. The works of the flesh are unmistakable: immorality, impurity, debauchery, idolatry, black magic, feuds, discord, jealousy, anger, quarrels, conflict, division, envy, drunkenness, wild behaviour, and things like these. I am warning you, as I warned you previously: those who act like this will not inherit the kingdom of God.

Galatians 5:16-17,19-21

Close

Sovereign God, for the many ways I fail to live as one of your people, forgive me. Guard me from temptation and teach me to live by your Spirit. Through Jesus Christ my Lord. Amen.

Lovingly restored

Read

Have nothing more to do with all these things: rage, anger, malice, slander, abusive language and deceitful behaviour, for you have renounced the old self with its associated practices and become a new person, your minds being renewed into the likeness of the one who created you.

Colossians 3:8-10

Ponder

The analogy drawn yesterday of a disfigured work of art was incomplete, representing only half the story, for although the situation looked hopeless, the painting in question was lovingly and painstakingly restored to its original splendour.

Once more, we can draw parallels in our own life, for although we disfigure what God intended us to be, he is constantly at work to restore and remake us. Although we may despair of ever changing, God never gives us up as a lost cause. He is continually striving to recreate us in the likeness of Christ – a transformation that, thank God, depends not wholly upon our own efforts, important though those are, but upon his grace.

Ask yourself

Do you still believe that Christ is able to change you, despite your repeated failure to live as his disciple?

Pray

Sovereign God, I thank you for the way you are at work in my life, constantly looking to refashion me into your image. I praise you that, despite my lack of faith, my many faults and my sometimes wilful disobedience, you never give up, patiently looking to recreate me through the power of your Holy Spirit. Come to me now in all my weakness, and by your grace, renew, redeem and restore me in the likeness of Christ, for his name's sake. Amen.

Remember

Just as we have borne the image of the man of dust, so we will likewise bear the image of the man from heaven.

1 Corinthians 15:49

Close

Gracious God, take what I am and remould me by your grace, so that I will bear the image of Christ within me, and live to his glory. Amen.

More than we deserve

Read

There is no distinction, since all have sinned and fall short of the glory of God; they are now justified by his grace as a gift, through the redemption that is in Christ Jesus.

Romans 3:23-24

Ponder

My son, Samuel, has a clear sense of right and wrong, to the point sometimes that, having been naughty, he will deny himself a subsequent treat. 'No,' he says, 'I don't deserve it.' No amount of argument can persuade him to believe otherwise. Even when he has said sorry and we tell him whatever he did wrong is over and done with, his resolution remains undiminished.

There is something of that attitude in all of us when it comes to receiving the grace and forgiveness of God. We want to believe in it, but we are so ashamed of our mistakes and so conscious of our unworthiness that we find it hard to accept. We feel that we must suffer some further penance; that we need to punish ourselves before we can even begin to earn forgiveness. That may be *our* way but it is not *God's*. Forgiveness is not earned; it is given. None of us deserve it, yet all can receive it. We need only to acknowledge our mistakes and confess to being truly sorry. He asks no more!

Ask yourself

Have you appreciated the extent of God's grace and the fact that he is always ready to forgive, however often or hopelessly you may fail him?

Pray

Sovereign God, if you treated us as we deserve, none could stand before you, but you are a God of infinite mercy, full of love and goodness. You came to our world in Christ, and you died for us while we were yet sinners. You reached out through him to those who knew themselves to be unworthy, deserving of punishment, yet, through your grace, you brought acceptance, wholeness and renewal.

So now, I open my life to your generous pardon, your unfailing love and your undeserved blessing. Receive my praise for all you so freely and wonderfully give in Christ, for his name's sake. Amen.

Remember

Now to someone who works, any reward is not regarded as a gift but as something owed, but to the one who trusts him who justifies the ungodly irrespective of works, such faith is reckoned as righteousness.   *Romans 4:4-5*

Close

Loving God, I have no claim on your love, no entitlement to your mercy, and yet your nature is always to forgive and forget. Open my heart to your grace, and help me to receive the new life you long to give me. Through Jesus Christ my Lord. Amen.

Living with doubt

Read

They brought the child to him. Seeing him, the spirit immediately convulsed the boy, and he fell to the ground, rolling about and foaming at the mouth. Jesus asked the father, 'How long has this been happening to him?' And he said, 'From infancy. Many times it has hurled him into flames or water, to destroy him, so if there is anything you can do, for pity's sake help us.' Jesus said to him, 'The question is, can *you* do anything – all things are possible for the one who believes.' And immediately the father of the child cried out, 'I do believe; help me deal with my unbelief!'

Mark 9:20-24

Ponder

'I believe in God, the Father Almighty, creator of heaven and earth . . .' The opening words of the Apostles' Creed have been accepted and repeated across the centuries as a summary of the faith of the Church. And most of us most of the time are happy to add our voices to those who have gone before us. Yet there are times when it's not that simple, when we find ourselves wracked with doubt. To make things worse, such moments are often compounded by a sense of guilt. The result can be a lonely struggle in the wilderness, crushed by a sense of isolation, failure and shame.

Yet, we are not the only ones to feel this way. Remember Thomas, nicknamed 'doubting Thomas' for his refusal to believe without proof. Above all, remember the father in the story above and his frank confession of where he stood. It wasn't that he didn't believe; it was just that there were some things he struggled to accept. Doubt may come to us all, however secure in faith we appear to be. Do not fear it, for it is not something to be ashamed of. Believe, rather, that God is able to take and use your questions to lead you into a deeper understanding of his purpose and a richer sense of his love. Do that, and you will discover that doubt is not the opposite of faith, but often an essential part of the journey of discipleship.

Ask yourself

What aspects of faith do you find difficult to accept or believe? Do you feel able to bring your doubt as well as your faith to God?

Pray

Gracious God, I come today confessing my faith, yet acknowledging also my doubt – the many things I don't understand, the statements of faith that don't make sense, the events of life that seem to contradict everything I believe about you. There are times when I am sure what I believe and times when I am uncertain.

Give me sufficient trust in you to acknowledge all my questions openly, and sufficient humility to offer each to you honestly in prayer. Save me from taking refuge in hollow words or empty ritual, but teach me rather to face the challenges life brings and to work through my faith in the light of them. Having been tested, may my faith grow stronger, able to face all and still to stand. Through Jesus Christ my Lord. Amen.

Remember

He said to Thomas, 'Put your finger here and see my hands. Reach out your hand and put it in my side. Do not doubt but believe.' Thomas answered him, 'My Lord and my God!' Jesus said to him, 'Have you believed because you have seen me? Blessed are those who have not seen and yet have come to believe.'   *John 20:27-29*

Close

Loving God, I come to you today, offering not just my faith but also my doubt, praying that you will use both to lead me closer to you. Amen.

Secret disciples?

Read

Joseph of Arimathea – a disciple of Jesus, albeit secretly because of his fear of the Jews – asked Pilate for permission to take away the body of Jesus. Pilate consented; so he went and removed the body. Nicodemus, who first came to Jesus by night, accompanied him, bringing with him a blend of myrrh and aloes, about a hundred pounds in weight. They took the body of Jesus and bound it, together with the spices, in linen cloths, following the burial custom of the Jews.

John 19:38-40

Ponder

Our first reaction, reading of Joseph of Arimathea and Nicodemus asking for the body of Jesus, is that it was too little, too late. A well-intentioned act, undoubtedly, but what use to Jesus was it now? If they'd stuck their necks out earlier, then how different things might have been. Yet is such an interpretation fair? Certainly open commitment from the start would have been better, but which of us would have acted differently in their place? To publicly declare allegiance to Jesus would have involved risk and, very likely, personal danger. For the ordinary people to follow him was bad enough in the eyes of the Jewish authorities; for a Pharisee it was unthinkable!

Many generations of Christians since have felt forced by persecution to be secret disciples: witness the catacombs of Rome or the story of Christians in the Soviet bloc before the demise of communism. For us, there is no such excuse. We have freedom of speech, freedom of conscience and freedom of belief. It's conceivable that we might suffer discrimination due to our faith but it's unlikely to be anything worse. Yet, how many of us are up-front about our faith, proud to acknowledge it, ready to nail our colours firmly to the mast? Or, to put it another way, how many of those we regularly come into contact with have any inkling that we are Christians or any idea of what our faith means to us? At least Joseph and Nicodemus had some reason to be secretive. Have we?

Ask yourself

Have you been guilty of secret discipleship, concealing your faith from others? Why?

Pray

Lord Jesus Christ, you tell us to walk in the light, and to be witnesses to it through the things we do and the people we are. You call us to let your light shine through us so that others might see the good works we do and give glory to God.

Forgive me that all too often I do the opposite, hiding my light under a bushel, even sometimes to the point of secret discipleship. Afraid of what others might think and concerned that admitting faith in you might prejudice my standing in this world, I keep my beliefs private. Forgive me the feebleness of my commitment and the weakness of my love. Help me to recognise everything you have done for me, and so teach me to acknowledge you proudly as the light of my life, whatever the cost may be. In your name I pray. Amen.

Remember

Everyone who acknowledges me before others, I will similarly acknowledge before my Father in heaven, but whoever denies me before others, I will likewise deny before my Father in heaven.   *Matthew 10:32-33*

Close

Lord Jesus Christ, you chose to identify yourself with us in all our frailty and sinfulness. Help me to gladly identify myself with you, proud to bear your name. Amen.

Closed minds

Read

He came to his native village and taught in the synagogue there in a manner that left all who heard him amazed, asking, 'From where did this man acquire such wisdom and the ability to perform such deeds of power? Surely, this is the carpenter's son? Isn't Mary his mother, and aren't James, Joseph, Simon and Judas his brothers? And don't his sisters live here among us? Where then did this man get these abilities?' And they took exception to him. But Jesus responded, 'A prophet is not without esteem, except among those of their own country or household.' And, due to their unbelief, his powerful deeds were few there.   *Matthew 13:54-58*

Ponder

Open-mindedness isn't always the quality it's cracked up to be. The way we use the term today, it is synonymous with an attitude of anything goes; anyone who dares to suggest that there are moral and ethical frontiers beyond which we should not venture being dismissed as bigoted, blinkered and out of touch with reality. The truth is, of course, that those who reason like this are themselves as narrow-minded as anyone, their minds steadfastly closed to the possibility that there could be limits to human freedom.

Open-mindedness doesn't necessarily mean that we accept everything; simply that we are ready to give a fair hearing to another's point of view, amenable to the possibility that we may need to reconsider our opinions in the light of their experience. If we are to grow in faith and mature as individuals, we all need to cultivate that quality. Those who think they have been given all they need to know and who refuse to have their horizons stretched may well find themselves in the position of the people of Nazareth, turning their backs on the truth when it was there before them.

Ask yourself

Where are your blind spots – those areas where you are closed to new ideas and insights?

Pray

Gracious God, you speak to me in all kinds of ways, through all kinds of people – forgive me that I am sometimes closed to what you have to say. I avoid that which challenges, disturbs or unsettles me, preferring to criticise and condemn rather than face the issues raised. Forgive me that I shut my ears to what I don't agree with, rather than listen to another point of view; that I am reluctant to accept new and unfamiliar ideas, taking refuge instead in what is tried and trusted. Forgive me that I can become so bogged down in what I think is right, so sure of my own convictions and set in my ways that I resent anything new.

Open my heart to the living reality of Christ, my mind to the sweeping breath of your Holy Spirit, and my soul to all that you would do and say, and so help me truly to live as one of your people, in the name of Christ. Amen.

Remember

Judge nothing prematurely, before the Lord returns, for he will shed light on those things hidden in darkness and reveal the innermost thoughts of people's hearts.

1 Corinthians 4:5

Close

God of all, break through the barriers that shut my mind fast, and help me to see things both as they really are and as you can help them become. Move within me, in the name of Christ. Amen.

You can do it!

Read

I can do all things through him who strengthens me.

Philippians 4:13

Ponder

'I can't do it.' How often have you made that excuse when faced with a difficult and demanding challenge? Occasionally it may be justified but, more often than not, the truth is that we either don't want to do what's asked of us, or fear we may make a fool of ourselves if we attempt it. The task in question may well be within our capabilities, but we would rather not risk finding out, just in case it's not. Yet, unless we are prepared to face such situations head on, to have a go and never mind the consequences, we will never realise our true potential, held back instead by half-formed fears and uncertainties. Two old sayings make the point well: 'Nothing ventured, nothing gained'; 'Nothing succeeds like success.'

Ask yourself

Are there challenges you face that you feel are beyond you? Are you looking at them in terms of your own ability to meet them, or in the context of God's strength?

Pray

Sovereign God, the challenges you set before me may be very modest compared with those faced by others over the years, but they can seem daunting nonetheless. I feel inadequate to meet the task, acutely conscious of my lack of faith, the limitations of my gifts and my inability to serve you as I would wish. Yet, throughout history you have repeatedly taken the most unpromising of material and used it in ways defying all expectations. You have turned doubt into faith, weakness into strength, timid service into fearless discipleship, and you go on doing that today through the power of your Holy Spirit.

Give me, then, the faith to respond to your call, trusting that, whatever you ask of me, you will be by my side to help me see it through, to the glory of your name. Amen.

Remember

Humanly speaking, it is impossible, but not with God; all things are possible with God.   *Mark 10:27*

Close

Sovereign God, teach me to let go of my fears and to trust in your strength, this day and always. Amen.

Finding fault

Read

Seeing that he ate with tax-collectors and sinners, the scribes and Pharisees challenged his disciples, saying, 'How is it that he eats with such people?' And it happened that he was passing through some cornfields on the Sabbath, and as they made their way through these, his disciples began plucking some ears of corn. The Pharisees said to him, 'Look at what they are doing! Why do you allow them to do what is unlawful on the Sabbath?' And he entered a synagogue, and there was a man there with a shrivelled hand. And they watched him carefully, to see if he would heal on the Sabbath, looking for an opportunity to accuse him.   *Mark 2:16, 23-24; 3:1-2*

Ponder

It is easy when reading verses like these about the scribes and Pharisees to shake our heads and tut in disapproval at their misguided attitudes, yet to do that is to make the same mistake they did: to find fault. How often are we guilty of just that? – swift to see the worst, slow to see the best; eager to criticise, reluctant to praise. We ignore a thousand good things and focus instead on one bad point, we destroy and undermine rather than build up and encourage, yet so often the faults we pick up on are trivial compared to our own.

Perhaps more disturbing still is that this response came from the overtly religious, those who believed themselves to be right with God. In similar fashion, the Church across the years has frequently been associated with narrow and nitpicking attitudes rather than a joyful celebration of all that is good. Don't let such a carping and negative spirit find a place in your life, for not only does it cause pain to others; ultimately it makes us the biggest losers, blinding us not only to one another but, above all, to God himself.

Ask yourself

In what ways have you been guilty of finding fault? Is it time you offered someone a word of praise and encouragement?

Pray

Living God, forgive me that I find it so easy to see faults in others and so hard to see them in myself. Forgive me that I am so often negative and so rarely positive. Teach me to see strengths rather than weaknesses, to lift people up rather than put them down, to nurture confidence rather than crush spirits, to recognise the good rather than dwell on the bad. Put within me the Spirit of Christ, so that I may follow his way of love and acceptance, mercy and understanding. In his name I pray. Amen.

Remember

If you bite and devour one another, take care that you do not end up destroying one another.   *Galatians 5:15*

Close

Loving God, you always see the best in me; teach me to see the best in others, for the sake of Christ. Amen.

Rough justice

Read

The Lord is slow to anger but great in power, and will most certainly not overlook the guilty. Who can stand before his righteous anger? Who can endure the heat of his fury? The Lord is a sure stronghold in a day of trouble; he keeps safe those who seek refuge in him, even though a flood surges around them. He will obliterate his adversaries and pursue his enemies into darkness. Why, then, do you hatch plots against the Lord? He will put an end to it; no adversary will rise up twice.

Nahum 1:3, 6a, 7-10

Ponder

The book of Nahum is not an easy book to read, its theme one of undisguised glee at a catastrophe about to befall the enemies of Judah. Yet if we see beyond the prophet's apparent vindictive delight, his words carry an important message, for the point he makes is that justice will finally be done. That must have taken some believing for his hearers, since for generations the people of Judah had suffered under the mighty yoke of the Assyrian empire. Sure enough, however, within a few years this seemingly impregnable dynasty was to collapse, as a new super-power, Babylon, emerged to take centre stage in the ancient world.

In recent years we have seen events just as remarkable in the destruction of the Berlin Wall, the end of the Cold War, the removal of apartheid, and the successive overthrow of dictatorial regimes the world over. All this is not to say that everything in this life works out as it should, for there are times when it manifestly does not. Yet at the heart of our faith is the conviction that God is actively involved in human history, striving to establish his kingdom despite everything that conspires to frustrate his purpose.

Ask yourself

Do you feel troubled sometimes by the apparent injustices in life? Are there events in history, other than those mentioned above, which help restore your faith in justice in this world, as well as the world to come?

Pray

Almighty God, I find it hard sometimes not to despair of our world. When I look at its pain and suffering, sorrow and despair, hatred and division, evil and injustice, I fear for the future, and struggle to make sense of it all. Yet, I remember today that you too feel sorrow, more than I can ever begin to imagine. Unlike me, though, *you* never give up – your love willing to give everything, even your only Son, to redeem, restore and renew.

Inspire me, through that knowledge, and so may I continue to strive for the coming of your kingdom, until that day when all things are reconciled to you in Christ, and I am one with you and him, now and for evermore. Amen.

Remember

Hardness and impenitence of heart stores up wrath for you on the day God reveals his righteous judgement and anger, for God will give to every person according to the things they have done.   *Romans 2:5-6*

Close

Teach me, Lord, that you are constantly at work, striving against everything that frustrates your will and denies your love. Teach me to hold on to those moments in life when wrongs are righted and justice is done at last. Above all, teach me to look at the cross of Christ, and to draw strength from the victory of love over what had seemed to be the triumph of evil. Amen.

For God's sake

Read

Whatever your task, do it for God's sake rather than anyone else's, knowing that you will receive an inheritance from the Lord as a reward.   *Colossians 3:23*

Ponder

'For God's sake, stop doing that!' 'For Christ's sake, get it right!' How often have we heard words like those? The name of God or Christ is frequently invoked in such ways, yet the irony is that those who tend to invoke it have little or no religious faith, using it instead as an expression of exasperation to underline their feelings. The Apostle Paul uses the idea in a very different sense, urging us to see everything we do as literally done for God's sake. He is not just talking about 'religious' activities but every aspect of life: our work, rest, interests and relationships, our thinking, speaking and doing – each of them offered as a gift to God.

That is a message we would do well to consider, for we tend to compartmentalise life into the sacred and secular to the point that the two barely meet. We also tend to see some people as specially called to religious vocations and others as engaged in less spiritual activities. I don't think Paul would have been happy with such a dichotomy. For him, whatever we do should be sacred, consecrated to God as part of our daily discipleship. It may catch the eye, it may not, but that's not important. What matters is that we live each moment in such a way that all we do is truly done for God's sake.

Ask yourself

How much of what you do is consciously consecrated to God? What difference would dedicating your actions to him make?

Pray

Loving God, you ask me whatever I do, to do it for your sake – to offer my whole life, my every thought, word and action to your service, for your glory. Help me to understand what that really means – to see every part of each day as an opportunity to work for you, and to approach my work and my leisure in such a way as to bear witness to you.

Teach me to do everything in such a way that others may recognise your hand upon me, your Spirit with me and your love in my heart. Through Jesus Christ my Lord. Amen.

Remember

In the light of God's mercy, I therefore urge you, my friends, to offer your bodies in fitting service as living, holy and pleasing sacrifices to God. *Romans 12:1*

Close

Living God, I commit to you not just a part but all of my life, asking that you will take who and what I am, and everything I do, and dedicate it to your service, for your name's sake. Amen.

Shepherd of the sheep

Read

The Lord is my shepherd, I want for nothing. He makes me lie down in fertile pastures; he leads me beside tranquil waters; he restores my soul. He leads me in right paths for his name's sake. Even though I walk through the darkest of valleys, I fear no evil; for you are with me, your rod and staff a constant source of comfort. You prepare a table before me in the presence of my foes; you anoint my head with oil; my cup brims over. Surely goodness and mercy will accompany me all my days, and I shall dwell in the house of the Lord my whole life long.   *Psalm 23*

Ponder

Few words have brought greater comfort and inspiration across the centuries than the 23rd Psalm. It is one of the few passages of scripture that most people have at least some knowledge of, and one that resonates at some deep unconscious level. Perhaps one of the secrets of its enduring popularity is that David himself, in his youth, was a shepherd. In other words, when he wrote 'The Lord is my shepherd' he knew what he was talking about, the words rich with personal associations. Here was no sentimental comparison. It was rather the testimony of someone who understood the commitment and devotion that shepherding requires and who, in an outpouring of wonder, realised that here was an illustration of God's astonishing love for all his people.

For us, that love has been revealed all the more wonderfully through Jesus Christ and his willingness to offer his own life for our sakes. He is the one who walked through that darkest of valleys, the valley of the shadow of death, so that truly we need fear no evil. Nothing now, in life or death can ever finally separate us from the love of God expressed through him.

Ask yourself

The words of the psalm are familiar but have you stopped to take in what they are saying?

Pray

Loving God, time and again I have gone astray from you; time and again you have come looking for me, putting me on your shoulders and carrying me home. I tell myself that next time it will be different, but it's not; still I wander from your side. I am weak and foolish, undeserving of your love, yet still you reach out in love, drawing me back to you.

I praise you for the wonder of your grace, for your willingness through Christ to lay down your life for the life of the world. I thank you for your constant provision of all my needs. Have mercy on my repeated failures, and continue to guide me, watching over me even when I lose sight of you.

Lead me on through the changes and chances of this life, and through the valley of the shadow of death, until I am safely gathered into your kingdom and the journey is done. In the name of the shepherd of all, Jesus Christ my Lord. Amen.

Remember

I am the good shepherd. The good shepherd surrenders his life for the sheep; the hired hand, not being a shepherd and therefore the sheep not really mattering to him, takes one look at a wolf coming and runs for his life, and the wolf scatters the sheep and seizes them. I am the good shepherd. I know those who are mine and they know me, just as I know the Father and the Father knows me, and I surrender my life for my sheep.   *John 10:11-15*

Close

Lord Jesus Christ, help me to stay close to you as you stay close to me, for your name's sake. Amen.

All to the good

Read

We know that all things work together for good with those who love God, who have been called according to his purpose.

Romans 8:28

Ponder

There's no getting away from it – life is a strange paradox. At times it all goes smoothly, bringing joy and fulfilment, but, at others, it brings tragedy and sorrow, leaving us searching for answers, hopelessly bewildered as everything we put our trust in is turned upside down. How do we make sense of it? Can faith offer a solution? Some maintain that God plans everything down to the very last detail. They may be right but, personally, I believe the answer is more complex; that God constantly needs to adapt his plans as time and again they are frustrated. Yet, though life may be impossible to understand at the time, when we come to look back it is often possible to discern God's hand at work, taking even the most terrible of moments and weaving them into his sovereign purpose. In that, rather than any simplistic sense, we can truly say that all things work together for those who love God.

Ask yourself

Have there been times when you have found times of trial and difficulty leading on to unexpected blessing?

Pray

Lord, so often I don't understand what is happening to me. I am swept along by a tide of circumstances, and I look in vain to find any pattern that might give meaning to it all. This fleeting span of ours is a confusing riddle from which you can seem painfully absent. Yet, you are there even though I cannot see you, patiently weaving the broken strands of life into an intricate tapestry. Teach me, then, to trust in you and live by faith until that day when the picture is complete and I understand at last all the ways you have been working to bring order out of chaos, good out of evil, joy out of sorrow, and life out of death. In Christ's name. Amen.

Remember
We are not discouraged, for even though we seem outwardly debilitated, inwardly we are being renewed every day. For the inconsequential affliction we face currently is preparing for us an eternal weight of glory beyond measure.

2 Corinthians 4:16-17

Close
Gracious God, in the good and the bad, the happy and the sad, help me to keep on trusting you, confident that your purpose will win through and your love triumph. Through Jesus Christ my Lord. Amen.

MAY

Learning to forgive

Read

Peter approached him and said, 'Lord, how often should I let someone sin against me and still forgive them? As many as seven times?' Jesus said to him, 'Not seven times, but, I tell you, seventy-seven times.' *Matthew 18:21-22*

Ponder

I wrote earlier in this book about how hard we can find it to say sorry after we've made a mistake. To do that means swallowing our pride, overcoming our embarrassment and laying ourselves open to a possible rebuff. It is far easier, though far less satisfactory, to keep our head down and wait for the hurt to subside. But if 'sorry' can be the hardest word to *say*, there are three words, directly related, which can be even more difficult to *mean*: 'I forgive you.' We may be happy enough to say that; we may want to mean it and genuinely believe that we do, but to really forgive someone in the true sense of the word is a rare gift indeed. All too often a past mistake is dredged up again in the heat of anger; an error which we considered long-since forgotten suddenly thrown back in our face. Probably each of us is as guilty of doing that as any.

With God, it is different. When we confess our sins and are truly sorry, they are put behind us, over and done with, dealt with once and for all. No going back to them later; it is as if they never were. That's the good news. The bad news is this: God wants us to show that same level of forgiveness to others. It's a lot to ask and we will probably always finally fail, but if we are serious about discipleship we need to try. If God can forgive us, who are we not to forgive in turn?

Ask yourself

Do you hold a grievance against someone? What is stopping you forgiving them?

Pray

Gracious God, I have no reason to expect your mercy, for though I say I am sorry I go on letting you down time after time, making the same mistakes I have always made, ignoring your will, even wilfully rejecting your guidance. Yet you go on forgiving me, year in, year out, always ready to receive me back and to help me start again. I praise you for the wonder of your love, your goodness that is never exhausted.

Help me, having been forgiven so much, to forgive others, whose mistakes are so little by comparison. Give me a generous heart and a gracious spirit, the ability not just to speak of forgiveness but to display the truth of it in my life. Teach me to give those who have wronged me the opportunity to begin afresh, the past forgotten and the slate wiped clean. Through Jesus Christ my Lord. Amen.

Remember

If you forgive others their mistakes, your heavenly Father will forgive you in turn; but if you do not forgive others, neither will your Father forgive your mistakes.

Matthew 6:14-15

Close

Loving God, teach me to recognise how much I have been forgiven and so help me to reach out to others in turn, ready to show mercy, to forgive and to forget, for your name's sake. Amen.

Beyond the obvious

Read

The Lord does not see as people see, for they look at appearances, but the Lord sees into the heart.

1 Samuel 16:7b

Ponder

Have you come across the book *Timpson's England*? If you haven't, then you've missed a treat. Written by John Timpson, the radio broadcaster, it is subtitled 'A look beyond the obvious', and that captures the book's essence perfectly. Through words and pictures, the author highlights some of the things that most people tend to pass by without even noticing them; objects and items small in themselves – a corbel here, an inscription there, a plaque, signpost, house or monument – yet which add immeasurably to an appreciation of our rich heritage.

Such an ability to look beyond the obvious is not only important in relation to objects and places but also when it comes to people, for invariably there is more to those we meet than appearances may suggest. All too easily we make snap judgements based on appearances rather than first getting to know the person underneath. Once you take the time to do that, the majority of people prove to be full of surprises, revealing unexpected gifts and qualities. Thankfully, although *we* tend to see what is only superficial, God looks deeper. Let our prayer be to see with his eyes, and so to glimpse the hidden riches in one another that all too often we never begin to recognise.

Ask yourself

On what do you base the judgements you make about people? How often have you been surprised on getting to know someone better?

Pray

Gracious God, I know how foolish it is to judge by the outside, yet time and again I catch myself doing it. My mind says one thing, but my heart tells me another. Even when I think I am looking deeper, my conditioning makes me look at the world in a set way, deceived by superficial impressions, failing to see the good in some and the evil in others.

Help me to see with your eyes, to look beyond the obvious to the deeper realities of life, and to recognise the true worth of all those around me. Amen.

Remember

I, the Lord, examine the mind and search the heart.

Jeremiah 17:10a

Close

Gracious God, send me back to the world with your eyes rather than mine. Help me to see not only the bad but the good, not simply the ugly but the beautiful, not just the worst but the best. Give me wisdom and discernment so that I may look beyond outward appearances to the deeper realities so often concealed underneath. Through Jesus Christ my Lord. Amen.

Beginnings from endings

Read

Mary stood beside the tomb, sobbing. As she wept, she peered again into the tomb and saw two angels clothed in white sitting where the body of Jesus had previously been lying, one at the head and the other at the feet. They asked her, 'Woman, why are you crying?' She answered, 'They have taken away my Lord, and I have no idea where they have laid him.' Having said this, she turned round and saw Jesus standing there but she did not realise who it was. Jesus said to her, 'Woman, why do you grieve? Who are you looking for?' Imagining he was the gardener, she replied, 'Sir, if you are the one who has carried him off, tell me where you have put him, and I will take him away.' Jesus said to her, 'Mary!' Spinning round, she exclaimed in Hebrew, 'Rabbouni!' (which means Teacher).

John 20:11-16

Ponder

At first sight the story of Mary Magdalene in the garden is a little puzzling. How is it that, having been told Jesus has risen, and then seeing him face to face, she doesn't realise who he is? Yet is that really so strange? She'd watched as he drew his last breath on the cross, she'd seen him carried limp and lifeless into the tomb, she'd witnessed the stone being rolled across, and, understandably, she was convinced that it was all over, his life irrevocably extinguished. Anybody who has faced the apparent finality of the death of a loved one will understand those feelings.

Yet slowly the truth dawned: from that ending had come a new beginning, a beginning not just for Jesus but for her and everyone. Joy, hope, purpose, love, which had all been buried with Jesus in the tomb, came leaping back to life; the future that a moment before had seemed so empty was suddenly brimming over with promise. That is the truth of resurrection not just for Mary but also for us all. It does not only speak of life beyond the grave; it tells us that from what looks the bleakest of endings God is able to bring new beginnings beyond our wildest dreams.

Ask yourself

Are there areas in your life where you have given up believing in the possibility of starting afresh?

Pray

Lord Jesus Christ, you brought new beginnings out of what had seemed the end; new hope in what had seemed hopeless; new purpose in what had seemed to deny all meaning. I celebrate that truth, yet I confess that I find it hard sometimes to believe such new beginnings can apply to me; that I too can start again. I look at my own situation – the opportunities missed, hopes dashed, possibilities denied, dreams extinguished – and I see no prospect of life rising fresh from the ashes. Yet, as you came to Mary, the Apostles and countless others since, so you come now in your life-giving renewing power.

Teach me, however hopeless circumstances might seem, however much I may feel myself to be at a dead end, never to lose my sense of all that you are able to do. Remind me that endings can lead to new beginnings, that new life can spring from the old, and in that confidence may I look forward to everything you will yet do in my life. In your name I ask it. Amen.

Remember

Behold, I make all things new.   *Revelation 21:5*

Close

Sovereign God, open my eyes to your renewing power and so help me to see each apparent conclusion as the start of a fresh chapter in my life. Through Jesus Christ my Lord. Amen.

Rising to the challenge

Read

Following the death of the Lord's servant Moses, the Lord spoke to Joshua son of Nun, Moses' assistant, saying, 'My servant Moses is dead. Now advance with all the people of Israel and cross the Jordan into the land that I am giving them. I will readily give to you everywhere that you set foot, as I promised to Moses. From the wilderness and the Lebanon as far as the great river, the river Euphrates, all the land of the Hittites and on towards the Great Sea in the west shall be your territory. Nobody will be able to withstand you all the days of your life. Just as I was with Moses, so I will be with you; I will not fail or forsake you. Be strong and of good courage; for you will lead this people to take possession of the land that I swore to their ancestors to give them.'

Joshua 1:1-6

Ponder

Anyone who has ever been hill walking will know the experience of thinking one is nearing the summit, only to find, as one gets closer, that there is another stretch to climb . . . and another . . . and another! However far we progress, there is always that little bit further to go.

So it proved, in a rather different sense, for Joshua and the people of Israel following the death of Moses. After years of wandering in the wilderness, they had finally arrived at the border of the Promised Land, their long journey at last over. Or was it? A closer inspection revealed that others already occupied the land they thought was reserved for them. The task of making it their own had only just begun. No wonder Joshua, the newly chosen leader of Israel, felt overwhelmed by the sudden responsibility thrust upon him. His was the onerous challenge of rallying a people reeling from disappointment and inspiring them to new levels of enthusiasm and endeavour. Alone, he couldn't have done it; but he wasn't alone, for God had promised to be with him wherever he went. He goes on making that promise to us today – to anyone and everyone willing to serve him, however great a challenge that service may involve.

Ask yourself
Are you facing a challenge that is greater than you expected it to be? Have you sufficient faith and courage to see it through?

Pray
Lord, it's hard, faced with disappointment, to find new reserves and fresh inspiration to try and try again. When I've given my all and believe I've achieved something, when I've kept on battling despite the obstacles in my way, it hurts to accept that there are still more hurdles to face, yet more setbacks to overcome. Yet though I may sometimes feel weary at the demands, I know in my heart that life is made of such challenges; that no achievement, however special, is sufficient to answer all my dreams.

Renew me, then, through your Holy Spirit, and give me the faith and commitment I need to walk the pilgrim way, pressing on towards the prize. Amen.

Remember
Be strong and take courage. Do not be disheartened or dismayed.   *1 Chronicles 22:13*

Close
Living God, help me to meet difficulties and disappointments with confidence, knowing that you will equip me to respond to whatever may be asked of me. Amen.

Ears to hear

Read

Even the sweetest of songs is as vinegar poured on a wound
to one who is heavy in heart.   *Proverbs 25:20*

Ponder

How many times have you said the wrong thing at the
wrong time and felt yourself curl up with embarrassment
as you realise you've gone and put your foot in it again?
There are times when that happens through no fault of our
own, when the delicateness of a situation is unknown to
us. At other times, though, there is no such excuse: our
gaffe is due to the fact that we opened our mouths before
we stopped to think. How often have we been so full of our
own news in conversation that we scarcely listen to what is
being said to us in turn? How often are we busily framing
our response before someone has barely started to speak?
Little wonder, then, that we end up saying the wrong thing.
Sensitivity is not some magical gift possessed by the select
few; it comes from being slow to speak and ready to listen.

Ask yourself

Are you as good at listening as you should be? Are you more
intent on sharing your news than hearing what others are
telling you?

Pray

Loving God, forgive me all the times I have failed to listen
to others, too preoccupied with my own affairs to hear
what they were saying to me. Forgive me the hurt I have
caused, the need I have overlooked and the opportunities I
have missed to offer help, all because I have not had ears
to hear.

Teach me to be open to what people are saying and sensitive to their needs, and so may I be ready to respond in the right way, at the right place and at the right time. Through Jesus Christ my Lord. Amen.

Remember
It is important to understand this, my friends: be slow to speak and swift to listen. *James 1:19*

Close
Loving God, when you want me to hear your voice calling through another, open my ears, open my mind, open my heart, and close my mouth! Amen.

A friend in need

Read

Ruth said, 'Do not urge me to turn back and abandon you. Wherever you go, I will go; wherever you stop, I will stop; your people will be my people, and your God my God. Where you die, I will die and be buried. In God's name, I swear that not even death will part me from you!'

Ruth 1:16-17

Ponder

What kind of friend are you? Are you the sort who can be depended on in a crisis, or the fair-weather variety, swift to vanish into the night the moment there is any suggestion that commitment might cost you something? Naturally we all like to think we're the former – true, loyal, trustworthy – but ask yourself honestly: how many people are there you would be willing to make sacrifices for?

For the Christian, not only should friendships possess a special quality, but the very concept of friendship has been widened by Jesus to include those both near and far, those we are close to and those who will always be strangers. To demonstrate such friendship is hard indeed and few will get anywhere near it, but today we are reminded of the devotion of Ruth who, centuries before Christ, showed herself to be a friend in need. What is God saying to you about your service to others through her example?

Ask yourself

What kind of friend are you to others? How deep is the commitment you put into your relationships?

Pray

Loving God, I thank you that you are a God I can depend on, always there in times of need, my truest friend. I thank you for all those I count as friends – those who I know will stand by me even when life is difficult and my fortunes low – and I thank you for the fellowship I share in Christ with all your people.

Help me to show true friendship in my relationships with others: to offer support in times of crisis, encouragement in times of fear, comfort in times of sorrow and hope in times of despair. Help me to know you as my constant companion, standing with me in all that I face, and as you have been faithful to me, so help me to be faithful to you. Through Jesus Christ my Lord. Amen.

Remember

A friend is a loving companion at all times.

Proverbs 17:17a (NEB)

Close

Gracious God, teach me today the meaning of friendship, both in relation to others and in relation to you. Through Jesus Christ my Lord. Amen.

The folly of faith

Read

Having left the prison, they entered the house of Lydia, and having seen and exhorted their fellow Christians there, they went on their way.   *Acts 16:40*

Ponder

What do you think of today's reading? A bit dull, isn't it? Hardly the stuff to capture the imagination or stir the spirit? Think again, for in this almost incidental remark concerning Lydia welcoming the disciples into her home there lies an action of astonishing faith, courage and commitment. Lydia was a seller of blue cloth; in other words, a woman who, against the odds, had made it in the world of Roman business selling the fabric worn by the highest officers in the land. It couldn't have been easy to succeed in the world of her time and one whiff of something untoward could bring all she'd built tumbling down over her head. Yet, when Paul and his companions came preaching the gospel she responded immediately, confessing her faith and seeking baptism, never mind that Christians were already facing persecution for their faith. If that wasn't enough, a short while later Paul became embroiled in a public row concerning a young slave girl; a dispute that led to him being hustled with his colleagues before the civic authorities, committed to prison, and finally expelled from the town.

Now do you see the message in these verses? Despite all this, knowing the risks, she opened her home gladly to the Apostle and his friends. In the eyes of the world, it must have seemed madness and I am sure many among her friends must have upbraided her for her folly. They were wasting their breath, for Lydia had discovered in the folly of the gospel the power of God.

Ask yourself

In what do you put your trust: human wisdom or God's foolishness?

Pray

Living God, I do not risk much today in committing myself to you, yet I still do not find it easy, for there are many who pour scorn on the gospel, who ridicule Christianity and who mock those who profess faith in you. Still more are dismissive of you, not hostile but simply regarding Christian teaching and everything to do with the Church as an out-dated irrelevance, the preserve of those who still feel the need for some kind of religion. Such apathy and indifference are in some ways harder to cope with than outright rejection, for none of us likes being thought foolish, and the temptation is to compromise my convictions, to tone down my message or even to conceal my commitment.

Help me to remember that your wisdom is often counted by the world as foolishness, and to remember in turn that the wisdom of this world in reality is all too often folly. Give me the courage and dedication I need to stay true to you no matter what people may say or think – the faith, if necessary, to be a fool for Christ. Amen.

Remember

The word of the cross to those who are perishing is folly, but to us who are being saved it is the power of God.

1 Corinthians 1:18

Close

Lord Jesus Christ, grant me real insight, genuine under-standing, true wisdom, and teach me to hold on to that, however foolish it may seem. For your name's sake. Amen.

What's in a name?

Read

Those who had been scattered following the persecution that developed in response to the martyrdom of Stephen travelled as far as Phoenicia, Cyprus and Antioch, though preaching the word only to the Jews. Some among them, however, were Cypriots and Cyrenians, and when these came to Antioch they preached about Christ to Greeks as well. And God's hand was upon them in such a way that a great number of them believed and turned to the Lord. It was there in Antioch that disciples were first called 'Christians'.

Acts 11:19-21, 26b

Ponder

Do you know what your name means? Mine, apparently, means 'carried away in triumph' or 'borne away in victory'. A nice thought, but I'm still waiting, and there's no sign of much happening yet! The fact is, of course, that our names don't signify very much, chosen because our parents liked the sound of them rather than because they say anything about us. A nickname, by contrast, is different. Typically, it says something about a person; the name designed to encapsulate some distinguishing feature.

So it was for believers in Jesus who had fled to Antioch following persecution for their faith. There they proclaimed and lived out the gospel with such resounding success that they earned a nickname that has stuck ever since: 'Christians'. It wasn't just an empty label; it said something about them, highlighting the fact that these were people who followed the way of Christ. Would anyone today, I wonder, looking at our lives, think to label us 'Christians'? Would it stick out a mile that we are followers of Jesus? Many still call themselves 'Christians' but they don't see that as having any bearing on the way they live. It's up to us to show them differently.

Ask yourself
How far is Christ seen in you? Does your life measure up to the name of Christ?

Pray
Lord Jesus Christ, I bear your name and I profess to follow your way, yet there is little if anything different about me from anyone else. I have failed you in so many ways; my faith weak, my love poor and my commitment unpredictable. I have been half-hearted in your service, concerned more about my own interests than your glory. All too often my words say one thing but my deeds another, the message I proclaim belied by the way I live, so that instead of leading people towards you I lead them away.

Forgive me and help me to follow you not just in name only but in truth, proud to be identified with your cause and committing my life to the work of your kingdom. Lord, I ask it for your name's sake. Amen.

Remember
Let none of you suffer as a murderer, a thief, a doer of evil, or even one who meddles in the affairs of others. If any of you suffer, though, as a Christian, do not be ashamed by it, but give glory to God because you bear his name.

1 Peter 4:15-16

Close
Lord Jesus Christ, you have called me into the family of your people; help me, then, to live as a child of God, to the glory of your name. Amen.

The last resort?

Read

A woman, who for twelve years had endured a persistent haemorrhage and who had suffered greatly at the hands of numerous physicians, spending everything she had in the process yet getting worse as a result rather than better, heard about Jesus. Pushing through the crowd, she touched his robe, saying, 'If I can only touch his clothes, I will be healed.'
                                                            Mark 5:25-28

Ponder

I read this week the powerful story of a woman's battle against breast cancer. She had endured radical surgery, together with radio- and chemotherapy but to no avail; the disease was still progressing. Finally, she turned in desperation to alternative medicine, travelling across the world to Mexico to find a cure, and today, several years later, she is alive and well to tell the tale. It does not follow that natural remedies guarantee a cure, but this woman's despair drove her to explore a last resort that, in her case, proved successful.

The story in Mark is very similar, only this time the last resort was Jesus. She had tried everything else and spent a fortune in doing so; he was her last hope. Her faith was not disappointed. How often do we treat Jesus as a last resort? How often do we turn to him in prayer only when we've exhausted every other option? In so many aspects of life, it only occurs to us to seek his help when every other door has closed to us. We cannot guarantee that our prayers will be answered as we wish; it is often patently not so. Concerning the issue of healing, for example, many are not made well, as they hope. What we can guarantee, however, is that we will find strength, support, peace and wholeness no matter what we face. Don't leave Jesus as a last resort. Don't turn to him in prayer when all else has failed. Bring your needs to him and let his renewing grace touch your life.

Ask yourself

Why do we so often turn to Jesus as a last resort? Is there a need you are struggling with concerning which you have yet to seek his help?

Pray

Loving Lord, you are always looking to respond to my needs, constantly reaching out to touch my life with your love, yet all too often I fail to seek the help you long to give me. I trust in my own strength; I try this, that and everything else; and I only remember you when I reach the end of my tether and there is no one left to turn to.

Forgive me for relegating you to the periphery rather than putting you at the centre of my life. Forgive me for treating you as a last resort instead of a first recourse. Teach me to bring my needs to you, knowing that though you may not always respond as I want you to, you will always respond in love, providing for my needs, granting me peace and bringing me the wholeness that you alone can give. In your name I ask it. Amen.

Remember

Blessed be the Lord, for he has heard my cry for help.

Psalm 28:6

Close

Lord Jesus Christ, before I do anything else help me always to turn to you, and so may I know your hand upon me, this and every day. Amen.

When one door closes

Read

Having been prevented by the Holy Spirit from speaking the word in Asia, they travelled through the districts of Phrygia and Galatia. Coming towards Mysia, they attempted to go into Bithynia, but again the Spirit of Jesus did not allow them; so, passing by Mysia, they journeyed on to Troas. That night, Paul had a vision, in which a man from Macedonia stood begging him for assistance, saying, 'Come across to Macedonia and help us.' In the light of that vision, we immediately tried to cross over to Macedonia, being persuaded that God had called us to preach the good news there.   *Acts 16:6-10*

Ponder

When I first felt the call to Christian ministry there was one problem standing in my way: for some years, I had suffered from a speech impediment; a stammer that, at one point, reached such a peak that I could barely put two words together. Hardly the ideal qualification for a would-be public speaker, you might say! I was encouraged, however, to carry on and, though the problem never completely left me throughout my fifteen years' ministry, few would have guessed I had any difficulties. Towards the end of that time, however, I began to struggle rather more than previously, enough to make public events an ordeal rather than a pleasure. Eventually I felt I could not continue in pastoral ministry. Yet, as one ministry ended, another began with the publication of my first book. Since then the written rather than spoken word has been the vehicle for communicating my faith.

That experience brought home to me what the Apostle Paul had discovered centuries earlier as he tried first to enter Asia, and then Bithynia, before finally recognising a call to Macedonia: the simple fact that when one door closes God invariably opens another. Life rarely goes as smoothly as any of us would like – our hopes sometimes dashed, our plans often thwarted – but through it all God is able to provide fresh avenues of service and new possibilities to explore.

Ask yourself

Have doors seemed to close in your life? Could it be that God is looking to lead you in a new direction?

Pray

Sovereign God, I cannot always make sense of life, your purpose sometimes hard to understand and my experiences a puzzle. I feel frustrated when things don't work out as I had hoped, confused when the way you seemed to be leading me no longer feels right, troubled when doors that once had beckoned suddenly seem closed firmly in my face. I cannot be sure whether such moments are meant to happen or whether they run counter to your purpose, but what I know for certain is that where one door closes you are able to open another.

Help me, instead of regretting what has been, to look forward to what is to come and to be ready to grasp the future, responding to each opportunity you give me as it comes. In the name of Christ I ask it. Amen.

Remember

Coming with the gospel to Troas, I found the Lord had opened a door for me there.   *2 Corinthians 2:12*

Close

Loving God, through all that life brings and in all the challenges I face, help me to see the way forward and to follow where you would lead me. Through Jesus Christ my Lord. Amen.

Sowing the seed

Read

Jesus told the crowd many parables, including this one: 'A farmer went out to sow and, as he did so, some seed fell by the wayside, and the birds swooped down and devoured it. Other seed fell on rocky ground, where there was little soil and, though it sprang up quickly because the earth was so shallow, when the sun rose, it was baked and withered away, since it had no root. Other seed fell among thorns, which, as they grew, choked the seedlings, so that they yielded no grain. Other seed fell into good soil and brought forth grain, rising up and increasing and yielding thirty and sixty and a hundred-fold.' And he said, 'Let those with ears to hear listen!'

Mark 4:2-9

Ponder

What's the most important lesson to be drawn from the parable of the sower? Is it that our lives need to be like fertile soil, receptive to the word of God, so that we bear a rich harvest to his glory? It could be, for there's no doubt God wants to see that in our lives. Is a more important message that we need to beware of temptations that may insidiously destroy our faith before we realise what is happening? It could be that, too, for there's no denying how real and dangerous temptation can be. Could it be that the underlying theme is to guard against shallow discipleship, a faith rooted in a superficial and emotional response rather than grounded in body, mind and soul? That's certainly an important point, for how many people commit themselves to Christ for a moment in a surge of enthusiasm, only swiftly to fall away? We can even argue that Jesus is telling us that some people will never respond to the gospel no matter how often they hear it. True perhaps, though it would be foolish to judge the state of another's soul. The truth is, of course, that all of these points are equally valid.

Yet there is a further lesson in his words which is, perhaps, more important than any, and that, quite simply, is the need to sow. The seed may be the object of the story, but the sower has first to sow it, and for 'sower' read 'us'. *We* are the ones called to spread God's word, the responsibility of proclaiming the good news of Christ entrusted to *us*. We cannot guarantee the results of our efforts but one thing is certain: unless we sow the seed, whatever the ground, there will be no harvest.

Ask yourself

Have you taken seriously the call to share your faith? When did you last witness to Christ?

Pray

Lord Jesus Christ, you have called me to be your witness, to proclaim your name and make known your love, but, though I try to respond to that challenge, I find it so hard. When I speak of you I am met with indifference, even hostility. Though I keep on trying, in my heart I give up, no longer expecting lives to be changed by your word.

Teach me to look beyond appearances and to recognise that, though I may not always see it, the seed I may sow bears fruit in unexpected ways and places; that though much will fall on barren soil, some will find fertile ground and in the fullness of time bear a rich harvest. Help me to trust, not in my ability but in your life-giving power, confident that, if I play my part, you will play yours. In your name I ask it. Amen.

Remember

Go into all the world and proclaim the gospel to all creation.

Mark 16:15

Close

Lord Jesus Christ, I cannot make disciples on my own, but I can play my part in sowing the seed for you to nurture. Help me to do that faithfully, conscious of my privilege and responsibility, for your name's sake. Amen.

Learning to say thank you

Read

It is good to give thanks to the Lord, to sing praises to your name, O Most High, to declare your steadfast love in the morning, and your faithfulness by night. For you, O Lord, have made me glad by your work; at the works of your hands I sing for joy. *Psalm 92:1-2, 4*

Ponder

What is one of the first words we learn to say as a baby? After 'mama' and 'dada', I suspect it's probably 'thank you' or, more precisely, 'ta'. So now another question: What's one of the first words we forget to say as Christians? The answer, I suspect, is once again 'thank you'. Of course, *you* may be the exception that proves the rule, but, if you are anything like me, your prayers are long on 'please' and short on 'thank you'. We ask God for this, that and every-thing else, bombarding him day after day with a string of requests, but when he answers our prayers and provides for our needs, how many times, I wonder, do we make a point of showing our appreciation? When it comes to people, few of us would dream of not saying thank you for a kind-ness, if only out of politeness. Why should it be any differ-ent when it comes to God? As the psalm reminds us, 'It is good to give thanks to the Lord.'

Ask yourself

When did you last make time to thank God for something? Have you been guilty of taking God's gifts for granted?

Pray

Loving God, I have so much to thank you for – so much that is good and special. Day after day you bless me, week after week you answer my prayers, year after year you meet my needs. I cannot thank you enough for your great goodness, yet the truth is I rarely thank you at all. Forgive me for taking your gifts for granted, for letting familiarity blind me to how fortunate I am, and so failing to thank you for all you have given.

Forgive me for being swift to ask for your blessing yet slow to acknowledge your generous response when you give it. Teach me to receive your innumerable gifts with heartfelt gratitude, and to show my thanks not just in words but in my daily living – in a life that gratefully celebrates the wonder of your love. In Christ's name I ask it. Amen.

Remember

Come into his gates with thanksgiving and his courts with praise. Offer thanks to him and bless his name. For the Lord is good; his unfailing love endures for ever and his faithfulness to all generations.   *Psalm 100:4-5*

Close

Gracious God, help me not only to ask in faith but to receive with gratitude, through Jesus Christ my Lord. Amen.

Encouraging others

Read

Joseph – a Levite and Cypriot, by descent – who had been nicknamed Barnabas by the Apostles, meaning 'Son of Encouragement', sold the land that he owned and laid the proceeds at the Apostles' feet.   *Acts 4:36-37*

Ponder

When we read the pages of scripture, hear dramatic stories of testimony, or meet sparkling Christians, it's hard sometimes not to feel a little daunted. Few of us have eye-catching gifts and it is unlikely that any contribution we may make will hit the headlines. That's why stories like that of Barnabas are so important. He wasn't one of the Apostles, nor one whose name has gone down in history for stunning signs and wonders, but I suspect had you taken a poll among the early Christians as to who in the Church meant most to them, Barnabas would have been one of the leading contenders to come out on top. Why? Because he had that most precious of gifts: the ability to encourage. In the verses above, it was through his generosity. In Acts 9:26-27 we see it through his trust, introducing the newly converted Paul to the Apostles when others still doubted his conversion. In Acts 15:36-39 he did it again, this time bringing encouragement to John Mark, giving him a second chance when Paul felt it too risky. We see it, yet once more, in Acts 11:23-24, where we read, 'when he arrived and saw the evidence of the grace of God, he was glad and encouraged them all to remain true to the Lord'. His was an unsung gift but a vital one; the sort that releases all kinds of gifts in others.

Are we the sort of people who encourage others, or do we discourage instead: seeing difficulties, highlighting weakness, stifling enthusiasm? There is no excuse: we may not possess show-stopping gifts but all of us, without exception, can offer a ministry of encouragement.

Ask yourself

In what ways are you able to encourage others? Have you been offering as much encouragement as you should?

Pray

Gracious God, you call us to support one another, to offer comfort in times of need, reassurance in times of fear, inspiration in times of challenge, and confidence in times of doubt. Forgive me for so easily doing the opposite – finding fault, running down, criticising and condemning. Forgive me for seeing the worst instead of the best, for believing the bad instead of the good, for so often pulling down and so rarely building up.

Teach me to recognise people's gifts and nurture them, to understand their problems and share them, to acknowledge their successes and applaud them, to appreciate their efforts and affirm them. Teach me, through the faith I show in people, to help them attempt great things and expect great things; to look at life seeing not the obstacles but the opportunities, not the things they can't do but the things they can. So may I help them to believe in themselves, discover their abilities, appreciate their worth and fulfil their potential. Through Jesus Christ my Lord. Amen.

Remember

Let us consider how we might spur each other on in love and good works, not forgetting to meet together, as some have grown accustomed to doing; but encouraging one another, and doing so increasingly as you see the day approaching.

Hebrews 10:24-25

Close

As you encourage me, so may I encourage others, through Jesus Christ my Lord. Amen.

Food for our souls

Read

Pay attention, everyone who is thirsty, come and find water;
and you that have no food, come, buy and eat! Come, buy
wine and milk, not for money but beyond price. Why spend
your money on that which is not bread, and why offer your
labour for that which cannot satisfy? Listen carefully to what
I say, and you will eat what is good, delighting yourselves in
the richest of food.   *Isaiah 55:1-2*

Ponder

One of the hardest aspects of parenting must surely be getting one's children to eat. Offer them a bar of chocolate or
a bag of sweets and there's no problem, but give them a
healthy balanced meal and they will sit there picking at it
for all the world as though you're trying to poison them!
Sometimes we just don't know what's good for us!

That's not just true of children but all of us. When it
comes to nourishing our souls, we all tend to be addicted
to junk food rather than that which can truly satisfy. We cram
so much into our lives in an effort to find fulfilment, yet still
cannot fill the aching void deep inside. It's nothing new:
countless generations have done the same since time im-
memorial. As the prophet Isaiah knew all too well, we are
hopelessly addicted to instant satisfaction; to that which
instinctively appeals to our senses yet cannot begin to meet
our innermost needs. We need to make time for God, space
for prayer and reflection, and room in our lives for spiritual
sustenance. Fail to do that and, though our stomachs may be
full to overflowing, our emaciated souls will slowly starve
within us.

Ask yourself

Do you still hunger and thirst to know God better? With
what do you feed and nurture your faith?

Pray

Living God, you have taught us that we should long to know you better: not just to want that but to urgently, passionately and wholeheartedly yearn for it, striving with all our being to understand your will and fulfil your purpose. You have told us that those who hunger and thirst after righteousness shall be filled.

Teach me the secret of such hunger. Instead of cluttering my life with so much that can never satisfy, teach me to empty myself so that I may be filled by you; to desire your kingdom, seek your will and study your word, earnestly, eagerly, expectantly. However much I know of your love, however richly you may have blessed me, teach me to keep that hunger alive, to thirst always for a deepening of my faith, a strengthening of my service and a greater awareness of your purpose. Through Jesus Christ my Lord. Amen.

Remember

Blessed are those who hunger and thirst for righteousness, for they will be satisfied.   *Matthew 5:6*

Close

Lord Jesus Christ, nourish me through your word, nurture me through your grace, feed me through your Spirit, fill me with your love, for your name's sake. Amen.

Sharing the load

Read

Bear one another's burdens, and so fulfil the law of Christ.

Galatians 6:2

Ponder

To say it was heavy was an understatement: it was like a lead weight – a suitcase crammed full to overflowing as I set off to the railway station to catch the train back to college. Unsurprisingly, the handle could not cope. A hundred yards up the road and it came off in my hand, the case crashing down and bursting open, spilling the contents everywhere. How glad I was, having stuffed everything back in again and bodily wrestled with the load for the rest of the journey, to be offered a helping hand by one of my fellow-students as I lugged it up to my room. Such a weight was too much to carry by myself and I learned never to try it again.

There are few people who do not carry a burden of some sort. It may not be a physical load but it is no less difficult to bear for that. The weight of guilt, fear, sorrow, despair, anxiety and pain, to name but a few examples, can be equally crushing and far more so. We cannot shoulder such burdens for others, much though we might sometimes wish we could, but we can share them, not least through listening and showing we care. To be there to share the load in such a way means more than we might imagine.

Ask yourself

Are there burdens you know of that you could help to share? Do you readily respond to those who need your help? Do you struggle too often to manage on your own instead of asking for help?

Pray

Living God, there are times when I feel weighed down by the stresses and strains of daily life – oppressed by worry, unable to throw off my anxieties, held captive by a multitude of secret fears. I thank you for all those who help me through such moments, who offer a shoulder to lean on, an arm to steady and a hand to share the load. Teach me in turn to bear the burdens of others, doing all I can through listening, understanding, caring and sharing, to offer them my help. As you have reached out to me, so teach me to reach out in turn, expressing your love and showing your care, to the glory of your name. Amen.

Remember

Encourage one another and build each other up, as indeed you are doing.   *1 Thessalonians 5:11*

Close

Lord Jesus Christ, you bore my sins on the cross, carrying there the burden of all the world. Teach me to bear the burdens of others, in your name. Amen.

Bearing our burdens

Read

Humble yourselves under the mighty hand of God so that, in due course, he may exalt you. Cast all your burdens upon him, for it matters to him what happens to you. So then, let us come boldly before his throne of grace, so that we may obtain mercy and find grace to help in time of need.
1 Peter 5:7; Hebrews 4:16

Ponder

It's often said that we should bear one another's burdens. That's all very well, and in an ideal world it would no doubt provide most of the support we could ever have need for. Only this isn't an ideal world, and there are problems that we either feel unable to share, or that no one can help with, or that people simply do not want to know about. I imagine we've all been in situations when we've felt utterly overwhelmed by a situation and haven't known who to turn to; hence the existence of organisations like the Samaritans.

Thankfully, we do not depend merely on human support for assistance – we are able to share our cares and burdens with God. Do that and, though the problems will not magically disappear, we will find a new perspective on them, an inner peace whatever our trouble, rest for our souls.

Ask yourself

Are you struggling with what seems an insurmountable problem, feeling that there is no one and nowhere you can turn to for help? Have you understood what it means to place your burdens into the hands of God?

Pray

Loving God, I pray for all who are bearing heavy burdens – those facing difficulties and problems to which they can see no solutions; wrestling with inner fears and phobias; racked by anxiety for themselves or loved ones; troubled about money, health, work or relationships – all those who crave rest for their souls but cannot find it. I pray for them and for myself, acknowledging that there are times when I too feel crushed under a weight of care. Speak to me and to all in your still small voice, and grant the peace and quiet confidence that only you can bring; and so may our burdens be lifted and our souls refreshed. Lord, in your mercy, hear my prayer, through Jesus Christ my Lord. Amen.

Remember

Take my yoke on you and learn from me, for I am tender and lowly in heart and you will find rest for your souls – for my yoke is easy, and my burden is light.

Matthew 11:29-30

Close

Sovereign God, when I can carry on no longer, my burdens too heavy to bear, take hold of me, take hold of them, and carry all in your loving arms, through Jesus Christ my Lord. Amen.

Shutting our ears

Read

Stephen, being full of the Holy Spirit, gazed up into heaven and saw there the glory of God and Jesus standing at his right hand, and he said, 'Look! The heavens are open and I see the Son of Man standing at the right hand of God.' Then they cried out with a loud voice, and shut their ears, and, in one mind, they rushed upon him.   *Acts 7:57*

Ponder

Have you ever been banned from a church? I have. It was many years back, during my time as a student, and I was preaching in a church in one of the Welsh valleys. My theme was Jonah and the whale, and as part of my exposition I enthusiastically went into the various scholarly interpretations of the story, ranging from affirmations of its literal truth to the suggestion that it might be a parable designed to counter bigotry and intolerance. I went away feeling the sermon had gone rather well, but a few months later I was summoned into the principal's office to learn otherwise. Not only had my words caused offence, but on no account was I ever to return there again!

Should I have aired theological debate in a sermon? I'm still not sure, though probably it was the wrong time and place. What that experience brought home to me, however, was how easily we close our ears to that which we'd rather not hear. Don't think I'm condemning, for I'm as guilty as any. We all have our set ideas from which it is hard to shift us, however open we may think ourselves to be. Like those who listened to Stephen as he testified to his faith, we shut out anything that challenges our preconceived ideas, preferring to silence it rather than face its challenge. It may be, of course, that our point of view is right all along; it may equally be that it is wrong or in need of modification. Unless we are willing to listen, we will never know.

Ask yourself

Are you open to ideas that may stretch and challenge your own or do you shut your ears to anything that contradicts your point of view? Is that a sign of faith or of underlying doubt?

Pray

Loving God, we do not want to be tossed around by every wind of change or swayed by every passing idea, but neither do we want to be so set in our ways that we are closed to new insights into truth and fresh perspectives on your word.

Forgive me those times when I have been just that, so convinced of my own rightness that I have refused to hear what others are saying – closing my ears to that which unsettles me and shying away from the possibility that my horizons need to be broader. Give me true humility to listen to other opinions, to explore different possibilities, to face searching questions, and to adapt my views where appropriate, confident that truth is strong enough to be tested and to emerge the stronger for it. In the name of Christ I ask it. Amen.

Remember

Hearing him speak of the resurrection of the dead, some poured scorn on him, but others said, 'We will hear you again concerning this matter.'   *Acts 17:32*

Close

Lord Jesus Christ, give me wisdom to hold on to truth but also humility to recognise that I do not have a monopoly on it. Open my heart to your challenging and illuminating word, from wherever that might come, for your name's sake. Amen.

Slipping back

Read

Thus says the Lord: If people fall, do they not get up again?
If they go astray, do they not return to the right path? So
why are my people continually backsliding, forever falling
away? We need to pay ever more attention to everything we
have heard, so that we do not let it slip.

Jeremiah 8:4-5a; Hebrews 2:1

Ponder

The other day brought an unexpected and unwelcome
surprise. On what ostensibly was the first day of spring we
had some of the heaviest snow of the year; even here in the
West Country the streets were briefly covered by a treacherous
layer of slush that made walking difficult. What should have
been a pleasant stroll became a tortuous journey, everyone
picking their way gingerly in case their feet should go from
under them.

At least, though, the danger was clear, so everyone knew
to take extra care. There are times on the road of Christian
discipleship when the going becomes slippery yet with no
outward indication of the fact. Instead of being like snow it
is more like black ice. We can be progressing serenely along
our way, sure of our footing and confident of reaching our
destination when, before we have time to realise what's
going on, we find that we have taken a tumble and slipped
over. Our confidence is shaken and our faith undermined
such that we are uncertain where to take our next step. It
all happens so easily and quickly. If we are not to find ourselves sliding back, we need to be vigilant and awake to the
things that might cause us to fall. Most of all, we need to
focus on God and seek his guidance, for he finally is the
one who can direct us safely along our path.

Ask yourself

Have you slipped back in your faith? Are there things that you know cause you to stumble?

Pray

Living God, I have committed myself to the path of discipleship and I want to walk it faithfully, but I know how easy it is to slip back. Help me to be alert to dangers, able to recognise those things that might trip me up. Help me to keep my eyes on you, knowing that you will lead me safely through the pitfalls and obstacles in my path. And when I do stumble or find myself slipping, hold on to me, keep me steady and direct my footsteps so that I will find the path once more and continue safely on my way until my journey's end. In Christ's name I ask it. Amen.

Remember

My steps have held fast to your paths; my feet have not slipped.   *Psalm 17:4*

Close

Lord Jesus Christ, my Saviour, able to keep my foot from slipping and to present me faultless and brimming over with joy into the glorious presence of God, to you be glory and majesty, dominion and power, now and for evermore. Amen.   *Jude v. 24 (adapted)*

A never-failing spring

Read

Again, the Lord spoke to me: Because this people have turned their backs on the gently flowing waters of Shiloah, the Lord will bring up the mighty floodwaters of the Euphrates against it, the king of Assyria and all his glory. It will rise ever higher and burst its banks, and it will sweep on as a mighty flood into Judah, spilling over until it reaches neck height. Its outstretched wings will fill every part of your land, O Immanuel.

Isaiah 8:5-8

Ponder

There was chilling news announced today: a warning from Tearfund that within the next 25 years over two-thirds of the world's population will be facing an acute shortage of water. As never before, water is becoming a precious commodity, bought and sold on international markets, and the trend is set to continue as nations compete for supplies of this life-giving resource. The 'waters of Shiloah' that the prophet Isaiah spoke of was, on one level, precisely the same, but was also a metaphor for a different and yet more vital resource. It refers to a canal that flowed gently but irrepressibly into Jerusalem, fed by the spring of Gihon and culminating in the Pool of Siloam. It was hugely valued – understandably so, given the arid climate of Israel – for not once had it been known to dry up; indeed, the spring still supplies water for Jerusalem to this day.

For Isaiah, though, it was more than simply an unfailing source of water, it was also a symbol of the faithful, enduring and unceasing love of God; a love that never stopped flowing out to his people but which they had now turned their backs on. The result, he warned, would be an unstoppable disaster in the form of Assyrian oppression, which, in contrast to God's quiet provision, would engulf them all in turmoil.

The theology may be crudely simplistic, but the underlying message is sound: if we put our faith in God, his love will sustain us, whatever may be thrown against us. If we look elsewhere for something on which to base our lives, we may find we have unleashed more than we bargained for.

Ask yourself

Do you put your trust in the loving provision of God, or do you base your security and happiness on something else?

Pray

Gracious God, I thank you for the many ways you provide for me, the love you so faithfully show and the blessings you give beyond my deserving. Forgive me for taking your goodness for granted instead of appreciating it as I should. Forgive me for failing to trust you despite all you have done, trusting instead in other people or other things. Teach me to put my faith in you, knowing that whatever I may be up against you will provide the help I need to face it. Through Jesus Christ my Lord. Amen.

Remember

Jesus said to her, 'Anyone who drinks this water will be thirsty again, but the one who drinks of the water I give will never thirst again, for that water will become a spring of water within, gushing up to eternal life.   *John 4:13-14*

Close

Loving God, just as you have provided over the years for my deepest needs, so help me today to trust for the future, knowing that your love will not fail. Amen.

It won't wash

Read

Nothing is hidden that will not be revealed; nor is there any secret that will not come out into the open and be known by all. Cleanse me from my secret faults.

Luke 8:17; Psalm 19:12

Ponder

Do you know what the term 'Greenwash' means? I didn't until recently. Apparently, it's a term used to describe the efforts of large industries and corporations to present their products as environmentally sensitive, even when they may be anything but. Have you noticed, for example, how virtually every detergent you buy today is labelled eco-friendly, how every foodstuff is farm-fresh, how every packaging is recycled and recyclable? Such claims are not necessarily groundless, many firms having done much to clean up their act, but green labels and marketing have become useful promotional tools in the hands of some who are less than scrupulous.

However, it's not just faceless corporations who dress things up; we all do it. We each have a public face we wear for the world and each seek to present ourselves in the most flattering light, putting the best gloss possible on those less-desirable aspects of our character. It's understandable that we should and, to a point, we can get away with it when dealing with people – but not with God. It is useless being anything other than honest with him, for he discerns the thoughts of our heart, the attitudes and motives that lie behind our actions. We may think we're being straight with him, but are we really? The image we have of ourselves is one thing; what God sees may be quite another.

Ask yourself

In what ways do you put on a mask for the world? Are you sometimes less than honest with God?

Pray

Living God, you know me inside out down to the last detail. You see me not as I would like to be, nor as I pretend to be, but as I am: the good and the bad, the faithful and the unfaithful, the lovely and the unlovely. With you, there can be no deception, no hiding behind a public face, and yet still you love me, despite all my faults.

Living God, remembering that truth, help me to be honest with you; confessing my faults, acknowledging my weaknesses and seeking your grace. Through Jesus Christ my Lord. Amen.

Remember

We have renounced shameful things that we prefer to keep hidden, no longer walking in craftiness or adulterating the word of God, but through the genuineness of our actions, commending ourselves to people's conscience before God. Judge nothing before the time, until the Lord comes, for he will both bring to light the hidden things of darkness and expose the thoughts of the heart: and then God will give praise to each one as appropriate.

2 Corinthians 4:2; 1 Corinthians 4:5

Close

Gracious God, help me to face the flaws everyone knows of and those I try to hide even from myself, knowing that your nature is always to have mercy and to help me start again. Take me and make me new, for Christ's sake. Amen.

Open our eyes

Read

Look at the birds of the air; they do not sow or reap or store away in barns, and yet your heavenly Father feeds them. Are you not much more valuable than they? See how the lilies of the field grow. They do not labour or spin, yet I tell you that not even Solomon in all his grandeur was clothed like one of these. If that is how God clothes the grass of the field, which is here today yet tomorrow is thrown on to the fire, will he not much more clothe you, O you of little faith?

Matthew 6:26, 28-30

Ponder

You may recall that a little while back 3-D pictures were all the rage. Open virtually any magazine or newspaper, it seemed, and you would be confronted with a curious pattern of dots and colours, which, we were told, would reveal a wonderful three-dimensional image when focused in in a particular way. Could you ever see it? I never did. That's the thing about sight; we don't all see things in quite the same way. An old saying puts it well: 'Two men looked out through prison bars; one saw mud, the other saw stars.' I like that. Where one sees ugliness another sees beauty, where one sees despair another sees hope. That's not to say that everything is subjective; rather that on occasions we have to have our eyes opened to the wonder of something before we appreciate it.

That is what Jesus was saying to the crowd gathered to hear his teaching: look properly at the ordinary things of life – something as commonplace as a flower in the meadow – and you will see God's hand behind it. To the eye of faith, life takes on a whole new dimension, speaking not just of the beauty of this world but also of the loving purposes of God. Let our prayer each day be that he might open our eyes to glimpse a little more clearly his presence all around us.

Ask yourself
In what ways do you see the hand of God in the world around you?

Pray
Creator God, I thank you for the world you have given us: so full of beauty, so touched with wonder. I praise you for its ability to move, astound and refresh us, and above all for the way it speaks of your love and purpose. Forgive me that I sometimes lose sight of those deeper realities, failing to look beneath the surface. Open my eyes afresh, and help me to see your hand in creation and your love in the daily routine of life. Through Jesus Christ my Lord. Amen.

Remember
The heavens extol the glory of God; and the firmament testifies to his handiwork. Day after day bears eloquent witness, and night after night communicates knowledge, without any need of speech, language or any other voice. Their music pervades all the earth; their words reach out to the furthest parts of the world. Do you have eyes, but fail to see? Do you have ears, but fail to hear? *Psalm 19:1-4; Mark 8:18*

Close
Sovereign God, open my soul to your living presence, and so may I glimpse your glory and discover the sacredness of every moment. Through Jesus Christ my Lord. Amen.

A childlike faith

Read

People brought their children to him so that he might touch them, but the disciples spoke harshly to them. When Jesus saw this, however, he was angry and said to them, 'Let the little children come to me; do not stop them; for the kingdom of God belongs to such as these. I tell you this, whoever does not receive the kingdom of God like a little child will never enter it.' And he embraced them, laid his hands on them, and blessed them. *Mark 10:13-16*

Ponder

To spend quality time with a young child is a profoundly moving experience. Yes, they can drive you to distraction sometimes, yet in the honesty, openness, innocence and simple trust of the very young, coupled with their unquenchable zest for life, there is something uniquely precious. Every parent will know the feeling of wanting to preserve those qualities for ever, safeguarding them against the ravages of time. We can't do that, of course – each of us has to become worldly-wise in order to survive in the harsher realities of daily life.

Yet while much that is childish is by necessity outgrown, there are certain childlike qualities we lose at our peril. However old we are, we still need to look at the world with wonder, glimpsing God within it, if our souls are not to be starved of nourishment. We need to trust God even when we do not understand what is happening to us. We need to approach life with that same sense of openness and that same hunger to learn, seeking God's help and guidance in our unfolding journey. It is one thing to be childish, quite another to be childlike. Have we lost sight of the difference?

Ask yourself

Have your experiences of life left you cynical and disillusioned? Have you made faith too complicated, losing your sense of childlike trust?

Pray

Gracious God, I thank you for the great adventure of life in all its endless diversity and richness. I thank you that there is always more to learn, more to explore and more to experience. Keep my mind open to that special truth for, as the years pass, I sometimes lose my sense of childlike wonder and fascination, becoming worldly-wise or blasé about life, taking for granted those things which once had the power to stir my imagination, and so sinking into an ever-deeper rut of cynicism and over-familiarity.

Help me to recapture something of the innocence and spontaneity of my childhood years; the ability to look at the world with open eyes, to trust in the future and to celebrate the present. Gracious God, give me faith in life and faith in you. Through Jesus Christ my Lord. Amen.

Remember

He sat down, called the twelve, and said to them, 'Whoever wants to be first must be last of all and servant of all.' Then he took a little child and put it among them; and taking it in his arms, he said to them, 'Whoever welcomes one such child in my name welcomes me, and whoever welcomes me welcomes not just me but the one who sent me.'

Mark 9:35-37

Close

Gracious God, grant me the wisdom of advancing years, together with the innocent enthusiasm of a little child, and by your grace help me to keep both untarnished. Through Jesus Christ my Lord. Amen.

All in God's time

Read

When they had brought them, they had them stand before the council. The high priest questioned them, saying, 'We gave you strict orders not to teach in his name, yet here you have filled Jerusalem with your teaching and you are determined to bring this man's blood on us.' But Peter and the Apostles answered, 'We must obey God rather than any human authority.' Then a Pharisee in the council named Gamaliel, a teacher of the law, respected by all the people, stood up and ordered the men to be put outside for a short time. He said to the council, 'Fellow Israelites, consider carefully what you propose to do to these men. I urge you to keep away from these men and let them alone; because if this plan or this undertaking is of human origin, it will fail; but if it is of God, you will not be able to overthrow them – in that case you may even find you are fighting against God!'
Acts 5:27-29, 34-35, 38-39

Ponder

Don't jump to conclusions – we have been told that time and again, yet sometimes we just can't seem to help ourselves. Instead of giving time for cool and calm reflection, we succumb to the knee-jerk response, the instinctive reaction, usually based more on our personal likes and dislikes than the merits of a given situation. So it was for the Apostles in the early days of the Church as they sought to proclaim their new-found faith to their fellow Jews. Few were willing even to consider their message, such was their hostility towards anything to do with Jesus. Their sole desire was to silence the Apostles by any means possible. One man, though, was different: the Pharisee Gamaliel. Where others jumped in to condemn, he urged caution. Time will tell, he argued; the will of God shall ultimately triumph.

We can push that argument too far, of course, using it to justify the *status quo* as God's purpose, yet there is nonetheless enormous wisdom in it. Before we rush in to criticise what is new and unfamiliar, before we rubbish anything that does not fit in with our preconceptions, we should stop and ask whose response this reflects: our own or God's? If it is the former, then we should stand back, take time, and give God the chance to confirm what he thinks rather than what we assume his response will be.

Ask yourself
How many times have you jumped to conclusions? Do you tend to jump in with both feet rather than allow time for reflection?

Pray
Lord Jesus Christ, you have told us not to judge lest we be judged. Yet so often I cannot help myself. I jump to conclusions, I am coloured by the prejudices of others, I am closed to all opinions other than my own.

Lord Jesus Christ, give me the wisdom of Gamaliel to recognise that I do not have all the answers, and help me to be patient, assured that in the fullness of time you will make your way clear to me. Amen.

Remember
There is only one lawgiver and judge able to save and destroy. Who, then, are you to judge your neighbour?

James 4:12

Close
Lord of all, teach me to listen to your voice before I speak, and to seek your will before attempting to impose my own. Through Jesus Christ my Lord. Amen.

Celebrating our diversity

Read

Now there are various gifts but the same Spirit; various ministries but the same Lord; different types of service but the same God working through all of them. Just as the body is a unit having many members, with all the members, though many, being part of the one body, so it is with the body of Christ. If the foot were to say, because I am not a hand I am not part of the body, would it be any less a part of the body? If the ear were to say, because I am not an eye, I am not part of the body, would it not be part of it? If the whole body were an eye, how would we hear? If all were given over to hearing, how would we smell? God, however, has arranged every part of the body as he wants it to be. If there were only one part, how could we talk of a body? The fact is that there are many members, but only one body.

1 Corinthians 12:4-6, 12, 15-20

Ponder

My wife and I did some decorating recently. The room we were working on was gloomy, in need of a lift, so we decided to go for a creamy yellow. Decision made? Don't you believe it! The range of creamy yellows is unbelievable – 'Porcelain Bowl', 'Sunrise', 'Narcissus', 'Laughter', 'Buttermilk', 'Wicker', 'Ivory', 'Straw', to name but a few. These were all shades of yellow, yet they were all different, each with its own subtle nuance.

It doesn't take much to see where I'm going next, does it? Unity in diversity – what the Church is all about, or at least what it should be. We're all Christians – Anglican, Roman Catholic, Baptist, Methodist, Salvation Army, house church, and countless others – but we each have our own distinguishing characteristics. Within each denomination and individual fellowship, the same applies: an enormous variety of gifts, temperaments and experiences represented in every one of them. Is that a weakness? It can be, if we let it divide us, but it should be quite the opposite: a source of strength as we celebrate our unity in diversity. Imagine if there were just one shade of yellow – what an infinitely poorer place the world would be. So with the Church: we all profess Christ as Lord and all seek to follow him, but I doubt any two of us are the same. Thank God for that wonderful, astonishing and enriching diversity!

Ask yourself
Do you see different ideas and different understandings of faith as a gift or a threat?

Pray
Loving Father, I thank you for the richness of your family. I praise you that you have called people with contrasting experiences of your love and a bewildering assortment of gifts and characters to be your people, bound together in Christ. Teach me to celebrate that diversity and to rejoice in the variety you have given. Help me to learn from others, and so may my faith grow and deepen as I continue along my individual pathway of faith and on my pilgrimage together with others. Through Jesus Christ my Lord. Amen.

Remember
Speaking the truth in love, we must grow in every aspect into him, who is the head; that is, into Christ, through whom each part of the body is joined and knitted together by every supporting ligament, so that every part of the body may function as it should, building itself up in love.

Ephesians 4:15-16

Close
Lord Jesus Christ, help me to see differences in others not as a threat but as an opportunity, and so help me to live in unity with all your people, to the glory of your name. Amen.

Coming and going

Read

Coming together, they asked him, 'Lord, is this the time when you will restore the kingdom of Israel?' He replied, 'It is not for you to know the time or seasons that the Father has laid down by his own authority, but you will receive power when the Holy Spirit comes upon you and you will be my witnesses both in Jerusalem, and all Judea and Samaria, and to the ends of the earth.   *Acts 1:6-8*

Ponder

It's a law of nature that what goes up must come down; we cannot have one without the other. In similar fashion, we talk of give and take, and of getting out what we put in. Certain concepts belong together. There is one pair of words, however, that – in the Christian life at least – we don't perhaps associate as much as we should do: 'coming' and 'going'. We have no trouble with the first, so much of the gospel about coming to Christ, receiving his love, enjoying his presence. How often, though, does that *coming to* him result in *going for* him? Too easily what we call discipleship becomes a personal and private affair between us and him, faith turned inwards instead of outwards.

Such an understanding bears little relationship to the call given by Jesus throughout his ministry. His call involved following him in sacrificial service, going out to proclaim the gospel and bringing light to others. We need to come to him first – of that there is no question – for only then can we find the resources we need to follow his way, but if our relationship ends there, then we need to look at it very carefully, or we may find it ends there in more ways than one.

Ask yourself

Is your faith more about what God can do for you than what you can do for him? Does it result in practical service as well as personal blessing?

Pray

Lord Jesus Christ, you do not simply call me to *believe* the good news; you call me to *share* it. Forgive me that I so often fail to do that. I am happy to *come* to you but reluctant to *go out* in your name, afraid of what might be asked of me and unsure of my ability to respond to the challenge.

Help me to understand that discipleship without service is no discipleship at all, and that faith without witness is a denial of everything I claim to believe. Teach me, then, not only to rejoice in the love you have shown me but, through word and deed, to share it with those around me, for your kingdom's sake. Amen.

Remember

I heard the Lord's voice, saying, 'Who can I send? Who will go for me?' I answered, 'Here I am, send me!'   *Isaiah 6:8*

Close

Living God, I have come to you seeking your word and guidance. Now help me to go for you in joyful service to work for your kingdom, share your love and make known the gospel. Through Jesus Christ my Lord. Amen.

It's your choice

Read

Look, I present you today with a straight choice between life and death, good and evil. If you obey the commandments of the Lord your God that I am giving you today – loving the Lord God, following his ways and keeping his commandments, instructions and laws – then you will live and prosper, and the Lord God will bless you in the land you are about to take possession of. If, though, you turn your hearts away and refuse to listen, misguidedly paying homage to other gods and offering them service, I tell you straight that you will perish; you will not live long in the land you are crossing the Jordan to occupy and possess. I invoke heaven and earth to witness against you today that I have presented you with a choice between life and death, blessings and curses. Choose life, so that you and your descendants may live. Love the Lord your God, obey him and hold fast to him.   *Deuteronomy 30:15-20a*

Ponder

You will probably have noticed the plethora of television programmes recently featuring robots. There's *Techno Games*, *BattleBots*, and the queen of them all, *Robot Wars*. It all makes for good viewing, particularly the sight of various high-tech creations smashing the living daylights out of each other. I'm tempted to say that it can't be much fun for the robots but, of course, the robots simply don't care either way. The day of the thinking, feeling robot is, we're told, on the way, but for the time being robots simply do what they're programmed to do, with no feeling, no emotions, no will and no purpose of their own.

I suppose God, if he'd wished, could have made us like that – mindless automatons at his beck and call. There would have been no disobedience then, no sin to spoil the world, but then again there wouldn't have been any pleasure or fulfilment either; not for us anyway. For that, you need free will, with all its associated dangers and problems. We can abuse that gift, as we often do, or we can use it wisely, seeking God's help and guidance in the decisions we make. He invites us to respond, but he will not take decisions from our hands or seek to control us – it's our choice.

Ask yourself

Do you use your free will wisely? What does choosing God's way involve?

Pray

Living God, you do not compel me to serve you but you invite me rather to respond to your love. You do not impose your will upon me or dictate the course I should take, but instead you offer your guidance, giving me signposts to walk by, but ultimately leaving the decisions I must make in my hands.

I thank you for this wonderful expression of trust, this freedom to choose and discover for myself, and I ask that you will help me to use it wisely, trusting you, in return, and seeking, so far as I understand it, to honour your will. Give me wisdom and courage to make the right decisions, at the right time and in the right place, to the glory of your name. Amen.

Remember

If you would rather not serve the Lord, then choose this day whom you will serve, whether the gods your ancestors served in the region beyond the Euphrates or the gods of the Amorites in whose land you are living; but as for me and my household, we will serve the Lord.   *Joshua 24:15*

Close

Lord Jesus Christ, you have shown me the way to life and invited me to follow. Freely I respond, in your name. Amen.

Praise where praise is due

Read

You are worthy, O Lord our God, to receive glory and honour
and power, for all things were made by you, their creation
and existence down to your will. Worthy is the Lamb that
was slain to receive power and riches and wisdom and
strength and honour and glory and blessing!

Revelation 4:11; 5:12

Ponder

It's always nice to receive praise, isn't it? Or is it? Actually,
I think there are times when it is the last thing we want.
When we've done something well, given of our very best,
then praise is indeed welcome and we feel justifiably disappointed if it is withheld. If, though, someone offers it to us
when we know it to be undeserved, then we feel patronised,
embarrassed, even angry. As we rightly say, 'Praise where
praise is due'.

With God there is never any question as to that. We owe
all we are to him, all that is and all that ever shall be. He is
the giver of life now and of the life to come, the power
behind the universe, the provider of all our needs – and so
we could go on. So, likewise, with Christ – the one who gave
his life for all, who brings hope and healing to a broken
world, who represents the ultimate embodiment of love.
Words cannot begin to tell of what we owe. Neither God
nor Jesus *need* our praise, but they *welcome* it as an expression
of our commitment, a token of our gratitude and a sign of
our faith. We do not offer that praise because we have to,
or because it is expected of us, but simply because it is
appropriate, the natural response to everything we have
received; the only response that will do.

Ask yourself

How often do you make a point of praising God? What things do you have to praise him for?

Pray

Great and wonderful God, I join with the great company of your people on earth and in heaven, to celebrate your majesty, to marvel at your love and to rejoice in your goodness. You are my God, and I praise you. I acknowledge you as the Lord of heaven and earth, ruler of space and time, creator of all, sovereign over life and death. You are my God, and I praise you. I salute you as the beginning and end of all things, the one who is greater than I can ever begin to imagine, higher than my highest thoughts, beyond human expression. You are my God, and I praise you. I affirm you as all good, all loving, all gracious, all forgiving. You are my God, and I praise you. I bring you now my worship, my faith and my life, offering them to you in grateful adoration. You are my God, and I praise you, through Jesus Christ my Lord. Amen.

Remember

I will call upon the Lord, who is worthy of all praise.

Psalm 18:3

Close

To God who is higher than my highest thoughts, yet closer than my closest friend, be thanks and praise, glory and honour, this day and for evermore. Amen.

Acknowledging our mistakes

Read

I will get up and go to my father, and I will say to him,
'Father, I have sinned against heaven and before you; I no
longer deserve to be called your son; regard me instead as
one of your hired hands.'   *Luke 15:18-19*

Ponder

'Someone who has committed a mistake and doesn't correct
it is committing another mistake' – so said Confucius. He
was right, wasn't he? Attempt to cover up some error of
judgement or pretend it never happened and, before we
know it, one thing leads to another until a situation spirals
horribly out of control. Yet, true though we realise that to
be, we continue so often to do precisely that: making excuses
for our behaviour, sweeping our mistakes under the carpet
or dismissing them as unimportant. It takes courage to
admit we've done wrong and to seek forgiveness. We manage
it sometimes with God, though even there we are probably
more selective than we might think, there being some
things we are loath to admit even to ourselves.

When it comes to others it is infinitely harder, especially
when it means facing up to someone we have wronged.
Many prefer to brazen it out rather than lose face, even
though that may mean adding one mistake to another. Is it
enough simply to confess our sins to God, or does true
confession need to involve acknowledging our mistakes
and saying sorry to those we have sinned against? It's a
more costly and demanding path for, unlike with God, we
have no guarantee of being forgiven, yet it is often the only
way to healing and reconciliation. Do we have the fibre to
admit our mistakes, even when it involves embarrassment
and humiliation? Are we ready, where necessary, to put our

hands up and to candidly confess, with no excuses or reservations, I was wrong?

Ask yourself
Are there mistakes you have made that continue to haunt you? Is it time that, as well as acknowledging them before God, you admitted them to those your mistakes directly affected?

Pray
Sovereign God, I find it so hard to acknowledge my mistakes, to admit that I am as fallible as the next person. I know I have done wrong, my errors all too evident, yet I run from the truth, unwilling or afraid to face facts. I deny my faults or attempt to excuse them. I concern myself with outer appearances rather than with inner reality, attempting to convince myself that all is well, even though I know in my heart that all is not as it should be.

Forgive me my dishonesty and cowardice. Help me not just to take the easy way out in confessing my mistakes to you but to confess them also to others so that I may be able to put them behind me and start afresh. Through Jesus Christ my Lord. Amen.

Remember
Confess your faults to one another, and pray for one another, so that you may be made whole.   *James 5:16*

Close
Sovereign God, when I do wrong, give me courage to acknowledge it before you and others, so that I may know your forgiveness and open a way to the healing of the wounds my mistakes have caused. Through Jesus Christ my Lord. Amen.

Equipped for battle

Read

Don the whole armour of God, so that you may be able to withstand the ruses of the devil. For we do battle, not with flesh and blood, but with the rulers, authorities and cosmic powers of darkness – with the spiritual forces of evil in high places. So then, take up the whole armour of God, so that you may be able to resist on that evil day, and, having done everything, resolutely still to stand. Stand, therefore, and secure the belt of truth around your waist, and put on the breastplate of righteousness. Shoe your feet with a readiness to proclaim the gospel of peace. Above all, grasp the shield of faith, with which you will be able to smother the flaming arrows of the evil one. Take also, by prayer and supplication, the helmet of salvation, and the sword of the Spirit, which is the word of God. *Ephesians 6:11-18a*

Ponder

One of the biggest box office hits of recent years is *Gladiator*, a film that graphically depicts the fate of those who had to do battle against man or beast in the amphitheatres of the Roman Empire. Imagine what it must have been like to be one of those unfortunate individuals, pitted against a lion with only a net for protection, or a fully armed soldier with a trident as your only weapon. What chance would you have had?

Ironically, though, in the Christian life, we can put ourselves in a similar situation, not in terms of our physical safety but of our spiritual welfare. There is so much that comes into conflict with the way of Christ, both within and outside us. Each day brings a succession of temptations, influences, demands and pressures that threaten to undermine our faith. Little wonder, then, that the Apostle Paul, in his letter to the Romans, spoke of two selves warring within him. Yet, unlike those early gladiators, we do not need to go into battle defenceless, for, as Paul reminds us again, God has given us the resources we need to defend ourselves. Do we make time for prayer and the reading of God's word? Do we look for ways to share the gospel? Do we walk in faith and seek after truth? It is not enough to stroll casually through life trusting that God will protect us. We have a part to play, and we neglect it at our peril.

Ask yourself

Do you make sufficient time and space in your life to put on the armour of God?

Pray

Living God, teach me never to underestimate the forces that conspire against my faith, but also never to neglect or undervalue the resources you put at my disposal to stand firm against their onslaught. Keep me awake to the power of temptation and aware of the many pressures that can lead to inner conflict. Teach me to put you at the centre of my life, meeting you in your word, relating to you in prayer, proclaiming you with my lips and honouring you with my life. So may I be equipped for battle and ready to defend myself against whatever I may face. Through Jesus Christ my Lord. Amen.

Remember

The night is nearly over, daybreak is near, so let us put on the armour of light. *Romans 13:12*

Close

Living God, I thank you that, wherever I am, whatever I face, you are with me through Christ, constantly by my side, travelling with me and looking to lead me forward into new experiences of your love. Receive my praise, through Jesus Christ my Lord. Amen.

Raise your sights

Read

Who has measured the waters in the hollow of his hand and marked off the heavens with a span, enclosed the dust of the earth in a measure, and weighed the mountains in scales and the hills in a balance? Who has directed the spirit of the Lord, or as his counsellor has instructed him? Whom did he consult for enlightenment, and who taught him the path of justice? Who taught him knowledge, and showed him the way of understanding? Even the nations are like a drop from a bucket, and are accounted as dust on the scales.   *Isaiah 40:12-15a (NRSV)*

Ponder

How many grains of sand are there on a beach? How many stars in the universe? None of us knows the answers to such questions, but I expect any guess we might make would fall well short of the correct number, for we are dealing here with a scale that stretches human comprehension to the limit.

There is something of that idea in the wonderful picture of God given by the prophet Isaiah. His words were addressed to a people in crisis: a people who, after years of exile in Babylon, had concluded that God was either unwilling or unable to help them. They considered themselves beyond forgiveness. They feared that their God must be inferior to the gods of Babylon. They felt powerless, defeated and bereft of hope. Into their despair, Isaiah brought a simple but profound message: raise your sights! Unwilling to forgive them? Think again, he says: God is more than ready to pardon. Inferior to the gods of Babylon? Think again: he is the creator of the ends of the earth, ruler over space and time. The future bleak? Think again: he will renew their strength and restore their hope. Here is a glorious reminder of the sovereignty of God; the God who is more loving, more powerful and more gracious than we can ever begin to imagine.

Ask yourself

Is your God too small? Have you put your own picture of God in place of the God we see revealed in scripture?

Pray

Eternal and sovereign God, with awe and wonder I worship you. You are all-powerful, ever present; shaping the pattern of history, transforming my life. You are all good, ever merciful; showering me with your blessings, forgiving my faults. You are always true, ever constant; daily fulfilling your purpose with the same dependability. You are all holy, ever perfect; just and righteous in all you do.

Forgive me that I have not worshipped you as fully as I should, that I have not praised you with heart and soul and mind, that I have glimpsed so little of your greatness. Forgive me for failing to appreciate your mercy, for forgetting your countless blessings and for losing my sense of awe and wonder before you. Open my eyes afresh to your splendour, my heart to your love, my mind to your purpose and my spirit to your presence, and so may I thrill to the wonder of all that you are, in the name of the living Christ. Amen.

Remember

Those who wait for the Lord shall renew their strength, they shall mount up with wings like eagles, they shall run and not be weary, they shall walk and not faint.

Isaiah 40:31 (NRSV)

Close

Almighty God, forgive me the smallness of my vision and the feebleness of my faith. Open my eyes to the wonder of all that you are, and may that knowledge sustain and inspire me all my days. Through Jesus Christ my Lord. Amen.

A god of our own making

Read

Their idols are silver and gold, fashioned by human hands.
They have mouths, yet cannot talk; eyes, yet cannot see.
They have ears, yet cannot hear; nostrils, yet cannot smell.
They have hands, yet cannot feel; feet, yet cannot walk; no
sound comes from their throats. Those who make them
become like them; and so does everyone who trusts in them.

Psalm 115:4-8

Ponder

Of all the offences against God it is possible to commit,
few are censured more frequently in the Old Testament than
the worship of idols. Throughout its pages a succession of
leaders and prophets pour scorn on anybody foolish enough
to pay homage to an inanimate object fashioned by
human hands, and, reading their scathing condemnations,
it is tempting to imagine we could never make a similar
mistake, the very idea unthinkable.

Yet such self-righteousness is ill-advised, for though we
would never consciously consider worshipping a man-made
idol, there are insidious ways in which we do just that. The
idols of our time are not carved in wood or moulded in
metal, but they are no less real – money, success, power,
sex, these are just a few of the modern-day 'gods' which
hold sway today. And though we may not like to admit it,
we figure more prominently among their devotees
than we care to admit. All too easily we shape our understanding of God to fit with what we want to believe. The
result may seem more comfortable to live with, but in the
final analysis it offers nothing for, quite simply, we are left
with no God at all.

Ask yourself

In what ways do you create false gods today? Where does
your true allegiance lie?

Pray

Sovereign God, you are the Creator of all, the Lord of history, ruler over space and time. You are greater than my mind can fathom, your ways not my ways nor your thoughts my thoughts. You alone deserve praise and worship. Yet all too often, without realising it, I pay homage to other gods; idols of material wealth and worldly satisfaction that have no power to satisfy.

Forgive me for my folly, for inadvertently bringing you down to my level and losing sight of who you are. Help me to open my life to your living and searching presence, and so may I honour you in all I am and all I do. Amen.

Remember

To whom, then, will you liken God, or with what likeness will you compare him? An idol? It is cast by a workman and a goldsmith gilds it and casts silver chains for it. The one unable to afford that selects wood that will not rot and seeks out a craftsman to create an idol that will not topple over. *Isaiah 40:18-20*

Close

Sovereign God, Lord of creation, remake me in your image and save me from trying to mould you to my own. Through Jesus Christ my Lord. Amen.

JUNE

Living the good news

Read

I therefore, a prisoner of the Lord, urge you to lead a life commensurate with the calling to which you have been called, patiently dealing with one another with humility and kindness in love, striving always to maintain the unity of the Spirit in the bond of peace.   *Ephesians 4:1-3*

Ponder

What would you make of it if the former US President, Bill Clinton, were to produce a book called *My Life as a Monk*, or if the Archbishop of Canterbury were to come out with a title *The A to Z of Safebreaking*? You would, I think, rightly surmise that you were being taken for a ride. If, however, these were to produce the respective titles *The Lewinsky Affair: My Side of the Story* and *Joys and Sorrows of an Archbishop*, then you'd take the books seriously, for you'd know that each author was writing from experience. It's all a question of credibility, and the same is true when it comes to living and witnessing to the Christian life.

We are told by Christ himself to share our faith, to witness to the truth of the gospel, and that is an important part of discipleship, but the effectiveness of our outreach will always depend on the transparency of our lives: how far what we say measures up to what we do. If our words say one thing but our lives another, then our testimony will always be taken with a pinch of salt, however much we urge people to judge the message rather than the messenger. We cannot hope, of course, to present anything like a perfect picture but we cannot afford to put across one radically different from the one we purport to represent. Do that, and no matter what we say or how often we say it, there will be few people willing to listen.

Ask yourself

What aspects of your life reinforce the gospel? What aspects undermine it?

Pray

Loving God, through Christ you demonstrated the wonder of your grace, living among us, sharing our humanity and giving freely of yourself. You didn't just speak of love; you showed it in action. Forgive me for so rarely doing the same, my life instead belying my words.

I talk of forgiving others, yet I nurse grievances; of being content, yet I am full of envy; of serving others, yet I serve self; of loving truth, yet I deal falsely. I speak of commitment, but I am careless in discipleship; of faith, but I am full of doubt; of vision, but I am narrow in my outlook; of being a new creation, but I continue in just the same way as before. Forgive me and help me not simply to talk about faith but to demonstrate it through the person I am. Grant that my words and my deeds may be one, so that I may witness effectively to your renewing, redeeming power. Through Jesus Christ my Lord. Amen.

Remember

Conduct yourselves wisely in relation to those who do not share the faith, making the most of every opportunity.

Colossians 4:5

Close

Living God, help me to proclaim the gospel not just through words but deeds – through what I say, what I do and who I am. Take what I am, and make me what I long to be, so that others, when they meet with me, meet also with Christ and know his living presence for themselves. Amen.

Cruel to be kind

Read

Well intended are the wounds inflicted by a friend, but effusive are the kisses of an enemy.   *Proverbs 27:6*

Ponder

'Be truthful, now – what do you think?' How many times have you been asked a question like that? And the chances are, when it came, your heart sank, for you knew full well that the judgement you were being asked to make would cause upset, if not outright offence. The truth can hurt. Few of us find it easy to be honest in awkward situations like those, and fewer still relish having the truth spoken to them.

Yet sometimes we need people with the courage to do just that if we are to see ourselves as we really are and so find the spur we need to rectify our faults. In the words of the Greek philosopher Socrates: 'Think not those faithful who praise all thy words and actions, but those who kindly reprove thy faults.' Have you the courage to speak the painful truth to others? More important still, are you willing to hear it spoken to you in turn?

Ask yourself

Are you open to criticism, or do you automatically attempt to defend yourself rather than contemplate unpleasant truths?

Pray

God of truth, you know me better than I know myself. You search my heart and mind, seeing me as I really am and confronting me with my true self. Forgive me that all too often I shy away from what is hard to accept, refusing to countenance anything that contradicts my self-image. I find it so difficult to be honest, closing my ears to truths I would rather not hear. I avoid those who challenge and disturb me, preferring instead those who soothe and flatter my ego.

Thank you for all those with the rare gift of speaking the truth in love; not spitefully, vindictively, or harshly, nor from any ulterior motives, but because they genuinely care. Thank you for those who are willing to risk my resentment, retaliation or rejection, in order to help me grow as an individual.

God of all, give me true humility and meekness of spirit, so that I may be ready to listen and examine myself, ready to ask searching questions about who I am and to change where necessary, ready to face the truth. Through Jesus Christ my Lord. Amen.

Remember

Whoever takes note of good advice is on the path to life, but those who reject a rebuke go astray. Those who ignore good advice despise themselves, but those who heed reproof grow in understanding. *Proverbs 10:17; 15:32*

Close

Gracious God, help me to open my life to your searching gaze and so open my heart to your redeeming love. Through Jesus Christ my Lord. Amen.

Daring to be different

Read

God saw that the earth was corrupt and filled with violence. And God said to Noah, 'I have seen the wickedness of humankind, and how the whole earth is violated because of them. I have resolved, therefore, to destroy them along with the earth. Make yourself an ark of cypress wood; make rooms within it, and cover it inside and out with pitch. Noah did just this, precisely following God's instructions.

Genesis 6:11, 13-14, 22

Ponder

Few of us like to stand out from the crowd, least of all when it involves being different. The occasional foible is one thing, eccentricity quite another. No one likes being thought odd. When Noah, though, set to work building an ark in the middle of the wilderness he must have looked exactly that – a strange character if ever there was one. We can scarcely imagine the ridicule he must have endured day after day as he laboured on his extraordinary enterprise with no sign of rain let alone flood.

Noah, though, was no stranger to being thought different, for, as the book of Hebrews (11:7) reminds us, his righteousness set him apart from others; his determination to stay true to God, whatever the pressures to the contrary; a rarity in his time just as it is in ours.

Given all that, it is tempting to suggest he had the last laugh, but I suspect laughter was the last thing on his mind after the tragedy that followed. The story of Noah is not about saying 'I told you so' to a cynical and hostile world. It is rather about having the courage to be different in the hope that someone, somewhere, may perhaps take notice.

Ask yourself

In what ways should Christians stand out from a crowd? In what ways do you stand out? Why do people ridicule and even persecute those who seem different?

Pray

Loving God, you call us to distinctive discipleship, a way of life that sets us apart from others. Not a self-righteous superiority based on judgemental intolerance, but a quality of love and a willingness to serve that shows itself in everything we say and do.

Forgive me that I fall so far short of that calling, compromising what I believe for fear of mockery. Forgive me that I go along with the way of the crowd rather than follow the demanding way of Christ. Speak to me now, challenge my complacency, and give me courage to be different. Amen.

Remember

Do not love the world or the things of this world. The Father's love is not in those who love the world; for everything in the world – the desires of the flesh, the craving of the eyes, the illusory riches of life – does not come from the Father but from the world. The world with its desires is passing away, but everyone who does the will of God will live for ever. *1 John 2:15-17*

Close

Gracious God, help me to be fully involved in this world and yet to live also in the light of the world to come, and so may my life be a witness to your sovereign purpose and your saving love. Through Jesus Christ my Lord. Amen.

The missing ingredient

Read

If I speak in the tongues of people or angels, but do not have love, I become nothing more than a blasting trumpet or a clashing cymbal. If I have the gift of prophecy and understand all mysteries and all knowledge, and if I have faith such as to remove mountains, yet do not have love, then I am nothing. If I dispense all my goods and surrender my body to be burned, yet do not have love, it profits me nothing.

1 Corinthians 13:1-3

Ponder

It looked good, it smelled good and, as I set the meal on the table, I was confident that it would taste good as well. But it didn't. Instead of setting the taste buds tingling as I'd anticipated, it was bland, lifeless, unappetising; a culinary flop rather than a cordon bleu masterpiece! Why? Because instead of adding chilli powder I'd mistakenly put in paprika – the vital ingredient was missing.

The analogy may be different, but the Apostle Paul was talking along much the same lines in his celebrated words on love to the Corinthians. He sets out what looks to be the perfect recipe for Christian discipleship: faith to move mountains, spiritual and human gifts, generosity and commitment to the point of unreserved self-sacrifice – what more could you possibly want? Yet, says Paul, without that one vital ingredient of love, it counts for nothing. We may have heard that message innumerable times, but we still need to hear it again, for it is impossible to overestimate its importance. We turn faith so easily into a matter of outward observance: of thinking or believing this, of doing or supporting that – the deed more important than the motive behind it. Don't let that happen. Whatever you do, whatever you count important, never confuse the incidentals of Christian discipleship with the one ingredient that really matters.

Ask yourself
How far is love the motivating factor behind all your actions?

Pray
Lord Jesus Christ, you summed up the law in one simple word: 'love'. Forgive me that though I often talk about love I rarely show it in practice. Forgive me everything in my life that has denied that love: the angry words and unkind comments; the thoughtless deeds and careless actions; the sorrow I have brought rather than joy, and hurt rather than healing; the care I have failed to express, support I have refused to offer and forgiveness I have been unwilling to extend.

Help me to look to you who showed love in action – a love that bears all things, believes all things, hopes all things, endures all things – and help me truly to realise that unless I have that then all my words, faith and religion counts for nothing. Amen.

Remember
This is the message that we have heard from the very beginning: that we should love one another.   *1 John 3:11*

Close
Gracious God, take the little love I have. Nurture, deepen, and expand it, until I have learned what love really means, until your love flows through my heart, until love is all in all. Through Jesus Christ my Lord. Amen.

With all we have

Read

What then, O Israel, does the Lord your God ask of you? Simply to fear the Lord your God, to follow in all his ways, to love and serve him with all your heart and soul, and, for your own good, to observe the Lord's commandments and decrees that I am giving you today.   *Deuteronomy 10:12-13*

Ponder

I watched the University Boat Race recently – a gripping battle in which both teams fought to the last. What always catches my eye in such encounters is not just the rowers but also the cox in each boat. They seem superfluous at first sight, an extra weight that the crew could well do without, yet their role is vital. As well as keeping the strokes synchronised, they also encourage the crew to greater effort, summoning every last ounce of energy from them. Their job is to ensure that every competitor doesn't just give a little but gives their all.

So it should be when it comes to loving God. Our relationship with him is not one we can breeze in and out of; not simply a vague feeling of thankfulness or adoration, nor merely a matter of the intellect, recognising that God deserves our worship. We are called to love God with all we have – body, mind and soul. It involves the will and the heart, acting on impulse and dogged determination, joyfully responding and actively seeking. Our prayers, our hymns and our worship talk a lot about loving God, but what do we actually mean by that? Is it simply pious sentiment, or are we committed to giving everything to make the relationship really work?

Ask yourself

In what ways do you work at your relationship with God? In what ways do you need to work at it further?

Pray

Sovereign God, I say I love you yet all too often my life says something else. I am casual and careless in my relationship with you, relegating you to the periphery of my life instead of placing you at the centre. I make time for you as an after-thought, fitting you in as and when the opportunity arises, and if I cannot find time, I lose little sleep over the matter. My prayer life is erratic, my study of your word lackadaisical, my commitment half-hearted.

Forgive me for imagining this is sufficient, for somehow thinking that our relationship can take care of itself. Forgive me for loving you so little and then wondering why I do not feel as close to you as I should. Teach me what it means to love you with body, mind and soul, and help me to be as committed to you as you are to me. Through Jesus Christ my Lord. Amen.

Remember

Be very careful to love the Lord your God.   *Joshua 23:11*

Close

Gracious God, take the little love I have and fan it into a mighty flame so that I may love you as you deserve, to the glory of your name. Amen.

Love your neighbour

Read

A lawyer questioned Jesus, hoping to catch him out. 'Teacher,' he asked, 'which of the law's commandments ranks first?' Jesus answered him, 'You shall love the Lord your God with all your heart, and with all your soul, and with all your mind. This is the first and greatest commandment. The second is similar: You shall love your neighbour as yourself.' On these commandments hang all of the law and the prophets.   *Matthew 22:35-40*

Ponder

The whole law encapsulated in two commandments revolving around one word: love – it all sounds so easy, doesn't it, so wonderfully straightforward. Or at least it does until we realise that the neighbours Jesus refers to are not just those who live next door or nearby, but everyone, everywhere; and then, suddenly, we feel overwhelmed by the scale of the challenge and the enormity of our responsibility.

Far from reducing the demands God places upon us, this suddenly intensifies them, for instead of giving us a list of things to avoid, it challenges us to explore what we are able to do. The list is endless, for there is virtually no limit to the human need within our world. In our own society and beyond there is a multitude crying out for support and help, desperately in need of a little kindness and compassion. We cannot, of course, respond to them all, and I don't for a moment expect that Jesus intends us to, but how far do we respond to any? Our response to others must always be the acid test of our commitment; indeed, it is cited in the first letter of John as the truest yardstick of our love for God. Faith begins with God's love for us and our love for him in response, but it cannot end there, for wherever our neighbour is in need God is in need too, asking us to tend his wounds.

Ask yourself

In what ways do you love your neighbour? How far does your neighbourliness extend?

Pray

Lord Jesus Christ, forgive me that so often I love only myself, my every thought for my own welfare, my own ends, my own esteem, my own pleasures. Forgive me that, at best, I reserve my love for the exclusive few – family, friends and relations.

Teach me to reach out to this troubled, divided world, recognising the call of my neighbour in the cry of the needy. Teach me what it means to belong not just to the community of faith but to the family of humankind, and in serving there may I serve you also, to the glory of your name. Amen.

Remember

Each of us should seek to please our neighbour, for the good purpose of building them up.   *Romans 15:2*

Close

Sovereign God, teach me to hear your voice in the cry of the poor, the hungry, the sick and the oppressed, and teach me, in responding to them, to respond to you. Through Jesus Christ my Lord. Amen.

Love your enemies!

Read

You have heard that it was said, 'You shall love your neighbour and hate your enemy.' But I tell you, love your enemies and pray for those who persecute you, so that you may become children of your Father in heaven; for he causes his sun to rise on the evil and the good, and the rain to fall on the just and the unjust.

Matthew 5:43-45

Ponder

There was a young man during my time at senior school who made my life a misery. At any and every opportunity he would hit, punch, or kick anyone unfortunate enough to cross his path. Like many others, I lived in fear of his approach. So one day, when I saw him making a beeline towards me, you can imagine how I felt – petrified. Even when he greeted me with a beatific smile, clasped hold of my hand and started to pour out apologies for all his past behaviour, I was convinced this sudden friendliness was just a front concealing some devious plan. But it wasn't. The change was real and remarkable, the remorse genuine, and from that day to the time he left school to go out into the mission field as an evangelist, I received only kindness and consideration from his hands. Yet, for all that, I still automatically flinched whenever I saw him, and still found myself waiting for the bubble to burst.

Love your enemies? It's hard enough, even when they stop being that and extend the hand of friendship. To love those who continue to hurt us – it's asking a lot, isn't it? Yet, that is the way of Christ. It doesn't mean liking them, or even feeling affection; that, surely, is expecting too much. It means being ready to forgive, to meet rejection with acceptance, to wish good rather than evil, to recognise our common humanity and the needs that tie us together.

Can you do that? I'm still not sure I can but I am sure I should. One look at the world, with all its tensions and conflicts, violence and division, prejudice and intolerance gives us a bleak picture of the alternative.

Ask yourself

What do you think loving your enemies involves? Are you able to meet that challenge?

Pray

Lord, we are told that the strongest survive, that in this world it's a question of never mind the rest so long as we're all right. Yet, you call us to another way – the way of humility, sacrifice and self-denial. You stand accepted wisdom on its head, claiming that the meek shall inherit the earth and that those who are willing to lose their lives will truly find them.

Lord, it is hard to believe in this way of yours, and harder still to live by it, for it runs contrary to everything I know about human nature, yet I have seen for myself that the world's way leads so often to hurt, sorrow and division. Give me, then, faith and courage to live out the foolishness of the gospel, and so to bring closer the kingdom of Christ, here on earth. In his name I ask it. Amen.

Remember

I say to all who are willing to listen, 'Love your enemies, do good to those who hate you, bless those who curse you and pray for those who abuse you.'   *Luke 6:27-28*

Close

Gracious God, teach me the secret of a love that goes on loving, despite all it faces. Through Jesus Christ my Lord. Amen.

Love yourself

Read

There was a man named Zacchaeus – a chief tax-collector and wealthy – who was trying to see who Jesus was, but because he was short in stature he could not see through the crowd. He ran ahead, therefore, and climbed a sycamore tree to get a better view, knowing Jesus was going to pass by that way. When Jesus reached the spot, he looked up and said to him, 'Zacchaeus, come down quickly, for I feel it right to stay at your house today.' Zacchaeus hurried down and joyfully welcomed him.   *Luke 19:2-6*

Ponder

Love yourself! Surely our problem is that we love ourselves overmuch already, too full of our own importance, own interests and own ideas. Perhaps so, but are such things the same as loving oneself? On the contrary, selfishness is often not so much a sign of self-love as of self-loathing. A shopping, eating or drinking binge can represent a desperate attempt to disguise a sense of inner emptiness. The know-it-all may be trying to deny, even to themselves, their deep-seated insecurity. The reality is that few people, for all the material blessings they may enjoy, feel at one with themselves, many wrestling permanently with a debilitating negative self-image.

I suspect Zacchaeus felt much the same. For all his wealth, he was clearly looking for something else in life, evidenced by the lengths he went to in order to see Jesus. No doubt he went more in hope than expectation, but hope was vindicated, for instead of the usual rejection he received he was treated as a person, an individual in his own right. For the first time in many years he was able to face himself and, in consequence, to let go of the prop of money he had clung to for support. There was guilt and shame, certainly, but there was also a recognition that God valued him and was ready to accept him as he was. Yes, there are things about ourselves that we would all like to change and some things we need to change, but we should never forget how much we mean to God, warts and all. Until we learn to love ourselves we can never truly love others.

Ask yourself

Is it true that we tend to be our own sternest critics? Do you dwell on your bad points at the expense of the good?

Pray

Gracious God, I do not find it easy to love myself, despite the way it may seem. I find it hard not to dwell on my weaknesses rather than my strengths, not to brood about mistakes and failures rather than rejoice in the things I have achieved. I look at myself and I see the faults and ugliness that I try to hide from the world, and I find the reality too painful to contemplate, so I try to push it away once more.

Gracious God, I thank you that *you* love me despite all this, that you value me not for what I might become but for what I am. Teach me to live each day in the light of that incredible yet wonderful truth that you love me completely and want me to be at one with myself. Through Jesus Christ my Lord. Amen.

Remember

You shall not seek vengeance or nurse a grievance against any of your people, but you shall love your neighbour as yourself: I am the Lord.   *Leviticus 19:18*

Close

Gracious God, I thank you for loving me before I ever loved you, and for continuing to love me even when I find it hard to love myself. Teach me to accept what I am and so to grow into what I can become. Through Jesus Christ my Lord. Amen.

Changing course

Read

In those days John the Baptist appeared in the wilderness of Judea, proclaiming, 'Repent, for the kingdom of heaven has come near.' Then the people of Jerusalem and all Judea went out to him, and all the region along the Jordan, and they were baptised by him in the River Jordan, confessing their sins.

Matthew 3:1-2

Ponder

Repent. It's not a word we use much nowadays, but there are few words that better express the message at the heart of the gospel. To become a Christian is not just about accepting a truth, confessing our faith in Christ. Nor is it simply an acknowledgement of wrongdoing and seeking of forgiveness. It is about a change of direction, a reorientation of life, pursuing a different course. That is the message at the heart of the gospel: that we need to turn from our old way to the way of Christ. For some that change, initially at least, may be more marked than others, their past lifestyle standing in stark contrast to their new-found faith, whereas those who have been brought up within the circle of the Church may find the outward change needed so negligible as to be almost imperceptible.

Repentance, though, is not a one-off thing – if only it were! We go on making mistakes every day of our life, inadvertently going astray with monotonous regularity. Before we know it, we are on the wrong road again; in all likelihood heading back the way we have come. Yet again, we find ourselves called to repent. The word may be archaic but the meaning is not. Whoever we are, whatever we have done, however many times we may have done so before, it is never too late to change course.

Ask yourself

In what ways do you still go astray? Are you ready to change direction?

Pray

Lord Jesus Christ, you have called me to faith and gratefully I have responded, committing myself to walking your way, yet I am conscious of my repeated failure, my inability to keep faith. I mean to follow, but I am weak and foolish, so easily deflected from my path, and eventually I despair of ever staying on my chosen course.

Assure me at such times that your patience is never exhausted, your love never withdrawn and your grace never denied. Teach me that you long to lead me forward again, waiting only for me to acknowledge where I have gone wrong and to reach out in faith for your forgiveness.

So I come, in true repentance, asking you to turn me round and lead me forward, in your strength and for your name's sake. Amen.

Remember

He is patient with you, his will being that none should be lost but that all might come to repentance. *2 Peter 3:9*

Close

Gracious God, whenever I lose my way, call me back and help me to turn again to the living way, through Jesus Christ my Lord. Amen.

Something to share

Read

Then they summoned them in again and ordered them not to speak or teach at all in the name of Jesus. But Peter and John responded, 'You must decide for yourselves whether it is right in God's eyes to obey you rather than him. The fact is that we cannot help speaking about the things we have seen and heard.'

Acts 4:18-20

Ponder

What is the first thing you do if you have a bit of good news? Unless you're very different from me, I expect your immediate reaction is to want to share it? Whether you've just got engaged, had your first child, earned promotion, come up on the premium bonds, or won a dream holiday, the natural and instinctive response is to rush round to a loved one, pick up the telephone or put pen to paper. We may even end up sharing our news with a complete stranger, such is our excitement. To keep such a thing to ourselves just doesn't seem right.

What, then, of the greatest news of all, the message of Christ? Do we burn to share that? Do we find we simply can't stop ourselves talking about it sometimes? That's what Peter and John found, in the days of the early Church. They knew the risks of speaking out and if they had entertained any lingering doubts these must surely have been dispelled by their reception at the hands of the chief priests and elders. Yet, despite every effort to silence them, they knew that they could not keep quiet. The problem we have today, of course, is that the gospel is not news in quite the same way; most people are aware of the Christian message even if they have little knowledge of what it is actually all about. We are confronted by a world convinced that it's old hat, and a world in which what's news today is forgotten tomorrow. We will not get far standing on our soapbox and quoting the Bible at people, nor through reciting parrot-fashion the creeds or central tenets of faith. We need to take a leaf out of the Apostle's book and tell of the things *we* have seen and heard; in other words, to share what faith means to us and what Jesus has done in our life, and to do that honestly, naturally and spontaneously.

Ask yourself

Do you still see the gospel as good news? What would you say if someone asked you what Jesus means to you?

Pray

Loving God, I thank you for all those who have had the faith and courage to tell others of their faith, even at a cost to themselves. I thank you for those who, having heard the Good News, have been determined to share it. May I through Jesus discover the truth of your love for myself, and in turn pass it on to others so that they too may hear and know the reality of Christ in their life, day by day. Amen.

Remember

I bring you joyful news for all people . . . a Saviour has been born for you who is Christ the Lord.   *Luke 2:10-11*

Close

Living God, you have given glad tidings, good news for all people. Save me from keeping it to myself, in the name of Christ. Amen.

Righting wrongs

Read

When you spread out your hands in prayer, I will hide my eyes from you; even if you offer many prayers, I will not listen. Your hands are full of blood; wash and make yourselves clean. Take your evil deeds out of my sight! Stop doing wrong, learn to do right! Seek justice, encourage the oppressed. Defend the cause of the fatherless, plead the case of the widow.

Isaiah 1:15-17

Ponder

In my garden is a small area that for a few months every year is overrun by fungi. The reason is very simple: it sits next to an old tree stump that has long since died but that I have been unable to dig out. I can treat the area with fungicide as much as I like, dig up the fungi until the cows come home, but it will make no difference – the problem will always return unless I succeed in tackling that root cause.

There are parallels here with world hunger and poverty. It has increasingly been recognised in recent years that the only way to resolve the growing gap between rich and poor, and to give what we call the Third World real hope, is to address the underlying factors of inequality. Short-term relief is vital but more needs doing if we are to see anything approaching a genuine solution. So where does that leave us? Are we left powerless in the face of impersonal economic forces or international government bureaucracy? Not at all! Ordinary people can make their voices heard. Through the way we shop or invest our money, the causes we support and the products we boycott, through more direct measures – such as petitioning our MP or lobbying multinational companies – we can call for change. The Jubilee 2000 campaign was a classic example of what can be achieved through concerted effort. Should Christians involve themselves in such matters?

Isaiah reminds us that a hunger for justice and a commitment to the poor is not an optional extra in the Christian faith but a responsibility at its very heart.

Ask yourself
What practical steps have you taken to work for a more just world? Do you steer clear of such issues, claiming it is out of your hands or none of your business? Is this what you genuinely feel or are you using it as an excuse to avoid the issue?

Pray
Loving God, I am reminded today that in terms of this world's resources I am one of the lucky ones – one of those with food in my belly and a roof over my head, with ample water and medicine, and with access to education, technology and so much else, my life brimming over with good things.

Forgive me my complacency in the face of the world's evils and my share in an order that not only perpetuates the divide between rich and poor but that actively widens the gap. Hear now my prayer for the millions less fortunate than me – those for whom hunger is a daily reality and a lifetime of poverty all that the future seems to offer. Teach me to give sacrificially in response to their need but, more than that, teach me to work for change, to do all in my power to help build a fairer world until that day when your kingdom dawns and all wrongs are righted. I ask it in the name of Christ. Amen.

Remember
The righteous plead the cause of the poor; the wicked feel no such concern.   *Proverbs 29:7*

Close
Lord of all, may my worship of you be reflected in a commitment to others and a passion for justice. Through Jesus Christ my Lord. Amen.

The unseen hand of God

Read

You are the one who drew me from my mother's womb and who led me to safety at her breast. I was dependent on you from birth, and since my mother bore me you have been my God. Do not be far from me, for trouble is at hand and I have no one to help me. You have rescued me from the horns of wild oxen. I will proclaim your name to my kinsfolk and I will praise you among the congregation. All who fear the Lord, praise him! For he did not spurn or despise the suffering of the downtrodden; he did not hide his face from me, but responded when I cried to him.

Psalm 22:9-11, 21b-23a, 24

Ponder

'Life must be lived forwards, but it can only be understood backwards.' So remarked the Danish theologian, Søren Kierkegaard, and there's a lot of truth in his observation. So often we cannot make sense of our existence one day to another. We look for a purpose but see only a riddle. We try to see where God's hand is at work but draw a blank. We cry out for help but none seems forthcoming. At such times, faith can be tested to the limit, as we struggle to understand why God seems remote and unmoved by our plight. Yet, as is so often the case in life, time can make all the difference. Weeks, months, even years later, we look back and we recognise with amazement how God was at work in our lives just when we were least aware of it. Experiences that seemed cruel, situations that looked bleak, days that felt hopeless, turn out to be formative moments in our journey of faith, leading us forward to new insights and horizons.

Remember that next time you feel God has forgotten you. Remind yourself that, though you may not see it now, the time will surely come when everything fits into place and you realise that God's unseen hand has been leading you safely onwards, through the good and the bad.

Ask yourself
Are there experiences you have had that puzzled you at the time but in which you later recognised God was at work?

Pray
Living God, there are times when I find it hard to make sense of life and when your purpose is difficult to fathom. I am puzzled by my experiences, confused by so much that seems to contradict your will and deny your love, and I wonder why you seem so distant, so unconcerned about my needs.

Yet experience has taught me that you are often at work in ways I do not recognise, responding to my cry and guiding my steps even though I have no inkling of it at the time. You have been with me in the darkest moments, holding on to me even when I do not see your hand. May that truth inspire me when life proves testing again, so that however far you may seem I will know that you are near, and so stride out in that confidence. Through Jesus Christ my Lord. Amen.

Remember
Even though I walk through a valley as dark as death I fear no evil, for you are with me, your staff and your crook are there to comfort me.   *Psalm 23:4*

Close
Sovereign God, when I cannot discern your hand or glimpse your presence help me to understand that you are no less near than you have ever been, and that, seen or unseen, you continue to work out your purpose. Through Jesus Christ my Lord. Amen.

One step beyond

Read

They were on the road leading to Jerusalem. Jesus was walking ahead of them, and they were amazed for, as they followed, they were afraid. He took the twelve aside once again, and began to tell them what was going to happen to him.

Mark 10:32

Ponder

What would you do if someone told you to lie on a bed of nails, walk across hot coals, bungee-jump off the Severn Bridge or parachute off the Empire State Building? If you've any sense, you wouldn't do it – I know I wouldn't! But how about if the person who posed those challenges promised to do each of them first, so that you could watch and learn from their experience, assured that each could be done before you followed suit? Well, I still wouldn't be convinced, but it's just possible that some of you bolder souls out there might have a try! When someone is willing to lead the way it makes a big difference, giving some people at least the courage they might not otherwise have had.

That willingness to take the lead characterised the life and ministry of Christ. It's there in our reading, Jesus knowing that his journey to Jerusalem was going to lead to his death, yet, far from holding back, dragging his feet or making an excuse to go no further, we see him leading the way, one step ahead of his disciples. We see it again following his resurrection, women going to the tomb to anoint his body, only to be told, 'He is not here. He has been raised from the dead and has gone ahead of you to Galilee. There you will see him.' (Matthew 28:6a, 7b) The message holds for whatever we may face. Whether it be a time of testing or blessing, darkness or light, tears or laughter, we can be sure that Jesus is with us; not simply by our side but leading the way, one step beyond.

Ask yourself

Are you feeling anxious about the future, afraid of what you might have to face? Have you lost sight of the fact that Jesus will be there, ahead of you?

Pray

Lord Jesus Christ, I praise you for your willingness to share our humanity with everything that means. I thank you that you endured the darkness of death, knowingly offering your life. I rejoice that you rose again, and that you were there once more, leading the way to life in all its fullness.

Teach me that, whatever I may face, you will guide my footsteps, showing me the path I must take and assuring me that nothing can ever separate me from your presence. Lord Jesus Christ, I praise you for that promise, and I put my trust in you, this day and always. Amen.

Remember

In my Father's house are many mansions: if it were not so, I would have told you. I go to prepare a place for you.

John 14:2 (AV)

Close

Living God, send me back to my journey of discipleship redeemed in love, renewed in faith, restored in strength and refreshed in spirit, in the name of the risen Christ who goes before me. Amen.

The inescapable call

Read

The word of the Lord came to Jonah, son of Amittai, saying, 'Go straightaway to Nineveh, that mighty city, and speak out against it; for their wickedness is an affront to my eyes.' But Jonah set off instead to Tarshish, wanting to escape from the presence of the Lord.   *Jonah 1:1-3a*

Ponder

In 1916 a law was passed in Britain making it compulsory for all unmarried men between the ages of 18 and 41 to enlist in the army and fight in the First World War. Not long after, married men were included too. In 1941, during the Second World War, women were compulsorily conscripted for the first time. The practice of conscription was only abolished in this country in 1962, a change in the law for which I personally give thanks.

How does all this compare with the story of Jonah? At first sight, there seem to be clear parallels – it almost looks as though God conscripted Jonah – but this is to misunderstand the story. God's call is not like that, for he will never compel us to do something against our will. What he *will* do, however, if he has a particular purpose for us, is keep on calling for as long as it takes us to respond. We may attempt to deny his call – thrusting it to the back of our minds, making excuses, convincing ourselves that we have misunderstood – but we will not find peace that way, for God will go on challenging us, day after day, year after year. The option is always ours to resist, as resist some do, but if God has chosen us for a particular task, then we will find that ultimately we cannot escape that call.

Ask yourself

Are you running from God's call? Is it time you faced up to the challenge?

Pray

Living God, I praise you that you have called me to faith in Christ, to fellowship in your Church, to Christian discipleship. I thank you that you keep on calling me to new avenues of service, new ways of serving you, new ways of working towards your kingdom. Forgive me that I am sometimes slow or unwilling to respond: I do not always understand what you are asking of me, I resist when your call is too demanding, I run from that which I would rather not do.

Living God, I praise you that though I ignore or disobey your call, still you seek me out, gently and lovingly leading me back to your way and entrusting to me, despite my faithlessness, the message of the gospel. I praise you that you are a God full of mercy: slow to anger, abounding in steadfast love, your nature always to forgive – a God who is always ready to give a second chance, repeatedly showing your patience, demonstrating your awesome grace time and time again. Help me to hear your voice clearly, to accept your will humbly and to respond to it gladly. In the name of Christ. Amen.

Remember

Where can I escape from your spirit? Or where can I run away from your presence? If I rise up to heaven, you are there; if I make my bed in Sheol, once again you are there.

Psalm 139:7-8

Close

Gracious God, I thank you for your call: the invitation to be part of the work of your kingdom. I thank you that you welcome me as I am – with all my faults and doubts – and that though I fail you repeatedly, still you want to use me in your service. Gracious God, I praise you for that inescapable sense of call that you give; help me to respond. In the name of Christ. Amen.

The graciousness of God

Read

The people of Nineveh believed God's message. They announced a public fast and clothed themselves in sackcloth, from the least to the greatest. When God saw their response, how they renounced their wicked ways, he decided against bringing the punishment on them he had intended and he did not do it. Jonah, however, was piqued, and flew into a rage. He prayed to the Lord and said, 'O Lord! Is this not what I feared would happen back in my own country? This is the reason I took flight to Tarshish when you first called; for I knew you to be a gracious God, merciful, slow to anger, and overflowing in the constancy of your love, and all too ready to surrender thoughts of punishment. Now Lord, I implore you, take my life from me, for I'm better off dead than alive.'

Jonah 3:5, 10-4:3

Ponder

Many of the characters in the Old Testament seem almost too good to be true. We can feel daunted by the depth of their piety, devotion and commitment. But not with Jonah. One of the great appeals of this short book is the raw humanity of this reluctant prophet. Irascible, cold-hearted and petulant, he is just about the last person you would expect God to call into his service; his faults, if only he could see, equally as great as of those he was called to preach to. But that is the beauty of this story, for it vividly portrays God's amazing grace in action. No one in the narrative remotely deserves his blessing, yet all end up receiving it.

The same holds true for us. We may pray 'Forgive us our trespasses as we forgive those who trespass against us', but thankfully God is willing to go a good deal further than that. The consequences, if he wasn't, don't bear thinking about!

Ask yourself

Is God calling you to be more forgiving towards others? Have you underestimated the extent of his grace, towards both them and you?

Pray

Gracious God, I thank you for the awesomeness of your love and the wonder of your grace. Day after day, you show me mercy, accepting my feeble faith and hesitant discipleship, understanding my weakness, putting my faults behind me and helping me to start again. However much I fail you, your patience is never exhausted, your love refuses to be denied. I deserve so little, yet you give so much; my love is so weak, yet you respond so richly; my faith is so small, yet you bless me so constantly.

Gracious God, if you dealt with me according to my deserving I could not hope to escape punishment, for I have failed you in ways too many to number. Help me to recognise that your grace is greater than I can ever begin to imagine, and may I rejoice in the wonder of your love that embraces all. Amen.

Remember

We have redemption in him through his blood, our sins forgiven through the riches of his grace that he heaped upon us.   *Ephesians 1:7-8a*

Close

Sovereign God, for your grace that thrills my heart, your mercy that transforms my mind, your peace that floods my soul and your love that flows through my life, receive my praise. In the name of Christ. Amen.

Perseverance

Read

So then, since we are surrounded by so great a crowd of witnesses, let us discard everything that encumbers us and the sin that clings so closely, and let us run with perseverance the race set before us, looking to Jesus, the beginning and end of our faith, who, focusing on the joy set before him, endured the cross, disregarding its shame, and has taken his seat at the right hand of the throne of God.

Hebrews 12:1-2

Ponder

When I was a student at Bristol Baptist College, the students of the local Methodist College challenged us to a cross-country run. The day dawned grey and drizzly but I was young, fit and raring to go. As I jogged comfortably along, I held secret hopes of dashing triumphantly over the finishing line in first place. Then we reached it: a steep climb fully half a mile long. I swear to this day that it was the Methodists' secret weapon, carefully chosen as part of the route. It may even be that they had prayed for rain! Whatever the case, the slope was so slippery that, after a couple of steps, my feet gave way and I slid wretchedly back down the hill to where I had started. Before long I was joined by a succession of fellow-Baptists in similar plight. Strangely, the Methodists had no such problem; they sailed up that bank as though they had sprouted wings. Did I ever conquer it? Eventually, yes, but only after some of my colleagues had inspired me through their heroic efforts to persevere for the sake of those following.

The Christian life can be equally demanding sometimes. We start off thinking it's plain sailing but suddenly unexpected obstacles appear in our path. At times we can feel like giving up, but we have the example of those who have gone before us to inspire us onwards, and a responsibility to future generations to lead the way in turn. Whether the race is easy or hard, we need to persevere, looking to Jesus and the joy set before us. For me, that day, the incentive was very simple – a hot shower and a cup of tea! The joy we look to through him is something far more wonderful – too wonderful for words.

Ask yourself
Can you and will you be able to make the testimony of the Apostle Paul (see *Remember* below) your own?

Pray
Lord God, you know that life isn't always easy. There are times when I feel exhausted, overwhelmed and defeated. Remind me then of those who have gone before, keeping the faith and running the race with perseverance. Remind me of Jesus, his willingness to endure the cross for my sake. Remind me of my responsibility to those who will come after me.

So, give me the strength to battle on, faithful to the last, in the knowledge that you are waiting to receive me and to grant me the joy of your kingdom, the prize of everlasting life. Through Jesus Christ my Lord. Amen.

Remember
I have fought the good fight, I have finished the race, I have kept the faith. From now on there is reserved for me the crown of righteousness, which the Lord, the righteous judge, will give to me on that day, and not only to me but also to all who have longed for his approaching.

2 Timothy 4:7-8

Close
Lord Jesus Christ, inspire me through your love and the great company of those who have gone before me, to persevere and run the race, to the glory of your name. Amen.

Hitting home

Read

The Lord sent the prophet Nathan to David, and he came before him saying, 'There were two men in a certain city, one rich and the other poor. The rich man owned numerous flocks and herds, whereas the poor man could afford just one young ewe lamb. He hand-reared this so that it grew up with him and his children. It ate out of his meagre resources, drank from his cup and lay in his arms, treated as though it was his own daughter. One day, however, a traveller visited the rich man and, reluctant to use one of his own animals to prepare a meal for his visitor, he took the poor man's lamb and prepared that for his guest instead.' On hearing this, David was incensed at the man's behaviour. He said to Nathan, 'As the Lord lives, the man who did this deserves to die; in recompense for his deed and in punishment for his lack of pity, he shall pay for that lamb four times over!' Then Nathan said to David, 'You are the man!'   *2 Samuel 12:1-7*

Ponder

Have you ever been asked to confront someone with an awkward truth? If so, then you will appreciate just how hard that is. Over the years, the lot seems to have disproportionately fallen to me more often than I would have wished, the reason being, according to others, that I am more diplomatic than most. It's a kind thought, but entirely misplaced. The reality is that I skirt gingerly around the subject, treading on eggshells rather than cause offence, vainly hoping that the penny may drop. Occasionally, a softly-softly approach such as that may succeed but, more often than not, it will fall on deaf ears. It's far better sometimes to speak the truth candidly. Yes, it may hurt, raise people's hackles, even make an enemy for life, but, if it helps someone grow as an individual, it is ultimately a kindness.

Nathan had that sort of courage. The message God gave him to speak was not an easy one, almost bound to meet with a hostile reception, yet the words needed saying if David was to recognise the error of his ways and find forgiveness. There are times when we need to confront individuals or society as a whole with unpalatable truths. Have we the courage of Nathan to meet that challenge?

Ask yourself

Have there been times recently when you have kept quiet rather than speak out against what you know to be wrong?

Pray

Living God, it isn't easy to speak out against wrong. We prefer to mind our own business rather than get involved; to keep our heads down for fear of the possible consequences should we intervene. More than that, we hold back for fear of hypocrisy, being all too conscious of our own faults and failings, and so feeling that we have no right to judge others. For good or bad reasons, from the best or worst of motives, we are sometimes silent, allowing evil to go unchallenged, rather than lifting up our voices against it.

Help me to know when it is not only right but necessary to speak, and when such moments come, give me wisdom, sensitivity and courage, so that I will know the words to say and be enabled to say them. Give me that rare ability to speak the truth in love. Through Jesus Christ my Lord. Amen.

Remember

Put off falsehood; let each of us speak the truth to our neighbour, for we all belong together. *Ephesians 4:25*

Close

Loving God, help me to speak your challenging, reforming and renewing word of truth, for your name's sake. Amen.

Cancelling our debt

Read

God forgave us all our sins, cancelling the debt written against us in the ledger with all its legal requirements, irrevocably doing away with it by nailing it to the cross.

Colossians 2:13

Ponder

Have you ever been in debt? Apparently, this is the most widespread social problem of our time. It's a horrible situation to be in and one that I've always taken care to avoid since my days living on a student grant. Each term I would end up forty, fifty, even one hundred pounds overdrawn, and though that may seem a relatively small amount today, at the time it felt like a giant millstone around my neck. At Oxford, with no grant at all, and reliant upon a number of small trusts and the generosity of my home church, it was harder still. I spent many a sleepless night tossing and turning as I brooded over how far I could stretch the overdraft and how I could ever hope to repay it. It is not just financial debts, however, that can eat away at our peace of mind. To owe even an apology to someone can weigh heavily upon us and to owe recompense that we cannot possibly make is harder still.

It is such a debt that we owe to God, for we have all failed him in innumerable ways, each deserving of punishment according to the Law of Moses. No matter how hard we try, we can never pay what is due, no amount of good works able to earn our salvation. Yet, that is where we come to the heart of the gospel, the good news of God's gracious mercy in cancelling the debt. We do not need to wrestle with that burden of shame or guilt, for he has taken it from us, nailed with Christ on the cross and buried in the tomb; unlike him, never to return. There are no easy answers to owing money; somehow or other it has to be paid or a black mark put against our name if it is written off. Thank God the debt we owe to him is freely and lovingly cancelled; we need only to ask.

Ask yourself

Are you troubled by a sense of guilt or unworthiness? Have you understood the implications of Christ's sacrifice on the cross?

Pray

Lord Jesus Christ, you paid the price that I could never begin to pay. You gave your all to cancel the debt I owe, securing my freedom through your suffering and death. I celebrate again the awesomeness of that sacrifice and the generosity of that gift, and I praise you that you make no extortionate demands in return for forgiveness, nor impose stringent conditions before you are ready to grant it. You ask me simply to acknowledge my need and to accept your mercy, trusting in what you have done on my behalf.

Lord Jesus Christ, such grace is beyond my comprehension, but I respond to it with joyful praise and heartfelt worship, offering you my love and service, not as a repayment but as a token of my glad thanksgiving. To you be glory and honour, blessing and adoration, now and for evermore. Amen.

Remember

God was in Christ, reconciling the world to himself, no longer holding people's offences against them, and he has committed to us the word of reconciliation.

2 Corinthians 5:19

Close

Sovereign God, I owe you everything, yet by your grace I owe you nothing! Great is your name and greatly to be praised! Amen.

Me! Prejudiced?

Read

If someone wearing gold rings and fine clothing enters your synagogue, followed by a shabbily dressed person, and you pay attention to the one in fine clothing, saying, 'Sit here in the best place', while you tell the poor person, 'Stand over there or sit beneath my feet', are you not showing discrimination and presuming to judge unfairly?

James 2:2-4

Ponder

A while back I watched the TV highlights of England playing a World Cup qualifying match in Eastern Europe. The result went in England's favour, but overshadowing the game were fears of a repeat of the racial harassment that had marred the Under-21 game the night before. According to the authorities in the country concerned, it was the first time many in their country had seen black people playing football – a feeble excuse, though, of course, it is not so long ago that black players in England faced similar abuse, week in, week out. The fact is that prejudice runs deep, and although sport in this country has largely succeeded in rooting out racism, all kinds of prejudice continue to scar the face of society. All kinds of measures have been adopted in an attempt to correct this, at times leading to a political correctness that borders on the ridiculous, but the fact is that legislation is sometimes the only way to protect the interests of those discriminated against.

In the Church there should be no place for prejudice but let us not fool ourselves that it has no foothold in our lives. It may not be overt discrimination on the grounds of race, gender, religion or sexuality – though sadly that is still sometimes seen – but there are other more subtle prejudices we find it hard to escape from, scarcely aware even of their existence within us. We need to recognise that danger and to ask for God's help in seeing beyond colour, culture and creed to the person underneath – a person he loved enough to send his Son to die for them.

Ask yourself

In what ways do prejudice and discrimination still have a hold in your life?

Pray

Loving God, I talk about all people having a place in your kingdom, but I do not always live as though I believe it. I try not to pigeonhole people according to the colour of their skin, their religion, their age or their gender, yet I have preconceived opinions about what is acceptable and unacceptable, and I write off anyone who does not conform to my ideas. I see differences as a threat rather than a gift, the prejudices within me running deep, poisoning my very soul.

Teach me to look at people with your eyes, seeing the good and the bad, the lovely and the unlovely, the strengths and the weaknesses, yet seeing above all our common humanity. Open my heart and mind to others, and so, in turn, to you. Through Jesus Christ my Lord. Amen.

Remember

God has shown me I should not call anyone impure or unclean. I recognise now how true it is that God does not show partiality, but accepts people from every nation who fear him and do his will. *Acts 10:28a, 34b-35*

Close

Living God, teach me that you did not just make some but all people in your likeness, and so teach me to value and respect everyone in the family of humankind. Through Jesus Christ my Lord. Amen.

Following my leader

Read

Walking beside the Sea of Galilee, he saw two brothers, Simon, known as Peter, and Andrew his brother, casting a net into the lake – for they were fishermen. And he said to them, 'Come and follow me, and I will make you fishers of people.' Straightaway they left their nets and followed him.

Matthew 4:18-20

Ponder

A friend reminded me recently that Jesus only talked once during his ministry of being born again but spoke of the need to follow him on innumerable occasions. There is an important point behind that observation, for there is a danger sometimes of making the moment of conversion all-important and forgetting that discipleship is, or should be, an unfolding journey. Peter and Andrew, together with the rest of the Apostles, followed Jesus not knowing what he was calling them to or where their response might lead. They responded in faith, trusting that he would guide them and, apart from Judas, they kept on following even when it led to sacrifice, hostility, rejection and the death of their Master on a cross. How many of us would have followed through all of that? Would we still have been there by his side after the first altercation with the Pharisees? Would we have had second thoughts when Jesus spelt out the cost of discipleship?

Even the Apostles' faith had its limits, of course, on the night of Gethsemane each briefly failing to follow. It needed the risen Christ to greet them once more, speaking his word of peace and reaffirming his call, before they felt able to resume their journey once more. We too may encounter moments when faith is tested and we no longer follow as we should, but Jesus will always be there, summoning us forward once again. Committing ourselves to Christ is a necessary step for all of us, whether that involves a dramatic experience of conversion or a gradual coming to faith, but it is only a first step. Don't mistake it for more.

Ask yourself

Do you still look to Jesus for guidance, or have you decided where you are going in life and how you intend to get there?

Pray

Lord Jesus Christ, it is not easy to follow you; not if we are serious about discipleship. You challenge our whole perspective on life, calling us not just to a statement of belief but to a way of life. You are always leading us forward, eager to guide us into new experiences of your love and a deeper understanding of your purpose, yet so often we refuse to follow where you would have us go.

Forgive me for losing the sense of direction with which I began my path of discipleship. Forgive me for trusting you when all goes well but doubting the moment life fails to conform to my expectations. Forgive me for thinking that I have done all that needs to be done, imagining that one simple confession of faith suffices for a lifetime. Lord, you are still calling, inviting me to respond. Help me to follow. Amen.

Remember

Then Jesus spoke to them again, saying, 'I am the light of the world: whoever follows me will not walk in darkness, but will have the light of life.'   *John 8:12*

Close

Sovereign God, rekindle my vision, revive my faith and renew my resolve to take up my cross and follow where you would lead me. Show me the way in Christ and give me faith to follow, for his name's sake. Amen.

Following suit

Read

If then there is any encouragement in Christ, any reassurance
in love, any belonging together in the Spirit, any compassion
and empathy, make my joy whole: be of the same mind,
having the same love, being in complete harmony and of a
common mind. Let the same mind be in you that was in
Christ Jesus.   *Philippians 2:1-2, 5*

Ponder

Lovers of card games like bridge, whist, solo or piquet will
know that there is one rule that must always be observed:
following suit. If a heart is laid, you must lay a heart; if a
spade, then a spade; the only exception being when you
have no cards of that suit left in your hand. Ignore this rule
and it is impossible to play the game: it is a recipe for chaos.

When it comes to Christian commitment, we must again
follow suit, though in a rather different way. We are called,
so far as possible, to follow the lead of Christ in all our
actions, showing the same love, compassion, dedication and
devotion as he did. We may sometimes struggle to do so –
indeed, without his help, we will often find it impossible –
but that nonetheless should be our goal, for in this case it
is not a game we are talking about but life, and how far our
lives point others to Jesus. Are you following suit as carefully as you should be?

Ask yourself

In what ways can you honestly say you are following the
example of Christ? In what ways do you fail to follow suit?

Pray

Lord Jesus Christ, I want to follow your example and I
strive to do so, but so often my weakness gets the better of
me. I talk of serving others but live instead for myself; I

speak of self-sacrifice but indulge my self-interest; I profess loyalty to your cause, yet repeatedly deny it through the way I live. I have preferred my ways to yours, more concerned with my own advancement than your kingdom. I have been weak in my commitment and half-hearted in offering my service.

Forgive me all the ways my life fails to reflect your goodness and all the ways my faithlessness betrays your grace. Touch my life afresh and fill my heart with your love so that I may truly live for you, making known your love and bringing closer your kingdom. In your name I ask it. Amen.

Remember

Christ suffered for us, leaving us an example, so that we should follow in his footsteps.   *1 Peter 2:21*

Close

Lord Jesus Christ, help me to grow in you so that something of you may grow in me, for your name's sake. Amen.

Following through

Read

As you therefore have received Christ Jesus the Lord, continue to live your lives in him, rooted and built up in him and established in the faith, just as you were taught, abounding in thanksgiving.
Colossians 2:6-7

Ponder

There was a time when I had delusions of mastering the game of golf. I hacked my way eagerly round a variety of municipal courses, dreaming one day perhaps of attaining a reasonable standard but, sadly, my skill never matched my enthusiasm. To put it bluntly, I was hopeless. Instead of soaring majestically down the fairway, my ball would dribble a few yards into a divot, veer wildly into the rough or dip disconsolately into the nearest water hazard. What was the problem? There were all too many, but one was an inability to follow through. Where I should have continued after the ball in a graceful arc, I instead chopped down on it with a vicious stab, burying my club in the turf and all but breaking my wrists in the process.

It's not just in sport that following through is important but in so much of life and faith. It's easy enough to start something; a different matter to finish it. So often we start something full of enthusiasm, only then to lose interest. Many likewise commit themselves to Christ, impulsively responding to the message of the gospel, but soon realise that they have taken on more than they first anticipated. Is that true of us? We may have professed our faith in Christ and started off on the journey of discipleship but that finally is not what counts. It's whether we complete the course that matters; whether having put our hands to something we are ready to follow it through.

Ask yourself

Is your faith as real as it used to be, or has your commitment grown cold?

Pray

Lord Jesus Christ, you call me, as you called your first disciples, to follow you: not simply to believe, nor merely to declare my faith and confess you as Lord, but to keep on following wherever you lead. Help me to follow you faithfully, walking wherever you might lead. Help me to follow your example, pursuing the way of love and accepting the road of sacrifice. Help me to follow through the life of discipleship, not allowing myself to become distracted, nor to lose heart so that I wander away from you, but keeping faith to the end.

Lord Jesus Christ, you call me, as you call all your people, to follow you. Teach me what that means, and by your grace help me to respond and be a follower of your way, to the glory of your name. Amen.

Remember

You, who were estranged from God, opposed to him in thought and deed, have now been reconciled through his giving of his earthly body in death, through which he is able to present you as holy, blameless and irreproachable, so long as you continue in the faith – grounded, resolute and unshakeable in the hope of the gospel.

Colossians 1:21-22

Close

Living God, fill my heart with your love and draw near in your grace, so that my faith may stay as fresh today and every day as the day it first began. Through Jesus Christ my Lord. Amen.

The best-laid plans

Read

Come now, you who say, 'Today or tomorrow we will go to such and such a town and spend a year there, doing business and making money.' You do not even know what tomorrow will bring. What is your life? For you are a mist that appears for a little while and then vanishes. Instead you ought to say, 'If the Lord wishes, we will live and do this or that.'

James 4:13-15

Ponder

Even the best-laid plans, they tell us, go to waste. It is, though, in the nature of humankind to plan ahead. We want to know what life has in store, we feel the need for a clear sense of direction, and we do everything in our power to ensure that the future measures up to our expectations.

There is no shortage of encouragement to such a way of thinking. Pension firms urge us to plan for retirement, insurance companies offer cover against each and every eventuality, whilst banks and building societies offer us all manner of investment schemes that promise bumper tax-free pay-outs ten, fifteen, twenty-five years into the future. All of course have their place for those who can afford them, as part of a sensible stewardship of their resources, but neither these nor anything else can guarantee the future. We never know what tomorrow may bring. Whilst it is necessary in life to look ahead it is also vital to live each day as it comes, valuing it for what it is, and being open to what it may bring.

Ask yourself

In whom or what do you place your trust for the future? Are you open to the possibility that God's plans may not be the same as yours?

Pray

Living God, I do not find it easy to live by faith. I want some idea of what the future holds, some assurance that things will work out as I hope. I like to feel in control of my life, and want to be able to shape events and influence my circumstances. To an extent, I can do that and yet my hold over anything is so tenuous, what seems certain today under threat tomorrow; what seems safe in my hands one moment plucked from my grasp the next.

I need to plan, not just for myself but also for my loved ones and so much else in life, and I ask for your help in doing that, so that I may make wise decisions for the future. Help me also, though, to recognise that the future is ultimately in your hands rather than mine, and so help me to seek your will before all else and to trust that you will always lead me. Through Jesus Christ my Lord. Amen.

Remember

The plans of the mind belong to mortals, but the answer of the tongue is from the Lord. The human mind plans the way, but the Lord directs the steps. The human mind may devise many plans, but it is the purpose of the Lord that will be established.   *Proverbs 16:1, 9; 19:21*

Close

Loving God, I do not know what lies ahead, except that there will be a mixture of good and bad, joys and sorrows, but what I know for certain is that, in life or in death, you will be with me, waiting to enrich my life, to bestow your blessing and to fulfil your sovereign purpose. In that faith I commit the future to you, through Jesus Christ my Lord. Amen.

A God both near and far

Read

You, Lord, are enthroned high over all the earth, exalted above all gods. Your constant love is higher than the heavens and your truth reaches up to the skies. To you be glory, O God, high enthroned in heaven. Let your glory illuminate the earth.   *Psalm 97:9; 108:4-5*

Ponder

'So near, yet so far.' How often have we heard that said? It's an expression we use when someone nearly achieves something but not quite: an athlete, perhaps, pipped at the post in an important race, or a student who has just missed out on passing an exam. With God we can use that expression in a different sense, not as one contradicting the other but as two points in a single spectrum. On the one hand, the Bible portrays God as the sovereign creator, the ruler of space and time, mighty and mysterious, beyond human comprehension – one to be served with fear and trembling. On the other hand, he is a God who draws near, who walks and talks with his people and who has shared our humanity in the person of Christ. It is a wonderful paradox, both aspects of God's nature vital to recognise if we are to have a balanced picture of who he is. We need a sense of his transcendence so that we do not end up shaping him in our image but we need also an awareness of his immanence if faith is to have any bearing on our life.

So, what sort of picture do we have of God? Do we still feel a sense of awe in his presence, a feeling of privilege that we are able to come before him? We should do. Yet, do we also see him as an intimate friend, involved in every aspect of our life, and wanting us to approach him with our hopes and fears, joys and sorrows? Ours is a God whose greatness is beyond expression and yet who delights to hear our prayer, who longs to bless us and who is passionately concerned about our lives – a God both near and far!

Ask yourself

Do you have a proper sense both of God's sovereignty and of his closeness? Do you succeed in balancing the two?

Pray

Almighty and everlasting God, with awe and wonder I come to worship you. You are higher than my highest thoughts but always close by my side; greater than I can ever imagine yet made known to me in Christ; all powerful but nurturing me as a mother tends her child; constantly at work in human history yet having a special concern for every one of us. Though I stretch imagination to the limit I barely begin to glimpse how wonderful you are. Though you sometimes seem distant, always you are near.

Almighty and everlasting God, give me humility to acknowledge my weakness beside your greatness, faith to trust in you despite my doubts, joy in knowing you despite the limitations of my understanding, and peace in serving you, knowing that you are the Lord of all, a God both near and far. In Christ's name I ask it. Amen.

Remember

You are near, O Lord, and all your commandments are true. The one who vindicates me is near. Seek the Lord while he may be found, call upon him while he is near.

Psalm 119:151; Isaiah 50:8; 55:6

Close

Sovereign God and Father, enthroned in splendour yet here by my side, I bring my worship, I bring myself, and I ask you to help me glimpse both your meekness and your majesty. Through Jesus Christ my Lord. Amen.

One day at a time

Read

Anxiety weighs down the human heart, but a good word
cheers it up.   *Proverbs 12:25*

Ponder

I recently came across two wonderful quotations. The first
was from Corrie Ten Boom: 'Worry does not empty tomorrow of its sorrow; it empties today of its strength.' The second
was from William R. Inge, one-time Dean of St Paul's:
'Worry is interest paid on trouble before it falls due.' What
wisdom there is in those words, yet how hard we find it to act
upon them. We know that worry is futile, not only failing
to achieve anything but actually undermining our ability
to face life's problems, yet sometimes we just can't seem to
help ourselves. To a point, that is natural, however sure our
trust in God. When our welfare is threatened, or our loved
ones are in any kind of danger, we would be less than
human not to worry about it. Yet to worry about what
might happen when there are no grounds to fear it, to fret
about possibilities rather than certainties, is foolhardy.
There is time enough to deal with these if and when they
arrive without facing them several times over beforehand.

Few things have the power to crush the human spirit
like worry, yet the irony is that most of the things we worry
about never materialise and those that do are often less
awful than we imagined. For the Christian there is the added
confidence that, even when our worst fears are realised, God
will be there to support us. Nothing can destroy the future
he holds for us; don't let worry destroy the present.

Ask yourself

Are you worrying about things you cannot change? What
effect has this had on your life?

Pray

Gracious God, you have promised to all who love you a peace that passes all understanding. Forgive me that I have failed to make that my own. I rush about, my mind pre-occupied by my problems. I brood over situations that I cannot hope to change, magnifying them out of all proportion. I worry about what the future may hold instead of focusing on the present moment and living each day as it comes.

Teach me that you hold all things in your hands and that, even when my worries prove justified you will give me strength to get through. Whatever clouds may appear on the horizon and whatever storms life might throw against me, may my mind be at rest, my spirit at peace and my heart untroubled. Through Jesus Christ my Lord. Amen.

Remember

Which of you by worrying can add one cubit to your stature? Therefore do not worry about what tomorrow will bring; there will be time enough for worrying when tomorrow comes. Let the problems of one day be sufficient.

Matthew 6:34

Close

Gracious God, I praise you for what has been, I thank you for what is, and I commit to you what shall be, in Jesus' name. Amen.

Where is your God?

Read

Tears are my food day and night, while people keep on saying
to me, 'Where is your God?'   *Psalm 42:3*

Ponder

Where is your God now? Has anyone ever asked you that?
They may not use those words exactly but they mean much
the same thing. People ask the question for a variety of
reasons. Some are only too eager to do faith down, looking
for any and every opportunity to say, 'Look at that, I told
you so.' Others have a very different motive, having begun
to explore the claims of Christianity for themselves and
maybe even tentatively committed themselves to Christ, only
to find their faith shattered by experiences they cannot
make sense of. Sometimes, and hardest of all to cope with, it
may be us posing the question ourselves, unable to reconcile
what we see in the world with the things we believe. Are
there any easy answers at such times? Well, if there are, I
don't know of them.

Yet there is an answer, and like so much in our faith, it
comes back to the cross of Christ. As he hung there in
agony, there were some gathered to gloat, some watching
in disbelief, and even Jesus himself asking why God had
forsaken him. The scribes and elders called out in mockery,
'He trusts in God; let God come and deliver him if he so
wishes', or, in other words, 'Where is your God now?' It
seemed proven beyond doubt that the God Jesus trusted in
simply wasn't there, and yet we know that he was *there*
most of all, reconciling the world to himself, opening the
way to life for all. We will still be asked the question sometimes, we will still occasionally ask it ourselves, and we will
still struggle to answer, yet we hold on to the conviction

that even when we can least see him God can be most powerfully at work.

Ask yourself

Do you find faith tested by your experiences of life? Does it help you to know that others have faced similar testing and come through the stronger for it?

Pray

Eternal God, mighty and mysterious, sovereign over all, it is beyond the power of human words to express your greatness, for you are higher than I can ever begin to imagine. I praise you for that truth, yet I confess, also, that it can be hard to live with, for it can make you seem remote, distant, detached from my situation, oblivious to my need. I thank you that such times are rare, but they *do* come – times when you seem so mysterious, so far removed from my situation, that I question whether you are there at all. I seek, yet I do not find; I ask, but I do not receive; I cry out for help, but you do not answer. Help me in such moments to gain inspiration from those who have felt the same beforehand. Assure me of your continuing purpose, your enduring love and your final triumph. Through Jesus Christ my Lord. Amen.

Remember

Not to us, O Lord, not to us, but to your name bring glory, for the sake of your unfailing love and your constancy. Why should the nations ask, 'Where is your God?' Our God is enthroned in the heavens; he does whatever he wishes.   *Psalm 115:1-3*

Close

Lord Jesus Christ, when I look for God but do not find him, help me to look to you and so recognise that, seen or unseen, he is at work, fulfilling his sovereign purpose. In your name I pray. Amen.

The bitter end

Read

Get rid of all bitterness, rage, temper, backbiting and insults, together with all malice, and be kind to one another, compassionate, forgiving one another as God in Christ has forgiven you. Be vigilant, in case anyone should fail to grasp the grace of God, ensuring that no root of bitterness springs up to spread unrest among you, through which many may be brought to ruin. *Ephesians 4:31-32; Hebrews 12:15*

Ponder

Few of us in our lifetime will be fortunate enough to escape being badly let down or hurt by someone. A close relationship may end in acrimony, a trusted friend betray a confidence, a broken promise deny us a long-dreamed of opportunity, or a moment's carelessness wreck our lives.

How do we cope with such experiences? There are two options: either we face them for what they are, working through the pain until we finally come to terms with it, or we can dwell on the injustice of life, licking our wounds and wallowing in self-pity. The latter reaction is perfectly understandable but ultimately tragic, for it succeeds only in adding insult to injury, robbing life of its joy and beauty. Few people are lonelier than those who are bitter in spirit. Get rid of your bitterness, then, through bringing it openly and honestly to God, before bitterness has the chance, metaphorically speaking, to get rid of you.

Ask yourself

Have you grown bitter about life? What has such bitterness done to you as a person?

Pray

Gracious God, I have so much to thank you for, and yet there are times when I lose sight of that, dwelling instead on the disappointments and frustrations of life. I brood about the things that didn't work out as I hoped, the hurts inflicted upon me, the mistakes made, the opportunities denied, and I allow these to fester within me, poisoning me from within, eating away at my happiness until I think of nothing else.

Forgive me my foolishness and help me to regain a proper sense of proportion. Teach me to put the past behind me and to embrace the present moment, recognising that what's done is done but that you are constantly making all things new. Save me from that sourness of spirit that finally will destroy me more than anything. Through Jesus Christ my Lord. Amen.

Remember

The heart knows its own bitterness and no stranger shares its joy.   *Proverbs 14:10*

Close

Gracious God, make me generous of heart, warm of spirit, forgiving in attitude and sunny of disposition. Through Jesus Christ my Lord. Amen.

Watch your tongue

Read

We all make mistakes. Anyone who can open their mouth without putting their foot in it must be perfect, able to rein in their whole body. We do that with horses, putting bits into their mouths to make them obey us and so guiding their whole bodies. Similarly, with ships – despite being so large that it takes a mighty wind to drive them, a tiny rudder steers them and the pilot directs them as he wills. So also the tongue, though a little member, can do great things. No one is able to tame the tongue – it is uncontrollably evil, full of deadly venom. Out of the same mouth we both praise God and curse one another. *James 3:2-5, 8-9*

Ponder

I have always been fascinated by the power of words. A simple proverb can express the profoundest of truths; a piece of poetry can inspire us or move us to tears; a good book can capture our imagination, making us feel part of another world; a well-chosen word of thanks or appreciation can lift the spirit. However, there is a negative side to this truth. Words can too easily be used to hurt and destroy, cheat and deceive, ridicule or revile. We will all be able to recall times when we opened our mouths without stopping to think, or when we spoke cruelly, intent on wounding. We will all have encountered those who never stop talking, wearing us out with their incessant empty chatter. We will all equally be aware of the way words have been used to incite hatred and intolerance, violence and war.

Words are God's gift, but they are a gift that needs to be handled with care, for they have a tendency to run away with us, and an astonishing capacity for both good and evil. Unless we learn to watch our tongues, we may well find that words become our master instead of us theirs.

Ask yourself

When did you last open your mouth and wish you hadn't? How often do you speak without thinking?

Pray

Lord, I thank you for the wonderful gift of words, the ability through language to communicate with others; to express our thoughts and feelings; to share information; to move, challenge and inspire; to offer ideas; to bring comfort.

Forgive me for the way I turn something so special into something so ugly, capable of causing such devastation. Teach me to think more carefully about what I say and to speak always with the intention of helping rather than hurting. Help me to use words wisely, in the name of Jesus Christ, the Word made flesh. Amen.

Remember

Reckless words are like sword thrusts, but a wise tongue brings healing. Those who watch their tongues preserve their lives; those who speak without thinking come to ruin. A gentle answer soothes tempers but an unkind word arouses anger. The tongue of the wise bestows knowledge, but the mouth of fools gushes with folly.

Proverbs 12:18; 13:3; 15:1-2

Close

Lord, I have heard it so many times before, but I ask it again for myself: May the words of my mouth and the thoughts of my heart be acceptable in your sight. Amen.

Asking in faith

Read

Ask, and it will be given to you; search, and you will find; knock, and the door will be opened for you. For whoever asks receives, and whoever searches finds, and to whoever knocks, the door will be opened. Would any among you, should your child ask for bread, give a stone? Or if asked for a fish, would you give a snake? If then, you who are flawed, know how to give good gifts to your children, how much more will your heavenly Father give good things to those who ask him! *Matthew 7:7-11*

Ponder

'Seek and you will find.' At least that's what Jesus tells us. It sounds good, doesn't it? And it is, no question. Yet, like most attractive promises, we need to be aware of important qualifications, for what Jesus was offering here was not a blank cheque, a guarantee that whatever we look for in life will be ours if only we look hard enough. On the contrary, many will seek after goals like status and success, fame and fortune, but never find them. The seeking Jesus has in mind is of a different kind – a search for meaning, for truth, for God. It is more than the perennial quest for happiness, though that is part of it. It is more than a striving after personal fulfilment, though that too is an integral aspect. It is a search for the infinite, the root and goal of our being, the purpose behind the universe and life itself; a journey of discovery that reaches its destination in Christ.

Seek in that way, openly and honestly, and, like the wise men long ago, you will find. Open your life to him and you will discover life in abundance, the answer to your deepest needs, the one before whom we too, as the magi before us, can only fall down on our knees in worship.

Ask yourself

What are your goals in life? Do you have your priorities right?

Pray

Loving God, you long to shower me with blessings, to fill my life with good things, yet there are times when, through my weakness of faith, I frustrate your gracious purpose and deprive myself of the inexpressible riches you so freely offer. I do not seek, so I do not find. I do not ask, so I do not receive. I concern myself with the fleeting pleasures of the moment and so fail to grasp treasures that endure for eternity.

Forgive me the shallowness of my values and the limitations of my understanding. Teach me to set my heart on those things that have the power to truly satisfy, which you so yearn to share with me. In the name of Christ I ask it. Amen.

Remember

If you appeal to me in prayer, I will hear you; if you search for me, you will find me; if you seek me with all your heart, I will ensure you find me, says the Lord.

Jeremiah 29:12b-14a

Close

Lord Jesus Christ, guide my thinking, my living and my praying, that I may discern your will, follow your way and receive your blessing. Amen.

Glimpsing the kingdom

Read

The kingdom of God is comparable to having scattered seed on the ground. Those who sow it sleep and wake night and day, and the seed sprouts and grows, though they have no idea how. The earth brings forth a crop by itself, first a shoot, then the head, then the full ear of grain. When, though, the grain is ripe, they set to work at once with their sickles, because the time for harvest has come.'

Mark 4:26-29

Ponder

In 1516 Sir Thomas More wrote *Utopia* in which he set out his vision of a society marked by peace, justice and harmony. Here was a picture of the way life could and ought to be. In 1949 George Orwell wrote *Nineteen Eighty-four*, a novel about the nightmare scenario of a totalitarian state in which every thought and action is regulated, encapsulated in the stark warning 'Big Brother is watching you'. Here was a picture of the way life could but mustn't be. What vision, I wonder, do we have of the future? Do we look forward with hope or fear, with anticipation or dread? What of the future beyond this life? Do we believe there is meaning to our existence even beyond death, or do we regard the grave as the end of all our striving?

Most of us would like to think the world can be a better place and we probably all want to believe in an afterlife but, as the years pass, our confidence can take a battering. The harsh realities of life seem to contradict the idealistic dreams of youth. The first flush of faith fades to a mere shadow of what it used to be. Yet, as so many of the parables of Jesus remind us, if we only have eyes to see, the signs of the kingdom are all around us. Not only is it coming but, in a real sense, it is here already, the miracle of changed lives taking place every day and every moment. To know Christ is to be given a foretaste of all that is yet to come; not simply a vision of what might be but a promise of what will be. If we cannot see signs of his coming kingdom, perhaps we are looking in the wrong place or for the wrong things!

Ask yourself
In what ways can you see God at work around you? What are you doing to bring his kingdom closer?

Pray
Lord Jesus Christ, we talk so often about the coming of your kingdom that we can forget, in a very real sense, it has come already, here all around us in a host of ways. In numerous expressions of love and kindness you are here, working out your purpose, serving and being served. In countless lives being changed every day, you are here, calling, cleansing, renewing, restoring. In the prayers, the work and the worship of your people, you are here, bestowing and making known your love.

The fulfilment may be yet to come, but the kingdom is here among us, dawning a little more brightly day by day. Help me to play my part in its growth, to do what I can to make it more real on earth, until that day when I dwell with you and all your people in your eternal kingdom, and yours is the power and glory for evermore. Amen.

Remember
Fortunate are your eyes, for they see, and your ears, for they hear. I tell you truthfully, many prophets and saints longed to see what you see, yet never saw it, and to hear what you hear, yet never heard it.'   *Matthew 13:16-17*

Close
Loving God, help me to see around me the seeds of your kingdom, and to nurture them lovingly until that day dawns when your will is done and you are all in all. Amen.

JULY

A world to explore

Read

I have not stopped praying that . . . your eyes may inwardly be enlightened so that you may know the hope to which he has called you, the glorious riches of the inheritance he has reserved for you among the saints, and his matchless power he grants to us who believe. *Ephesians 1:16b, 18-19a*

Ponder

One of my distant relations, so I am told, was Colonel Percy Fawcett, an intrepid explorer hailing from Torquay in Devon whose travels took him on several dangerous journeys into the region of Mato Grosso where in 1925, together with his eldest son, he disappeared without trace. Some may recall the television series about him a couple of years ago, or even have read the book *Exploration Fawcett*. Sadly, I cannot claim to have inherited any of Percy's adventurous spirit but in one sense I am involved in an exploration; namely, the unfolding journey of faith. Hopefully, we all feel the same, for we should always be moving forward into uncharted territory, discovering new experiences of God's love, fresh insights into his grace, innovative paths of service and a revitalised vision of his purpose. However established our faith, there is always more to learn. However rich our experience, there is always more to discover. Like any good explorer, the more we see the more we realise there is still to learn.

So it was that Paul, Apostle and celebrated teacher, could yet speak of the indescribable wonder of God, the mysteries yet to be unravelled, the knowledge still to be gained. Far though he had come, he knew that he had not arrived and would never do so in this life. Whatever joys he had known, whatever truths he had grasped, there were still inexhaustible riches to be unearthed – a world to explore.

Ask yourself

Has faith for you become a journey or a destination? Are you still open to new horizons?

Pray

Living God, thank you for everything that speaks of your loving purpose; all the ways you teach, guide and challenge, calling me forward in faith. Forgive me that I sometimes lose sight of the great things you have done and the wonders you have yet to reveal. Draw near in love, and open my heart to all the ways you are at work, my eyes to your glory all around me, my ears to your living word, and my mind to your truth.

So may I grasp each day a little more of who and what you are, acknowledging your greatness, marvelling at your love, rejoicing in your blessings and celebrating your inexhaustible mercy. Through Jesus Christ my Lord. Amen.

Remember

O, the depth of the riches of the wisdom and knowledge of God! How unfathomable are his judgements, and mysterious are his ways! Who has known the mind of the Lord, or who can claim to have been his counsellor?

Romans 11:33-34

Close

Lord Jesus Christ, save me from thinking I have arrived in my faith. Show me that, however far I have come, there is always further to go and more to be revealed, for your name's sake. Amen.

Practice makes perfect

To read

Do you not know that those running in a race all take part, but only one receives the prize? Run, therefore, so that you may be the one who obtains it. Athletes wrestle to discipline their bodies, so that they may receive an award that ultimately perishes, but we strive for an imperishable award. In consequence, I do not run aimlessly, nor do I box as though I am pummelling thin air, but I subject my body to punishment to make sure that, having announced the race to others, I am not disqualified from it myself.

1 Corinthians 9:24-27

Ponder

What makes a champion? How is it that some people reach the top of their sport while the majority struggle along in the ranks of the average? Part of the answer, of course, lies in training and part in talent, but probably the most important thing is practice. As the old saying has it, practice makes perfect. In the world of sport, as in almost every other sphere of entertainment, what the spectator sees is the result of countless hours spent toiling away behind the scenes, building up fitness, mastering techniques, refining skills and working on temperament.

So it is with Christian discipleship. We cannot simply sign up and leave the rest to God, nor can we reach a certain point and then ease off. Faith involves determination, and commitment to a cause. It demands a constant programme of prayer, Bible study, reflection and worship; a daily striving to overcome our weaknesses and eliminate our mistakes; a hunger to achieve ever more in the service of Christ. God does not leave us to work alone. He has given the power of the Spirit within us to strengthen, instruct and motivate, but that can only do so much. Unless we play our part we will find ourselves struggling round the first lap wondering why others seem to have progressed so far in their faith, and we will have only ourselves to blame.

Ask yourself

Are you serious about your faith, treating it as a lifetime commitment, or is it more like a casual hobby – something you dip into as the fancy takes you?

Pray

Living God, I talk of commitment, yet so often I am casual about my faith and complacent in discipleship. I neglect your word and fail to make time for prayer or quiet reflection, thus giving myself little opportunity to hear you. Instead of seeking to grow in faith, I assume I have advanced as far as I need to.

Forgive me my feeble vision and lack of dedication. Instil in me a new sense of purpose and a greater resolve to fulfil it, and so help me to achieve the prize to which you have called me in Jesus Christ, for his name's sake. Amen.

Remember

I want to know Christ and the power of his resurrection and what it means to participate in his sufferings through identifying with him in his death; if, through that, I may somehow attain to the resurrection from the dead. Not that I have already achieved this or reached such a goal, but I endeavour continually to make it my own, just as Christ Jesus has made me his own. Friends, I do not claim to have yet secured this for myself; but what I do is this: forgetting what is past and straining forward to what is yet in store, I strive to reach the goal of the prize of God's heavenly call in Christ Jesus.   *Philippians 3:10-14*

Close

Lord Jesus Christ, give me a vision of your kingdom and show me the part you would have me play in bringing it closer. So help me to strive each day towards that goal, for your name's sake. Amen.

The God who sets us free!

Read

If you continue in my word, and truly live as my disciples, then you will know the truth and the truth will set you free.

John 8:31b-32

Ponder

A while back, a story made the news of a man who masqueraded as a doctor for several years, even conducting minor operations, before he was finally exposed as an impostor. Such tales give us a clue to understanding the words of Jesus above. At first sight, we may wonder in what way the truth can set us free. Surely, a key, hacksaw or crowbar would be a far more useful tool in securing freedom. This, though, is to misunderstand the sort of imprisonment Jesus has in mind; the freedom he speaks of is very different to a release from physical incarceration. It concerns the need for an inner liberation, and, in that sense, we all live a lie, just as surely as the charlatan above; not through any deliberate deceit but because we are estranged from our true selves, prevented from being the people we could and should be by our alienation from one another and our deeper alienation from God.

As St Augustine once said of God, 'You stir man to delight in praising you, because you have made us restless for yourself, and our heart is restless until it rests in you.' A book on psychotherapy that I have been working on today illustrates the point well, speaking of the widespread search among people for a sense of identity, an awareness and acceptance of their true selves. In Christ, we find that unconditional acceptance, that sense of purpose and the fulfilment that so often seems to elude us. Through him we discover the freedom we long for to be ourselves and to live life to the full, both now and for all eternity.

Ask yourself

Have you discovered the freedom God wants you to experience? If not, what things still hold you captive?

Pray

Merciful God, you do not love me for what I might become but for what I am, with all my faults and weaknesses. You do not dwell on my failures, but instead invite me to acknowledge them openly before you in order to receive your pardon and then to move on.

Teach me to do just that – to accept your offer for what it is and, rather than wallow in guilt, to rejoice in your mercy. Teach me to let go of the recriminations, doubt and fears that hold me captive and to accept the freedom you have won for me in Christ. So, help me not simply to talk about new life but to live it joyfully, receiving each moment as your gracious gift, in the name of Christ. Amen.

Remember

The law of the Spirit of life in Christ Jesus has freed you from the law of sin and death.   *Romans 8:2*

Close

Lord God, light of the minds that know you, life of the souls that love you, strength of the wills that serve you, help me so to know you that I may truly love you and so to love you that I may fully serve you, whose service is perfect freedom, through Jesus Christ my Lord. Amen.

Gelasian Sacramentary

Believing the best

Read

Love is patient and kind; it is not jealous or puffed up with its own importance, vaunting itself before others, nor does it knowingly cause offence. It does not seek its own well-being, is not easily provoked, and does not think evil or rejoice in wrongdoing but rejoices rather in the truth. It embraces all things, believes all things, hopes all things, endures all things.   *1 Corinthians 13:4-7*

Ponder

Many years ago I was given a copy of a poem, the author of which I have never discovered, on the subject of friendship. It speaks of someone 'who will not run away . . . but will stop and stay', even when they see our darker side, the aspects of our character we prefer to keep hidden: 'a friend who far beyond the feebleness of any vow or tie will touch the secret place where I am really I'. I like that, for it speaks not only of true friendship but also of love. We bandy the word around so much, don't we – in church as much as anywhere – yet we rarely get close to understanding what it means. Another poem, this time by William Shakespeare, encapsulates the qualities at its heart: 'Love is not love which alters when it alteration finds . . . O no! it is an ever-fixed mark'.

Yet neither of these two examples can quite match the timeless words of Paul in his letter to the Corinthians. There is enough here to reflect on for a lifetime and still not exhaust it, but, for me, one thing about love stands out in what Paul says: its willingness to believe the best. We see this exemplified in the ministry of Jesus. Where others saw reason to condemn, he offered forgiveness; where others saw evil, he saw good. He knew the worst of people yet he saw also the best. Isn't that what should mark us out as

Christians? We are not called to be naively idealistic, pretending people are better than they really are, nor expected to ignore their faults and attribute non-existent virtues. What we *are* asked to do, though, is to see the positive as well as the negative, the potential for good as well as the capacity for evil. Do that, and we will begin to understand what it means to love and why love is so special.

Ask yourself
Do you bring out the good in people or the bad? Do you help them to discover their potential or crush their confidence?

Pray
Gracious God, I marvel today at the wonder and extent of your love; the fact that you came in Christ not simply to a few but to all: good and bad, lovely and unlovely, deserving and undeserving. You reached out and accepted me as I am, with all my doubts and fears, faults and weaknesses. You look deep into the hearts of all, and where I see ugliness, you see someone infinitely precious, so valuable that you were willing to endure death on a cross to draw them to yourself.

Forgive me that I find it so hard to accept others in turn, seeing the worst rather than the best, putting down rather than building up. Break through my narrow judgemental attitudes and help me to see the special in people as well as the ordinary, loving others as you love me. Amen.

Remember
Let us mull over how to spur each other to love and good deeds, not overlooking the need to meet together, as some tend to do, but encouraging one another, especially since you see the Day approaching.   *Hebrews 10:24-25*

Close
Lord Jesus Christ, as you have seen the good in me, so help me to see the good in others, for your name's sake. Amen.

The God who never sleeps

Read

I will look up towards the hills – from where will my help come? It comes from the Lord, maker of heaven and earth. He will not allow your foot to stumble, for he who keeps you will not slumber. The one who guards Israel never slumbers and never sleeps. The Lord is your guardian; a shelter at your right hand. The sun will not beat upon you by day, nor the moon by night. The Lord will protect you from all evil; he will watch over you, body and soul. The Lord will guard your going out and your coming in, now and always. *Psalm 121*

Ponder

Are you any good at working into the small hours of the morning? In the process of writing this book, I've found myself doing that a few times recently, but I'm finding it increasingly difficult. Despite my resolve, my eyes begin to droop and head to nod, until reluctantly I have to turn in for the night. Few of us are able to stay awake too many hours before the urge to sleep proves irresistible.

According to the writer of Psalm 121, God is different. He is the one who never slumbers, the one who, by day or by night, is constantly watching over us, guarding us against evil. That does not mean nothing unpleasant can happen to us or that we are safe from danger, for Christians have no more guarantee of that than anyone else. What it does mean is that God will be there when we need him, to give us strength and to surround us with his love. Whatever we may face and however things may seem, he will be with us – at all times, in all places, always!

Ask yourself

Have you lost sight of the fact that God is always keeping watch? Have you mistakenly imagined he has turned his back on you or is no longer interested in your welfare?

Pray

Living God, help me to remember that you are a God who never sleeps; a God on whom I can depend in any and every situation. When I feel lost and alone, teach me that you are there. When I feel overwhelmed by trouble, unsure of my ability to get through, help me to remember that you are close by. When I feel uncertain of the way ahead, fearful of what the future may hold, teach me that you are watching over me. Help me to understand that, whatever I may face, you will guide and guard, protecting me from evil and enfolding me in your everlasting arms, and in that knowledge may I meet every day with quiet trust and glad thanksgiving, in Christ's name. Amen.

Remember

Finding them sleeping on his return, he said to Peter, 'Are you asleep, Simon? Couldn't you even stay awake for one hour?'

Mark 14:37

Close

Gracious God, for the constancy of your love, the faithfulness of your guidance and the certainty of your help, receive my praise, in the name of Christ. Amen.

No comparison

Read

The heavens acknowledge your mighty deeds, O Lord; and the congregation of the holy ones proclaims your constancy. For who on high can compare to the Lord? Who among the heavenly host is like the Lord, a God revered in the assembly of the holy ones, great and awesome above all those around him?

Psalm 89:5-7

Ponder

Can you remember being taught in your schooldays about metaphors and similes? You remember: a simile is a comparison using the word 'like' or 'as', whereas a metaphor is a comparison that treats the thing being spoken of as if it is that which it resembles. As a writer, I'm always on the lookout for an effective comparison since, well used, they can bring a piece of writing to life. They are not, however, always easy to find, and an inappropriate comparison can have the opposite effect, destroying a carefully created atmosphere through appearing forced and artificial, or even coming across as faintly ludicrous.

When it comes to God, comparisons are not just difficult but impossible, for every metaphor or simile we may use can, at best, point to a fraction of the truth, each concealing as much as it reveals. However many words we may pile up to speak of his power, love, grace or goodness, they will always be inadequate; the reality invariably goes far beyond them all put together. Never forget that. However great you consider God to be, however lofty a picture of him you may have, he is infinitely greater than you can ever begin to imagine – truly beyond comparison!

Ask yourself

Do you still have a sense of the sovereignty of God that

defies human expression, or have you grown casual and complacent in his presence?

Pray

Almighty and most wonderful God, unsearchable and inexhaustible, greater than I can ever imagine, higher than my highest thoughts, enthroned in glory and splendour, I offer again my worship, recognising that your ways are not my ways, nor your thoughts my thoughts.

Forgive me for forgetting that sometimes, imagining that I know all there is to know about you. Forgive me my narrow vision and closed mind; the way I have tied you down to my own understanding, closing my heart to anything that challenges my restricted horizons, and so losing sight of your greatness. Remind me that you have always more to say, more to reveal and more to do. Open my eyes, my mind and my heart to who and what you are, and so fill me with awe and wonder, joy and thanksgiving, praise and worship, now and for evermore. Amen.

Remember

No one among the gods is like you, O Lord, nor are any deeds like yours. All people that you have made will come and bow in homage before you, O Lord, and give glory to your name, for you are great and do breathtaking things. You alone are God.   *Psalm 86:8-10*

Close

Almighty God, I acknowledge again that yours is the hand that created the universe, the power that shapes the course of history, the love that moves through all things and the grace that opens up the way to life, yet having said all that I have barely begun to exhaust the riches of your greatness. Receive my praise, and open my heart to know you better each day, until that day when I meet you face to face and rejoice in the wonder of your presence, through the grace of Christ. Amen.

We'll meet again

Read

Now Christ has been raised from the dead, and become the first fruits for those who have fallen asleep. For, just as death came through one man, so also the resurrection of the dead comes through one man. As in Adam all die, so also in Christ will all be brought back to life. Listen and I will tell you a mystery. We will not all sleep for ever, but at the last trumpet we will all be changed, in a moment, in the twinkling of an eye, for a trumpet will sound and the dead will be raised to immortal life, and we shall be changed!

1 Corinthians 15:20-22, 51-52

Ponder

During the dark years of the Second World War there was a song that was to become a firm favourite among troops and civilians alike, bringing solace, encouragement and inspiration to those separated from friends and loved ones. That song, of course, sung by the forces sweetheart Vera Lynn, was 'We'll meet again'. Tragically, many never did meet again, thousands losing their lives in the far-flung fields of battle. That conflict, like the one that had preceded it such a short time before, starkly brought home the reality of death to innumerable families, few untouched by the loss of a son, husband, brother or other relation.

Today, by contrast, we can push our mortality under the carpet; death, as has often been observed, is the great social taboo of our time. So how do *we* view it? Is it something to dread, a step into a terrifying unknown? Is it a cause for despair; the last enemy that makes a mockery of all our hopes and striving? It is for many, but it shouldn't be, for the message of the gospel is that death has been defeated; Christ has won new life for all through the cross and the empty tomb. Naturally, the prospect of dying remains unwelcome, whether it be our own death or that of our loved ones, for it still entails the heartbreak of separation and ensuing sense of isolation for those who are bereaved. Words can never express the pain and inner turmoil that losing someone close to us involves. Yet, we believe it is not the end of the story but rather the start of a new chapter; a chapter in which, one day, we'll meet again.

Ask yourself

Have you grasped the full wonder of the victory Christ has won over death?

Pray

Loving God, I praise you that in Jesus you experienced not just life but also death – that you endured the darkness of Gethsemane, the agony of the cross and the finality of the tomb, triumphing over everything that keeps us from you. I thank you that where the world saw only defeat, you brought victory, nothing able to stand against your sovereign purpose. May that knowledge bring hope to all for whom life is overshadowed by death; a new perspective bringing light and hope into the pain and sorrow of such moments. Grant the assurance that death is not the end but a new beginning; a stepping stone into your glorious kingdom in which death shall be no more and where all will rejoice in the wonder of your love, for evermore. Amen.

Remember

Death has been swallowed up by victory. Where, death, is your victory? Where, death, is your sting?

1 Corinthians 15:54b-55

Close

Living God, teach me to look beyond the apparent finality of death to the new life you hold for all your people, and help me to rest secure in the knowledge that nothing can finally separate me or those I love from your sovereign purpose in Jesus Christ my Lord. Amen.

The turn of the tide

Read

God, rescue me, for the waters have risen to my neck. I sink in a deep swamp, where I can find no footing; I have slipped into deep waters, and the flood engulfs me. Lord, I bring you my prayer. In your own time, O God, and out of the greatness of your unfailing love, answer me. Faithfully hear me, once more, and rescue me from sinking in the swamp; deliver me from my adversaries and from the deep waters. Do not let the flood overwhelm me, or the deep swallow me, or the pit close up over my head.   *Psalm 69:1-2, 13-15*

Ponder

The waves were pounding in and smashing against the sea wall, cascading high into the air before splashing down in a sea of spray. It was hard to believe that the defences could take it much longer, such was the remorseless ferocity of the assault, yet still the water rose ever higher, threatening to engulf the whole stretch of coastline. We returned next morning, wondering what we were going to see, but the scene could hardly have been more different. The waves were diminutive now, breaking gently on to an open stretch of sand, and the sea beyond was like a millpond, a more tranquil picture hard to imagine. The tide had turned!

How often have we felt caught up in a storm, wave after wave beating against us and threatening to sweep us away? Like the psalmist, we feel all at sea, looking back wistfully to better days and wondering why God doesn't seem to help us. Yet, just as certainly as high tide follows low and low high, so it will be for us too. After the storm, there will come peace; after turmoil, quietness; after sorrow, joy. We may not see it at the time, there seeming no prospect of respite or any sign of change, but God will always be there with us, holding our head above the water until, in the fullness of his time, the tide will turn and the waters recede.

Ask yourself

Do you feel overwhelmed by trials and troubles? Have you the faith to trust in God, confident that the tide will turn?

Pray

Sovereign God, it is easy to trust you when life is good, but when circumstances change then faith is suddenly put to the test. When one problem, one anxiety, one sorrow follows another, I feel overwhelmed, swimming against a current that sweeps me deeper and deeper into difficulty.

Teach me that however fierce the storm, it can never finally swamp me, for you will be there to rescue me in my time of need. Teach me to hold firmly to you knowing that you will keep hold of me until the storm is past and calm returns. In Jesus' name I pray. Amen.

Remember

He stretched down from on high and took hold of me, lifting me out of the seething waters. If the Lord had not been on our side . . . then the flood would have swept us away, the torrent would have overwhelmed us and the raging waters gone over our heads.   *Psalm 18:16; 124:1a, 4-5*

Close

Lord Jesus Christ, when the waters rage and the waves threaten to engulf me, support, strengthen and keep me safe, until the tide turns and the sun shines once more. Amen.

The road to nowhere

Read

Utterly pointless, says the Teacher, a waste of time. Everything is utterly futile. What do people gain from all the toil at which they toil under the sun? A generation goes, and a generation comes, but the earth remains for ever. The sun rises and the sun goes down, and hurries to the place where it rises. The wind blows to the south, and goes round to the north; round and round it circuits before it finally returns.

Ecclesiastes 1:2-6

Ponder

Occasionally in life we have a clear sense of purpose, a goal that we feel able to strive towards with single-minded determination. Often, though, it is very different. Like the Teacher in the book of Ecclesiastes, we feel we are going round and round in circles, treading the same old ground, trapped on a road to nowhere. Somehow, we cannot seem to find the fulfilment we anticipated, even when we succeed in that goal of ours. We find ourselves in a rut from which there seems to be no escape, overwhelmed by a sense of helplessness and futility in the face of the constant grind to help pay the bills, meet the mortgage and so on.

If that's how you feel, then the book of Ecclesiastes may come as a breath of fresh air. These are not the sort of words we usually associate with scripture – indeed, we might well wonder how they got into the Bible at all – but get in they did and thank God for it. The stark realities that we prefer to brush aside are exposed here, forcing us to reflect on the deeper meaning of life. For the Teacher that finally brings him back to God – the one who is before all, behind all and beyond all. The Christian is able to take things one stage further, for in Christ we have been given a new sense of purpose: a kingdom that we daily work towards in faith, a goal of growing closer to Christ, the promise of eternal life. Whether it's the words of the Apostle Paul about pressing on towards the goal; of Hebrews concerning the city of God; or of Jesus about the coming of the kingdom of heaven – each time the message is the same. We are not on the road to nowhere but on a journey that leads us to the ultimate destination – into the very presence of God!

Ask yourself

Have you lost your sense of direction in life? Do you feel as though you're going round in circles? Is it time to recommit yourself afresh to the journey of faith?

Pray

Gracious God, as the years have passed, so my energy and enthusiasm for life have passed with them. Though some of my goals have been realised, many have not and probably never will be, and the idealism of my youth has slowly been replaced by a world-weary cynicism. Instead of eagerly anticipating the future, I am content now simply to get by, living from one day to the next. Yet, in Christ, you have given a hope that never fades and a purpose that endures for ever, opening up a life of infinite possibilities and constant new beginnings.

Open my eyes to that wonderful truth, and so, whatever hopes may be dashed or goals thwarted, may I continue always to travel in faith, looking forward to that day when your kingdom shall come and your will be done, in the name of Christ. Amen.

Remember

Thomas said, 'Lord, we do not know where you are going, so how can we know the way?' Jesus answered him, 'I am the way, the truth and the life.'   *John 14:5-6a*

Close

Lord Jesus Christ, may the promise of your kingdom and your call to share in building it continue to inspire me, today and every day. Amen.

Living water

Read

On the final day at the climax of the Feast, Jesus stood and proclaimed for all to hear, 'If any of you are thirsty come to me and drink. As the scripture has said, "Streams of living water will flow from the heart of whoever believes in me."'

John 7:37-38

Ponder

Given recent disappointing summers, it's hard to believe that a few years back we were experiencing periods of drought and warnings that our ponds, rivers and springs may dry up, perhaps for ever. I can still, however, remember times when I looked out on my parched garden and actually longed for it to rain! Such moments in this usually sodden country of ours are rare, but in Israel, as elsewhere in the Middle East, they are all too common, water a precious and treasured resource. For those in such places, its scarcity is not just an inconvenience but also a threat to life itself, and hence every spring, oasis or well is accorded almost sacred status.

This is the context in which Jesus promised a stream of living water to anyone who is thirsty, a claim made all the more remarkable by the occasion he chose to make his pronouncement. It was the Feast of Tabernacles – a day on which the Jews remembered God's provision of water from a rock during Israel's time in the wilderness – and the highlight of events was a ceremonial pouring out of water as a symbol of that time when God had turned despair to hope, doubt to faith, and almost certain death to a celebration of life. What Jesus promised now was all this and more besides: a quality of life beyond anything they had dreamed possible; an inner fulfilment and peace, coupled with a new sense of purpose, that would offer life a new dimension in every sense. It is a promise that holds as much today as ever – in a world thirsty for meaning, Jesus tells us to come and never thirst again.

Ask yourself

Do you still thirst for a sense of meaning in your life? Have you received the gift Jesus offers, or do you look to other things for fulfilment?

Pray

Lord Jesus Christ, I have no need to be thirsty, for I have tasted the water you offer and experienced first-hand its power to satisfy, yet sometimes I turn my back on the life-giving spring you offer. I seek fulfilment elsewhere – in money, material possessions, work, friendships – forgetting that none of these, however much pleasure they may bring, can meet my deepest needs.

Help me to enjoy the blessings you have given, the innumerable good things in life, but help me also to keep a proper sense of perspective, recognising that you are the one who gives meaning to all. So may your living water well up within me and overflow in joyful praise, loving service and spontaneous witness, to the glory of your name. Amen.

Remember

Never again will they hunger or thirst, neither will the sun or any scorching heat beat on them, for the Lamb at the centre of the throne will be their shepherd, and he will guide them to springs of living water, and God will wipe away every tear from their eyes.   *Revelation 7:16-17*

Close

Living God, as you have promised that water will gush forth in the wilderness and streams bubble up in the desert, so may the living water of Christ flow in me and through me, this day and always. Amen.

The kingdom within

Read

Asked by the Pharisees concerning the coming of the kingdom of God, he replied: 'The signs of God's kingdom cannot be observed, nor will anyone say, "Look here!" or "Look there!" – for the kingdom of God is within you.'

Luke 17:20-21

Ponder

I remember as a child reading the tale of a little boy (thankfully fictitious) with a tendency to daydream. Instead of looking where he was going, this unfortunate lad was forever gazing absent-mindedly into space, his thoughts elsewhere, the result being a series of ever-greater catastrophes. There is danger that we as Christians can make a mistake not unlike that; namely of being too heavenly-minded to be of any earthly use. We've all met Christians who seem so pious that they come across as divorced from the real world, and we've probably all heard sermons that cry out for some down-to-earth application that can focus the point being made in terms of daily experience rather than remain suspended in the rarefied atmosphere of spiritual niceties. Unless faith is about everyday life and able to make a difference there, then it isn't much use to anyone.

That, to me at least, is the point Jesus was making to the Pharisees when they questioned him about the kingdom of God. Yes, its fulfilment is in the future, at some date that we cannot and do not need to know, but it is also here and now, having begun the moment Jesus entered the world in the stable of Bethlehem. The implications of that truth are immense. We cannot wash our hands of this world in the hope of another kingdom to come; neither can we sit back and leave everything to God. We all have a role in his purpose, a part to play in helping to bring it to fulfilment.

Unless we have a sense of his kingdom already within us, and unless we do what we can to bring that kingdom closer, then we may look forward to its final establishment in vain, for we will not recognise it when it comes.

Ask yourself
Do you see the kingdom of God as something that will come in the distant future or as already having begun here on earth? What are you doing to help make that kingdom more real?

Pray
Loving God, there are some things in life I look so hard for that I cannot see them even when they are right under my very nose. Your kingdom is like that. I look forward to the time when Christ shall return and I repeat the words of the prayer he taught us, 'Your kingdom come', but I forget that he also proclaimed your kingdom is already here.

Loving God, teach me what that means. Help me to understand that though the kingdom has been initiated through him, it must continue through me and those like me – through the service I offer and the life I live in his name. Save me from being so concerned with what will be that I lose touch with what is, for his name's sake. Amen.

Remember
He said to them, 'When you pray, use words like these: "Our Father in heaven, to you be praise and honour. May your kingdom come and your will be done, here on earth as it is in heaven."'   *Matthew 6:9-10*

Close
Lord Jesus Christ, instead of looking for your kingdom, may I help to build it, through your grace. Amen.

Standing at the door

Read

Look, I stand at the door and knock. I will go in and eat with whoever hears my voice and opens the door, and they will eat with me.   *Revelation 3:20*

Ponder

I like to think that the pastoral visits I made during my time in the ministry were generally welcomed but, on one occasion at least, my presence was definitely superfluous to requirements. I was calling to see someone who, though a member, had drifted to the fringe of church life and whose husband was ambivalent, if not hostile, to all things Christian. My ring at the doorbell met with no response so, having popped a calling card in the door, I was making my way back down the garden path when I happened to glance back. There, looking furtively out the window was the husband in question, checking to make sure the coast was clear. For a second our eyes met before, with an expression of utter dismay, he dived in desperation behind the settee, determined to avoid me at all costs. Realising I was not wanted I turned and walked nonchalantly away, pretending I'd spotted nothing untoward.

What reaction, I wonder, does Jesus receive when he stands at the door of our lives? Do we fling the door open wide and welcome him in, or is our response more guarded? Do we open it a little way but keep the security latch fixed, in case he asks more of us than we want to give? Do we open the door briefly, only to show him out again when commitment doesn't suit us? Or do we sometimes even keep it firmly closed, pretending we're not in when we'd rather not be disturbed? It's our choice, for Jesus will never force his presence upon us if it is not wanted, but equally he will never give up knocking until the door is opened.

More patient than any saint, more persistent than any salesman, more ardent than any suitor, he will always be there seeking entry, so that he can share our life and, more important, so that we can share his. Is it time you let him?

Ask yourself
Have you assumed that once you open the door to Jesus it is open for ever? Does your experience suggest otherwise? Is there some area of your life he is still seeking access to?

Pray
Lord Jesus Christ, forgive me the times I have kept you out of my life, preferring to do my own thing in my own way and believing I have no need of your help. Forgive the times I have kept you standing on the doorstep, not wanting to face your challenge or to have my comfortable lifestyle questioned. Forgive the times I have welcomed you for a moment only to show you the door later, faith proving incompatible or hard to reconcile with certain aspects of my life.

Help me open the door of my heart without reserve and to keep it open, come what may. Come now and make your home in me so that I may dwell in you always and rejoice in your constant presence and unfailing love. Amen.

Remember
I tell you in truth that whoever does not enter the sheepfold through the door but gains entry another way is a thief and a robber, but the one who enters by the door is the shepherd of the sheep.   *John 10:1-2*

Close
Lord Jesus Christ, when you knock at the door and I fail to let you in, knock harder, until I open. Amen.

A firm foundation

Read

Everyone who hears my words and acts on them will be like a wise person who built his house on rock. The rain fell, the floods came, and the gales blasted and battered against that house, but it did not collapse, because its foundations were on rock. On the other hand, everyone who hears my words and fails to act on them will be like a fool who built his house on sand. The rain fell, and the floods came, and the winds blasted and battered against that house, and it collapsed – and what a collapse it was!   *Matthew 7:24-27*

Ponder

A while back, I watched a series of television programmes called *Heartbreak Homes*. Among the properties featured were a number along the Norfolk coast; homes that, on paper, looked idyllic yet that, in reality, were under sentence, the sea inexorably eating its way into the cliffs towards them. It isn't just a matter of a few inches every decade or so, but rather of several feet every few months, so much so that numerous houses have toppled over the edge within the last few years. The former occupants were understandably distraught, having had little inkling of the rate of erosion when they had first moved in. Global warming, coupled with new sea defences further up the coast, had exacerbated what previously had been considered an essentially long-term problem. The foundations had looked secure enough but they had been ruthlessly exposed.

Reading the familiar parable of Jesus concerning the wise and foolish builders, we may feel it goes without question that we are those who have built on rock, but the above experiences counsel caution. Remember that Jesus didn't say, 'Everyone who hears my words will be like a wise person who built his house on rock', but, 'Everyone who hears my words *and acts on them'*. The two are very different. It's not hearing the words of Jesus that matters, not even accepting they are true; it's whether they make a difference to who we are, whether they change the way we live. Are we still so sure we've built our house on rock?

Ask yourself

Can you truthfully say that you have heard the words of Jesus *and acted upon them*?

Pray

Lord Jesus Christ, I like to think I have founded my life firmly upon you, but the reality may not be as I imagine. Though I declare my faith and profess your name, though I talk of commitment and speak of service, there is a danger of this being all show and no substance, a matter of words rather than deeds. I fail to listen to what you would tell me, I am slow to reflect on what discipleship really means, and I offer you only a part of my life, keeping the rest back for fear of what you might ask of me. Like the foolish builder, I hear your words but do not act upon them, my good intentions never translated into action.

Forgive me, despite your guidance, for building my life on sand rather than rock. Open my ears, my mind and my heart, so that I may not only hear what you would say to me but also respond with body, mind and soul, to the glory of your name. Amen.

Remember

By the grace God has given to me, I laid a foundation like a skilled master builder, and someone else is building on it. Every builder must carefully decide how to build on it, for no one can lay any foundation other than that already laid, which is Jesus Christ.   *1 Corinthians 3:10-11*

Close

Lord Jesus Christ, speak again and help me to listen, so that your words may inspire me to deeds, for your name's sake. Amen.

Power for living

Read

I pray that your eyes may be inwardly opened so that you may understand the hope to which he has called you, the wonderfully rich inheritance of the saints and his matchless power for us who believe. That power is like the astonishing strength he demonstrated when he raised Christ from the dead and exalted him to his right hand in the heavens, far above all rule and authority, power and dominion, and any title that can be given him, not only in this current age but also in the age to come.   *Ephesians 1:18-21*

Ponder

It was my big moment: my first official public engagement as an author, and the opportunity to create a good impression. The journey to get there had been a long one, necessitating an early start; so early, in fact, that I had taken the precaution of having a shave the night before, knowing time would be short the next day. My plan was to spruce myself up with my electric shaver when I arrived in order to look as presentable as possible. It didn't work that way: the shaver gave a cursory buzz and then subsided into silence. Fool that I was, I'd forgotten to charge the batteries!

So often, we find ourselves short on power when we most need it. In moments of crisis or opportunity, challenge or difficulty, we look for those extra reserves only to find there's nothing else to draw on. Whoever we are, however strong a character we may be, we all have our limitations. That, though, is to reckon without Jesus and to forget his promise of power for living, the power that the Apostle Paul speaks of so wonderfully in his letter to the Ephesians. This is not power as the world understands it, demonstrated in brute force or show of strength, but is seen rather in weakness: through humility, service and self-sacrifice. It is the power of love, the gift of Christ through his Spirit, able to change lives as nothing else can begin to and to release untold potential in each one of us. With that strength within us we will find, whatever the challenge before us, we have more than sufficient reserves to meet it.

Ask yourself

Do you attempt to meet life in your own power or through the power that God has promised?

Pray

Living God, I imagine sometimes that my life is in my own hands, mine to shape as I will. I fondly believe myself able to meet the rough with the smooth, to withstand adversity and bounce back after disappointments. On occasions it's true, but equally there are times when it's patently false, experience painfully teaching me how fragile is my hold on happiness and how limited my resources to face life's demands.

Teach me to remember that true power lies in you – not as the world understands it in any show of strength but in an unshakeable confidence, an inner peace and a living faith through which your Spirit is able to work and move beyond all expectations. Open my heart to that mighty and mysterious presence, and so may I discover power for living, in Jesus' name. Amen.

Remember

God has not given us a spirit of fear but of power, love and self-control.   *2 Timothy 1:7*

Close

Lord Jesus Christ, grant by your grace that the power of the Spirit may flow through me to the glory of your name. Amen.

A treasure beyond price

Read

Jesus said again, 'Truthfully, I tell you that I am the gate for the sheep. Whoever enters by me will be saved, and will come in and go out and find pasture. The thief comes to steal, kill and destroy but I have come that you may have life and live it to the full.'

John 10:7, 9-10

Ponder

Money we are told, can't buy us happiness. Do you believe that? Probably most of us will nod our heads sagely as if to say, 'How true!' but when it comes to it, few of us would turn our backs on a fortune, or even a small bonus, were we to be offered it – I know I wouldn't.

Money can, of course, buy us many things that we find it hard sometimes not to covet, and if it cannot buy happiness, it can certainly keep at bay some things that may prevent us from being happy. Yet the fact remains that the most important things in life are beyond price: things like friendship, health, self-esteem, motivation, peace of mind and fulfilment. Some of these, indeed, may be lost rather than gained through financial riches.

One kind of riches however, *can* offer happiness, even though it has nothing to do with earthly wealth. It is God's gift of new life in Christ; a gift not restricted to the few, nor granted through a lottery, but open to all, simply waiting for us to claim it. The more we know and love him, the more we will recognise him as our truest friend, and so discover the wholeness, sense of worth and purpose, rest for our souls and inner contentment that only he can bring. Here is treasure indeed; the one kind of riches that guarantees lasting happiness, now and for all eternity.

Ask yourself

To whom or what do you look for happiness? What do you see as true fulfilment?

Pray

Loving God, thank you for your great gift of life in all its fullness – everything you have given to enjoy, celebrate and live for. Thank you for the innumerable blessings you shower upon me every day: love to share, beauty to enthral, health to enjoy, food to eat and so much more – a world to excite, fascinate and savour. Above all, thank you for the life you have given me in Christ; a life that you want me and all people to enjoy not just now but for all eternity.

Teach me to celebrate your love in all its richness, to rejoice in your gifts in all their abundance and to celebrate life in all its fullness, to the glory of your name. Amen.

Remember

For God so loved the world, that he gave his only begotten Son, that whosoever believeth in him should not perish, but have everlasting life.   *John 3:16 (Authorised Version)*

Close

Living God, for your love beyond price and your goodness beyond measure, receive my praise, in the name of Christ. Amen.

Just as I am

Read

As he reclined in the house, many tax-collectors and sinners came and reclined with him at table. Seeing this, the Pharisees challenged his disciples, 'Why does your teacher eat with tax-collectors and sinners?' Hearing this, Jesus responded, 'It is not the healthy who need a physician but those who are sick. Leave us alone and mark this, "I desire mercy rather than sacrifice, for I came not to call the righteous but sinners."'

Matthew 9:10-13

Ponder

Some years ago there was a powerful song in the charts sung by Gloria Gaynor, titled: 'I am what I am'. The song was a bold affirmation of self in the face of the many pressures from individuals and society as a whole to pretend to be something that we're not. We all feel the need to put on a good face, be socially acceptable, conform to the latest fashion, measure up to what others consider attractive, and so on. The modern industry in liposuction, breast enlargement, nose jobs and other kinds of cosmetic surgery is a case in point, and in much more subtle psychological ways we bow to public opinion in our craving for acceptance.

In similar fashion, many people feel there is no way that God can possibly accept them as they are. They imagine that they must somehow prove themselves first, live lives that are whiter than white and cleaner than clean. They couldn't be further from the truth, for the message of the gospel is that God accepts us as we are, with all our faults and failings, guilty secrets and ugly habits, fragile faith and hesitant commitment. God's love is not dependent on anything we do but is shown out of sheer grace, defying all human reason. If we wait until we are perfect before we feel he can possibly accept us, then we will wait for ever.

The astonishing, wonderful truth is that we can come to him now, just as we are, and find him waiting to welcome us with open arms.

Ask yourself
Do you still, deep down, feel that you must earn God's forgiveness? Do you impose your own measures of acceptability and unacceptability?

Pray
Lord Jesus Christ, like so many others I yield to pressures to conform in my yearning for acceptance. I wear a socially acceptable mask, say the right words and do what's expected of me rather than risk rejection, even when it means pretending to be what I'm not. I am so used to acceptance being conditional that I find it hard not to approach you in the same way, feeling that I must measure up to some yardstick of what is pleasing to you.

Teach me that your love is not like that. Help me to recognise that even when I fail you, your love is not withdrawn. May the knowledge that you accept me as I am help me each day to become more fully the person I can be, through your saving grace. Amen.

Remember
God's love is shown to us in this, that Christ died on our behalf while we were yet sinners.   *Romans 5:8*

Close
Gracious God, you know what I have been, you know what I want to be, but above all you value what I am. May that great truth teach me to value myself and others, and above all to value you and your redeeming love in Christ. Amen.

A master plan?

Read

Human beings may plan their way, but it is the Lord who will guide their steps. The human mind may formulate many ingenious plans, but the Lord's purpose will always triumph. The Lord orders all our steps; how then can mere human beings make sense of the path we travel?

Proverbs 16:9; 19:21; 20:24

Ponder

Over the last year, by courtesy of the Internet, I have resumed a love affair with the game of chess that first began when I was in my mid-teens at school. At a prearranged time each week I log on to the appropriate website, my brother in Birmingham doing the same, and we enjoy a lightning battle in cyberspace. Usually, I come off best in those encounters, but on the rare occasions I test my wits against my 'Chessmaster' computer program, it's a different story. Suddenly, I find myself out of my depth. Whatever move I make, the computer – or should I say the programmer behind it? – comes up with a devastating riposte.

In some ways, there are parallels here with life. We do our best to plan for the future, carefully considering the various options open to us, but there are other forces in play that are beyond our control. Some would push the analogy further and suggest that everything is ultimately part of God's master plan, nothing happening that does not fit in with his will. Are they right? Personally, I cannot go along with such a view, for where does it leave free will, and how can we square it with the evil and suffering we so often witness around us? I do not believe God has every move planned any more than a chess player knows exactly how a game will unfold. At any moment, there are always an infinite number of possibilities open to us, and God will not force our hand as to which we choose. The wonder is – and this I firmly believe – that, whatever we do, he is able to adapt to it in such a way that his purpose – not just for us but also for all creation – cannot be thwarted. Whatever may frustrate or fight against his will, his purpose will finally emerge victorious. Thanks be to God!

Ask yourself
What do you understand to be God's purpose? In what way does your life affirm or deny this?

Pray
Living God, I thank you that you are always at work, striving to establish your kingdom and to enfold all things in your love. I praise you for the way you work in my life – guiding, teaching, enabling, equipping – constantly looking to draw me closer to yourself. But I thank you also that you have given me free will; the ability to make my own decisions and respond knowingly to your love. Forgive me when I abuse that freedom, flouting your commandments and deliberately going against the purpose that you have revealed in Christ. Forgive me when the decisions I take contradict my faith and deny the gospel.

Take my life, with all the mistakes I have made and continue to make, and work within and through me towards the fulfilment of your will, to the glory of your name. Amen.

Remember
I know, O Lord, that humans cannot control the future nor determine the course their life will take.   *Jeremiah 10:23*

Close
Living God, because of or despite me, for or against me, with my help or my hindrance, your will be done in my life and all things, by the grace of Christ. Amen.

Breaking down the barriers

Read

In Jesus Christ you who were once distanced have been brought close by his blood. For he is our peace, having made two groups into one by destroying through his flesh the barrier between us – that is, the dividing wall of hostility. He has done away with the law with its commands and regulations, in order to create in himself one new humanity out of two, thus making peace, reconciling both groups to God in one body through the cross and putting hostility to death through it. He came and preached peace to those who were distant and those nearby, for through him we both have access to the Father by the one Spirit.

Ephesians 2:13-18

Ponder

10 November 1989 was a truly historic day – a day that saw the first steps in the demolition of the Berlin Wall. Few of us who watched the events of that night unfolding on television ever thought we'd live to see that moment, so entrenched had positions become, so deep the suspicion between East and West. For years the world had lived in fear of that divide spilling over into world conflict, but suddenly everything changed overnight. Of course, bricks and mortar can be destroyed relatively easily; ingrained attitudes of intolerance, hatred and prejudice take much longer. So it was in the time of the Apostle Paul, only this time the tension was between Jew and Gentile, and the resulting divisions threatened to drive a deep wedge into the early Church.

For Paul, all such divisions have their root in one thing: our separation from God – a barrier that no amount of effort on our part can ever hope to overcome. Yet, what *we* can never do, Paul tells us, God has done for us in Christ; everything that keeps us estranged from him done away with, nailed with Jesus on to the cross. The one who broke down barriers throughout his life – welcoming the outcasts, mixing with 'sinners', overthrowing social convention – has broken down the greatest barrier of them all. If he has done that, isn't it time we broke down the walls that still divide us from one another – in the Church, in society and in our own relationships?

Ask yourself
What things do you still allow to separate you from God? What things create divisions in your daily relationships?

Pray
Sovereign God, there is so much in my life that separates me from you and others – my selfishness, pride, greed and envy; my thoughtless actions, foolish words and selfish nature; my narrowness of outlook and built-in preconceptions – so much that runs contrary to your will and denies your love.

I thank you that, through Jesus, you have broken down the barriers that divide person from person and humanity from you. Help me and all your people to live in such a way that we reflect that truth in all we are and do. Stir the hearts of all, so that the day may come when the worth of everyone will be recognised, their rights observed, their dignity respected and their good pursued. In Christ's name I ask it. Amen.

Remember
There cannot now be either Jew or Greek, slave or free, male or female, for you are all one in Christ.

Galatians 3:28

Close
Lord Jesus Christ, reach out in love to this foolish, faithless world and, by your grace, tend our wounds. Come again to all who are hurting and all who are hating, and overcome the things that still keep us apart, for your name's sake. Amen.

The God who seeks us out

Read

What woman having ten silver coins, if she loses one of them, does not light a lamp, sweep the house, and search carefully until she finds it? When she has found it, she calls together her friends and neighbours, saying, 'Rejoice with me, for I have found the coin that I had lost.' Just so, I tell you, there is joy in the presence of the angels of God over one sinner who repents.

Luke 15:8-10

Ponder

There was a time when I used to play the occasional game of golf, but I haven't played now for several years. The fact is that I simply couldn't afford to. No, it wasn't the green fees that I found prohibitive but the cost of replacing lost balls. You see, so abysmal was I that my shots invariably ended up in the rough, the water or even out of bounds. At first, I used to hunt assiduously for the errant ball, waving players past as I continued my search, but eventually, since I was invariably way over par, I scarcely bothered to look at all – just a cursory glance into the undergrowth before taking out another ball and moving on.

Few of us are willing to look for anything for too long, even if something is valuable to us. The exception, of course, is if a child or loved one should go missing. Then we would go on searching for as long as it takes. That is how God feels about us. As Jesus so tellingly put it in the parable of the lost coin, he is like the woman who searches carefully *until she finds it*. When we go astray, God doesn't just look for a moment before losing interest; he goes on looking for as long as it takes, never resting until he finds us. Whoever we are, whatever we may have done, we matter to him, enough for him never to abandon his search; enough even to rescue and redeem us through the offering of his Son.

Ask yourself

Do you feel, having gone astray, that there is no way back? Do you set limits to God's patience or love?

Pray

Lord Jesus Christ, it is wonderful enough that you bother to look for me at all; more wonderful still that you keep on looking day after day, year after year, until you have found me. No matter what I do or how often I fail, still I matter to you, enough for you never to rest until I am restored to your side.

Teach me to recognise the astonishing breadth of your love, and to respond with gratitude in faithful service and joyful praise, to your glory. Amen.

Remember

The Son of man came to seek and save that which was lost.
Luke 19:10

Close

Gracious God, I rejoice in the knowledge that though I so easily give up on you, you will never give up on me. For that great truth, I praise you, in the name of Christ. Amen.

Living with disappointment

Read

Hope unfulfilled makes the heart sick.   *Proverbs 13:12a*

Ponder

There is an old saying, 'It is better to have loved and lost than never to have loved at all'. No doubt that's true, but to experience joy and then to lose it, or to have high hopes only to see them dashed, can be a bitterly painful experience. Disappointment is a crushing emotion, for a time blotting out all else. Indeed, there can come a point when any ability to believe in the future is extinguished altogether, so powerful is the fear of being hurt once again.

As Christians, we are not immune from such experiences, but we have one we can turn to who will never disappoint us, come what may. Through Christ, we discover meaning and purpose, a hope worth committing our lives to and a joy that will surpass all our expectations. More than that, we know that he will give us strength to live with life's disappointments and to bounce back from them, the darkest and bleakest of moments transformed into a gateway to new beginnings.

Ask yourself

On what do you found your hopes? Can you put your trust in this, or are you ultimately setting yourself up for disappointment?

Pray

Loving God, so many things in life have promised much but delivered little. I have set myself targets but failed to hit them. I have achieved goals only to find they did not yield the satisfaction I expected. I have been let down by others and, worse still, I have let myself down on more occasions than I care to remember. So often, hope ends in disappointment, exposed as wishful thinking, misguided ambition or sheer naivety.

Teach me, before all else to trust in you, confident that your love will never fail or disappoint. Teach me to base my life on your living word that promises so much yet delivers even more than I can ever ask or imagine. In Christ's name. Amen.

Remember

We give glory in our troubles, knowing that troubles inculcate fortitude, and fortitude breeds character, and character produces hope, and hope does not disappoint us, because the love of God has been poured into our hearts through the Holy Spirit that has been given to us.   *Romans 5:3-5*

Close

Living God, when life fails to measure up to my expectations, remind me of the hope I have in Christ, through which I can expect fulfilment beyond measure, by his grace. Amen.

An absolute certainty

Read

I am not ashamed to suffer for his cause, for I know the one I have believed in, and I am certain that he is able to guard that which I have entrusted to him, until that day. The foundation laid by God stands sure, carrying this guarantee: 'The Lord knows those who are his'.

2 Timothy 1:12; 2:19a

Ponder

When I first decided to turn to writing and freelance editing full time, my wife was understandably concerned. We'd been used to paid employment with a guaranteed wage each month, but suddenly all that was gone. Instead, once one contract was finished, I had to wait in hope for the next phone call that would signal more work was on its way. As for my books, there was no way of knowing whether these would be successful or otherwise, though we both realised that the chances of making even half a living out of Christian writing were remote. It was a difficult decision, then, and one that we both found hard to get used to.

But the fact is that for all of us, to some extent, life is uncertain. None of us knows what the next day will hold, and nothing is guaranteed, however definite it may seem. There is, though, one thing we can depend on come what may, and that is the love of God in Christ. Whoever we are, whatever we may face, whenever it may be, we know that he will be with us to equip and strengthen, and to lead us ultimately into his eternal kingdom. All else may change but his promise will not – that alone is certain!

Ask yourself

What things concerning the future do you feel most uncertain about? Do you feel sure of your ultimate destiny?

Pray

Gracious God, I thank you that you are here by my side, wanting to meet me, greet me and teach me. I thank you for being with me everywhere – at every moment, every place and every occasion – watching over me as a father watches over his child. Day by day, you stay close – recognised or unrecognised, remembered or forgotten, obeyed or disobeyed, acknowledged or taken for granted. Though my response to you is varied and my commitment wavering, you are always the same: ever-faithful, all-loving, always true.

I have no way of knowing what the future may hold, whether for good or ill, but what I do know, and hold on to, is that you will remain the same, always there when I need you, and that nothing finally can ever separate me from your love in Christ. For that assurance, receive my praise, in his name. Amen.

Remember

Humans swear by what is greater than they are, an oath by way of confirmation ending all argument. Similarly, when God resolved to make the reliability of his purpose yet more evident to the heirs of his promise, he reinforced it by an oath, so that through two unchangeable things, in which he cannot possibly prove false, we who have sought refuge in him might take heart and grasp the hope set before us. This is an anchor for our soul, sure and dependable, through which we can enter the inner shrine behind the curtain.   *Hebrews 6:16-19*

Close

Living God, in the unpredictability of this life, faced with the apparent fickleness of fate, teach me to trust completely in the sure and certain hope you have given in Christ, for his name's sake. Amen.

Recognising the signs

Read

The Pharisees came and engaged in debate with Jesus, testing him by asking for some sign from heaven. He sighed deeply in his spirit, saying, 'Why does this generation seek a sign? I tell you bluntly that no sign will be given to this generation.'

Mark 8:11-12

Ponder

All of us will have been asked at some point for proof of our identity. When applying for a passport or driving licence, for example, we need to produce a signed photograph and an official document, such as a birth or wedding certificate, before this can be issued. Increasingly, today, we are asked for evidence that we are who we claim to be. Many, similarly, wanted proof concerning the identity of Jesus. They knew that his followers believed him to be the Messiah but before they could even consider such a claim, they wanted some concrete corroboration. One cannot help sympathise a little with their request. It was, after all, an astonishing assertion that Jesus was making. Add to that the fact that many had come previously claiming to be Messiah, and we can at least begin to understand their hesitation.

So why was the response of Jesus so curt, according to Matthew's Gospel (12:39) even more brusque than that recorded by Mark? The answer is that he had already given innumerable signs, if only they had eyes to see them. Everything in his life and ministry pointed to who he was, testifying to the hand of God upon him. If they couldn't see the truth that was staring them in the face, then they would never see it, no matter how many more signs they were given. We, like the Pharisees, may sometimes wish there was less need of faith and more certainty in Christian belief. We may crave for some sign to put paid to any lingering doubts we may have. I suspect, though, that Jesus' answer to us would be the same: the signs are all around those with the humility, the insight and the faith to discern them.

Ask yourself

Are you so preoccupied with questions that you fail to see the answers all around you? Have you missed the signs God has given of his renewing love and transforming power?

Pray

Living God, you are at work in so many ways, if I could only see it. Forgive me everything that blinds me to the breadth of your activity – my closed mind and rigid pre-conceptions; my limited understanding and lack of faith, my asking the wrong questions and looking in the wrong places for the wrong things.

Open my eyes to your presence, my mind to your truth, and my soul to your Spirit, and so may I glimpse you in the daily events of life and in the affairs of the world, this and every day, in Christ's name. Amen.

Remember

Do you still not understand or realise what is happening? Have your hearts become so hardened that despite having eyes you cannot see and having ears you cannot hear? Do you not remember? Do you still not understand?

Mark 8:17-18, 21

Close

Lord Jesus Christ, open my eyes to all you have done and all you are doing, and so help me to glimpse all you are yet able to do by your sovereign grace. Amen.

A time to be still

Read

He persuaded his disciples to board the boat and cross to the other side ahead of him, while he dismissed the crowds, and having done that, he went up the mountain by himself to pray. As evening fell, he was there alone.   *Matthew 14:22-23*

Ponder

We watched spellbound as it appeared out of the undergrowth, making its way cautiously up the lawn to the supply of food left out for it in anticipation. It was our first, and so far only, sighting of a badger in the wild, and the few minutes we spent watching it feed made it a holiday to remember. I could have watched for longer, but as I shifted position to get a better view, it caught sight of my movement and, in a trice, it was gone. Watching wildlife requires stillness and patience, the ability to stay quiet for some length of time. Fail to do that, and the object of our search remains hidden, tantalisingly out of sight.

There are parallels here with glimpsing God, although we should not push the analogy too far. He is with us all the time, everywhere at every moment, yet most of the time we are unaware of it, too caught up in the hustle and bustle of life. It is often only when we pause for a few moments, making time to be still and reflect, that the full wonder of his presence dawns on us. Even Jesus, who seems to have been in tune with God throughout his life, recognised the need to draw aside from the crowds and spend a quiet time in prayer. If Jesus needed such times to focus his thoughts on God, how much more do we need them in turn!

Ask yourself

When did you last make time to be still in the presence of God? When did you last focus your thoughts entirely upon him?

Pray

Living God, too often I rush from one thing to the next, preoccupied with the demands and responsibilities of each day, and wondering where I might find the strength to see me through. Yet instead of turning to you I struggle on as best as I can.

Teach me to create space in my life for you, to make a few moments every day in which I can be quiet and still, and teach me to do that not as an afterthought but as a prerequisite, recognising that when I give you your proper place, everything else will fit into place as well. In Christ's name I ask it. Amen.

Remember

Be still, and know that I am God.   *Psalm 46:10*

Close

Living God, whatever the pressures and duties of the day, teach me to find time for stillness, and in seeing you there may I see you always and everywhere, through the grace of Christ. Amen.

The courage to fail

Read

You will tell them all these things, but they will not listen to you; you will challenge them, but they will not give you a hearing.

Jeremiah 7:27

Ponder

Nothing succeeds like success, so they say, and we've all seen the truth of that on countless occasions. A sportsperson or team looks down and out, hopelessly beaten, until an unexpected point, goal or run brings fresh heart and the tables are turned. A business is struggling to survive, its shares plummeting on the stock market, but then a new product captures the imagination and investors are suddenly queuing up to be part of its success story. An author struggles for years to make a living, virtually unheard of, only for a book out of the blue to shoot to the top of the bestseller list, and from then on everything he or she produces is like gold dust. Success breeds success, but what we can forget is that success also involves the courage to fail. The last-ditch effort of the sportsperson may backfire, leading to almost certain defeat; the innovative product pioneered by the firm may turn out to be a flop; the author's new book may fare no better than previous offerings, ending up on the back shelf of some cut-price bookshop. It takes courage to risk failure and, in consequence, many of us never even attempt to find success.

The prophet Jeremiah could have been similarly defeatist for he knew from the outset of his ministry that few would listen to him and that many would be overtly hostile to his message, yet he carried on regardless in the hope that one or two might hear and respond. We, in turn, need that same faith and courage in the service of God; a willingness to accept apparent failure and not be deflected from our path, to take on new initiatives and attempt great things, even though they may seem beyond us. Another familiar proverb sums it up well: 'If at first you don't succeed, try and try again.'

Ask yourself

Is the memory of past failure preventing you from trying something again? Are you allowing the fear of failure to deny the possibility of success?

Pray

Living God, I don't like failing at something. It hurts my pride, destroys my confidence and undermines my self-esteem. Far better, I tell myself, to cut my losses, admit defeat and focus on the things I know I can do well. Yet you have shown me through those like Jeremiah that success is not always won easily; that there are times when I must work for it despite setbacks, persevering come what may.

Teach me, then, never to lose heart, but to take the leap of faith in times of adversity, confident that ultimately the victory will be yours through Christ my Saviour. Amen.

Remember

We are afflicted in every way, but not crushed; bemused, but not driven to despair; persecuted, but not abandoned; struck down, but not destroyed; always bearing in the body the death of Jesus, so that the life of Jesus may be revealed likewise in our bodies.   *2 Corinthians 4:8-10*

Close

Living God, when what you ask seems beyond me, help me to trust in your purpose, and if I meet with failure, teach me not to lose faith but to try and keep on trying, in Christ's name. Amen.

A personal response

Read

When Felix, who had a good knowledge of the Way, heard these things, he postponed judgement, saying, 'When Lysias the tribune comes down, I will come to a decision then.' Some time later, when Felix came with his wife Drusilla, who was a Jewess, he sent for Paul and heard him out concerning his faith in Jesus Christ. As Paul debated with him concerning righteousness, moral responsibility and forthcoming judgement, Felix grew agitated and responded, 'Go your way for the present. I will send for you in due course.'

Acts 24:22, 24-25

Ponder

When I first started this book, it was my intention to write the prayers in the first person plural; in other words, the prayer below would have started, 'Loving God, forgive us our failure to listen to your voice' rather than 'forgive *me my* failure to listen to your voice'. However, it was suggested that the first person singular should be used to emphasise the personal devotional nature of the book. An apparently small change, yet one that brought home to me how easy it is to come out with fine-sounding sentiments when they are not applied directly to oneself. The use of 'I' and 'me' suddenly meant that the prayers were *my* prayers in a way they hadn't been before: they spoke of, questioned and examined *my* response, *my* faith, *my* witness, *my* love or lack of it – and the experience was both unsettling and salutary.

We see something similar in the response of Felix to Paul's defence of his faith. Felix, we read, was well informed about the Way of Christ, and he probably felt more than able to hold his own in conversation about its merits. Had conversation been kept on an abstract level, perhaps he could have, but Paul had other ideas. He faced Felix fair and square with the challenge of the gospel, the result being that though Paul was the one on trial, Felix was the one writhing and squirming. Many of us are happy to talk about Jesus and nominally follow him so long as it does not impinge upon our private life or ask too much of us. Such a response may be comfortable but it has little to do with faith. True discipleship means allowing our lives to be examined and transformed, opening ourselves to the searching gaze of Christ and listening to what he has to say, even when his message is unwelcome and disturbing. We may like to think we've done that already, but there's no harm in making sure!

Ask yourself

Is your faith a theoretical exercise or a life-changing experience? Are you willing to let it speak directly to your life rather than talk generally about all?

Pray

Loving God, forgive me for refusing sometimes to listen to your voice. Deep down in my heart of hearts I know you are speaking to me, but I would rather not hear. When your message is too demanding, when you ask of me what I would rather not face, when your words make me feel uncomfortable, striking too near the mark, I stubbornly resist, closing my ears and pushing you away.

Yet however hard I may try, I will never finally silence your voice – not until I have listened and responded. Help me then to hear what you would say to me, and act upon it. Amen.

Remember

What about you? Who do you say that I am?   *Luke 9:20a*

Close

Lord Jesus Christ, save me from simply knowing *about* you; help me truly to know you as my Lord, Saviour and friend, through your grace. Amen.

Travelling light

Read

You have received freely; give freely in turn. Take no gold, silver or copper coins in your belts, no wallet for your journey, no spare tunic, sandals or a staff, for workers deserve their food.   *Matthew 10:8b-10*

Ponder

What's the best thing about moving house? For me, one of the big plusses is sorting out all the clutter that has accumulated over the years and consigning it to the tip. The task may seem anything but a blessing at the time, yet once the sifting is over and the paraphernalia discarded, there comes a wonderful sense of liberation; until, that is, we settle down and accumulate it all once again! Most of us have a compulsive tendency to buy things we do not really need and then to hoard them, just in case they should come in useful one day. But does our store of possessions bring us happiness? I suspect that more often than not the opposite is true, those possessions a millstone round our neck instead of a source of pleasure.

Contrast that with the picture painted by Jesus as he sent out his Apostles into the mission field. They were to travel light – not only without possessions but also without money, equipped with only the most basic of requirements – essentially living by faith. I do not think we can take that picture as a model for life today, for the context is completely different. The way may be right for some but it would be poor citizenship were we all to follow it. There is, nonetheless, a vital lesson here. To be effective in discipleship, to grow in our faith and to discover lasting happiness we need to break free of the stranglehold of possessions, recognising that our ultimate security lies elsewhere. We need to set our goals elsewhere, and to use our resources in the service of Christ rather than self. It's easy to imagine we have done that, but how much, I wonder, would we be willing to renounce should we be put to the test?

Ask yourself
How much do possessions mean to you? How far does your life reflect this?

Pray
Living God, I like to imagine that possessions are not important to me but the reality is different. I surround myself with all kinds of belongings and I am constantly seeking more. Some contribute much to my life, others yield nothing, but all of them can so easily come between me and you, closing my eyes to what is ultimately important in life.

Forgive me the time, money and resources I waste in accumulating what I do not need. Forgive the selfishness and the wasted opportunities to give to or serve others that so often lie behind it. Teach me to travel light, recognising where true fulfilment lies, and so may my service be deepened and my relationship with you enriched, through the grace of Jesus Christ. Amen.

Remember
All the believers shared everything together, selling their possessions and goods, and distributing them among each other, as anyone had need. As it is written, the one that gathered much had nothing over, while the one that gathered little lacked nothing.   *Acts 2:45; 2 Corinthians 8:15*

Close
Lord Jesus Christ, help me to use my possessions in your service rather than allowing them to possess me. Amen.

A surprising contribution

Read

Looking out upon and surveying the vast crowd that had gathered around him, Jesus said to Philip, 'Where can we buy bread to feed this number?' He said this to test him, knowing full well what he intended to do. Philip answered, 'Even if we had two hundred denarii, it would barely be enough to give each one a morsel.' Then Andrew, one of his disciples and the brother of Simon Peter, said, 'There's a lad here who has five barley loaves and a couple of fish, but what use are they among so many?' Jesus said, 'Get the crowd to sit down and make themselves comfortable.' It was a grassy spot, so they settled themselves down there, about five thousand of them in all. Then Jesus took the loaves and, having given thanks, he distributed them to the reclining crowd, together with the fish, each having as much as they wanted. When they were filled, he said to his disciples, 'Gather up the pieces left over so that nothing is lost. They gathered as instructed, and filled twelve baskets with the pieces of barley loaf left uneaten.   *John 6:5-13*

Ponder

What contribution can I make to God's kingdom? What difference can anything I may do possibly make to people's lives? Have you ever asked yourself questions like those? It's natural enough that we should, for we are all fallible, finite human beings, only able to do so much, no matter how committed we might be. Yet, if we imagine this excuses apathy or disillusionment, think again, for, as the story of the feeding of the five thousand so graphically illustrates, that is to reckon without the love of God in Christ. In this astonishing incident, we witness in action the God who takes what seems to be a little and turns it into something great; the God who is able to take an apparently wholly inadequate response and use it in a way that defies human understanding.

The young lad in the story could so easily have reasoned that his loaves and fishes could achieve nothing among so many, but he didn't, offering them instead to be used as Jesus saw fit. We all know the results of that action. Let us, in turn, never undervalue the little we have to offer, but instead let us remember that in God's hands it can yield the most unexpected of results.

Ask yourself
Do you withhold your money, your gifts or your service because you feel it can make no difference? Have you left God out of the equation?

Pray
Loving God, I haven't much to give, and of what I do have I give you only a fraction. To think that you can use it stretches credulity to the limit, and yet, across the years, you have taken what the world regards as insignificant and repeatedly used it to transform situations.

Teach me, then, to look not at the feebleness of my resources, nor the awesome scale of human need, but to recognise instead your sovereign power, and so, in faith, may I offer my money, witness and service in the name of Christ, to the glory of your name. Amen.

Remember
'Do not worry,' said Elijah . . . 'Make a little cake from what you have and bring it out to me, and then make something for your son and yourself. For this is the word of the Lord, the God of Israel: "The jar of flour shall never be exhausted nor shall the flask of oil run dry, until the Lord sends rain on the land."'   *1 Kings 17:13-14*

Close
Lord Jesus Christ, teach me that a little in your hands can achieve more than a fortune in mine, and so inspire me to give generously of myself in your service, to the glory of your name. Amen.

Walking in faith

Read

Jesus said to them, 'You are going to have the light just a little longer. Walk while you have the light, before darkness overtakes you. Those who walk in darkness do not know where they are going. Put your trust in the light while you have it, so that you may become children of light.

John 12:35-36

Ponder

A man was out walking on the Lake District mountains, enjoying the wonderful views and revelling in an exhilarating sense of freedom, when suddenly the clouds drew in and the hills were enveloped in a thick cold mist so dense that he could see only a few paces ahead. He struggled on for a time only to realise, to his horror, that he had somehow strayed from the path. He did not want to risk staying up on those hills all night, yet he knew there were sheer cliffs all around him and that one false step could lead to injury or even death. Then, through the mist, he caught sight of a pile of stones, and he remembered reading something about stone cairns, placed at intervals along the main footpath as a guide to the walker. He inched towards it and then cautiously followed the line of cairns back down to the town below and hence to safety.

There are times when life is a little like that – one moment everything going smoothly and the next plunged into chaos such that we do not know which way to turn next. We feel caught between the devil and the deep blue sea, unsure whether to take a step backwards or forwards, or to dig in where we are. That walker had to place his faith in stones arranged along the footpath; we are called to place our faith in Christ, and to trust him for guidance. We may not know where the path may lead from one day to the next, but we are assured of our ultimate destination. Are we ready to walk in faith?

Ask yourself

What 'signposts' has God given you to guide you on your journey of faith? How often do you follow these? What causes you to ignore them?

Pray

Lord Jesus Christ, you call me to walk in faith, but I so rarely do that. I follow for a time, but I am quickly led astray. When your message is too demanding, when you ask from me what I would rather not give, and when your words make me feel uncomfortable, striking too near the mark, then I turn away from you, resisting your call. When other interests conflict with discipleship, when the demands and responsibilities of each day crowd in upon me, I am swift to forget you, ignoring your will in preference to my own. When life is hard and things do not go as I'd hoped, faith gives way to doubt and I lose sight of your promises.

Forgive that shallowness of my commitment, and grant light to my path, so that I may step forward in faith and travel onwards wherever you might lead, through Jesus Christ my Lord. Amen.

Remember

Blessed are those who have learned to acclaim you, who walk in the light of your presence, O Lord.   *Psalm 89:15*

Close

Lord Jesus Christ, help me to walk the journey to which you have called me, keeping faith in your saving purpose. When I grow weary, revive me; when I go astray, direct me; when I lose heart, inspire me, and when I turn back reprove me. Keep me travelling ever onwards, trusting in your guidance and certain that you will be there at my journey's end to welcome me home into your eternal kingdom. In your name, I ask it. Amen.

After you

Read

If there is any comfort in Christ, any consolation of love, any fellowship of the Spirit, any pity or compassion, complete my joy by having the same love, being one in mind and soul, doing nothing out of personal ambition but in humility, counting others better than yourselves and being concerned more about their well-being than your own.

Philippians 2:1-4

Ponder

The mention of humility automatically calls to mind the 'so very 'umble' Uriah Heep of Charles Dickens fame. That fictional character has probably done more to devalue the word 'humble' in popular understanding than anyone else, many subconsciously associating it with a smug, sanctimonious piety. There are Christians like that, convinced that they should be timid, submissive and diffident, but I do not believe Paul had those characteristics in mind when he wrote to the Philippians. The words he might have chosen, had he been asked to enlarge on his meaning, would, I think, have been 'modest', 'unassuming', 'unpretentious', 'gentle' – the sort of attributes we see displayed so often and so wonderfully throughout the ministry of Jesus. We see it in his birth in a stable, his mixing with social outcasts, his response to the sick and untouchable, his welcoming of little children, his washing of the disciples' feet, his quiet agony on the cross and, finally, in his forgiving renewing word of peace as the risen Saviour. The Son of God and Lord of all, yet the one who has time for all, however high or low they may be. We cannot hope to emulate him fully, but we should strive nonetheless to show similar humility: putting self second and others first.

Ask yourself

In what ways do you put others first? In what ways do you put them down?

Pray

Lord Jesus Christ, you came into our world as the King of kings and Lord of lords, but you came also as the servant of all. You came deserving praise and worship, yet willingly accepting mockery, rejection and suffering for my sake. You came to bring life in all its fullness, yet you offered your life to redeem the world.

Teach me to recognise the values of your kingdom that turn human values on their head. Help me to understand that I discover self when I lose sight of it, that I serve you when I respond to others, that I am lifted high when I am brought low, and may that realisation shape the kind of person I am and the life I live, to the glory of your name. Amen.

Remember

Therefore, let God bring you low under his mighty hand, so that, in due course, he may lift you up.　　*1 Peter 5:6*

Close

Loving God, go with me now and help me to offer the worship you most desire – to do justice, to love kindness and to walk humbly with you every step of the way, in the name of Christ. Amen.

That's rich!

Read

He told them a parable, saying, 'The land of a wealthy man yielded a plentiful harvest, such that he thought to himself, "What ought I to do? I have insufficient space to store my crops." Then he decided, "Here's what I'll do – I'll demolish my barns and build bigger ones, and store all my grain and my goods there. I will say to my soul, 'Soul, you have more than enough possessions to last you many years; take it easy – eat, drink, and make merry.'" But God said to him, "You fool! This very night your soul will be asked of you, and all these things you've prepared, whose will they be then?" So it is with anyone who stores up lavish personal treasures, but who is not generous towards God.'

Luke 12:16-21

Ponder

What must people in the Third World think when they hear Christians in the West talking about true riches, treasure in heaven and the like? We talk so glibly about not valuing wealth, and self-sacrifice, yet for the starving in Somalia, the displaced in Mozambique, the shanty-town dweller in Brazil, it must be hard not to think, 'That's rich, coming from them!' What do we really know about poverty or need? Precious little. And, for all our talk, most of us spend our lives in either the pursuit of more, or the safeguarding of what we already have. Believe me, I'm as guilty as any.

The stark parable told by Jesus of the rich fool challenges us to a radical reappraisal of life and wealth. It tells us that true riches are only found through sharing them with God. What does that mean? Putting our bit in the collection plate on Sunday? In part, yes, but it is more than that, for didn't Jesus make plain to the rich young man who came to him seeking eternal life that giving to God must be expressed through giving to others? We *do*, of course, respond to those in need. I suspect Christians have been at the forefront in terms of giving to all those situations mentioned above, and many besides. Yet have we given as we should or as we prefer; sacrificially, or simply what we feel we can spare? When we learn to deny ourselves and give from our plenty, that *is* rich!

Ask yourself
Are you as generous as you could be towards God? What does this mean in practice?

Pray
Gracious God, I have enough and more than enough, but I know there are many deprived of even the basic necessities of life: who go hungry while I eat my fill, who have nothing to drink or wear, no place to call their home, no access to medicine or hospital care and no opportunity to improve their lot. Teach me not only to pray for them but to respond to their plight by giving generously from my plenty, in Christ's name. Amen.

Remember
Urge those who are wealthy in this life not to think of themselves as superior to others, nor to base their hopes on the uncertainty of riches, but to base them rather on the God who so richly provides everything for our enjoyment. They are to do good, be rich in good works and be ready to share generously, thus setting in place the fundamentals of enduring treasure, such that they may take hold of the life that really is life. *1 Timothy 6:17-19*

Close
Gracious God, you became poor so that we might become rich. Help me to become a little poorer so that I might discover true riches. Amen.

Joyful faith

Read

I have said these things to you so that my joy may be in you, and that your joy may be complete.

John 15:11 (NRSV)

Ponder

'If you want joy, real joy, wonderful joy, let Jesus come into your life' – so run the opening lines of a chorus that was very popular some years back. The theology may be a bit simplistic, yet it emphasises an aspect of the gospel that we can sometimes lose sight of: that what God wants for us more than anything is joy. He is not a stern forbidding God looking to judge, nor a dictatorial demanding God, more concerned with what we shouldn't do than what we should. He is a God who desires our happiness, who loves to see us celebrate, who wants us to experience a joy that will never fade or lose its sparkle.

Whatever he may ask of us, we need always to set it in this context, remembering that everything he has done for us in Christ was done for one purpose: to make our joy complete, not only in this life but for all eternity.

Ask yourself

How much does joy figure in your faith? Do people see in you that faith is something to celebrate?

Pray

Loving God, I praise you that you do not just give me happiness, but joy; a sense of celebration that bubbles up within me, irrepressible and indestructible. I thank you that even when life is hard, even when I am confronted by tragedy and disaster, there is always an underlying sense of joy, springing from a confidence in your eternal purpose.

Help me to open my life more fully to you each day, so

that my joy may be complete and communicate itself to others in such a way that they too may come to rejoice in your love and experience your blessing. Through Jesus Christ my Lord. Amen.

Remember
May the God of hope fill you with all joy and peace in believing, so that you may abound in hope by the power of the Holy Spirit. *Romans 5:17 (NRSV)*

Close
Living God, for the joy of life, the joy of faith, the joy of knowing you, I give you my grateful praise. Amen.

AUGUST

Digging deeper

Read

The Lord said to Samuel, 'I want you to go to Jesse in Bethlehem, for I have chosen one of his sons to be king.' Samuel
followed the Lord's instructions, and went to Bethlehem.
The moment he spotted Eliab he thought, 'This must be
the one God has chosen to be anointed.' But the Lord said
to Samuel, 'Don't be taken in by good looks or physique,
because I have rejected him. The Lord does not see as people
see, for they look at appearances, but the Lord sees into the
heart.' Then Jesse called Abinadab, and made him pass before
Samuel, but he said, 'No, this isn't the Lord's chosen one.'
Then Jesse presented Shammah, but again Samuel said, 'No,
he's not the chosen one either.' Jesse made seven of his sons
pass before Samuel, but Samuel said, 'The Lord has not
chosen any of these.' Finally, Samuel asked Jesse, 'Are all your
sons here?' He answered, 'There is one more, the youngest,
but he is out looking after the sheep.' Samuel said to Jesse,
'Send for him; we will not sit down until he's here.' Jesse
sent for him to be fetched in. He was handsome, with glowing
cheeks and shining eyes. The Lord said, 'Get up, and anoint
him; for this is the one.' So Samuel took the horn of oil,
and anointed him in the presence of his brothers.

1 Samuel 16:1b, 4a, 6-13a

Ponder

Some years ago, a newspaper ran an advertising campaign
based on the slogan 'One million . . . readers can't be wrong'.
The implication was that if enough people subscribe to
something, it must be right. It is human nature to want to
follow the crowd. Those who question the established
norms of society are branded as heretics, eccentrics or even
revolutionaries, their challenge conveniently side-stepped
through the use of such dismissive labels. Sometimes,

questions may be misplaced, but equally there are times when they need asking, faith having to take a critical look at the values the world takes for granted if it is to be true to itself.

So it was for Samuel, sent by God to the house of Jesse to anoint a new ruler over Israel. He went there, imagining he was a shrewd judge of character, well able to discern God's will. He came away recognising he had much still to learn about the ways of God, who sees far deeper than most of us even begin to see. His experience counsels us never to judge by appearances and never to imagine we have understood all there is to understand.

Ask yourself

Are you taken in by appearances? Is God calling you to think again about decisions or judgements you have made?

Pray

Gracious God, I know it is foolish to judge by the outside, yet I catch myself doing it time and again. Even when I think I am looking deeper, I am still conditioned to look at the world in a way that I find almost impossible to escape from. All too often, I let superficial impressions deceive me.

Help me to see with your eyes, to look beyond the obvious to the deeper realities of life, and to recognise the true worth of all those around me, for Christ's sake. Amen.

Remember

Do not base your judgements upon outward appearances, but upon the truth. *John 7:24*

Close

Living God, before I jump to conclusions and pass judgement on others, help me to look again, and with your help to look deeper, recognising that you alone can judge the heart. In Christ's name, I pray. Amen.

Christian clothing

Read

As God's chosen ones, therefore, holy and greatly loved, clothe yourselves with compassion, kindness, humility, meekness and patience, being merciful to one another and forgiving any quarrel you may have; in other words, forgive as the Lord forgave you. Above all, clothe yourselves with love, which binds everything together in perfect harmony.

Colossians 3:12-14

Ponder

What sort of clothes do you wear? Are you the daring flamboyant type or one who prefers a little more restraint; the kind of person who likes to dress casually or who only feels comfortable when more formally attired? Clothes, we are told, say something about the people behind them, giving an insight into their character and disposition.

All of which takes us to the heart of what Paul was saying in his letter to the Colossians. Having just discussed various undesirable characteristics that we should strive to put off, he moves on here to the qualities we need to put on, and the language he uses is carefully chosen. He doesn't just say be compassionate, kind, humble and so on, but urges the Colossians to clothe themselves with such things, or, to put it another way, to make those attributes so much a part of themselves that they are self-evident to all they meet, the first thing people will see; unmistakable, eye-catching. Compassion, kindness, humility, meekness, patience, mercy and love – the essential ingredients of every Christian's wardrobe. This is not, of course, an exhaustive list, but it gives us a clear idea of what God wants and expects to see in our lives. Are these the 'clothes' we wear, the qualities that mark us out, or are we still more often than not turned out in the uniform of pride, greed, envy, bitterness and other such garments of the old self? If the latter, then isn't it time we heeded those wonderful words of Paul, and started measuring up?

Ask yourself

What Christian qualities are visible in your life? What do people see of Christ in you?

Pray

Living God, I know what my life ought to be like, I know what it is, and I am ashamed at the difference between the two. Where I ought to reveal Christ, I show only myself. Where I ought to bear witness to his life-changing power, I demonstrate instead how little has actually changed. So much about me denies rather than affirms the gospel, leading people to dismiss its claims rather than to explore them further.

Forgive me for all that is wrong and, by your Spirit, clothe me with joy, peace, patience, kindness, generosity, faithfulness, gentleness, self-control, and, above all, love. Work in my life, and so work through me to speak to others, through the grace of Christ. Amen.

Remember

All of you, be subject to one another, and clothe yourselves with humility, for God resists the proud but gives grace to the humble.   *1 Peter 5:5b*

Close

Living God, help me before all else to clothe myself with Christ and so to make him known through word and deed, to the glory of his name. Amen.

The first and the last

Read

Then the mother of the sons of Zebedee approached him with her sons and, kneeling before him, she asked him to do her a favour. He responded, 'What is it you wish for?' She answered, 'Say that these two sons of mine will sit with you in your kingdom, one at your right hand and one at your left.' Jesus answered, 'You don't know what it is you are asking. Are you able to drink the cup from which I am about to drink?' They said to him, 'We can.' He continued, 'You will indeed drink from that cup, but to sit at my right and left hand is not mine to grant; it is for those for whom my Father has prepared it.' Overhearing this conversation, the remaining ten disciples were incensed at the two brothers' behaviour. Jesus, however, beckoned them across to him and said, 'You are well aware that the rulers of the Gentiles and those who are elevated to positions of authority lord it over their people. Don't let it be like this among you; for whoever wishes to be great among you must be your servant, and whoever wishes to be first among you must be your slave.'

Matthew 20:20-27

Ponder

Reading this account, it is hard not to think of modern-day parents thrusting their precocious children into the public eye through talent shows, beauty contests and the like. Were James and John similarly pushed forward by a doting, domineering mother? Well, not exactly, because for one thing they were grown men, well capable of speaking for themselves. It is more likely that they got their mother to speak on their behalf, voicing a concern held by all of the Apostles as to whether their loyalty would be rewarded, but which each was embarrassed to ask about outright.

Before we tut in disapproval at their pushiness, we do well to ask ourselves if we are any different. Is our faith wholly altruistic, concerned solely with the service of Christ, or is there more than a hint of safeguarding our ultimate destiny, guaranteeing future blessing in the life to come? There is probably an element of that in everyone's faith, but we are called to serve Christ for his sake rather than our own, to seek his kingdom rather than our welfare. If faith becomes just another way of putting ourselves first, then it is time to think again, for whatever else it may be, that is not faith at all.

Ask yourself

Do you follow Jesus for what you can get out of your faith or for what you can put in? Are you more concerned with securing future blessing than offering present service?

Pray

Lord Jesus Christ, I want to serve you, and I like to believe I do, but unwittingly I can turn even my faith into a way of serving myself. I gain strength through fellowship and worship, but neglect your call to mission. I focus on my own concerns in prayer and forget about the world beyond. Even my deeds of kindness can finally be more about my own sense of righteousness than the needs of those I think I am serving.

Lord Jesus, overcome the stranglehold of self and help me to understand that true discipleship brings its own reward, for the more I give the more I shall receive. In your mercy, hear my prayer. Amen.

Remember

Whoever wishes to be first, will be the last of all and the servant of all.   *Mark 9:35b*

Close

Lord Jesus Christ, teach me the values of your kingdom and the joy of knowing you, and so may I put you first and self second, to the glory of your name. Amen.

The folly of envy

Read

Who is wise and discerning among you? Show by the quality of your life and works a sensitivity stemming from wisdom. If your hearts are filled with sourness, envy and selfish ambition, do not take pride in it and flout the truth. Such wisdom is not God-given, but is earthly, secular and fiendish, for where there is envy and self-centred ambition there will correspondingly be turmoil and evil of every kind.

James 3:13-16

Ponder

When I was training for the ministry at college there was a certain poster very much in vogue among my colleagues. It was a cartoon depicting four cows in adjoining fields, each leaning over their neighbour's fence to munch the grass in their field. And the caption? Well, there was no need for one, was there? It delightfully illustrated that old saying about the grass always being greener on the other side, and, illusory though that greener grass may be, it is so true of the way we think. Instead of being content with what we have we just can't help looking jealously at those around us, eyeing up their latest acquisition, their comfortable lifestyle, their beautiful house, and wishing it was ours. A daily bombardment of advertising wards off any possibility of us coming to our senses.

Occasionally, of course, the grass *is* greener, in material terms anyway. But if we allow ourselves to get sucked into the whirlpool of envy, then the quality of our lives will spiral downwards, for in time our view of everything and everyone will be contaminated by its poison.

Ask yourself

Are there possessions you covet or people you envy? In what way are such people richer than you? Would having what they have bring you happiness?

Pray

Living God, you have given me so much; forgive me that I still want more. I have so many blessings to rejoice in; forgive me that instead I dwell on the pleasures I do not have. Above all, forgive me for the way I allow envy to poison my attitudes and colour my judgement, insinuating itself into the way I think, feel, speak and act towards others.

Teach me to appreciate everything that is good in my life, and to rejoice equally with others in the things that are good in theirs, and, beyond all else, teach me to celebrate the love that you give freely to all, beyond measure, without reserve, now and for all eternity, through the grace of Christ. Amen.

Remember

Wrath is forbidding, anger is overwhelming, but who is able to stand before envy?   *Proverbs 27:4*

Close

Gracious God, instead of coveting the things I don't have, help me to appreciate the treasures I do. In the name of Christ. Amen.

Showing off?

Read

Conduct yourselves wisely in your dealings with those outside the faith, making the most of every opportunity. May your speech always be gracious, seasoned with salt, in such a way that you know how to respond appropriately to everyone.

Colossians 4:5-6

Ponder

How would you feel if you'd spent a fortune on a wonderful new hairstyle, only for no one to notice? Or how about if you rolled up to work one day in a spanking new Rolls-Royce and no one batted an eyelid? You'd be disappointed, wouldn't you? How about, then, if you were dining in a top-notch restaurant and you spilled soup down your front, or if you were about to meet someone on a first date and suddenly your mother turned up with a scrapbook of you as a baby – how would you feel then? Pretty embarrassed, to say the least! There are some things in life we like to show off and others we definitely don't!

Which brings us to the words of Paul to the Colossians, for what he was effectively telling them to do was to show off. Not in the sense we usually use that expression – blowing our own trumpet, being puffed up with our own importance – but instead, showing the love of Christ and his renewing transforming power. Don't be shy about your faith, said Paul. Let people see what you're made of, what you have to offer in Christ, what a difference he has made to your life. Let your honesty, sincerity, compassion and genuine concern for others set you apart, serving as a beacon to others. Is that showing off? Not in the way the world understands it, no – it's more a matter of letting it show; and that brings us to the crunch question we all do well to ask ourselves. We may make time for devotions such as these, we may attend church on a Sunday, we may commit ourselves day after day to the service of Christ, but when we get out into the world, into the routine business of life, how far will any of that show itself in action?

Ask yourself

Are you concerned with boosting your own image and self-esteem or bringing glory to Christ? Do you seek to draw attention to your achievements or point rather towards God's? How far could someone speak of you in the way Paul speaks of the Church in Rome in Romans 1:8 (see below)?

Pray

Lord, I'm good at talking about faith, at making the right noises and saying the right words. I'm not bad either at looking the part – turning up at church, looking respectable, getting involved in Christian activities. Yet, when it comes to living the faith, so often my life shows much of me and little of you. Forgive me when the things I say and do deny rather than affrim the gospel. Forgive me when I conceal my discipleship for fear of what others may think.

Help me to follow you faithfully, reflecting your love, demonstrating your compassion and responding to your guidance. Touch my heart and strengthen my faith, so that in the days ahead I may live and work for you, and bring glory to your holy name. Amen.

Remember

I thank my God through Jesus Christ for you all, because your faith is spoken of throughout the world. *Romans 1:8*

Close

Lord Jesus Christ, grant that everything I am, and all I say and do, may resound to your praise and glory, for your name's sake. Amen.

Grasping the moment

Read

Running up to the chariot, Philip heard [the eunuch] reading
Isaiah the prophet, so he asked him, 'Do you understand
these words you're reading?' The eunuch answered, 'How
can I possibly do that unless someone explains them to
me?' And he urged Philip to come up and sit with him. The
eunuch asked Philip, 'Tell me, who is the prophet talking
about here? Does he refer to himself or someone else?'
Then Philip, beginning with that passage of scripture,
talked to him about Jesus. *Acts 8:30-31, 34-35*

Ponder

The question caught me entirely by surprise. I was on a train
journey during my time as a theological student, when
suddenly a young man sitting opposite me, spotting the
textbook I was poring over, leant across and asked me what
I made of Jesus. Have you ever had an experience like that,
asked out of the blue to summarise what your faith means
to you? If you have, then, like me, you may well have found
yourself caught on the hop, unable to make the most of the
opportunity. Contrast that with the story of Philip and the
Ethiopian eunuch. For years, the eunuch had been searching
the scriptures seeking enlightenment, recognising that they
pointed to something truly special yet unsure quite how to
interpret them. Philip found himself in the right place at
the right time but, more important, he turned out to be the
right *person*, using the God-given moment to win this man
to faith. Interested enquiry rapidly turned into enthusiastic
commitment, and all it took was a willingness to get alongside and bear witness to Christ.

How, then, should we apply this today? I don't think it's
about memorising words of testimony until we have them
off pat – that will cut little ice with anyone. Nor would I

advocate immersing ourselves in statements of doctrine, creeds, or other kinds of theological jargon, in the hope that we can trot them out parrot-fashion whenever the need arises – that would prove even more counter-productive. What is important is that we take time to reflect on our faith, and to ask ourselves honestly what Jesus means to us and what difference he has made to our lives. Do that and, when the opportunity comes to speak out for Christ, we shall not be found wanting.

Ask yourself

How would you reply if someone asked you today what Jesus means to you? What impact does your faith make in your life?

Pray

Lord Jesus Christ, you have called me to bear witness to what you have done and on occasions there come opportunities to do just that. You don't expect me to be a gifted evangelist, but you do ask me to speak naturally of you when the chance presents itself. Yet, more often than I care to remember, when that time has come I have wasted it, uncertain what to say, worried about making a fool of myself, afraid of being misunderstood. Forgive me all the occasions I have let you down, failing to share the joy I have found in you. Teach me to reflect on your goodness, to recognise all you have done for me, and so to make the most of every opportunity you give me to proclaim your love and make known the good news. In your name I ask it. Amen.

Remember

[Pray] for me, that the right words may be put into my mouth, so that I may boldly make known the mystery of the gospel. *Ephesians 6:19*

Close

Lord Jesus Christ, when anyone speaks *to* me of you, by your grace speak *through* me to them, for your name's sake. Amen.

Resisting temptation

Read

Joseph was fine-looking and attractive, and in time his master's wife cast her eyes on Joseph and said, 'Make love with me.' But he refused and said to her, 'I need to consider my master. He has no worries concerning the affairs of his household, having entrusted its administration into my hands. My authority here is second only to his, and he has withheld nothing from me except you, since you are his wife. How, then, could I repay him with such wickedness, and sin also against God?' Although she made insinuations to Joseph every day, he refused to lie beside her or even to be with her alone.

Genesis 39:6b-10

Ponder

Temptation comes in many shapes and forms. For some it is sex, for others money; for some drugs, for others power. All of us have our Achilles' heel – a vulnerable spot where temptation unerringly strikes – and though we may resist for a time, it is hard not to succumb when faced by temptation's repeated assaults.

The same must have been true for Joseph, faced by the flirtatious advances of Potiphar's wife – he would have been less than human had he felt no stirring within him. Yet however attracted he may have been, he did not succumb, because he knew that to do so would be to compromise everything he believed. Sold into slavery he may have been, rejected by his own brothers, and faced with an uncertain future in a foreign land; it didn't matter – the principles that underpinned his life and the faith that sustained these still held good. For Joseph, the all-important factor was not what *he* desired but what *God* required. It is a principle that all of us, faced with temptation, do well to follow.

Ask yourself

In what areas of life do you find yourself most vulnerable to temptation? Do you take steps to avoid such temptation, or do you put yourself in situations where you know it will strike?

Pray

Loving God, you know what it is to be tempted, for you took on human flesh, making yourself frail and vulnerable, just as I am. You know what it is to lose everything, for you gave your only Son for the life of the world. For my sake, you became poor, enduring humiliation, and yet you stood firm, refusing to be swayed or to contemplate compromise.

Teach me, in turn, to hold fast, come what may. When temptation comes, help me to seek your will rather than follow my own inclinations, to seek your kingdom rather than pursue my gratification. Show me the way you would have me take, and help me to walk it faithfully, now and always. Amen.

Remember

Keep watch and pray, so that you do not find yourself drawn into temptation – the spirit indeed is willing but the flesh is weak.   *Matthew 26:41*

Close

Living God, lead me away from temptation and deliver me from evil, for your name's sake. Amen.

The God who opens doors!

Read

I will remain at Ephesus until Pentecost, because a great door for valuable work has opened to me, and there are many who oppose me.   *1 Corinthians 16:8-9*

Ponder

'It's not what you know but who you know.' How often have we heard that expression? Times may have changed, but in some areas of life it's still probably the case that a friend in high places or a mention of the old school tie can mean more than all one's qualifications and credentials. Put simply, knowing the right people opens doors. In the context of graft, corruption, and nepotism, that is a fact we may deplore, yet there is a sense in which this saying accurately describes the essence of being a Christian, for at its heart faith is not about what you know but who you know. We do not become a Christian from learning dogma or memorising scripture but through a personal encounter with the living Christ.

The analogy, though, can be pushed further, as Paul's words to the Corinthians make clear. Commitment to Christ does not open doors to fame and fortune but it opens doors nonetheless. It brings opportunities for service and gateways into new experiences of his grace and power. It offers fresh avenues and new possibilities to explore, opening up directions that we may never before have thought possible. What we may consider beyond us, Christ can equip us to meet. What we deem impossible he renders feasible. Where we see no means of entry he shows the way through. Christian discipleship is not about arriving at a safe destination but about discovering doors into uncharted territory. We cannot open such doors on our own, but thankfully, we don't have to; for us, more than anyone, it's not *what* we know but *who* we know. Thank God for that!

Ask yourself

Is God urging you to explore new opportunities for service? Is there something you feel called to do but see no way of achieving? Have you lost sight of God's ability to open doors?

Pray

Gracious God, help me always to remember that you are able to transform situations in a way beyond my expectations, overcoming obstacles, offering strength, equipping with gifts and shaping circumstances to make the impossible become possible. Remind me of the innumerable ways you have acted across history, taking the most unlikely of people and using them in even unlikelier situations to make known your love and fulfil your purpose.

Save me, then, from closing my mind to the opportunities that you might present. Teach me, in my turn, to be alert to your call and ready to respond wherever you might lead, to the glory of your name. In Christ's name I ask it. Amen.

Remember

From Attalia they sailed back to Antioch, where they had been committed to the grace of God for the work they had now completed. Having arrived there and gathered the church together, they related everything God had done through them and how he had opened a door of faith to the nations.   *Acts 14:26-27*

Close

Living God, show me the doors you have opened and teach me to walk through them in faith, trusting in your guidance and power, this day and always. Amen.

Under the carpet

Read

Hatred stirs up strife, but love covers over all offences.

Proverbs 10:12

Ponder

Sweeping things under the carpet – it's not a good idea, is it? Whether we're speaking literally or metaphorically, attempting to keep something hidden rather than tackling it head on only stores up extra trouble in the future.

So, how do we make sense of the words above? At first sight, they seem to suggest love does something much like this, sweeping our mistakes from public view, but this is only half the story. Leave it there, and our faults would always be lying beneath the surface, waiting to be dragged out and used against us at any time. Love is different – it not only covers over our offences but does away with them so completely that when the carpet is lifted there is no trace to be found. Such love is rare in human relationships – few of us, however devoted we may be, are able to forgive and forget – but that is the love God has for us, and the love that he calls us to strive towards in turn.

Ask yourself

Are you willing to forgive and forget, or do you brood over hurts inflicted on you, allowing them to fester deep inside? Is God calling you to put an end to some long-running grievance or dispute?

Pray

Gracious God, once more I thank you for the wonder of your love and the awesome extent of your mercy. I have failed you in so much, repeatedly ignoring your will and breaking your commandments, yet, despite my betrayal, you not only forgive but also put my mistakes behind me.

However often I go astray, however great my faults and however feeble the love I show in return, you are always willing to forget and move on.

Teach me the secret of such love. Touch my heart with your goodness and so may I learn to let go of past hurts and build instead for the future. May I be an agent of your healing, redeeming and renewing grace, to the glory of your name. Amen.

Remember

Above anything else, ensure that your love for one another continues undiminished, for love covers over a multitude of sins.   *1 Peter 4:8*

Close

Lord Jesus Christ, as you have forgiven me, teach me to forgive others, wholly and unreservedly, for your name's sake. Amen.

A prayer from the heart

Read

When praying, do not pile up empty words in the way the Gentiles do, imagining they will be heard because of their eloquence. Do not copy them, for your Father knows everything you need before you even ask him. Pray instead like this: Our Father in heaven, may your name be honoured, your kingdom come and your will be accomplished, on earth as in heaven. Give us the things we need and forgive our debts as we also have forgiven our debtors. Do not bring us into temptation but rescue us from evil.

Matthew 6:7-13

Ponder

Towards the end of my time at secondary school, I wrote what I considered to be one of my best essays, so it was with some excitement that I presented it to my English teacher, fully expecting an enthusiastic response. I was to be disappointed, his only observation being, 'It's a bit long-winded, isn't it.' You'd have thought I might have learned my lesson after that, but a few years later at theological college I received back an assignment from my Old Testament tutor with the following terse appraisal: 'Pompous and verbose.' You may well be sharing his sentiments! Many of us use more words than necessary to get our point across, and that can be especially so when it comes to prayer, not because of any innate wordiness but because we somehow feel we must spell everything out if God is to answer us. We've probably all sat through services in which the prayers are longer than the sermon, or through prayer meetings that seem to go on for ever.

Contrast such experiences with the simple model of prayer given by Jesus, and his equally direct advice on the subject. God knows what we need, Jesus tells us, even before we ask him, prayer being for our benefit rather than his. It's the thought rather than the words that matters most to him. Of course, words have their place but we should never get hung up on them, still less worry that God will not hear us if we don't get them right. Indeed, it's worth asking whether we fail to hear him answer sometimes because we're too busy speaking to listen!

Ask yourself

Do you struggle to find the words in prayer? Does it matter? How far do words help and how far do they hinder?

Pray

Living God, you invite me to share *with* you in prayer but instead I talk *at* you. You invite me to seek your will but I attempt rather to impose my own. You tell me that you know all my needs, yet I present you with a list of demands and requests.

Forgive me the way I misunderstand and abuse prayer. Teach me not only to speak but also to listen, not just to seek but also to find, not simply to bring my requests but also to respond to your call. Remind me that there is a time for words and a time to keep silent, and help me to make room for both. In the name of Christ I pray. Amen.

Remember

Tread carefully when you enter the house of God. Better to draw near and listen than to offer the sacrifice of fools, for they cannot keep themselves from doing evil. Never be in a hurry to talk and do not let your heart speak hastily before God, for God is in heaven and you are upon earth. So, then, let your words be few.   *Ecclesiastes 5:1-2*

Close

Lord Jesus Christ, like your disciples long ago, my prayer today is simply this: Teach me how to pray. Amen.

Being there

Read

Judas and Silas, being prophets themselves, encouraged and built up the fellowship in Antioch. After they had been there some time, the believers sent them back in peace to those who had sent them. However, it seemed right to Silas to remain there. Similarly, Paul and Barnabas, and many others, stayed in Antioch, teaching and preaching the word of the Lord.

Acts 15:32-35

Ponder

If I said the names 'Paul' and 'Silas' in the same breath, which one would you immediately recognise? The answer, of course, is Paul, the celebrated Apostle who did so much to further the gospel during the early days of the Church. We can overlook the fact that for many of his missionary journeys he was accompanied by Silas, but though *we* might forget the contribution Silas made, *Paul* never did.

What was it, then, that made Paul value Silas so much? For one thing, Silas may have acted as his scribe, recording his letters as he dictated them. For another, he clearly had gifts in his own right, regarded as a leader of the Church among Christians back in Jerusalem. Perhaps, though, what stood out above all else was, quite simply, his willingness to be there when needed. Whatever Paul came up against, he knew that Silas would be ready to face it with him. Imprisoned, beaten, attacked, insulted, it made no difference – he remained a friend in need, someone to lean on in moments of crisis. Never underestimate that gift, for it is one of the most precious there is, and one that each of us can show in our turn. It may not seem much – simply being there – yet for someone going through the mill it can mean more than any words or action.

Ask yourself

Is there someone you know of who is in need of a friend to stand alongside them? Have you underestimated the importance simply of being there, imagining instead that there is something you need to do or say if you are to offer help?

Pray

Loving God, thank you for always being with me, whatever I may face, to strengthen, encourage, comfort and protect. Thank you for those around me who I can count on to be there when I need them. Teach me through their simple yet vital ministry – their willingness to share my troubles and bear my burdens – that there is nothing I need face alone. Teach me to share that ministry in turn, ready to draw alongside those in any kind of need and to offer support and companionship. Help me to understand that it is not so much the things I say or do that matter at such times, but simply being there.

So may I give expression to your love and bring home your presence, to the glory of your name. Amen.

Remember

With the help of Silas, whom I regard as a faithful brother, I have written to you briefly, encouraging you and testifying that this is the true grace of God. *1 Peter 5:12*

Close

Lord Jesus Christ, as you have been there for me, help me to be there for others, for your name's sake. Amen.

Done and undone

Read

There is, then, no condemnation now for those in Christ Jesus, because the law of the Spirit of life has set us free from the law of sin and death. I am convinced that nothing can separate us from Christ's love. Neither death nor life, nor angels nor demons, nor the present nor the future, nor any powers, nor height nor depth nor anything else in all creation, will ever be able to separate us from the love of God that is ours in Christ Jesus our Lord.

Romans 8:1-2, 38-39

Ponder

Why is it that a piece of string, no matter how carefully you put it away in a drawer, always ties itself into knots? Even more perplexing, how is it that children's shoelaces, however painstakingly you may tie them, manage to come undone within a few paces? Whoever succeeds in answering such mysteries will be a rich person indeed! It's not just string and shoelaces, however, that become tangled into knots or come undone; we find the same in so much in life. Tackle a pile of washing up or ironing, mow the lawn or weed the garden, clean the car or paint the house, and before you know it the job needs doing again, but make one simple mistake and, however hard we try, we can't undo it. Or can we?

At the heart of our faith lies a triumphant message of something both done and undone. On the one hand, nothing can undo what God has done in Christ. Through his death and resurrection, he has destroyed the power of evil and opened the way to life for all. What needed doing has been done, and nothing can ever change that! Yet, on the other hand, through that decisive act, everything else done can be undone, for God is always ready to put the past behind us and to help us start again. To assume that we are bound by what has gone before is to deny the glorious resurrection message. Whatever we are, or have been, we can always be a new creation! The past is done with, the future is open – thanks be to God!

Ask yourself

Do you feel tied down by past mistakes? Have you recognised that God has dealt with these once and for all in Christ?

Pray

Living God, there are times when I feel dismayed that nothing seems to change for the better. I go on making the same mistakes I've always made, and all around there seems to be as much sorrow and suffering, hatred and evil as there has ever been.

Help me to hold on to the conviction that things can change, remembering how, in the resurrection of Christ, you overcame the power of sin and death. Help me to remember that, though everything may seem to conspire against your purpose, you have won the victory through him – a victory that nothing can ever undo – and so may I trust in your ability to transform and renew all things, by his grace. Amen.

Remember

In all these things we are more than conquerors through him who loved us.   *Romans 8:37*

Close

Lord Jesus Christ, for the victory you have won over sin and death, and the victories you continue to win in my life, receive my praise. Amen.

A faith to die for

Read

Full of the Holy Spirit, [Stephen] gazed into heaven and saw there the glory of God with Jesus standing at his right hand, and he said, 'Look, the heavens are open, and I can see the Son of Man standing at God's right hand.' Then, crying out with a mighty roar of rage and shutting their ears to his words, they fell upon him with one mind. They cast him out of the city and stoned him, and as they stoned him he called out in the name of Christ, saying, 'Lord Jesus, receive my spirit.' Then, falling on his knees, he cried out in a voice all could hear, 'Lord, do not hold this sin against them.' And, having said this, he fell asleep.

Acts 7:55-58a, 59-60

Ponder

Nearly 400 years ago, the world of medicine was plunged into controversy by an English physician, William Harvey, who contradicted established wisdom by suggesting that blood is pumped from the heart to the lungs, back through the heart and then out via the arteries before returning to the heart through the veins. The theory was spot on, but at the time it aroused a storm of protest from medical, scientific and religious 'authorities'. At around the same time, Galileo caused yet greater consternation with his hypothesis that the earth orbits the sun rather than vice versa. So shocking was this considered that he was forced to recant and put under house arrest for the remainder of his life. Each of these two men, however, continued with their work, refusing to sacrifice their beliefs despite intolerable pressures.

There are parallels here with the story of Stephen, the first Christian martyr. On trial for his faith, it must have been tempting to tone down his message, even opt for secret discipleship, for he knew well enough the consequences should he refuse to back down. Yet, instead he spoke out boldly, conscious that many would take their lead from him. Had he and others like him given in and denied their faith, who can say where the Church would be today – whether indeed the gospel message would have died an early death there in Jerusalem. It is unlikely that any of us will ever be called upon to die for our faith but how ready are we to live up to it in a sceptical and sometimes hostile world?

Ask yourself

How easily would you compromise or even abandon your faith? Does Jesus mean to you what he should?

Pray

Lord Jesus Christ, thank you for staying true to your calling to the very end, refusing to compromise your mission in any way. Thank you for all those who have followed in your footsteps, giving their all for the sake of the gospel.

Teach me to walk faithfully in your way rather than follow the course of least resistance, to stand up for what I believe rather than go along with the crowd. Help me to understand all you have done for me, and so may my life be spent in your service, to the glory of your name. Amen.

Remember

Anyone who denies me before others, I in turn will deny before my Father in heaven. *Matthew 10:33*

Close

Teach me, good Lord, to serve you as you deserve. To give and not to count the cost, to fight and not to heed the wounds, to toil and not to seek for rest, to labour and not to ask for any reward, save that of knowing that I do your will, through Jesus Christ my Lord. Amen.

Prayer of St Ignatius Loyola

Letting go

Read

As he prayed, his face was transformed and his clothes became a dazzling white. Then two men appeared, Moses and Elijah, talking with him. Peter and those who were with him, having fallen asleep, were startled into wakefulness and they saw his glory and the two men alongside him. As these two departed Peter said to Jesus, not really knowing what he was saying, 'Master, it is good for us to be here. Let us make three tents: one for you, one for Moses and one for Elijah.'

Luke 9:29-30, 32-33

Ponder

Some moments mean so much to us that we wish we could pop them into a bottle and preserve them unchanged so that the happiness they bring never fades. I feel like that as I write, having spent a wonderful weekend with my family, away from it all – no work, no telephone, no pressures – an opportunity to unwind, spend some quality time with the children and rejoice in the indescribable beauty of this world God has given us. The memories of that time are still fresh in my mind as I sit now in my garden, the last rays of the sun dipping below the trees and a blackbird singing its heart out nearby. If I could put time on hold, I couldn't choose a better moment than this. Yet, if I could do that, how long would my joy remain untarnished? Unpalatable though it is to admit it, familiarity would soon rob the moment of its magic. In this world, life must move on if it is to keep its sparkle.

That was a truth Peter was to learn the hard way at that mysterious event we call the Transfiguration. He recognised the moment as special and wanted to keep hold of it, to the point of suggesting that he and his colleagues build tents so that Jesus, Moses and Elijah could remain there a little longer. It wasn't to be, though. Life had to move on. Jesus had to walk the way of the cross for which he had been born; Peter and his fellow Apostles had more to learn, more to experience and more to understand. The lesson holds true for us today. One day we will savour a joy that will never fade or end but, until then, we must treasure every God-given moment for what it is and then move on. We cannot preserve any moment, no matter how special. Attempt to do so and far from holding on to it, we will destroy it instead.

Ask yourself

Are you attempting to hang on to the past rather than move on to the future? Have you the faith to believe that God holds the best things yet in store?

Pray

Loving God, occasionally there are moments that I never want to end, moments so special that I wish time would stand still so that I could hold on to them for ever, but I know that neither life or faith is like that, instead always needing to move on if it is not to grow stale.

Help me, then, to be open to new experiences of your love and new insights into your greatness, so that I may know you better each day, until that time I rejoice in your presence for all eternity, in the joy of Christ that will never fade or perish. In his name I ask it. Amen.

Remember

Jesus said, 'Mary!' She turned to him and said 'Rabbouni!' (which is Hebrew for 'My Master'). Jesus said, 'Do not cling to me, for I have not yet ascended to the Father. But go to my brothers, and tell them that I am now ascending to my Father and your Father, my God and your God.'

John 20:16-17 (NEB)

Close

Lord Jesus Christ, save me from so dwelling on all that has been that I overlook your blessings now and your promise of joy to come. Amen.

Theory and practice

Read

Put the trumpet to your lips! A vulture soars over the sanctuary of the Lord, because they have broken my covenant and defied my law. They appeal to me for help, crying, 'We know you, Lord God of Israel.' But Israel has rejected what is right, and in consequence will be pursued by the enemy. They established kings against my wishes; they set up leaders without my knowledge; they have created idols of silver and gold for themselves.   *Hosea 8:1-4*

Ponder

Take an exam today and the chances are that you will find a much greater emphasis upon practical work than was once the case. Increasingly, it is recognised that while theory is important, it is equally important to know how to use it; to be able to apply knowledge to daily life. On paper, we may know everything there is to know about a subject, yet we barely have a clue how to act upon it. On the other hand, in some tests the emphasis upon theory has been stepped up. Enrol now for a driving test and as well as showing the examiner that you know how to drive you must also display a sound knowledge of the Highway Code. The fact is that both theory and practice are important, each complementing the other.

Sadly, when it comes to serving God, that is all too often forgotten. So it was with the people of Israel in the days of the prophet Hosea. They believed that they knew God inside out but they were mistaken. They knew *about* him – what he had done and what he promised to do – but they no longer acted upon it. Faith had become divorced from life, with disastrous consequences. The danger is just as real today. We can all too easily become nominal Christians, professing faith in Christ and yet showing no evidence of commitment in terms of the way we live. Equally, we can turn commitment into a matter of doing good works, loving others and working for a better society, forgetting the underlying message of the gospel. We need to make room for both if faith is to be authentic, spending time in prayer, study and reflection in order to know God better, but also acting upon what we learn of him and his will for our lives. Theory and practice – don't let either one get the better of the other.

Ask yourself
In what ways do you nurture your faith, seeking opportunities to know God better? In what ways does your faith show itself in action?

Pray
Gracious God, I do not know you or serve you as I should, my faith sometimes short both on theory and practice. I am careless in making time for you, rarely stopping to read your word or seek your will. I am casual in discipleship, more concerned with serving myself than you or others.

Help me to know you better and to love you more deeply, and may that in turn help me to prove my love for you in action, showing the sincerity of my faith by practising what I preach, to the glory of your name. Amen.

Remember
Brothers and sisters, what use is it for people to claim they have faith if they have no works to show for it? Can that faith save them?   *James 2:14*

Close
Lord God, light of the minds that know you, life of the souls that love you, strength of the wills that serve you, help me so to know you that I may truly love you, and so to love you that I may fully serve you, whose service is perfect freedom, through Jesus Christ my Lord. Amen.

Gelasian Sacramentary

Shoulder to shoulder

Read

Then I will cleanse the lips of the nations, that all people may call on the name of the Lord and serve him shoulder to shoulder.

Zephaniah 3:9

Ponder

Just a few years after the death of Jesus, Roman legions under the leadership of the emperor Claudius sailed across to Britain from Gaul and, before long, added the bulk of these shores to their already vast empire – another addition to a long list of successful conquests. So, what lay behind their astonishing success? Numerous factors were involved but few were more important than the simple yet highly effective tactic they followed in battle: the tactic of standing shoulder to shoulder and fighting as a co-ordinated unit. Not for them the wild undisciplined attacks of the Britons; instead, their success was built on teamwork, on working together come what may.

There is something of that idea in the wonderful words of the prophet Zephaniah as he looked towards a new era in which God's people would stand shoulder to shoulder in God's service; a time when instead of looking to their own interests, each would strive first for the kingdom of God. We can apply that picture to discipleship today. However great our resolve, there is little way we can grow as Christians without the stimulus and support of others. However great our faith, there is still less we can achieve in God's service on our own. If we are to make any impact on society, any significant difference to the world we live in, then we need to work together, both with those in our own fellowship and within the wider Church. Solitary discipleship may have its attractions, but ultimately it sells both God and self short. We are part of a new people, a holy nation, that

God has called into being to serve him shoulder to shoulder in one faith and in the common cause of Christ.

Ask yourself

Are you playing your part in the life of the Church? Do you stand in solidarity with fellow-Christians in your own fellowship and beyond?

Pray

Loving God, you have called me into the fellowship of the Church, to work alongside your people for the growth of your kingdom. You have called me into a family through which I can find support, encouragement, strength and inspiration. Forgive me the many times I have lost sight of that truth, neglecting my responsibilities towards others and overlooking the contribution they can make to my life in turn.

Forgive me for going it alone rather than standing with my brothers and sisters in Christ; for allowing apathy, selfishness, mistrust or differences of opinion to obscure the unity we should share in the gospel. Open my eyes to everything I can give and receive, and so may my faith be enriched and my service renewed, to the glory of your name. Amen.

Remember

Whatever happens, conduct yourselves in a manner befitting the gospel of Christ, so that, whether I come and see you for myself or only hear reports concerning you in my absence, I will know that you stand resolute in one spirit, striving together with a common purpose for the faith of the gospel.   *Philippians 1:27*

Close

Living God, teach me that I need others just as they need me, and so may I discharge my responsibilities faithfully within the great company of your people, to the glory of your name. Amen.

A point of reference

Read

I, the Lord, do not change.   *Malachi 3:6a*

Ponder

Searching through my bookshelves the other day, I came across a couple of books about my home town, Southend-on-Sea – *Southend Past* and *Edwardian Heyday*. The two comprise a fascinating collection of photographs showing the town in bygone days, and to see the difference that just over a century has made is truly astounding. Take the area of Prittlewell, where I spent most of my childhood years and where my parents still live. Today, it is a busy, feature-less area with little to distinguish it from the urban sprawl that has swallowed it up, but 120 years ago it was the main habitation in the area and a truly delightful village full of timber-framed cottages and rustic charm. Were it possible to travel through time, a visitor from the past would imagine they had come to the wrong place, except for one feature: the parish church of St Mary's that still presides majestically over its centre – a welcome point of reference in a forever changing landscape. Not that you have to go back a hundred years to notice changes: almost every shop I remember as a boy has either closed down or changed its use, and once quiet roads are now busy thoroughfares.

The case of Southend, of course, is repeated in towns up and down the country, and is but one more example of the way life itself is in a constant state of flux. As the years pass, not only places change but us with them, our attitudes, opinions, beliefs and convictions repeatedly challenged and shaken, if not completely undermined. Many find themselves not knowing what to believe in, life apparently without meaning or direction. Yet, as the prophet Malachi reminded the people of Judah centuries ago, there is a point of reference for us all in the one true God; the God who tells us, 'I, the Lord, do not change.' That is a promise which generations of believers across the years have found to be true, in a world where everything else seems never to stay the same.

Ask yourself

Do you feel overwhelmed by changes taking place in your life, or depressed by the rapid pace of change around you? Have you lost sight of the revelation of God in Christ – the same yesterday, today and tomorrow?

Pray

Living God, even in my lifetime so much has changed, so many of the things that I took to be enduring features turning out to be passing shadows. It is hard not to be unsettled by it all, and harder still not to question whether anything is permanent, even your love. I find myself all at sea, like a ship without an anchor, overwhelmed by a sense of helplessness in stemming the relentless flow of time, and I look around in desperation for something to support me; a lifeline to keep me afloat.

Teach me to look to you, the one unchanging reality in a world that is constantly moving on. Teach me that you alone offer a hope that endures and a life that defies the ravages of the years, and so may I keep my eyes fixed on you, come what may, assured that though all else may fade away, your love will remain the same, unchanged and unchangeable. In Christ's name I ask it. Amen.

Remember

He himself has said, 'I will never leave you or forsake you.'
Hebrews 13:5b

Close

Living God, help me in this uncertain and fleeting world to keep my eyes fixed on you, knowing that though all else may change, you will not. Amen.

A changed life

Read

A certain young man accompanied him, wearing nothing but a linen cloth. They grabbed hold of him, but he wriggled out of the cloth and ran off naked.　　　*Mark 14:51-52*

Ponder

Who was the young man who ran off naked into the night at the time of the arrest of Jesus? That question has fascinated scholars across the years and although no definitive answer has been given, the general consensus of opinion favours John Mark, the writer of the gospel in which this enigmatic character is mentioned. It's an intriguing thought, isn't it – both heart-warming and inspiring to think that someone so desperate to disassociate himself from Jesus could, in the space of a few years, become the writer of what most regard as the earliest of all the gospels, eagerly testifying to his faith in the risen Christ.

If the conjecture is right, was this, I wonder, the first time that Mark had faced up to the incident? Presumably so, for why else refer to it so obliquely? It seems he still couldn't bring himself to come clean completely, yet he wanted to testify to what for him must have been the most marvellous truth in the already unforgettable gospel message: the fact that Jesus had changed *him*, turning his life inside out and upside down. The same testimony, together with a similar sense of wonder, can equally be ours! No one is outside the transforming power of his saving love and no mistake is beyond his forgiveness. He is constantly at work in the lives of all who will receive him, to redeem, renew and restore. Whoever you are, Jesus can change you!

Ask yourself

Have you learned to let go of former mistakes, recognising that they are past history? Are you open to the difference Jesus can make in your life?

Pray

Loving God, there are some things in my past I would rather forget but that return to haunt me – foolish actions, hasty words, evil thoughts, wasted opportunities – things I should have done but haven't or that I shouldn't have done but have. I find it hard to forgive myself, harder still to think that others can do so and hardest of all to believe that you can ever forgive me. Yet, though *I* may condemn myself, and others do the same, *you* repeatedly show me how you are able to change lives, not just forgiving past mistakes but also making people new, renewing them from within through your Holy Spirit.

Help me, then, to bring all the feelings of guilt and shame that hold me down, and to open my life to your renewing touch in Christ, for in his name I ask it. Amen.

Remember

You, who were dead in your sins and the uncircumcision of your flesh, he has brought to life with him, having forgiven you all your sins. *Colossians 2:13*

Close

Lord Jesus Christ, help me always to remember that you are able to change not just other people's lives but mine too, and so renew me day by day through your redeeming grace. Amen.

Seeking God's glory

Read

Let your attitude be the same as that which distinguished Christ Jesus, who, though he was in the form of God, did not regard equality with God as something to be exploited. Instead, he emptied himself, taking the form of a servant and sharing our humanity, and, having taken on human form, he humbled himself to total obedience, even to the point of death – death on a cross. For that reason, God highly exalted him, giving him the name that is above every name, so that at the name of Jesus every being in heaven, on earth and under the earth should kneel, and every tongue should acknowledge that Jesus Christ is Lord, to the glory of God the Father.   *Philippians 2:5-11*

Ponder

During my ministry in Cheltenham, I had the opportunity once of touring a local radio station, and I got into conversation with the presenter of the station's Christian and religious programmes. It gave me a fascinating insight not only into the world of a radio presenter, but also into an aspect of human nature. The station, it turned out, operated on a tight budget, so much so that there was no way it could pay most of the people who appeared on its programmes. Presenters relied instead on individuals wanting to hear their voice on radio, eager to enjoy their few minutes of fame, and the system was eminently effective – there was never any shortage of applicants! Personally, the thought of being interviewed in any public forum fills me with cold dread, but I can understand the line of reasoning well enough. We all like to feel important, don't we? A bit of praise, appreciation, even admiration warms the cockles of one's heart, and there's nothing necessarily wrong with that – praise where praise is due has its place.

Yet, as Christians, we need to beware, for we are not in the business of drawing attention to ourselves. We can slip into that more easily than we might think; self-righteousness and self-congratulation being beguiling traps for the unwary. Paul points us instead to Jesus, the one who more than any other had reason to point to himself, but always his concern was to point to the Father and bring glory to him. Is that our concern too, the goal to which all our efforts are directed? Or is our faith, for all its outward piety, ultimately more about our own self-image; about what others may think of us rather than him? 'To God be the glory', says the old hymn. How far do our lives echo those words?

Ask yourself

Whose glory are you most concerned with: your own or God's. To whom does your life point?

Pray

Gracious God, I don't mean to put myself before you; it just happens. I talk of your glory, but it is my own that concerns me. I speak of bringing honour to your name, yet I waste so much energy nursing or nurturing my ego instead.

Forgive me the pride that lurks deep within, claiming the praise that is rightfully yours. Forgive me my failure to follow and learn from Christ. Teach me, as he did, to humble myself under your mighty hand, so that in your own time you may lift me up. Amen.

Remember

Those who speak of themselves seek their own glory, but he who seeks the glory of the one who sent him, this one is true, and there is no unrighteousness in him.   *John 7:18*

Close

Living God, help me to live for you so that your life may shine through me, to the glory of your name. Amen.

A life of prayer

Read

Epaphras, from among your number and a servant of Jesus Christ, sends greetings. He is always wrestling on your behalf in prayer, asking that you may stand firm, mature and fully assured of the will of God.

Colossians 4:12

Ponder

'I'll pray for you.' Countless individuals must have made that promise innumerable times across the years, but what does it actually mean? Sometimes it is little more than a platitude; a suitably pious-sounding way of avoiding the need to offer any more concrete help. Usually, though, we offer it in all sincerity, but, despite our best intentions, fail to act upon it. We mean to pray, but there are so many needs to pray for and so little time in which to do it. Meaningful prayer tends to go out of the window, reduced to a few cursory and general words. Contrast that with the tribute paid by Paul to the man at the centre of our reading today: Epaphras, a man who was 'always wrestling in prayer' for the Philippians. Of all his gifts, this, in Paul's opinion, was what made Epaphras stand out – his dedication to prayer.

So what can we learn here? First, for Epaphras prayer wasn't a casual take-it-or-leave-it activity; it was part of his life, a privilege and responsibility he wrestled with day by day. It wasn't a vague activity, either. He knew whom he was praying for, what he was praying about and why he was praying. Equally, prayer wasn't simply concerned with his own affairs or his immediate circle. It reached out to others, concerned with their needs and ultimate welfare. Finally, and most important, he acted upon his prayers. 'I can personally testify,' Paul went on to say, 'that he works tirelessly, both for you and for those in Laodicea and Hierapolis.' What exactly he did, we are not told, but it is clear that

Epaphras didn't leave it all to God; he played his part in ensuring his prayers were answered. 'I'll pray for you.' It's a wonderful promise if we really mean it. How many of us actually do?

Ask yourself
What do you find hardest about prayer? In what ways have you ever wrestled in prayer?

Pray
Loving God, I am good at talking about prayer but poor when it comes to praying. I find that the words just don't come or I find myself repeating the same old things. I speak of a conversation, but the reality is more typically a monologue, and on the rare occasions I make time to listen, I struggle to hear your voice. The result is that I give up, prayer pushed to one side, conveniently forgotten, until some tragedy or crisis awakens me to my need of you.

Forgive me for abusing prayer, using it as an excuse to avoid real service. Forgive me my misguided prayers, looking only to my ends rather than yours. Forgive me my neglect of prayer, my reluctance to take it seriously or to devote time to you. Teach me what it means to wrestle in prayer and what it means to act in faith, and so may I use your gift as you intended, to the glory of your name. Amen.

Remember
Persevere in prayer, remaining constantly alert in it with thanksgiving.   *Colossians 4:2*

Close
Living God, grant that not only my words but everything I am and do may be offered to you as a living prayer, in the name of Christ. Amen.

A glimpse of glory

Read

As I looked, a stormy wind came out of the north: a great cloud with brightness around it and fire flashing forth continually, and in the middle of the fire something like gleaming amber. In the middle of it was something like four living creatures. In the middle of the living creatures there was something that looked like burning coals of fire, like torches moving to and fro among the living creatures; the fire was bright, and lightning issued from the fire. As I looked at the living creatures, I saw a wheel on the earth beside the living creatures, one for each of the four of them, their construction being something like a wheel within a wheel. Over the heads of the living creatures there was something like a dome, shining like crystal, spread out above their heads. And above the dome over their heads there was something like a throne, in appearance like sapphire; and seated above the likeness of a throne was something that seemed like a human form. Like the bow in a cloud on a rainy day, such was the appearance of the splendour all around. This was the appearance of the likeness of the glory of the Lord.

Ezekiel 1:4-5a, 13, 15, 16b, 22, 26, 28 (NRSV)

Ponder

The more established we become in our faith, the more fixed our picture of God can become. It's not that we consciously let this happen; it's simply that we settle into a rut – and the deeper we sink, the harder we find it to escape. The vision that once fired our imagination becomes blurred; the sense of God's love and power that previously excited us becomes just another article of faith.

Just occasionally, however, something happens that brings God sharply back into focus. That's what happened to the prophet Ezekiel, carted off to exile in Babylon. For him and his fellow Judeans it must have been a desperate time. How could God allow it to happen? The experience was deeply disturbing, but the divine encounter that resulted from it was to change Ezekiel's life for ever, for through his extraordinary, mind-boggling vision he came to realise that God was far greater than he had ever dared imagine, more wonderful than the mind can even begin to fathom!

Ask yourself

Why does it sometimes take a crisis to focus your mind again on God? Have you lost the sense of wonder you once felt in his presence?

Pray

Gracious God, you are above all, beneath all, beyond all, within all. You are God of past, present and future; of space and time, heaven and earth; of all people, all creatures and all creation.

Forgive me for sometimes losing sight of those awesome realities, settling instead for a fragmented picture of who you are shaped by my narrow horizons and flawed and limited understanding. Stir my imagination, and help me to see a little more clearly each day the wonder of your glory. In Christ's name I ask it. Amen.

Remember

Now to the God and Father of us all, be glory, now and for evermore. Amen.   *Philippians 4:20*

Close

Sovereign God, open my heart afresh to the wonder of your presence, the awesomeness of your power, the breadth of your love and the extent of your purpose, and so may I live each day to the glory of your name. Amen.

A clean sheet

Read

In the year King Uzziah died, I saw the Lord enthroned on high, exalted over all; and the hem of his robe filled the temple. Seraphim waited upon him, each having six wings; two of which they used to cover their faces, two to cover their feet, and two to fly. They called back and forth to one another, saying, 'Holy, holy, holy is the Lord of hosts; the whole earth is full of his glory.' At the sound of their voices the threshold shook and the house was filled with smoke. And I cried out, 'Woe am I! I am lost, for I am a man of unclean lips, living among a people of unclean lips; yet with my own eyes I have seen the King, the Lord of hosts!' Then one of the seraphim flew to me, holding in his hand a burning coal taken from the altar with a pair of tongs. The seraph touched my mouth with it and said, 'Since this has touched your lips, your guilt is no more and your sin is done away with.' Then I heard the voice of the Lord saying, 'Whom shall I send? Who will go for me?' And I said, 'Here I am; send me!'

Isaiah 6:1-8

Ponder

One of the tragedies of the Church is that it has acquired a reputation for being smug, self-righteous, holier than thou. How this has happened I do not know, for while some in the Church are more than ready to sit in judgement, by far the majority are too aware of their own faults to point the accusing finger at others. Such, at least, has been my experience. The heart of the Christian message is one of forgiveness rather than judgement; about the God who is ready to accept us as we are, rather than as we should be. Of course this involves a desire to change, but it begins and ends with God rather than ourselves. The truth of that is most clearly demonstrated through Christ, but it was discovered centuries before by countless others.

So it was that a young man, worshipping in the temple of Jerusalem, suddenly found himself faced by the call of God. Hopelessly inadequate though he felt, burdened by a profound sense of unworthiness, Isaiah discovered that God is always ready to take the initiative in offering us a fresh start. All that he needed to do was respond, and with that began one of the most remarkable prophetic ministries of all time, his words touching the hearts of generations across the centuries. All we need to do is respond in turn, to discover the new beginning God longs to bring us, a new beginning not of our own making but entirely of his grace.

Ask yourself
Have you accepted the forgiveness of God, recognising that he wants to use you as you are?

Pray
Gracious God, I have no claim on your goodness, no reason to expect your mercy. Despite my best intentions, I repeatedly fail you, preferring my way to yours. I say one thing, yet do another; I claim to love you, yet openly flout your will. Forgive me, for, try as I might, I cannot help myself.

Renew me through your Spirit, redeem me through the grace of Christ, and remake me through your great love, so that I might live and work for you, to the glory of your name. Amen.

Remember
If you, Lord, should keep account of our sins, which of us could hold up our head before you? In you, though, is forgiveness, and consequently we worship you.

Psalm 130:3-4a

Close
Loving God, teach me what it means to be made new, and help me to receive each moment as a fresh start, through the grace of Christ. Amen.

The spitting image

Read

He is the image of the invisible God, the firstborn of all creation, because through him all things in heaven and on earth were created, both visible and invisible, whether thrones, dominions, rulers or powers – each has been created through him and for him. He is before all, and everything holds together through him. In him, God was pleased fully to dwell, and through him to reconcile all things to himself, whether on earth or in heaven, by making peace through the blood of his cross.   *Colossians 1:15-17, 19-20*

Ponder

'Isn't he like his dad!' we often say, or 'Isn't she like her mum!' 'Look at those eyes, that nose – the spitting image of his father! Look at her chin, her mouth! A dead ringer for her mother!' The similarities between parent and child can indeed be remarkable, and that usually extends further than mere physical resemblance. Like it or not, our gestures, mannerisms, temperaments and attitudes all betray our origins, far more than we might realise. Not that two people are ever the same, but there can be remarkable likenesses between them. However great these may be, though, they are nothing compared with the likeness Paul speaks of in his letter to the Colossians: that between Jesus and God. Here is a parallel unlike any other, closer and more striking even than perfectly identical twins, for the Son does not just resemble his Father; he fully and completely makes him known. To know Jesus is to know God, to look at his life is to see God at work, to experience his love is to be touched by God's love in turn, and so it goes on.

It is a startling claim at any level, but altogether astonishing when we recall that the God we are talking about here is the same God who, according to the Old Testament, is enthroned in righteousness, mighty in power, greater than the human mind can comprehend and so holy that nothing impure can stand before him. A yawning gulf had separated him from humankind, any knowledge of him partial and once removed, but suddenly it is different – God made flesh, sharing our humanity and inviting us to share his life. That is the truth at the heart of the gospel, the message we celebrate today and every day. We are not limited simply to knowing *about* God; we are invited to know him for ourselves in a daily relationship with Christ – the spitting image of the Father!

Ask yourself

What sort of God do you see in Jesus? What attribute stands out most clearly in his life?

Pray

Living God, I know that your ways are not my ways, or your thoughts my thoughts. I know that you are sovereign over heaven and earth, ruler over space and time – above, beyond, before and after all. Yet, you have made yourself known to me in Christ, revealed your love, demonstrating your mercy, granting your blessing and sharing your life.

In him, I glimpse something of your majesty and experience the wonder of your grace. From him, I receive peace and fulfilment that passes all understanding. Through him, I offer my thanks and give to you honour and worship, praise and glory, now and for evermore. Amen.

Remember

No one has ever seen God, but the only Son of the Father – the one closest to him – has made him known to us.

John 1:18

Close

Lord Jesus Christ, make me one with you, just as you are one with the Father. Remake me in his image, so that something of him may shine from me, to the glory of his name. Amen.

In Christ, in . . . ?

Read

From Paul, by God's will an apostle of Jesus Christ, and Timothy our brother, to the holy and faithful brothers and sisters in Christ in Colossae: grace and peace to you from God our Father. Whenever we pray for you, we always thank God, the Father of our Lord Jesus Christ, because we have heard of your faith and love for all the saints, springing from the hope stored up for you in heaven that you heard about in the word of truth, the gospel that has come to you. So then, having received Christ as Lord, continue to live in him, rooted and growing in him, established in the faith taught to you, and overflowing with thanksgiving.

Colossians 1:1-6a; 2:6-7

Ponder

For today's reading I could just as easily have chosen the opening words of any of Paul's letters, for they all have one thing in common – they each relate to a specific group in a specific place called to a specific task. One or two letters were intended as circulars, to be passed on to other groups in a similar situation, but the underlying intention was always the same – Paul wrote to encourage Christians in a variety of locations to work out their faith *where God had put them*.

It may seem a small point but it's a vital one, for it earths faith in reality, underlining the need for commitment to be visible in the routine business of daily life. We can all be Christians in church on a Sunday. We can all make the right noises in our personal devotions, locked comfortably away in the privacy of our own homes. We can all seem suitably devout in our concern for the needs of the world or the ills of society in general. All such things are important but they are second to what really counts: to putting our faith into practice here and now, wherever we find ourselves. This is the acid test of commitment and the yardstick whereby we will be judged by others: whether the faith we profess is reflected in the things we do; whether the person we *are* corresponds to the person we *claim* to be; whether the love we talk about is seen in action. We may profess the name of Christ as often as we wish, but what Paul would want to ask us is this: is our commitment evident to others?

Ask yourself

Are there ways in which you can express your faith through involvement in your local community or neighbourhood? Is there someone in your street, or perhaps even in your family, who needs your help and support? How far could anyone use Paul's words to the Thessalonians (see below) to describe the daily outworking of your faith?

Pray

Lord Jesus Christ, help me to show my faith not just in abstract love for the world but also in practical service to those around me. In my daily relationships – at home, at work, at leisure, at church; whenever and wherever it might be – teach me to live out my faith in such a way that my life embodies the claims and truth of the gospel, to the glory of your name. Amen.

Remember

We continually remember before our God and Father your work produced by faith, your labour prompted by love, and your endurance inspired by hope in our Lord Jesus Christ.   *1 Thessalonians 1:3*

Close

Living God, you have made yourself real to me in Christ. Help me now to make you real to others, demonstrating the reality of my faith through the person I am, the service I offer and the life I lead, to the glory of your name. Amen.

Pot-bound Christians?

Read

He gave some to be Apostles, some prophets, some evangelists, and some pastors and teachers, to prepare God's people for practical service and to build up the body of Christ until we are united in faith and the knowledge of the Son of God, attaining maturity corresponding to the full measure we see in Christ. Then we will no longer be like children. Instead, speaking the truth in love, we will in every respect grow into the one who is the Head; that is, Christ.

Ephesians 4:11-14a, 15

Ponder

I couldn't work it out at all. It has been doing well until then – a beautiful healthy plant growing with seemingly inexhaustible vigour – but now something was wrong; the once glossy leaves a listless yellow, new growth sparse and the stems spindly. I tried feeding, watering, pruning it, but to no avail – the malaise continued to worsen. Then, suddenly, I realised the problem, a tangle of roots protruding from the base of the container providing the vital clue. The plant was pot-bound, crying out for space in which to spread its feet. A few weeks later, repotted with a liberal supply of fresh compost, it was romping away with all its former exuberance.

The analogy with faith is clear enough. When we start out in discipleship growth is rapid, everything new and exciting, so much to learn and discover – our commitment seeming to blossom with every passing day. Imperceptibly, however, the process stutters, slows, stops, until, instead of growing in faith, our devotion starts to shrivel and our enthusiasm to fade. We become comfortably ensconced in the same old soil, resenting any disturbance, unaware that our faith is being starved and suffocated, inexorably sucked dry. If it is not ultimately to die, we need to be open to new horizons, receptive to ideas other than our own, and ready to explore new avenues of service. You may have grown once, you may think you are growing still, but the reality may be that you've become a pot-bound Christian. The more vehemently you reject that possibility, the more likely it may be.

Ask yourself
Are you still open to new ideas and insights? Do you still expect to grow in your faith?

Pray
Living God, I thank you for the seed of faith you have sown within me and for the way it has grown across the years, but I confess also that there are times when all is not as it should be. Instead of continuing to flourish, my commitment starts to flag and my vision to wilt, cramped by the narrowness of my horizons, suffocated by complacency and starved of space in which to expand.

Forgive me for allowing that to happen and accepting it as the norm. Help me to open my life to you so that you can feed me through your word, nourish me through your Spirit and nurture me through the gracious love of Christ, in whose name I pray. Amen.

Remember
Grow in grace and in the knowledge of our Lord and Saviour Jesus Christ.   *2 Peter 3:18a*

Close
Living God, teach me that whatever I have learned about you and however established my faith may be, there is still more to discover and further to grow. Open my life, then, to new horizons, through Christ my Lord. Amen.

An unwitting mistake

Read

You know my folly, O God; there can be no hiding my
wrongs from you.   *Psalm 69:5*

Ponder

'Robot Wars' pyjamas! – it was just what we were looking
for, so we hung them on the pushchair and continued our
look round the store. Some time later and several shops
further on, we looked down in horror, for there were the
pyjamas, still hanging where we'd put them earlier. Somehow, we'd paid for everything else but clean forgotten
about these, walking away with them, security tag and all!
Luckily, I was able to rectify my mistake, hurrying back to
the shop to settle up, but that experience brought home to
me how easy it is inadvertently to make a mistake. A moment
of carelessness, a word thoughtlessly spoken, or simply a
case of sheer forgetfulness such as mine, and we can find
we've done wrong though it was the last thing on our mind.

Is it right to call such errors sin? Not in a pejorative,
judgemental sense, no, yet unintended mistakes can be as
destructive as any premeditated wrongdoing. They are also,
by definition, the hardest mistakes to avoid, since we do not
even know we are making them. Perversely, we can be harder
on ourselves over our unintended blunders than God will
ever be. Where he, as always, is ready to forgive, we chastise
ourselves for not having seen the pitfalls. Such concern may
be understandable and, if it helps avert repeating our errors,
it has a place, but we will never eliminate every misjudge-
ment from our lives. In this, as in everything, we depend on
his grace – a grace that knows us and loves us as we are.

Ask yourself

What inadvertent mistakes have you made recently? What caused them? What might have avoided them? Have you put them behind you?

Pray

Living God, there are times when I deliberately disobey you, but more often than not I inadvertently let you down, failing both you and others. Save me from punishing myself over innocent mistakes, but grant me also wisdom and insight, so that I may awake to temptation, alert myself to pitfalls and be sensitive to situations. Direct my steps, and so help me to walk in your way, by your grace. Amen.

Remember

I have wandered astray like a lost sheep. Seek out your servant, for I have not forgotten your commandments.

Psalm 119:176

Close

Living God, flawed and fallible though I am, work within me by your grace to do your will and fulfil your purpose, through Christ my Saviour. Amen.

A meaningful offering

Read

Looking up, he saw well-to-do people putting their gifts into the treasury, and also a poor widow offering two small copper coins. He said, 'Mark my words, this poor widow has put in more than all of the others; for they have contributed out of their plenty, but she, despite her poverty, has put in everything she had to live on.'

Luke 21:1-4

Ponder

'And now the collection will be received.' It's surprising how often you hear announcements like that in church. Even more common is to hear members of the congregation use the same terminology. It may be innocent enough, but, personally, it makes me wince, for it can subconsciously encourage a fundamental misunderstanding of what Christian giving is all about. The implication is that we give out of duty: not because we may but because we must, because it is expected of us. What a contrast between that and the widow at the treasury. Humanly-speaking her gift was pathetic, barely worth the bother of counting it, but as far as God was concerned it was a priceless treasure, because it was given not as a collection but as an offering. She gave it because she wanted to, because she was eager to respond, and she gave sacrificially because she wanted to tell God how much he meant to her.

We can apply her example not only to the giving of our money but also of our time, our prayers, our love and our service. Do we truly *offer* those to God, or do we give them mechanically, half-heartedly, grudgingly? Do we bring them out of routine or habit, or as a spontaneous expression of love and thanksgiving? 'It's the thought that counts,' we are often told. In terms of our response to God, those are words well worth pondering.

Ask yourself

Do you give your best or your leftovers to God? Is the faith and love you profess for him backed up by your giving?

Pray

Gracious God, you give to me out of love, pouring out ever more blessings day after day. Forgive me for sometimes giving to you out of habit or duty. I bring an offering in worship because it is expected. I make time for personal devotion because I feel I ought to. I respond to others only when my conscience pricks. The result may seem worthy enough, but the true value is small.

Teach me instead to give joyfully, not because I must but because I may. Teach me to offer my money, my worship and my service as a gesture of love and an expression of my gratitude. Help me to understand that it is not the gift that matters so much as the spirit in which it is given, and may that awareness inspire me to offer myself freely to you, in Christ's name. Amen.

Remember

I will pay you for it. I will not bring to the Lord my God an offering that has cost me nothing.   *2 Samuel 24:24*

Close

Loving God, you gave without counting the cost, your sole desire to share your love and impart your joy. Help me to give back to you in return, not as a duty or an afterthought, but as a joyful privilege, a giving of my best, an offering from the heart. Take what I am and consecrate it to your service, in the name of Christ. Amen.

A second chance

Read

A few days later, Paul suggested to Barnabas, 'Let's pay a return visit to every city where we have announced the word of the Lord, to see how the believers are getting on there.' Barnabas wanted to take John Mark with them, but Paul felt it inappropriate to take someone who had deserted them in Pamphylia and failed to accompany them in their work. A sharp disagreement ensued, as a result of which they parted company; Barnabas took Mark with him and sailed to Cyprus, while Paul, having chosen Silas, set out on his journey, commended by the believers to the Lord's grace. He went through Syria and Cilicia, affirming the work of the churches there.   *Acts 15:36-41*

Ponder

'Once bitten, twice shy', we sometimes say, and so it was for the Apostle Paul. He'd set off on the first of his missionary journeys with Barnabas and John Mark as his trusted companions, these two clearly those he especially looked to for support, encouragement and inspiration. Mark, though, had found the going tough; so tough, in fact, that midway through their itinerary, he felt compelled to call it a day, no longer able to cope with the endless demands and privations. It was an understandable reaction from a young man at the end of his tether, but for Paul it was unforgivable. In his view, Mark had jeopardised his God-given mission, and he was in no mood to make allowances.

Barnabas was different. Whereas Paul felt unable ever to trust Mark again, he was ready to give him a second chance.

I can't help feeling that Paul should have known better; after all, hadn't he once been given a second chance himself, enabling him to start a new life? Like Mark, like Paul, like every Christian, we too have been given not only a second chance but as many chances as it takes; God's love and patience is never exhausted. Unlike Paul, are we ready to give those who have let us down a second chance?

Ask yourself
Have you closed your heart to someone because they've let you or someone else down? Is it time to give them another chance?

Pray
Gracious God, I don't find it easy to give someone a second chance, especially when they've let me down personally. It's hard to overcome feelings of hurt and anger, and harder still ever to trust that person in the way I used to. Yet *you* go on giving me another chance day after day and, despite my repeated failure, you are willing still to trust me with the work of your kingdom.

Teach me, then, instead of dwelling on faults, to look for strengths; instead of putting people down, to lift them up; and instead of consigning them to the scrap heap, to give them the benefit of the doubt. Help me to forgive others as you forgive me, in Christ's name. Amen.

Remember
If a brother or sister sins against you, rebuke them, and if they repent, be ready to forgive. If that same person sins against you seven times in one day, and each time comes back and says, 'I'm sorry', you must forgive them.

Luke 17:3b-4

Close
Gracious God, your gracious love keeps no score of wrongs, no record of past mistakes. Teach me to let go in turn, and to believe the best of others as you have believed the best of me. Amen.

Faith and understanding

Read

O Lord, my heart is not lifted up, my eyes are not raised too high; I do not occupy myself with things too great and too marvellous for me. But I have calmed and quieted my soul, like a weaned child with its mother; my soul is like the weaned child that is with me. *Psalm 131:1-2 (NRSV)*

Ponder

Space, so the experts tell us, is circular. Travel out into the furthest reaches of the universe and, if you keep on going for long enough, you will eventually return to where you started. Frankly, that makes no sense to me whatsoever, for if space has any kind of boundary, then what lies behind it? Surely, more space! Yet how can something go on and on, without ever reaching an end? That, too, seems to defy all reason. The whole concept of infinity is truly mind-boggling. The fact, though, that I can't get my head round it doesn't alter the truth; it simply highlights the limitations of my mind.

There is a lesson here when it comes to questions of faith. While I would never for a moment encourage Christians to avoid wrestling with complex issues relating to belief, I would equally urge caution in rejecting truths simply because we cannot understand them. There comes a point when we have to admit the limitations of our intellect – our inability, in this life at least, to fathom the deepest realities of life. Baffling questions, such as the existence of suffering and evil, can all too easily lead us to question everything, but we need to learn to live with paradox. In the words of George Rawson's great hymn:

> We limit not the truth of God
> to our poor reach of mind,
> by notions of our day and sect,
> crude, partial and confined . . .

Who dares to bind to his dull sense
the oracles of heaven,
for all the nation's tongues and climes
and all the ages given?
That universe, how much unknown!
That ocean unexplored!
The Lord has yet more light and truth
to break forth from his word.

Ask yourself

Have you allowed questions you cannot answer to undermine your faith? Do you need to recognise your limitations and God's greatness?

Pray

Sovereign God, stronger than I can ever comprehend, greater that I can ever imagine, wiser then I can ever understand and more loving than I can ever dream, teach me to consecrate my mind to you, as well as my heart, using my intellect to wrestle with questions of faith and to grow in understanding. Yet, teach me also when I need to recognise the limitations of the human mind. Show me when I need simply to trust, knowing that you are a God above all gods, made known through Christ my Lord. Amen.

Remember

See, God towers above us in his majesty; who can begin to be a teacher like him? Who has decreed the way he should take, or who can say, 'You have done wrong'? Surely God is so great that we cannot know him; the number of his years is beyond our reckoning.   *Job 36:22-23, 26*

Close

Living God, teach me always to seek for understanding, but always to recognise how little I have understood. Amen.

The valley of tears

Read

Then they went to a place called Gethsemane, and Jesus said to his disciples, 'Sit here while I pray.' He took Peter, James and John along with him, and he began to be deeply distressed and troubled. 'My soul is overwhelmed with sorrow to the point of death,' he said to them. 'Stay here and keep watch.' Going a little farther, he fell to the ground and prayed that if possible the hour might pass from him. 'Abba, Father,' he said, 'everything is possible for you. Take this cup from me. Yet not what I will, but what you will.'

Mark 14:32-36 (NIV)

Ponder

'I shouldn't be feeling like this. I know it's wrong but I just can't help it.' I've lost count of the times I've heard comments like that from people feeling guilty about being depressed or miserable. The idea that they've anything to be ashamed of is ridiculous, of course, yet there are subtle pressures in the Church today that can make us feel we should banish all negative thoughts from our minds. Much modern worship focuses upon themes such as joy, praise and celebration, to the exclusion of other emotions, and this emphasis seems to be reinforced by verses like Philippians 4:4, which states: 'Rejoice in the Lord always; again I say it: rejoice!' If we're not careful, the sorrowful and downhearted can feel excluded, even to the point of regarding their feelings as a sin. They feel that they should somehow be able to rise above sorrow; that, even though they are not immune from tragedy, it should not hit them in quite the same way that it does non-believers.

That is one reason why the story of Gethsemane is so important, for here we see God identifying himself with human sorrow. 'My heart is ready to break with grief,' said

Jesus; as the New International Version puts it, 'My soul is overwhelmed with sorrow to the point of death.' Here is a reminder that God himself, through Christ, has shared in our blackest, bleakest moments. He is a God who not only understands what grief and heartbreak mean but also empathises with those experiencing them. Above all, he is a God who stays close to us through such times and who, finally, will bring hope after despair, laughter after tears and joy after sorrow.

Ask yourself

Does your faith make room for sorrow as well as joy?

Pray

Loving God, I remember today all who mourn, their hearts broken by tragedy, tears a constant companion, laughter and happiness seeming a distant memory.

Reach out into their pain, heartache and sadness, and give them the knowledge that you understand their pain and share their sorrow. May your arms enfold them, your love bring comfort, and your light scatter the shadows, so that they may know joy once more and celebrate life in all its fullness. Amen.

Remember

I am tired of my misery; every night I soak my bed with tears; I saturate my couch with my weeping. My eyes waste away because of sorrow; they grow feeble because of all my enemies. May those who sow in tears reap with shouts of joy. *Psalm 6:6-7; 126:5*

Close

Living God, when life is hard and sorrows are many, lead me safely through the valley of tears until the horizon opens, the clouds lift and the sun shines once more, by the grace of Christ. Amen.

Getting in deep

Read

A woman of Samaria came to draw water, so Jesus asked
her, 'Give me a drink.' The Samaritan woman responded,
'How can you, a Jew, ask me, a woman of Samaria, to give
you a drink?' (Jews have no dealings with Samaritans.)
Jesus answered her, 'If you knew the gift of God, and who
has asked you, "Give me a drink", you would have made
the request to him, and he would have given you living
water.' The woman replied, 'Sir, the well is deep and you
have no bucket, so where will you get this living water?'
Jesus said to her, 'Anyone drinking the water here will thirst
again, but whoever drinks the water I will give them will
never be thirsty.' The woman said to him, 'Sir, give me this
water, so that I need never thirst or come here again to
draw water.'
John 4:7, 9-11, 13-15

Ponder

When I first started college at Oxford, I decided to join a local
student orchestra. I'd played the flute regularly during my
schooldays, and also occasionally during my time at Bristol,
but I wanted now to take things a little more seriously. The
day of the first practice arrived, and I eagerly picked up a copy
of the music, only to freeze in disbelief. There was no way I
could begin to play such a complex piece, yet my fellow-
flautists launched into the work without a moment's hesitation. Clearly, I had bitten off more than I could chew – and
that, I'm afraid, was the end of my musical ambitions.

The woman at the well was to find that she also had
taken on more than she'd bargained on, though in a rather
different sense. Approached by a stranger asking for a
drink, the next thing she knew he seemed to be offering
her an inexhaustible source of water of her very own. No
wonder she was excited, for it must have been hard work

toiling to and from that well each day. She wanted to take things further, to gain access to this personal spring, and only slowly did the truth dawn that Jesus was talking about something very different. She suddenly found herself drawn into a searching examination of her life, facing facts that she had never questioned before. Meeting Christ is like that, or at least it should be. It involves a penetrating and ongoing challenge that draws us into ever-deeper waters. Unlike my ill-fated musical aspirations, however, we will never be out of our depth, for our ability to meet the challenge depends not on us but him. Through meeting Jesus, the Samaritan woman met herself as never before. Are we prepared to do the same in turn?

Ask yourself

Are you open to the word of Christ that challenges your preconceptions and leads you into previously uncharted waters?

Pray

Lord Jesus Christ, I talk of following you but much of the time I expect you to follow me. I want you to conform to my own wishes. I ask you to meet my list of requirements. I decide the way I want you to work, attempting to mould your purpose according to my own narrow horizons.

Lord Jesus Christ, break through the chains I put around you, and help me to face the challenge you daily bring me, if only I have eyes to see and ears to hear. Amen.

Remember

Search me, O God, and know my heart; test me and know my thoughts. See if there is any misguided way in me, and lead me in your eternal path.   *Psalm 139:23-24*

Close

Lord Jesus Christ, open my heart to your searching presence, and teach me to respond to your challenging word, however unsettling that might be. Amen.

SEPTEMBER

Daring to hope

Read

See, a day is coming for the Lord, when the plunder taken from you will be divided in your midst. On that day there shall not be either cold or frost. And there shall be continuous day (it is known to the Lord), not day and not night, for at evening time there shall be light. On that day living waters shall flow out from Jerusalem, half of them to the eastern sea and half of them to the western sea; it shall continue in summer as in winter. And the Lord will become king over all the earth; on that day the Lord will be one and his name one. *Zechariah 14:1, 6-9 (NRSV)*

Ponder

To have our hopes raised only to see them dashed again is a cruel experience. The result can be to plunge us into a deeper sense of despair than anything we faced previously. So it was for the people of Israel after they returned to Judah following their time of exile in Babylon. An initial mood of jubilation soon gave way to an overwhelming feeling of anticlimax, as the Utopia that people had expected to dawn failed to materialise. It wasn't just hope that took a battering in consequence; for many it was their faith. Where was the glorious new kingdom God had promised his people?

Today the kingdom we expect may be different, but the question can seem equally valid. We look forward to the day when God's purpose will be fulfilled, when his will shall be done and his kingdom come on earth, but when will that be? Do we have the courage to keep on hoping, even when everything around us seems to undermine belief?

Ask yourself

In what ways does faith bring you hope? Should you pin all your hopes on some future kingdom or does faith give grounds for hope in this life too?

Pray

Gracious God, I thank you that you are always with me, in the bad times as well as the good, the difficult as well as the easy, the sad as well as the happy. I thank you that though I have sometimes been unsure of the way ahead, you have always been there to guide me; though I have felt discouraged, you have offered me fresh inspiration; though I have been in despair, yet you have given me hope. Through all the changing circumstances of life, I have found from personal experience that your steadfast love never ceases and that your mercies are new every morning.

May the knowledge of all you have done give me confidence in the days ahead, so that whatever problems I face, whatever disappointments I experience, whatever sorrows may befall me, I will still find reason to look forward, reason to believe in the future and reason to hope. Lord of all hopefulness, hear my prayer, in the name of Christ. Amen.

Remember

I will hope continually, and will praise you more and more each day. *Psalm 71:14*

Close

Gracious God, when I am uncertain of the way ahead give me guidance, and when I feel discouraged give me fresh inspiration. May the knowledge of your unfailing love give me confidence that whatever problems I might face and whatever sorrows might befall me, I shall still find reason to believe in the future and reason to hope. Amen.

Truly committed?

Read

Come to him, a living stone rejected by mortals yet chosen and precious in God's sight, and, like living stones, allow yourselves through Jesus Christ to be built into a spiritual house, a holy priesthood offering spiritual sacrifices acceptable to God.

1 Peter 2:4-5

Ponder

I like to think of myself as a supporter of Southend United Football Club. In my mid- to late-teens I watched them play most weeks, my home being just a couple of minutes' walk from the ground and, although I moved away from the town twenty-five years ago, I still follow the team's fortunes with interest. Indeed, I have even taken to looking up the club's official website to catch the latest match report or news. Sadly, though, I haven't watched the team play for over ten years, and that, I'm afraid, exposes my 'support' for what it is – an empty illusion. The truth of the matter is that I'm *interested* in Southend rather than a supporter, for support needs to show itself in action. Unless I am there on the terraces, cheering on the players, or contributing to the club's finances through paying at the turnstiles, my so-called support means precious little.

The parallel between this and nominal discipleship is not hard to spot. Many of us claim to be Christians, but when was the last time we darkened the door of a church, turned the pages of a Bible, approached God in prayer or expressed our faith through practical service? Yes, we may tune in to the occasional TV *Songs of Praise* or 'God slot' on the radio, but if that's as far as it goes, then something is wrong. I'm not saying that you have to go to church to be a Christian, or that there is a certain lifestyle that must be rigidly adhered to in order to be counted such – therein lies the road to bigotry, hypocrisy and legalism. What I am saying, as much to myself as anyone, is that being a Christian – that is, *belonging* to Christ rather than simply being *interested* in him – must necessarily make a difference to the way we live. If that isn't the case, then it's time we asked ourselves if we're actually Christians at all.

Ask yourself

In what ways does Christian commitment make a difference in *your* life? How far does your faith show itself in action?

Pray

Lord Jesus Christ, I talk about belonging to you and offering you my service, but so often reality falls short of the ideal. Instead of making you an integral part of my life, I treat you as an optional extra, there to turn to as and when it suits me. Instead of working for your kingdom, I strive solely to serve my own interests. Instead of involving myself in the life of your people, I stay on the fringes, reluctant to commit myself wholly to your cause. My deeds deny my words; my life betrays my lack of faith.

Forgive me and save me from confusing nominal Christianity with living discipleship. Teach me what it means to belong to you and to be part of your Church, and so may I serve you as you deserve, to the glory of your name. Amen.

Remember

If any are hearers rather than doers of the word, they are like those who view themselves in a mirror, only immediately to forget what they look like the moment they turn away. By contrast, those who look into the perfect law of freedom and persevere in it, living not as forgetful hearers but as committed doers, their deeds will be blessed.

James 1:23-25

Close

Gracious God, teach me to be as committed to you as you are to me. Amen.

Thinking of you

Read

Tychicus will pass on all the news about me; he is a much-loved brother, a faithful minister, and a fellow servant in the Lord. I have sent him to you with one aim in mind: to let you know how we are and to encourage your hearts through him. He will come with Onesimus, that faithful and beloved brother from among your own ranks. Together, they will let you know what's been happening here. Aristarchus, my fellow-prisoner, greets you, as does Mark, Barnabas' cousin, about whom you have been instructed – if he comes to you, welcome him. Similarly, Jesus, also known as Justus, sends you greetings. *Colossians 4:7-11a*

Ponder

How often have you promised to write to somebody and then not done so; or assured a friend that you will pray for them, only for it to slip your mind? If you are anything like me, you will have done so more times than you care to remember. Such forgetfulness is perhaps understandable but it is also regrettable, for it does us all good to know that someone is thinking of us. I remember receiving a letter several years ago from an old friend whom I had not seen since student days. What prompted her to write I have no idea, but it was heartwarming to know that the experiences we had shared at university so long ago still meant something. No doubt, we can all testify to similar experiences, when an unexpected card, letter or phone call brought us encouragement and inspiration.

The Apostle Paul recognised how much it meant for someone to stay in touch, as his many letters in the New Testament illustrate. He wrote for a variety of reasons, but his chief concern was simply to let those churches he had been instrumental in setting up know that he was thinking of them. However difficult their circumstances may have been, however severe a time of testing they were facing, he wanted them to know that they were not alone. How far do we make a point of remembering those we can no longer be present with in the flesh? More important, how often do we let those people know we are thinking of them? We talk often in high-flown language about love, fellowship and service without actually doing much to make these real. Staying in touch with someone and showing we care is a very simple yet meaningful way of putting such words into practice.

Ask yourself

Is there someone who needs to know you are thinking of them? In what ways can you show your concern for and interest in those you are unable to be present with in person?

Pray

Lord, I talk of being part of your family, of sharing in a special bond that nothing can break, yet so often such claims are only fine-sounding words. When circumstances change and I am separated from those I considered myself close to, I soon drift apart from them, scarcely sparing them a second thought. I know this is sometimes inevitable, but I know also that there are those to whom just a word or note to let them know I am thinking of them would mean so much.

Awaken me, then, to the opportunities I have to express my continuing concern, and in showing *I* care may they know *you* care too. In Christ's name I ask it. Amen.

Remember

All those who are with me send greetings to you. Greet those who love us in the faith. Grace be with you all.

Titus 3:15 (NRSV)

Close

Lord Jesus Christ, as you are always thinking of me, reaching out in love, so teach me to reach out to others, for your name's sake. Amen.

A changed man

Read

Peter sat outside in the courtyard, and a servant-girl approached him saying, 'You also were with Jesus the Galilean', but he denied it before them all, saying, 'I've no idea what you're talking about'. He went out to the porch, where another servant-girl saw him, and she said to those gathered there, 'This man was with Jesus of Nazareth.' He denied it once again, with an oath, 'I do not know the man.' Shortly afterwards, the bystanders came up and confronted Peter, 'There's no doubt that you also are one of them, for your accent gives you away.' Then he began to curse and swear, 'I do not know the man!' At precisely that moment, the cock crowed, and Peter remembered what Jesus had said: 'Before the cock crows, you will deny me three times.' He stumbled outside and wept bitterly.   *Matthew 26:69-75*

Ponder

A few months ago my wife attended a reunion of former classmates. She found it a fascinating experience. A few had hardly altered but the majority had changed beyond recognition. In our verses today, we encounter a man in whom there was to be a truly remarkable change. We meet him first as an ordinary fisherman going about his daily business, but following the call of Christ he quickly emerges as the leader of the Apostles. All that, though, must have rung somewhat hollow on that awful night when, just as had been predicted, he denied Jesus three times.

Yet, when we turn to the book of Acts, what a different story we find. It is Peter, in Acts 2, who boldly speaks out for Christ on behalf of the Apostles following the baptism of the Holy Spirit. Later, when his persistent testimony lands him in hot water with the authorities, he responds, 'Make up your own minds whether it is right in God's eyes to obey you rather than him. The fact is we cannot help but speak concerning everything we have seen and heard' (Acts 4:19-20). From one afraid to be associated with Christ, Peter had changed to one proud to bear his name; from one whose only thought had been his own safety to one heedless of the cost of discipleship. Here is an astonishing testimony to the way Jesus is able to change lives. The change in us may not be quite so dramatic, but the message of Peter's story is clear: if Jesus could change his life, he can change anyone's!

Ask yourself
Are you open to the changes God wants to make in your life? Do you recognise that he is equally able to transform the lives of others?

Pray
Lord Jesus Christ, I remember today how you changed the life of Simon Peter, turning fear into courage, uncertainty into confidence, denial into affirmation. Remind me that as you changed him, so you can also change me; that you are constantly at work nurturing my faith, strengthening my commitment and deepening my experience of your love.

Open my heart to the movement of your Spirit, so that I may give you freedom to mould and shape me to your will, and so make me the person you would have me be, to your praise and glory. Amen.

Remember
We were buried with him through baptism into death, so that, just as Christ was raised from the dead, we too might walk in newness of life.   *Romans 6:4 (NRSV)*

Close
Lord Jesus Christ, take what I am and have been, and by your renewing, redeeming touch direct what I shall be, to the glory of your name. Amen.

Counting our blessings

Read

The blessings of your father are stronger than the blessings of the eternal mountains, the bounties of the everlasting hills.

Genesis 49:26 (NRSV)

Ponder

Sometimes in life something happens to remind us of how much we have to celebrate – the many blessings and gifts that God so freely showers upon us. Sadly, such moments can be all too rare. More often than not, we lurch from one demand, one crisis, one responsibility to another, scarcely finding time to draw breath and reflect on the reasons we have to give thanks. If we are not careful, we end up brooding on the things we haven't got, sucked into a vicious circle of self-pity, the more sorry we feel for ourselves the more grounds there seem to be for such feelings.

We need to stop occasionally and, in the words of the old hymn, make time to 'count our blessings', for when we do that, life seems very different. There is so much that is not only good but indescribably wonderful, beautiful beyond words. The words above were concerned not with God's blessing but with Jacob's blessing to his sons, but they could speak more appropriately of all God has done for us. Make time to consider such things and, far from feeling sorry for yourself, you will realise how much reason you have to give thanks.

Ask yourself

How often do you make time to thank God for all he has given? Do you have life's joys and sorrows in their proper perspective?

Pray

Lord, I have so much to thank you for, yet all too often I take it all for granted. Instead of counting my blessings, I dwell on my frustrations. Instead of celebrating everything you have given, I brood about the things I don't have. In pursuit of illusory dreams of happiness, I lose sight of the gifts that each day brings, the countless reasons I have to rejoice.

Forgive me for forgetting how fortunate I am, and help me to appreciate the wonder of all I have received from your loving hands. Amen.

Remember
Blessed be the God and Father of our Lord Jesus Christ, who has bestowed on us in Christ every spiritual blessing in the heavenly realms.   *Ephesians 1:3*

Close
Sovereign God, for your blessings too many to number, and your goodness too wonderful for words, I give you my praise. Amen.

A proper perspective

Read

I say to everyone among you, by the grace given to me, not to have a misplaced sense of your own importance, but to appraise yourselves judiciously, each according to the degree of faith that God has granted to you.   *Romans 12:3*

Ponder

One of the things my children most enjoyed on a recent holiday was a visit to a hall of distorting mirrors. They ran from one to the other with peals of laughter and squeals of delight, repeatedly calling us to come and see what they looked like. It is truly remarkable what an effect a few kinks in a mirror can have on your reflection, rendering you short and squat one moment and with the legs of a gazelle and neck of a giraffe the next!

Such distortions, though, are as nothing compared to those we can create in our own minds. Sometimes we belittle ourselves to the point of feeling we are of no stature at all, yet, conversely, we can develop such an inflated picture of ourselves that our ego is in danger of bursting. What compounds the problem is that we are usually unaware of our mistake, tending to confuse illusion with reality. Pride is a danger that numerous passages of scripture rightly warn us against, for there are few human traits less desirable yet more common. Equally, we should beware of devaluing who and what we are. God wants each of us to have a proper sense of our intrinsic worth and, similarly, an appreciation of the worth of others. We are all flawed, yet all special, none of us perfect but none irredeemable. Don't build yourself up, don't do yourself down – it's advice we would all do well to heed.

Ask yourself

In what ways do you think too highly of yourself? In what ways do you have a negative self-image? What is God saying to you about both?

Pray

Lord Jesus Christ, you do not want me to think too much or too little either of myself or of others. You want me to recognise that everyone is important to you – none more so, none less – each of us unique in your sight, valued for what we are.

Help me to keep a sensible balance in life; to have a due sense of my own worth and that of others. Above all, give me a constant awareness of your greatness, before which I can only bow in wonder, acknowledging my weakness beside your strength, and may that realisation give me a proper perspective on all. In your name I ask it. Amen.

Remember

Pride goes before an undoing, and an arrogant spirit before a fall. It is better humbly to take a seat among the poor than to divide the spoil with the proud. Let someone else flatter you, not your own mouth – someone you don't know rather than your own lips.   *Proverbs 16:18-19; 27:2*

Close

Gracious God, teach me that you value everyone not for what they might become but for what they are, and so give me a proper respect for myself and for all, in the name of Christ. Amen.

Taking it on the chin

Read

All the people, high and low, approached the prophet Jeremiah and said, 'Ask the Lord your God to show us where we should go and what we should do.' The prophet Jeremiah said to them, 'Fair enough, I will pray to the Lord your God as you ask, and I will pass on to you whatever answer the Lord gives. I will hold nothing back from you.' They responded to Jeremiah in turn, 'May the Lord be a steadfast and implacable witness against us if we do not act exactly as the Lord your God indicates to us through you. Whether it is welcome or unwelcome, we will obey the voice of the Lord our God to whom we send you, so that it may go well with us; we will obey his voice.'

Jeremiah 42:1b-2a, 3-6

Ponder

When did you last ask somebody for a straight answer? More important, when did you last seriously reflect on an answer that went against what you wanted to hear? We don't like being told to do something we'd rather not do and we resent advice that undermines our established opinions. The same is true when it comes to God. Although we may say, 'Your will be done', most of us are probably like those who approached Jeremiah, asking him to seek God's guidance for the future. They sounded sincere enough, and they probably were, but when Jeremiah delivered God's answer, suddenly a very different attitude became evident. 'You are lying!' they said; 'The Lord our God has not sent you to forbid us from making our homes in Egypt. Baruch, son of Neriah, has turned you against us so that we may be put in the power of the Babylonians, and that they may kill us or deport us to Babylon' (Jeremiah 43:2b-3). Their response was perfectly understandable, for, faced by Babylonian occupation, they preferred to shape their own future rather than have it imposed upon them. The result was that they dismissed anything they didn't want to hear.

We talk much in the Church today about seeking God's will but often it is more about shaping God to our will than letting his will shape us. The truth is that he doesn't always fit in with our expectations, and his guidance may be anything but welcome. It is at such times that faith is tested, and shown to be genuine or otherwise. Are we any more willing than the people of Jeremiah's day to listen to what God wants to say to us?

Ask yourself

Are you guilty of putting your own words and ideas into God's mouth? Are you ready for God to answer your prayers in a way that challenges rather than reinforces your ideas, attitudes and preconceptions?

Pray

Living God, forgive me my superficial understanding of prayer – the way I abuse and distort it, using it as a personal lever to coerce you rather than a personal encounter through which I might grow closer to you each day.

Teach me to seek what you will, rather than what I desire; to be open to your guidance, however much it may conflict with my own wishes. Teach me to obey your voice. Amen.

Remember

Your kingdom come, your will be done, on earth as it is in heaven.   *Matthew 6:10 (NRSV)*

Close

Living God, whether your way is easy or hard, your word comforting or disturbing, your will welcome or hard to accept, teach me to listen, to learn and to follow faithfully, for Christ's sake. Amen.

Learning to say no

Read

I deemed it necessary to send to you Epaphroditus – my brother, co-worker and fellow-soldier, and your messenger sent to minister to me in my need – since he has been pining for you all and troubled that you heard about his illness. He was indeed so ill that he came close to death, but God had mercy on him, and not only him but me also, sparing me yet another sorrow. I therefore readily sent him to you, so that you may rejoice at seeing him again and I may be less anxious. Welcome him, then, in the Lord with all joy, and treat him with respect, because he risked his life for the work of Christ and came close to death in order to offer service to me that you were unable to provide.

Philippians 2:25-30

Ponder

It was the church AGM and we'd reached the point every member dreads: a couple of posts had yet to be filled causing the minister to pronounce those dreaded words, 'Any volunteers?' Needless to say, the posts went unfilled! Ask for a volunteer when a job needs doing and the chances are you'll be wasting your time. Paradoxically, if you ask someone face to face, there's every prospect of a different response, for when we're put on the spot it's surprisingly hard to say no; in fact, some of us find it virtually impossible. It may be a cliché but it is also true that 'if you want something done, ask a busy person'.

What the saying fails to add is that the extra task taken on may just prove to be the straw that breaks the camel's back. If you are the sort of person who takes on ever more jobs, responsibilities and demands, even when you're already flagging under the strain of others, take note. Paul's words afford us a glimpse of Epaphroditus, a man who quite clearly took on too much and nearly paid for it with his life. He learned the hard way that we all have our limitations beyond which it is foolhardy to push ourselves. It may seem the Christian thing to say yes, but if that causes our health to suffer, endangering the happiness of our loved ones and preventing us from fulfilling our responsibilities as we would want to, then perhaps it's time we learnt to say no. All of us can do something; none of us are called to do everything!

Ask yourself

Have you taken on too much or accepted responsibilities that you are unable to fulfil? Is there something you are being asked to do that you should politely but firmly refuse?

Pray

Living God, it is hard sometimes to say no. I do not want to let people down. I like to appear on top of things, capable of meeting every challenge, and I am reluctant to admit my limitations. I am afraid of being thought selfish, unwilling to put myself out. For a whole variety of reasons, I find it easier to say yes even when I know I should decline.

Teach me that there are times when I owe it to myself, my family or my friends to say no, and times also when saying yes will mean a job is not done properly, if at all. Help me to do what I can, both in your service and in the service of others, but to recognise also what I can't do, and then grant me the courage I need to say no. In Christ's name I pray. Amen.

Remember

Are all Apostles, all prophets, all teachers, all equipped with great powers? Do we all have the gift of healing, or tongues, or interpretation?   *1 Corinthians 12:29-31a*

Close

Lord Jesus Christ, teach me when to say yes and when to say no, and help me not only to take those decisions but also to stick to them once taken. Amen.

Against all odds

Read

The Philistine [Goliath] said to David, 'Am I a dog, that you approach me with sticks?' and he swore at David using the name of his gods. 'Come on,' he taunted, 'attack me, and I will give your flesh to the birds of the air and to the beasts of the field.' But David responded, 'You confront me with sword, spear and javelin, but I confront you in the name of the Lord of hosts, the God of the armies of Israel, whom you have defied.' When the Philistine advanced towards him, David darted forward to do battle with him. Reaching down into his bag, he took out a stone, slung it, and struck the Philistine on the forehead; the stone sank into his forehead, and he collapsed face downwards on the ground.   *1 Samuel 17:43-45, 48-49*

Ponder

It's always pleasing, isn't it, when a midget turns the tables on a giant. Whether it be a non-league football team defeating its premier league relations, a village store fighting off competition from an out-of-town supermarket, or a local pressure group resisting the plans of a multinational company, our hearts warm to tales of the underdog come good.

Little wonder, then, that the tale of David and Goliath has stood the test of time, told and retold by countless generations across the years. Their celebrated encounter is a classic example of the underdog coming out on top, triumphing against all the odds. There can be few plots more extensively used by writers throughout the centuries, but what makes this story so wonderful is that it is not fiction but fact. It offers an enduring testimony to the way God is able to help each one of us measure up to the obstacles we face and, no matter how great they may be, to emerge victorious over them.

Ask yourself

Is there a situation you have given up on because you have looked at it only from a human perspective? Is it time you reappraised things in the light of what God is able to achieve?

Pray

Gracious God, there are times in my life when I feel up against it and when everything seems to conspire against me. I look at the problems confronting me, and I feel small and helpless, powerless to do anything about them. Yet, you are a God who time and again has used those who seem insignificant in this world to achieve great things; a God who has overcome the strong through the weak and who is able to accomplish within me far more than I can ask or even imagine.

Help me, then, when I am faced by obstacles that seem insurmountable, to put my trust in you, knowing that you will give me the strength I need, when I need it. Amen.

Remember

Strengthen the weak hands and steady the trembling knees. Say to those of a fearful disposition, 'Be strong, have no fear! Your God is here. He will bring retribution and terrible recompense. He will draw near and save you.'   *Isaiah 35:3-4*

Close

Sovereign God, instead of seeing what *I* can't do, teach me to see what *you* can, through Jesus Christ, my Lord and Saviour. Amen.

A clean breast of it

Read

Happy is the one whose wrongdoing is forgiven, whose faults are covered. Happy is the one to whom the Lord ascribes no guilt, and in whose spirit there is no pretence. While I remained silent, my body grew weary with my constant groaning, for day and night your hand weighed heavily upon me; my strength dried up like sap in the heat of summer. Then I acknowledged my sin and did not conceal my guilt from you; I said, 'I will confess my disobedience to the Lord', and you absolved me from my guilt and sin.

Psalm 32:1-5

Ponder

In the mid-1990s, an issue came to dominate British politics – the question of sleaze. Scarcely a week went by, it seemed, without some sordid scandal emerging about an MP or public figure; so much so that this matter in large part contributed to the humiliating defeat of the Conservative government in 1997. Countless prominent people had cause to wish they had come clean when they could, rather than have their guilty secrets splashed out later on the front pages of the tabloids. The reason they kept quiet, of course, was that they were afraid honesty might jeopardise their careers.

Fear can similarly come to rule *our* lives. The stakes involved may not be quite so high, but we hesitate to admit to past errors or present indiscretions for fear of losing face, endangering a relationship, or causing hurt to others and embarrassment to ourselves. At the time, sweeping a mistake under the carpet may seem an attractive option. It is only later that we learn how wrong we are, as guilt eats away at our conscience and the fear of being found out nags away at the back of our minds. Saying sorry is never easy and can prove costly, but it is also the only way to resolution and reconciliation. Refusing to admit our mistakes may ultimately prove more costly still.

Ask yourself
Is there some guilty secret nagging away at the back of your mind? Have you faced up to it before God? Have you faced up to it with those concerned and asked for forgiveness?

Pray
Gracious God, I'm not bad at confessing my mistakes to you, but I'm hopeless when it comes to confessing them to others. I make excuses for my behaviour rather than admit the truth; I prevaricate and deceive, rather than acknowledge my weakness. Instead of admitting where I've gone wrong and seeking forgiveness, I go on digging an ever-deeper hole for myself, making it harder and harder to go back and start again.

Give me courage when I fail to confess my mistakes to those affected by my actions, and help me to do all in my power to make amends. Teach me to face the truth so that the truth may set me free, in Christ's name. Amen.

Remember
No one who conceals mistakes will prosper, but whoever confesses and turns from them will obtain mercy.

Proverbs 28:13

Close
Lord Jesus Christ, teach me to be honest with you, with myself and with others, and so may I know the peace of a clear conscience and a right relationship with you and others. Amen.

The mighty acts of God

Read

Come and see what God has done, how awesome his works on our behalf! He turned the waters into dry land so that his people might pass through them on foot. Come and rejoice in him. He rules for ever by his power, his eyes watch the nations. How wonderful are the works of the Lord, pondered on by all those who delight in them. They are majestic and glorious; his righteousness endures for ever. He has gained renown through his awesome deeds; the Lord is gracious and rich in mercy.

Psalm 66:5-7; 111:2-4

Ponder

What is it that makes someone famous? The answer, of course, lies in the special things they have done, the scale of their achievements, the way they stand out from the ordinary. The adulation accorded to modern-day stars can come very close to worship, and in a sense there is a parallel here to our worship of God, for at heart this is about the great things *he* has done. To this day, Jewish worship revolves around past events: deliverance from Egypt, the crossing of the Red Sea, manna in the wilderness – and nowhere is this celebration of God's mighty acts more evident than in the psalms. 'Sing a new song to the Lord, for he has done marvellous things' (Psalm 98:1a). 'Give thanks to the Lord of lords, for he alone does great wonders.' (Psalm 136:3-4)

If the psalmists could write like that all those years ago, then how much more cause have we to rejoice today, for we can celebrate the coming of Christ, the history of the Church and our personal experience of the Holy Spirit! Take time to remember what God has done, in the world, the Church and your own life. Reflect on his mighty acts – all he has done, is doing and has yet to do – and so let us echo the psalms once more in declaring: 'The Lord has done great things for us and we are glad!' (Psalm 126:3)

Ask yourself

When did you last stop to consider the wonderful deeds of God, both in creation and throughout history? When did you last reflect on the things he has done in your life?

Pray

Almighty God, you have done more for me than I can ever begin to acknowledge. You have done so much throughout history, more than words can ever fully express. So I come once more in grateful and heartfelt worship. I praise you for the wonder of the universe, the loveliness of the world, and the beauty of your creation. I thank you for the joy of life, with all there is to delight, fascinate, challenge and enrich. I rejoice in the new life you have given me in Christ – the hope, strength, peace and inspiration you grant me each day through him. I praise you for the constancy of your love, the breadth of your purpose and the awesome extent of your mercy. You have blessed me beyond my deserving, showering me with good things, and yet you still hold the best in store.

Almighty God, for your mighty acts and sovereign deeds, I give you my worship and offer you my life in glad response. Through Jesus Christ, my Lord. Amen.

Remember

Great is the Lord and supremely deserving of praise; his greatness is beyond measuring. One generation will proclaim your works to another; they will acknowledge your mighty acts. *Psalm 145:3-4*

Close

Sovereign God, I look back in wonder, I look forward in confidence, and so I look to you now in worship, through Jesus Christ, my Lord. Amen.

Because we may

Read

Let everyone give as their heart leads them to do, not reluctantly or because it is expected of them – for God loves a cheerful giver.

2 Corinthians 9:7

Ponder

There are few things we like less than having something done for us out of duty. What might otherwise have been a valued act of service brings instead a sense of humiliation; what appeared to be an act of friendship becomes a cause of rancour; what seemed a hugely generous gift feels suddenly like a tarnished trinket, all but worthless. We want people to respond to us not because they feel they should but because they want to. We want their dealings with us to be transparent rather than hiding some ulterior motive. What we *don't* want, above all, is to be patronised.

We do well to bear that in mind when it comes to our dealings with God, for all too easily the service we offer him becomes a matter of duty rather than privilege. We don't intend it to happen, nor are we always conscious of doing so, but little by little the sparkle in our faith fades and the spontaneity that once characterised our relationship with God has become a routine of going through the motions. We bring our offering because it is expected of us; we read the Bible because we feel guilty if we don't; we say our prayers because we feel we ought to – and we hope God won't notice. Is that what he wants from us? Of course not. He wants us to love him, serve him and worship him not because we must but because we may. He wants us to offer our discipleship not because we should but because we can. If we bring it for any other reason, it is time to stop and think, for it might be that God feels just as we would in his place – that he'd rather we didn't bring it at all.

Ask yourself

Is your faith about duty or joyful response? Do you worship, pray, read the Bible and go to church because you feel you ought to or because you want to?

Pray

Loving God, I bring you my worship not because I must but because I may; not because I have to but because I want to. I come not out of duty but privilege; not because it is expected of me but because you have graciously invited me to respond.

Receive my joyful worship and glad thanksgiving, my love, my faith and my service, for I offer them freely to you just as you offered yourself freely for me, through my Lord and Saviour, Jesus Christ. Amen.

Remember

Remember the words of Jesus, 'It is more blessed to give than to receive.'
Acts 20:35b

Close

Living God, teach me to give as gladly and as lovingly and unreservedly to you as you have given to me. Amen.

Idle hands

Read

I passed by the field of one who was lazy, by the vineyard of someone with no sense; and I saw that it was all overrun with thistles; the ground strewn with weeds, and its stone wall in ruins. I took careful note of what I saw; I looked and received instruction. A quick doze, a brief nap, a little folding of the hands to rest, and poverty will come upon you like a thief, and want like a brigand. *Proverbs 24:30-34*

Ponder

For some people the very thought of hard work makes them go weak at the knees, to the point that they keep on putting it off, *ad infinitum*. Others simply get stuck in, and in no time at all the job gets done. Most of us are probably somewhere in between. We do what's expected of us – most of the time anyway – and perhaps just occasionally, if we're feeling especially virtuous, we do that little bit extra; yet somehow there's always a few things left undone, just enough to niggle away in the back of the mind and disturb our peace. We know we've got to do it, but we just can't summon up the enthusiasm. We realise it will have to be done eventually, yet we invariably succeed in putting it off one more day.

Is it worth it? We may buy ourselves a little time – an evening together away from the children, an all too rare morning lie-in, an afternoon on the beach, but the thought of that job is always there, haunting us like some tantalising spectre. The longer we leave it the worse the prospect becomes and the less we feel inclined to do it. If we are not careful, we slip into a self-perpetuating downward spiral, achieving ever less as we prevaricate all the more. The warnings of Solomon in the book of Proverbs may seem somewhat over the top, but beware, the danger may be more real than you think.

Ask yourself

'The devil tempts all, but the idle person tempts the devil'.
Is that true? If so, is it true in your life?

Pray

Lord, you have given me a multitude of gifts and opportunities; forgive me that I sometimes fail to use them. I don't
think of myself as lazy, but time and again I avoid tasks
which I ought to tackle, at cost to myself, to others and even
to you. So many possibilities are wasted and so much peace
of mind lost because I prefer to put off till tomorrow what
I ought to do today.

Teach me to make the most of each moment, to use my
talents to the full, and to tackle every task as it comes, for
both my sake and yours. Amen.

Remember

As a door turns to and fro on its hinges, so it is with a
[lazy] person in bed. They thrust a hand into a dish, but
can't be bothered to bring it back up to their mouth. The
indolent man is wiser in his own eyes than seven who can
answer discreetly.   *Proverbs 26:14-16*

Close

Gracious God, teach me to recognise time as your gift, held
in trust by your grace, and so help me to use it wisely rather
than squander a priceless treasure. In Christ's name I ask it.
Amen.

Inner peace

Read

Peace I leave with you; my peace I give to you. I do not give to you as the world gives. Do not let your hearts be troubled, and do not let them be afraid. *John 14:27 (NRSV)*

Ponder

A common marketing ploy today seems to be to promise peace of mind. Take out a pension plan or an insurance policy and you can put your worries behind you. Go on holiday to the sun and get away from it all. Buy a new car, washing machine or stereo system and take the stress and strain out of life. Anything and everything, it seems, promises us a more relaxed and happy existence. Sadly, however, statistics don't bear this out. We may have more leisure time and money today than previous generations, and we may enjoy all the latest hi-tech gadgetry, yet we live in a world where stress is rife and where countless people yearn for a sense of inner peace. Peace, like happiness, cannot be bought; indeed, the quest for money, possessions and status is often what destroys the little peace that we have.

We can find a degree of peace in this world in the sense of briefly getting away from it all, but for the Christian real peace comes ultimately from another source – from an awareness of God's love made real through the inner presence of his Holy Spirit. We cannot create such peace ourselves, but we can cultivate it through making time for God, creating a space in our lives for prayer and reflection, and being open to what he would do within us. Such peace involves letting go and seeing life from another perspective than that typically adopted, but it also means taking hold of a prize greater than anything the world can give – a peace that passes understanding.

Ask yourself

Do you feel at peace with yourself? Is your life based on the things that really matter?

Pray

Living God, I have so much to celebrate, more than previous generations would have imagined possible, yet it does not bring me peace. I still worry about the future and brood over the past; still fret over money, work or loved ones, and still wrestle with pressures, fears, anxieties and questions. For all their sophistication and ingenuity, the technology and wealth of modern society cannot meet my deepest needs nor calm the storm within.

So I come to you who alone can nourish my soul and renew my being – the one in whom I find not the extras of life but life itself. Teach me to measure all else against who and what you are, and, in getting that into perspective, may I discover the peace you promise to all who know you. Through Jesus Christ my Lord. Amen.

Remember

I will lie down and sleep in peace; for you alone, O Lord, make me lie down in safety.   *Psalm 4:8*

Close

Loving God, wherever I am, wherever I go, whatever I do, however I feel, I know that you will be with me, to hold, to heal, to guide and to bless. So, I will go in peace, assured of your unfailing love. Amen.

Use for the 'useless'

Read

Consider the nature of your calling. Not many of you were wise in human terms; not many were important; not many were well born. God, however, chose the foolish of this world in order to shame the wise, the weak to shame the strong, the lowest and the despised – those considered as nothing – to quash those who consider themselves something, so that nobody may boast before him.   *1 Corinthians 1:26-29*

Ponder

It looked to me like a pile of old junk – a curious assortment of bric-a-brac and cast-offs barely worth a second glance. Clearly, however, some people saw things differently, for there was a queue outside waiting for the doors to open and the mad scramble to begin. I never felt altogether comfortable at those jumble sales, for I was keenly aware that for some people the goods on sale there represented all they could afford, yet in my first church they were a fact of life – the only way to keep the doors open and keep me in a job. I learned something useful, however, from the experience; namely, that what might seem useless to one person can be anything but to another; a lesson that is equally applicable when it comes to assessing people. All too easily, we write people off, judging them by our own set of values and concluding that they fail to pass muster.

Strangely, we can do the same of ourselves, convinced that there is no way God can possibly use us. God, however, invariably has other ideas, able to use people in the most unexpected and surprising of ways. Never consider that you or anyone else is useless, for as far as God is concerned, 'useless' is a word that doesn't exist.

Ask yourself

Are there people you have dismissed because you did not see how God could use them? Have you underestimated the way that God might be able to use *you*?

Pray

Living God, I have been guilty of devaluing both others and myself. I have seen weaknesses and failed to consider strengths. I have dwelt on failures and ignored success. I have looked at the outside instead of searching deeper beneath the surface. Forgive me for overlooking my own potential and closing my mind to that in those around me. Forgive me for finding it so easy to put people down and so hard to build them up.

Teach me to recognise that everyone has a place in your purpose and a contribution to make to your kingdom, and so help me to be open to everything you are able to do. Through Christ my Lord. Amen.

Remember

To this point, we have become the refuse and cast-offs of this world.   *1 Corinthians 4:13*

Close

Living God, teach me that my judgement and yours are rarely the same, and so awaken me to all you are able to do, through others and through me, however unlikely it may seem. In Christ's name. Amen.

The everlasting arms

Read

The eternal God is your dwelling place, and underneath are the everlasting arms. *Deuteronomy 33:27 (RSV)*

Ponder

Anyone who has had children will never forget the magical moment when they first began to walk. It was probably a few stumbling steps, no more, but it marked another stage in the journey of life. For such steps to happen, however, one thing is usually needed – a mother or father close at hand with arms outstretched, waiting to catch their child should they start to totter and fall. The knowledge that someone is there to offer support is all important, giving children the confidence they need to take not just their first faltering steps en route to walking but also their first steps in so much else – exploring new horizons, meeting new people, starting a new school, taking on new responsibilities and so on. Sometimes this will lead to success; at other times to failure; but always there will be – or at least should be – the knowledge that a mother or father is there for them, ready to pick them up, offer a comforting embrace, and urge them onwards.

So it is with God. He is always there watching over us, ready to offer a helping hand in times of need, to lift us up when we stumble, to comfort us in sorrow and reassure us in times of fear. Even in death, those arms are there, enfolding us as we meet the last enemy and leading us to life eternal. God delights in us as much as we do in our own children, and whether we see it or not, we rest secure in his everlasting arms.

Ask yourself

Do you feel vulnerable and alone? Are you scared of what the future might hold? Have you lost sight of the encircling arms of God?

Pray

Loving God, I know I shouldn't be afraid but sometimes I am – afraid of what the future might hold and whether I will have the strength to meet it. Thank you for the assurance that whatever I may face, you will be there beside me. Thank you for your promise to lift me up and help me to start again, however often I may fail. Thank you for the times you have reached out in the past, the experiences I can look back on when your arms have been there to support me when I needed them most.

Teach me to trust you more completely and so to step out in faith, confident that, though I may stumble, you will set me on my feet once more. Amen.

Remember

He will feed his flock like a shepherd; he will gather the lambs in his arms and carry them in his bosom, and gently lead those that are with young.   *Isaiah 40:11 (RSV)*

Close

Living God, embrace me in your arms, encircle me with your grace and enfold me in your love, for Jesus' sake. Amen.

Declaring our loyalties

Read

Anyone who is ashamed of me and my words, the Son of Man will be ashamed of in turn when he comes in his glory and the glory of the Father and the holy angels.

Luke 9:26

Ponder

I mentioned a little earlier in this book that it's almost ten years since I last watched Southend United, my hometown football team, in action. What I didn't mention is why I haven't been to any of their matches since then. To get to their home matches would clearly be impossible – the journey from Somerset is simply too long and expensive to contemplate – but how about away-games? I could have gone to watch Southend play Exeter, Torquay or Bristol Rovers – all relatively near – but one experience has put me off: the memory of the last away-match I attended. It was against Swindon Town during Southend's best-ever spell in their history; the club pressing, believe it or not, for a place in the Premier League, and I was there with my brother Julian to cheer on the team. Frustratingly, though, it was Swindon who scored first, and as an almighty roar erupted around us, we realised to our horror that we were entirely surrounded by home supporters. Another goal, another roar, and we nervously struggled to hide our disappointment. Eventually, Southend managed to score, but our instinctive whoop of delight died in our throats as a thousand malevolent stares bore down upon us. Discretion proved the better part of valour! We weren't ashamed of the team – far from it – but we were afraid to declare our loyalties, worried about the possible repercussions.

How often is the same true of our relationship with Christ? We sit quiet when we ought to speak up; we turn a blind eye when we ought to make a stand; we compromise our convictions when we ought to stay true. With a football team it's understandable, no club, however special, worth risking one's safety for, but can there be any such excuse with Jesus? The cause is far greater and, ironically, today at least the danger less great. Can we ever justify failing to declare our loyalty to him?

Ask yourself
Have you ever hidden or played down your faith? Why? How will you respond the next time you are put to the test?

Pray
Lord Jesus Christ, when I think of your commitment to me and your willingness to face suffering and death on my behalf, I am ashamed of my disloyalty to you and my failure to stand up for your kingdom. I keep quiet about my faith for fear of embarrassment. I close my eyes and ears to wrongdoing, rather than risk unpopularity. I water down my principles for the sake of an easy peace. I avoid getting involved in needs around me, claiming they are none of my business. In so many ways, I let you down, offering you an empty, secret discipleship.

Forgive me my weakness and cowardice, and give me courage to stand up for what I believe in and proudly to declare you as Lord of my life, to the glory of your name. Amen.

Remember
I am not ashamed of the gospel, for it is the power of God leading to salvation for everyone who believes, to the Jew, first, and also to the Gentile.   *Romans 1:16*

Close
Living God, teach me to show in my life the loyalty I declare with my lips. Amen.

Peacemakers

Read

Blessed are the peacemakers, for they will be called children of God.
Matthew 5:9 (NRSV)

Ponder

Last week, a nightly news bulletin featured one of the most moving stories I've heard in a long time. It was just a few days after the appalling suicide bombing of an Israeli wedding reception had left several people dead and countless others maimed and injured – men, women and children, one moment enjoying a family celebration and the next caught up in the most unspeakable carnage. Few incidents better sum up the depth of hatred between Jew and Arab, the level of atrocities on both sides seeming to know no bounds.

The story I have in mind, though, was very different. It concerned the father of a young man killed in an accident. Distraught with grief, the father agreed to donate his son's organs to a hospitalised patient in urgent need of a transplant. Nothing extraordinary about that, you might think, except that the donor was an Arab and the patient an Israeli! 'I wanted my son's death to bring life,' explained the father, 'whether it be to Jew or Arab.' The contrast could hardly be more poignant nor the example more challenging. A small act but a massive gesture that, for a few hours at least, spoke of peace and reconciliation. Would we have acted the same in that man's place? I wonder. Our situation may be far removed from his, but in innumerable ways we have the opportunity every day to act as peacemakers or to perpetuate the things that cause division. We can show forgiveness or nurse grievances, swallow our pride or thrust ourselves forward, admit mistakes or refuse to bend, make the first move or resist every advance. All of us have the opportunity in our daily relationships to work for harmony and reconciliation, but few of us take the opportunity as often as we should. Which are we: peacemakers or peace-breakers?

Ask yourself
What qualities characterise a peacemaker? How far are any of these evident in your life?

Pray
Loving God, I talk so glibly of peace but find it so hard to pursue it. I speak of breaking down barriers and living in harmony, but when it comes to being a peacemaker, I so often fall short. Forgive the many things within me that make for conflict – my pride, greed, envy and intolerance; my nursing of petty grievances and unwillingness to forgive, my preoccupation with self and lack of time for others – so much that pulls apart rather than draws together.

Make me an instrument of your peace. Teach me to heal wounds rather than create them, to unite rather than divide, to reconcile rather than separate. Put a new spirit within me – a spirit of love and openness, acceptance and understanding, healing and reconciliation. May the peace I so often pray for begin here and now with me, in the name of Christ. Amen.

Remember
So then, let us pursue the things that make for peace and the building up of one another. *Romans 14:19*

Close
Lord Jesus Christ, teach me not just to be *at* peace but to work *for* peace, to the glory of your name. Amen.

Reversing the roles?

Read

Tread carefully when you enter the house of God. Better to draw near and listen than to offer the sacrifice of fools, for they cannot keep themselves from doing evil. Never be in a hurry to talk and do not let your heart speak hastily before God, for God is in heaven and you are upon earth. So, then, let your words be few.   *Ecclesiastes 5:1-2*

Ponder

How many of us, if we went to hospital for a consultation with a specialist, would refuse to listen to the diagnosis, insisting that we know better? Which of us, if we had to call out the AA, would tell the mechanic how to do his or her job? Or, again, how many of us, if by some mischance we found ourselves on trial in the high court, would presume to advise our barrister as to the best way to conduct the case? In all of these situations, to stick our oar in and refuse to bow to a greater authority would be the height of folly, yet the words of Ecclesiastes warn us that we can often be guilty of doing something very similar when it comes to God. We claim that he is sovereign over all, ruler of heaven and earth, and Lord of space and time, but so often, having done that, we calmly proceed to present him with a personal wish list, without the slightest sense of incongruity. 'Grant me this', we say; 'do that', 'do the other', as if we fully expect him to be at our beck and call.

The problem is that some passages in scripture concerning asking in faith appear, on a superficial reading, to encourage such an approach, but think about the implications were that true: it would be tantamount to putting ourselves in God's place! Of course there will be times when something matters so much to us that we will beg him to listen, and of course there will be times when he readily does so, but if

God is who we say he is, surely the right approach in prayer has to be to listen to what *he* wants before listing what *we* desire. Prayer is not finally something *we do*, but something *he* invites us to *share in*. Lose sight of that, and we're in danger of losing sight of him.

Ask yourself

How often in prayer do you make time to listen to what God might be saying? How far are your prayers about your wishes and how far about God's will?

Pray

Almighty God, yours is the purpose that brought the world and universe into being, and yet I try sometimes to impose my will on yours. You are the Lord of heaven and earth, yet I imagine sometimes that I know best. Yours is the hand that has led your people across the ages, yet I assume sometimes that my wish is your command.

Forgive me for reversing the roles and setting myself up in your place, seeking my ends rather than your will. Teach me not just to speak of faith but to live by it, trusting in your way, listening to your voice and working for your kingdom. Through Jesus Christ my Lord. Amen.

Remember

Much dreaming and many words are empty. Therefore, stand in awe before God.   *Ecclesiastes 5:7*

Close

Gracious God, I know that you are always ready to listen, but teach me first to hear what you would say before I start to speak myself. Amen.

Past put behind us

Read

The people said to Samuel, 'Intercede before the Lord your God for us, your servants, so that we may not die; for we have compounded our many sins by the evil of demanding a king for ourselves.' Samuel said to the people, 'Do not be afraid. Yes, you have done evil, but don't let that deflect you from honouring the Lord. Rather, serve him with all your heart. Do not experiment with false gods that can neither profit nor save, for they are useless. For his sovereign name's sake, the Lord will not cast you off, because it has pleased him to make you his own people.'

1 Samuel 12:19-22

Ponder

Have you ever made a mistake that you have rued ever since? It is a rare person indeed who has no regrets, but the question is, how do we respond to them? Two wrongs, we are told, don't make a right, yet all too often our response to one mistake is to make another, until life ends up spiralling out of control.

The situation underlying our reading from Samuel was much like that, the people of Israel in danger of abandoning their trust in God and going their own way. On the surface, there is nothing so terrible in their so-called 'mistake'; what was so wrong, after all, in asking for a king? The answer lies in the thinking behind their request; namely, their desire to follow the way of the world rather than the way of God. They preferred an earthly ruler they could see and touch, however fallible he might be, to a heavenly ruler who seemed remote and isolated. Now, having seen their mistake, they felt God must surely have abandoned them, but they came to Samuel with one last desperate plea, and his reply offers an enduring message as applicable today as it was then. Yes, you made a mistake, he tells them, but in God's eyes, it's over and done with, already forgotten. Don't dwell over the past; look forward to the future and make the most of the present. God doesn't brood over what's been and gone, but puts it behind him. If he can do that, isn't it time we did as well?

Ask yourself

Are you troubled by the memory of past failures? Do you fear God may be punishing you for mistakes made long ago? Have you fully grasped the true meaning of forgiveness?

Pray

Living God, though I have let you down in so many ways, teach me that you do not judge as I do, but that you are truly willing to forgive and forget. Teach me to put the past behind me and to accept the new life you so freely offer, and so may I live each day as your gift, nurtured by the love of Christ and renewed through your Holy Spirit, to your praise and glory. Amen.

Remember

If you, Lord, were to keep an account of our sins, who could lift up their head before you? In you, though, is forgiveness, and so it is that you are worshipped.   *Psalm 130:3-4*

Close

God of past, present and future, teach me let go of my yesterdays, to trust in your tomorrow, and so to rejoice today, celebrating the fullness of life that you have given through Jesus Christ my Lord. Amen.

21 SEPTEMBER

Like little children

Read

They brought little children to him so that he might touch them, but the disciples scolded them. Seeing this, Jesus was angry and said to them, 'Let the little children come to me; do not impede them; for the kingdom of God belongs to such as these. I tell you this, whoever does not receive the kingdom of God like a little child has no hope of entering it.' Then he enfolded them in his arms, laid his hands on them, and blessed them.

Mark 10:13-16

Ponder

Few parents will be at risk of sentimentalising the teaching of Jesus concerning children and our need to become like them. Children are by no means all sweetness and light – not even little ones. They can be mischievous, bad-tempered, spiteful, temperamental and much else besides. Yet, at the same time, few people who have raised a family will be at risk of missing the innate truth in what Jesus said, because there is something in children that is very special. It is hard to put that something into words, but it has to do with innocence and enthusiasm for life, total trust and unreserved love, and that amazing ability to be brawling one moment and to forgive and forget the next – just some of the qualities that make being a parent such a joyful and rewarding responsibility. One look, one word or one gesture after an exhausting day that has driven you to your wits' end suddenly makes it all seem worth it a thousand times over. No child is perfect, but, given the love and the opportunity each deserves, all have precious gifts and characteristics this far untarnished by the world. We need to recapture those qualities in terms of our relationship with God if we are truly to become his children.

Ask yourself

What sort of childlike qualities might Jesus have had in mind when he spoke about becoming like children? How far are these evident in your life? Which qualities do you think we most commonly lose when we get older?

Pray

Lord Jesus Christ, I remember your words to the disciples that the kingdom of heaven belongs to little children, and I remember also your warning that unless we become like children we can never hope to enter that kingdom. Teach me what that means. Grant me the childlike qualities I need to grow in faith – a child's innocence and hunger to learn, a child's love and total trust. Help me, like them, to step out gladly into the great adventure of faith, to the glory of your name. Amen.

Remember

Sitting down, he called the twelve, and said to them, 'Whoever wants to be first must be last and the servant of all.' Then, taking a little child, he put it among them and, encircling it in his arms, he said to them, 'Whoever receives one such child in my name receives me, and whoever receives me receives not just me but the one who sent me.'

Mark 9:35-37

Close

Living God, grant me the wisdom of the years and the enthusiasm of childhood, the discernment of adulthood coupled with the innocence of youth. Help me to rediscover the child in me and so grow to maturity in you. Through Jesus Christ my Lord. Amen.

The faith to ask

Read

Jesus entered a house intending to keep his presence there hidden, but he could not escape notice. A woman whose little daughter had an unclean spirit immediately heard about him, and she came and prostrated herself at his feet. The woman was a Gentile, by birth a Syrophoenician. She implored Jesus to rid her daughter of the demon, but he said to her, 'Let the children be fed first, for it would not be right to take the children's bread and throw it to the dogs.' 'Ah yes, sir,' she retorted, 'but even the dogs under the table eat the children's crumbs.' Jesus answered her, 'For an answer like that, you may go – the demon has left your daughter.' The woman went home, and found the child lying on the bed, the demon having gone.   *Mark 7:24-30*

Ponder

There's no denying it – scripture can be hard to understand sometimes. Take this encounter of Jesus with the woman of Syrophoenicia. To put it kindly, his response comes across as abrupt and aloof; to be more blunt, it appears down-right rude; a dismissive, heartless rejection of an earnest plea for help. So what was Jesus thinking of? Why react like he did? One possibility is that Mark exaggerated the severity of Jesus' reply; another, that Jesus wanted to test the woman's faith to ensure she was genuinely seeking help rather than just inventing a story to get near him. I don't seriously believe either.

In my view, he recognised this woman's sincerity straightaway, and saw in her an opportunity to illustrate a fundamental truth at the heart of faith. According to Jewish teaching, the woman, as a foreigner, had no claim on his help; he knew it, she knew it. Yet she came, nonetheless, not because she deserved anything from him but because she understood both what he had to give and that he would be ready to give it. That's the point here: Jesus is saying to the crowds, 'Look at this woman. She understands who I am even if you don't. She knows that I delight to respond, not because of any worth on your part, but because of who and what I am.' It's a message we need to learn in turn. None of us has any claim on his goodness or any right to demand his love, but he is ready to hear our prayer and to meet our innermost needs. All we have to do is ask, and mean it!

Ask yourself

Does God seem to ignore *your* requests sometimes? Were you serious in what you asked for, or did you ask half-heartedly, not really sure what you wanted and even less certain that God would answer?

Pray

Lord Jesus Christ, it is hard to keep faith when you do not seem to answer my prayers; harder still when you seem remote and disinterested, seemingly unmoved by my pleas. Teach me that, sometimes, you are speaking precisely through that apparent lack of response, challenging me to look more deeply into my situation and to broaden my horizons. Yet teach me also to trust that you do hear and delight to respond, and so may I never be discouraged from asking, in your name. Amen.

Remember

Whatever you pray for in faith, you will receive.

Matthew 21:22

Close

Lord Jesus Christ, though I deserve so little, teach me that you are always ready to give much, provided I am truly ready to seek. Amen.

Speaking their language

Read

Standing in the middle of the Areopagus, Paul said, 'People of Athens, I perceive that you are deeply religious, for as I walked by I couldn't help noticing your objects of worship, among which I spotted an altar on which was inscribed "To an unknown god". What you worship as unknown, I now proclaim to you. The God who created the world and all things in it, the Lord of heaven and earth, does not live in shrines made by human hands, nor is he served in the sense of being dependent on anyone. Rather, he gives breath and life to all things. He created all nations that live on earth from a common ancestor, and he established the times and limits of their existence so that they will search for God and, should they grope after him, eventually find him – although ultimately he is not far from any of us. In him we live, move and have our being, as indeed some of your own poets have said, "For we also are his offspring".'

Acts 17:22-28

Ponder

If someone were to regale you with Einstein's theory of relativity, how long would it be before you excused yourself? Unless you happened to be a physicist, I expect you would look for the earliest opportunity. The subject may be fascinating to experts, but to most of us it is virtually another language. Communication is about speaking to people in terms they can relate to.

This perhaps accounts for the astonishing success of the Apostle Paul throughout his ministry. Look at the way he addressed the people of Athens. As a Jew, his inclination must have been to talk of Jesus in terms of Old Testament prophecy, and, as a Pharisee, in terms of the Jewish Law; but he did neither, because he knew such concepts would mean nothing to his Greek listeners. He needed to speak to them in terms of their own faith and culture, and that is precisely what he did, quoting, in a masterstroke, from Epimenides and Eratus, two of their own poets – in other words, talking their language. Do we do that when we share our faith, or do we slip into the language of jargon? Effective testimony takes two things: a willingness to speak honestly about what God means to us, and a sensitivity towards those we are talking to, so that God may speak in turn to them.

Ask yourself

When you attempt to share your faith, do you talk *to* people or *at* them?

Pray

Lord of all, you call me to witness to Christ; to share with others what he has done for me. Help me to do that wisely, sensitively, honestly and faithfully. Teach me to speak from personal experience rather than by empty rote; to present the simple message of the gospel rather than the intricacies of doctrine or dogma; and to be conscious of those I am talking to, instead of conscious of myself. Whenever and wherever the opportunity presents itself, teach me to witness in a way that is relevant and alive, and so may your love be made known to all, in the name of Christ. Amen.

Remember

I have become all things to all people, so that I might exploit every possibility to save them. Everything I do is for the sake of the gospel, so that I too may share in its blessings.

1 Corinthians 9:22b-23

Close

Lord, you have given me good news to share. Help me to remember not just the message but the people you want me to share it with, and so may I speak the words you would have me say in the way you would have me say them. Amen.

The beginning of wisdom

Read

Happy is the one who finds wisdom and who acquires understanding, for wisdom profits more than silver, and brings gain better even than gold. She is more precious than jewels, and nothing you might name can compare with her. Long life is in her right hand, and in her left are riches and honour. Her ways bring pleasure, and all her paths bring peace. She is a staff to those who lay hold of her; a source of happiness and security to those who hold her fast.

Proverbs 3:13-18

Ponder

What do Plato, Aristotle, Darwin, David Attenborough, Monty Python, and the writers of Proverbs and Ecclesiastes have in common? They have all explored questions concerning the meaning of life. How did life start? Why are we here? What does the future hold? The way to answer such questions, according to the book of Proverbs, appears straightforward enough – namely, to seek wisdom – but what is wisdom and how do we find it? For some, the answer lies in academic study. Others claim it is through the university of life. Others still maintain that the solution is to let go of the world and lose oneself in mystical speculation. According to the author of Proverbs, however, the answer is much simpler: 'The fear of the Lord is the beginning of wisdom' (Proverbs 1:7; 9:10) – a contention echoed in the psalms (Psalm 111:10). Gain insight into the ways of God, and we will discover the true meaning of life.

Does this leave a place for the intellect, the wisdom we can gain through study and daily experience? Of course it does. The range of topics covered in Proverbs is surprisingly down to earth, yet do not confuse the message given there with mere worldly wisdom. Faith is concerned with the daily stuff of life, yes, and thank God for that, but it brings to it a new dimension and a different perspective that often stands accepted wisdom on its head – a different kind of wisdom ultimately exemplified through the folly of the Cross, through which true meaning is found for all.

Ask yourself

Where do you look for wisdom and understanding? Does life, despite all you have learnt, or perhaps even because of it, sometimes seem without purpose? Have you confused divine and human wisdom?

Pray

Loving God, I thank you for all there is to explore in this wonderful world and fascinating universe you have given us. I thank you for all those whose study and research have unlocked so many of the secrets concerning the origins and development of life, and I thank you that you have given me a mind with which to think, enquire and learn. Teach me to apply my mind to gaining understanding, but teach me also that, however much I may learn, true wisdom concerning ultimate realities lies not in human ingenuity, but in you, the beginning and end of all. Amen.

Remember

The sayings of the wise are sharp as goads, and their collected sayings are like nails driven home, for they come ultimately from one shepherd. Beware of anything beyond these, my child. There is no end to the books you might consult, but too much study will wear you out. The end of the matter, once everything has been heard, is this: fear God and keep his commandments; no one should be expected to do any more than this. For God will judge every deed, and every secret thing, whether good or evil.

Ecclesiastes 12:11-14

Close

Living God, teach me the secret of true wisdom, in knowing and serving you, through Christ my Lord. Amen.

The silences of God

Read

The Lord was passing by, and a gust of wind arose, so strong that it shook the mountain and shattered rocks before him, but the Lord was not in the wind. After that came an earthquake, but the Lord was not in the earthquake, and after the earthquake came fire, but the Lord was not in the fire; and after the fire there was simply the sound of silence. When Elijah heard that, he hid his face in his cloak, went out and stood at the entrance of the cave. Then a voice came to him that said, 'Why are you here, Elijah?'

1 Kings 19:11b-13

Ponder

The story of Elijah's encounter with God on the slopes of Mount Horeb has inspired countless sermons and innumerable prayers, not to mention the celebrated hymn, 'Dear Lord and Father of mankind, forgive our foolish ways'. What, though, is it all about, and what, in particular, is the significance of the 'sound of silence', or the 'still small voice', as other translations put it?

There are probably several equally valid answers to those questions, but one that occurred to me rereading these verses is that perhaps this incident has something to say concerning those times when God seems far away. Elijah looks for God in the mighty wind, surely a sign of his power, but no, he is not there. He looks again in the mighty earthquake, but again, no. Then there is the fire, reminiscent of the cloudy pillar that guided the people of Israel, and you can almost imagine Elijah thinking, 'This must be him!' – but yet again it isn't. Yet, just when the prophet may have been giving up hope, there comes that voice like a gentle whisper – so unpretentious, so insignificant, you could almost miss it. Was this God's way of telling Elijah he is present in the ordinary and unsensational moments of life even when it doesn't look like it? I may simply be clutching at straws here, but I like to think there is a grain of truth in such an interpretation, for, let's face it, occasions when God is dramatically at work are few and far between. The fact is that he is equally present in the humdrum business of daily life, even when we struggle to catch sight of him; perhaps there most of all.

Ask yourself

Is there some prayer of yours that God doesn't seem to have answered? Could it be that you haven't heard his voice in the silence?

Pray

Loving God, there are times when, no matter how I call, you seem silent, when I cannot hear your voice no matter how I listen for it. Grant me courage in those moments to ask if I have closed my heart and mind to what you would say, but help me also to understand that there are times when you expect me to get on with the business of discipleship without you directing my every step.

Help me to see that your silence may not be a sign of my faithlessness or your displeasure but rather of your love, offering me the opportunity to grow towards Christian maturity. Help me then to remember all those times you have spoken unmistakably, to me and to others, and let those moments sustain and direct me until your word comes again, in the name of Christ. Amen.

Remember

The Lord has listened to my plea; he will accept my prayer.

Psalm 6:9

Close

Gracious God, help me to hear again your still small voice, your word even in the silence, and so to recognise that, however little I may see it, you are always there and always active, through Jesus Christ my Lord. Amen.

The mind of Christ

Read

Who has known the mind of the Lord and who can presume to instruct him? Yet we have the mind of Christ.

1 Corinthians 2:16

Ponder

How far do you think it's possible to read someone's mind? Personally, I've always been sceptical about the idea, but there can be no denying that sometimes a person can have a special bond with another; a general sensitivity that borders on telepathy. When we are truly close to someone and have grown to know them inside out, there are times when we can be pretty sure what they are thinking and how they will react in a given situation.

For me, that is the key to Paul's extraordinary statement to the Corinthians; a claim that, at first glance, seems to border on the blasphemous. The last thing Paul is suggesting is that we can know what Jesus is thinking – that would be tantamount to making ourselves God. The idea, rather, is of becoming so close to him and making him so much a part of our life, that his will becomes our will and his way our way. It speaks of a personal relationship, of knowing Christ in such a manner that it influences our whole way of thinking. In the final analysis, the picture becomes not us reading his mind but him being able to shape ours.

Ask yourself

How far is your faith about a personal relationship? What things keep you from having the mind of Christ?

Pray

Lord Jesus Christ, there is so much within me that is not as it should be: thoughts, attitudes, desires and fears that alienate me from others and from you and that disturb, divide and ultimately destroy. I long to be like you: to feel the same love and compassion that you felt, to experience the same closeness with God, and to know the same inner wholeness and harmony. Alone, though, I cannot achieve it, no amount of effort sufficient to help me emulate your example.

Draw closer to me through your grace, and fill me in body, mind and soul. Speak to me, teach and guide, so that I may know you better. Work within my heart, transforming the clay of my life into a new creation, moulded by your hands. In your name I ask it. Amen.

Remember

Let the same mind be in you that was in Christ Jesus.

Philippians 2:5 (NRSV)

Close

Prince of Peace, heal me. Lamb of God, redeem me. Shepherd of the sheep, guard me. Light of the world, lead me. Lord Jesus Christ, touch my life by your grace, and help me to live and work for you, to your glory. Amen.

You can say that again!

Read

As I said to you before, I say to you once more, 'If anyone preaches any gospel other than that which we have received, a curse be on them!'

Galatians 1:9'

Ponder

When I first had the idea of putting together this book, I thought it would be a relatively straightforward job. I had plenty of material to adapt from my time in ministry and numerous new ideas mulling in the back of my mind, so a few months at most and I would be finished. Instead, as I write this, I'm already several months past the date I first promised to complete the book and I have worked into the small hours virtually every night over the last twenty or so weeks. The reasons are many, but chief among them has been a concern that I might end up repeating earlier material, inadvertently perhaps using the same reading, prayer or thought for the day. No, I'm not using that as an excuse to do just that here, but would it matter if I did, for isn't there a sense in which we've been doing that anyway as Christians for the past two thousand years?

Of course the words haven't been precisely the same, but just think of the countless sermons that have been preached and Bible passages discussed during that time, all on essentially the same message. There will have been different approaches, different texts, and different nuances of interpretation, but essentially the concern of each has been to proclaim the good news of Jesus Christ. All this points us to the wonder of the gospel – that though we may hear it again and again, it still has the power to speak to us in new and challenging ways, and still has the power to change lives. I'm not going to repeat myself word for word in this book – not on purpose anyway – but I hope in a sense I have repeated myself on every page in testifying to the renewing life-giving power of God revealed in Christ. For there, if ever there was one, is a message that will be as fresh tomorrow and every day as the day it was first spoken; a message concerning which we can happily declare, without hesitation, 'You can say that again!'

Ask yourself

Can you recall moments when a familiar verse or passage of scripture has suddenly leapt out at you, possessed of new meaning? Do you still read the Bible and share in worship, expecting God to speak to you?

Pray

Loving God, I thank you for the way your word has spoken across the centuries and continues to speak today. I praise you that the gospel has changed the lives of innumerable individuals, and that it has changed my life in turn.

Teach me never to lose sight of that message or its transforming power; never to forget that, however familiar it may be, it can still speak in new and exciting ways to my heart and experience. Help me, this and every day, to be open to your voice and to hear you speaking, and, above all, help me to respond, through Christ my Lord. Amen.

Remember

This is the message that you have heard from the beginning: that we should love one another.   *1 John 3:11*

Close

Living God, ever old, ever new, speak *to* me and *through* me of your great love in Jesus Christ, always the same yet never exhausted. Amen.

Stewards of creation

Read

The Lord is a great God, a great king over all gods. In his hands are the depths of the earth, as well as the hills and valleys. The sea is his, he made it, together with the dry land, fashioned by his hands. Come! Let us prostrate ourselves in worship, let us kneel before the Lord who made us, for he is our God and we are his people, the flock that he shepherds.

Psalm 95:3-7a

Ponder

Probably few people were overly surprised when George W. Bush, on his accession to the US presidency, promptly cancelled American support for the Kyoto agreement on greenhouse gases and climate change. Given his record as a state governor, it was pretty much par for the course, yet even the most hardened observers must have caught their breath at the stunning cynicism of his actions. The world today is facing intolerable pressures, and the threat of ecological catastrophe is all too real, yet the richest country in the world, responsible for well over half of all greenhouse gas emissions, saw fit to turn its back on the most important international agreement on the environment so far negotiated.

The reason? Money. And there, in a nutshell, is the issue at the heart of environmental change. Most of us claim to be concerned about the environment, yet we baulk when it comes to paying more for a truly green product. We say we abhor waste, yet make little effort to recycle rather than throw things away. We wring our hands over pollution, yet we think nothing of hopping into the car rather than walk or cycle. If we really believe this is God's world held by us in trust, can we ever justify such carelessness? As Christians, we not only need to add our voices to the mounting calls for a sensible stewarding of creation; we also need to live in such a way that we give a lead through our actions. To fail in that is to betray the responsibility God has placed into our hands.

Ask yourself

What practical steps are you taking to be a more faithful steward of creation? In what ways are you still guilty of wasting or exploiting the resources God has given?

Pray

Lord of all, I forget sometimes that your love involves responsibility as well as privilege; a duty not just to you but to the whole of your creation to nurture and protect rather than simply exploit it. Forgive me my part in a society that has too often lived for today with no thought of tomorrow. Forgive me my unquestioning acceptance of an economic system that plunders this world's resources with little regard as to the consequences. Help me to live less wastefully and with more thought for those who will come after me.

Challenge the hearts and minds of people everywhere, that both they and I may understand more fully the wonder and the fragility of this planet you have given us, and so may we honour our calling to be faithful stewards of it all, in Christ's name. Amen.

Remember

The world is established, firm and immovable; the Lord will judge the peoples justly. Let the heavens be glad and the earth exult, the sea roar and all that is in it, the fields and everything in them rejoice. Then the trees of the forest will sing for joy before the Lord, for he will come to judge the earth. He will judge the earth with righteousness and all people fairly. *Psalm 96:10b-13*

Close

Loving God, forgive me for taking your many gifts for granted – forgetting, squandering and even abusing them. Help me to rejoice in all you have given and to steward it wisely, to your glory. Amen.

Reaping what we sow

Read

Do not be taken in: God will not be made a fool of. Whatever someone sows, that person will also reap; the one
who sows what the body wants will reap corruption, but
the one who sows what the Spirit desires will reap eternal
life through that same Spirit. So, then, let us never grow
weary of doing what is right, for, provided we do not give
up, we will reap at harvest-time. *Galatians 6:7-9*

Ponder

Several years back, my wife took a fancy to the Welsh poppy,
deciding that it was something we ought to grow, so every
time we visited a garden centre, we looked for a specimen.
Eventually, we found one and with eager anticipation we
planted it in the border. We were not disappointed; the plant
flowered its heart out for month after month. The following year, though, we were in for a shock, for suddenly we
didn't have *one* Welsh poppy, we had *hundreds* – another
sprouting, so it seemed, wherever we cared to look! Here
was a classic case of reaping what you sow, even if we hadn't
physically scattered the seeds ourselves. A little more research
and we would have known exactly what we were letting
ourselves in for.

How far, though, can we apply this principle to life? Hard
work is not always rewarded, honesty doesn't always pay,
effort doesn't guarantee success, and love doesn't guarantee
love in return. Yet, having said that, there is another level at
which we *do* reap what we sow, both in this life and
beyond. The rewards associated with Christian discipleship
may not be tangible, but they are there nonetheless. The
rewards for loving others, offering our service and pursuing
good may not be quantifiable in human terms, but they
are no less real. Similarly, wrongdoing and injustice, though

they may seem to go unpunished, carry their own cost. We can sow with no thought of tomorrow if we wish – God will not stop us – but he tells us repeatedly throughout the scriptures that the time will come, whether in this life or the next, when we will reap the harvest. What, then, will we sow? It's our choice.

Ask yourself

What apparent injustices in life trouble you most? Have there been particular moments that have restored your faith in the purposes of God? What were they? What, for you, are the rewards of knowing and loving God?

Pray

Sovereign God, I can't help wondering sometimes about the fairness of life. When I see the good suffer and the wicked prosper, my faith is shaken such that I inevitably start to question. There is so much that doesn't seem to make sense; so much that appears to deny everything I believe about you.

Teach me, despite the apparent contradictions of life, to keep faith that you are there, striving against everything that frustrates your will and denies your love. Teach me to hold on to those moments when I see wrongs righted and justice done. Above all, teach me to look at the cross of Christ and to draw strength from the victory there of love over what had seemed to be the triumph of evil. Amen.

Remember

They sow the wind and reap the whirlwind. Sow righteousness and you will reap steadfast love.   *Hosea 8:7a; 10:12a*

Close

Living God, as you have sown your word in me, help me to sow your word among others, to the glory of your name. Amen.

Words from the heart

Read

While [Paul] was making his defence, Festus exclaimed, 'You've taken leave of your senses, Paul! All your learning has driven you insane.' Paul replied, 'I am not insane, most excellent Festus; what I am telling you is the truth and sound common sense. The king knows well enough about these things, which indeed is why I speak to him freely; for I am quite sure none of these matters escaped his notice, none of them having been done in a corner. King Agrippa, do you believe the prophets? I know that you believe.' Agrippa said to Paul, 'Do you think you can persuade me to become a Christian in such a short time?' Paul answered, 'Whether it take a short or a long time, I pray God that not only you but all who are listening to me today might become such as I am – except for these chains.'

Acts 26:24-29

Ponder

A few years ago a fascinating television documentary series asked the question 'What makes a great speaker?' Using archive film of great orators such as Lloyd George, Winston Churchill, Martin Luther King, Billy Graham and Donald Soper, suggestions were made as to the essential qualities for any speaker. These included posture, gestures and manner-isms, power and inflection of voice, well-chosen pauses, eye contact, tempo, repetition and humour. I watched those programmes eagerly, hoping that next time I delivered a sermon the congregation would leap to their feet in wild and spontaneous applause, and that before long crowds would be flocking to my church in their droves! Sadly, it never happened and, of course, I never seriously imagined that it would, truly gifted speakers being a rare breed.

One such speaker, however, was clearly the Apostle Paul. In part, this was due to his willingness to talk the language of his listeners, but he had another quality that we can all emulate – quite simply, a transparent sincerity. There was no artifice about Paul, none of what, in modern politics, we have come to refer to as 'spin'. In his trial before Festus and Agrippa, instead of toning down his message as many would have done in his place, he gave a frank and honest life history, telling of the personal pilgrimage that had led him to Christ. None of us will achieve anything like Paul achieved, nor speak with a fraction of his authority, but all of us can speak with sincerity, and if we do that, we may find that the results are far greater than we ever dared to expect.

Ask yourself
What things hold you back from sharing your faith? Who or what was it that won you over to Christ, and what was it that most spoke to you then?

Pray
Loving God, you do not call everyone to be an evangelist or a preacher of your word, but you do call us all to be witnesses, telling others what Jesus has done for us. Through the Apostle Paul, you have shown that what really counts, if we are to do that effectively, is not using clever words or care-fully rehearsed arguments, but simply speaking openly and honestly from the heart. Loving God, as I have heard, so help me to tell, to the glory of your name. Amen.

Remember
Do not worry about what you are to say, but when the moment arrives speak of whatever comes into your heart, for it will not be you speaking but the Holy Spirit.

Mark 13:11b

Close
Lord Jesus Christ, whenever I speak for you, save me from trying to be clever; help me simply to be genuine. Amen.

Our sufferings, however, was certainly the 'good faith' in part, this was due to its willingness of life that inspired of the literature, and inured to other quality. It is the 'small and the - quite simple - it has extraordinary care. They are no matter about Paul, none of what is modern politics we have come to take to account. It is still better to be had a surprise. Instead of torturgdom, his message is really would have done to his pure believes react and honour the human writing of the perpetual pilgrimage that had to be done to God - those of us with believe anything, the Paul achievement not easy with a faith of this authority but all our Europe and with sincerity, and if we do not, we may find that the resistance far greater than we ever need to expect.

Ask yourself

* What things that you reckoned during your faith. What so that was it that works towards the Christ and of what that most noble to you that.

Pray

* In this God, you do not call everyone to be an evangelist. A particular to you and as far you do call to offer in this witness through the - which Paul has done to us. Through the Apostle Paul, you have shown that after the discipline it we come to do that effectively, in a little together, much of our faith expressed in prayer and but in his hope and loving. Through us, help us, through it, meek in a loving - today, I have, there I so help me O Tell, to the glory of Christ our Lord. Amen.

Remember

* Do not worry about what you attend to say when the hour is and answers speak of a human I am of a true vindication, but it will then be you speak of, but the Holy Spirit.
  Luke 12:11

Advice

* Should hesitate and whenever I speak to you, so, I see how trying to be clever, help me again to beg anew my Amen.

OCTOBER

Taking stock

Read

Assess yourselves to check that you are living in the faith. Test yourselves to make sure. Do you not realise that Jesus Christ is in you? – assuming, of course, that your faith is not a sham.

2 Corinthians 13:5

Ponder

The very mention of the two words in our title today is enough to send a shiver down some people's spines. For them, stocktaking conjures up images of mad panic and frenetic activity; hours counting and recounting, scouring warehouses and checking manically through computer records, wondering just how so much has gone missing. For any business, though, taking stock is essential, not only in checking against theft and fraud but also in assessing how well and in what areas the firm is succeeding.

That is a principle we do well to apply to ourselves as Christians, as the words of Paul to the Corinthians powerfully remind us. 'Examine yourselves,' he says, 'and see whether you are living in the faith.' In other words, stop and take stock; make time for a long hard look at your life, some serious soul-searching. Don't just muddle through. Don't assume that everything is automatically ticking along as it should be. Don't imagine that once you've got the ball of Christian discipleship moving you can leave it to take care of itself. Nothing could be further from the truth. It's all too easy to get lost along the way: to take a false step here, a wrong path there, until instead of making progress you're slipping backwards, unsure of where you're going and why. How far have you honoured the vows you once made? How far have you lived up to your commitment? How far have you achieved the things you once set out to achieve? In short, what have you made of your life?

Stop and take stock. You may not like what you find, but at least you will know where you stand and, with God's help, have the chance to do something about it before it's too late to put matters right.

Ask yourself

Have you made the most of the gifts, guidance and opportunities God has given you? Is your faith still growing as it should be? When was the last time you stopped to take stock?

Pray

Living God, forgive me for being content to drift along with little sense of direction or purpose; for assuming it is enough to get by, and failing to ensure that I do even that. Give me courage to examine myself honestly, to take stock of my life carefully and prayerfully, and so to see myself as I am and glimpse what I could and should be with your help.

Help me to face the things I prefer to push aside, pretending they are not there – to recognise my weaknesses as well as my strengths, my faults as well as my virtues. So may I grow each day in faith and live more fully to your praise and glory, through Jesus Christ my Lord. Amen.

Remember

Much will be required of those who have been given much, and those who have had much entrusted to them will find even more demanded. *Luke 12:48b*

Close

Teach me, Lord, to take stock, thoughtfully, honestly and prayerfully, and help me to see myself as I really am rather than as I imagine myself to be. Amen.

The assurance of things hoped for

Read

Some will say, 'How can the dead be raised and what sort of body will they have?'   *1 Corinthians 15:35*

Ponder

Faith, we are told, is one of the great qualities of the Christian life, an essential ingredient of genuine discipleship. But living with faith is far from easy, for most of us prefer cast-iron certainties to promises we must accept on trust. Nowhere is this more so than when it comes to the fact of death and our hope of eternal life. We believe in the resurrection and the kingdom of heaven, but we can't help wishing we knew a bit more about it. Where will it be? How will we get there? When will it come? What will it be like? These and a host of other questions all too easily play on our minds, insidiously undermining our confidence. 'If only we knew,' we tell ourselves. 'If only we could see, then it would all be so much easier.' But the fact is we do not need to see anything more than God has already revealed, for true faith should be based on what we experience today as much as what we're promised tomorrow. When God is an ever-present reality in our life, we need no proof as to the future.

Ask yourself

Is your faith dependent on what happens now and on things you can see and touch? Have you tied God down to this world rather than caught through him a glimpse of the world to come?

Pray

Lord, you call me to live by faith, not by sight. You tell me to trust in things unseen, in realities I cannot grasp. I do my best, but it's not easy, for I like to have everything cut and dried, spelt out for me down to the finest detail. I struggle to cope with uncertainties in relation to everyday matters, the routine business of life, let alone my eternal destiny. Yet I know deep down that there is no other way, for the joys you hold in store for me are beyond my imagining, too awesome for the human mind to comprehend.

Teach me, then, to leave all things in your hands, trusting for tomorrow through what I know of you today. Teach me to work for your kingdom until that day I enter into the wonder of your presence. Amen.

Remember

We are always in good heart, knowing that while we are at home in the body, we are absent from the Lord – for we walk by faith and not by sight.   *2 Corinthians 5:6-7*

Close

Lord, even when I cannot see you, when life seems dark and hope seems to be in vain, teach me to keep faith with you knowing that you will keep faith with me. Amen.

About turn

Read

You will have heard of my former conduct within Judaism – how I vigorously persecuted and laid waste the church of God and how I progressed in Judaism beyond most of my contemporaries, defending the tradition of my fathers with a fanatical zeal. When, though, the one who elected me from my mother's womb chose by his grace to reveal his Son through me, so that I might preach him among the nations, I did not discuss it with anyone, or go to Jerusalem to meet with those who were Apostles before me, but went away to Arabia before returning to Damascus. I was unknown then except by name to the churches of Judea, they having heard only that their former persecutor was now preaching the faith, and they praised God because of me.

Galatians 1:13-17, 22-24

Ponder

Early in her term as prime minister, Margaret Thatcher made a proud boast that was to become a trademark catch-phrase: 'The lady is not for turning.' Was that a quality or a flaw, a sign of strength or a weakness? The answer, I suspect, is a bit of both. It takes courage to hold on to our convictions, not least in politics. On the other hand, there may be times when we need to listen to other opinions, explore other avenues and even change direction altogether.

We see the last of those options graphically illustrated in the life of the Apostle Paul. Imagine the courage it must have taken for him, the archetypal Pharisee and destroyer of the Church, publicly to declare he had got things wrong. You might have expected him to keep his conversion quiet, adopt a low profile, but not Paul. Instead, he pursued his new faith with the same vigour he had pursued his old. Conversion for us may be a far less dramatic experience, yet nonetheless there is a change for us all – turning our backs on the old self and embracing the new. As with Paul, it is a two-fold response, involving not just a moving *away* from our former ways but a moving *towards* Christ. It takes courage to accept that all is not as it should be and to commit oneself to a lifetime of discipleship. It takes more courage still, having made that initial step, to recognise that the job, far from being finished is only just begun. Conversion is not a one-off experience but an ongoing process – a turning and turning again to Christ.

Ask yourself

How far do you find your old self asserts itself, despite you having committed yourself to Christ? Is it time you turned again *to* Christ as well as *away from* your old life?

Pray

Living God, I turned to you once and, naively, I imagined I had done all that needed doing; that from then on I would say goodbye to my old self and live in newness of life. The reality is that two selves war within me.

Help me, then, to turn to you once more, and to go on doing so for however long it takes. Help me, each day, to put off the old self and to be renewed in body, mind and spirit through your grace, until in the fullness of time you have finished your redemptive work and made of me a new creation. Through Jesus Christ my Lord. Amen.

Remember

You have been taught in Christ to put off your old self and your former conduct, corrupted by all kinds of deceitful desires, and to be renewed in your inner mind, putting on the new self created in the likeness of God, in righteousness, holiness and truth.

Ephesians 4:21b-24

Close

Lord Jesus Christ, teach me not simply to turn from my old ways, but to embrace the new, celebrating life as you desire and living to your praise and glory. Amen.

Not as bad as it seems

Read

Ahab told Jezebel everything Elijah had done, and how he had put all her prophets to the sword. Then Jezebel sent a messenger to Elijah, saying, 'Let the gods do the same to me, and worse besides, if by this time tomorrow I do not take your life as you took theirs.' Then Elijah was afraid. He arose and ran for his life, and coming to Beersheba, in Judah, he told his servant to remain there while he himself went on another day's journey into the wilderness. He sat down under a solitary broom tree, and asked God to let him die: 'It is enough; now, O Lord, take my life, for I am no better than my ancestors.' Suddenly the word of the Lord came to him, saying, 'What are you doing here, Elijah?' He answered, 'I have worked passionately for the Lord, the God of hosts; for the Israelites have forsaken your covenant, torn down your altars, and put your prophets to the sword. I alone am left, and now they want to take my life in turn.'

1 Kings 19:1-5a, 9b-10

Ponder

There's an old Arabian proverb that is a particular favourite of mine: 'All things are less dreadful than they seem.' That is the truth learned by Elijah in the story above. He had just experienced one of the high spots in his ministry, when the prophets of Baal were humiliated on Mount Carmel, but, as is so often the case, a high quickly gave way to a low. Presumably, Elijah had imagined that, following his earlier triumph, his troubles were over; that Jezebel and her prophets would have to admit defeat. Instead, he discovered that she had renewed her campaign against him with an even greater ferocity. As far as Elijah was concerned, it was him and God against the world, and he was fed up with fighting a one-man battle. God, though, had a surprise up his sleeve, for Elijah was shortly to discover that he was anything but alone – that, in fact, there were seven thousand people in Israel who had not bowed the knee to Baal.

There is a continuing message in this for us today. In the Church, we can feel up against it, struggling to keep the doors of our buildings open, demoralised by lack of members, disheartened by the limited impact of our efforts. As individuals, we can feel we are ploughing a lonely furrow, or simply find that life is getting on top of us. Through the experience of Elijah, God is saying, 'Don't be dismayed; all things are less dreadful than they seem.' However isolated you may feel, he has not left you to carry the load alone. Seen or unseen, there are others playing their part and working for his kingdom. Seen or unseen, he is always there to strengthen, to support and to see us through.

Ask yourself
Is life looking bleak at present? Do you feel it is beyond redemption? Have you forgotten to put God into the equation?

Pray
Gracious God, when life is testing and your purpose is hard to fathom, help me to remember that you are able to see me through. When I feel overwhelmed by the challenge before me, yet see nowhere and no one to turn to, remind me to reach out to you, knowing that whenever I need you, you will be there. Teach me that, with you, no situation is beyond hope, and that no darkness can ever fully extinguish the light, and in that confidence may I walk each day in faith, to the glory of your name. Amen.

Remember
If God is at work on our behalf, who can prevail against us?
Romans 8:31

Close
Living God, no matter how helpless or hopeless I may feel, teach me that with you by my side, all things are always less dreadful than they seem. Amen.

Take aim

Read

This is what we pray for: that you may become perfect.

2 Corinthians 13:9 (NRSV)

Ponder

'Aim for perfection' – it's ridiculous, isn't it, for which of us can possibly hope to achieve anything approaching that? Put in those terms, there's no denying it – the goal is utterly and hopelessly beyond us – but look again and we will see that Paul isn't suggesting we *will* be perfect; simply, that we should make that our aim. It is a small but vital difference, well illustrated by my misspent days at college. When I wasn't playing table tennis, space invaders or snooker there, I used to enjoy the odd game of darts. Unfortunately, I wasn't all that good, so I developed a strategy of aiming at the lower-left quadrant of the board where a number of average point-scoring segments are clustered together. The strategy didn't work all that well, largely because I tended to miss the board altogether, but it was doomed to failure anyway, since I was purposely aiming low and so had little hope of getting anywhere near a maximum score, except by a sheer fluke.

How often in Christian discipleship do we do something similar, settling for second best instead of striving to become more like Christ? We are afraid of committing ourselves fully in case we cannot measure up to the challenge. We are reluctant to respond with body, heart and soul, in case God asks more of us than we feel able to give. We tell ourselves that there is no way we can serve him properly but that he would rather have partial, half-hearted service than nothing at all. The reality, of course, is that if we aim low, we will probably end up hitting a mark even lower. We have set ourselves up for failure before we have even begun. I don't think for a moment we will ever be perfect in this life, but that doesn't excuse us from trying. It isn't reaching the goal that counts but striving towards it. Can we settle for less?

Ask yourself
Do you strive in your discipleship to become more like Christ, or have you settled for second best?

Pray
Lord Jesus Christ, so often I let you down because I don't seriously aim to follow you. I am afraid of what unreserved commitment might involve. I tell myself that you will understand if I tone down what you expect from me; that, since you will make allowances for my mistakes, I needn't try too hard to live up to your example.

Forgive me for abusing your grace and twisting the gospel, making excuses to evade your challenge. Forgive me for effectively denying your transforming power through the narrowness of my vision and weakness of my faith. Teach me to focus on your grace and goodness, so that though I may still never come anywhere near what I ought to be, I may at least have the chance of getting closer. In your name I ask it. Amen.

Remember
Finally, my friends, whatever is true, honest and just, whatever is pure, lovely or commendable, if there be anything good and worthy of praise, consider such things. Keep on doing what you have learned, received, heard and seen in me, and the God of peace will be with you.

Philippians 4:8-9

Close
Living God, help me not to look at what I am, nor at what I can do, but rather at what you can achieve within me by your grace, through Jesus Christ my Lord. Amen.

Picking up the pieces

Read

I had become like a broken pot but you heard my pleas when I cried out for help. The Lord is close to the broken-hearted and he saves those who are crushed in spirit. He mends the broken in spirit and tends their wounds.

Psalm 31:12b, 22b; 34:18; 147:3

Ponder

What would you do if you smashed a prized ornament? The answer, of course, depends on the extent of the damage but the chances are that you would try to pick up the broken fragments and glue them back together. Consider, though, if it was a clay flowerpot you had dropped; what would you do then? Almost certainly, you would sweep up the shards and discard them without a second thought. It is only when something means a lot to us that we take time to try and repair it.

All of which helps us to appreciate the testimony of psalms like those quoted above. Like David in Psalm 31, we too can feel battered and broken by life, shattered beyond repair. Can God possibly care enough about us to spend time rebuilding our lives, putting the pieces back together again? It seems impossible, doesn't it, yet God does precisely that. However long it takes, however painstaking a process it may be, he is always looking to heal and renew us, to make us whole. No matter how broken we may be, we are never beyond his restoring touch.

Ask yourself

Are there areas of your life where your faith, your dreams or your confidence have been broken? What does it mean to be made whole?

Pray

Lord Jesus Christ, I remember today how throughout your ministry you looked to bring healing and wholeness. I remember how you touched the lepers, restored sight to the blind, cured the sick, and helped the lame to walk; how you brought hope to the broken-hearted and those crushed in spirit, peace of mind to those who were troubled, and forgiveness to those burdened by guilt or failure.

Lord Jesus Christ, I bring you my life, and I pray for your healing and renewing touch in body, mind and spirit, this and every day. Restore me and make me whole, by your grace. Amen.

Remember

The spirit of the Lord God is upon me, for the Lord has anointed me. He has sent me to announce good news to the oppressed; to bind up the broken-hearted, to proclaim freedom to those held captive and release for all who are imprisoned; to proclaim a year of the Lord's favour and a day of our God's vengeance. He has sent me to comfort those who grieve, to adorn them with garlands instead of ashes, oil of gladness instead of mourners' tears, a garment of praise instead of a heavy heart.   *Isaiah 61:1-3a*

Close

Lord Jesus Christ, take the bruised, battered and broken pieces of my life and, by your grace, make me whole. Amen.

In light inaccessible?

Read

Moses said, 'Show me your glory, I pray.' God answered, 'I will cause all my goodness to pass before you, and I will pronounce my name, "The Lord", in your hearing. I will be gracious to whom I will be gracious, and I will be merciful to whom I would show mercy. However, you cannot see my face, for no one can see my face and live.'

Exodus 33:18-20

Ponder

Recent years have seen some stunning pictures of the planets in our solar system, most particularly Mars and Jupiter, revealing details about them never seen before. Such pictures, however, wonderful though they are, have only served to highlight the vastness of space and the massive limitations on our ability to explore it. Most of our solar system is millions of light years away, so even if we could send out a space probe now to distant stars, it would not yield any information for centuries to come. So much of the universe is tantalisingly inaccessible, and can only be understood through piecing together the various clues given us.

In a sense, the same was true for the Israelites when it came to God. He appeared remote in his holiness, awe-inspiring in his sovereignty; a God who inspired fear as much as love. If he could be known, it was only at a distance; not in the sense of a living and daily personal relationship. For us, all that is different thanks to Christ. *In* him, God has shared our humanity, becoming one with us. *Through* him, he has broken down whatever keeps us apart. *From* him, we receive life – the very life of God himself. It is the same God as before, enthroned in splendour over all, yet a God whom we can know as friend and companion, whom we can relate to one to one and whom we can approach in confidence, knowing that his nature is to love and forgive. In contrast to that warning given to Moses, not only do we see God in Christ, but through doing so we discover the way to life in all its fullness.

Ask yourself

Do you have a sense of the magnificence and sovereignty of God, or has your relationship with him become too cosy? Do you have a sense of the closeness of God, present with you each day in Christ through his Spirit, or is your relationship with him too detached?

Pray

Great and wonderful God, with awe and wonder I worship you, for you are greater than my mind can fathom, beyond my highest thoughts, sovereign over all. I worship you in your holiness, and yet I also greet you as a friend, for you have shared my humanity, identifying yourself wholly with our world and demonstrating the awesome extent of your love. You have broken down the barriers that keep us apart, and so I know you with me day by day – constantly by my side.

Great and wonderful God, give me a sense of your greatness and your grace, your power and your gentleness, your otherness and your nearness. Remind me each day that your eternal purpose spans all creation yet includes my life, here and now. So, may I give you glory, through Jesus Christ my Lord. Amen.

Remember

In Christ Jesus our Lord, we have access to God in boldness, and confidence through faith in him.   *Ephesians 3:12*

Close

Living God, remind me that though you are far above all human thought you are always near, made known through Christ and dwelling within through your Holy Spirit. Receive my grateful praise. Amen.

A living testimony

Read

Since many undertook to compile a record of the events
fulfilled among us, just as they were passed on to us by those
servants of the word who, from the start, were eyewitnesses
to them, it seemed right for me, after carefully checking all
my sources, to write an accurate account for you, most
excellent Theophilus, so that you might know the truth
concerning everything you have been taught.   *Luke 1:1-4*

Ponder

To believe in something we haven't seen for ourselves isn't
easy, especially when that something stretches credulity to
the limit. If I were to tell you, for example, that I just
looked out of the window and saw a Martian spaceship
alighting on my lawn, you wouldn't believe me, would
you? So why should we believe the gospel records concerning
Jesus, with their startling claims of God made flesh, nailed
to a cross and rising from the tomb? For me, nowhere is
there a better reason for believing such claims than that
given at the beginning of Luke. Unlike Matthew and John,
Luke wasn't one of the original Apostles; indeed, so far as
we know he didn't meet with Jesus at all during his earthly
ministry.

So how did Luke know so much about Jesus? Quite simply
through the testimony of others. Luke found himself in
much the same situation as we are in today, dependent upon
other people's words of witness for everything he knew
about Jesus. Would he just have accepted this unthinkingly?
I don't think so. On the contrary, both in his gospel and
his sequel to it, the book of Acts, he clearly took pains to
check his facts before setting them down on paper. That's
one reason to accept his testimony, but there's another, more
important still. Eyewitness accounts alone wouldn't have

been sufficient to win Luke to faith; they needed to be backed up through experience. Luke doesn't write simply as a historian but as someone who has experienced the reality of the risen Christ in his own life and who enjoys an ongoing relationship with him. Though he never met with Jesus in the flesh, he clearly met with him in Spirit, enough to change his life for ever. That's why he wrote his gospel: to let others know what Jesus meant to him. And that's why we can believe his words and the testimony of others to the life-changing power of Christ – because we too can know and experience his presence for ourselves.

Ask yourself

Is your faith based upon the acceptance of historical facts, or first and foremost upon a personal encounter? Does the testimony of scripture to Jesus ring true in your own life?

Pray

Lord Jesus Christ, I thank you that though I wasn't at the stable like the shepherds, I can experience new birth in my life. I praise you that though I wasn't able to see you healing the sick, I can still be made whole by your touch. I marvel that though I was not there as you suffered on the cross and rose from the tomb, nonetheless you died for me so that I might rise with you.

For the awesome truth that I can know you as meaningfully today as any of those who witnessed your earthly ministry, I give you my worship. Amen.

Remember

Blessed are those who have not seen me and yet have come to believe.   *John 20:29b (NRSV)*

Close

Lord Jesus Christ, though I cannot physically see or touch you, help me so to know you that I may truly love you, and so to love you that I may faithfully serve you, to the glory of your name. Amen.

Eyes to see

Read

As Jesus and his disciples were leaving Jericho, followed by a large crowd, a blind beggar, Bartimaeus, the son of Timaeus, was sitting by the roadside. When he heard that it was Jesus of Nazareth passing by, he started to cry out, saying, 'Jesus, Son of David, have mercy on me!' Many in the crowd rebuked him, telling him to be quiet, but he called out yet more loudly, 'Son of David, have mercy on me!' Jesus stopped in his tracks and said, 'Call him here.' They called the blind man, saying to him, 'Take heart and get up, for he is calling you.' So, throwing off his cloak, he leapt up and came to Jesus. Then Jesus said to him, 'What do you want me do for you?' The blind man answered, 'Teacher, grant that I may see again.' Jesus said to him, 'Go; your faith has healed you.' Immediately, he regained his sight and followed him on the way.   *Mark 10:46-52*

Ponder

There is a supreme irony in the story of Bartimaeus, just as there is in the account of the blind man by the Pool of Siloam in the Gospel of John. Both stories concern a blind man seeking help from Jesus and in both cases there is, initially at least, hostility from the crowd. In Mark's story, this is directed against Bartimaeus for presuming to bother Jesus; in John's, it is directed against Jesus for presuming to heal and forgive sins. What unites both accounts is the contrast between this misguided response and that of the one Jesus heals: Bartimaeus believes that Jesus has time for everyone, and he is not disappointed. The result is that he ends up following the way of Jesus. The blind man in John's Gospel falls on his knees in worship and declares his faith in Jesus as the Son of God (John 9:38).

The blindness that both evangelists want us to think

about is not so much the absence of physical but spiritual sight. The crowds think they see but they don't. The two men know they cannot see, but in recognising their need of Jesus they see more than anyone else, not just with their eyes but with their souls. For us, too, there is more to life than our eyes tell us. The problem is that many of us do not or will not see it. We need to follow the example of Bartimaeus and to ask Jesus, 'Grant that I may see'.

Ask yourself

When did you last gain new insight into the wonder of God as revealed in Christ? Are you always looking, by his grace, to glimpse a little more of his glory?

Pray

Loving God, I thank you for the gift of sight; for everything of beauty, inspiration and interest that I see each day. Forgive me, though, that too often I see only with my eyes, failing to look beneath the surface to deeper truths underneath. Open the eyes of my soul, so that I may see where you would lead me and look at the world in a new light, through Jesus Christ my Lord. Amen.

Remember

Jesus said, 'My coming into this world brings judgement: those unable to see being given sight, yet those who believe they see everything exposed as seeing nothing.' Hearing his words, a group of Pharisees alongside him exclaimed, 'Can we not see, then?' Jesus answered, 'There's no blame in being unable to see. Your guilt lies in claiming to see when you can't.'

John 9:39-41

Close

Lord Jesus Christ, send me back to the daily business of life with eyes open to see you, ears open to hear you, a mind open to receive you and a heart open to serve you, for your name's sake. Amen.

A question of sovereignty

Read

If you confess with your lips that Jesus is Lord and believe
in your heart that God raised him from the dead, you will
be saved. *Romans 10:9 (NRSV)*

Ponder

For many years now a controversial issue in political debate
has been how far Britain should move towards integration
within the European Union. Some feel that we need to take
a step back, distancing ourselves from federalistic tendencies;
others argue that the only way forward is to develop ever-
closer ties. It is a vexed issue, guaranteed to stimulate lively
debate, the thrust of which will invariably revolve around
the question of sovereignty: are we to be answerable to
Europe or to ourselves, and will joining make any difference
either way? For my part, like many others, I'm undecided,
my heart telling me one thing but my head another.

Few people like giving up their sovereignty, but there is
a sense in which, as Christians, we have to do just that, for
coming to faith involves decisions concerning not national
but ultimate sovereignty. Who is Lord of our lives? Who is
the one finally in control? Whom do we answer to? To say
Jesus is Lord is not just a formal expression, like some oath
we take before being admitted to some secret society. It is
an acknowledgement that Jesus has first place in our lives.
It is a pledge to devote time and energy in the service of his
kingdom. Yes, we declare it with our lips, but we need to back
that up in our lives. How many of us can honestly say, 'Jesus
is Lord', and point to our lives to prove that we mean it?

Ask yourself

In what way is Jesus the Lord of your life? Are there aspects
of the way you live that deny his Lordship?

Pray

Lord Jesus Christ, I claim to follow you and, with my lips, I have declared you to be Lord and King of my life, but all too often my actions deny my words. I have broken your commandments, betrayed your love and ignored your guidance, my faith fickle and my allegiance poor. Forgive me all the ways I fail you, through thought, word and deed. Forgive me my limited understanding of your greatness and the narrowness of my vision. Forgive my inability to grasp the values of your kingdom, still less to base my life upon them.

Lord Jesus, I come before your throne, throwing myself upon your grace, and asking you to receive my homage and service, poor though these may be. Rule in my heart and use me for the growth of your kingdom, to the glory of your name. Amen.

Remember

God has highly exalted him, giving him the name that is above every name, so that at the name of Jesus every being in heaven, on earth and under the earth should bow down, and every tongue should acknowledge that Jesus Christ is Lord, to the glory of God the Father.   *Philippians 2:9-11*

Close

Lord Jesus Christ, may my life proclaim what my lips confess: that you are King of kings and Lord of lords, to the glory of your name. Amen.

What God requires

Read

He has told you, O mortal, what is good; and what does the Lord require of you but to do justice, and to love kindness, and to walk humbly with your God?   *Micah 6:8 (NRSV)*

Ponder

A few years ago, the government of the day embarked on a programme that it called 'Back to Basics'. As with so much concerned with politics, the public treated it with a healthy dose of scepticism, which was just as well given that the initiative was to backfire in truly spectacular fashion. Nonetheless, in theory, at least, the idea was a good one, for there are times when we become so absorbed in details that we lose sight of the simple principles that underlie our convictions. As Christians we are not exempt from that danger – in fact, many would say we are most vulnerable to it, since there are so many things that people within the Church feel strongly about, to the point of making them articles of faith. All too easily, we make the gospel more complicated than it really is. Some insist on assent to certain creeds, others on a particular style of worship, others again on church structures and organisation, and so it goes on. Nor are these the only distractions, for we can just as easily become bogged down in questions of doctrine or over-concerned with the minutiae of faith.

At such times, we need reminding of what serving God is all about, just as the people in Micah's day needed reminding. Of course, doctrine is important, but don't let it obscure the basics. Of course, worship, fellowship and theology matter, but not if they hinder rather than further the work of God's kingdom. I'm reminded of the celebrated words of the theologian Herbert Butterfield: 'Hold fast to Christ, and for the rest be uncommitted.' Or, as Micah puts it, 'do justice, love kindness and walk humbly with your God'. Get that right, and the rest can take care of itself.

Ask yourself

Has your faith become over-complicated? Have you lost sight of the essentials of Christian service, allowing yourself to become sidetracked by peripheral issues?

Pray

Loving God, you call me to live as one of your people: to walk each day by your side, seeking your will, pursuing what is right and showing your love in my attitudes towards others. Forgive me that I sometimes make your call so complicated, losing sight of the things you really require. Forgive me that I become preoccupied with the trappings of faith rather than focusing on the essentials.

Help me to offer you the sort of life you want to see and to be the person you would have me become. Teach me what you require and, by your grace, may I live to the glory of your name. Amen.

Remember

Pure and unspoilt religion before God the father is this: to visit the orphans and widows in their affliction and to keep oneself untarnished by the world. *James 1:27*

Close

Gracious God, teach me to offer the worship you desire: to do justice, to love kindness, and to walk humbly with you, every step along the way. Through Jesus Christ my Lord. Amen.

Life's riddle

Read

O Lord, how long must I cry to you for help before you will listen? How long must I cry, 'Violence!' before you will save? Why do you let me witness wrongdoing and endure trouble? Destruction and aggression are all around me; conflict and disputes spring up everywhere. The law is watered down such that justice has no chance of winning through. The righteous are surrounded by wickedness, and so justice is perverted. *Habakkuk 1:2-4*

Ponder

I like the book of Habakkuk. There's something hugely refreshing about the honesty with which it tackles the enigmas of life. No pious acceptance here that every event must somehow be God's will; no tortuous attempt to find a spiritual explanation for whatever happens – for this prophet the world presents deep puzzles for which he seeks some answers.

Those who find his questions disturbing may prefer to gloss over them, turning instead to the less controversial passages that follow, but to do that is to bury one's head in the sand. Avoiding the issues helps no one, for the challenge does not go away. Simplistic answers are equally unhelpful, in the end doing more harm than good. Personally, I believe God prefers an honest cry of confusion to a faith that deals with life's riddles by sweeping them under the carpet.

Ask yourself

What do you find most difficult to reconcile with your faith in God? Is your relationship with him such that you feel able to share your confusion honestly and openly?

Pray

Eternal God, there are times when I find life a puzzle, your purpose a mystery and experience seeming to contradict everything I believe about you. I try to make sense of it all, but without success, satisfactory answers always seeming to elude me.

Teach me at such moments to trust in you, recognising that what the world counts as folly is often true wisdom. Help me to live with riddles and apparent paradox, and to keep on searching for truth, confident that in the fullness of time you will make all things clear. In the name of Christ, I ask it. Amen.

Remember

Though the fig tree fails to blossom or the vines to bear fruit; though the olives produce nothing and the fields yield no food; though the flock is cut off from the fold and there is no herd in the stalls, yet will I rejoice in the Lord; I will give praise to the God of my salvation. God, the Lord, is my strength; he makes my feet like those of a deer, and helps me to scale the heights.   *Habakkuk 3:17-19*

Close

Lord of all, despite everything that conspires against you, help me to hold on to the conviction that good will finally conquer evil, and your love ultimately triumph over all. Amen.

A passionate God

Read

In this is love, not that we loved God but that he loved us and sent his Son to be the atoning sacrifice for our sins.

1 John 4:10 (NRSV)

Ponder

What things are you truly passionate about? The question was put in a sermon I heard recently, and it opened up a dimension of faith that I'd never really considered before – the idea of a God who is *passionate* about us! The word is from the Greek παθημα meaning 'emotion', 'passion' or 'sacrifice', which, in turn, derives from the word πασχω, meaning 'to suffer' or 'to endure evil'. Emotion, suffering and sacrifice – all three are deeply interwoven, for to care passionately about someone means you are ready to suffer for them, to make personal sacrifices to secure their happiness.

Such is the love God has for us. It is not just a vague feeling of benevolence or a general concern and affection; it is a passionate and consuming love that gave all, even his own Son, to restore our broken relationship with him, to draw us closer to himself. It is the 'love divine, all loves excelling' spoken of by the hymn writer; the 'love that will not let us go'. We're not used to thinking of God in terms of high emotion – or, at least, *I'm* not – but we should be, for the wonder of the gospel is not simply that God loves us but that he loves us passionately!

Ask yourself

Have you realised how much God loves you? Do you forget, sometimes, how passionately he cares?

Pray

Gracious God, I praise you that, above all else, you are a God of love – not of judgement, anger or vengeance, but constant and total love. Though I repeatedly fail you, turning my back on your goodness, still you continue to love me, fiercely and wholeheartedly. Though I turn away from you, wilfully rejecting your guidance and repeatedly betraying your trust, still you long to take me back, to restore a living, loving relationship with you.

For this awesome love, greater than words can express, deeper than I can begin to understand and more passionate than anything else I shall ever experience, I give you my thanks and offer my worship, in the name of Christ. Amen.

Remember
He who did not hold back his own Son, but sacrificed him for our sake, will he not with him freely give all things to us? *Romans 8:32*

Close
Living God, may your love flow to me, reaching down to bless and within to bring joy. May your love flow through me, reaching upwards in worship and outwards in service. May *your* love kindle *my* love, to the glory of your name. Amen.

Faith in adversity

Read

As Pharaoh drew near, the Israelites looked back and spotted the Egyptians coming after them. They cried out to the Lord in terror, and said to Moses, 'Was it because there were no graves in Egypt that you have brought us here to die in the wilderness? Isn't this just why we told you in Egypt to leave us alone and let us serve the Egyptians? We would rather have served the Egyptians than die in the wilderness.' 'Do not be afraid,' answered Moses. 'Stand firm, and see the deliverance that the Lord will bring you today, for you will never again see the Egyptians whom you see here today. The Lord will fight for you; you have only to keep still.' Then Moses stretched out his hand over the sea, and by a strong east wind throughout the night the Lord drove the sea back, turning it into dry land as the waters divided. The Israelites passed through the sea on dry ground, the waters forming a wall to their right and left. Then the Lord said to Moses, 'Stretch out your hand over the sea, so that the water may come back upon the Egyptians, their chariots and their chariot drivers.' So Moses stretched out his hand over the sea, and, as dawn broke, the sea returned to its place.

Exodus 14:10-14, 21-22, 26-27a

Ponder

We talk sometimes of experiencing a roller coaster of emotions, and if ever that phrase was appropriate, it must surely be in describing the story of the crossing of the Red Sea. Imagine the ups and downs those involved must have gone through. First suspense and excitement as they left Egypt to face an unknown but exciting future. Then dismay and despondency as it became apparent that Pharaoh had changed his mind and the Egyptians were coming after them. After this, sheer amazement at the sight of the waters opening before them and then, finally, having crossed safely to the other side, an overwhelming sense of relief and exultation.

There is a lesson for us here. Life does not always go smoothly; it brings its fair share of challenges, even times when the future looks hopeless but, come what may, God is with us, in both the good and the bad. Remember that next time trouble strikes. Whatever the obstacle confronting you, God is able to lead you safely through.

Ask yourself

Are there times when God has overcome seemingly immovable obstacles in your path? How did he help you?

Pray

Lord, it is easy to follow you when life is going well; much harder when I come up against problems. Forgive me for the weakness of my faith, for being a fair-weather disciple, swift to turn back when the going gets rough.

Help me to recognise that there are times when I must face challenges and overcome apparently insurmountable obstacles, and teach me that you are as much there in those times as at any other. Give me courage to walk wherever you lead, confident that you will never forsake me. Amen.

Remember

Who shall separate us from the love of Christ? Shall trouble or hardship, persecution or famine, nakedness, peril or sword? As it is written, 'For your sake we are being put to death all day long, and reckoned as sheep for the slaughter.' In all these things, however, we are more than conquerors through him who loved us.   *Romans 8:35-37*

Close

Lord, whatever I may face, teach me that your power is sufficient for all my needs. Teach me, then, to walk in faith, confident that you will show me the way forward. Through Christ my Lord. Amen.

The key to contentment

Read

Do not exhaust yourself in an effort to get rich; be sensible enough to avoid that trap, for though you see it one minute, it will be gone the next; suddenly taking wings to itself and flying off into the sky like an eagle. The miser rushes to get rich, apparently ignorant of the fact that loss is sure to come. Whoever loves money will not be content with money; nor the one who loves wealth, with gain.

Proverbs 23:4-5; 28:22; Ecclesiastes 5:10

Ponder

In 1957 the then Prime Minister, Harold Macmillan, informed the British public, 'Most of our people have never had it so good.' Nearly half a century later, we in the Western world have it better still in terms of material possessions. We live today in a country more prosperous than it has ever been; a society that enjoys a standard of living that our forebears could only have dreamt of just a few decades ago. So, are we correspondingly happier than those who lived before us, more content and fulfilled than previous generations? Paradoxically, the answer is no. If anything, the opposite is true, a deep sense of emptiness pervading the lives of many. All that, of course, is not to deny that possessions can bring pleasure, nor that they make life easier in a whole variety of ways, but they can never meet our deepest needs.

It remains true that you cannot buy happiness. To discover that, we need to look deeper: we need to nurture our soul rather than our body, to unearth treasure that will last when all else has faded away. It is treasure such as this that Jesus promised to all those who follow him.

Ask yourself

How far have possessions brought you contentment? Have there been times when they have brought the opposite? What do you value most in your life?

Pray

Lord Jesus Christ, I know that true riches do not lie on earth and yet I find it hard truly to accept that fact. Day after day, I strive to put a bit of extra money into my pocket, and I yearn to splash out a little, to treat myself to those few extra luxuries, to afford my dream holiday, car or home. I find it hard to see beyond the alluring pleasures of this material world, even though I know that so much of what it seems to offer is illusory, unable to satisfy for more than a few moments, let alone to meet my deepest needs.

Open my eyes to true riches: to the blessings you have given me and to all that you yet hold in store. Help me to appreciate the joy and fulfilment that you alone can offer, the inheritance beyond price that comes through knowing and serving you. I ask it in your name. Amen.

Remember

There is great gain in godliness combined with contentment; for just as we brought nothing into the world it is certain that we can take nothing out of it. So, then, if we have food and clothing, we will be satisfied with these. I have learned to be content in all circumstances.

1 Timothy 6:6-8; Philippians 4:11b

Close

Gracious God, teach me to celebrate all I have received, but to set my heart first on your kingdom and to show my gratitude for all your many gifts by offering back my life in your service, to the glory of your name. Amen.

Waste disposal

Read

Put to death whatever is earthly within you: sexual immorality, depravity, lust and other evil desires, including greed, which is a form of idolatry, because the wrath of God will come on account of such things. You once followed ways such as this, in your former way of life, but now you must get rid of all such things – anger, wrath, malice, slander, and abusive language from your mouth.   *Colossians 3:5-8*

Ponder

What is the most exciting vehicle on today's roads – a fire engine, police car or ambulance, perhaps; a digger, crane or car-transporter; or perhaps a Porsche or BMW? When my son was a little boy there was one vehicle that ranked higher than any of these: the municipal waste disposal truck. Each collection day, we had only to say the magic words 'Bin lorry!' and Samuel would be there, eyes glued to the front window as he watched the lorry's progress with rapt attention. Waste disposal – hardly a thing to get excited about, you might think, and yet, of course, without it our streets would soon become clogged with rubbish resulting in all kinds of threats to health and public safety. When waste is allowed to accumulate, the consequences can be dire.

This leads us to what Paul was striving to get across to the Colossians, as indeed in so many other of his letters. He had spoken a little earlier of the grace and mercy of Christ, but here he breaks off for a moment, in case his words might be misconstrued. Don't use that goodness, he says, as an excuse to ignore the build-up of undesirable characteristics in your life. Don't let thoughts and deeds that have no place gain a foothold once again, for if you do they will poison from within the new life you have found in Jesus as surely as rubbish left to accumulate will contaminate its surrounding environment. We may not be able to identify with all the vices Paul lists, but there are probably a few we can relate to well enough. Get rid of them, says Paul, before they get rid of you! Don't let them gain a hold, or you may find that though God has time for you, you no longer have time for him.

Ask yourself

What characteristics of the old self do you still need to 'put to death'?

Pray

Living God, I know that much in my life is not as it should be; that I have allowed thoughts and deeds to creep back in that inexorably eat away inside, poisoning my attitudes, and subtly destroying my relationship with you.

Help me to recognise that though you are always ready to forgive, such things slowly prevent me from recognising my need for forgiveness. Teach me that, though I cannot dispose of my faults or weaknesses by myself, with your help I can be awake to their presence and find strength to resist them in times of temptation. In Christ's name I pray. Amen.

Remember

The works of the flesh are self-evident: sexual immorality, depravity and dissipation; idolatry and sorcery; hatred, conflict and anger; jealousy and envy; quarrels and disputes; drunken revelling; and things like these. I warn you, as I warned you previously, that those who do such things will not inherit the kingdom of God. *Galatians 5:19-21*

Close

Living God, cleanse me from within and purge me from everything that keeps me from you. Through Jesus Christ my Lord. Amen.

Praying in faith

Read

While Peter was kept in prison, the Church prayed earnestly to God for his safety. The very night that Herod intended to send for him, Peter, bound with two chains, was sleeping between two soldiers, a watch also being kept at the front of the prison door. Suddenly, an angel of the Lord appeared and a light filled the building. Touching Peter on the side, he woke him, saying, 'Get up quickly!' The chains fell from his wrists, and the angel said to him, 'Fasten your belt and put on your sandals.' He did so. Then he said to him, 'Wrap your cloak around you and follow me.' Peter went out and followed him. He went to the house of Mary, the mother of John Mark, where many had gathered in prayer. When he knocked at the porch door, a maid called Rhoda came to answer. On recognising Peter's voice, she was so overjoyed that, instead of opening the door, she ran back inside and announced that Peter was standing at the gate. They said to her, 'You've taken leave of your senses!', but she was so insistent that it was him that they said, 'Perhaps it's his angel.' Meanwhile Peter carried on knocking; and when finally they opened the door and saw him, they were amazed.

Acts 12:5-9a, 12-16

Ponder

Ask any Christian what they find hardest in the Christian life and they will probably say prayer. We find it hard to give prayer proper time and harder still to find the words for what we want to say, but perhaps most difficult of all is coming to terms with the many times when we do not seem to receive an answer or when the answer given is not quite what we hoped for. Faith tells us one thing, experience another, and eventually it is experience, often all too painful, that tends to win the day. There was a time, perhaps, when we would have asked for something, fully confident that God would grant it, but as the years pass and that fails to happen, we find it increasingly hard to keep on believing. As a result, our prayers become mechanical, offered more out of duty than expectation.

Yet God *does* hear and *does* respond, our failure to hear his answer often due to our failure to listen or the strait-jacket we subconsciously set upon him. It may be that his answer is 'no', or 'not yet', but it may also be that he has already answered 'yes', if only we can throw off the shackles of doubt and bring ourselves to believe it.

Ask yourself

When did you last pray, expecting God to answer? Have you allowed a fear of abusing prayer to lead you to abandon it altogether?

Pray

Gracious God, I don't have to tell you how weak is my prayer life, for you know it already, or how weak is my faith, for you can see that clearly. I am afraid to pin too many hopes on prayer, in case you do not grant my requests. I am hesitant to ask in case I am seeking the wrong things.

Teach me that you are a God who listens and delights to respond. Save me from the lack of trust that frustrates your purpose, preventing me from recognising your hand at work. Give me ears to hear, eyes to see, and a heart that truly believes. Through Jesus Christ my Lord. Amen.

Remember

Truly, I tell you this: whatever you ask the Father in my name, he will give you. Until now, you have not asked for anything in my name. Ask, and you will receive, so that your joy may be complete.   *John 16:23b-24*

Close

Living God, give me the faith I need to pray, and teach me to pray to you in faith. Amen.

Truly committed?

Read

Your hearts must be fully committed to the Lord our God, to live by his decrees and obey his commands, as at this time.

1 Kings 8:61

Ponder

If you were at the ground of a football team riding high in the Premiership, or enjoying an extended run in the FA Cup, the chances are that you would hear a jubilant chant from the fans along the lines 'We'll support you evermore!' If you were watching a team in mid-table, having just drawn a cup match that they should have won, you may well hear a few jeers and catcalls from increasingly disgruntled spectators. If you were watching a team at the bottom of the table enduring yet another 6-0 thrashing, you probably wouldn't hear much at all, because most of the 'fans' will long since have deserted the club and stayed at home. True commitment is hard to find; most of us are fair-weather supporters.

Sadly, that's often also the case when it comes to our commitment to God – a truth reflected in those words of Solomon above. He spoke at a time of celebration, the people of Israel having excitedly gathered to dedicate their new temple, and, understandably, spirits were high and the enthusiasm of the crowd contagious. It was easy at such a time to make bold declarations of faith and sweeping promises of loyalty, but Solomon knew how easily those could be forgotten once people returned to the routine business of life. The danger is just as real today. Many start out as Christians, bubbling over with enthusiasm, full of everything God has done for them and everything they plan to do for him, only to lose interest when life doesn't quite work out as expected. Once the first flush of faith has faded, the novelty is over and the initial excitement of conversion has passed, discipleship doesn't hold the attraction it once did. It's easy to start out on the journey of faith and to walk it when all is going well, but are we ready to follow even when it proves costly or demanding? Are we truly committed?

Ask yourself

Are you as committed to Christ as you once were? Has your commitment ebbed and flowed with changing fortunes? Is it time you recommitted yourself to his service?

Pray

Gracious God, I have committed myself to your service, but I am all too aware of how weak my commitment is and how often I fail to honour it. When my allegiance has been tested, my loyalty put on the line, I have repeatedly been found wanting, more concerned with my own interests than with serving Christ. When discipleship has involved cost, and service meant putting myself out on behalf of others, my good intentions have swiftly evaporated, exposed as little more than fine-sounding ideas.

Gracious God, I want to serve you better, but I know that I will fail again, just as I have failed before, my faith flawed and my love imperfect. Have mercy on me, and teach me through Christ, and his faithfulness to the last, to stay true to you whatever life may bring. For his name's sake I pray. Amen.

Remember

May the Lord our God be with us as he was with our fathers; may he never leave or forsake us. May he turn our hearts to him, to walk in his ways.   *1 Kings 8:57-58a*

Close

Living God, help me to walk as closely with you as you walk with me. Through Jesus Christ my Lord. Amen.

God in the darkness

Read

When it was the sixth hour, darkness fell over the whole land until the ninth hour. And at the ninth hour, Jesus cried out in a loud voice, 'Eloi, Eloi, lama sabachthani?' which translated means, 'My God, my God, why have you forsaken me?'

Mark 15:33

Ponder

How many of us are scared of the dark? Probably few of us are afraid in the sense we once were as children, yet there is still something about darkness that makes us associate it with the sinister, evil and unknown. It is not surprising, then, that if there is one thing we associate with God and one symbol used for him more than any other, it is light. 'The Lord is my light and my salvation,' says Psalm 27; 'of whom shall I be afraid?' Or again, in Psalm 36, 'With you is the fountain of life; in your light we see light.'

So we could go on, piling one text on top of another. Yet, while all this is true, it is not the complete picture, and it's a good thing it isn't, for there are times when life seems dark, bleak, grim and forbidding; when even God seems far away such that we cry out in despair – times described by St John of the Cross as 'the dark night of the soul'. What do we make of moments like those? Has God no place in them? Must we face them alone? Not if the words of the gospels concerning the death of Christ are to be believed, for there we read of how darkness descended on the land as Jesus hung on the cross. It seemed, even to Jesus, as though God wasn't present but the reality, of course, was different. It was here that God was supremely and astonishingly at work, offering himself for the life of the world, paying the price that would set us free. Though darkness seemed to have overtaken the world, the reality was that the light of

God's love was shining brighter than ever and nothing would be able to overcome it. There are times when, for the Christian as much as any other, life seems dark and God seems far away, but never feel that God has abandoned you, for sometimes it is in the darkest moments that he is there most of all.

Ask yourself

Does life seem dark at present, devoid of hope or meaning? Does God seem far away and unconcerned? Have you lost sight of the fact that he can be at work in the darkness to bring yet greater light into your life?

Pray

Living God, I praise you for the promise that nothing can ever overcome your light. I thank you that even when life seems dark and hopeless, when I search but cannot glimpse your presence and call yet cannot hear your voice, still you are with me, the light of your love inexorably burning off the clouds until it breaks through once again, bathing me in sunshine.

May that knowledge sustain me through the bleakest moments, bringing the assurance that good will triumph over evil, hope replace despair, joy come after sorrow, and life triumph over death – that even the deepest darkness will be turned to light. Through Christ my Lord. Amen.

Remember

If I say, 'Surely darkness will come upon me, and daylight become as night', even the darkness is not dark to you; the night is as bright as day, for darkness is as light to you.

Psalm 139:11-12

Close

God of light, be with me in my darkness, until night passes and your light breaks through. In the name of Jesus Christ, my Lord and my Redeemer. Amen.

Introducing Jesus

Read

The woman left her water-jar and returned to the city. She said to the people there, 'Come and see a man who told me everything I had ever done. He cannot be the Messiah, can he?'

John 4:28-29

Ponder

We will all, at some time or other, have been in a situation when a friend or acquaintance says to us, 'Let me introduce you to so and so'. This can, of course, be nothing more than a formality, an expected social nicety, but it can mean a great deal more. A simple introduction can lead to a fascinating encounter and even a lasting friendship as two people move from being complete strangers towards getting to know each other.

Consider that in relation to the words of the Samaritan woman in John's Gospel. This may not be an introduction, in the strict sense of the word, but it had much the same effect, inducing those she was addressing to meet Jesus for themselves – to talk with him and enter into a personal encounter. The result? 'Many Samaritans from that city believed in him, because of the woman's testimony' (John 4:39). There is an important lesson here when it comes to Christian testimony. We can try sometimes to argue people into faith, imagining that we need to answer all their questions before they can come to belief. What is actually required is something far simpler: merely to introduce people to Jesus – to ensure that they know of him and about him. We must do our part; the rest is down to him.

Ask yourself

Have you sometimes fallen into the trap of trying to preach at people instead of simply introducing them to Jesus?

Pray

Lord Jesus Christ, just as others have introduced you to me, so help me in turn to introduce you to others; not preaching at them, nor seeking to ram my beliefs down their throat, nor trying to argue with them or convince them of the claims of the gospel, but simply pointing at who and what you are. Help me to speak of all that you mean to me and of everything I have found you to be, and so may others come to meet you and know you for themselves, through your grace. Amen.

Remember

Philip found Nathaniel and told him, 'We have found the one written about in the law of Moses and the prophets: Jesus of Nazareth, the son of Joseph.' Nathaniel responded, 'Can anything good come out of Nazareth?' Philip answered, 'Come and see.'   *John 1:45-46*

Close

Lord Jesus Christ, show me when and where to speak for you, but remind me, having spoken, that you are also able to speak for yourself. Amen.

An unbreakable bond

Read

I appeal to you, brothers and sisters, in the name of our Lord Jesus Christ, agree among yourselves and avoid any division, so that you may be perfectly joined, of the same mind and united in a common purpose.   *1 Corinthians 1:10*

Ponder

Have you ever tried sticking metal with wood glue, or plastic with wallpaper paste? If you have, then you'll know you were wasting your time, for you were using the wrong tool for the job. Different glues are designed for different tasks, and what works for one may not work for another. Get it right, however, and you will create a bond to last.

Such *should* be the effect of the love we are meant to share as Christians. The reality, sadly, is very different. For all the moves in recent years towards Church unity, there are as many if not more divisions today than ever, splinter groups breaking away over questions of doctrine, worship and church practice. Individual fellowships are equally marred by gossip, cliques, personality clashes, backbiting and so on. All too often, instead of testifying to the love of Christ, our relationship with other Christians speaks instead of our human fallibility, turning people away from the Church instead of drawing them towards it. There will always, of course, be differences of opinion and outlook among us, for we are all individuals with unique experiences of Christ. Similarly, there will be those we are more naturally drawn towards than others; that is a simple fact of life. If, though, we are truly 'in Christ', then the faith we share should transcend such differences, the love that unites us more powerful than anything that may divide.

Ask yourself

Are you open to Christians of other denominations and theological persuasions? Are your relationships with Christians in your own church what they should be, or have there been disagreements that have come between you?

Pray

Gracious God, for all my talk of love and fellowship, I am not very good at loving others, too easily allowing divisions and differences to sour my relationships. For all my talk of being part of your family, I close my mind to so many brothers and sisters in Christ.

Forgive me, and open my mind to the unity of faith that I share with your people in every place. Give me a concern for and openness to all. Fill your Church with love, and so bind us together, to the glory of your name. Amen.

Remember

Strive eagerly to preserve the unity of the Spirit in the bond of peace. Above all else, put on love, this being the bond that holds everything together.

Ephesians 4:3; Colossians 3:14

Close

Gracious God, forgive me when differences drive me apart from others, and so fill me with the love of Christ that I may share a common and unbreakable bond with all your people, in the name of Christ. Amen.

The God of love

Read

Dear friends, let us love one another, because love comes from God; all those who love are born of God and know God. Whoever does not love knows nothing of God, for God is love. God demonstrated his love like this – he sent his only Son into the world in order that we might live through him. In this is love, not that we loved God but that he loved us and sent his Son to be the expiation for our sins. God is love, and all who dwell in love dwell in God, and God dwells in them.   *1 John 4:7-10, 16b*

Ponder

On my shelves at home I have a variety of dictionaries and thesauri which I have cause to consult on innumerable occasions, and one of the things that invariably surprises me is the sheer complexity of words. A single term can have a wide range of nuances, and many have several completely different meanings. Even everyday terms can prove surprisingly difficult to define. You would have thought, then, that one word in particular would be harder to define than any – the word 'God' – and in a sense that is true, for you could probably find as many interpretations as there are people. Some would stress his holiness, others his power, others, again, his ineffability – so many aspects of God that could justifiably be highlighted.

Yet, in our reading today, we see another approach that, in the light of all of the above, is truly remarkable, for according to John, one word says it all: God is *love*! For some, such a definition is far too loose; so vague and insipid that it ends up saying nothing. Yet, the fact is that, when it comes to God, no other word will do, for God *is* love! It's as simple and straightforward as that – the one description that says it all, and if we lose that one simple truth, we lose everything. He longs to bless, not punish; to give, rather than take away; his nature always to have mercy, show kindness and fill our lives with good things. No, we don't deserve such goodness, for we continue to fail him, day after day, but that's what makes God's love so special, for, despite the feebleness of our response, it goes on cleansing, renewing, restoring, forgiving – refusing to let go, come what may. One word to describe the one true God, but what a word and what a God!

Ask yourself

What word would first spring to mind were you asked to describe God? Have you grasped the full extent of his love? Is that love reflected in your life?

Pray

Lord God, so many words are used to describe you, in an attempt to sum up just who and what you are. We speak of your power, might and majesty to express your greatness. We label you eternal, everlasting, infinite, to convey your timelessness. We speak of your justice, righteousness and holiness to encapsulate your otherness. We call you Creator, Father, Redeemer to articulate your goodness. Yet, all these words fall short, pointing to part but not all of the truth.

I praise you, though, that there is one word that says it all – that little word 'love'. Overworked, misapplied, misunderstood it may be, but it is your whole nature, your whole purpose and your whole being. In that knowledge may I live each day, assured that, whatever may be, your love will always enfold me until it finally conquers all. Lord God, I praise you, through Jesus Christ my Lord. Amen.

Remember

How precious is your constant love, O God! All people may take refuge under the shelter of your wings.   *Psalm 36:7*

Close

Gracious God, I go on my way knowing that your love is all in all, now and for evermore. Amen.

Learning to love

Read

Beloved, since God so loved us, we also ought to love one another. No one has ever seen God; if we love one another, God lives in us, and his love is made complete in us.

1 John 4:11-12 (NRSV)

Ponder

There's a hymn I used to sing as a boy, with the chorus: 'They'll know we are Christians by our love, by our love; yes, they'll know we are Christians by our love.' What a beautiful picture that paints, and how special life would be were it true. Sadly, most of the time it's not. Although we warm to everything Jesus said about loving others – even our enemies – and although we want to love more than anything, most of the time we are not very good at it. The truth is that we find it hard to *like* some people, let alone *love* them.

We can't change that by ourselves, of course; no amount of effort on our part can make us feel something we don't, but when we open our lives to God's grace we catch a glimpse of what love is really all about. None of us deserves that love, and yet God glimpses in each one of us something that is special – precious enough to die for. If he can see that in us, surely we can see it in others.

Ask yourself

Would anyone know you are a Christian by *your* love? What do you find hardest about loving?

Pray

Gracious God, I marvel that you can love someone like me, for there is so little about me that deserves it. I look into the mirror of my soul and I am ashamed of what I see there, for the image is marred by greed, pride, selfishness, envy and so much else that destroys not just others but myself too.

Yet, incredibly, you value me to the point that I am precious in your sight, special enough even to die for. If you can accept me, despite everything, teach me to do the same and, in learning to love myself as you do, help me also to love others and love you. Through Jesus Christ my Lord. Amen.

Remember

This is my commandment – that you love one another as I have loved you. *John 15:12*

Close

Lord Jesus Christ, come to me, live in me, love through me. Amen.

Grappling with God

Read

Jacob was left alone; and a man wrestled with him there until dawn. When the man saw that he had not defeated Jacob, he struck him on his thigh as they wrestled, such that he dislocated Jacob's hip. He said, 'Let go of me, for dawn is breaking', but Jacob responded, 'I will not let you go, unless you bless me'. 'What is your name?' he asked. 'Jacob,' came the reply. Then the man said, 'You will no longer be called Jacob, but Israel, for you have contended both with God and with humans, and prevailed.' Then Jacob asked him, 'Please tell me your name.' 'Why do you ask my name?' he said, but then he gave him his blessing. So Jacob called the place Peniel, saying, 'I have seen God face to face, and yet my life has been spared.' The sun rose upon him as he passed Peniel, limping because of his hip.

Genesis 32:24-31

Ponder

Grappling with God – it's a strange idea, isn't it? Very different from the more traditional picture of humbly and obediently accepting God's will. Yet that is what we find in one of the most dramatic if enigmatic incidents in the Bible. The imagery is crude, if not shocking – a mysterious stranger who accosts Jacob by the ford at Jabbok turning out to be none other than God himself. More puzzling still, so tenaciously does Jacob hold fast during the ensuing test of strength that God is unable to extricate himself without first granting a blessing. As Alice might have said, 'It all gets curiouser and curiouser'.

Yet it is precisely the primitiveness of this encounter that, for me, makes it so compelling. There is no false piety here, no alabaster saint as far removed from our human condition as it is possible to be. Here is an individual like you or me, coming warts and all before God and struggling to come to terms with the complex realities of life and faith. Who knows quite what Jacob wrestled with in the darkness of that night – doubt, fear, pride, guilt? – you name it and it was probably there! Symbolic the whole story may be, but its power remains undiminished, giving hope and encouragement to all those who grapple with God in turn.

Ask yourself
With whom do you think Jacob was grappling in his strange encounter: himself or God? With what aspects of faith do you find yourself wrestling?

Pray
Almighty God, I have no claim on your love, no reason to feel I deserve it, for I am false and faithless in so much, but I want to know and serve you better; to glimpse your glory, understand your greatness and receive your blessing. I want to taste more of your goodness and experience more of your grace, to know your power within me, and so I come, resolved to take hold of the new life you have promised, and determined to struggle for it despite all that gets in my way. Respond to me, I pray, and, as I have come to you, so come to me, through Jesus Christ my Lord. Amen.

Remember
You must work out your own salvation with fear and trembling, recognising that God is at work in you so that you will be able to understand and accomplish his good purpose.

Philippians 2:12b-13

Close
Gracious God, teach me to wrestle with my sin, my doubts, my fears and my weaknesses, and, in battling with those, may I find I have taken hold of you, through Christ my Lord. Amen.

Telling the news

Read

As it says in scripture, 'No one who puts their faith in him will be put to shame.' For there is no differentiation between Jew and Greek; the same Lord is Lord of all and generous to all those who call on him. As it says again, 'Everyone who calls on the name of the Lord will be saved.' How, though, can they call on one in whom they have not believed, and believe in one of whom they have never heard? How can they hear without someone to proclaim him, and how can anyone proclaim him unless they are sent?

Romans 10:11-15a

Ponder

According to Stephen Pile's *The Book of Heroic Failures*, Hiroo Onoda, a lieutenant in the Japanese army, still believed he was fighting the Second World War until 10 March 1974, twenty-nine years after the war had ended! How did he not know peace had been declared? He was stationed on a remote island in the Philippines, and although 'Come home' letters had been dropped from the air, no one bothered to tell him in person that the war was over.

It's a remarkable story that takes some believing, but the principle behind it is clear enough and it is one we do well to heed as Christians. 'How can they call on one in whom they have not believed, and believe in one of whom they have never heard?' asked Paul, and, of course, they couldn't. Unless people are told about Jesus, they will never come to faith. There was a time when those words were a rallying call to mission overseas. Today, they are also a call to mission at home, for there are many here in our country who have little knowledge of Christ, their awareness limited to the few smatterings they may have heard in assemblies and religious instruction at school. The temptation is that we leave the telling to someone else – and the danger is that no one else will tell them! We may not all be sent as missionaries or evangelists, but we all have a story to tell and a faith to proclaim. Can we afford not to share it?

Ask yourself

Is there someone who has not heard the message of the gospel, whom you could have told? Have you kept silent when you should have spoken up?

Pray

Lord Jesus Christ, you call me, as you call all your people, to go out and proclaim the gospel. Forgive me for failing to honour that calling; for being only too ready to come to you but less willing to go out in your name; eager to receive but reluctant to give. Help me to recognise my responsibility towards others – to understand that if I leave it to someone else to tell them about Jesus, they may never hear the good news.

Fill me, then, with new vision and resolve, so that when the opportunity comes to speak for you, I may do so – faithfully, honestly, sensitively and joyfully – to the glory of your name. Amen.

Remember

How lovely on the mountains are the feet of the messenger who announces peace, who brings good news, who announces salvation, calling to Zion, 'Your God is king.'

Isaiah 52:7

Close

Living God, may my lips speak of you, my deeds honour you, and my life proclaim you, through Christ my Lord. Amen.

Bodybuilding

Read

You, my friends, building yourselves up on your most holy faith and praying in the Holy Spirit, keep yourselves in the love of God, and look forward to that day when, in his mercy, our Lord Jesus Christ will give us eternal life.

Jude vv. 20-21

Ponder

In the paper this morning, I spotted a truly grotesque picture. It related to an article concerning the possible inclusion of bodybuilding as an official Olympic sport, and featured two muscular bodybuilders, biceps bulging, sinews stretching and veins popping. All right, so I wouldn't have minded a few of those muscles myself, but not to the point of becoming an Arnold Schwarzenegger look-alike!

There is, though, a sense in which we all need to build ourselves up, and that is in terms of our relationship with Christ. Faith is not something that grows automatically, like some seed that we can plant and then forget about until the fruits start to appear. It needs to be nourished and nurtured, so that it will develop in the way it should, strong and healthy. That means more than the occasional prayer or quick dip into our favourite Bible verses, feeding ourselves the same lesson day after day. It requires a diet that will both sustain and help us to grow further, until we reach something of the measure of the stature of Christ. That, though, is only half of it, for faith also needs to be exercised if it is to stay in shape, put through its paces in the daily treadmill of life. We may not aspire to become Christian heavyweights but what is our goal in discipleship? Are we content to be spiritual weaklings, or do we hunger to grow strong in the Lord?

Ask yourself

Does your faith need building up? Is it in need of some exercise? What are you going to do about it?

Pray

Living God, I thank you that you provide me not only with daily bread but with the bread of life – inner nourishment that means I need never go spiritually hungry again. You offer me so much through which to nourish my faith – your love in Christ, the inner presence of your Holy Spirit, and the testimony of the scriptures – and yet all too often I fail to feed myself as I should. The result is that I grow weak instead of strong, my faith starved, emaciated, wasting away – a pale shadow of what it ought to be.

Forgive me, and teach me to nurture my faith so that I may be strong in your service, to your glory. Amen.

Remember

So, then, I commend you now to the Lord and to his word of grace that is able to build you up and give you your inheritance among all those who are sanctified. *Acts 20:32*

Close

Lord Jesus Christ, save me from a flabby couch-potato faith, so out of condition that it is doomed finally to collapse and die. Teach me to put faith into action, so that it may be stretched and grow, and equip me for service in your kingdom. Through Christ my Lord. Amen.

The litmus test of faith

Read

When the Son of Man comes in his glory, together with his angels, he will sit in state on his throne, with all the nations gathered before him, and he will separate people one from the other as a shepherd separates the sheep from the goats, putting the sheep to his right and the goats to his left. Then the king will say to those on his right, 'Come, those who my Father has blessed – inherit the kingdom prepared for you from the foundation of the world. I was hungry and you gave me something to eat, thirsty and you gave me a drink, a stranger and you made me welcome, naked and you clothed me, sick and you visited me, in prison and you had time for me.' Then the righteous will answer, 'Lord, when did we see you hungry and give you food, or thirsty and give you a drink? When did we see you a stranger and make you welcome, or naked and clothe you? When was it that we saw you sick or in prison and visited you?' Then the king will answer, 'I tell you the truth, whenever you did it to the least of your brothers and sisters, you did it also to me.'   *Matthew 25:31-40*

Ponder

Do you remember your first chemistry experiment at school? Almost certainly it involved a piece of litmus paper, dipped into a test-tube of liquid to see if it turned red or blue, indicating acid or alkali. There is something of that test in the words of Jesus concerning the sheep and the goats, only this time the test concerns something very different – how faithfully we have responded to Christ.

What are the distinguishing features we should look for? Doctrinal soundness? Faith that can move mountains? Gifts of the Spirit? An impeccable record of church attendance? Not according to this parable, they're not. What counts, rather, is whether we have responded to people in need; whether we have shown our faith in action, expressing through our care and compassion the love of Christ. That, we are told, is the litmus test of Christian discipleship. Of course, we need to consider such words in the light of Christ's teaching concerning mercy and forgiveness, but we should not use that to evade or tone down their challenge. Faith may not depend on works but it ought to result in them, at least in part. The warning here is not so much that Jesus will reject us but that, through turning our back on others, we may find that *we* have rejected *him*.

Ask yourself
In what way have you served Christ recently through serving others? In what way have you ignored him through ignoring others?

Pray
Lord Jesus Christ, all too easily I turn serving you into a matter of private devotion and personal fulfilment, more concerned with what I will receive from you than what I should give to others. Forgive me for turning the gospel on its head, tailoring it to suit my own ends rather than allowing it to shape my life. Forgive me for being so preoccupied with heaven that I forget needs here on earth.

Teach me that, though I can never earn my salvation, I need to show the reality of my faith through the way I live. Show me where you would have me serve, and help me to love you as you love all, for your name's sake. Amen.

Remember
Those who exploit the poor insult their Maker, but those who respond to the needy do him honour.   *Proverbs 14:31*

Close
Lord Jesus Christ, as you have shown *your* love to me, help me to show *my* love to others. May my deeds speak as clearly as my words, my life speaking of you, to the glory of your name. Amen.

Rising to the challenge

Read

The Lord said, 'I have witnessed the misery of my people in Egypt; I have heard their cry at the hands of their taskmasters. Yes, I know how much they are suffering, and I have come down to deliver them from the Egyptians, and to lead them out of that country to a fine and extensive land; the land of the Canaanites, Hittites, Amorites, Perizzites, Hivites, and Jebusites, flowing with milk and honey. The cry of the Israelites has reached my ears and I have seen how the Egyptians oppress them, so come, and I will send you to Pharaoh to bring my people Israel out of Egypt.' But Moses retorted, 'Who am I that I should go to Pharaoh and bring the Israelites out of Egypt?' God answered, 'I am with you.'

Exodus 3:7-12a

Ponder

When did you last face a challenge that seemed completely beyond you but from which there was no escape? Anyone who has been in such a situation will have at least some insight into how Moses must have felt when God turned up in a burning bush ordering him to confront Pharaoh and demand the release of his people. It was a lot to ask of anyone, but for someone like Moses, by all accounts nervous and hesitant in speech, it was little short of purgatory. This was one request he could do without! The trouble was, God apparently couldn't do without him.

The verses above are but the start of one of the most astonishing conversations between God and man recorded in scripture. On the one hand, we have the sheer humanity of Moses, coming up with reason after reason why he was the least suitable candidate for the job, and, on the other, we have God countering every argument with an unanswerable riposte. It's hard not to feel sorry for Moses as finally he is almost browbeaten into submission, but it's equally impossible not to be inspired by the way that, having finally risen to the challenge, God provided him with all the resources he needed, and more besides. Remember, then, next time you face an apparently impossible challenge, that though it may be beyond you, it's not beyond him!

Ask yourself

Have you been asked to undertake something that you feel incapable of doing? Do you feel overwhelmed by the demands being made on you? Have you lost sight of what God can do, even if you can't?

Pray

Lord, there are so many challenges in life, so many obstacles I feel unable to face. Whether it is the everyday pressures of life or the unique responsibilities of Christian discipleship, I question sometimes whether I can cope, convinced that I lack the necessary qualities, courage and commitment to meet them successfully. Yet you have promised that whatever you ask anyone to do, you will enable them to fulfil it, your Spirit always there to encourage and your hand to guide.

Inspire me, then, to respond in faith, confident that, in your strength, no task is too hard to take on, and no challenge so daunting that I cannot meet it. In Christ's name I ask it. Amen.

Remember

Wait for the Lord; be strong, let your heart take courage, and wait for the Lord.   *Psalm 27:14*

Close

Sovereign God, teach me that though much is beyond me, nothing is beyond you. Amen.

629

Finding God

Read

The word of the Lord came to Nathan: Go and tell my servant David, 'This is the word of the Lord: Are you the person to build a house for me to live in? Down to the day I brought Israel up out of Egypt, I have never lived in a house, but have journeyed in a tent and a tabernacle. Wherever I journeyed with Israel, did I ever ask any of those I appointed as leaders to shepherd my people Israel: "Why haven't you built me a house of cedar?"'

2 Samuel 7:4-7

Ponder

Where do we find God? The answer, of course, is everywhere. Yet, though we know that to be true, we can act sometimes as though the reality is otherwise. We treat 'church' as if God is especially present there; as if meeting together gives us special access in a way no other situation can offer. It is an understandable mistake, for in worship we set time aside for God and so may well be particularly conscious of his presence, but, as those fascinating words of Nathan to David show us, this runs the risk of getting things back to front.

David wanted to build a glorious temple in Jerusalem where God could be honoured by all his people, but instead God sent Nathan to remind him that he had never been tied to one place, instead having travelled with his people in all the ups and downs of their history. Wherever they had been, whatever they had faced, he had been there by their side. For the Israelites, that presence was symbolised by the Ark of the Covenant that they carried with them; for us today it is experienced yet more closely through the indwelling of the Holy Spirit. Where do we find God? In church, certainly; in times of quiet prayer and reflection – then too; but the fact is that he is present every moment of our lives, involved in every aspect of every day. Wherever we are, whatever we experience, he is there, waiting to meet us!

Ask yourself
Do you tend sometimes to focus on God on Sundays and forget about him for the rest of the week? Have you understood that God is involved in every moment of every day?

Pray
Living God, I thank you for opportunities to share in the worship of your people and to focus my thoughts on your presence, but save me from mistakenly imagining you are more there than anywhere else.

Teach me that you are by my side wherever I may be and whatever I may be doing, involved in every aspect of my life and every part of the world. May that knowledge illumine the affairs of each day and enrich each moment as I realise that you are there, waiting to meet with me, speak to me, lead me and bless me. Teach me to consecrate not just a few moments each week but all of my life, to the glory of your name. Amen.

Remember
Be strong and determined, neither afraid nor anxious about anything, for the Lord your God is with you wherever you go.   *Joshua 1:9*

Close
Gracious God, open my eyes to your presence, and just as you walk with me, help me to walk with you. Through Christ my Lord. Amen.

A new heart

Read

These are the words of the Lord God: I will give them a different heart and put a new spirit into them; I will take the
heart of stone out of their bodies and give them a heart of
flesh. Then they will conform to my statutes and keep my
laws. They will become my people and I will become their
God.   *Ezekiel 11:17a, 19-20*

Ponder

In December 1967, Dr Christiaan Barnard performed the first
human heart transplant at Groote Schuur Hospital in South
Africa. It was an operation that stunned and enthralled the
world, few having believed it could ever be achieved.
Today, it is almost a routine operation. In the early days,
life expectancy for the donee was relatively short; today,
such surgery means a new beginning and a fresh chapter in
life. The words of Ezekiel are figurative rather than literal, yet
the transplant they speak of is no less dramatic – if anything,
it is more so – for what the prophet is talking about is people
being changed not on the outside but deep within. Can it
really happen? Not according to worldly wisdom. 'A leopard
cannot change its spots,' we say; 'Once a thief always a thief.'
It's hard as life goes by not to share such a cynical view of
the world.

The people of Ezekiel's day felt much the same, greeting
his words with scepticism if not outright scorn. Quite simply,
they'd heard it all before. Experience had taught them that
they would go on making the same mistakes in the future
as they had in the past. Ezekiel, though, believed differently, confident that God had the power to change people
deep within. His words were, of course, to find their fulfilment in the coming of Jesus and the gift of the Holy Spirit.
Through Christ, the work of renewal has begun; work that

will continue until the day we are united in the kingdom of God. Never lose sight of that promise. Never forget what God has done or what he shall yet do.

Ask yourself

Do you despair of ever changing? Are you focusing too much on trying to change yourself rather than allowing God to transform you in Christ?

Pray

Gracious God, you know how much I want to serve you. I have resolved to live more faithfully so many times that I have lost count, yet, somehow, when the moment of challenge comes, I am found wanting. Despite the good which I long to do, I fall victim yet again to the same old weaknesses, unable to conquer the feebleness of my sinful nature.

Have mercy, O God, and renew me through your Holy Spirit. Cleanse me through the love of Christ, and put a new heart and a right spirit within me, through Jesus Christ my Lord. Amen.

Remember

This is the covenant I will make with the house of Israel after that time, says the Lord: I will place my law within them, and write it on their hearts; I will be their God and they will be my people. They will no longer need to teach each other to know the Lord, for each one of them will know me, from the least to the greatest, says the Lord; for I will forgive their disobedience, and remember their sin no more.   *Jeremiah 31:33-34*

Close

Gracious God, take what I can never change, and, by your grace, make it new. Amen.

Small world

Read

Wanting to justify himself, [the lawyer] asked Jesus, 'And who is my neighbour?' Jesus replied, 'A man was going down from Jerusalem to Jericho, and fell into the hands of robbers, who stripped him, beat him, and went away, leaving him half dead. Now by chance a priest was going down that road; and when he saw him, he passed by on the other side. So likewise a Levite, when he came to the place and saw him, passed by on the other side. But a travelling Samaritan came near him; and when he saw him, he was moved with pity. He went to him and bandaged his wounds, having poured oil and wine on them. Then he put him on his own animal, brought him to an inn, and took care of him. The next day he took out two denarii, gave them to the innkeeper, and said, "Take care of him; and when I come back, I will repay you whatever more you spend." Which of these three, do you think, was a neighbour to the man who fell into the hands of the robbers?" ' He said, 'The one who showed him mercy.' Jesus said to him, 'Go and do likewise.'   *Luke 10:29-37 (NRSV)*

Ponder

'It's a small world.' Today that seems more true than ever. We can travel across the globe in a matter of hours, watch events live by satellite from thousands of miles away, and talk to people in distant continents almost as if they are in our own front room. That fact brings enormous blessings but also new responsibilities and demands. 'Who is my neighbour?' the lawyer asked Jesus. The answer was anyone and everyone.

Two thousand years ago that challenge must have seemed daunting enough; today it is massive, for suddenly every person in every country has become our concern;

every disaster, our disaster; every*one* our neighbour. When floods strike Bangladesh, we know; when famine hits Sudan, we know; when students are massacred in Tiananmen Square, we know. Day after day, pictures of emaciated children confront us as we sit down to our meal of plenty; of the homeless as we sit in the warmth and comfort of our homes; of the poor as we enjoy an ever-rising standard of living. All these are our neighbours in today's small world. Charity may begin at home but it cannot end there. By ourselves, of course, we cannot put all the world's ills to right, nor respond to every place of need, but neither can we turn our backs and pretend that they are none of our business. 'Which of these,' said Jesus, 'was a neighbour to the man?' 'The one who showed him mercy,' came the answer. 'Go and do likewise!'

Ask yourself

No one can respond to every need, but is there a situation in which you can make a difference? Is it time you responded to someone far away as well as close to home?

Pray

Lord Jesus Christ, your words concerning love for our neighbour sound so wonderful, until I stop to ask what they mean, and then, suddenly, the scale of the challenge and the likely cost of discipleship dawns on me, and I wonder how I can even begin to respond.

Teach me that, though I can't do everything, I can do something. Teach me that a little offered by many can achieve much by your grace. Fill me, then, with your love so that I may love in turn, to the glory of your name. Amen.

Remember

The whole law is encapsulated in one simple commandment: Love your neighbour as yourself. *Galatians 5:14*

Close

Living God, teach me that this small world is your world, and so show me where in responding to others I can respond to you. Amen.

NOVEMBER

All Saints

Read

Remember your leaders, those who spoke the word of God to you; consider the outcome of their way of life, and imitate their faith.

Hebrews 13:5

Ponder

In 1492, as we will all have learned at school, Christopher Columbus set off from Spain in the *Santa María*, sailing west on a journey that he hoped would take him around the world to India. His crew were terrified, convinced that, since the earth was flat, they would eventually fall off the edge to their deaths. Of course, nobody fell off anywhere, the ship eventually reaching what came to be known as the West Indies. The destination may have been other than intended, but the voyage proved conclusively that the world was not flat at all but round. Once done, many followed the same journey, and a thriving trade route was soon established. As so often in life, it took someone to show the way, someone to convince the doubters of what could be done.

That, for me, takes us to the heart of All Saints' Day, a day that celebrates those who have gone before us in faith, and whose Christian discipleship has inspired subsequent generations. It's not about holier-than-thou men and women adorned by a halo, such as we might see in a church stained-glass window, but about ordinary people like you and me whose lives serve as an extraordinary example. Remember such people, take note of their way of life, and learn from them, for they have shown what can be done and what God waits to do, here and now, in your life today.

Ask yourself

Who, to you, epitomises what faith is all about? In what ways are you striving to be more like them?

Pray

Living God, I thank you for all those who have run the race and kept the faith before me; all whose example, across the centuries, has given encouragement and inspiration to your people in their personal journey of faith. I thank you for those whose life and faith have spoken to me – uplifting, instructing, challenging and guiding; leading me forward into new experiences of your love. Forgive me that I sometimes forget such examples, losing sight of all you have done and all you continue to do.

Teach me to learn from the great company of saints to which you have called me to be a part. Speak, so that my love may grow, my faith be deepened and my resolve to serve you be strengthened. So may I live always to your praise and glory, through Jesus Christ my Lord. Amen.

Remember

Let your speech, behaviour, love, faith and purity serve as an example to believers. *1 Timothy 4:12*

Close

Living God, encourage me through all who have gone before me, so that I in turn may encourage those who travel after me, along the way of Christ. Amen.

Continuing in the faith

Read

From that time, many of his followers turned back, no
longer walking with him.

John 6:66

Ponder

Looking through the bargain section of our free paper, I
was struck by certain items that kept reappearing: musical
instruments, golf clubs, fish tanks and so on. It didn't need
much imagination to work out why these were for sale: they
had clearly been bought by someone in a fit of enthusiasm,
convinced that they offered an exciting new hobby, only
for the novelty to wear off and their new 'toy' to be discarded.
They had started but they couldn't continue.

That, I'm afraid, is true of many who commit themselves
to Christ. They too start out bursting with enthusiasm but,
as soon as the first flush of excitement fades, they quickly lose
interest. No, I am not just talking about others; the fact is that
such a scenario can be as true of us as anyone. We may think
we are just as committed as we used to be, yet in reality we
may simply be going through the motions, our faith going
nowhere. In our hearts, like the followers of Jesus mentioned
in John's Gospel, we may have turned back so that we no
longer walk with him. The initial act of commitment is
easy; it's when the cost of discipleship and level of commitment required become clear that the real test comes. I'm
reminded of the catchphrase immortalised by Magnus
Magnusson in the TV quiz *Mastermind*: 'I've started, so I'll
finish.' That's what faith is all about, what it means to be a
disciple of Jesus. Can we honestly echo those words?

Ask yourself

Are you still following Jesus with the same enthusiasm
with which you started out? Are you moving forwards or
slipping backwards?

Pray

Lord Jesus Christ, you know that I want to follow you, but you know also how hard I find it to do so. Despite my good intentions, I repeatedly slip back into my old ways, pursuing my own ends rather than your will. Instead of working and witnessing for you, I am lukewarm in service and weak in discipleship. Instead of growing, my faith has become stale and tired, no longer challenging or inspiring me as in the days when I first believed.

Forgive me for falling away so easily. Cleanse, renew and restore me by your redeeming touch, and help me to live for you today, tomorrow and every day, sure and steadfast, to the glory of your name. Amen.

Remember

Observe, then, the kindness and the severity of God: his severity towards those who have fallen away, but the kindness he shows to you, provided you continue in that kindness. If not, you too will be cut off.   *Romans 11:22*

Close

Living God, by your grace, equip, enable and enthuse me, so that I may faithfully walk the way of Christ, and finish what I started. Amen.

Standby Christians

Read

Jesus drew near and said to them, 'All power in heaven and earth has been given to me. Go, then, and make disciples of all people, baptising them in the name of the Father, the Son and the Holy Spirit.'

Matthew 28:18-19

Ponder

Did you know that the power used to keep televisions and electrical appliances in the UK on standby for just one day would be sufficient to provide electricity for a small town? It's a sobering thought, isn't it, all that power going to waste, achieving nothing.

Perhaps equally sobering is the thought that we as individuals and, together, as a Church, might be guilty of wasting a different sort of power – the power of God. 'You will receive power,' said Jesus, 'when the Holy Spirit comes upon you.' What he envisaged there was the power of the Spirit so flowing through us that we shall make a difference to the world we live in, changing lives through our work and witness. Some, of course, do just that, but, all too often, our efforts are devoted simply to keeping our own affairs ticking over. We look to our own journey of discipleship, our own relationship with Christ, and no further. As churches, we look inwards rather than outwards, concerned with servicing our plethora of committees, maintaining the fabric and supporting church events. Instead of surging out, God's power becomes trapped in an internal loop. It is as though we are put on standby, rarely if ever used for the purpose we were designed for. If the power stored in all those appliances on standby could meet the needs of a town, so the power at our disposal could meet the needs of the world, if only we had the will and courage to release it.

Ask yourself

Does your faith look inwards or outwards? Are you open to God's power working *through* you as well as *in* you?

Pray

Living God, I praise you for your sovereign power through which you have transformed my life, bringing strength, joy, hope and peace. I thank you for the power that flows within me through Christ and the living presence of the Holy Spirit, equipping me to see life in a new way and to meet each day with confidence. Yet, I am conscious that you want your life-changing power to flow through me, reaching out into the world beyond.

Forgive me that I have failed to let that happen, so concerned with self that I have forgotten my responsibility to others. Forgive the narrowness of my vision that has led me to become a holding station rather than a conduit of your renewing grace. Move within me, and open my life to all that you are able to do, so that in your name I may live and work for you. Through Jesus Christ my Lord. Amen.

Remember

The kingdom of God depends not on words but on power.
1 Corinthians 4:20

Close

Lord Jesus Christ, may your power flow in me, through me and from me, to the glory of your name. Amen.

Behind the scenes

Read

Give my greetings to Mary, who laboured so hard on your behalf. Greet Urbanus, our fellow-worker in Christ, and my beloved friend Stachys. Greet Apelles, who has proven himself in Christ. Greet Tryphena and Tryphosa, those women who have also worked so hard in the Lord. Greet my dear friend Persis, who has toiled in so much for the Lord's sake. Greet Rufus, chosen in the Lord, and his mother, who has been a mother to me, too. Greet Asyncritus, Phlegon, Hermas, Patrobas, Hermes and the brothers with them. Greet Philologus, Julia, Nereus and his sister, and Olympas and all the saints with them.   *Romans 16:6, 9-10a, 12-15*

Ponder

How often do you read the credits at the end of a film or television programme? The answer is probably never; most of us switch off our attention the moment the action has ended. Those credits, however, remind us that more people are involved in a production than simply those who appear onscreen. Producer, director, camera-crew, musicians, make-up department, lighting technicians and numerous others – all play a part in perfecting the finished article. Bear that in mind when you come to the lists of names, such as the one above, that typically end the letters of Paul. The temptation is to skim through these – particularly given the tongue-twisting nature of some of them! – yet that is to miss an important point. The people referred to may not have gone down in history as spiritual giants, yet their contribution was nonetheless vital. These, if you like, were Paul's backroom staff; those who encouraged, supported, nurtured or worked alongside him behind the scenes. Paul may have made the headlines but, without their tireless involvement, he couldn't have functioned as he did.

We do well to remember that today; it is easy to overlook those working in the background. Unglamorous tasks such as cleaning, catering, cooking, washing-up, preparing the minutes, arranging flowers and so on – do we ever show our appreciation for such things? All too often, we take such work for granted. A word of thanks may mean more than we might imagine. Conversely, you may be one of those undertaking such work. If so, never underrate the part God has called you to play, for it is as important as any other. We all have different gifts and different roles – let's remember to value them all.

Ask yourself
Is there someone in your church or your life whose contribution you have failed fully to appreciate?

Pray
Lord, I am so wrapped up in myself that I forget sometimes all I owe to others: the support, love, encouragement and inspiration I receive from so many. I am swift to complain when things are not done but slow to express gratitude when they are; good at criticising but poor in showing appreciation.

Help me to recognise everything others do for me and to make a point of acknowledging it. Help me to play my part in turn, contributing to their lives with equal commitment and dedication. In Christ's name I pray. Amen.

Remember
Our gifts differ according to the grace given to us. If our gift is prophecy, let us prophesy; if serving, let us serve; if teaching, let us teach; if encouraging, let us encourage; if giving, let us give; if leading, let us lead thoughtfully; if showing compassion and empathy, let us do so cheerfully.   *Romans 12:6-8*

Close
Living God, whatever you call me to, help me to perform it faithfully, gladly and wholeheartedly, to the glory of your name. Amen.

Remembering what was

Read

Remember what the Lord your God did. Remember the way that the Lord your God has led you.

Deuteronomy 7:18; 8:2

Ponder

Of all the months of the year, November seems to be a time for remembering. First, there comes All Saints' Day followed by All Souls' – occasions that remind us of those who have gone before us in the faith. Then, there is Guy Fawkes' Night; not, of course, a Christian festival but part of British folklore, reminding us of a long-distant plot against Parliament that reflected the religious tensions of that time. Next, there comes Remembrance Day, as we recall the sacrifice of so many in two World Wars and other conflicts. So much to remember, so much to learn from, so much that calls us to build for the future in the light of the past.

For the people of Israel, remembering was an integral part of their faith; the story of how God had delivered them from Egypt and led them safely through the wilderness to the Promised Land repeated by parents year after year, to their children and children's children. The memory of God's goodness and guidance across the years sustained, enriched and encouraged their faith. For the Christian, too, remembering has a special place. 'Do this in memory of me,' said Jesus (1 Corinthians 11:24). Such words remind us that our faith is not based on wishful thinking or idle speculation, nor on some clever deception or well-intentioned philosophy, but is rather rooted in history, in what God has done. Make time, then, to remember – not just today or on those days given over to remembering, but every day.

Ask yourself

Do you forget sometimes how much God has done for you? Do you make time, through prayer and the reading of God's word, to remember his faithfulness across the ages?

Pray

Almighty God, teach me to remember all you have done and to give you the praise you deserve. Teach me each day to recall your creative acts, your mighty deeds throughout history, and your faithful dealings with your people across the years. Above all, teach me to remember your graciousness in Jesus Christ – your coming, living, dying and rising among us, so that we might have life in all its fullness. For the memory of such things, and the constant reminder of them I receive each day, I give you my thanks and praise, through Jesus Christ my Lord. Amen.

Remember

Remember Jesus Christ, raised from the dead.

2 Timothy 2:8

Close

Gracious God, always you remember me. Teach me to remember you. Amen.

Remembering the poor

Read

All they asked was that we should continue to remember the poor; precisely what I was determined to do.

Galatians 2:10

Ponder

We are told that in Britain, over the last twenty years or so, the rich have grown richer and the poor have grown poorer. If that's true here, it's all the more true in the world as a whole, the gap between the 'haves and the have-nots' having widened to enormous proportions. The figures are truly staggering: well over three-quarters of the world's resources are enjoyed by less than a third of its total inhabitants. Is this simply a matter of academic concern? For anyone who claims to follow Christ the answer must be no. Throughout his ministry, Jesus showed what Archbishop David Shepherd termed in the title to his controversial book, a *Bias to the Poor*; and his words show that a concern for the poor is not just an optional part of discipleship but integral to it; an inescapable challenge to all who would follow him.

So it was that the early Church, racked by a time of controversy concerning the relationship of Jews and Gentiles, came up with one simple requirement – to remember the poor. Yes, there's a danger of seeming patronising, or of giving to charity to salve our consciences, but there's a much greater danger of using such reservations as an excuse to avoid the challenge and forgetting the poor altogether. Forget their needs and the gospel seems strongly to suggest that we have forgotten Jesus as well.

Ask yourself

How far do you see concern for the poor as integral to the gospel? In what ways can you and do you meaningfully express that concern?

Pray

Gracious God, I long for the day when your world will be as you want it to be: a world in which you lift up the lowly and fill the hungry with good things; in which love and justice will triumph, evil be ended and the meek inherit the earth. Give me confidence that such a day will come, and, more than that, give me the resolve to help make it happen. Help me to respond as best I can to the many millions who cry out for help, and so to play my part in bringing the dawn of your kingdom closer and turning vision into reality. In Christ's name I ask it. Amen.

Remember

He has filled the hungry with good things, but sent the rich away empty . . . The spirit of the Lord has anointed me to proclaim good news to the poor . . . Go out quickly into the streets and alleys of the town, and bring in the poor . . . Sell all you have and give the proceeds to the poor, and you will have treasure in heaven. *Luke 1:53; 4:18; 14:21; 18:22*

Close

Lord Jesus Christ, who became poor for my sake, teach me, having so much, to remember the many who have so little, and in responding to them, may I respond to you. Amen.

A master touch

Read

The centurion sent friends with a message for Jesus, saying, 'Lord, do not trouble yourself further, for I do not deserve to have you come under my roof. That's why I didn't presume to come to you in person. Just speak the word, and let my servant be made well. Like you, I am a man set under authority, with soldiers under me. I tell one, "Go", and he goes, and another, "Come", and he comes. Similarly, I say to my slaves, "Do this", and they do it.' When Jesus heard this, he was astounded, and turning to the crowd that followed him, he said, 'I tell you truthfully, I have not found any faith to equal this, even in Israel.' When the messengers returned to the house, they found the slave restored to health.

Luke 7:6b-10

Ponder

It wasn't a big job – just a few screws to be removed so that an old wooden partition could be taken out. All right, so the threads were a little worn, but I was confident that I could finish the task in no time. If nothing else, it would save the builders – who were fitting a window in the attic – a little time, if not save us a little money. Four hours later, I was still hard at it; sweat dripping down my chin, blisters raw on my hands. It was time to admit defeat and let the experts take over. Two minutes later, the job was done! The lesson is clear enough. Sometimes we need to recognise that we need help.

So it was with the Roman centurion who asked Jesus to heal his slave. He was a man in authority, used to giving orders, accustomed to getting things done, but this time he recognised the need for a higher authority, someone who could do what he couldn't. There are times when we need to do the same. We should not underestimate the gifts that

God has given, however, for there may often be times when the answer to our prayers lies in our own hands, and it is up to us to use those gifts as God directs. At other times, though, we need to recognise our impotence, and throw ourselves entirely upon the power of God. Above all, perhaps, we need his guidance in getting the balance right.

Ask yourself

Are you trying to do things that you need God's help to finish? Are you seeking God's help for what he has already given you the gifts to achieve?

Pray

Sovereign Lord, there are things I can do by myself and things only you can do. There are times when I have the resources within me to cope with a situation and times when I depend utterly on you for help.

Teach me to know the difference and help me to remember that though my reserves may run dry, yours never will. Give me, then, an appreciation of my abilities, but above all, an appreciation of yours. Through Jesus Christ my Lord. Amen.

Remember

So, then, let us come boldly before his throne of grace, so that we may obtain mercy and find grace to help in time of need. *Hebrews 4:16*

Close

Living God, for the help you have given and the assistance you are always ready to give, receive my praise, in the name of Christ. Amen.

Meaningful membership

Read

Now you are the body of Christ, each having your own place as members within it.   *1 Corinthians 12:27*

Ponder

Four years ago I joined the Society of Authors. It seemed a good idea at the time, if only because here was a body concerned with defending and promoting authors' rights. Every year since then, though, I have wondered whether it is worth renewing my subscription, not because of any fault on the society's part but because I have made no use whatsoever of my membership. I have been to none of its seminars or any of the regional get-togethers. I haven't met a single fellow-member, and due to the constant pressure of work I haven't even had time to read the society's quarterly magazine. In fact, all I do is stump up my £80-a-year membership fee. Effectively, I am a nominal member, no more than a name on a bit of paper.

Such membership, of course, is meaningless, for belonging to any organisation should mean being involved and playing a part, all of which is worth bearing in mind when it comes to being part of the Church. We may carry the label 'Christian' but that by itself means nothing. We need to meet together, worship together and work together, united in the common cause of Christ. We need to offer not just our money but our time and effort, looking for ways in which our gifts can be used for the good of all. Above all, we need to make time for one another, so that we are not simply members on paper but a family in practice. To be a Christian means to be part of the body of Christ. Are we fulfilling our role within it?

Ask yourself

What do you put into the life of your local church? What do you receive through being part of God's people?

Pray

Gracious God, I thank you for the great honour of belonging to Christ and of being part of his body. Teach me what that means. Help me to contribute to the life of your people, through offering my time, money, gifts and service. Help me to make time for fellowship, so that I may know the strength that comes through sharing joys and sorrows, joining in prayer and worship, and learning through the experience of others. Help me to appreciate the enrichment that comes through being an active member of your family, and so may I make that membership more real each day. Through Jesus Christ my Lord. Amen.

Remember

When one member suffers, all the members suffer with it; and when one member is exalted, all the members rejoice with it.   *Ephesians 5:30*

Close

Lord Jesus Christ, may I not simply belong to you in name only, but be one with you and all your people, working together for your kingdom, to the glory of your name. Amen.

Papering over the cracks

Read

This is what the Lord said to Jeremiah: 'Go down at once to the potter's house, and there I will speak to you.' So I went down to the potter's house, and there I found him working at the wheel. Occasionally, one of the vessels he was shaping from the clay was spoiled in his hands, and then he would start again and rework it into another vessel more to his liking.

Jeremiah 18:1-4

Ponder

Last night I did some wallpapering. This morning I wished I hadn't, for it looks a complete bodge! The wall in question is an old one, pitted with cracks, lumps and bumps, but I had spent considerable time filling these in and sanding them down to what I thought was a relatively smooth finish. A good thick lining paper, I reckoned, and it would look good as new. How wrong I was!

It is often much the same story in life. We attempt to cover over our weaknesses rather than tackle and eradicate them. We know all is not as it should be, but we vainly imagine that, through our own efforts, we can make the best of a bad job. The truth is that we can't. What my wall needs is replastering. What *we* need is remaking, and only God can achieve that. Don't paper over the cracks. Don't settle for a ham-fisted make-over. Acknowledge before God what's wrong with your life, and let him put right what you can't start to tackle yourself.

Ask yourself

Are there things wrong in your life that you need to face up to? Is it time you stopped trying to conceal the truth and allowed God to reshape your life?

Pray

Living God, there is so much in my life that is not as it should be, yet all too often I stubbornly refuse to admit it. I pretend there is nothing really wrong; that any minor aberrations are superficial, hardly worth bothering about. Even when I am more honest with myself, I still believe that I can put matters right through my own efforts; that all it needs is a greater resolve on my part. Yet, despite all my attempts to start afresh, the old mistakes and weaknesses soon show through, as unsightly as ever.

Teach me that I need your help if I seriously hope ever to change. Put a new heart and a right spirit within me, and recreate me from within. Take me and mould me in your hands, so that I may be the person you would have me be. By the grace of Christ my Lord. Amen.

Remember

Show penitence and turn away from all your disobedience; otherwise evil will be your ruin. Cast away from you all the wrongdoing that you have been guilty of against me, and get yourselves a new heart and a new spirit!

Ezekiel 18:30b-31a

Close

Lord Jesus Christ, renew, remake, remould, reshape me. By your grace, redeem and restore, reclaim and refashion, to the glory of your name. Amen.

Questions and answers

Read

If you cry out for insight, and raise your voice for understanding, if you seek for it as for hidden treasures – then you
will understand the fear of the Lord and find the knowledge
of God. For the Lord gives wisdom; from his mouth come
knowledge and understanding.   *Proverbs 2:3-6*

Ponder

Many of us will recall the radio quiz shows *Twenty Questions*
and *What's my line?*. It's fun to work out the answer
through a process of deduction, even though the questions
themselves may be very simple. Such games are, in fact, a
microcosm of life, for the chief way we learn anything is
through asking questions. My daughter Kate is currently at
that stage of repeatedly asking 'Why?' about anything and
everything. It can be exhausting, even infuriating at times,
but it is an essential part of growing up and the sign of a
healthy enquiring mind.

Sadly, when it comes to faith some Christians feel guilty
about asking questions, almost as though they feel they are
being disloyal or sinful in entertaining them. Many feel that
they must unquestioningly accept every item of Christian
doctrine and dogma. Such unthinking acceptance, however,
is a dangerous business, not least because Christians themselves cannot agree about what should and shouldn't be
accepted, as witnessed by denominational and theological
divisions, and other splits over worship and church practice.
Words have different nuances and events can be interpreted
in various ways; few things are as clear-cut as they might
seem. We all see some of the answers but no one sees them
all. Far from discouraging questions, I believe God wants
us to ask them, so that our minds may be stretched and
our understanding of his loving purpose may grow. That

doesn't mean that we should reject what we cannot make sense of, nor that we set up scientific or human wisdom as the yardstick by which all is measured, but it does mean that we search and keep on searching for deeper understanding and greater enlightenment, always open to the new insights that God waits to reveal.

Ask yourself

Are there areas of Christian belief you find hard to understand or difficult to accept? Have you acknowledged these openly before God?

Pray

Gracious God, I thank you for all you have revealed to me in Christ and for the faith you have put into my heart, but I thank you also that there is more to understand in my continuing journey of discovery.

So I bring you the things I don't understand, the statements of faith that don't seem to make sense and the events of life that seem to contradict what I have been taught of you. I bring you my certainty and my uncertainty; those areas where faith is sure and those where it hangs by a thread. Give me sufficient trust to acknowledge my questions openly and to offer them honestly to you in prayer. Save me from taking refuge in ritual or dogma, but teach me rather to face the challenges that life brings and to work through my faith in the light of them, so that, having been tested, it may grow the stronger, able to face all and still to stand. Through Jesus Christ my Lord. Amen.

Remember

Of first importance is to acquire wisdom; to gain understanding, though it may cost you all you have. *Proverbs 4:7*

Close

Gracious God, give me courage to ask questions, faith to live with them, and grace to grow through them, to the glory of your name. Amen.

Lest we forget

Read

We have heard for ourselves, O God, our predecessors have told us the deeds you performed in their time, how in bygone days you saved us from our enemies.   *Psalm 44:1, 7a*

Ponder

'Do you remember the time we came here before?' asked my mother. I racked my brains, trying to recall it, but it was no good; the occasion was clean forgotten, as though it had never been. We do remember many things, of course, but we forget many others, as probably all of us can testify from bitter experience. Points we ought to remember have that infuriating habit of disappearing from our minds just when we need to recall them most, and so we resort to such props as a knot in a hankie or a memo-board in the kitchen, hoping that these may jog our memory.

Such, increasingly, is the rationale behind Remembrance Day. Every year, the number of those who lived through one or both of the two World Wars diminishes, yet for that reason the occasion becomes more rather than less important. We have only to witness the horrors of Bosnia, or the continuing violence in the Middle East and so many other parts of the world, to realise that things haven't changed as much as we might like to think. Some even dare to suggest that the horrors of the Holocaust never actually happened, thus dismissing, at a stroke, the suffering, terror and anguish experienced by so many millions. The fact is that we cannot afford to forget the past. Remembrance Day does not glorify war but rather recalls the price of peace, reminding us of the evil and inhumanity that people can stoop to, and the sacrifice so many made to ensure that such tyranny did not triumph. It purposely thrusts such things back into our consciousness – lest we forget.

Ask yourself

Do you forget sometimes how much you owe to those who fought for the freedom of this country? Why do we need to remember, and what lessons can we learn?

Pray

Almighty God, on this day of remembering, help me to learn the lessons of the past: to understand the cost of war, the price of peace, the scope of human depravity and the extent of human self-sacrifice. Help me to learn those lessons – to live and work for peace, to stand up against evil, to serve and not to count the cost, to work in whatever way I can for a better world.

Forgive me that I do not remember as often as I should, forgetting how fortunate I am to live in freedom and how lucky to enjoy peace; forgetting those who still suffer from the wounds of battle and others who even now mourn their loved ones. Speak to me today and help me not only to say the words but truly to mean them: 'We will remember them.' Amen.

Remember

There is no greater love than this: to give your life for another.

John 15:13

Close

Living God, teach me to remember the lessons of the past, so that I may appreciate the present and work always for a better future, in the name of Christ. Amen.

Singing his praises

Read

Praise the Lord! Praise the Lord, O my soul! I will praise the Lord as long as I live; I will sing praises to God all my life long. How good it is to sing praises to our God; for he is gracious, and a song of praise is fitting.

Psalm 146:1-2; 147:1b (NRSV)

Ponder

How do you feel when someone offers you praise? Do you nod in eager agreement and ask them to continue? I doubt it, unless perhaps you are trying to hide your embarrassment. While a little praise every now and again is undeniably welcome, too much is hard to handle, especially if we're in the company of others at the time.

What about God? Is he any different? Does he positively revel in praise, lapping it up and asking for more? Does he not only enjoy but also expect it? The words of scripture, and indeed of public worship, can give that impression sometimes, but I think it's misleading, for, like so much else in prayer, the opportunity to praise God is given as much for our benefit as his. It gives us the opportunity to put our feelings into words, to express the sense of thankfulness and joy that bubbles up within us, and in so doing it reminds us of what God has done and who he is. It is a way of responding; of telling him we haven't just taken his goodness for granted but that it is special to us. I've no doubt God takes pleasure in such words but I don't for a moment think that he demands them. We offer him praise not because we ought to but because we can; because, truth be told, we cannot help ourselves.

Ask yourself

Do you see praising God as a duty or a privilege? Do you offer praise as often as you should?

Pray

Living God, I know that you do not need my praise, but I want to give it to you nonetheless, for you have blessed me in so much. I want to acknowledge your goodness and thank you for the constancy of your love. I want to show my appreciation for the wonder of life and tell you how much it all means to me. I want to express my gratitude for your unfailing grace, the forgiveness you so freely and faithfully offer.

Living God, I do not simply *want* to say these things; I *need* to, for my heart burns within me in joyful celebration. So I come to you again now in grateful adoration and heartfelt worship. Hear my prayer and receive my praise, in the name of Christ. Amen.

Remember

I will bless the Lord at all times; his praise will constantly be upon my lips.

Psalm 34:1

Close

Sovereign God, I cannot praise you too much. Forgive me that I fail to praise you enough. Amen.

An eternal promise

Read

We can confidently say, 'The Lord is my helper, I will not be afraid; what can anyone do to me?'
Hebrews 13:6

Ponder

Sitting there in the dentist's waiting room, contemplating yet more fillings and other equally hideous forms of legalised torture, those words suddenly rang rather hollow. 'What can anyone do to me?' Well, a great deal, actually. All right, so a visit to the dentist is not so dreadful, but you have only to read the account in Hebrews 11 of the sufferings inflicted on God's people in days gone by to realise the atrocities that can be perpetrated by our fellow human beings: 'They were stoned to death . . . sawn in two . . . killed by the sword . . . persecuted, tormented'. Nor does being a Christian in any way guarantee an exemption from physical suffering. For many it has been the opposite; their commitment to Christ has directly brought suffering, if not death itself. That is not to say God will not give us strength to face such times, for he has clearly done just that on countless occasions, but if we see faith as some kind of insurance policy for health and happiness, then we may be in for a bitter disappointment.

What the writer to the Hebrews had in mind when he said so confidently, 'What can anyone do to me?', was not our immediate fate but our eternal destiny. He knew well enough what Christians can go through, and yet he also knew what God has promised. That is precisely why he wrote as he did. None of us knows what we may face in this world, whether good or ill. What we do know is that God's love is with us, not just now but for all eternity, and that nothing will ever finally be able to come between us and that promise. We too, then, can confidently say, 'The Lord is my helper, I will not be afraid. What can anyone do to me?'

Ask yourself
Do you feel up against it at present? Are you finding it hard to make sense of what you're going through? Have you kept in mind the eternal dimension of faith?

Pray
Loving God, I thank you for all the ways you are with me and all the ways you grant your blessing. I thank you for the guidance you give, the strength you supply, the mercy you show and the love with which you surround me. Above all, though, I thank you that your purpose is not just for this life but also for all eternity, for you are still holding the best in store.

Teach me to walk with you each day and to know you are always by my side, and so may I trust you for the future, keeping hold of the everlasting hope you have given me in Christ, that nothing shall destroy. Amen.

Remember
Having been justified by the grace of Jesus Christ our Saviour, we have become heirs to the promise of eternal life. You may safely trust in these words.   *Titus 3:7-8a*

Close
Living God, for the knowledge that whatever this life may bring, you hold new life in store, I give you my thanks and praise. Amen.

Partners in prayer

Read

In the same way, the Spirit identifies with us in our weakness. We do not know how to pray or what to pray for, but the Spirit pleads on our behalf with entreaties that are beyond words, and the one who searches our hearts knows the Spirit's mind, because he intercedes constantly on behalf of the saints seeking the fulfilment of God's purpose.

Romans 8:26-27

Ponder

A while back, I was asked to speak at an event for Christian leaders on the subject of personal prayer. The invitation came as something of a surprise, for although I have written innumerable prayers, I still consider myself anything but an expert on the subject. Like the vast majority of Christians, prayer does not always come easily to me, nor am I as disciplined about it as I should be. If my spiritual well-being and relationship with God were entirely down to me, frankly it wouldn't be up to much. Thankfully, it's not; neither for me nor any one of us.

The Holy Spirit articulates our thoughts to God, even when *we* find it impossible to do so. More than that, Christ himself is constantly interceding on our behalf, bringing our unspoken needs and requests before God. Prayer may start with us but it doesn't end there. However much it may sometimes feel like it, we are never alone when we attempt to pray. That's not to encourage casualness or complacency, for prayer is ultimately given for our own benefit as much as God's, but if you can't quite find the right words, and if you genuinely can't find the time you'd like to give, don't punish yourself, your prayer will get to him nonetheless.

Ask yourself

Do you worry sometimes that your difficulty in finding the right words for prayer may mean you are not heard? Do you fear that you have missed someone or something out? Are you aware that Jesus and the Holy Spirit are always interceding on your behalf?

Pray

Living God, there are times when I pray but the words just won't come, and times when I simply don't know what to pray for. There are times, too, when I forget to pray, or when my prayers are casual and half-hearted, squeezed in as an afterthought at the end of the day. I thank you that I am not alone then in prayer, and that your response does not depend solely on my own efforts.

I thank you for the work of the Spirit within, articulating my deepest thoughts and needs, and I praise you for the faithfulness of Christ, constantly interceding on my behalf. Living God, hear *my* words and *their* prayer, and in your mercy reach out in love. Amen.

Remember

[Jesus] is able to save those who approach God through him, since he lives constantly to make intercession for them.

Hebrews 7:25

Close

Lord Jesus Christ, when I cannot or do not say the things I mean to, speak for me, through your Spirit, in the presence of God. Amen.

Patience, patience

Read

It is better to be patient in spirit than proud in spirit.

Ecclesiastes 7:8

Ponder

The meeting was going on longer than expected, and I was growing increasingly impatient. 'Get to the point!' I felt like saying, but of course I didn't say anything; I just sat there stewing. At last, I was on my way home, but what was this? A slow driver ahead of me, pottering on as though he had all the time in the world, and not a chance of over-taking. Again, there was nothing for it but to grit my teeth as my blood rose to boiling point! I got past eventually and put my foot down, hoping to make up for lost time, but it was no good: first a set of roadworks, then a diversion, and so it went on – patience frayed to the limit.

Was it worth getting so worked up? Of course not. When I eventually arrived home, my head ached, my hands were tense and my mind in a whirl; several hours spoiled for the sake of a few minutes. All too easily, life is like that. We rush from one thing to the next, one eye on the clock, begrudging every wasted moment, yet in trying to save a few seconds we end up frittering away far more of our lives. We need to learn that every moment is God's gift, whatever we are doing, and to make the most of each one while we have it.

Ask yourself

Do you tend to lose your patience? Does rushing to do things that bit faster help or hinder?

Pray

Lord, I know it's foolish, that impatience gets me nowhere, but I just can't seem to help it. I try telling myself, 'What's the hurry?' I do my best to take it easy. I remind myself of what really matters. Yet, before I know it, I find myself fretting once more about a few moments wasted here, a little delay there.

Touch me by your grace and teach me to receive every moment as your gift, living each one for what it is. Put a tranquil spirit, a quiet mind and a patient heart within me, and help me to learn that the more I worry about time, the less I will enjoy the time I have. Amen.

Remember
Those who are in too much of a hurry miss the way.

Proverbs 19:26

Close
Sovereign God, when I start to fret over the loss of a single minute, remind me that your love will continue for all eternity. Amen.

Speaking out

Read

Balak said to Balaam, 'What have you done to me? I brought you to curse my enemies, but now you have done nothing but bless them.' He answered, 'Must I not take care to say what the Lord puts into my mouth?'

Numbers 23:11-12 (NRSV)

Ponder

The writer, Alexander Solzhenitsyn, spent eight years of his life, between 1945 and 1953, in prison. His 'crime' was to speak out against the way Stalin had acted during the Second World War. Twenty-one years later he was arrested again and sent into exile for having dared in his book *The Gulag Archipelago* to document the era of Stalinist terror. More dramatic still is the story of Nelson Mandela, who in 1961 was imprisoned for his campaign against apartheid, spending the next twenty-nine years in prison until his eventual release in 1990.

For me, the example of Balaam calls to mind the courage of those two men. Summoned by Balak, king of the Moabites, to pronounce a curse on the Israelites, he did the very opposite and pronounced a blessing. That must have taken some doing, for he was well aware of the reaction this would provoke, but he spoke the words that he believed God wanted him to say. We may not be put on the spot quite like any of these individuals, but there will be times when we know it is right to make a stand, either in support of good or against evil. What will we do then? Will we say what people want us to say, for the sake of a quiet life, or will we, instead, have the courage to speak out?

Ask yourself

Have there been times when you have kept silent when you should have spoken up? Do you go along with the crowd rather than risk a hostile response?

Pray

Living God, it is uncomfortable sometimes having to choose. I prefer to sit on the fence, to hedge my bets, to take the path of compromise in the hope of pleasing all. Even when I know the right way, I turn aside from it, fearful of the cost that may be involved. Yet, deep down, I know this simply won't do; that failing to decide *for* you means deciding *against* you.

Help me to recognise when I need to make a choice, and then give me courage to stand firm in faith, whatever it may cost. Amen.

Remember

Pray also for me, that the right words may be put into my mouth, so that I may boldly make known the mystery of the gospel, for which I am currently an ambassador in chains. Pray that I may courageously declare it, as I ought to speak.

Ephesians 6:19-20

Close

Sovereign God, when you give me your word, give me the courage I need to speak it. Amen.

Unlikely choices

Read

You did not choose me; I chose you.   *John 15:16*

Ponder

Imagine that you had just been handed a freshly opened box of chocolates. Which would you choose? It would be a tough decision, wouldn't it? If you're anything like me, though, there would be options you wouldn't even consider. You know the sort – the coffee creams, toffee cracknel or nougat that always end up left over at the end of every box. When you have a choice, you can afford to be choosy. All of which makes the words of Jesus in John's Gospel the more remarkable, for he is telling his disciples here that of all the thousands of people he could have chosen to be his Apostles, he chose them! Not that he was wrong to do so – history has more than vindicated his judgement – but, to put it kindly, they were not the obvious choice; hardly those you would expect anyone to choose if they planned to start a world-changing movement.

Yet Jesus had selected these above all others, recognising qualities in them that he could take and use towards the fulfilment of his purpose. So it continues today. We do not *choose* to follow Jesus; we *respond* to his call. He is the one who takes the initiative in establishing a relationship, not us. Why does he do that? Because, once again, he sees in us something special, something that he infinitely values. The greatest wonder of all is that he leaves no one out when choosing, no rejects at the end of the pile. Though many will reject him, he has a place for everyone who is ready to receive him. Do you sometimes question whether you have any place in his kingdom, any right to call yourself a Christian? Then remember this: before you even knew there was a choice to make, Jesus chose you.

Ask yourself

Do you find it hard to believe that God can use you? Have you forgotten that he chose you through Christ?

Pray

Living God, I praise you for the knowledge that you have chosen me to be a part of your people. I rejoice in everything that means: that you did not just accept me because you had to, because no one else would respond; that you did not accept me reluctantly, hesitant because of my faults and weaknesses; and that you did not accept me provisionally, dependent upon whether I measure up to your expectations.

Instead, I know that you welcome me freely, gladly and unequivocally, opening your heart to me without hesitation or reserve, glad to embrace me as your child and to call me one of your family. For the wonder of that truth, I offer my grateful worship, in the name of Christ. Amen.

Remember

You are a chosen race, a royal priesthood, an elect nation, set apart by God as his own people.   *1 Peter 2:9*

Close

Lord Jesus Christ, whenever I question my worth, teach me that you believe in me totally, enough even to die for me so that I might enter into your kingdom, and in that knowledge may I live each day, at one with myself and at one with you. Amen.

Ready to receive

Read

Sin pays a wage, and the wage is death, but God gives freely, and his gift is eternal life in union with Christ Jesus our Lord.   *Romans 6:23*

Ponder

It is more blessed, we are told, to give than to receive. We can interpret that in two ways. Most of all, of course, it is an encouragement to generosity, reminding us of the joy that comes through giving to others, but if we turn that around, there is another truth beneath the surface, for it can actually be surprisingly hard to receive. When someone presents us with an unexpected gift, or perhaps helps us out of financial difficulties, we can feel embarrassed and indebted. 'You shouldn't have done that!' we say, or, 'I can't possibly accept that'. We want to do something in return. Some go further, actually feeling angry, refusing to accept what they see as charity. Most of us have an innate feeling that we need to earn something rather than have it given.

Such a way of thinking easily spills over into our relationship with God. Although we talk of being justified by faith, deep down we feel that we must do something to show we deserve it and to win his approval. That, though, is to forget the key message of the gospel: that God's love is not earned but is freely given through Christ. We do not have to prove our worth or pay God back. He asks us simply to receive.

Ask yourself

Do you still feel that you must somehow put yourself right with God? Do you see salvation as something you have to earn?

Pray

Living God, I know that I have no claim on your love and no reason to expect your goodness, for I fail you day after day, week after week, yet I celebrate once more the glorious truth that you love and accept me as I am. Though I deserve so little, you give me so much; though I serve you so poorly, you bless me so richly, your grace never exhausted, your love refusing to be denied. I know that I can never earn such love or ever begin to repay it, but I praise you that you do not ask me to, your gift of new life in Christ truly being free. Help me then, humbly, gladly and gratefully, to receive what you offer, and to give you the glory. Amen.

Remember

If one man's sin brought death to many, how much more has the grace of God and the free gift that comes through the grace of one man, Jesus Christ, abounded for many.

Romans 5:15b

Close

Gracious God, teach me that before I can give anything, I need first to receive, and so open my life to your saving renewing love, through Christ my Lord. Amen.

The God who is ready to welcome

Read

He set off and went to his father. But while he was still far off, his father saw him and was filled with compassion; he ran and put his arms around him and kissed him. Then the son said to him, 'Father, I have sinned against heaven and before you; I am no longer worthy to be called your son.' But the father said to his slaves, 'Quickly, bring out a robe – the best one – and put it on him; put a ring on his finger and sandals on his feet. Get the fatted calf and kill it, and let us eat and celebrate; for this son of mine was dead and is alive again; he was lost and is found!'

Luke 15:20-24 (NRSV)

Ponder

Have you ever sat in a waiting room, wondering when you will be seen to? It's all too common, isn't it, as anyone who has sat in a hospital casualty department or DSS office will know. How much longer will we have to wait? Is there some problem? Will we be seen at all? Such questions inevitably cross one's mind. Even worse, though, is sitting as a child outside the head teacher's office, waiting to be summoned after committing some misdemeanour – not that I would know, of course! What sort of reception will we get? What kind of punishment is in store for us?

Some people approach God like that, wondering whether he will receive them and afraid of the consequences if he does. 'Can he truly have time for someone like me?' they ask themselves. 'Of course not! Can he possibly forgive my many mistakes? It beggars belief.' If that's how you feel, then look again at the parable of the lost son, for there we see one of the most memorable pictures of God in the whole Bible; a God who waits to greet us while we are still far off, reaching out to embrace us in love. With him, there is no question of being kept outside, left to stew and finally made to suffer. On the contrary, we need only make the first tentative steps of approach and he is there waiting to receive us, longing to welcome us home.

Ask yourself

Do you worry how God will respond to you? Have you understood that he is always waiting to receive you, no matter what you have done?

Pray

Loving God, I do not know why I go astray, for I want so much to stay true. I yearn to offer you faithful and committed service, but somehow I always fall short, and I fear sometimes that one day even your love will be exhausted, my disobedience pushing your patience too far.

Remind me, at such times, of your infinite grace that goes on reaching out to me, come what may. Remind me that you are a God always ready to forgive and forget, longing to lift me up and carry me safely home on your shoulders. In Christ's name I thank you. Amen.

Remember

God will ransom my soul from the power of Sheol. He will receive me. *Psalm 49:15*

Close

Gracious God, just I am, I come, committing myself to your loving mercy, through Jesus Christ my Lord. Amen.

Going under?

Read

Thus says the man: 'I am weary, O God, I am weary, O God.
How can I prevail?'   *Proverbs 30:1 (NRSV)*

Ponder

There are times when life gets on top of us, the pressures
and demands too much to bear, and for most of us such
moments are nearer than we might imagine, for who can say
what tomorrow might bring? We may feel everything is
under control, life running along smoothly, but one setback
or disappointment can change our whole perspective,
sending us spiralling into a vortex of chaos and confusion.
Suddenly problems seem to engulf us from every side, suck-
ing us in ever deeper. Most of us can survive such pressures
for a time, but there comes a point when our strength gives
out and we feel ourselves going under. All too many can
testify to the mind-numbing, strength-sapping effect of
stress and its capacity to drive us to the brink of despair
and beyond.

Faith does not provide easy solutions to such times, but it
does offer a resource to hold on to; namely, the knowledge
that whatever we may face, nothing will finally be able to
overcome God's purpose or separate us from his love. Put
our trust in him and, though we may feel utterly overwhelmed, we will find his hand is there to hold our heads
above the water until the storm subsides and calm returns.

Ask yourself

Do you feel up against it? Are you struggling to cope with
the demands life brings? Have you the faith to let go of your
problems and place them in God's hands, confident that
nothing will finally come between you and his purpose?

Pray

Living God, I like to think that I am one of this world's survivors, able to meet whatever life may throw at me and emerge unscathed, but, in my heart, I know that I am as vulnerable as the next person, my composure and confidence hanging on a thread that can be broken at any time. A crisis, difficulty, disappointment or personal tragedy, and the whole edifice I have so carefully constructed can come tumbling down around my ears. Most of the time I succeed in shutting out such thoughts, finding them too uncomfortable to contemplate, but sometimes they force their way into my consciousness, and I can escape them no longer.

Save me from running away in a vain attempt to deny the truth; from taking a road that leads only to the fears mounting and gaining a firmer hold. Teach me instead to share my burdens and anxieties with you, and so to find strength, peace, hope and courage even when the storm rages about me, secure in the knowledge of your eternal love made known through Jesus Christ my Lord. Amen.

Remember

We are afflicted in every way, but not crushed; perplexed, but not driven to despair; persecuted, but not forsaken; struck down, but not destroyed; always carrying in our body the death of Jesus, so that the life of Jesus may also be made visible in our bodies.   *2 Corinthians 4:8-10 (NRSV)*

Close

Lord Jesus Christ, when I find myself overwhelmed by life's problems and struggling to stay afloat, be there to still the storm and to grant your peace. Amen.

Christ in you!

Read

I have been crucified with Christ, so that it is no longer I who live but Christ who lives within me. The life that I now live in the flesh is lived by faith in the Son of God, who loved me and gave himself up for me.

Galatians 2:19b-20

Ponder

'What's got into you?' When did someone last ask you that? It may be that you woke up like a bear with a sore head, snapping and snarling at everyone you met. Equally, you may have been on top of the world, full of the joys of spring, to the point that you seemed positively to radiate sunshine.

I suspect that many in the days of the early Church must have been asked something very similar. Take the day of Pentecost, for example, when the Apostles were filled with the Holy Spirit and began powerfully to preach the gospel; a number of the crowd looked on incredulously, suggesting they were drunk or out of their minds. Or consider Paul, changed overnight from being a persecutor of the Church to one of its most ardent proponents. Again, people must have reacted with disbelief, wondering what could have brought about such a change. So it must have been for countless others – one moment devout Jews, followers of the gods of Greece and Rome, or having no faith at all, and the next declaring a personal relationship with Christ; a relationship that had made an unmistakable difference to their lives. To anyone who asked what had got into them, the answer was very simple: it was Jesus. As Paul was to put it in his letter to the Colossians, 'Christ in you, the hope of glory.'

Remember those words, for they remind us that the gospel at its heart is not about us striving to be like Jesus, but about Jesus working within us. Yes, he wants us to become more like him so that our lives speak to others, but that all comes down not to our own efforts but his presence within us, and the renewing work of his Holy Spirit. Open our heart and soul to his grace and people may indeed look at us and say, 'What's got into you!'

Ask yourself

Is it evident to others that Christ lives within you? Have you recognised that faith begins with opening your life to his love rather than any attempt to become more like him through your own efforts?

Pray

Lord Jesus Christ, I thank you that discipleship is not finally about what I can do for you but about what you have done for me. I praise you that your love does not depend on my works but on your grace.

I celebrate with wonder your presence within me; the way you have come into my life to offer your guidance, strength, peace and joy. Fill me a little more each day, so that I may know you better and become more like you, my life testifying to your sovereign and renewing power. Amen.

Remember

God chose to make known among all nations the glorious riches of this mystery, which is Christ in you, the hope of glory.   *Colossians 1:27*

Close

Lord Jesus Christ, teach me that if I would be in you, you first must be in me. Amen.

Self-service?

Read

Brothers and sisters, you were called to freedom. Make sure, though, that you do not use that freedom to indulge the flesh, but, in love, become servants of one another.

Galatians 5:13

Ponder

We live today in a self-service world. Whether we're popping in to our local supermarket, filling up at the petrol station or eating in a canteen, the chances are that we will serve ourselves, and our only contact with a member of staff will be to pay the bill. All this, of course, reflects the wishes of consumers who, by and large, enjoy having the freedom to choose what they buy and value not having to queue too long to buy it. I would be the first to endorse those benefits, yet I can't help thinking sometimes that this trend reflects an underlying and less desirable facet of human nature that arguably has become more apparent over recent years in Western consumer society as a whole: the idea of putting self before all others, looking after number one.

To find people willing to give up their time voluntarily for others is becoming increasingly difficult. Many once-flourishing movements, for example, committed to serving the community are now struggling to survive. This is not down purely to greed and self-interest; hard economics makes it necessary for many couples to work long hours simply to pay the mortgage and make ends meet, thus yielding little time for anything and anyone else. Yet most of us, if we are honest, could still afford a little more time, interest, support and money than we are willing to give. As Christians, we are called to serve others, putting their needs before our own. Can we claim to have responded to that challenge, or are we children of our time: self-service Christians?

Ask yourself

In what ways do you serve yourself? In what ways do you serve others? In what ways could you serve them if you had the mind to?

Pray

Lord Jesus Christ, I'm good at talking about service but not very good at showing it. I speak of your love for the helpless and hopeless, but I all too rarely translate concern into action. Forgive me for the way I have neglected so many opportunities to help others, through deeds large or small. Forgive the selfishness that has obscured love, the greed that has denied compassion and the laziness of body, mind and spirit that has so often prevented any meaningful response.

Show me where and how I can serve in your name, and inspire me to reach out in love, offering something of myself to others, even as you offered your all for me. By your grace, I ask it. Amen.

Remember

So then, if I, your Lord and master, have washed your feet, you also ought to wash each other's feet. I have set an example for you to follow, so that you might do to others what I have done to you. I tell you this: servants are not greater than their master, nor are those who carry messages greater than the one who sent them.   *John 13:14-16*

Close

Lord Jesus Christ, teach me not to serve myself but others, not to seek my own ends but your will, and so may all I am and all I do bring glory to your name. Amen.

No contest!

Read

This is the word of the Lord to Zerubbabel: Not by might, nor by power, but by my Spirit, says the Lord of hosts.

Zechariah 4:6 (NRSV)

Ponder

In the right corner: Hercules; in the left corner: Mr Bean! It's an incongruous thought, isn't it, a greater mismatch hard to imagine, yet it is no greater than the situation that faced Israel in the days of Zechariah. After many years exiled in Babylon, they had returned to rebuild Jerusalem and restore the temple, but what hope did they realistically have? Compared to the numerous other countries that surrounded them, let alone the mighty empires of their day, they were puny, with scarcely a hope of defending themselves should they be attacked. So it had been for the bulk of their history; a small country surrounded by marauding giants. Humanly speaking, they had no chance, but the words of Zechariah were not about human things but about God and what he could do through his Spirit.

The situation was not so different for the Apostles gathered together on the day of Pentecost. How could they possibly fulfil the call of Jesus to make disciples of all nations? The answer, of course, is that *they* couldn't, but *God* could! Without him, they were powerless; with him, all things were possible. We need to remember that today when we feel up against it. When we look at the needs of society and feel overwhelmed by our inability to respond, when we are faced by apathy concerning the gospel and wonder how we can even begin to share our faith, we need to recall and trust in that promise: 'Not by might, nor by power, but by my Spirit, says the Lord of hosts.'

Ask yourself

Do you approach situations from the perspective of what you feel able to do, or of what God is able to do with your help?

Pray

Sovereign God, I praise you for the way you have demonstrated your strength across the centuries, working in circumstances that seemed hopeless and through people that seemed powerless to do anything. I praise you that you are able to transform situations in a manner that defies human logic, giving strength to the weak and achieving great things that look impossible.

Teach me never to measure a solution by the way things seem and never to back away from a challenge because I consider myself unable to meet it. Help me to look to you and to trust in your strength that is stronger than any earthly power, recognising that whatever you set out to accomplish, you will do. Through Jesus Christ my Lord. Amen.

Remember

The Lord is the strength of his people, a safe refuge for his anointed.   *Psalm 28:8*

Close

Living God, teach me to trust in you, knowing that what I can't do, you can! Amen.

Stepping back, stepping forward

Read

He told his disciples to get into the boat and go on ahead
of him to Bethsaida, on the other side, while he dismissed
the crowd. After taking leave of them, he went up on the
mountain to pray . . . In those days he went out to the mountain to pray; and all night he continued in prayer to God.

Mark 6:45-46; Luke 6:12

Ponder

Have you ever heard of Henry the Hermit or St Cuthbert?
Both are associated with the magical coast of Northumberland. St Cuthbert made his home on Lindisfarne, otherwise
known as Holy Island – a small rocky outcrop connected
to the mainland by a narrow causeway that for most of the
day is submerged by the sea. Henry was even more of a
recluse, spending his days in prayer and meditation on an
island some distance offshore. Few of us will feel called to
quite such an austere way of life, but we can learn something
from their example, for there are times when we too need
to get away from it all, if only for a few moments, in order
to hear God's voice. It's not that he's removed from the
daily round of life – far from it – but sometimes pressures
can build up in such a way that they obscure his presence.
When writing this book, for example, there have been
many times when I struggled for inspiration, becoming
increasingly agitated when none was forthcoming. At one
time, I would have soldiered on regardless, spending hours
and even a whole day on one paragraph, yet getting
nowhere. Experience, though, has taught me to get up and
walk away; to take a stroll in the garden, or to reflect on a
different passage, or simply to spend a few moments doing
nothing. Through stepping back, I am able to step forward.

It is noticeable that Jesus himself, at key moments in his life, made time for quietness, drawing away from the crowds, spending time alone high in the hills so that he could focus on the presence of God, away from the innumerable pressures and demands put upon him. It is not always easy to do that, I know. When the children are screaming and there's a pile of washing-up to see to, when there's another meeting to attend and another deadline to meet, stepping back can seem a luxury we can ill afford. Yet, the fact is, it is a necessity; a step we sometimes need to make if we are to have any hope of progressing further.

Ask yourself
Is it time you let go of something you are wrestling with and handed it over to God? Do you make enough time in your life to step back so that God can lead you forward?

Pray
Living God, in the rush and bustle of each day I all too often lose sight of you, my mind occupied by the responsibilities, demands and difficulties confronting me. Instead of turning to you, I get sucked in ever deeper, getting these out of all perspective and denying myself the strength I need to meet them.

Teach me to find time for you, if only for a few moments, so that I may hear your voice and discern your will. Teach me to step back and take stock, so that I may then step forward, renewed in faith, strengthened in spirit, and equipped for whatever you may ask, in Jesus' name. Amen.

Remember
Now, more than ever, the word spread about Jesus, and large crowds would gather to hear him and be healed of their illnesses, but he would withdraw to remote places and pray.   *Luke 5:15-16*

Close
Living God, help me to find time for you, and so to find time for all. Amen.

685

An unfading hope

Read

When the chief shepherd appears, you will win the crown of glory that never fades away.   *1 Peter 5:4 (NRSV)*

Ponder

It was a fascinating display – a wonderful collection of tools and machinery from years gone by. Steam engines, ploughs, tractors, threshing machines, wagons and horse-drawn carriages, and much more – a wonderful reminder of yesteryear. It struck me, though, walking round and looking at the dates of the various items, that yesteryear was not so long ago. The earliest vehicle was barely a century old; in other words, dating back just a couple of generations. What today are obsolete museum pieces would have been state-of-the-art technology in my great-grandparents' time, the treasured possession of some proud new owner. It was a stark reminder of the transience of life and the pace of change.

What a contrast between that and the hope of the gospel, as summed up in those words above. New life in Christ is not here today and gone tomorrow but is a gift for all eternity. Though everything else may change, it will not. Though generations come and go, it remains the same. The promises of God will not tarnish, and our hope will never fade, for the kingdom of God, unlike this world, is built to last; to endure not simply for our brief lifespan but for all eternity.

Ask yourself

In which does your hope ultimately rest: this life or the life to come?

Pray

Eternal God, I praise you for the faithfulness of your love and the constancy of your purpose. I thank you that though all else may change, you stay the same; that though heaven and earth may pass away, your word endures for ever.

Teach me to live each moment in the light of that assurance, recognising that your promises in Christ will never fail and that the new life he has won for me will never fade. Help me to enjoy all the many blessings of this life, celebrating everything you have so richly given, but help me finally to put my trust in your eternal kingdom; in the one hope that will never disappoint me. Through Jesus Christ my Lord. Amen.

Remember

This is what he has promised us: eternal life.

1 John 2:25 (NRSV)

Close

Living God, in all the fluctuating fortunes of this life, teach me that your love and the life you hold for me in Christ endures for ever. Amen.

As white as snow

Read

Come now, let us talk this through together, says the Lord:
though your sins are like scarlet, they will be as white as
snow; though they are red like crimson, they will become
like wool.   *Isaiah 1:18*

Ponder

Are you the sort of person who dreams of a white Christmas?
I am. Yes, I know snow can be a nuisance and a hazard, but
I just can't help myself. There's something magical about
the way a heavy snowfall transforms the world into a picture
postcard scene, like something from a Christmas card or a
fairy story. It doesn't last, of course. Before long, it's churned
up into piles of slush and muddy footprints, but for a few
moments all the greyness and ugliness of winter disappear.

For me, that idea is echoed in those unforgettable words
of the prophet Isaiah. We all know that our lives are not
what they could and should be, that there is so much which
prevents us from being the people that God intended. Yet,
says the prophet, with God's help things can change, not
by our own efforts but through his grace. If we are ready to
turn to him and admit our mistakes, he is ready to forgive
and wipe the slate clean. No doubt, we will soon muddy
the picture again, just as with that fresh fall of snow, but
this time it is different, for the offer is always there to start
again, however often we may fail.

Ask yourself

Have you lost sight of the unreserved forgiveness God
offers to all in Christ? Does that still make you catch your
breath in wonder?

Pray

Almighty God, I have no claim on your love and no right
to expect forgiveness, yet you constantly reach out in love,

eager to forgive and forget. Day after day, your nature is to have mercy, putting the past behind me and helping me to begin again. I thank you for the awesomeness of your love and I ask for your help in opening my life to your redeeming grace.

Teach me to confess my sins and to commit myself again to your service, and so may I receive the cleansing, renewal and forgiveness you alone can bring. Through Christ my Saviour. Amen.

Remember

Sprinkle me with hyssop, and I will be clean; wash me, and I will become whiter than snow.   *Psalm 51:7*

Close

Lord, forgive what I am and have been, and bless what I shall be, to the glory of your name. Amen.

Only human?

Read

God is greater than any human being.   *Job 33:12*

Ponder

'Oh well, we're only human.' I expect we have all heard words similar to those more often than we can begin to remember. The fact that we are 'only human' is taken to explain, and indeed even justify, all kinds of foolish actions and errors of judgement. Few of us would argue with the assertion that human nature, despite all its potential for good, is fundamentally flawed. Yet, are we right to talk about being *only* human? Some passages in scripture seem to suggest so, none more than the bald statement above from the book of Job. In fact, throughout the Old Testament, and also in the New, there is a strand of tradition asserting the total sovereignty of God – the fact that he is unlike any other, beyond human comprehension, so holy that no one can see God and live.

Surely, then, there can be no argument. Well, not quite, for there are also passages like Genesis 1 speaking of God creating humankind in his own image; or Luke 12:7 in which Jesus speaks so eloquently of the value God places on each one of us; or Psalm 8 where human beings are said to be just a little lower than God himself. God, in other words, doesn't see us as *only* human but as wonderfully so, lovingly fashioned by his hands and infinitely important. Yes, we all know what we mean by the expression 'we're only human', but don't let's push it too far and, above all, don't let's allow it to colour our understanding of what it means to be human. We all have our faults, but we all also have our worth, our strengths and our God-given potential. Though *we* may sometimes overlook that, God never will.

Ask yourself

Do you use being 'only human' to excuse your weaknesses and mistakes, or do you strive to fulfil your human potential in Christ?

Pray

Living God, I am guilty sometimes of overstepping my humanity, minimising the gulf between us and setting myself up in your place. Yet, at other times I am guilty of the opposite mistake, devaluing my humanity and belittling that of others. I see weakness rather than strength, failure rather than potential, and errors rather than achievements. I write people off rather than recognise their true worth; I expect the worst rather than believe the best; I fail to appreciate all that you are able to do in people's lives, including my own.

Living God, I understand so little of what it means to be human. Speak to me now and in glimpsing your greatness may I discern more clearly my own worth and the worth of all. In Jesus' name I ask it. Amen.

Remember

When I gaze at the heavens, your handiwork, the moon and stars that you brought into being, what are human beings that you should consider them, mortals that you value them? Yet, you have made them scarcely lower than God and crowned them with glory and honour. You have given them authority over your creation and put all things under their feet.   *Psalm 8:3-6*

Close

Living God, teach me to value both others and myself as much as you value us all. Teach me to respect what it means to be human and so to consecrate everything that I am to your service, in the name of Christ. Amen.

Glimpsing the kingdom

Read

The disciples approached him and asked, 'Why do you speak to them in parables?' He answered, 'Because though it has been given to you to know the secrets of the kingdom of heaven, it has not been given to them, yet those who have will have much more given to them, whereas those who have next to nothing will lose even that. In other words, I speak in parables, because though they look they see nothing, and though they hear they neither listen nor understand. In them is fulfilled the prophecy of Isaiah saying: "You will hear but not understand, and see yet not perceive. For this people's heart has grown complacent, their ears hard of hearing, and their eyes closed; they see nothing, hear nothing and understand nothing that might make them turn to me so that I might heal them." Blessed, though, are your eyes, for they see, and your ears, for they hear. I tell you this, many prophets and righteous people longed to see what you see, but did not see it, and to hear what you hear, but did not hear it.'

Matthew 13:10-17

Ponder

'Much of what we see depends on what we are looking for.' In other words, we often miss something that is staring us in the face, either because we are closed to the possibility of seeing it or because we are preoccupied with something else. Jesus was aware of that problem, his use of parables designed to break through people's preconceptions so that they might see the world in a new light.

That need is as real today as ever, especially when it comes to understanding the kingdom of God. All too easily, we relegate that kingdom to some far-off place and time. Certainly, the final consummation of God's purpose must come later, but, as Jesus proclaimed at the very start of his ministry, 'The time is fulfilled, and the kingdom of God has come near' (Mark 1:15). The fact is that the kingdom has already dawned, if only we have eyes to see it. Like yeast or a mustard seed, it is slowly growing, its presence evidenced in countless lives being changed every day, in numerous expressions of love and service, in the work and worship of the Church, and in so much more. As well, then, as looking to the future and praying 'Come, Lord, come', we need to nurture the seeds that Jesus has already sown, ensuring we do all in our power, through his grace, to see them grow.

Ask yourself
Are there ways in which you unconsciously dismiss this world, looking instead to a world to come?

Pray
Gracious God, you do not want me to see your kingdom as a time and a place confined to the distant future; you want me to recognise that it is already present and to commit myself to helping it grow here on earth. Inspire me through all those who have caught a vision of what life can be, and who have had the faith and dedication to translate that vision into reality. Help me to learn from them and to understand that you are at work in this world. Teach me to offer my service, as best I may, working with your people everywhere to see your will done and your kingdom come in all its glory. Through Christ my Lord. Amen.

Remember
Despite not having seen him, you love him; and although you do not yet see him, you believe in him and rejoice with an inexpressible and wonderful joy, for you are obtaining the fruits of your faith, the salvation of your souls.

1 Peter 1:8-9

Close
Living God, open my eyes to all you are doing now, and so may I glimpse all you shall yet do. Through Christ my Lord. Amen.

The light of life

Read

In him was life, and that life was the light of all. The light shines in the darkness, and the darkness could not overcome it.

John 1:4-5

Ponder

During my time with Toc H, a charity dedicated to breaking down barriers of prejudice and intolerance in society, I was privileged to visit the place where the movement started: Talbot House, in Belgium. It was here that the Revd Philip Clayton, known affectionately as 'Tubby' to friends and colleagues, started a club for soldiers serving in the front line, a club open to all – irrespective of colour, culture, creed or rank – that was to shine as a beacon of light in a world that seemed to have been plunged into darkness.

Walking today among the mass rows of gravestones that dominate the landscape in that part of Belgium, it is astonishing that anyone managed to keep hope and faith alive amid scenes of such dreadful carnage, yet somehow the light could not be extinguished. As Tubby Clayton put it, 'All the darkness in the world cannot extinguish the light of one candle' – another way of expressing those wonderful words from the beginning of John's Gospel.

There is much in life that seems to suggest sometimes that darkness has gained the upper hand and that evil has defeated good, but faith reminds us that from the darkness of Calvary dawned the day of resurrection – light that can never be extinguished. However dark life may seem, God has promised that his light will ultimately break through.

Ask yourself

Do you find it hard sometimes to keep believing, faced by so much apparent darkness in the world? Do you still hold on to the conviction that God's light will shine through?

Pray

Gracious God, I read in scripture of light shining in the darkness, yet sometimes the reality appears very different. Day after day, I hear stories of poverty, sickness, sorrow and suffering – some from far afield, some on my own door-step. All around me there seems to be so much injustice and oppression, hatred and evil. I try to trust in your purpose, but the reality of this world seems to belie your love and contradict the gospel.

Reach out, I pray, wherever there is darkness, and grant that the light of your love may shine in my heart and in the hearts of all, to the glory of your name. Amen.

Remember

The people who walked in darkness have seen a great light; those who lived in a land of deep darkness – on them light has shined. For a child has been born for us, a son given to us; authority rests upon his shoulders; and he is named Wonderful Counsellor, Mighty God, Everlasting Father, Prince of Peace. His authority shall grow continually, and there will be endless peace for the throne of David and his kingdom. He will establish and uphold it with justice and with righteousness from this time onward and for evermore. The zeal of the Lord of hosts will do this.

Isaiah 9:2, 6-7 (NRSV)

Close

Gracious God, even when all seems dark, teach me that your light will always shine through. Amen.

An unwelcome surprise

Read

You have exhausted the Lord with all your talk, yet you ask, 'In what way have we wearied him?' By claiming that those who do evil are good in the sight of the Lord, and that he takes pleasure in them, and by asking, 'Where is the God of justice?' 'Look,' says the Lord of hosts, 'I am sending my messenger to prepare the way for me, so that the Lord whom you seek will suddenly come to his temple. The messenger of the covenant whom you so eagerly anticipate is coming, but who can endure the day of his coming or stand when he appears? For he is like a refiner's fire and fullers' soap; he will preside as a refiner and purifier of silver, and he will purify the descendants of Levi. I will approach you in judgement, and be swift to bear witness against the sorcerers, the adulterers and those who bear false witness; against those who exploit their hired workers, the widow and the orphan, who thrust aside the alien, and who do not fear me,' says the Lord of hosts.   *Malachi 2:17-3:3a, 5*

Ponder

Anyone who has ever listened to Handel's *Messiah* will be familiar with those words of the prophet Malachi. They make sobering reading, not least because those to whom they were first addressed were convinced they were more than ready to welcome God's promised deliverer, and assured of his approval when he came. From Malachi came the call to think again – a warning that the day of the Lord would be anything but welcome. Why? Because their lives were a pale shadow of what the Messiah would expect from them. Their expectation of God's blessing had become divorced from their daily lives, and the result, warned the prophet, would be an unpleasant shock.

There is a danger that we today can make the same mistake. We may believe that we are ready to face God's judgement, whenever and however that may come, but before we sit back complacently we would do well to examine our consciences, assess our lifestyles and ask whether everything in our life is quite as it should be. Fail to do that, and we may find the day of the Lord not quite the occasion we like to imagine.

Ask yourself

How far does the service you offer to Jesus measure up to the faith you profess in him? If he were to walk into the room tomorrow, would he recognise you as one of his followers?

Pray

Lord Jesus Christ, you call me to test myself and to ensure that I am still in the faith. Help me to take that challenge seriously, for I so easily imagine all is well when much in fact is wrong. I talk of listening to *your* voice, but hear what *I* want to hear. I speak of seeking *your* will, yet prefer *my* way, expecting you to conform to *my* expectations.

Draw close to me and fill me with your Spirit, so that my faith may be as real and as fresh today as the moment I first believed. Prepare me for your coming again, so that I may be ready to receive you and found faithful in your service, to the glory of your name. Amen.

Remember

For this very reason you should make every effort to support your faith with goodness, and goodness with knowledge, and knowledge with self-control, and self-control with endurance, and endurance with godliness, and godliness with mutual affection, and mutual affection with love. For if these things are yours and are increasing among you, they keep you from being ineffective and unfruitful in the knowledge of our Lord Jesus Christ.   *2 Peter 1:5-8 (NRSV)*

Close

Living God, save me from a life that proclaims one thing, but displays another. Amen.

DECEMBER

Vision for the future

Read

The wolf shall live with the lamb, the leopard shall lie down with the kid, the calf and the lion and the fatling together, and a little child will lead them. The cow and the bear shall graze, and their young lie down together; and the lion shall eat straw like the ox. The nursing child shall play over the hole of the asp, and the weaned child will put its hand on the adder's den. They will not hurt or destroy on all my holy mountain; for the earth will be full of the knowledge of the Lord as the waters cover the sea.

Isaiah 11:6-9 (NRSV)

Ponder

A vision of the future or sentimental nonsense? What do you make of these words of Isaiah? Are they poetic imagery or prophetic foresight? In terms of this life, at least, both those appraisals contain an element of truth. In recent years we have seen startling moves towards peace in some quarters of the world, yet there have also been unspeakable atrocities and mind-boggling inhumanity. Sadly, for every reason to hope there seems to be still more cause to despair, and, eventually, disillusionment sets in. We'd like to believe in a world such as the prophet paints – a new age of peace and harmony when violence, discord and hatred will be a thing of the past – but most of us take such claims with a strong pinch of salt. Life, we tell ourselves, is just not like that.

Such an attitude is understandable given the lamentable record of human history and the continuing divisions in our world today, yet it cannot finally be acceptable. *We* may abandon the world to its fate – God never will. He will not rest until his will is done and his kingdom established, on earth as it is in heaven. It may seem light years away from the world as we know it today, but we must never lose that vision of what life can become, nor stop working towards it.

Ask yourself

Is there any hope of Isaiah's vision being fulfilled in this world, or must it wait until the world to come? What practical steps can you take to promote peace and reconciliation?

Pray

Gracious God, I look at the world sometimes, and I despair. I see its greed, corruption, hatred and violence, and I can't help asking, 'How will it ever change?' I want to believe, and occasionally my hopes are rekindled by moves towards peace, yet it is hard to keep faith when, time after time, such initiatives come to nothing.

Gracious God, help me to recognise that my way of looking at the world is not the same as your way, and that where I see no prospect of change, you are able to transform situations beyond recognition. Teach me never to lose sight of all that you are able to do and all that you are already doing. Inspire me, therefore, to pray for and, in my own small way, work towards peace and reconciliation. Through Jesus Christ my Lord. Amen.

Remember

Then I saw a new heaven and a new earth; for the first heaven and the first earth had passed away, and the sea was no more. And I heard a loud voice from the throne saying, 'See, the home of God is among mortals. He will dwell with them; they will be his peoples, and God himself will be with them; he will wipe every tear from their eyes. Death will be no more; mourning and crying and pain will be no more, for the first things have passed away.'

Revelation 21:1, 3-4 (NRSV)

Close

Sovereign God, I have asked it so many times before, but I ask it again, together with all your people: 'Your kingdom come, your will be done, on earth as it is in heaven.' Amen.

Be prepared

Read

As for times and seasons, my friends, there is no need to write to you, for you are well aware that the day of the Lord will come upon you as a thief in the night. Just when people are saying, 'Relax, all is well', destruction will strike them as labour pains grip hold of a pregnant woman, and no one will escape. You, though, my friends, are not in the darkness such that the day should overtake you like a thief, for you are all children of light and of the day rather than of night and darkness. So, then, do not sleep like others, but be watchful and clear-headed. Those who sleep, do so in the hours of darkness just like those who get drunk, but since we are of the day let us remain clear-headed, putting on the breastplate of salvation through our Lord Jesus Christ, who died for us so that, whether we wake or sleep, we shall live together with him.   *1 Thessalonians 5:1-10*

Ponder

'Be prepared!' Two words that all Scouts, past or present, will have indelibly printed on their minds. In theory, they should never be caught short, ready instead to respond to every eventuality. But life, of course, has a habit of catching us on the hop, and although that can be a problem, it is also a blessing. Imagine how dull life would be if we could know everything that was going to happen and had exhausted its ability to offer new horizons and experiences.

It is not just life, however, that can surprise us but, above all, God. Take, for example, his coming to the world in Christ. For years, the people of Israel had looked forward to his coming, yet when the moment arrived many failed to see it. They thought they understood what God would do and were unprepared for anything else. The words of Paul to the Thessalonians suggest that *we* can do much the same. At first sight, they seem to be concerned simply with the return of Christ, but that is to miss the point, for Paul stresses that we do not know when that day will be, or what it will involve. We should live each day in a sense of expectation, recognising that God is at work in a host of ways, constantly able to surprise us. Do that and whenever Christ comes we will be ready to meet him. Strictly speaking, we can't be prepared for the unexpected, but we can be open to the possibility that God may speak to us and work through us in ways we have not even begun to imagine. Be prepared!

Ask yourself

Do you still expect God to reveal new things about himself? Are you open to your faith being stretched and your experience of his love deepened?

Pray

Lord Jesus Christ, I remember today that though your people looked forward for so long to your coming, many were not prepared, failing to recognise you when you came.

Forgive me that I am equally closed sometimes to your coming into my life, forcing you into a mould I have made for you, presuming your thoughts and your ways are the same as mine. Forgive me that my expectations are small and limited, shaped by looking at life from a human rather than eternal perspective. Forgive me, and help me to be prepared. Teach me to examine myself – my words and deeds, thoughts and attitudes – and so to live each day open to what you would do in me and through me, to the glory of your name. Amen.

Remember

A voice crying in the wilderness, 'Prepare a way for the Lord; make ready a straight path for him.'   *Luke 3:4*

Close

Lord Jesus Christ, prepare my heart to welcome you now, and so may I be ready to welcome you when you come again. Amen.

From small beginnings

Read

From you, Bethlehem of Ephrathah, small though you may be among the clans of Judah, shall emerge one who is to rule in Israel, whose roots go back into history, from the earliest of times. Therefore, he will give up his people only until the time when she who is in labour bears a child; then the remnant of his people will return to their kinsfolk in Israel. He will stand and feed his flock in the strength of the Lord, in the majesty of the name of the Lord his God. Thus, they will live in safety, for at that time his greatness will extend to the ends of the earth; and he will be the man of peace.

Micah 5:2-5a

Ponder

'Every oak has been an acorn.' 'Small is the seed of every greatness.' 'Great weights hang on small wires.' 'Great engines turn on small pivots.' These are just some of the innumerable proverbs reminding us that unpromising beginnings need not be a barrier to success; and that, similarly, is a theme which runs throughout the Old Testament, from Moses taking on the might of Egypt to David killing Goliath, from Elijah triumphing over the prophets of Baal to Daniel facing up to the terrors of the lions' den.

The prophet Micah adds one more unforgettable picture to the list in the little town of Bethlehem. It is hard today to appreciate how extraordinary it must have seemed to hear God's promised Messiah associated with this insignificant town, notwithstanding its associations with King David. Jerusalem, surely, was the only place fitting for someone of such stature! In human terms, this may have been true, but not in God's. As so often before and since, God proves himself to be a God of the unexpected. In his kingdom the first invariably find themselves last, and the last first.

Ask yourself

Are there times when you have surprised yourself by achieving something you thought yourself incapable of even attempting? Are you guilty sometimes of judging strength and success by outside appearances?

Pray

Sovereign God, time and again you have overturned human expectations, using the most unlikely of people in yet more unlikely surroundings. You have shown beyond doubt that no situation or person is outside the scope of your purpose – that each one can be used by you.

Teach me, then, to be open to everything you would do through those around me, and to recognise also all you can do through me, working in ways I would never dare to contemplate and can scarcely imagine. Sovereign God, you recognise the potential of everyone and everything – help me to do the same. Amen.

Remember

To what can we liken the kingdom of God, or what parable can we use to explain it? Think of it as a mustard seed. When sown in the soil, there is no seed on earth smaller, yet, having once been sown, it shoots up and becomes the greatest of all shrubs, putting out branches so large the birds of the air can make nests in its cover.   *Mark 4:30-32*

Close

Living God, teach me that you can do more with a little than I could hope to achieve had I the whole world at my disposal. Amen.

Called to account

Read

At that time I will search Jerusalem with a lantern, and I will punish those who sit smugly over the last of their wine, assuring themselves, 'The Lord won't do anything to us, either good or bad.' Their wealth shall be plundered, and their homes laid waste. Though they build houses, they will never live in them; though they plant vineyards, they will drink no wine from them. The great day of the Lord draws near, rushing ever closer upon us; the sound of that day will be bitter, and the warrior will cry aloud there. It will be a day of wrath, of misery and hardship, ruin and desolation – a day of clouds and thick darkness, of trumpet blast and battle cry against the fortified cities and lofty battlements.   *Zephaniah 1:12-16*

Ponder

The older one gets, the more one comes to recognise that life isn't fair. The heady idealism of youth gives way to the hard-headed realism of middle age, as the truth slowly dawns that, in this life at least, people don't always get what they deserve. Honesty may be the best policy when it comes to peace of mind, but it is not necessarily the most lucrative; the unpleasant truth is that all too often cheats *do* prosper.

Coming to terms with facts like this is a painful business and one that can test faith to the limit, just as it did in the time of Zephaniah. There were many in his day who, faced by the apparent injustices of life, concluded that God was either disinterested in human affairs or powerless to intervene. It was an understandable mistake, but one that the prophet had no time for. In God's time, he warns, justice will be done, and seen to be done by all. We lose sight of that at our peril.

Ask yourself

Do you think God's justice is reserved for a Last Judgement and future life, or is there a sense in which he calls people to account for their actions today? How would you fare if you were called to account now for your actions?

Pray

Sovereign God, I cannot help wondering sometimes about the justice of life. I see so much that is wrong, so much that I cannot make sense of, and I ask myself why you stand by and let it happen. Day after day, I watch helplessly as truth is trodden underfoot, love exploited, and the innocent suffer, while those who least deserve it seem to flourish.

Help me, confronted by such enigmas, not to lose heart. Teach me to recognise that loving you brings its own rewards, greater than any this world can offer, and remind me also that the time will come when everyone will answer to you, and justice will prevail. Amen.

Remember

Everyone will have to give an account to him who stands ready to judge the living and the dead.   *1 Peter 4:5*

Close

Lord Jesus Christ, teach me to live each day in such a manner that I would be happy for you to walk in and find me. For your name's sake. Amen.

The fullness of time

Read

In the fullness of time, God sent his own Son, born of a woman and born under the law, so that we who were subjects of the law might be redeemed, and, through adoption, become his children.   *Galatians 4:4-5*

Ponder

Some people claim that there could have been no more opportune moment for the coming of Jesus than the time God actually chose. The Roman empire, they argue, brought unparalleled peace and stability, an opportunity to travel as never before, and an intermingling of cultures that brought an openness to new ideas – just the sort of world in which the gospel could quickly spread. It's a beguiling argument, but it doesn't work, for the fact is there are many other times in history for which an equally strong case could be made. If Jesus had come today, for example, how much more of an impact might he have made? Using modern technology, he could have relayed his message around the world in seconds. Instead of preaching to small crowds on the hillside, he could have addressed whole nations live by satellite. Surely, if any era qualifies for the label 'the fullness of time', it should be the twenty-first century!

Yet God didn't choose this or any other date we might suggest – he chose that day in the reign of the Emperor Augustus when Mary and Joseph had gone to Bethlehem to be taxed. Why then? We cannot say, for we do not know the workings of God's mind. His timing is of his choosing, no one else's. There is a lesson here concerning not just the birth of Christ but the whole of life. We may wonder some-times why our prayers are not answered as quickly as we would like. Equally, we may find that God is calling us to grasp the moment when we want to hang back, reluctant to commit ourselves. Advent reminds us that God's timetable and ours may not be the same, and it asks us if we are ready to put his timing first.

Ask yourself

Do you feel impatient with God sometimes, or do you feel, on the contrary, that he is pushing you too fast? Is it time you considered his timetable, rather than your own?

Pray

Eternal God, ruler over space and time, before all, in all, and beyond all, I worship and acknowledge you, recognising afresh that your ways are not my ways nor your thoughts my thoughts. Forgive me for sometimes losing sight of that fact, presuming that *I* know better than you; even expecting you to do my bidding rather than me do yours. Teach me that you are beyond my greatest imagining, higher than my loftiest dreams, and that you do things in your own way and time.

Teach me, then, to trust in your timing even when it conflicts with my own; to accept my part in your scheme of things, and to leave the rest to you. Through Jesus Christ my Lord. Amen.

Remember

It has pleased him to make known to us the mystery of his will, set forth in Christ – that, in the fullness of time, he might unite all things, in heaven and on earth, in him.

Ephesians 1:9-10

Close

Living God, help me to recognise that what may seem the right time may be wrong, and what may seem the wrong time may be right. Teach me to seek your guidance, and to respond as you direct. Amen.

The rising sun

Read

The sun will rise over us from heaven, to shine on those sitting in darkness and in the shadow of death; to guide our feet into the way of peace.   *Luke 1:78-79*

Ponder

There's something wonderful about dawn, isn't there? It speaks of new beginnings, a fresh start – another day set before us, full of promise and opportunity. It is precisely ideas such as these that lie behind the wonderful words of Zechariah in Luke's Gospel; words that capture something of the wonder, joy and hope associated with the coming of Christ. Here was one who would bring joy where there was sorrow, hope where there was despair, love where there was hatred, and peace where there was division; not just a fresh chapter in history but also the possibility of a similar renewal in every human life that can only be compared to the rising of the sun; a new dawn!

That is what God offers to you and me today, to anyone and everyone willing to turn to Christ; a fresh start, a new day, and though darkness may sometimes seem to threaten once again, this sun will never set, but go on shining for all eternity.

Ask yourself

Have you opened your life to the light of Christ? Do you, through him, see each moment as a new beginning?

Pray

Loving God, I praise you that the light which dawned in the life of Zechariah and Elizabeth, that transformed the future for Mary and Joseph and that lit up the sky on the night of the Saviour's birth, continues to shine today. I thank you for the new beginning you have brought in my life, and the light that continues to guide me.

Teach me to walk in that light day by day, and so may each moment be a new dawn, a new beginning, rich in promise and filled by your love. Through Jesus Christ my Lord. Amen.

Remember

There will be no more night, nor the light of lamp or sun, for the Lord God will be their light, and they will reign for evermore. *Revelation 22:5*

Close

Lord Jesus Christ, may the flame of faith burn brightly within me, and your light shine in my heart, so that I, in turn, may bring light to others, to the glory of your name. Amen.

Believing the impossible

Read

An angel of the Lord appeared to Zechariah, standing on the right-hand side of the altar of incense. On seeing him, Zechariah was awestruck and paralysed by fear, but the angel said to him, 'Don't be frightened, Zechariah, for your plea has been heard. Your wife Elizabeth will bear you a son, and you are to call him John. He will bring you joy and gladness, and many will rejoice at his birth, for he will be great in the eyes of the Lord. He will turn many of the people of Israel to the Lord their God, and he will go out in the spirit and power of Elijah to turn the hearts of parents to their children, and those who have gone astray to the wisdom of the righteous – to prepare people so that they are ready for the Lord.' Zechariah said to the angel, 'How can I know this is true? For I am an old man, and my wife also is getting on in years.' The angel replied, 'I am Gabriel. I stand in God's presence, and he has sent me to tell you this good news, but now, since you have not believed my words that in due course will be fulfilled, you will be struck dumb, rendered mute until the day these things happen.'

Luke 1:11-15a, 16-20

Ponder

'Impossible! It can't be done!' That was the response of Zechariah to the news that his wife Elizabeth was to give birth to a son. Whether she was beyond childbearing years is not clear, but there is no doubt that any hopes the couple might have had of her conceiving were long since gone. They were reconciled to their disappointment, so, to be told that a child was to be born to them after all must have seemed too good to be true. From a human point of view, it was a perfectly understandable response, but here we are talking about God. That is what Zechariah failed to account for, and that is what made all the difference, for with God all things are possible.

Do we believe that? There will be times when we find God's promises hard to accept; times when we look at our life or the life of the world, and we feel that both are beyond redemption. Humanly speaking, that again is perfectly understandable, but once more we fail to account for God – the God who lived and died among us in Christ, raising him from the tomb; the God who has repeatedly shown that nothing is beyond him, however much it may seem beyond us!

Ask yourself

Have you set limits to what God is able to do? Have you lost your sense of his sovereign power and purpose?

Pray

Loving God, for all my protestations of faith there are some things I consider to be not only beyond me but beyond you as well. Hope says one thing but realism another, and in consequence I set limits on the way you are able to work in my life. Forgive me for doubting your power and questioning your ability to work in my life. Remind me of the way you have overturned human expectations throughout history, demonstrating that all things are possible for those who love you.

Teach me, then, to look beyond the obvious and immediate, and to live in the light of your sovereign grace, which is able to do far more than I can ever ask or imagine; through Christ my Lord. Amen.

Remember

What is impossible for people is possible for God.

Luke 18:27

Close

Living God, though I can do nothing, teach me that you can do everything. Through Christ my Lord. Amen.

Preparing the way

Read

The angel said, 'Don't be frightened, Zechariah, for your plea has been heard. Your wife Elizabeth will bear a son, and you are to call him John. He will turn many of the people of Israel to the Lord their God, and he will go out in the spirit and power of Elijah, to turn the hearts of parents to their children, and those who have gone astray to the wisdom of the righteous; to make ready a people prepared for the Lord.'
Luke 1:13, 16-17

Ponder

Go to watch any star or celebrity in concert, and, almost certainly, they will have a supporting cast. Turn to the first two chapters of the gospel of Luke, and you will find something rather similar. The chapters are concerned primarily with the birth of Jesus, but there's another birth entwined with his, another character who figures prominently in his story, and that, of course, is John the Baptist. In fact, John is given a mention in the early chapters of all four gospels, so, clearly, his role was important, but what exactly was that role and what can we learn from it?

The answer is very simple, and it's there in those words from Luke, chapter 1: 'to make ready a people prepared for the Lord.' This was John's task: to prepare the way of Christ; not in the sense of being a warm-up act, but rather as one who would get people ready to welcome Jesus when he came. For John that was to mean speaking out concerning the kingdom Christ would bring. It meant also following a distinctive lifestyle to reinforce his message. It meant pointing away from himself and towards Jesus. The lesson for today could hardly be clearer. We need to echo John's example in our own lives. Like him, we are called to prepare the way of Christ so that others today may meet him for themselves.

Ask yourself

What are you doing to prepare the way of Christ? Does your life testify to your faith?

Pray

Lord Jesus Christ, I thank you for all those who prepared the way for your coming, both in Bethlehem and in countless hearts since that day. I think especially of John the Baptist – his courage to speak the truth no matter what the cost; his readiness to point away from himself and towards your light; his willingness to live in such a way that everything he did testified to the truth of his message in a manner that words alone could never do.

Help me to prepare your way in turn, witnessing to your renewing power and demonstrating your compassion, so that the hearts of many may be ready to receive you today. In your name I ask it. Amen.

Remember

You, child, will be called the prophet of the Most High; for you will pave the way of the Lord, to bring knowledge of salvation to his people through the forgiveness of their sins.

Luke 1:76-77

Close

Lord Jesus Christ, make me always ready to serve you, and so may I prepare the hearts of others to welcome you. Amen.

Rediscovering the word

Read

While they were fetching the silver that had been brought into the house of the Lord, the priest Hilkiah discovered the book of the law of the Lord that had been given through Moses. Hilkiah said to the secretary Shaphan, 'I have discovered the book of the law in the house of the Lord'; and he gave the book to Shaphan who brought the book to the king and informed him, 'The priest Hilkiah has given me a book, and he read it out aloud to the king. When the king heard what was in the book of the law, he tore his clothes, saying, 'Great is the anger of the Lord, poured out on us because our forebears did not obey the commandments of the Lord or do what is written in this book.'
2 Chronicles 34:14-16b, 18b-19, 21b

Ponder

Reading the Bible today is something we take for granted, all too literally. We have all kinds of translations to choose from, and a host of material designed to help us better understand whatever passage we are reading. Most of us will have a Bible in our home, if not several, but how often do we make time to read it? In all too many households, the Bible is left to gather dust, serving more as a talisman than a word to live by.

If that is true for us, we do well to consider the reaction of Josiah when, early in his reign, the book of the law was discovered in the temple, having been hidden away there and forgotten for many years. A regrettable oversight, some might have called it, but not Josiah. For him it was a calamity that had immediately to be addressed, for in his eyes this neglect of God's word was tantamount to throwing one of God's most precious gifts back into his face. Are we guilty of doing the same today? A Bible sitting on the shelf helps no one; it's reading it that counts!

Ask yourself

Do you still make time to read the Bible? Do you just skim through a few verses or do you make time to study it, asking what it is saying to you?

Pray

Gracious God, you have spoken not just through the law, but through the prophets, through words of wisdom, history and psalms, and through the testimony of Evangelists and Apostles to Jesus Christ, the Word made flesh. I can turn to the Bible whenever I wish to and read it freely in my own tongue. I can read new translations that help bring the age-old message to life, and I have access to all kinds of resources designed to deepen my understanding of what I read.

Forgive me that all too often I leave your word sitting on a shelf, unopened, unexplored. Help me to recognise the priceless treasure you have given me in the scriptures, and teach me in the clamour of each day to make time to read them reverently and thoughtfully, so that your voice may speak again, offering light to my path and the way to life in all its fullness. Amen.

Remember

So now I commend you to God and to the message of his grace, a message that is able to build you up, and to give you the inheritance among all who are sanctified.

Acts 20:32 (NRSV)

Close

Living God, you have given me the word of life; forgive me that I fail to read it and then wonder why you fail to speak to me. Amen.

God's active word

Read

'I am God, and there is no other. I am God and there is none like me, pronouncing the end at the beginning and speaking at the dawn of time of things yet to be done, proclaiming, 'My will shall prevail, and I will fulfil my purpose. I have spoken, and I will make it happen; I have planned, and I will accomplish it.'

Isaiah 46:9-10, 11b

Ponder

Look at the label on any medicine and you will see there a list of active ingredients. Without them, your prescription would be useless, a mere placebo. There is a parallel here with the words of Isaiah, the prophet able to speak with conviction of the ultimate fulfilment of God's purpose because he knew that when God says he will do something he does it, his word always active! There is never any question of him saying one thing and doing another, making a promise and then forgetting to honour it. He is wholly dependable, a God in whom we can put our trust.

That is the truth we celebrate at Advent and Christmas. These are seasons concerned with what God has done – not just what he promised but what he achieved! They speak of the God who has acted decisively in human history, wonderfully and unmistakably putting his words into practice! God didn't just wish the world well and then leave it to get on with its own affairs. He didn't just tell us what we need to do and then expect us to struggle on as best we can. He didn't give fine-sounding promises that remained only promises. He revealed love in action, the Word made flesh. That living Word continues to be active today, in our lives and in our world, and, through him, we know indeed that what God has pledged to do, he will accomplish!

Ask yourself

Do you expect God to act in your life? Do you read God's word, believing that it continues to have the power to speak and change lives today?

Pray

Sovereign God, I thank you that you are a God I can depend on, a God in whom I can put my trust. What you promise, you do; what you purpose, you accomplish. Throughout history you have honoured your promises, and above all in the coming of Jesus, and his living, dying and rising among us. I thank you for everything that means for me today – for the assurance it brings that I can live each moment with confidence, knowing that, though all else may fail, you will not; though heaven and earth may pass away, your words will endure for ever.

So I put my trust in you, secure in your love, confident in your eternal purpose and assured that your will shall be done. Receive my thanks, in the name of Christ. Amen.

Remember

The Word became flesh and lived among us, and we have seen his glory, the glory as of a father's only son, full of grace and truth.   *John 1:14*

Close

Living God, teach me to trust that you will do everything that you have promised, your word continuing to work in my life and the life of the world until your purpose has been fulfilled. Amen.

God's living word

Read

For, as it is written . . .   *Matthew 2:5b*

Ponder

'As it is written' – those words run like a thread throughout the Gospel of Matthew and, indeed, throughout much of the New Testament, the message of the law and the prophets seen as fulfilled in the birth, life, death and resurrection of Christ. So what is it saying? On one level, it reinforces the theme we explored yesterday of God's word always being active, never exhausted until it has fulfilled its purpose. There is, though, a second truth that can be drawn from these words, which takes those observations a little further, for the fascinating fact is that the scriptures cited as being fulfilled were, more often than not, initially addressed to a very different situation in an altogether different time. Suddenly, though, with the coming of Christ, they took on new meaning; imbued with fresh power and fulfilled in a yet more wonderful way. God's word of old was speaking again to a new time and situation.

Countless generations across the years can testify to that same truth in their own lives, words of scripture initially concerned with events and people long past having leapt out of the page as though God was speaking directly to them. Here is the wonder of the Bible: that words so very old can seem so startlingly new. That is why we call it God's word, for, difficult though it may be sometimes to understand – occasionally dry, often complex, frequently mystifying – God nonetheless can speak through it today to you, to me, to everyone.

Ask yourself

Do you still expect the Bible to speak directly to your life? Are you open to familiar passages of scripture speaking to you in new ways, or do you breeze through them too quickly to give them any chance of doing so?

Pray

Living God, break through the stranglehold of familiarity and complacency, and open my heart to your word, so that it may speak afresh to my life. Teach me to read the scriptures as Matthew read them, recognising that your word continues to find fulfilment in Jesus Christ, and so may I read with hope, faith and expectation, hearing your voice and seeing your hand in the world today. Amen.

Remember

Now all this took place so that what was spoken of the Lord by the prophet might be fulfilled.   *Matthew 1:22*

Close

Living God, teach me to read your word not as some record of past events but as a message that goes on being realised in new ways today, both in my life and in the life of others, by the grace of Christ. Amen.

The God who believes in us!

Read

For God so loved the world that he gave his only Son, so that everyone who believes in him may not perish but may have eternal life.   *John 3:16 (NRSV)*

Ponder

'I believe in God, the Father almighty, maker of heaven and earth'. So say the opening words of the Apostle's Creed, a statement of faith designed to encapsulate the essential convictions of Christian belief; to summarise what we believe, or, at least, what we are meant to believe. Yet, all such creeds leave one thing out; a statement that, for me, is more important than any other, and that is the affirmation that God believes in us! We are talking, of course, about a different kind of belief, though it is not as different as you might at first think. What we see in the birth of Jesus is God firmly and resoundingly declaring: 'I believe in humankind!'

To understand the full wonder behind that statement we need to remind ourselves what, in the biblical sense, it means to say, 'I believe'. It doesn't mean accepting the existence of something, in the sense that we might believe in ghosts or flying saucers. It means belief in the sense of trust, putting one's faith in something, and being ready, if necessary, to stake one's name and reputation on the object of one's belief. Seen in that light, how many people do we truly believe in? Yet, that is the belief God has in us. He doesn't see us through rose-coloured spectacles. He is not blind for a moment to our fallibility and sinfulness. Yet, despite all that is wrong in our lives, he sees something precious in us, special and worth saving – even worth dying for! In the stable in Bethlehem, the child in a manger, and the life, death and resurrection that followed, we see God's emphatic 'yes' to humankind, his affirmation of our worth! The creeds are important, don't get me wrong, but they don't quite say everything, for it seems to me that if we haven't understood that God believes in us, we haven't really understood what it means to say, 'I believe in God'.

Ask yourself

Does a sense of your faults and failings lead you some-times to question your own worth? Do you realise that God believes in you, even if you don't?

Pray

Living God, when I look at my life, I see so much that is wrong and so little that is right. I see selfishness and greed, envy and bitterness, rather than the fruits of the Spirit that I so much long to show. I see narrowness of mind, weakness of faith and feebleness of commitment rather than the vision, trust and dedication that you expect from me. I want to live and work for you, yet I seem incapable of doing so, and I despair of ever changing.

Help me to remember that you can achieve what I cannot hope to do by myself; that you love me and died for me even before I knew you. Teach me that *you* believe in me, even when *I* don't. In Christ's name I pray. Amen.

Remember

When the time was right, Christ died for the ungodly in all their weakness. It is exceedingly rare for someone to die for anyone, even a righteous person, though perhaps if they're sufficiently good someone might actually dare to do so, but God proved his love for us in that while we were yet sinners, Christ died for us.   *Romans 5:6-8*

Close

Gracious God, help me to believe in you as much as you believe in me. Amen.

The start of it all

Read

In the beginning was the Word, and the Word was with God, and the Word was God. He was in the beginning with God. All things came into being through him, and without him not one thing came into being. What has come into being in him was life, and the life was the light of all people. The light shines in the darkness, and the darkness did not overcome it. He was in the world, and the world came into being through him; yet the world did not know him. He came to what was his own, and his own people did not accept him. But to all who received him and believed in his name, he gave power to become children of God, who were born not of blood or of the will of the flesh, or of the will of man, but of God. And the Word became flesh and lived among us, and we have seen his glory, the glory as of a father's only son, full of grace and truth.

John 1:1-5, 10-14 (NRSV)

Ponder

There is something unusual about the Gospel of John. Unlike Matthew and Luke, John does not start with Mary or Joseph, nor does he refer to Bethlehem, a stable or a manger; in fact, there is no mention of a Christmas story at all. Unlike Mark, he does not start with the ministry of Jesus either, though he soon moves on to this. He takes us instead to the dawn of time and the events of creation, as he reminds us of God's sovereign will there at the beginning of it all. Despite everything that would frustrate him and deny his love, he tells us, God's gracious purpose was there from the start, the living Word later to be embodied in the Word made flesh. For John, the coming of Christ is not God's attempt to make up for a ghastly mistake; it is the natural expression of a love constantly at work, revealed in history, declared through prophets, and finally lived out in flesh and blood. John's testimony calls us to reflect on all God has yet to do in the light of everything he has already done.

Ask yourself

Does your faith begin and end with the New Testament? Are you doing justice to the God whose purpose in Christ has been at work since the beginning of time?

Pray

Gracious God, despite our repeated disobedience, your love continues undiminished, reaching out to us every moment of every day. Despite the rejection of the world, still you go on seeking to draw us to yourself, until every broken relationship with you is mended. So it is now and so it has always been from the beginning of time, your nature always to have mercy.

Help me to appreciate the enormity of your faithfulness, and to use this season of Advent to open my heart more fully to your grace. Through Jesus Christ my Lord. Amen.

Remember

Before the world was founded, he chose us in Christ to be holy and without blemish in his sight, filled with love, and he destined us, according to his will and pleasure, to be adopted as his children through Jesus Christ.

Ephesians 1:4-5

Close

Loving God, teach me that your gracious purpose goes back to the beginning of time, and that it will endure until the end of time, and beyond. Through Jesus Christ my Lord. Amen.

A time for rejoicing

Read

How lovely on the mountains are the feet of the herald who proclaims peace, who brings good news, who announces deliverance and who says to Zion, 'Your God reigns!' Listen! Your watchers lift up their voices and together they sing for joy.
Isaiah 52:7-8a

Ponder

Some years ago a prominent newsreader bemoaned the fact that only bad news seems to make the headlines. Sadly, nothing much seems to have changed; daily bulletins are still dominated by news of another riot, murder, disaster or tragedy somewhere in the world.

The seasons of Advent and Christmas, however, remind us of another kind of news, for the events they speak of were marked from the very start by a mood of rejoicing. When Mary and Elizabeth met for the first time since Mary became pregnant, Elizabeth exclaimed: 'The moment I heard you call in greeting, the child in my womb leapt for joy' (Luke 1:44), and Mary's response was to joyfully proclaim 'I rejoice with all my heart because of God my Saviour' (Luke 1:47). So it was to continue after the birth of Jesus, as angels appeared to shepherds with the message, 'See – I am bringing you good news of great joy that is for all people: today a Saviour has been born to you in the city of David, who is Christ, the Lord' (Luke 2:10b-11). Finally, when the wise men at last reached their destination and entered the house where Mary and Joseph had taken lodging with their child, 'they were overwhelmed with joy' (Matthew 2:10). This is not to say that sorrow was at an end – the slaughter of children in and around Bethlehem ordered by Herod was to show this was far from the case. Yet, within the trouble and pain of the world, the tragedies and trials that beset us all, God had brought joy that nothing finally could overcome – good news that we continue to celebrate today.

Ask yourself
In all the bad news of this world, do you lose sight sometimes of the good news of Christ? Have you experienced the joy that comes through knowing him?

Pray
Gracious God, I thank you for the joy you have brought to so many through the birth of Jesus; the joy you gave to Mary, shepherds and magi as you entered the world in Christ, that you have brought to subsequent generations of believers across the centuries and that you bring now to me.

I praise you that whatever I face, I have your love to support me, the grace of Christ to enrich me, and the presence of your Spirit to equip me. Inspire me afresh each day with the good news of Christ, and so may I go on my way rejoicing, now and always. Amen.

Remember
Now may the God of hope fill you with all joy and peace in believing, so that hope may blossom within you, through the power of the Holy Spirit.   *Romans 15:13*

Close
Living God, you have given me news of great joy – teach me to celebrate that truth each day. Amen.

Magnifying the Lord

Read

Then Mary said, 'My soul magnifies the Lord, and my spirit exults within me in God my Saviour, for he has looked on the lowliness of his servant. From now on and for all time, people will call me blessed, because the Mighty One has done great things for me. Holy is his name!'   *Luke 1:46-49*

Ponder

When I was a child I was given a magnifying glass; not just any old magnifying glass, but one so powerful that when I looked through it I could see things in enormous detail. I can still remember how it opened up a whole new world that I had never imagined existed before. A moss-covered wall near my home became a thick and lush jungle, and the tiny ant crawling through it became a terrifying monster rampaging through the undergrowth. Everywhere I looked, I saw things in a different light and on an altogether different scale.

What, you may ask, has all that to do with the song of Mary? The clue is there in that opening line: 'My soul magnifies the Lord.' The expression is an old-fashioned one, so much so that many newer translations have altered it, but, in so doing, they have lost an important part of what it is saying. On one level, it is talking simply about God, but, on another level, it is also about Mary and the way God had taken on a new significance in her life. Suddenly, a new world has opened up for her – a world in which she glimpsed God's greatness and goodness as never before, recognising that he was actively involved in her life and the life of the world. For Mary, of course, the circumstances were special, yet the coming of Christ, and his coming again to each one of us through his Spirit, means that we too can taste that joy and experience a similar sense of wonder. Advent calls us, then, in turn, to catch sight of the awesomeness and sovereignty of God, so that we might thrill to his presence and join with Mary in declaring: 'My soul magnifies the Lord, and my spirit exults within me in God my Saviour.'

Ask yourself
Do you need to broaden your understanding of the greatness and majesty of God? When did you last give him the praise and honour he deserves?

Pray
Gracious God, I praise you for this season of Advent; this time for rejoicing and celebration, praise and worship, exulting in your goodness. I praise you for coming in Christ, bringing in a new kingdom and anticipating an era of peace and justice when the poor will have plenty, the hungry be fed, and the lowly be lifted up. I praise you that you want me to be a part of that; not just to share in it but also to play a part in bringing it to pass.

Forgive me that I sometimes lose sight of your purpose and underestimate your greatness. Open my eyes to the breadth of your love, the wonder of your mercy and the extent of your goodness, and so may I give you the worship and adoration that is due to you, this and every day. Through Jesus Christ my Lord. Amen.

Remember
O magnify the Lord with me, and let us lift up his name together. I will praise the name of the Lord in song; I will magnify him with thanksgiving.   *Psalm 34:3; 69:30*

Close
Sovereign God, give me today a deeper sense of who and what you are, and may I acknowledge your greatness through word and deed, to the glory of your name. Amen.

A costly response

Read

Simeon blessed them and said to Mary, Jesus' mother, 'This child is destined for the fall and rise of many in Israel, and will be a sign that many will speak against, revealing their inner thoughts – and a sword will pierce your own soul too.'

Luke 2:34-35

Ponder

How much will you be spending on Christmas this year? Probably a lot more than you might think. Not only will there be presents to buy, which themselves represent a sizeable expense, but there will also be the Christmas dinner, boxes of sweets and chocolates, perhaps a few bottles of wine, not to mention Christmas cards, a tree, decorations and all the other odds and ends that go to make up what we see as a traditional Christmas. There's no doubt about it, Christmas is becoming an increasingly costly time, to the point that some people pay into a Christmas kitty each week so as to spread the expense over a year.

There was, however, another cost involved in the very first Christmas, which perhaps we can sometimes overlook. We see it partly in the response of Mary to God's call; her willingness to surrender her body to God's will. That alone, alongside the joy and privilege, entailed making a sacrifice, for life from that moment was never to be the same again. Yet it went further than that, for just a few days after the birth of her son there were to come those words of Simeon warning of a sword that would pierce her soul; words that must have cast a lengthening shadow across her life as Jesus inexorably took the way that led to the cross. It was Mary's willingness to accept the cost of service, as well as the rewards, that made possible God's gift of life. How willing are we to accept the cost of discipleship, in turn?

Ask yourself
Have you understood the true cost of Christmas? How much are you willing to give back to God in return?

Pray
Gracious God, I forget sometimes that alongside the blessings of discipleship there is always the cost – sacrifices that will be asked of me; demands upon my time, energy, gifts and money; responsibilities I will be asked to accept.

Help me to respond gladly to whatever you may ask, knowing that, however great the price may be, the rewards are infinitely worth it. Teach me to offer to you all that you ask from me, until that day when I rejoice in everything you hold in store for all your people. Through Christ my Lord. Amen.

Remember
Standing near the cross of Jesus were his mother, and his mother's sister, Mary the wife of Clopas, and Mary Magdalene.
John 19:25b (NRSV)

Close
Gracious God, as I think of the gifts I will buy for others, teach me what it cost to make possible the gift of new life for all through your Son – the greatest gift there could be. Amen.

Who? Them!

Read

This is what happened concerning the birth of Jesus Christ. While his mother, Mary, was engaged to Joseph, but before they lived together, she became pregnant, through the Holy Spirit. Being a good man unwilling to expose her to public disgrace, Joseph planned to end the engagement quietly. However, just when he had made this decision, an angel of the Lord appeared to him in a dream and said, 'Joseph, son of David, do not be afraid to take Mary as your wife, for the child conceived within her is from the Holy Spirit. She will bear a son, and you are to call him Jesus, for he will save his people from their sins.' All this took place to fulfil what the Lord had spoken through the prophet: 'Look, the virgin will conceive and bear a son, and they will call him "Emmanuel", which means, "God is with us."' After waking from his sleep, Joseph did as the angel of the Lord had instructed, taking Mary as his wife, but he had no sexual relations with her until she gave birth to a son; and he named him Jesus.   *Matthew 1:18-25*

Ponder

If there's one thing harder than accepting that God can use *you*, it's accepting he can use someone else, especially when that 'someone' is close to you. We think we know all about them, and, almost certainly, their faults and weaknesses are clearer to us than to most people. Any suggestion that God has singled them out for a special purpose is often met with more than a raised eyebrow. When those faults are writ large, then it's all the harder to believe.

What must it have looked like then, to Joseph, when Mary broke the news that she was expecting, only to tell him in the next breath that the child she carried was not the result of some illicit liaison but had been conceived by the Holy Spirit? How would you have responded in his shoes? A little scepticism was perfectly understandable. Yet Joseph, like Mary, was willing to let God overturn his preconceptions; ready to accept that God should use this girl he thought he knew in the most remarkable of ways. The circumstances in this case were, admittedly, unique, but the principle holds nonetheless for us all. We need to be open to God working through those we might least expect him to; and, above all, through those we are so close to that we mistakenly imagine we know everything there is to know about them. It may be that it is time to think again!

Ask yourself
Are you open to God working through your family, friends and acquaintances? Are you really as open as you might like to think you are?

Pray
Living God, forgive me for imagining sometimes that I know all there is to know about people; for presuming to judge their abilities and qualities on the basis of what I understand about them. Forgive me for questioning what you can do through them because I fail to see their true potential. Teach me that you are able to use anyone and everyone in ways I have not even begun to consider.

Open my eyes, then, to what you are doing in those around me, and help me to recognise what you may be saying to me through them. In Christ's name I ask it. Amen.

Remember
I tell you truthfully, no prophet is accepted in his or her own town. *Luke 4:24*

Close
Gracious God, teach me that if you can use me, you can use anyone. Through Jesus Christ my Lord. Amen.

Unlikely choices

Read

Here is an account of the genealogy of Jesus the Messiah, the son of David, the son of Abraham. Abraham fathered Isaac, who fathered Jacob, who fathered Judah and his brothers, who fathered Perez and Zerah by Tamar. Perez fathered Hezron, who fathered Aram, who fathered Aminadab, who fathered Nahshon, who fathered Salmon, who fathered Boaz by Rahab. Boaz fathered Obed by Ruth, and Obed fathered Jesse who was the father of King David. David was the father of Solomon by the wife of Uriah.

Matthew 1:1-6

Ponder

The opening chapter of Matthew's Gospel is surely one of the least inspiring in the Bible – or is it? At first sight, it looks like nothing more than a list of names, but appearances can be deceptive. Look deeper, and a different story emerges – for four of the names are anything but dull: Tamar, who conceived twins by her father-in-law Judah, through deceiving him about her identity; Rahab, the prostitute in Canaan who sheltered Joshua and his colleagues when they were spying out the Promised Land; Ruth, the Gentile from Moab who married Boaz and settled in Israel; and 'the wife of Uriah' – Bathsheba– who had an illicit affair with King David that led indirectly to the death of her husband. It was unusual in Jewish circles to mention women in a genealogy; more unusual still to mention Gentiles, and as for those like Rahab, Tamar and Bathsheba who had been caught up in tawdry sordid affairs – frankly, they'd have been seen as an embarrassment.

So what's going on here? The answer is simple and wonderful. Here is a graphic demonstration of God's grace in Christ, even before he was born. He came, not through the morally perfect or ritually clean, nor through the accepted and expected routes, but through those deemed imperfect, unsuitable and unworthy. The pattern was wonderfully continued in the choice of Mary, an insignificant girl in Nazareth; in the selection of rough and ready shepherds as the first to hear the good news; in the call of fishermen, a tax-collector and a zealot as his disciples; and in the willingness Jesus showed to mix with 'tax-collectors and sinners' throughout his ministry. Here is the God who has time for anyone, whoever that person may be; who has time for everyone, whatever they may have done. Here is the God who has time for you!

Ask yourself
Do you feel unworthy of God's love? Have you understood that no one is beyond his saving grace or outside his loving purpose?

Pray
Loving God, remind me again that you are a God of grace, reaching out to the bad as well as the good, to sinners as well as saints. Teach me that you chose Mary, representative of the powerless; shepherds, examples of the socially marginalised; and countless others across the years; and that, in turn, Jesus reached out to those whom society had rejected.

Help me, then, to turn to you, acknowledging my faults and weaknesses, knowing that, despite them all, you have a place for me in your kingdom. Through Jesus Christ my Lord. Amen.

Remember
Jesus said to them, 'It is not those who are healthy who need a physician but those who are sick. I have come not to call the righteous but sinners.'   *Mark 2:17*

Close
Living God, teach me that your grace is wider than I can begin to imagine, and your love wonderful beyond words. Amen.

One with us

Read

The Word became flesh and lived among us, and we have seen his glory, the glory as of a father's only son, full of grace and truth.   *John 1:14 (NRSV)*

Ponder

Despite its message of joy and celebration, Christmas is a time of mixed emotions, meaning different things for different people. For some it will indeed be a time of celebration, bringing family get-togethers, parties, the giving and sharing of presents, the laughter of children, feasting and merriment. For others, by contrast, it will bring pain. It may be the memory of a loved one who has recently died that hurts, or of an earlier bereavement around Christmas. It may be the recollection of bygone years before children grew up and left home to start a family of their own. It may be the burden of sickness, disability or terminal illness. Or it may be the continuing suffering of countless millions across the world facing the ever-present reality of poverty, homelessness, hunger and disease. Many will have little, if anything, to celebrate, in worldly terms. Christmas may be a time of joy, but not everyone will be rejoicing.

Yet it is precisely here that we glimpse the true wonder of the Christmas message, for at its heart is the proclamation that God became flesh, taking on our humanity. In other words, he understands what we are going through, whatever it might be. He doesn't just sympathise with our pain and sorrow; he empathises. He doesn't stand aloof from the daily round of life, for he has shared in it himself and is involved in our human situation. Christmas *is* a time of joy, but it is not just for the joyful; it *is* a time of celebration but it is not reserved for those who are celebrating. It is a time of good news for all, whether they laugh now or weep, rejoice or despair. God has entered our world so that, in the fullness of time, we may enter his kingdom where all, indeed, will rejoice.

Ask yourself
Does Christmas fill you with mixed feelings, or even with a sense of dread? Have you felt able to bring your pain and hurt to God, knowing that he wants to help you bear it?

Pray
Gracious God, I thank you for the astonishing love you showed in Christ, sharing our humanity through him. I praise you that you became flesh and blood like me, experiencing the same temptations I face, torn by the same fears, suffering the same pain and tasting the same joys and sorrows.

For the assurance this brings – the knowledge that you understand the worries, concerns, doubts and problems that confront me each day – receive my worship, in the name of Christ. Amen.

Remember
Unquestionably great is the mystery of our faith: God revealed himself in flesh, was vindicated in the Spirit, was seen by angels, is proclaimed among all nations and believed in throughout the world, and has been taken up in glory. *1 Timothy 3:16*

Close
Gracious God, teach me that you shared my humanity from birth to death, so that I might share your eternity. Through Christ my Lord. Amen.

The forgotten person?

Read

He was in the world, and though the world was made through him, the world did not recognise him. He came to that which was his own, but his own did not receive him.

John 1:10-11

Ponder

Have you finished writing and posting your Christmas cards? If you haven't, then you'd better get a move on if you want to ensure that they will be delivered before Christmas Day. Yet, even when you've posted the last one, you can just about guarantee an unexpected card will arrive from someone you've completely forgotten about. Embarrassing, isn't it!

That person, though, may not be the only one you forget about, for there's someone else we all too often overlook, and that, astonishingly, is Jesus himself! We may sing about him, read about him and hear about him time and again, yet fail actually to stop and meet him. We can be so busy with our festivities, even our carol services and celebrations, that we miss out on the personal encounter that Christmas offers. Instead of offering a welcome, the doors of our lives are firmly barred. Instead of going in heart and mind to Bethlehem, we stay wrapped up in our own little world. Instead of receiving the greatest gift ever offered to humankind, we find ourselves asking why it hasn't quite felt like Christmas. Don't let that happen to you. Whatever else, don't forget the one who Christmas is ultimately all about and don't forget to respond to him.

Ask yourself

Will you make time to remember Christ this Christmas? Will you place him at the heart of your celebrations as he deserves?

Pray

Loving God, the great festival of Christmas is drawing nearer and we are busy preparing for it – choosing presents, writing cards, planning get-togethers, buying food – so much that has become an accepted and expected part of this season. Yet, in all the bustle, we so easily forget what matters most: responding to the gift of your Son.

Forgive us for so easily relegating Jesus to the periphery of our celebrations rather than placing him at the centre where he belongs; for doing so much to prepare for Christmas on the surface yet so little to make ourselves ready within. Open our hearts to welcome the living Christ into our lives, and so may we rejoice in his love, not just at this Christmas time, but always. In his name we ask it. Amen.

Remember

She wrapped him in bands of cloth, and laid him in a manger, because there was no place for them in the inn.

Luke 2:7 (NRSV)

Close

O holy child of Bethlehem, be born in me today. Amen.

The God who comes to us

Read

I have come to bring light into the world, so that everyone who believes in me will not remain in darkness.

John 12:46

Ponder

There was a time when, should you feel too unwell to get to your local surgery, a doctor would come and see you. Not any more, or at least not as was once the case. There are some circumstances, of course, when a doctor will still come but the usual procedure out of hours is to get yourself to a duty doctor who will deal with your problem. The onus is on the patient to *go* because, quite simply, there aren't enough doctors to *come*.

We can tend to think of God in a similar sort of way – as one we have to *go to*, with the responsibility on us to make the first approach. Look, though, at the nativity stories in Matthew and Luke, or the opening verses of John's Gospel, and a very different picture emerges. Running through them all, like a common thread, is the message that it is God who first comes to us. He came to Zechariah, then Mary, then Joseph, and then to the shepherds out in the fields – the approach always at his initiative. He came bringing his word of promise, challenge, joy and hope, offering his love and his gift of new life – and so he continues to come today. Before we yet know him, before sometimes we even know our need, he draws near, reaching out in welcome, extending his grace. Yes, Christmas calls for a response, as we shall explore further tomorrow, but it is not finally about us coming to God; it is, above all, about him coming to us.

Ask yourself

What things prevent God from coming into your life? Are you so busy sometimes coming to God with your prayers and requests that you fail to realise he has already come to you?

Pray

Loving God, I thank you for the great truth at the heart of Advent and Christmas – your coming to our world in Christ. I praise you that you go on coming, day after day, not just to others but also to me, meeting and working within me through your Holy Spirit. Forgive me everything that obstructs your coming; all the trivia and irrelevancies with which I fill my life at the cost of time for you; all the cares, doubts and unbelief that prevent me sometimes from even glimpsing your presence.

Come afresh now, and break through all the barriers in my life, so that I may know you more nearly by my side and draw yet closer to you than I was before. Speak your word, grant your guidance, confer your power and fill me with your love, and so may I bring my service to you as faithfully as you have come in Christ to me. In his name I ask it. Amen.

Remember

He came and proclaimed peace to you who were afar off.
Ephesians 2:17a (NRSV)

Close

Living God, when I forget you, when I fail you and when I wander far from you, keep on coming to me by your grace, and open my heart afresh to your love. Through Christ my Lord. Amen.

RSVP

Read

To all who received him and believed in his name, he gave the right to become children of God; children born not of blood or any union of the flesh, nor of any human desire, but of God.   *John 1:12-13*

Ponder

RSVP – four letters through which we ask people to indicate their acceptance of an invitation or otherwise. It's a way of politely asking the recipient not to put the invitation away and forget about it, or to delay their reply until the very last minute, but to respond as soon as possible.

There is a sense in which we see something similar in the events of the birth of Christ, and indeed throughout his life and ministry. First, it was Mary, asked to respond to God's word pronounced by Gabriel, and her response was swift and unreserved: 'I am the Lord's servant. Let it be to me just as you say' (Luke 1:38). Next, it was Joseph, challenged to think again about breaking off his engagement, his response equally prompt: 'After waking from his sleep, Joseph did as the angel of the Lord had instructed, taking Mary as his wife' (Matthew 1:24). Then, it was the shepherds, told that a Saviour had been born to them in Bethlehem, and from them too there was no hesitation: 'They came with haste, and found Mary and Joseph, and with them the baby, lying in a manger' (Luke 2:16). Finally, there were the wise men, seeing the star in the east and immediately following it: 'They knelt down and paid him homage. Then, opening their treasure chests, they offered him gifts of gold, frankincense, and myrrh' (Matthew 2:11). The coming of Christ was an invitation to respond, and it is an invitation that God continues to extend today – to you, to me, to everyone. It's no good just receiving it and then putting it away; no good thinking we can put off a decision until some other time, for God is asking you, as he asked so many all those years ago and as he has asked so many since: RSVP.

Ask yourself
Have you responded to God's love in Christ? Have you made a response, only to go back on it, slipping back or falling away in faith?

Pray
Gracious God, I thank you for your gracious invitation in Christ to know your love and share your life. I praise you for coming in him, so that I can come to you. Teach me that I need to go on making my response day after day; that it is not a one-off thing, once done and then forgotten, but an ongoing renewal of commitment, a consecrating of all I am and all I do to you.

So, once more, I bring you my worship, I offer you my service and I dedicate my life, in Jesus' name. Amen.

Remember
'What must I do to be saved?' 'Believe on the Lord Jesus Christ, and you will be saved – you and all your household.'
Acts 16:30b-31

Close
Living God, teach me not just to know about your invitation to meet with Christ. Teach me to respond, and so to know him for myself. Amen.

A time for worship

Read

His father, Zechariah, was filled with the Holy Spirit, and spoke this prophecy: 'Blessed be the Lord God of Israel, for he has looked favourably on his people and redeemed them.'

Luke 1:67-68 (NRSV)

Ponder

What words should you use to address the Queen, another member of the royal family, a Lord or Lady, or even the Archbishop of Canterbury? Do you know? I don't – and the chances are, if I were to be introduced to anyone so eminent, I would clam up completely, unsure quite how I ought to respond. You may be feeling a little like that after the theme yesterday: the challenge to respond to God's love in Christ. 'I want to respond,' you might say, 'but how?' To answer that in full would take many pages, but one thing stands out above all others in the Christmas stories, and that is the response of worship.

When Zechariah regained the power of speech, the first thing he did was to praise God. When Mary realised the full wonder of what God had done for her, she burst into joyful song. When the shepherds had been to the stable and seen the child in the manger, they returned, glorifying and praising God for everything they had heard and seen. When Simeon and Anna saw Mary and Joseph bringing Jesus into the temple, they immediately cried out in praise. When the magi reached the house where Jesus was, they fell down and worshipped him! For each one there could only be one response to the coming of Christ, one response that would do: to offer their worship in glad and joyful praise. Of course, there's more to our response than that, for worship leads on to service and witness in a wide variety of ways, but this is where it starts – in recognising what God has done, in joyfully acknowledging his greatness and in humbly offering our grateful worship.

Ask yourself
How will you respond to God this Christmas? Will you put worship at the centre of your celebrations?

Pray
Sovereign God, I can never repay your goodness and never fully express my thanks, but I bring you again today my praise and worship, offered in the name of Jesus. Like the choir of angels on the night of his birth, I sing in adoration. Like the shepherds, returning from the manger, I give you praise for everything I have experienced. Like the magi, kneeling in wonder, I bring you my homage as a token of my love and a sign of my commitment.

All I think, all I do, all I say, all I am, I bring to you in reverent praise and joyful celebration. In the name of Christ. Amen.

Remember
All at once, there was with the angel rank on rank of other heavenly beings, praising God and saying, 'Glory to God in the highest heaven, and peace on earth among all on whom his favour rests!'   *Luke 2:13-14*

Close
To you, O God, be praise and glory, worship and adoration, today and always. Amen.

Making room

Read

It happened at that time that Caesar Augustus issued a
decree that a census should be taken of the entire world.
This was the first such census and occurred while Quirinius
was governor of Syria. All, therefore, went to be registered,
each to their appropriate town. Joseph, being of the house
and family of David, went from the Galilean town of
Nazareth to Judea, to the city of David called Bethlehem,
to be registered with his fiancée Mary, who was expecting a
child. While they were there, she went into labour and gave
birth to her first-born son. She swaddled him in strips of
cloth, and laid him in a manger, because there was no room
for them in the inn.   *Luke 2:1-7*

Ponder

Anyone who has ever commuted by train to London will
know all about the problems of making room. Carriages
are already full to overflowing as the train pulls into another
station heaving with yet more people. Or you may have
travelled to the coast on a bank-holiday weekend looking
for somewhere to stay, only to see the same sign in every
window: 'No Vacancies'. The situation must have been a little
like that in Bethlehem on the night of Jesus' birth. People
of the house and line of David had come from across Judea
to be enrolled in the Roman census, cramming into every
house, guest room and inn. We can scarcely imagine what
Mary and Joseph must have gone through as they searched
desperately for somewhere to stay overnight.

That experience, of course, was a symbol of things to come:
Jesus found no room in the hearts of many throughout his
ministry and continues to find no room in the hearts of
many today. We may imagine that *we* are different; that we
have opened the door of our lives and welcomed him in,

but let's not be complacent about it. The truth is that most of us only half-open the door, at best. We allow Jesus access to certain areas of our life but keep other areas ring-fenced. We make room when it suits us, but at other times give him our divided attention if any at all. It is easy to fool ourselves that such a response will do, when, in reality, Jesus is knocking at the door, still asking to come in.

Ask yourself

Do you make enough room in your life for Christ? Do you give him a central place or fit him in somewhere on the periphery? Are there areas of your life that faith doesn't touch?

Pray

Lord Jesus Christ, I remember today how you came to our world and found no welcome; how, from the very beginning, you were shut out, no room for you even in the inn. Forgive me that I am guilty sometimes of shutting you out in turn, failing to make room for you in so many areas of my life. Despite my words of faith and commitment, I turn my back on you when I would rather not face your challenge.

Forgive me, and help me to make room for you, not just this Christmas but always. Teach me to give you not merely a token place in my heart, but to put you at the very centre of my life. Come now, and make your home within me, by your grace. Amen.

Remember

He was in the world, and the world came into being through him; yet the world did not know him. He came to what was his own, and his own people did not accept him.

John 1:10-11 (NRSV)

Close

Lord Jesus Christ, show me those areas of my life where I still keep you out, and help me to open them to you fully, so that you may live in and work through me, to the glory of your name. Amen.

It *is* you!

Read

There were shepherds in that area, living in the fields and keeping watch over their flock during the night. Suddenly, an angel of the Lord appeared to them, and the glory of the Lord shone around them, and they were overcome with terror. However, the angel said to them, 'There's nothing to be frightened of; for see – I am bringing you good news of great joy that is for all people: today a Saviour has been born to you in the city of David, who is Christ the Lord. Let this be a sign to you: you will find a child swaddled in strips of cloth and lying in a manger.' All at once, there was with the angel rank on rank of other heavenly beings, praising God and saying, 'Glory to God in the highest heaven, and peace on earth among all on whom his favour rests!'

Luke 2:8-14

Ponder

Do you remember the advertising campaign, some years ago now, which preceded the launch of the National Lottery? It caused quite a controversy at the time: a giant hand hovering over the rooftops of a town before finally a finger reached down to single out one household as the lucky winner of the coveted jackpot, backed up by the words, 'It could be you!' The suggestion was that the hand of providence might one day select us to receive a fortune. Did you take the bait? Many have, and a number of people have become millionaires as a result, but the majority of participants will have spent a considerable amount of money with little if anything to show for it.

Contrast that with the events of Bethlehem that we are preparing once again to celebrate. Here was the promise not of money on earth but of riches in heaven; a prize not merely for this life but for all eternity – the greatest gift ever offered. Yet this was no lottery, dependent on the whim of fate. There was no question of it *could* be you if you happened to get lucky. The message of the angels, the evangelists and countless generations of faith since is quite simple: 'It *is* you!' The promise of God in Christ – his gift of new life with everything that means – is not reserved for the exclusive few, nor dependent on any quirk of chance. It is yours for the taking, waiting simply for you to claim it – for you, for me, for everyone!

Ask yourself

Have you recognised that the gospel is good news for you? Have you personally responded to it?

Pray

Gracious God, I praise you for the glorious message of this season – the glad tidings of great joy, ever old yet ever new. I thank you for the faith of Mary, the commitment of Joseph, the message of the angels and the response of the shepherds – the way you changed their lives that day in Bethlehem. Above all, though, I thank you that you have changed *my* life too; that the good news they heard and responded to is news for today as much as then, for *me* as much as anyone!

Teach me never to forget that wonderful truth; never to overlook the fact that you have come to me in Christ. May that knowledge burn brightly in my heart; a constant source of joy and inspiration, whatever life may bring. In his name I pray. Amen.

Remember

God chose to make known among all the nations the glorious riches of this mystery, which is Christ in you, the hope of glory.   *Colossians 1:27*

Close

Living God, teach me that the glad tidings proclaimed at Bethlehem all those years ago is good news for me today, here and now. Amen.

Seeing for ourselves

Read

When the angels had departed and returned to heaven, the shepherds said to each other, 'Let us go, then, to Bethlehem and see this event that has taken place, which the Lord has made known to us.'

Luke 2:15

Ponder

I learned something interesting recently. Apparently, many people claim that the artist, Picasso, was left-handed; to the extent that several websites dedicated to left-handedness cite him as a celebrated example of such. The fact is, though, that he was *right*-handed, as can be proven by an examination of the photographic and historical records. What was it, then, that caused so many people to think otherwise? The answer is that they took someone else's word as fact; assuming that what they were told had to be true. It's an understandable mistake, for we often have nothing but hearsay to go on, yet we need to be alert to the dangers, for ultimately there can be no substitute for first-hand experience. Until we have seen the truth of something for ourselves, either by witnessing it or testing its veracity, we cannot categorically say that we know something.

That is just as true when it comes to knowing God. We need to learn from the example of the shepherds, who, when told the good news that the Saviour had been born, went to find out for themselves. 'Let us go, then, to Bethlehem,' they said, 'and see this event that has taken place, which the Lord has made known to us.' We may have been taught about faith as a child; we may have been brought up in a Christian home; we may have sat in church and shared in countless services; we may even know the Bible back to front – it makes no difference. What matters is that we have met with Christ; that we have put our faith in him and discovered in practice the truth of his words and the reality of his presence.

Don't let your faith rest on someone else's experience, on what others have told you about Christ – turn to him, open your life to his love, and let the gospel be true for you!

Ask yourself

Have you made a personal act of commitment, or does your faith rest on what others have told you? Have you discovered for yourself the reality of Jesus in your life?

Pray

Loving God, challenge me through the example of the shepherds. Teach me that it is not enough to accept the claims of the gospel simply through what someone else has said, but that I need to experience the truth of it for myself.

Help me, then, to open my soul to the presence of Christ, and to welcome him into my life. Help me to know the reality of his Spirit at work within me, and to accept the message of the gospel, not just with my head but also with my heart. In his name I pray. Amen.

Remember

We know that he lives in us by the Spirit that he has put within us. *1 John 3:24b*

Close

Living God, teach me to base my faith not simply on the testimony of others, but on my own experience of Christ. Amen.

Something worth hurrying for

Read

So they came with haste, and found Mary and Joseph, and the baby lying in a manger.   *Luke 2:16*

Ponder

If you were to be told in church on Sunday that a wealthy philanthropist was in the street outside handing out wads of cash, how much time would you waste after the service before you went to find out if it were true? The chances are that you'd be out of the church like a shot the moment the final hymn had ended – if not before! Again, if you were out walking and spotted an excited cheering crowd ahead of you, rushing towards something, you'd probably quicken your pace, eager to see what was happening. Some things in life are worth hurrying for. So it was for the shepherds after hearing the news of the birth of Christ. It's only a small detail, but it's an important one: 'they came with haste'. Why? Because the news they'd heard was exciting, breathtaking, wonderful; news they and their people had been waiting so long to hear – almost too good to be true! There was no question of waiting until the next morning and then casually strolling down to Bethlehem after they'd knocked off work. This was news that had to be investigated at once, not something that could be postponed.

Do we, I wonder, still feel that sense of excitement at the Christmas message? Do we still marvel at what God has done for us in Christ? Do we still catch our breath in wonder at the miracle of the Saviour's birth – God made flesh? Do such things still capture our hearts and fire our imagination, not just at Christmas but also day after day and week after week? We may have responded; we may have discovered the truth for ourselves long ago – that doesn't matter: the message of Christmas is still one to get excited about!

Ask yourself
Do you still feel a sense of anticipation as you make time to meet with God? Do you still get excited about your faith?

Pray
Gracious God, I thank you that you have given me good news in Christ, a message that has thrilled generations across the years, uplifting, encouraging, challenging and renewing. I thank you for the way that message has spoken to me, showing itself to be glad tidings in so many ways. Yet, I confess that there are times when I lose my initial sense of awe and wonder, and no longer feel the urgent desire to respond to your love in the grateful service that I felt when I first started out on the path of discipleship.

Forgive me for becoming casual and complacent in my faith, failing to make time to worship you, and forgetting the need to nurture my relationship with Christ. Speak to me again, meet me through the living Christ, and open my heart to the renewing touch of your Holy Spirit. So may I catch again the sense of urgency felt by the shepherds as they rushed to Bethlehem, and may the wonder of your love burn within me each day, to your glory. Amen.

Remember
As they were going on their way, they came to some water, and immediately the eunuch said, 'Look, here is water. What is there to stop me from being baptised?'   *Acts 8:36*

Close
Sovereign God, in all the rush and bustle of life, teach me to recognise the one thing worth pursuing above all else – your awesome love revealed in Christ. Amen.

Something worth sharing

Read

Having seen it, they shared everything they had been told concerning the child, and all those who heard them marvelled at what the shepherds said.

Luke 2:17-18

Ponder

If I were to say to you the words 'made for sharing', what word or words would you automatically insert before them to make, what at one time at least, was a well-known catch-phrase? The chances are that you would think of that old advertisement, 'Quality Street, made for sharing'. I, though, have something very different in mind: the word 'Christmas'. You will see some logic in that straightaway, for Christmas is traditionally a time for sharing cards, presents and good wishes. It is a time also when families come together and share in a way that may not be possible during the rest of the year. For Christians, it is also a time for sharing in worship: nativity, candlelight and carol services.

Yet, special and important though all those are, they miss one thing out; something that we see in the example of the shepherds. 'When they had seen him, they spread the word' (Luke 2:17). Think about that for a moment, and then ask how far it is reflected in your life. Having seen Jesus, their instinctive response was to want to share it – to tell others the good news, to make sure that they too heard about what God had done. This wasn't something to keep to themselves, an event staged solely for their own benefit. In the words of the angel, it was 'news of great joy for all people'. I've no doubt we will share much this Christmas, and hopefully what we give will bring those nearest and dearest to us great joy, but will we share the greatest gift of all? Will we communicate what we have experienced of

God's gift in Christ? 'Christmas, made for sharing' – is that how you see it?

Ask yourself

How far, this Christmas, will you share the sense of joy and wonder that the shepherds had on that first Christmas in Bethlehem? Will anyone hear of the good news of Christ from you?

Pray

Living God, I remember today how shepherds responded to the message of the angels – how they hurried to Bethlehem and found the baby lying in a manger, and how afterwards they went on their way, sharing what they had seen and heard. Teach me to share my experience of Christ in turn. Help me to understand that your coming through him is good news for everyone, and that you want me to help make that known.

So, help me to live each day with joy in my heart and wonder in my eyes, as I share the love that you have shown me and make known the great thing that you have done in Christ. In his name I ask it. Amen.

Remember

Go back to your friends, and tell them the great things God has done for you and the mercy he has shown.   *Mark 5:19*

Close

Gracious God, as you have so freely given your love and spoken your word to me, so teach me to share both with others, to the glory of your name. Amen.

Think about it

Read

Mary stored these things up in her heart, pondering what they might mean.
Luke 2:19

Ponder

Still waters, we are told, run deep. They also have another quality: the ability to reflect. Both those qualities, though in a somewhat different sense, are amply evident in the example of Mary at the birth of Jesus, and we do well to ponder them. It must have been an exciting night for her, that night Jesus was born. For a start, there was the natural euphoria of giving birth and of holding her child close for the first time, but, alongside that, there was more. There was the memory of Gabriel, telling her that this child was the Son of God, and then, as if to confirm it, there came shepherds, no doubt blurting out their story of angels praising God and directing them to where a Saviour, the Messiah, had been born. She could so easily have been swept along by the tide of events, carried away by it all in such a way that she scarcely gave a thought to what was happening, but she didn't – she stored these things up in her heart, pondering what they might mean. In other words, she looked deeper, beneath the surface, and she reflected on what God had done in her life. She made time to consider and to understand.

Do we do that today? Christmas is an exciting time for us too, though for different reasons. It's an occasion for party-ing and celebrations, for family reunions and get-togethers, for giving and receiving, laughing and making merry. And why not? – those all bring some welcome happiness in the bleakness of winter. Yet, how many of us pause to reflect on what it's ultimately all about, on what we're celebrating and why, on the thing God has done for us that gives the season its name. Make time for fun and celebration, but, above all, make time to think and reflect on the true meaning of Christmas, for then you will truly find something worth getting excited about.

Ask yourself

Do you still make time to think about your faith? When was the last time you paused to reflect quietly on what God might be saying to you?

Pray

Gracious God, help me to learn from the example of Mary. Teach me this Christmas time, like her, to ponder all that you have said and done: to listen again to familiar readings and carols, and to hear again the story I know so well, but also to consider what it all might mean; what you are saying through it not just to others but also to me.

In all the celebrations and rejoicing, help me to be still before you so that I may open my heart to your living word, your renewing love and your redeeming power, and so know the presence of Jesus within me, by his grace. Amen.

Remember

Finally, my friends, whatever is true, what is honest, whatever is right, whatever is pure, whatever is lovely, whatever is commendable, good and worthy of praise, think about such things. *Philippians 4:8*

Close

Gracious God, teach me, like Mary, not just to see but to reflect on what I have seen, and thus to glimpse your hand at work. Through Jesus Christ my Lord. Amen.

A careful search

Read

Herod secretly summoned the wise men and ascertained from them exactly when the star had appeared. Then he sent them to Bethlehem, saying, 'Go and search carefully for the child; and when you have found him, bring word to me, so that I, in turn, may go and offer homage.'

Matthew 2:7-8

Ponder

Familiarity, it is said, breeds contempt, and if ever there is a danger of that it must surely be in relation to the Christmas message. We know the story so well – too well – having heard it so many times that we no longer take in sometimes what we are hearing. We listen to the words of scripture and sing well-loved carols, but they wash over us, no longer firing our imagination as they once did.

It is worth reflecting occasionally on those words of Herod to the magi as he sent them off to Bethlehem. The situation, of course, is different, in that they were seeking someone they had not yet met, encountering Jesus for the first time, but his words are nonetheless just as appropriate for those of us today who have known and followed Jesus for as long as we can remember. 'Go and make a careful search for the child.' Do that, not just today but every day, and what we find may still surprise us.

Ask yourself

Do you approach worship and personal devotion expecting to meet with Jesus, or have these become a matter of habit? Do you still search carefully for him in your times of prayer and reflection?

Pray

Lord Jesus Christ, teach me to search for you as eagerly and whole-heartedly as the day I first found you for myself, and so may you continue to surprise me with the wonder of your love and the awesomeness of your grace. Amen.

Remember
Seek the Lord while he may be found. Call upon him, while he is near.   *Isaiah 55:6 (NRSV)*

Close
Lord Jesus Christ, though the journey is long and I encounter obstacles along the way, help me to keep on searching to know you better, until that day when I enter your kingdom and meet you face to face. Amen.

The message that speaks for itself

Read

Jesus did many other signs before his disciples that have not been recorded here, but these things have been written so that you might believe Jesus is the Christ, the Son of God, and that, through believing, you might have life in his name.

John 20:30-31

Ponder

I worked out recently that during my time in the ministry I preached well over a thousand sermons. That statistic brought home to me how many millions of sermons must have been delivered over the years, thousands more being added to that number every week. Do any say anything new? I doubt it. More important, I doubt any set out to do so, for the goal of every preacher is, or should be, simply to proclaim the age-old message of the gospel. Certainly, each will attempt to bring home afresh the significance of that message for new generations, and this may well involve exploring different approaches and angles, but ultimately the heart of what any may say will have been said many times before. Sometimes a sermon will succeed in its aim – challenging, teaching, instructing, inspiring. At other times, it will leave its listeners cold, serving more to obscure than to illuminate.

No doubt, the same has been true of the reflections in this book, some having brought home the wonder of God's grace, others having left as many questions as answers. No one has a monopoly on truth, still less the ability to fathom the full riches of the gospel. Thankfully, scripture's ability to speak does not depend on any human agency, however helpful this may be at times. It has spoken across the years to countless generations and continues to do the same today, still having the power to transform lives and win people to faith in Christ. My aim in this book has been to provide an aid to reflection; a focus for prayer based on the words of scripture. It will only have succeeded in its purpose, however, if it has prompted the reader to delve further into the Bible so as to encounter the message that, thank God, is able to speak for itself!

Ask yourself

What passages of scripture have spoken most powerfully to you? Do you still expect God's message to speak, or do you fail to make time for it as you once did?

Pray

Gracious God, I praise you for the way your word has spoken to so many across the years, offering a lamp to walk by and a faith to live by. I thank you for the way your word has spoken to me, stirring my imagination, kindling and nurturing faith, confronting and questioning, yet also renewing and uplifting, each day assuring me of your constant love and gracious purpose.

Help me to hold on to the word of life, to reflect on the glad tidings, to stay true to the good news of Jesus Christ. Teach me, above all else, to make time for the message that speaks for itself. In Jesus' name I pray. Amen.

Remember

Jesus did countless other things; so many that, were every one of them to be listed, I doubt that the world itself could contain all the books that would have to be written.

John 21:25

Close

Living God, for your word that has spoken to so many, and continues to speak today, receive my praise, in the name of Christ. Amen.

SEASONAL
SUPPLEMENT

A positive response

Read

If, with Christ, you died to the elemental spirits of the universe, why do you live as if you still belonged to the world? Why do you submit to regulations, 'Do not handle, Do not taste, Do not touch'? All these regulations refer to things that perish with use; they are simply human commands and teachings. These have indeed an appearance of wisdom in promoting self-imposed piety, humility, and severe treatment of the body, but they are of no value in checking self-indulgence. So if you have been raised with Christ, seek the things that are above, where Christ is seated at the right hand of God. Set your minds on things that are above, not on things that are on earth.

Colossians 2:20-3:2 (NRSV)

Ponder

Tomorrow will be Ash Wednesday, the first day of Lent. What does the season mean to you? What sort of ideas does it conjure up in your mind? For many, it is associated with giving something up: an opportunity, perhaps, to kick that unwanted habit, go at last on that long-intended diet, or deny oneself those unnecessary extra luxuries. All such acts of discipline have their place, as the teaching of Jesus concerning taking up our cross makes clear, but they give a very one-sided view of Lent, for, if anything, it should be about taking something on; committing yourself, in the words of Jesus, to going the extra mile.

That doesn't mean taking work on for work's sake, or looking for extra duties, demands and responsibilities. Rather, it is about resolving to follow Christ more faithfully, determined to give him our whole-hearted discipleship. It might mean more disciplined devotion, perhaps more practical service, maybe more effective witness or possibly the offering of previously unused gifts. Whatever it is, it is more than giving something up; it is primarily giving something back to the one who gave us his all. Consider today what Christ has done for you; then ask what you can do for him, and use Lent as an opportunity to respond.

Ask yourself

What will your response to Lent be? Will you give something up in a gesture of self-denial, or will you look to take something on that will help you to grow in faith?

Pray

Living God, forgive me that, too easily, I slip into a faith of negatives, imagining that you are more concerned with what I shouldn't do than what I should. Teach me that although there is a very real place for self-denial there is also a place for affirming and celebrating life in all its fullness. Help me, then, to use this coming season of Lent as a time to grow and learn, to deepen my faith and strengthen my commitment; above all, a time to make more room for you, so that you can work in my life and enrich my experience of your love. Through Jesus Christ my Lord. Amen.

Remember

Let love be authentic; abhor what is evil, cling to that which is good; reciprocate each other's affection; outshine one another in showing honour. Do not drag behind in showing enthusiasm, but be fervent in spirit and serve the Lord. Exult in hope, be long-suffering in affliction and be steadfast in prayer. Give generously to the needs of the saints; offer hospitality to strangers.   *Romans 12:9-13*

Close

Lord Jesus Christ, teach me to take up my cross, but also to celebrate your gift of new life. Amen.

A thorough examination

Read

Assess yourselves to check that you are living in the faith. Test yourselves to make sure.   *2 Corinthians 13:5a*

Ponder

The older we get, the more it pays to keep a check on our health. That's not to say we should become morbid hypochondriacs; simply that we should keep an eye out for problems so that we can seek help to put them right before they take hold. If that is true medically speaking, it's true also when it comes to our spiritual health, for that can equally suffer as the years go by. Complacency, disillusionment or sheer weariness are all conditions that can steal upon us, sapping our faith of its natural vitality. Just as with our physical well-being, we need to be alert to the signs, regularly making time to examine ourselves.

Traditionally, Lent is such a time, calling us to reflect on our discipleship and to ask ourselves if everything is as it should be. None of us is perfect, of course, and the last thing God wants is to encourage a spirit of negative self-criticism. Rather, he wants us to conduct an honest self-appraisal, and then to seek his gracious help in bringing inner healing and renewal. The cure does not lie in us, any more than self-help remedies are the answer to every physical ailment. It lies in recognising something is wrong and seeking help from the one who alone is able to give us wholeness. If we are willing to admit our need, he will do the rest.

Ask yourself

When did you last reflect on the state of your discipleship? Have you been burying your head in the sand, aware that not all is well but reluctant to face it? Have you forgotten God's promise of forgiveness and renewal?

Pray

Almighty and all-seeing God, I thank you for this season of Lent: a time to reflect upon my discipleship, to consider my calling, to examine myself and to assess the health of my faith. Help me to be honest in this: to see myself as I really am with all my weaknesses, ugliness and sinfulness. Help me to face the things I usually prefer to push aside; the unpleasant truths I sweep under the carpet, pretending they are not there.

So may I come to you, acknowledging my faults, recognising my weaknesses and receiving your forgiveness, which alone can make me whole, through the grace of Christ. Amen.

Remember

Examine me, O God, and search me; test my heart and mind.   *Psalm 26:2*

Close

Lord Jesus Christ, touch my life with your healing forgiveness, and put a new heart and a right spirit within me, so that I may truly love you and faithfully serve you, to the glory of your name. Amen.

Changing our tune

Read

As he rode, people carpeted the road with their cloaks. Then, as he started the descent from the Mount of Olives, the whole multitude of the disciples began loudly and joyfully to praise God for the mighty deeds they had seen, saying, 'Blessed is the king who comes in the name of the Lord! Peace in heaven, glory in the highest heaven!' Some Pharisees in the crowd said to him, 'Teacher, rebuke your disciples and tell them to stop.' He answered, 'I tell you this, if they were to keep silent, the very stones would shout out.' As he caught sight of the city, he wept over it, saying, 'If only you recognised this day the things that make for peace! Instead, though, they are hidden from your eyes!'   *Luke 19:36-42*

Ponder

It was only a children's story but it made the point well. 'Who will help me sow my seed?' asks the chicken. 'Not I', comes the answer. 'Who will help me reap the harvest?' 'Not I', comes the answer again. 'Who will help me grind the flour? knead the dough? bake the loaf? 'Not I . . . not I . . . not I.' Then, finally, the all-important question: 'Who will help me eat the bread?' and, immediately, a change of tone: 'Me! Me! Me!' It is an illustration, of course, of the fickleness of human nature, our friendship and loyalty so often depending on what's in it for us.

So it was on that first Palm Sunday as Jesus entered Jerusalem to the acclaim of the crowds. 'Who will welcome me as king?' his actions seemed to be saying, and the answer was 'Me!' Who wants to share in the kingdom of God?' and again the answer is 'Me!' Yet, just a few days later when the crunch question comes – 'Who will follow the way of the cross?' – the response from many is so very different: 'Not I!' – or, to put it more accurately, 'We have no king but Caesar. Crucify! Crucify! Crucify!' Palm Sunday is a day that challenges us concerning our loyalty, asking how ready we are to follow when faith is demanding and the going gets tough. Thank God, it is also about the one who, however often we may change our tune, stays faithful to us to the point of death.

Ask yourself

Are you prepared to accept the cost as well as the rewards of service? Have you understood that the Servant King and the King of kings are one and the same?

Pray

Lord Jesus Christ, I am good at singing your praises when life goes as I want it to, but it's another matter when my expectations are overturned, my preconceptions challenged and my faith tested. I am eager to receive your blessings but reluctant to take the way of sacrifice. I am happy to proclaim you as King, but hesitant in offering my service. So often, my commitment is short-lived, superficial and self-centred, more about *my* well-being than *your* kingdom.

Forgive me, and by your grace, help me to offer you true allegiance, whatever you may ask, to the glory of your name. Amen.

Remember

My kingdom is not of this world.   *John 18:36a*

Close

Lord Jesus Christ, I thank you that though I am faithful to you in so little, you are faithful in so much; that though I repeatedly change my tune, your love never fails. To you be praise and glory, now and for ever. Amen.

Totally devoted to you!

Read

Then they came to Jerusalem.   *Mark 11:15 (NRSV)*

Ponder

Some years ago, there was a song in the charts from the hit musical *Grease* with the title 'Hopelessly devoted to you'. It was a song about love – a love sufficiently strong to overcome hurt and rejection in order to establish a lasting relationship. There is a sense, though on a far deeper level, in which that title perfectly sums up the attitude of Jesus towards the whole of humankind, nowhere exhibited more clearly than in the week leading up to the cross.

We see it, believe it or not, in those five simple words of our reading. They look simple enough, don't they? – but beneath the surface they bear eloquent testimony to the awesome love of Christ, for, humanly speaking, Jerusalem was the last place Jesus should have been heading for. The knives were out for him, his enemies determined finally to silence him, and Jesus knew it as well as anyone. Yet he carried on, setting his face towards Jerusalem, refusing to be deflected from his path. He went willingly to his death, despite all it cost him – despite the emotional, physical and spiritual trauma he endured, just like any other human being. Why? Quite simply, because he loves us, his devotion to us greater than any we might show to him. That song title could have been written about Jesus, except for one thing; his love wasn't hopeless – anything but – it brought hope, joy and life to all. What we see in Christ is something more wonderful still: the one who is totally devoted to you!

Ask yourself

Have you begun to realise how much Jesus loves you? Have you made your response?

Pray

Lord Jesus Christ, I am reminded today that you didn't just accept death for my sake but chose it; that you didn't simply let things happen but planned them in advance, knowing the way you would take, down to that final agony on the cross. You staked all, you gave all, and you did it willingly for the sake of people like me. Such love is too wonderful to comprehend, but I thank you for it with all my heart, and offer you my joyful praise in glad response. Amen.

Remember

Live in love, as Christ loved us and gave himself up for us, a fragrant offering and sacrifice to God.

Ephesians 5:2 (NRSV)

Close

Lord Jesus Christ, teach me to love as you love, and to offer you the devotion you deserve and that you so freely show to me. Amen.

Unsung disciples

Read

Jesus sent Peter and John, saying, 'Go and prepare the Passover meal for us that we may eat it.' They asked him, 'Where do you want us to make preparations for it?' 'Listen,' he said to them, 'when you have entered the city, a man carrying a jar of water will meet you; follow him into the house he enters and say to the owner of the house, "The teacher asks you, 'Where is the guest room, where I may eat the Passover with my disciples?'" He will show you a large room upstairs, already furnished. Make preparations for us there.' So they went and found everything as he had told them; and they prepared the Passover meal.

Luke 22:8-13 (NRSV)

Ponder

'First, I'd like to thank my wife and family for their faithful support; then, there's my manager, my agent, my friends . . .' We've all heard speeches like that, haven't we? Whether it's an Oscar winner, a sports personality having just won a prestigious event, an author awarded the Booker prize, or any other celebrity achieving recognition in their chosen field, the routine is much the same. And why not, for each of us, famous or otherwise, have people to whom we owe much; those who have helped make things possible. The speeches may often be boring, even embarrassing to listen to, but they nonetheless give well-deserved thanks to those behind the scenes.

There are no such speeches associated with Jesus in the days leading up to the cross, but there are hints of at least two people who played such an incognito role. The first was the owner of the colt upon which Jesus rode into Jerusalem. It only needed the disciples to say, 'The Lord needs it', for him gladly to let it go. The second was the owner of the upper room in which Jesus and the Apostles shared the Last Supper. Again, we have no idea who he was, but he also played his part in allowing Jesus to use his room in this way. These two shadowy individuals remind us that we can offer service in simple, practical ways that are no less valuable than 'spiritual' contributions. Our gifts may not be those that catch the eye, and it may be that we prefer it that way, but that does not mean we have nothing to offer. All of us have a part to play in God's kingdom and all have something to contribute in the service of Christ.

Ask yourself

Are you doing everything you can for the cause of Christ? Have you undervalued the contribution you are able to make?

Pray

Lord, you do not call me to a position of eye-catching responsibility in your service, but I have a part to play nonetheless. Whatever my gifts, I have a contribution to make which you can use in fulfilling something of your eternal purpose.

Teach me, then, to listen for your voice and, when you call, to respond gladly, offering whatever you ask whenever you need it, to the glory of your name. Amen.

Remember

Whatever you do, put yourself into it wholeheartedly, doing it for the Lord.   *Colossians 3:23*

Close

Lord Jesus Christ, teach me to serve you, not for any recognition I might receive but for the joy of contributing to your kingdom. Amen.

All talk?

Read

Simon Peter said to him, 'Lord, where are you going?' Jesus replied, 'You cannot follow me where I am going now, but you will some day.' Peter said, 'Lord, why can't I follow you now? I will lay down my very life for you. Even though everyone else might fall away, I will not.' Jesus responded, 'Mark my words: today, this very night, before the cock crows twice, you will disown me three times.' Peter, though, protested forcefully, 'Even if I have to die with you, I will never disown you.' The others all said the same.

John 13:36-37; Mark 14:29-31

Ponder

'A penny off income tax, cheaper fuel, more investment in the health service and education, higher pensions, tough measures on crime . . . ' We've heard it all before, haven't we? The words trotted out by politicians every four years or so as the country braces itself for another election. It's not that the politicians set out to deceive us (well, not most of them, anyway); rather that, swept along on the tide of the moment, they find that when it comes to it, they simply can't deliver – their fine words exposed as all talk.

So it was for Peter in the moments leading up to the cross. 'Even though everyone else might fall away, I will not. Even if I have to die with you, I will never disown you.' Rash, impulsive words, no doubt, but he meant every word and fully believed he could honour such promises. Events, of course, were to prove him wrong. So what is the message here for us? That we, like Peter, are false and faithless? That we are often prone to empty rhetoric? Both are probably true. The key detail, however, is that Jesus knew full well that Peter would fail him, that his words were all talk, yet still he loved him – enough to continue to the cross, enough to have chosen him as the rock of his Church. That's the wonder of this incident: that far from wanting him to punish himself afterwards for his failure, Jesus wanted Peter to know that he knew his weakness, understood he would fail, and yet still loved him. Here is the awesome message of the gospel – the message that gives hope to us all.

Ask yourself

Are you punishing yourself for past mistakes, burdened by a sense of guilt at your weakness and failures? Have you understood that Christ died for you as you are?

Pray

Lord Jesus Christ, I am reminded today that you chose Peter to be the rock of your Church – the man who, for all his protestations of loyalty, misunderstood and denied you. I am reminded that you chose ordinary, weak human beings to be your followers and that each in some way failed you when put to the test. I am reminded that you have called me in turn, just as weak, foolish and fallible, and yet, despite that, still you love me.

Lord, I praise you that though I see so little good within me, you see someone worth dying for and worth sharing life with for all eternity. Amen.

Remember

Here are words that you should trust and fully accept: that 'Jesus Christ came into the world to save sinners', I being the chief of such. Yet, I received mercy for that very purpose, that since I am the worst of sinners, Jesus Christ might display his supreme patience, making me an example to those who will gain eternal life through believing in him.

1 Timothy 1:15-16

Close

Lord Jesus Christ, by your grace, help me not just to talk of loyalty but to show it, as you have shown it to me. Amen.

Look both ways

Read

During supper, he took bread, and having given thanks he broke it and gave it to them, saying, 'Take this; it is my body.' Then he took a cup, and, giving thanks to God, he handed it to them; and they all drank from it. Then he said, 'This is my blood, the blood of the covenant, shed for many. I tell you the truth, I will not drink of the fruit of the vine again until that day when I drink it new with you in the kingdom of God.'

Mark 14:22-25

Ponder

There's a piece of advice we will all have received many times as children: 'Look both ways.' I refer, of course, to learning to cross the road, and to the advice of the Green Cross Code: 'Look right, look left, look right again.'

There is a sense in which Maundy Thursday invites us to do something very similar, only this time we are talking not about left and right but about the past and the future, and the difference those make to the present. 'Take this; it is my body,' said Jesus, and, as Paul reminds us in his letter to the Corinthians, these words are to serve as a constant reminder to Christians, calling to mind his suffering and death. Yet it was not all solemnity, for there was also a message of hope; a hint of joy to come in his words, 'I will not drink of the fruit of the vine again until that day when I drink it new with you in the kingdom of God.' Here, then, is a call to look backwards and forwards, to remember and to anticipate. It is a message not just for Maundy Thursday, nor simply for each time we break bread and share wine, but for each day and every moment. We are called to live here and now in the light of what God has done and what he promises to do.

Ask yourself

Are you unsure of your ability to face the present or uncertain of what the future might bring? Is it time you reminded yourself of what God has done in Christ, and what he promises still to do?

Pray

Lord Jesus Christ, I remember today everything you did to bring me life: the heartbreak you experienced, the fear you faced, the questions you wrestled with and the agony you endured. Save me from ever forgetting. I look forward to what you have promised: a day when I will share with you in your Father's kingdom where there will be an end to sorrow and suffering, sin and death. Save me from ever losing sight of that destiny.

I look back, I look forward, and thus I commit myself in confidence to your service here and now, knowing that you are the same Lord, yesterday, today and tomorrow – the one in whom I can safely put my trust. Amen.

Remember

The Lord Jesus, on the night he was betrayed, took bread, and having given thanks, he broke it and said, 'This is my body, broken for you. Do this in memory of me.' Similarly, he took a cup afterwards, saying, 'This cup is the new covenant in my blood. Whenever you drink, do this in memory of me.' For as often as you eat this bread and drink this cup, you proclaim the Lord's death, until he comes.

1 Corinthians 11:23-26

Close

Lord Jesus Christ, teach me to remember, teach me to look forward in faith, and so teach me to live each moment in the light of your love. Amen.

A straight choice

Read

The passers-by hurled insults at him, shaking their heads and saying, 'So, then, you who would destroy the temple and build it in three days: come down from the cross and save yourself!' The chief priests and teachers of the law joined in mocking him with similar taunts. 'He saved others,' they said, 'but he cannot save himself! Let this Messiah, the king of Israel, come down now from the cross, so that we might see and believe.'

Mark 15:29-32a

Ponder

'Many a true word is spoken in jest.' So the saying has it, and if you need convincing of that, take a look at the taunts faced by Jesus on the cross. 'He saved others, but he cannot save himself!' – words of mockery and derision aimed at adding to the suffering already experienced by Jesus, and you can imagine his tormentors smirking, chuckling, congratulating themselves on their own wit. Make him eat his words, they thought; now let's see how smart he is!

Yet, if they had but known, they could not have spoken more profoundly, for those words give voice to the stark choice faced by Jesus and the love he showed in taking the path he did. Could he have saved himself? Of course he could. Not only could he have steered well clear of Jerusalem in the first place, but for someone who had healed the sick, stilled the storm, fed the multitude, even raised the dead, to come down from the cross was nothing, positively straightforward by comparison. Yet to do that would have been to go back on his mission and deny his calling; for it was only through his accepting suffering and death that he could open up the way to life for others. It was a straight choice, an 'either/or' rather than 'both/and' situation, and he chose to save us rather than himself.

'He saved others, be he cannot save himself.' How wrong they were, yet how right!

Ask yourself

Have you appreciated the enormity of what Jesus did on the cross? Do you recognise the scale of the choice he had to make?

Pray

Lord Jesus Christ, I marvel again today at the astonishing truth that lies at the heart of this week – that you endured the humiliation of Gethsemane, the agony of the cross and the darkness of the tomb, not because you had to but because you chose to. I praise you that despite the jeers and ridicule you faced, your concern was always for others rather than yourself, and thus you freely chose the way of humility, service and self-sacrifice; the lonely path of the cross. Above all, I praise you for your faithfulness to the last – that though you could so easily have stepped down from the cross, you didn't; and though you could have saved yourself, you preferred instead to save the world.

Lord Jesus Christ, however often I hear it, still I am amazed by the magnitude of your love and the awesomeness of your sacrifice. Receive my praise and accept my worship, for your name's sake. Amen.

Remember

Surely he has carried our weaknesses and carried our afflictions; yet we reckoned him stricken, struck down and afflicted by God. He was wounded, though, for our misdeeds, crushed for our mistakes; he endured the punishment that made us whole and his bruises brought us healing. We have all gone astray like sheep, each going our own way, but the Lord has laid on him the offences of us all.

Isaiah 53:4-6

Close

Lord Jesus Christ, as you put *me* first, help me to put *you* first in turn. Amen.

He was dead

Read

Since it was the day of preparation for the Passover, the Jews did not want dead bodies left on the cross during the Sabbath, especially because that Sabbath was a day of special import, so they asked Pilate to have the legs of those who had been crucified broken and their bodies removed. Accordingly, the soldiers broke the legs of the first and then the second of those crucified with Jesus, but when they came to Jesus, they saw he was already dead so they did not break his legs. Instead, one of the soldiers pierced his side with a spear.   *John 19:31-34a*

Ponder

Some animals, when faced with danger, make use of a cunning trick. Instead of running or standing up to fight, they play dead, thus confusing their attacker, which is only interested in live prey. To hear some people talk, you might imagine that the crucifixion involved a similar trick. Maybe Jesus wasn't dead, after all, some suggest; perhaps in the coolness of the tomb he regained consciousness, and was subsequently whisked away by his followers under cover of darkness.

It's far-fetched, I know, but some people will believe anything rather than have their preconceptions challenged. The idea of resurrection simply goes against everything they believe about and experience in the world. Yet, one look at the gospels – and at the Gospel of John in particular – leaves us in no doubt about the truth. Jesus was dead, a spear thrust into his side to make doubly certain. He was laid limp and lifeless in a tomb, and a stone rolled against the entrance. Humanly speaking it was over, the end of a wonderful ministry and an unforgettable man. He had shared our life; he had shared our death. If the story was to continue, it was out of human hands – it was down now to God.

Ask yourself

Is there a danger sometimes, in the light of the resurrection, of forgetting that Jesus actually died, going the whole way on our behalf?

Pray

Lord Jesus Christ, I can lose sight sometimes of the darkness of Good Friday, living as I do in the light of Easter, but I remember today that for those who saw the life slip from you as you hung on the cross, there could be no mistaking the truth, no escaping the awfulness of the moment. You endured the pain of betrayal, the hurt of denial, the humiliation of mockery and, finally, the awful isolation of separation from your Father as you took our sins on your shoulders, and you did it for such as me.

Lord Jesus, I marvel at your love; at the fact that you were willing to go not just part of the way but the whole way to redeem the world. I marvel that you, in whom is life eternal, were willing to experience death so that I might taste that life. Teach me today to appreciate the wonder of that sacrifice and to recognise all that it means in so many ways. Amen.

Remember

That evening, a wealthy man from Arimathea, named Joseph, who was also a disciple of Jesus, went and asked Pilate for the body of Jesus, and Pilate ordered that it should be given to him. Joseph took the body, wrapped it in a clean linen cloth, and laid it in a tomb which he had hewn for himself in the rock. Then, having rolled a huge stone across the tomb entrance, he went away. Mary Magdalene and the other Mary remained there, sitting opposite the tomb. *Matthew 27:57-61*

Close

Lord Jesus Christ, you gave so much; help me to give to you, if only a little, in return. Amen.

From defeat to victory

Read

He is not here; he has risen!

Luke 24:5b

Ponder

'Oh well, that's it,' he said. 'No point in watching any longer.' And it genuinely looked like it. We'd allowed our little boy to stay up late that night to watch Manchester United in the European Cup Final but, with the disappointment increasingly evident in his eyes, we were beginning to wish we hadn't. Just a few seconds left – no, actually into injury time – and the German supporters were already saluting their team, the engraver poised over the trophy that was already decked out in their team's ribbons . . . and then it happened: a goal from nowhere, scenes of wild jubilation, and the game heading for extra time. But what was this? Another attack . . . a corner . . . a goal! From the jaws of defeat, Manchester United had snatched victory!

Unbelievable? Well almost. Yet not half so extraordinary as the event nearly two thousand years earlier, when three women made their way solemnly to their master's tomb. There were tears in *their* eyes too; not just of disappointment but utter devastation, for the one who had been the centre of their lives and on whom they had pinned all their hopes was dead; cruelly murdered on a cross. There was no hope of *him* coming back; it was over, finished. Until suddenly, the tomb was before them . . . empty . . . a stranger telling them Jesus had risen . . . and the Lord himself standing before them, greeting them as he'd greeted them so often before. Defeat had been turned to victory; a victory not just for them but for us, and one we share in not simply by proxy but first-hand – for it means new life for all, new beginnings, new hope – the assurance that whatever we might face, nothing can stand between us and the love of God in Christ. Unbelievable, yet true!

Ask yourself

Are there situations in your life that you despair of and in which you feel defeated? Have you forgotten that God is able to triumph in what seem the most hopeless of circumstances?

Pray

Lord Jesus Christ, I thank you for the great message of Easter – that in what the world counted defeat you won the greatest of victories. I praise you for your triumph over evil and death, and for everything that this has meant over the years to so many people. Most of all, I thank you for my own experiences of your resurrection power – the times you have brought me victory over the things that deny me the opportunity of living life to the full.

Teach me to live each day in the light of what you have done, confident that no situation, however dreadful it may seem, is finally beyond your power to redeem, and so may I put my trust in you always, for this life and the life to come. Amen.

Remember

Listen and I will tell you a mystery! Not all of us will die, but we will all be changed, in a flash, in the blink of an eye, at the last trumpet. For the trumpet will sound, and the dead will be raised imperishable, and we will be changed. For this ephemeral body must put on an eternal body, and this mortal body must put on immortality. When this is done, then the words of the saying will be fulfilled: 'Death has been swallowed up by victory. Where is your victory, death? Where is your sting?' Death's sting is sin, and sin's power lies in the law. Give thanks, then, to God who gives us the victory, through our Lord Jesus Christ.

1 Corinthians 15:51-57

Close

Living God, though I may feel crushed beyond redemption, teach me that your love will always overcome. Amen.

Too good to be true?

Read

Returning from the tomb, they related everything to the eleven
and those gathered with them – it was Mary Magdalene,
Joanna, Mary the mother of James, and other women with
them who told it to the Apostles – but their words seemed
like a foolish fancy, and they did not believe them.

Luke 24:9-11

Ponder

Do you know the hymn 'Can it be true?' It's not sung
today as often as it used to be, which is a pity, for it asks a
question central to Easter that many stumble over. The
question is essentially this (though the hymn puts it more
poetically): Can it be true that Jesus lived and died and
rose again? Most people have no problems with the first
two of those – that Jesus lived and died. But when it comes
to resurrection it's a different matter. Quite simply, for many
people it seems too good to be true. It's almost as though the
very fact that the idea is so special, by definition disproves
it. We're just not used to good news like that. It's the stuff
of daydreams, not for hard-headed realists of the twenty-
first century.

The funny thing is that it wasn't the stuff for hard-
headed realists of the first century either. When the women
who'd gone to the tomb burst in on the disciples with the
news that Christ had risen, their words, so we are told,
seemed like a foolish fantasy, or, as the *New International
Version* of the Bible so graphically puts it, 'like nonsense'.
These were no credulous romantics waiting to swallow any
old story; they were down-to-earth individuals, utterly convinced that it was all over; that Jesus was dead and buried.
Yet, each came not just to believe but to know that he was
alive and with them again through his Spirit; that knowledge

sufficient not just for them to recommit their lives to him but gladly to die in his service. It may have seemed too good to be true, but they were soon to discover that it wasn't. Have you discovered that too?

Ask yourself

Have you allowed the defeatism of this world to undermine your faith? Does your faith need resurrecting?

Pray

Sovereign God, sometimes it *does* seem too good to be true – the cross, the empty tomb and the promise of new life, not just now but for all eternity. There are times when, for all my faith, I struggle to accept it, not because I don't want to but because I want to so much, and I wonder whether I'm fooling myself, telling myself what I want to believe. Yet, you remind me today that this is precisely how the Apostles felt, until they met with the risen Christ and knew the truth for themselves, not as speculation but as an indisputable experience.

Rekindle my faith this Easter-time. Assure me, through experiencing again the presence of the risen Christ in my heart, that with you nothing is too good to be true, for you are able to do more than anyone could ever imagine. To you be praise and glory, now and for evermore. Amen.

Remember

They found the eleven and their companions assembled together, and saying to each other, 'The Lord has indeed risen! He has appeared to Simon!' While they were discussing this, Jesus stood among them in person and said to them, 'Peace be with you.'   *Luke 24:33b-34, 36*

Close

Living God, teach me that the gospel is not only wonderful-sounding news but it is also true! Amen.

The God who cannot be kept down

Read

The following day – in other words, the day after that of Preparation – the chief priests and the Pharisees congregated before Pilate and said, 'Your excellency, we recall how that deceiver said while he was alive, "After three days I will rise." Will you, then, order that the tomb be made secure until the third day? Otherwise his disciples may come and steal him away, and tell the people, "He has been raised from the dead" – a final deception that would be worse than the first.' Pilate said to them, 'You have a guard of soldiers; go and make it as secure as possible.' So they went and made the tomb secure by sealing it with a stone and leaving a guard in charge.   *Matthew 27:62-66*

Ponder

When my daughter was a baby she had a wonderful inflatable toy called 'Bopper Bear'. No matter how hard or how often you knocked it over, it would always bounce back up again. I don't know if Kate enjoyed it, but I did!

There is something of that idea in the story of the resurrection, for we see there a supreme demonstration of the God who cannot be kept down. The enemies of Jesus had conspired together, determined finally to do away with him, and as they cut him limp and lifeless from the cross, sealing him in a tomb, they must have been convinced they had succeeded. Even then, they placed a guard outside the tomb, just to make sure. They were leaving nothing to chance. Yet, it didn't matter, for the next day what did they find but the stone rolled away and the tomb empty, their worst fears realised. How could it be? What could have happened? These are good questions, which anyone who disputes the resurrection still needs to answer. Hatred had done its worst, but the love of God could not be kept down. Christ was risen! It's as true today as ever; ultimately there is nothing and no one that can frustrate the will of God. Though many may still try and sometimes seem to succeed, ours is a God who will finally triumph, and who gives us the victory in turn.

Ask yourself

Do you find it hard sometimes to believe in the ultimate triumph of God's purpose? Have you forgotten the astonishing events of that first Easter?

Pray

Living God, I praise you once more for the good news of Easter, the triumphant message of resurrection – new hope, new joy, new life! I praise you for the truth at its heart: that your love could not be kept down, your purpose could not be defeated and your mercy could not be destroyed. Teach me that what was true then is true now – that there is still nothing that can stand in the way of your sovereign power and redeeming grace.

Assure me, then, however things may seem and even when faith seems to fly in the face of reason, to trust in you, confident that your will shall be done and your kingdom come. Through Jesus Christ my Lord. Amen.

Remember

I am convinced that neither death nor life, nor angels or demons, nor the present or the future, nor any powers, nor height or depth or anything else in all creation, will ever be able to separate us from the love of God that is ours in Christ Jesus our Lord. *Romans 8:38-39*

Close

Lord Jesus Christ, as you rose victorious over death, so may hope, faith and love continue to triumph in my life over everything that conspires against them. Amen.

Better than expected

Read

That same day, there were two going to a village called Emmaus, about seven miles from Jerusalem, and they were discussing everything that had happened. As they conversed and talked together, Jesus himself drew near and walked with them, but somehow their eyes did not recognise him. He said to them, 'What was it you were discussing together as you walked?' They halted, looking dejected. Then one of them, called Cleopas, answered, 'Are you the only one visiting Jerusalem not to know the things that have happened there over recent days?' 'What things?' he asked. 'The things about Jesus of Nazareth,' they replied; 'a prophet mighty in word and deed before God and all the people; how our chief priests and leaders handed him over to be sentenced to death and then crucified him. We had hoped that he was the one who was going to redeem Israel.'   *Luke 24:13-21a*

Ponder

How often do plans work out as well as you hoped? There may be the odd occasion when they measure up to expectations, but, in my experience, our grand designs and dreams rarely yield in practice what they promise in theory. More often than not, hopes have a habit of falling horribly flat.

A similar sense of anticlimax, though infinitely more intense, was felt by the two disciples walking back along the Emmaus Road, their mood summed up in those plaintive words: 'We had hoped that he was the one who was going to redeem Israel.' For a time, they had dared to imagine that the promised day of the Lord had dawned, but their hopes had been dashed – another case, so it seemed, of reality not measuring up to expectations. Read on, though, and it's a different story; for suddenly, as they broke bread with this stranger, they realised who he was – not just the redeemer of Israel but the risen Lord, back from the grave, victorious over sin and death. Here, in miniature, is one of the great truths of the gospel: that Jesus does not simply fulfil our hopes but far exceeds them, offering joy and peace, hope and strength beyond anything words can begin to express. Thanks be to God!

Ask yourself

Have your hopes in life met with disappointment? Have you underestimated what Jesus is able to offer?

Pray

Lord Jesus Christ, I praise you today for the wonder of your mercy, the extent of your love and your great gift of life. I rejoice that you came into our world not just to be an earthly Messiah but a universal Saviour, the King of kings and Lord of lords. I thank you not only for everything you have done but for everything you have yet to do – the blessings I have yet to experience, the insights I have yet to discover, the joys that you yet hold in store.

Remind me each day that you are not simply able to meet my needs but able to give me far more than I can ever ask or imagine, and so may I look forward in hope, and live each day with joy in the light of your love. Amen.

Remember

No eye has seen, nor ear heard, nor any heart conceived of the things that God has prepared for those who love him.

1 Corinthians 2:9

Close

Living God, I thank you that however great I think you are, the truth is I have scarcely begun to understand the fullness of your gift in Christ. Amen.

Making waves

Read

We always thank God, the Father of our Lord Jesus Christ, because we have heard of your faith, and your love for all the saints, springing from the hope stored up for you in heaven that you heard about in the word of truth, the gospel that has come to you. Just as it has been bearing fruit and growing in the whole world, so, from the moment you first heard it and truly understood the grace of God, it has been bearing fruit among you.

Colossians 1:3-6

Ponder

From when he was a little boy, my son loved throwing stones into water – the bigger the better, since the more exciting the splash. Not that it needs a big stone to have a profound effect – just a tiny pebble tossed into the centre of a pool sends ripples radiating inexorably outwards until they reach the bank.

In a sense, the same could be said of the life, death and resurrection of Christ. It all began so quietly, in a stable in Bethlehem and a baby lying in a manger, and, even at the height of his ministry, the majority of the world's population would have been oblivious to his existence. What could one man hope to achieve through his life, death or even resurrection? In global terms, it was a drop in the ocean – but what a drop, for still today the ripples of Christ's coming are reaching outwards! Who would have believed two thousand years ago that the gospel would still be changing lives and the Church continuing to grow? It was beyond his enemies' worst nightmares and greater than his followers' wildest dreams. Yet that is the nature of our God; the God who, in his sovereign power, plunged himself into the pool of human history in such a way that the world would never be the same again.

Ask yourself

Do you doubt sometimes that God is able to make an impact in the world today? Have you forgotten the way the good news of Christ has changed countless lives across the years?

Pray

Sovereign God, I praise you today for the power of the gospel; the way across the centuries it has spoken to so many lives. I praise you for everything you achieved in Christ, transforming not just individuals but the very course of history through his life, death and resurrection. I praise you that you involved yourself in human history, not standing aloof from our need but sharing our humanity so that we might share your eternity.

For your life-giving grace and mighty strength that continue to reach out into the world and that will never rest until your will is done and your kingdom come, receive my glad and joyful worship, in the name of Christ. Amen.

Remember

By God's grace, I have become a servant of this gospel entrusted to me by the working of his power, so that now, through the Church, the rich and varied wisdom of God might be proclaimed to the rulers and heavenly authorities, in accordance with the eternal purpose he has fulfilled in Jesus Christ our Lord.   *Ephesians 3:7, 10-11*

Close

Sovereign God, through the power of your risen Son, continue to work within me and through me, to make your name known. Amen.

Truth will out!

Read

Some of the guards went into the city and told the chief priests what had happened. After the priests had called together the elders, they formulated a plan to give a generous bribe to the soldiers, telling them, 'You must say this, "His followers came during the night and made off with him while we were sleeping." If the governor gets to hear of this, we will reassure him and keep you out of trouble.' So the guards took the money and did as instructed.

Matthew 28:11-15a

Ponder

Truth will out, we are told, and so it repeatedly proves. There may be occasions when deceit goes unnoticed, but falsehood has an uncanny habit of being exposed; of weaving a web that finally traps the very one who spins it. We may suppress the truth, we may twist and distort it, but it is hard to keep it hidden for ever, as the death and resurrection of Christ make crystal clear. His enemies stopped at nothing to get their man, cynically employing false witnesses to secure the verdict they were looking for. Similarly, when they heard news of the empty tomb, they turned once again to deceit, slipping a backhander to the guards in a desperate bid to hush up events. They did all they could to stifle the truth, but it was no good, for first one person, then another, then another still, and so on in perpetuity, met with the risen Lord and knew the truth for themselves.

There is here both challenge and promise. On the one hand, there is a warning that deception will be uncovered however hard we try to conceal it; that all things will finally come to light. On the other hand there is assurance that right will triumph; that God's purpose will triumph. So we put our trust in Christ, the way, the truth and the life, knowing that his love is sure and his mercy dependable, now and always.

Ask yourself

Are you hiding behind half-truths or untruths? Is it time to be open with God, so that you might receive his mercy and know the peace of a clear conscience and a life right with him?

Pray

Lord Jesus Christ, I celebrate again today your triumph over falsehood and evil; the fact that all the attempts to discredit you and suppress the truth of your resurrection came to nothing, for it was impossible to deny the reality of your presence in the hearts of those who knew you.

Forgive me that I am not always as truthful as I should be, slipping so easily into white lies, hiding behind untruths or half-truths, or being economical with the truth. Remind me that *your* truth can set me free, and so teach me to receive it with joy, speak it in love and live by it in faith, trusting in your love that alone will never fail. In your name I ask it. Amen.

Remember

If we claim to have no sin, we are fooling ourselves and the truth has no place in us. If we confess our sins, he is just, and we can rely on him to forgive our sins and cleanse us from all evil.   *1 John 1:8-9*

Close

Living God, teach me that though all else may prove false, you will stay true. Amen.

A second chance

Read

When they had breakfasted, Jesus said to Simon Peter, 'Simon, son of John, do you love me more than these?' He said to him, 'Yes, Lord, you know that I love you.' Jesus said to him, 'Feed my lambs.' He said to him a second time, 'Simon, son of John, do you love me?' He answered, 'Yes, Lord, you know that I love you.' Jesus said to him, 'Look after my sheep.' He asked him a third time, 'Simon, son of John, do you love me?' It wounded Peter that he asked him a third time, 'Do you love me?', so he responded, 'Lord, you know everything; you know that I love you.' Jesus said to him, 'Feed my sheep.'

John 21:15-17

Ponder

Which of us haven't at some time wished we could have a time over again; that we could undo some thoughtless or angry word, some rash commitment or unwise judgement, or some careless mistake? If only we could have a second chance, an opportunity to put right the past!

If anyone longed for that it must surely have been Peter; for he must have felt helplessly and hopelessly burdened by past mistakes. The memory of his denial of Jesus – not once, not twice, but three times – must have haunted him without respite. What wouldn't he have given to undo those moments? Only, of course, he couldn't – or could he? For suddenly, here was Jesus asking, not once, not twice, but three times: 'Do you love me?' It took a while for the message to sink in, his initial reaction one of pique, but finally, I suspect, the truth dawned – for each time he'd denied him, Jesus was offering the opportunity to make amends, to put the past behind him and start afresh. No, we cannot put the clock back as such, and, yes, sometimes, in terms of others at least, we have to live with the consequences of our mistakes, but with God the opportunity is always there to move forward from what has been towards what shall be. We need only to acknowledge our faults and be truly sorry for resurrection to begin once again, here and now.

Ask yourself

Are you burdened by a sense of guilt? Do you feel there is no way God can forgive past mistakes? Have you understood what the resurrection means in terms of new beginnings now?

Pray

Gracious God, though I try to put the past behind me, all too often I am haunted by mistakes. Though I try to make amends for the wrongs I've done, I find it hard to escape a sense of guilt.

Remind me that you are always ready to offer free and total forgiveness, no matter how foolish I have been or how many opportunities I have wasted. Teach me that the past is done with and the future is open before me. Receive, then, my thanks and lead me forward, in the name of Christ. Amen.

Remember

In his divine mercy he had overlooked the sins of the past, in order to show that he is righteous and that he justifies the one who has faith in Jesus.   *Romans 3:25b-26*

Close

Lord Jesus Christ, teach me that new life does not begin in the distant future but here and now, and so may I receive your gracious gift with glad thanksgiving. Amen.

Still good news

Read

Now the eleven disciples went to Galilee, to the mountain to which Jesus had directed them. When they saw him, they worshipped him; but some doubted. And Jesus came and said to them, 'All authority in heaven and on earth has been given to me. Go therefore and make disciples of all nations, baptising them in the name of the Father and of the Son and of the Holy Spirit, and teaching them to obey everything that I have commanded you. And remember, I am with you always, to the end of the age.'

Matthew 28:16-20 (NRSV)

Ponder

Which of us haven't at some time wished we could have a time over again; that we could undo some thoughtless and angry word, some rash commitment or unwise judgement, or some careless mistake? Do those lines sound familiar? They should do, for you read them only yesterday. Like most things, when you've heard them once, you've heard them enough! The great wonder of Easter, by contrast, is that we can hear its message again and again, yet it goes on being as true and relevant today as it was yesterday, and as it will continue to be tomorrow and the next day, *ad infinitum*.

How different that is from typical modern-day news headlines. I discovered some of those the other day when I was lifting carpets in the course of redecorating. Beneath them were newspapers dating back three, four, even five years, the events emblazoned on the front pages seeming strangely remote. Not that you have to go back years for that to be true; in our high-tech media age, even yesterday's news is old hat. The good news of the resurrection is different. Why? Because it continues to change lives in the present, each day offering hope and new beginnings to believers across the world. Easter Day may be over, but we cannot consign the message it proclaims to the past. It is still good news, today and every day!

Ask yourself

Does the good news of the resurrection go on being true in your life each day? Have you underestimated the continuing power of the gospel to speak in people's lives today?

Pray

Sovereign God, I thank you that Easter is not just about events long ago but about now; not just about others but about me; not just about certain aspects of life but about life itself! I thank you for the truths of Easter I can continue to celebrate today: the victory of good over evil, love over hate, life over death; the turning of weakness into strength, fear into courage, doubt into faith; a new beginning where it had seemed like the end, hope where there had been despair; confidence where there had been confusion.

Help me to live each day in the light of Easter, with its joy bubbling up in my heart, its laughter shining from my eyes, and its message always on my lips. So may others, seeing the difference it has made to me, discover the difference it can make for them. Through Jesus Christ my Lord. Amen.

Remember

I am not ashamed of the gospel, for it is the power of God leading to salvation for everyone who believes, to the Jew, first, and to the Gentile.

Romans 1:16

Close

Lord Jesus Christ, may the message of your resurrection continue to stir my heart and change lives today, just as it has spoken to so many across the years. Amen.

The complete picture

Read

Coming together, they asked him, 'Lord, is this the time when you will restore the kingdom of Israel?' He replied, 'It is not for you to know the time or seasons that the Father has laid down by his own authority, but you will receive power when the Holy Spirit comes upon you and you will be my witnesses both in Jerusalem, and all Judea and Samaria, and to the ends of the earth.' Having said this, and while they were watching, he was lifted up, and a cloud hid him from their sight. While he was going and they were staring into the sky, suddenly two men clothed in white stood next to them. They said, 'Men of Galilee, why do you stand staring into the sky? This Jesus, who has been taken from you up into heaven, will come in the same way that you saw him go.'

Acts 1:6-11

Ponder

There are few things worse than reading a book and finding that a page is missing. It's worst of all when it's the last page. Few of us would even start to read a book if we knew it would be cut short, yet, with Jesus, we sometimes do something very similar, celebrating his resurrection, and the gift of his Spirit at Pentecost, but virtually overlooking his Ascension. One reason for this, perhaps, is that our account of the Ascension is caught in a time-warp, reflecting the cosmology of days gone by. God is seen as 'up there' and so Jesus is portrayed as vanishing *up* into heaven, the disciples staring stupefied into the sky. Such language serves to obscure the underlying message of Ascension as surely as the cloud hid Jesus from the Apostles' sight.

Yet, if the details of what happened are a mystery, the significance is clear enough. This was a watershed moment for the Apostles when they realised, for the first time, the full magnitude of who Jesus was. They had followed him during his ministry, believing him to be the Messiah; they had rejoiced at his resurrection, greeting him as the risen Lord; but now they recognised that he was the Son of God, the King of kings and Lord of all. Don't forget Ascension Day! Above all, don't forget what Ascension Day means, for it reminds us that Jesus is greater than words can begin to express, sovereign over all. It gives us the complete picture, without which our faith is infinitely the poorer.

Ask yourself

Do you feel a sense of awe in the presence of Christ? Do you worship him not just as a friend by your side through his Spirit, but also as the one enthroned in splendour?

Pray

Lord Jesus Christ, I thank you for the truth at the heart of this day – you were brought low yet have been lifted high; you were the servant of all yet are above all and beyond all; though you spent your life in Palestine and died in Jerusalem, your love has transformed lives in every country and continent, crossing barriers of culture, colour and creed.

With all your people in every age, I give you praise and glory, honour and thanksgiving, now and always. Amen.

Remember

Having taken on human form, he humbled himself to total obedience, even to the point of death – death on a cross. For that reason, God highly exalted him, giving him the name that is above every name, so that at the name of Jesus every being in heaven, on earth and under the earth, should bow the knee, and every tongue should acknowledge that Jesus Christ is Lord, to the glory of God the Father.

Philippians 2:7b-11

Close

Lord Jesus Christ, remind me of all that you are and equip me to live to your glory, until that day when I kneel in your presence and join in the worship of heaven, to the glory of your name. Amen.

A gift for all

Read

When the day of Pentecost dawned, they were gathered in one place. Suddenly, a sound like the rush of a mighty wind came from heaven, filling the house where they were sitting. After that, tongues of fire appeared that divided, so that a tongue rested on each of them. They were all filled with the Holy Spirit, and began to speak in various tongues, as the Spirit enabled them. This is what was spoken of by the prophet Joel: 'In the last days, God declares, I will pour out my spirit on all people; your sons and daughters will prophesy, your old men will dream dreams, and your young men will see visions. I will pour out my spirit even on male and female slaves in those days.'

Acts 2:1-4, 16-18a

Ponder

Have you stayed in the Hilton hotel, owned a Rolls-Royce or dined with the Queen? I haven't, and I very much doubt I ever will. Some things in life are reserved for the select few, while the majority of us have to make do with more run-of-the-mill facilities and occasions. The people of the Old Testament believed that this was true of the Spirit of God, convinced that it was a rare and special gift which only a privileged elite would experience. There was no way in the world *they* would be filled by that Spirit; such an honour went to those like Gideon, Samuel, Isaiah, Ezekiel and others of similar stature. For the rank and file, God would always be one step removed, access to him mediated by priest and temple. The words of the prophet Joel, wonderful though they sounded, must have raised more than a few eyebrows when first spoken, for they postulated an entirely new relationship with God.

Yet that is the relationship experienced by the Apostles on the so-called day of Pentecost, and it is a gift offered to us in turn. God is not remote and detached, but can be experienced as a living reality within – encouraging, teaching, empowering, guiding – ever at work in our lives. There is no favouritism with God. There is one privilege we can all enjoy: the inner presence of the Holy Spirit – surely the greatest privilege of all!

Ask yourself

Do you sometimes see God as distant, removed from daily life? Have you opened your life to the living presence of his Holy Spirit?

Pray

Gracious God, I thank you that I can know you for myself through the living presence of your Holy Spirit. I praise you that, by your Spirit, you meet my innermost needs, filling my soul to overflowing with joy, peace, hope and power. I celebrate the way you are always moving in my life, deepening my faith, enriching my experience, strengthening my commitment and enlarging my vision.

Help me to open my life more fully to the presence of your Spirit, so that I may know you better and be equipped to serve you more fully, to the glory of your name. Amen.

Remember

To demonstrate that we are his children, God has sent the Spirit of his Son into our hearts, crying, 'Abba! Father!' You are, therefore, no longer a servant but a child, and if a child, then also an heir, through God's doing.   *Galatians 4:6-7*

Close

Holy Spirit, unpredictable as the wind, unquenchable as fire, yet gentle as a dove, come now and breathe new energy into my life and new life into my soul, by your gracious power. Amen.

A glorious mystery

Read

Now there are various gifts, but the same Spirit; various ministries but the same Lord; different types of service but the same God working through all of them.

1 Corinthians 12:4-6

Ponder

Mention Advent, Christmas, Holy Week or Easter to most Christians, and you will see a sparkle of interest in their eyes, for these are well-loved festivals that speak in innumerable ways. Mention Trinity Sunday and you are more likely to witness a blank expression or complete lack of interest. It is an occasion that few people warm to, and one that in many nonconformist churches passes completely unnoticed. Why? You only need to look at the so-called Athanasian Creed to find out the answer. It goes like this: 'I believe in God the Father incomprehensible, God the Son incomprehensible, God the Holy Spirit incomprehensible' and so on, at great length. For many people the word 'incomprehensible' sums up both the Creed and the ideas about God it is trying to express. When it comes to the doctrine of the Trinity, we are out of our depth, struggling with concepts that baffle us, for how can it make sense to talk of three persons who are at once wholly distinct yet wholly one? It is, indeed, incomprehensible.

Yet that is the whole point, the very reason why Trinity Sunday is so important, for it reminds us of a truth we cannot afford to forget: that God is beyond the human intellect, defying expression, greater than we can ever conceive. We encounter him as a loving Father who is yet sovereign over all; as a human being who lived and died among us yet rose again and is exalted at the Father's right hand; and as an inner reality that fills us with peace, joy, hope and power.

We cannot explain how the pieces fit together but we know that they do, for we have experienced the truth for ourselves. If we imagine that we have solved the mystery and that the full wonder of God is firmly in our sights, then it is time to think again, for if we ever think that, then the truth is that we have lost sight of him altogether.

Ask yourself

Do you still have a sense of the mystery and wonder of God? Does the doctrine of the Trinity make sense to you as an experience, if not intellectually?

Pray

Mighty God, beyond all space and time, greater than my mind can grasp, ruler over all that is, has been and shall be – I worship you. Loving Father, kind and merciful, full of goodness and compassion, constantly watching over me and directing my steps – I praise you. Saviour Christ, flesh of my flesh yet the living image of God, sharing my humanity yet one with the Father, loving to the point of death yet bringer of life – I acknowledge you. Holy Spirit, free and mysterious, source of guidance and inspiration, filling my heart and mind – I welcome you.

Mighty God, Father, Son and Holy Spirit, with awe, joy and thanksgiving I celebrate all you mean to me and everything you have done in my life. To you be glory and honour, this and every day. Amen.

Remember

May the grace of the Lord Jesus Christ, the love of God, and the fellowship of the Holy Spirit, be with you all.

2 Corinthians 13:13

Close

Sovereign God, Father, Son and Holy Spirit, teach me to live with mystery, and simply to celebrate each day my many experiences of your love. Amen.

Getting it wrong

Read

What, then, are we to say? Should we continue to sin in order that grace may abound? By no means! How can we who died to sin go on living in it? Do you not know that all of us who have been baptised into Christ Jesus were baptised into his death? Therefore, we have been buried with him by baptism into death, so that, just as Christ was raised from the dead by the glory of the Father, we too might walk in newness of life. *Romans 6:1-4 (NRSV)*

Ponder

This was nice, I thought, as I lay in bed relaxing – a gentle tickle from my wife. Only then it dawned on me that she was busy reading, both hands holding her book. So if *she* wasn't tickling me, what was? With a mixture of trepidation and curiosity, I pulled back the duvet . . . and there it was – the biggest, hairiest spider I've ever seen, scampering up my armpit and on to my chest! Rarely have I moved so fast as at that moment. Rarely had the spider moved so fast either! Things were not what they had seemed; I had misread the situation completely.

So it was, in a very different sense, for the Church in Rome. Some there were suggesting that, since we are justified by faith in Christ, it doesn't matter how we live; that we can go out and do what we like, confident that God will forgive us. Some, indeed, pushed the idea even further, suggesting that we should purposely sin so that he might display his mercy yet more fully. I doubt any of us would consciously entertain thoughts like those for a moment, but we can nonetheless stray inadvertently down that road. It won't matter if I bend the rules just this once, we tell ourselves; God will understand. I needn't worry about the odd thing being wrong; God will forgive. I've no doubt he will, but we should never use that as an excuse for complacency. We are justified by God's grace, and for that let us daily give thanks, but we are also called to newness of life, and towards that let us daily strive – not in order to earn God's love but to thank him for it.

Ask yourself
Does the knowledge of God's forgiveness lead us to be casual and even blasé sometimes? Is there a point at which the life we live may effectively deny the faith we profess?

Pray
Living God, I thank you for your amazing grace, your love of me as I am, despite all my faults and weaknesses. I praise you that you accept me not through my own efforts or according to my own deserving, but through faith in Christ. Forgive me for abusing that truth sometimes, throwing your love back into your face through taking it for granted. Forgive me for assuming sometimes I can carry on regardless, secure in the knowledge of your mercy. Teach me to long to serve you better and to grow in the likeness of Christ, not in any attempt to justify myself but simply to express my love for you.

Fill me now with your Spirit, and so help me to live each day in newness of life, to the glory of your name. Amen.

Remember
Do not imagine that I have come to abolish the law and the prophets. I have not come to abolish but to fulfil them. I tell you this: so long as heaven and earth continue, not a letter or a stroke will disappear from the law until everything that needs to happen has happened.   *Matthew 5:17-18*

Close
Gracious God, though I can never hope to live as faithfully as I ought to, help me to try. Amen.

SCRIPTURAL
INDEX

Scriptural Index